Using Turbo Pascal® 6

2nd Edition

Michael Yester

Using Turbo Pascal® *6*, 2nd Edition

Library of Congress Catalog No.: 90-64405

ISBN: 0-88022-700-1

94 93 92 8 7 6 5 4 3

Interpretation of the printing code: the rightmost double-digit number is the year of the book's printing; the rightmost single-digit number, the number of the book's printing. For example, a printing code of 91-1 shows that the first printing of the book occurred in 1991.

Illustrations: Susan Moore

Cover Design: Dan Armstrong

Production Team: Jeanne Clark, Sandy Grieshop, Betty Kish, Bob LaRoche, Michele Laseau, Howard Peirce, Tad Ringo, Louise Shinault, Johnna VanHoose

Publishing Director
Richard K. Swadley

Publishing Manager
Joseph B. Wikert

Acquisitions Editor
Gregory Croy

Product Development
Ella M. Davis

Managing Editor
Neweleen Trebnik

Senior Editor
Rebecca Whitney

Production Editor
Susan Pink

Technical Editor
Chris Land

Composed in Garamond and OCRB
by Que Corporation.

About The Author

For the last ten years, Michael Yester has been involved in the design, development, and management of financial systems. He holds an M.B.A. in finance and an M.S. in computer science and has taught courses in both systems design and accounting. He is currently an independent consultant residing in Los Angeles.

Content Overview

Table of Contents

Part IV Reference

Trademark Acknowledgments

Que Corporation has made every attempt to supply trademark information about company names, products, and services mentioned in this book. Trademarks indicated below were derived from various sources. Que Corporation cannot attest to the accuracy of this information.

ANSI is a registered trademark of American National Standards Institute.

COMPAQ PLUS is a registered trademark of COMPAQ Computer Corporation.

IBM and IBM 8514/A are registered trademarks and IBM PC*jr* is a trademark of International Business Machines Corporation.

MS-DOS is a registered trademark of Microsoft Corporation.

Norton Utilities is a trademark of Symantec Corporation.

Turbo Pascal and SideKick are registered trademarks and Turbo Lightning is a trademark of Borland International, Inc.

SixPak Plus is a registered trademark of AST Research, Inc.

Acknowledgments

I would like to thank my friends (assuming any of them are still speaking to me) who somehow managed to tolerate me while I was working on this book.

I would like to thank also the editors and staff at Que Corporation for the support and guidance they provided during this project. Special thanks go to Pegg Kennedy and Allen Wyatt, who were willing to risk commissioning a first-time author; Greg Croy and Chris Land, who had to wade through impenetrable material; and especially Bill Nolan, who (miraculously) never lost faith.

Introduction

What Is Turbo Pascal 6.0?

Turbo Pascal 6.0 from Borland International is the latest stage in the evolution of the Pascal language. Turbo Pascal 6.0 is a powerful, integrated applications development package that offers support for a mouse, a multiple file editor capable of handling files up to 1M, an improved debugger, and a command-line version of the compiler. With Turbo Pascal 6.0, programmers can create highly readable, modular programs that generate fast, efficient, executable code.

Almost any high-level programming problem that can be expressed in English can be expressed in Turbo Pascal. In addition, Turbo Pascal is well suited for many low-level systems programming tasks, because of the ease with which it can access both PC hardware and the operating system.

Who Should Use This Book?

Using Turbo Pascal 6, 2nd Edition, is written for everyone with an interest in Turbo Pascal programming—from the new user to the seasoned veteran.

Using Turbo Pascal 6, 2nd Edition, takes a simple, linear approach. It begins with basic system installation instructions, proceeds through a course in Turbo Pascal programming, demonstrates how to use the unique features of the Turbo Pascal language, explains how to develop sophisticated systems-level applications such as memory-resident programs, and closes with an explanation of object-oriented programming techniques. This book is not intense, but it *is* thorough. No matter what your level of expertise, this book will be of interest to you.

What Is in This Book?

Using Turbo Pascal 6, 2nd Edition, is divided into four parts. Essentially, they form an introduction to Pascal programming, an introduction to Turbo Pascal programming in particular, an introduction to advanced Turbo Pascal programming applications, and a reference section. Practical software tools are presented throughout.

Part I, "Learning Turbo Pascal," introduces the fundamentals of the Pascal language and introduces the major features specific to the Turbo dialect. The design and operation of a typical Turbo Pascal program are examined, including how data is represented and controlled, how memory is organized, and how units are used.

- ❑ Chapter 1, "Getting Started with Turbo Pascal," leads the beginning Turbo Pascal user through the stages of installing the compiler on the PC and performing a step-by-step programming session.
- ❑ Chapter 2, "The Structure of a Turbo Pascal Program," introduces the components of the Pascal language—including reserved words, symbols, identifiers, numbers, and strings—and shows how they combine to form the basic structure of a Turbo Pascal program.
- ❑ Chapter 3, "Data and Data Types," discusses the nature of data. It also identifies the various groupings, called *types*, used to categorize data and shows how data types are used in a program.
- ❑ Chapter 4, "Expressions, Operands, and Operators," presents the instructions that control the flow of programming operations and manipulate and manage program data.
- ❑ Chapter 5, "Procedures and Functions," covers how to combine related data and code statements.
- ❑ Chapter 6, "Dynamic Data Structures," explains how the PC manages memory and how memory can be used to store data objects.

- Chapter 7, "Units," discusses the standard units of Turbo Pascal and describes Turbo's separate compilation feature.
- Chapter 8, "Debugging Your Programs," presents Turbo's integrated debugger and shows how you can use it to solve complex programming problems.

Part II, "Programming," demonstrates how to write Turbo Pascal programs using a variety of input and display options. This section also discusses directory and file management.

- Chapter 9, "Keyboard Input," explains the design, operation, and management of the keyboard and demonstrates how to read and interpret any key combination.
- Chapter 10, "Text Display," discusses the design, operation, and management of the text screen and how to develop programs that exploit such features as windows, colors, and intensity.
- Chapter 11, "Graphics Display," presents and demonstrates the extensive Turbo Pascal graphics subroutine library.
- Chapter 12, "Accessing DOS," describes how to access and control the operating system of your PC, including date, time, and sound commands. In addition, the chapter discusses the DOS environment and the program segment prefix (PSP) and demonstrates how to execute child processes and control program termination.
- Chapter 13, "File Handling," discusses the characteristics and management of text, typed, and untyped files.
- Chapter 14, "Directory Handling," discusses the management of collections of files in the form of directories and disk drives.

Part III, "Advanced Programming," provides an introduction to some of the advanced systems-level applications available with Turbo Pascal. It also covers object-oriented programming techniques and the user-interface toolbox, Turbo Vision.

- Chapter 15, "Overlays," demonstrates how to allow different parts of a single Turbo Pascal program to occupy the same internal memory locations.
- Chapter 16, "BIOS, DOS, and Assembly Language," describes how your program can access the major software services available in your PC and explains how to incorporate low-level assembly language instructions.

- Chapter 17, "The 8087 and External Devices," demonstrates the various ways Turbo Pascal lets you access all of the equipment connected to your PC, including hardware ports and both predefined and custom device drivers. The 8087 coprocessor is also discussed.
- Chapter 18, "Interrupt Service Routines," explains how DOS uses both the BIOS routines and its own subroutine library to maintain control of the PC. Further, the chapter explains how you can directly access those routines and even add to them for your own purposes.
- Chapter 19, "Memory-Resident Programs," reveals the procedures and techniques to develop memory-resident programs that either run continuously or are user-activated with hot keys.
- Chapter 20, "Object-Oriented Programming," introduces the concepts of object-oriented programming (OOP) and demonstrates how OOP is supported by Turbo Pascal.
- Chapter 21, "Advanced Object-Oriented Programming," discusses advanced OOP topics such as private object components, abstract and multilevel objects, and containment.
- Chapter 22, Turbo Vision," provides an introduction to Turbo Vision, Turbo Pascal's user-interface software toolbox.

Part IV, "Reference," provides a library of all the procedures and functions available in Turbo Pascal 6.0. The reference also includes a summary of the Turbo Pascal compiler directives, including conditional compilation instructions.

Part I

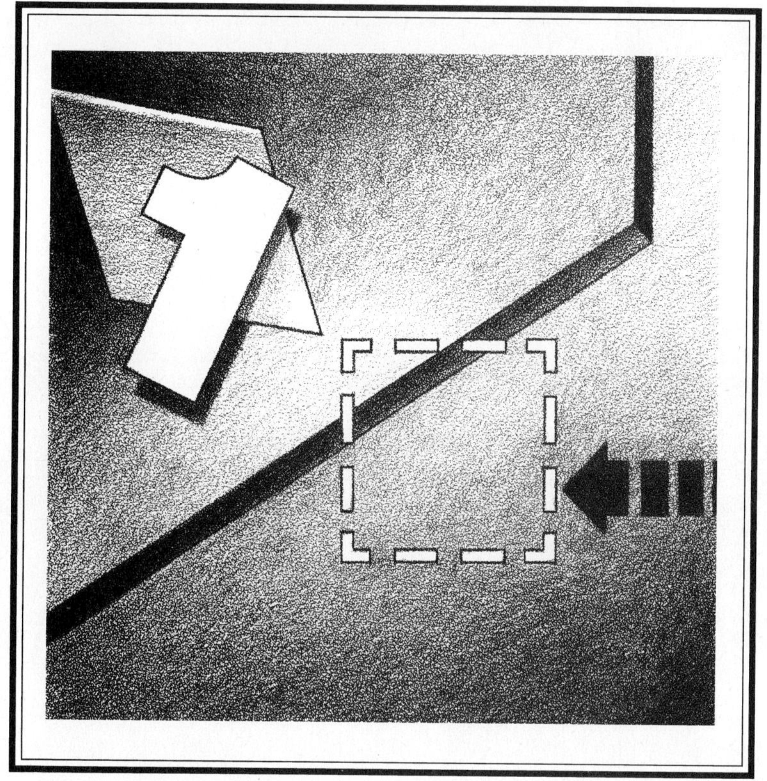

Learning Turbo Pascal

CHAPTER 1

Getting Started with Turbo Pascal

The success of Borland's Turbo Pascal is attributed to the compiler's speed, the implementation features, and the product's environment. Borland has updated the environment several times, offering more sophisticated versions. The latest update comes with version 6.0. The new Integrated Development Environment (IDE) offers text-based windows, supports the mouse and multiple files, and can edit files up to 1M (1 million bytes) in size. In addition to the IDE version of the Turbo Pascal compiler, Borland has offered, in the last few updates, a command-line version of the compiler, TPC.EXE. This enables quick compilations of programs, batch file operations that recompile programs, and the compilation of large programs. The Professional Pack of Version 6.0 offers two command-line compilers, TPC.EXE and TPCX.EXE. The latter version handles projects with huge files.

The IDE version is implemented in the TURBO.EXE program and offers the following features:

- Pull-down menus and dialog boxes
- Multiple overlapping windows
- Support for a mouse
- Multiple-file editor that handles files up to 1M
- Improved debugger
- Advanced on-line hypertext help

This chapter discusses the essential information you need to be up and running with Turbo Pascal in as short a time as possible. In addition, you take a brief tour of the integrated environment, learning every command and function you need to begin using Turbo Pascal. This chapter is written for those who are not current users of an earlier Turbo Pascal version. If you are already familiar with the process of installing the compiler, you should probably skim the next few pages.

The Turbo Pascal Package

The Turbo Pascal package contains four 360K diskettes and four manuals. The diskettes are labeled INSTALL/COMPILER, HELP, BGI/UTILITIES, and TURBO VISION/TOUR. Following are the major files in the distribution disks:

1. Contents of the INSTALL/COMPILER diskette (Volume INSTALL):

INSTALL.EXE	The Turbo Pascal installation program.
README	Text file containing information not included in the Turbo Pascal manuals.
README.COM	Program to display the README file.
TURBO.ZIP	Archive file containing the various versions of the Turbo Pascal compilers, TURBO.EXE and TPC.EXE.
UNZIP.EXE	Utility to unpack files.

2. Contents of the HELP diskette (Volume HELP):

HELP.ZIP	Archive file containing hypertext help and other on-line help.

3. Contents of the BGI/UTILITIES diskette (Volume UTILITIES):

BGI.ZIP	Archive file containing drivers (*.BGI), fonts (*.CHR), examples (*.PAS), and the BGI graphics library unit (GRAPH.TPU).
DEMOS.ZIP	Archive file containing the source code for the demonstration programs.
DOCDEMOS.ZIP	Archive file containing the complete programs mentioned in the manuals (especially the *Turbo Vision* manual).

ONLINE.ZIP	Archive files containing additional documentation not found in the Turbo Pascal manuals.
TCALC.ZIP	Archive files containing the source code for the MicroCalc spreadsheet program.

4. The contents of the TURBO VISION/TOUR diskette (Volume VISION):

INTRFACE.ZIP	Archive file containing the implementation section of the Turbo Pascal library units (including Turbo Vision).
TOUR.ZIP	Archive file containing an interactive tour of the Integrated Development Environment.
TURBO3.ZIP	Turbo 3.0 compatibility files, including the TURBO3.TPU and GRAPH3.TPU library units.
TVDEMOS.ZIP	Archive file containing the source code for programs and plug-in units that use Turbo Vision. The archived files are valuable and timesaving add-ons to your programs.
TVISION.ZIP	Archive file containing the compiled Turbo Vision library units. The source code for a few of these units is also supplied.

The first manual, *User's Guide,* discusses the installation of the software, the integrated environment, object-oriented programming, debugging Turbo Pascal programs, project management, the editor commands, and the command-line compilers. The second manual, *Programmer's Guide,* covers the language definition, the library cross-reference, assembly language and Turbo Pascal, and the compiler's error messages. The third manual, *Turbo Vision Guide,* teaches you how to program with Turbo Vision. The first part uses a cookbook approach in revealing Turbo Vision; the second part presents a reference to the various objects, data types, and variables that make up Turbo Vision. The last manual, *Library Reference,* contains the routines of the run-time library. Thanks to the new hypertext help of version 6.0, you most likely will have little use for the last manual.

Preparing Your Diskettes

After you open the package, the first thing you should do is read, sign, and mail Borland's No-Nonsense License Statement. Among other things, it explains that you have the right to make as many backup copies as you need for your own personal use. You should take advantage of this to safeguard your original diskettes; use them as seldom as possible. You prepare backups in three simple steps:

1. To prevent any possibility of accidental erasure, attach write-protect tabs to the four distribution diskettes.
2. Use the `DISKCOPY` command to make working copies of each of the original diskettes. (Consult your DOS manual if you are not familiar with this command.) Be sure to label each copy.
3. Store the original diskettes in a safe place. From now on, you need to use only the copies.

Next, insert your working copy of the Install/Compiler diskette in drive A, and enter the following:

```
A:
README
```

The README.COM program displays the contents of the README file, which contains supplementary information not found in the manuals. Because one of the topics README usually covers is installation procedures, now is the time to review its contents. It is generally a good idea to use the README.COM program to print a copy of the file so that you have a hard copy for future reference. Type **P** to begin. You can see a complete list of program options by pressing the F1 function key.

Installing Turbo Pascal Version 6.0

Turbo Pascal Version 6.0 comes complete with an installation utility, INSTALL.EXE, which considerably simplifies the process of configuring your system. This section discusses how to use INSTALL.EXE on hard disk and floppy-based systems. Read through the appropriate section before you begin. Remember that unlike some copy-protected software, Turbo Pascal can be installed as often as you want.

Throughout this discussion, it is assumed that your first and second floppy diskettes are drives A and B, respectively, and your hard disk (if you have one) is drive C.

Hard Disk Installation with INSTALL.EXE

When you use INSTALL.EXE to place the compiler on your hard disk system, a number of directories are created:

C:\TP	Stores the compiler files and the help files.
C:\TP\TVISION	Contains the Turbo Vision compiled library units.
C:\TP\TVDEMOS	Stores the source code for programs and plug-in units that use Turbo Vision.
C:\TP\DOCDEMOS	Contains source code for OOP examples in the *User's Guide* and *Turbo Vision Guide*.
C:\TP\DEMOS	Stores the source code for demonstration programs that are related to neither Turbo Vision nor the BGI system.
C:\TP\DOC	Contains the interface sections for the various standard compiled library units, the command-line utilities, and information on Turbo Vision.
C:\TP\BGI	Stores the BGI-related files for the drivers, fonts, library units, and examples.
C:\TP\UTILS	Contains the utilities (such as GREP and MAKE).
C:\TP\TURBO3	Contains the compiled library units that offer compatibility with Version 3.0.

If you want all of the Turbo Pascal files to reside on your hard disk, you need about 3.3M of free disk space. Many of the following files, however, are discretionary:

1. The C:\TP directory contains the README file, which contains the latest word from Borland on added features, typographical errors in the documentation, helpful hints, and so forth. It can be read and printed with the README.COM program. After you have done that, you can remove both files from your hard disk.

2. The C:\TP\DOC directory contains listings of unit headers. Although the headers are extremely informative, they do not need to be present for the compiler to run. (You should, however, print them and keep the hard copies as reference.) This directory also holds the HELPME!.DOC file, which contains answers to the questions the Borland Technical Support department receives most frequently. You should most definitely print and read this file, but again, it does not need to remain resident on your hard disk.

3. If you are using Turbo Pascal for the first time or if your programs are not based on source code from Version 3.0, you probably will not need the contents of C:\TP\TURBO3.

To install Turbo Pascal Version 6.0 on your hard disk with the INSTALL.EXE utility, follow these steps (it is assumed that your hard disk is drive C):

1. Insert your working copy of the INSTALL/COMPILER diskette in drive A, then enter

   ```
   A:INSTALL
   ```

   to begin. The first thing you see is the Turbo 6.0 Installation Utility sign-on screen, as shown in figure 1.1.

2. Press the Enter key to proceed. INSTALL.EXE asks for the drive you are using for diskettes. To accept the default of drive A, press Enter and proceed. If the installation disks are in drive B, type **B** and press Enter.

3. INSTALL.EXE then inquires about the desired configuration, as shown in figure 1.2. Choose the `Install Turbo Pascal on a Hard Drive` option.

4. Figure 1.3 shows the installation menu for the hard disk. Essentially, you are asked to confirm that the default directory names are acceptable. In addition, you should agree to `Unpack additional archives`, which means only that you want the files on the diskettes converted to a usable format. Press the F9 function key to start the installation process.

The INSTALL.EXE utility creates the named directories, then copies and unarchives files. The installation proceeds automatically. You will be asked to insert the other three Turbo Pascal diskettes. Follow the instructions on the screen.

Fig. 1.1. The main screen of the INSTALL.EXE installation utility.

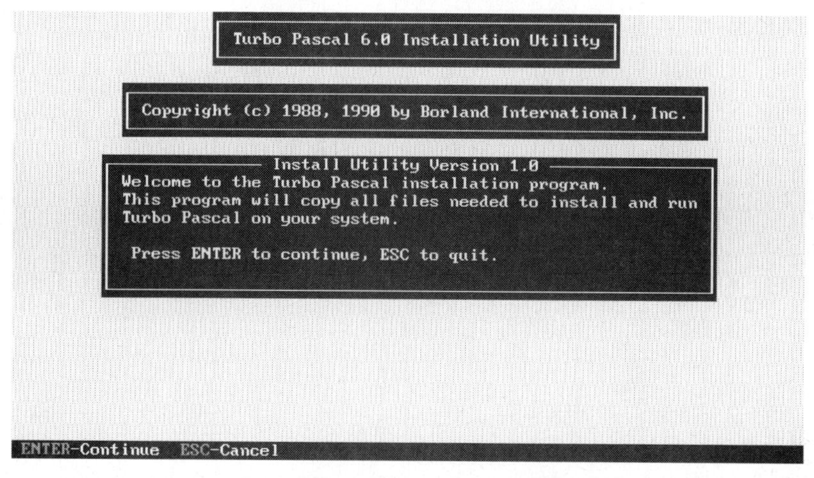

Fig. 1.2. The installation options of the INSTALL.EXE program.

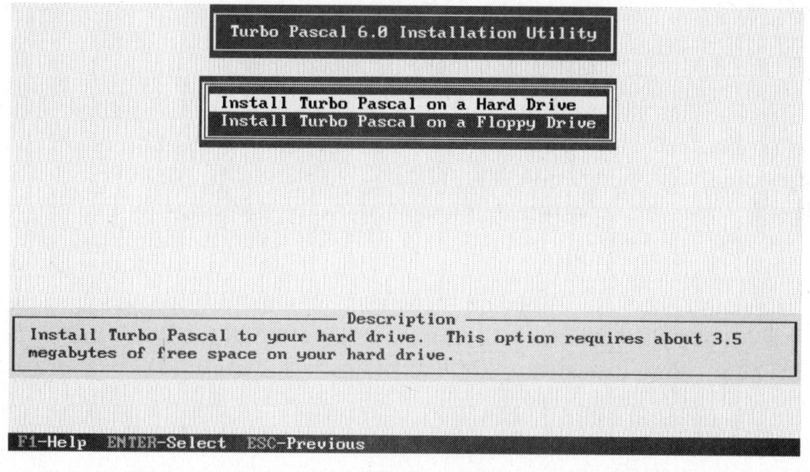

Fig. 1.3. Configuration options for installing Turbo Pascal on a hard drive.

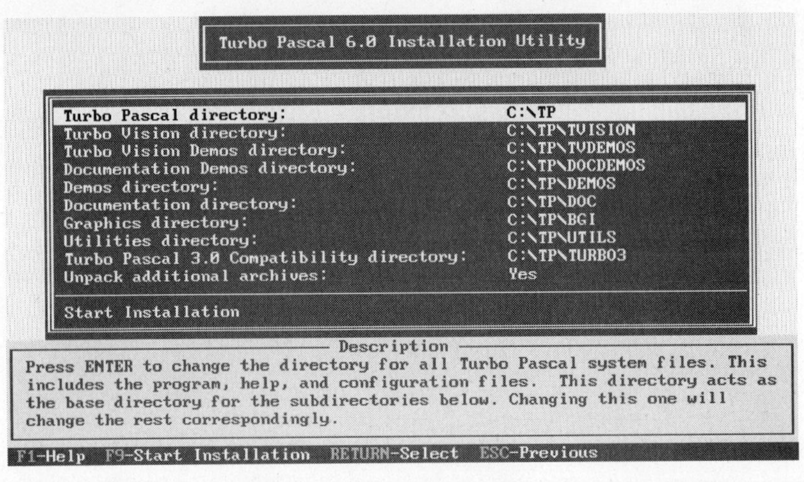

Floppy Diskette Installation with INSTALL.EXE

Using the INSTALL.EXE utility, you can install on floppy diskettes a bare bones Turbo Pascal system that includes either TURBO.EXE or TPC.EXE (the command-line version) and TURBO.TPL. How does the INSTALL.EXE utility handle the various diskette sizes and capacities? It simply assumes a worst case scenario of your having 5 1/4-inch diskette with a capacity of 360K. The INSTALL.EXE utility requires two 360K disks to install the IDE version, and only one 360K disk to install the command-line version. If you are using disks of another size or capacity, you need the same number of disks as those required for 360K disks.

To install Turbo Pascal Version 6.0 on your floppy diskette with INSTALL.EXE, follow these steps (it is assumed that your floppy diskette drives are A and B):

1. If you have a dual floppy system, you need formatted disks. To format a blank disk, insert it in drive B and insert your DOS disk in drive A. The blank disk in drive B is formatted using the following command:

   ```
   FORMAT B:
   ```

   Repeat this operation to format a second disk, if needed.

2. Place your working copy of the INSTALL/COMPILER disk in drive A, then enter

   ```
   A:INSTALL
   ```

   to begin. The first display is the Turbo 6.0 Installation Utility sign-on screen, as was shown in figure 1.1.

3. Press the Enter key to proceed. INSTALL.EXE asks for the drive you will use for the working diskettes. Press Enter to accept the default of drive A.

4. INSTALL.EXE then prompts you to select your configuration, as was shown in figure 1.2. Choose the `Install Turbo Pascal on a Floppy Drive` option.

5. Figure 1.4 shows the installation menu for the floppy diskette system. You can choose between the integrated environment compiler (TURBO.EXE) and the command-line compiler (TPC.EXE). The assumption here is that you prefer the integrated environment compiler, TURBO.EXE.

***Fig. 1.4.** Configuration options for installing Turbo Pascal on a floppy drive.*

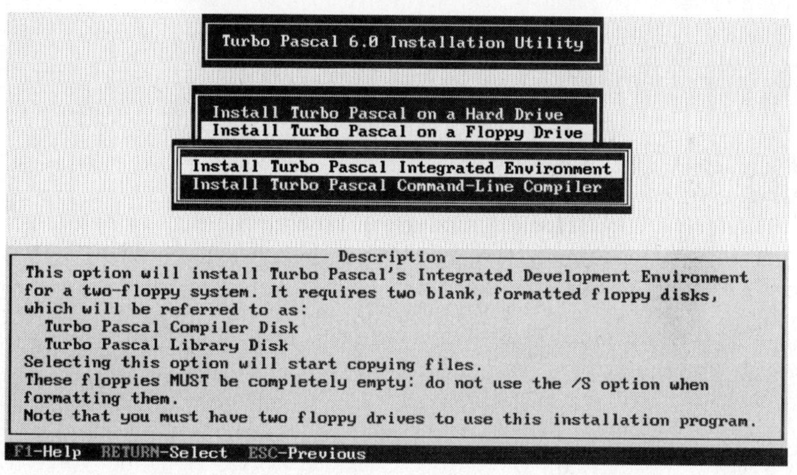

If you select to install the integrated environment compiler, INSTALL.EXE prompts you for two disks, the Turbo Pascal Compiler disk and the Turbo Pascal Library disk. TURBO.EXE is written to the first disk. Then you are prompted to insert the second disk in drive B. INSTALL.EXE writes the TURBO.TPL file to the second disk.

If you want to install the command-line version, choose the `Install Turbo Pascal Command-Line Compiler` option. INSTALL.EXE prompts you to insert the compiler disk in drive B. Both TPC.EXE and TURBO.TPL fit easily on one disk (they occupy just under 115K of disk space).

Configuring Your System

If your system executes an AUTOEXEC.BAT file when it is booted, you should initialize `PATH` to the TP and TP\UTILS subdirectories by including the following line:

```
PATH=C:\TP;C:\TP\UTILS;
```

If you already have a `PATH` statement, add the TP and TP\UTILS subdirectories as follows:

```
PATH=C:\DOS;C:\WP51;\C:\TP;C:\TP\UTILS;
```

You need to reboot the computer so that the operating system can reconfigure for the new CONFIG.SYS parameters. Now you are ready to run the compiler.

Running Turbo Pascal Version 6.0

After the Turbo Pascal compiler is installed, you can use it by following a few simple steps. The following discussion assumes that you have selected the TURBO.EXE integrated environment.

To bring up Turbo Pascal on a hard disk system, change to the Turbo Pascal subdirectory by entering the following command:

```
CD \TP
```

You may want to use the directory command, `DIR`, to verify that you are in the correct subdirectory. Next, invoke the compiler by entering:

```
TURBO
```

The computer then loads the compiler.

To bring up Turbo Pascal on a floppy diskette system, insert your Turbo Pascal System disk in drive A and enter the command

```
TURBO
```

The computer then loads the compiler.

Turbo Pascal Menu Displays

When the IDE compiler is invoked from your hard or floppy disk, a single line of text appears below the DOS prompt to display the copyright and Turbo Pascal version number. This line appears while the Turbo Pascal IDE is being loaded into memory. When this is done, the screen displays the empty Turbo Pascal desktop. Welcome to the integrated environment!

The menu bar offers a rich set of tools for developing, running, and debugging your programs. If you have a mouse installed, its cursor appears somewhere on the desktop. The empty desktop shows the menu bar at the topmost screen row, the status bar at the bottom screen row, and the empty half-tone desktop background. Figure 1.5 shows the Turbo Pascal desktop with the `About` dialog box showing the copyright and version information for Turbo Pascal.

***Fig. 1.5.** The main screen of Turbo Pascal.*

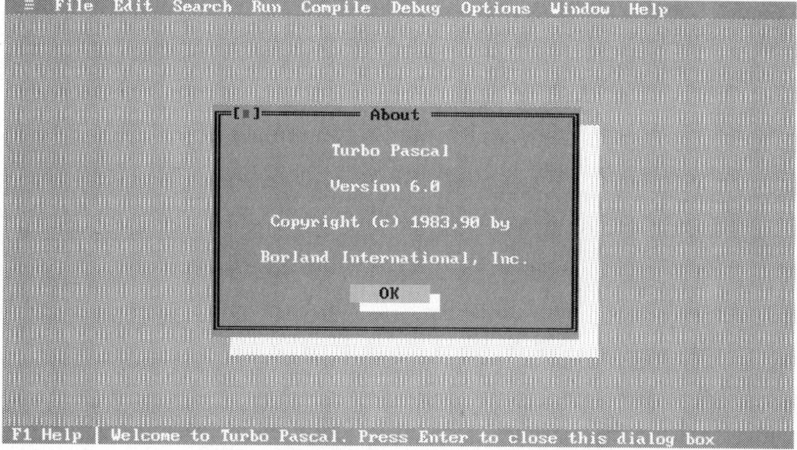

The first question you might ask is how to select the various menu options. A main menu option can be selected by several methods. You can select the `File` option, for example, in one of the following ways:

1. Press the Alt-F key combination to directly invoke the `File` option and pull down its menu. You press Alt-F because the letter *F* in *File* is highlighted by a red color.
2. Press F10 to put the program in the main menu. Next, press F (the highlighted letter of the `File` option) to select the `File` option and pull down its menu.
3. Move the mouse (if you have one installed) to the `File` option and click on the left button. This pulls down the File menu.

The various options of the File menu (shown in figure 1.6) are invoked by one of the following methods:

1. Each available option is associated with a hot key, displayed in red. An option is invoked by pressing the corresponding hot key.
2. Certain options are associated with shortcut keys that can be invoked from the editor. The shortcut keys are either function keys, alternate keys, or control keys. The shortcut keys are displayed along with the corresponding menu options. In the case of the File menu, the F2, F3, and Alt-X keys are shortcut keys for the `Save`, `Open`, and `Exit` options, respectively.
3. The up and down arrows can be used to select an option. Pressing Enter invokes the selected option.
4. The mouse can be used to select an option. Clicking on an option invokes it. If you hold the mouse's left button down while you move the mouse cursor up or down, you can move among the various menu options. When you release the mouse button, the current selection is invoked.

No menu selection method is best: you will develop your own preferences shortly. By the way, you now know four ways to end the operation of the compiler.

The Turbo Pascal menu options are context sensitive. Depending on the status of your work, certain options are available while others are not. The unavailable options are displayed in light gray.

Fig. 1.6. The File menu.

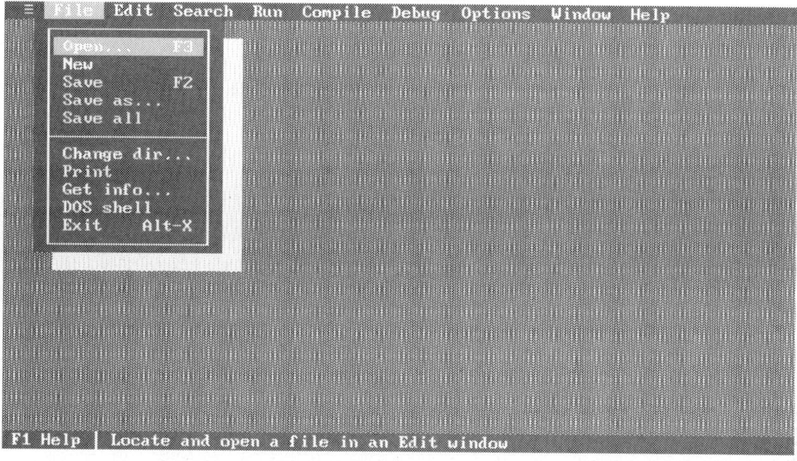

Let us briefly review the main menu options:

≡ — This menu contains the About option that shows the dialog box containing the copyright and version information. Other options refresh and clear the display.

`File` — This is your connection to the outside world. The `File` options enable you to open, save, and create program files; to select directories; and—with the `DOS shell` option—to suspend temporarily the execution of the compiler by returning to the operating system (you just type the `EXIT` command to return to Turbo).

`Edit` — You use this menu to cut, copy, and paste text in the Edit windows, restore a deleted line, and view the contents of the Clipboard window. (The Clipboard contains text that was cut or copied from an edited window.)

`Search` — This menu offers a powerful tool for searching and replacing text in the Edit windows; searching for procedures while debugging; finding run-time errors in your files; and jumping to specific line numbers in your file. The text search-and-replace options are highly versatile.

`Run` — You use this menu to compile and run a program, or single-step through a program for debugging.

`Compile` — Most of the time, you will want to run your programs immediately. Occasionally, though, you will prefer to compile and store them on disk so that you can run them later outside the integrated environment. The `Compile` option handles this for you.

`Debug` — The integrated environment comes complete with a sophisticated debugger that helps you look "under the hood" of your PC while a program is running. Debugging is discussed in Chapter 8.

`Options` — This menu enables you to fine-tune the settings for the Turbo Pascal compiler, the linker, the working directories, and the environment. The default settings are adequate for most programming tasks. For now, simply accept the default settings.

`Window` — You use the options in this menu to manage the various windows, especially if you are not using a mouse. Some `Window` options enable you to move, resize, close, and zoom on the active window; arrange the windows; invoke the debugging watch window; move to the next or previous window; view the user screen; and view a list of the current and most recently loaded windows.

`Help` — This is your door to the powerful on-line hypertext help system. You can obtain help by topics or by index.

Steps in Creating a Turbo Pascal Program

This section concentrates on the features you use in every session: entering, saving, opening, and running a program.

Entering and Editing the Program

One of the attractions of the integrated development environment is the built-in editor. To try it, choose the `File` option from the main menu and then select the `New` suboption. This opens a window with a default file name based title of NONAME00.PAS and invokes the editor, placing the cursor at the upper left window corner (this assumes that the desktop was clear). Enter the following program. (Except for the message in single quotation marks, capitalization and spaces do not matter.)

```
program First;
begin
    writeln( 'Hello, world!' )
end.
```

The `writeln` (pronounced "write line") statement instructs the compiler to display whatever it finds between the parentheses.

Notice that the window containing your program is made up of the following components:

1. A double-line frame forming the upper, left, and part of the bottom window edges.
2. A vertical scroll bar is the right edge of the window. A small rectangular character in the scroll bar indicates what portion of the file you are viewing.
3. A horizontal bar forms most of the bottom window edge. A small rectangular character in the scroll bar indicates the marginal shift of the text you are viewing.
4. The title bar is located at the center of the upper edge and contains the window title or the name of the file being edited.
5. The zoom box is located at the right side of the upper edge. When the character in the zoom box is an up arrow, the active window is viewed at the current size. When you click on that box, it zooms on that window and the character in the zoom box becomes the up/down arrow symbol. When you click on the zoom box with a mouse, it toggles between normal and zoomed views.
6. The close box is located at the left side of the upper edge. It always contains a solid block symbol. When you click on the close box with a mouse, it closes the corresponding window.
7. A window number is located at the right side of the upper edge, to the left of the zoom box.

To resize a window, you invoke the `Size/Move menu` suboption of the `Window` option and then use the Shift key with the up, down, left, or right arrow key to adjust the window size. (Press Esc to cancel any changes.) Press Enter when you are finished. If you have a mouse, you can resize a window by following these steps:

1. Move the mouse cursor to the lower right window corner.
2. Hold down the left button and drag the mouse cursor toward the center of the window to shrink it, or away from the center of the window to expand it.
3. Release the left button of the mouse when you have finished resizing the window.

To move a window, you invoke the `Size/Move menu` suboption of the `Window` option and then use the up, down, left, or right arrow key to adjust the window location. Press Enter when you are finished. If you have a mouse, you can move a window by following these steps:

1. Move the mouse cursor to the upper window edge.
2. Hold down the left button and drag the window to its new position.
3. Release the mouse button.

If you are familiar with the WordStar word processing package, you are already familiar with the basic Turbo Pascal editing functions. If you do not know WordStar—in fact, if you have never used a word processor before—you need to remember only a few things:

1. The cursor (the flashing underline character that marks your current position) can be moved around the screen with the arrow keys on your numeric pad. Whatever you type is inserted where the cursor is located when the key is pressed. The editor keeps track of the current line and column.
2. You end each line by pressing the Enter key.
3. If you make a mistake, move the cursor over the mistake and type any new material. If you need to erase a character, position the cursor over the unwanted character and press the Del (delete) key. You can remove several unwanted characters by holding down the Del key a bit longer.

Your screen should now look like the one in figure 1.7.

Fig. 1.7. The `Hello, world!` *program.*

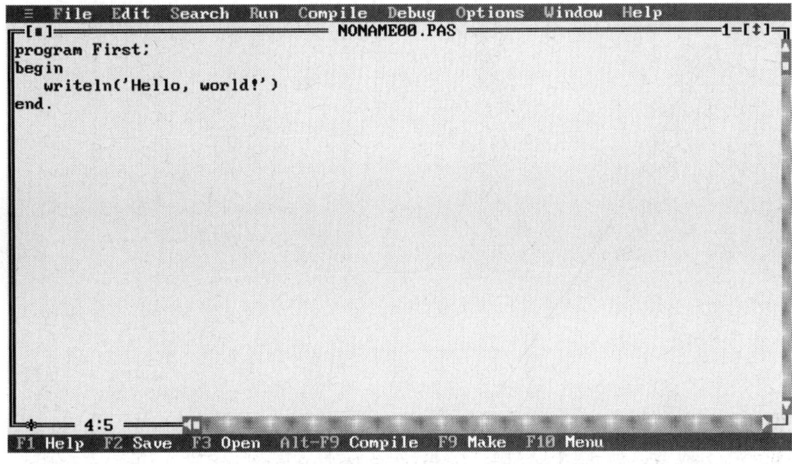

Although several additional editing features are available, these are the only ones you need to know for now. Editing is that simple. In fact, many experienced programmers use Turbo as their word processing system.

Running the Program

Now it is time to run your first program. Press the F10 function key to leave the editor and return to the main menu. Then select the `Run` option, as shown in figure 1.8. This instructs the integrated environment to compile and execute your program. (Alternatively, you could have gone directly from the editor to the Run menu by pressing Alt-R.)

Notice that the hot key for the `Run` option is Ctrl-F9. Even from the editor, your program will compile and execute if you press Ctrl-F9.

If you made a typing error, Turbo stops the compilation, returns to the editor, positions the cursor over the offending section of code, and tells you—in English—the problem it found. If this happens, correct the problem and rerun the program. If this does not happen, you may want to commit an error deliberately (omit a single quotation mark, for example) and see how the compiler helps you locate the error.

Fig. 1.8. The Run menu.

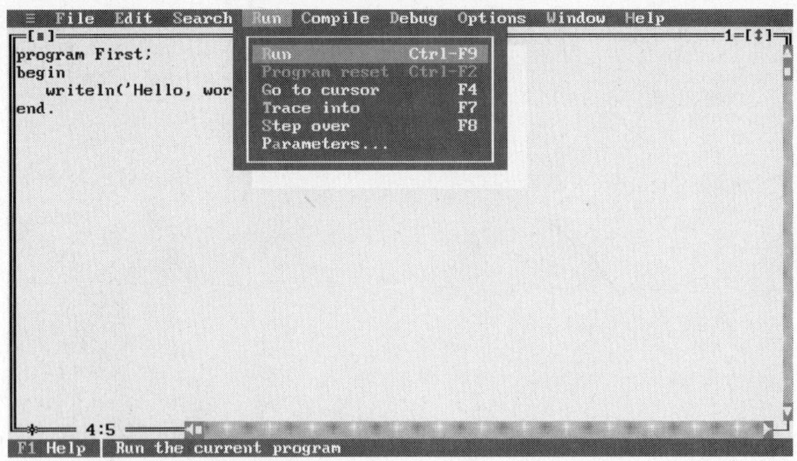

If you did not make any typing mistakes, you will probably notice that the screen flashes for a second, then returns you to the editor. You have probably figured out that the program is supposed to display a message, but where?

Press Alt-F5 (the shortcut key for the `Window/User screen` suboption) to view the user screen that is similar to figure 1.9. You can see your first message at the end of whatever was on the screen before you ran the compiler. Press any key to return to the integrated environment.

Saving the Program

Refer back to figure 1.7, and notice the characters NONAME00.PAS on the upper window frame. This is the name of the file when your program is saved; but in this case, you have not yet saved the program. Let us remedy that right now.

If you have been following the chapter closely, the current directory is the one you were in when you invoked TURBO, that is, C:\TP on a hard disk system or A:\ for a floppy diskette system. Select the `File` option. Notice that one of the options lets you change the current directory. As you write and acquire more programs, you will probably want to segregate some of your files. For now, just remember that the opportunity exists.

Fig. 1.9. Output from the `Hello world!` *program.*

```
C>turbo
Turbo Pascal  Version 6.0  Copyright (c) 1983,90 Borland International
Hello, world!
```

Now select the `Save as` option. You are prompted for a file name. Use **first** because it is also the name of the program. After you type the name but before you press the Enter key, your screen should look like figure 1.10. After you press Enter, you will notice that NONAME00 has been changed to FIRST. Note that you do not need to specify an extension; Turbo Pascal assumes that all program files use .PAS.

Fig. 1.10. Choosing a file name for the `Hello, world!` *program.*

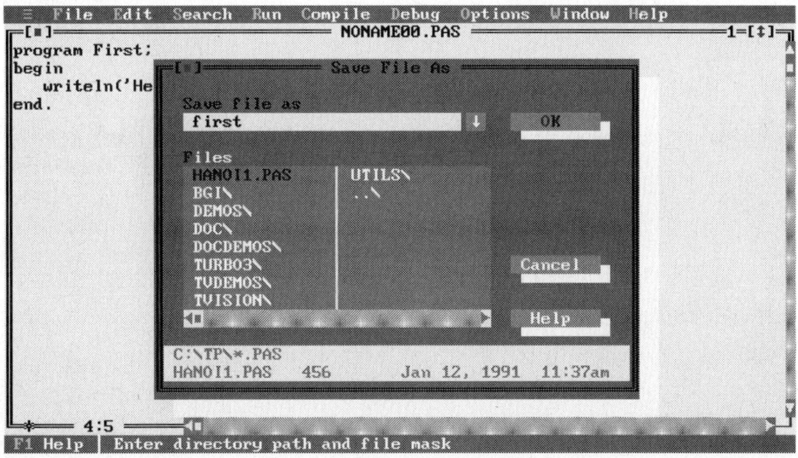

The `Write to` option is used only to create a file on the disk. From now on, if you edit the program and want to save its current version, you can simply select `Save` to store the file. Remember to save frequently. Most programs are considerably longer than the four-line demonstration you just created, and they are painful to lose. Note that the hot key for `Save` is F2; you can use this key to save your program at frequent intervals while you are editing.

Now exit the compiler by pressing the Alt-X hot key to select the `Exit` option. You are about to find out how to retrieve the program from disk.

Loading the Program

Again, invoke the compiler by entering **TURBO** at the DOS prompt. After the program loads, select the `File` option (as shown in figure 1.6). You are probably in the same subdirectory you were in when you invoked TURBO for the first time (C:\TP or A:\ in these examples). If not, now would be the time to select the `Change dir` option and specify the directory you are using to store your programs.

Now choose the `Open` option. The integrated environment responds as shown in figure 1.11, with a dialog box titled `Open a File`. The input line of the dialog box shows *.PAS. The file list box displays all of the .PAS files in the current directory, including your FIRST.PAS file, and all of the connected directories. Simply press the Enter key and accept the *.PAS default. FIRST.PAS, the first entry in the file list box, is now highlighted, as shown in figure 1.12. To select it, just press Enter. (If FIRST.PAS had not been the first file in the list, you would have used the arrow keys to select it.)

The FIRST.PAS program is loaded in a new window, titled FIRST.PAS. Edit the program by changing the word `world` to the word `again`. Remember that you position the cursor over the spot where you want to type new material or where you want to use Del to remove something. After you make the change, your program should look like the following:

```
program First;
begin
   writeln( 'Hello, again!' )
end.
```

Next, rerun the program. You can use F10 to return to the main menu, where you can select `Run`, or you can simply use the Ctrl-F9 hot key. The result can be examined with the `User screen` option (Alt-F5) in the

Window menu. Instead of the original `Hello, World!` message, you now see `Hello, again!` After viewing this output, press any key to return to the editor.

Fig. 1.11. Choosing the name of the next file you want to load.

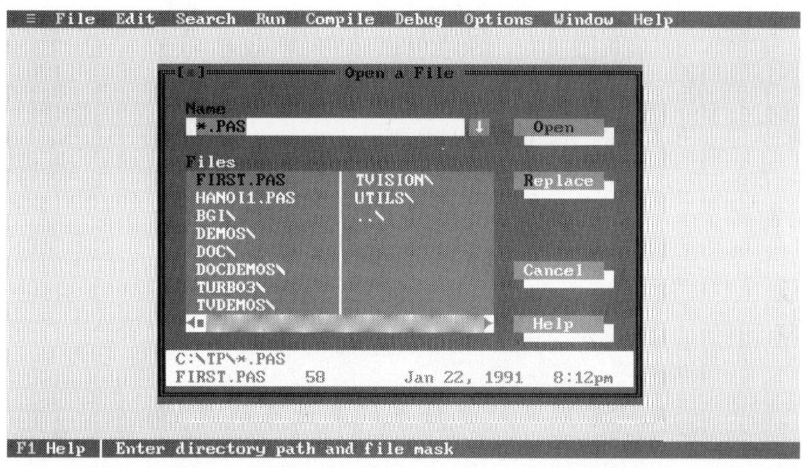

*Fig. 1.12. All files in the C:\TP directory that match *.PAS.*

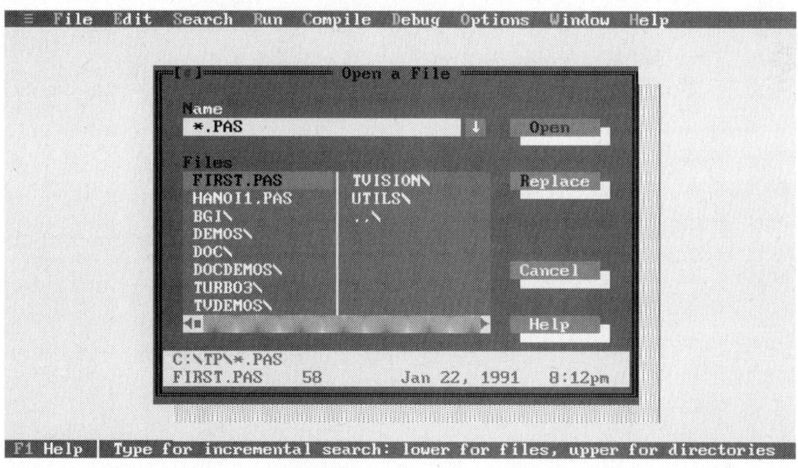

Now, quit the compiler by selecting the `Exit` option in the File menu or by using Alt-X. The compiler reacts with a warning, as shown in figure 1.13. Because you have changed the program, the integrated environment displays an `Information` dialog box and forces you to choose consciously to save the file or lose your work. You should save it, by pressing the Y key. To remind you that the file has been changed, the editor displays * in the bottom frame of the window to the left of the line:column numbers.

***Fig. 1.13.** Verifying whether to save or lose your changes.*

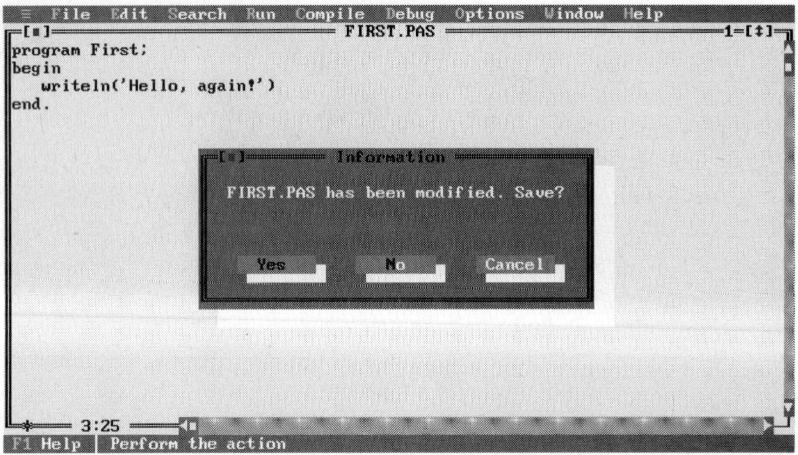

Consider what you just did. By telling the compiler to save the latest version of your program, you have told it to overwrite the previous contents of the FIRST.PAS file. The integrated environment will do that, but not before it copies FIRST.PAS to a new file, FIRST.BAK, in the same directory. Only one generation of your program is saved as backup (as BAK files are called). If you want more, you can save your files under different names. More than one professional programmer (and author) has used backup files to salvage work that otherwise would have been lost forever.

Running the Program Directly from DOS

So far, you have seen how to run a Turbo Pascal program in the integrated environment. But you may have written a utility program that is useful only when it is run directly from DOS. Or you may have written a game program that you want to share with a friend who does not have a copy of the compiler. You might even have developed a business application that will run on several PCs in your office.

Invoke the compiler by entering **TURBO** at the DOS prompt. After the program loads, select the `File` option, and load the FIRST.PAS program.

To run the program directly from DOS, select the Compile menu. The fourth option, `Destination`, enables you to choose between compiling to memory and compiling to disk. Select the `Destination` option and press the Enter key to toggle between the two choices; as shown in figure 1.14, you want to choose to compile to disk. Now select the first option, `Compile` (Alt-F9). The integrated environment responds with a status window similar to the one shown in figure 1.15. After you see the `Compile successful` message, press any key to return to the editor, then quit the compiler by pressing Alt-X.

***Fig. 1.14.** The Compile menu.*

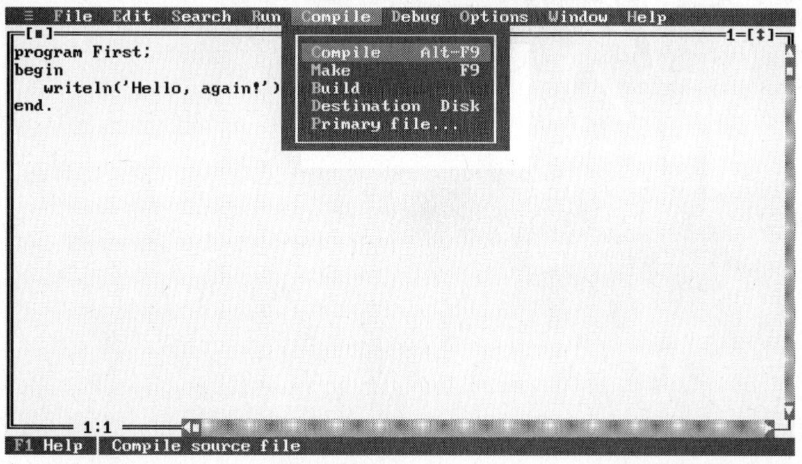

Refer to figure 1.16. If you enter the command `DIR FIRST`, you will find three files. FIRST.EXE is the executable file. FIRST.BAK is your original `"Hello, world!"` program, and FIRST.PAS is your current `"Hello, again!"` program.

Fig. 1.15. Progress messages when compiling to disk.

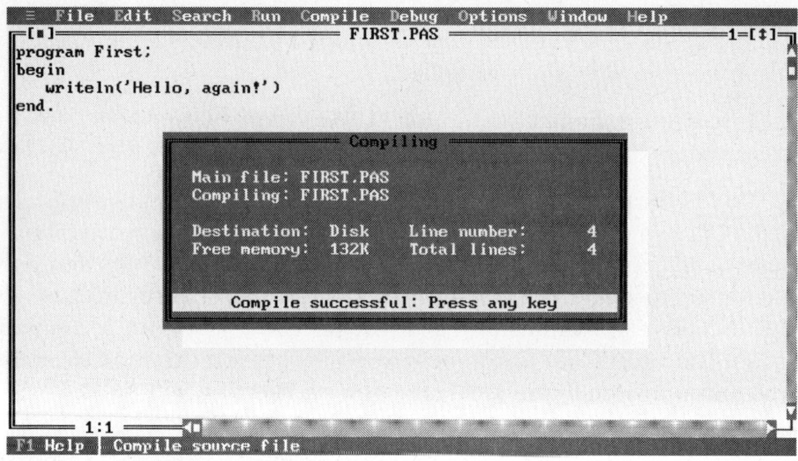

Fig. 1.16. The files created during the current session.

```
C>dir first.*

 Volume in drive C is ST CYR
 Volume Serial Number is 3831-17F6
 Directory of  C:\TP

FIRST    EXE      1936 03-29-91  10:41a
FIRST    BAK        58 03-29-91  10:38a
FIRST    PAS        58 03-29-91  10:41a
        3 File(s)   21798912 bytes free

C>first
Hello, again!

C>
```

The FIRST.EXE program can be run by entering the following command:

```
FIRST
```

This loads the program and displays the `Hello, again!` message.

Getting On-Line Help

The integrated environment of Turbo Pascal 6.0 uses hypertext technology to implement on-line help. This includes on-line reference for the predefined Turbo Pascal routines. For example, suppose that you want to know more about `writeln`, which was used in the FIRST.PAS program. How do you go about doing so?

The answer is surprisingly easy. First, load the FIRST.PAS program as described earlier. Second, move the cursor to any character of `writeln`. Finally, press Ctrl-F1, and there you have it! Figure 1.17 shows the help window giving you more information about `writeln`. If you scroll down the text in the window you will see a short Turbo Pascal example on how to use `writeln`. The help window can be resized and moved, just like any other window. You can resize and rearrange your program window and the help window, so that the latter remains in view while you edit your program.

Fig. 1.17. A sample on-line Help window.

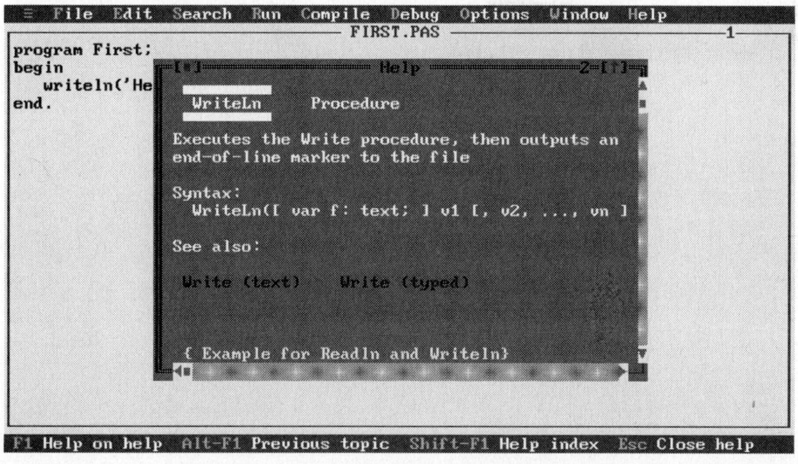

Multiple Windows

The Turbo Pascal 6.0 integrated development environment offers significant changes, for example, multiple text-based window support. You can now open more than one window to view the same file or different files. For example, you may want to display the same program in multiple windows (usually two) to use the information from one part to write statements in another part. When you open the same program in multiple windows and make a change to the program in one window, the programs in the other windows are automatically updated.

The first nine windows can be selected directly by pressing Alt-1 through Alt-9, respectively. Alt-0 pops up a list of active windows. Windows can be opened, closed, resized, moved, zoomed on, tiled, and cascaded. The one active window is marked by a highlighted white double frame; all other windows have a grey single frame.

You can switch quickly from one window to another by simply clicking on the new window with the mouse. Alternately, you can press F6 to select the next window. Using a mouse is highly recommended to maximize ease of navigation in the Turbo Pascal integrated development environment. You can, for example, quickly scroll through the viewed text by dragging the vertical scroll bar box with the mouse (while holding the left button mouse down).

Another change involves dialog boxes, which are special fixed windows that allow you to enter various kinds of input. Dialog boxes contain the following:

- Push buttons, such as the OK and Cancel buttons. To select a push button, click on it with the mouse, or press the Tab key followed by the Enter key.
- Input lines that allow you to enter data. Input lines often contain history boxes that are invoked by pressing the down-arrow button to the left of an input line. This pops up a small scrollable window that stores your most recent input. History boxes are a time-saver, because they allow you to select a previous input without retyping it.
- Radio buttons. These are special controls that allow you to select one of several options. You use the up and down arrows to select a radio button.
- Check boxes. These special controls enable you to select any applicable options. You use the up and down arrows to visit a check box. Use the space bar to toggle the mark, X, in the box.

Figure 1.18 shows multiple windows containing programs loaded from the \TP\DEMOS directory. This window layout required a sequence of file loading, window resizing, and window moving. Figure 1.18 is not a typical case; it is an extreme example to show the flexibility of the integrated environment of Turbo Pascal 6.0.

Fig. 1.18. *Programs loaded from the \TP\DEMOS directory.*

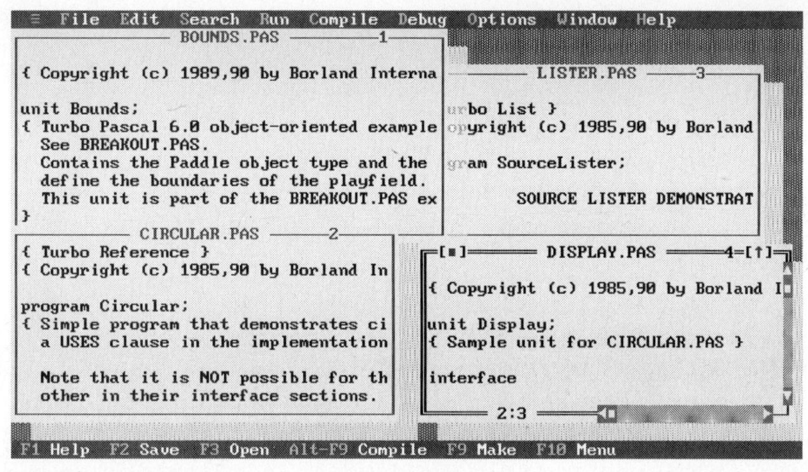

Summary

In this chapter, you learned everything you needed to know to take the Turbo Pascal compiler out of the package and

- ❑ Install Turbo Pascal on your PC
- ❑ Enter a program
- ❑ Edit a program
- ❑ Save a program
- ❑ Load a program
- ❑ Compile a program
- ❑ Execute a program in the integrated environment
- ❑ Execute a stand-alone program directly from DOS

- ❑ Obtain on-line reference information
- ❑ Stack multiple windows

This chapter also described the menu system of the Turbo Pascal integrated environment and familiarized you with the commands and options that you will begin to use routinely as you progress through the remainder of the book.

CHAPTER 2

Structure of a Turbo Pascal Program

This chapter introduces Pascal by presenting a fundamental overview that explains both the essential components and the overall structure of a program. At the end of the chapter, you look at a typical Turbo Pascal program.

If you are already familiar with Pascal, and especially if you are already familiar with the Turbo dialect, feel free to bypass the next few pages or skim through them. But if you have never written a Pascal program, this chapter is for you.

A word of advice before you continue; unless you try very, very hard, nothing you do in a Turbo Pascal program is likely to break your PC or damage any software. So feel free to try the examples, and do not worry about making errors. Soon you will be impressed with how protective and helpful Turbo can be. The most horrible situation you are likely to encounter is when your program "hangs" (in an infinite loop, for example). If this happens, just press the Alt, Ctrl, and Del keys simultaneously to reboot your PC. Remember that whatever you have not saved to disk will be lost—so save your work frequently!

For now, begin at the beginning.

What Is a Computer Language?

Think of a computer as a purely mechanical device—a pocket calculator with a program pushing the keys. (In many ways, a four-function pocket calculator is more sophisticated than the CPU of a personal computer.) A calculator is able to load, add, display, and store data by relying completely on its built-in circuitry. Pressing the plus key (+) triggers a sequence of events (adding the contents of the input buffer to main memory, displaying main memory, clearing the input buffer, and so on) comparable to what would be done by a computer performing a similar job.

Although the PC is capable of the same internal sequence of events as the calculator, its built-in functions, called *machine code*, are—individually, at least—far more primitive. Numbers can be input, added, stored, and displayed in several ways, and each method requires a complicated sequence of machine-code instructions to carry it out.

Rather than "reinvent the wheel" with each new program, computer languages such as Pascal collect these machine-code instruction sequences into standard routines. In Pascal, each one of these routines is called a *procedure* or a *function*, and each one has a name. If you look in the index of the *Library Reference*, you will see that Turbo Pascal has over 200 of them, with names such as `ClrScr`, `Write`, and `Sound`. These names are *standard*, which means that whenever one of these names appears in a program, the compiler automatically assumes that your intent was to execute the machine code in the underlying procedure or function.

A procedure is called by stating the name of the procedure followed by its parameters, if any, enclosed in parentheses. A function is called just as if the function name (along with its parameters, if any) were a variable.

A Note on Procedures and Functions
Procedures and functions are essentially identical; in fact, most functions can be rewritten in the more general form of a procedure. So for now, just think of them as collections of machine code.

What Is a Compiler?

A *compiler* is a program that takes program statements written in a computer language and rephrases them into instructions that the PC's microprocessor understands. The Borland Turbo Pascal compiler translates the lines of a Pascal program into the machine-readable code of the 8086-family microprocessor. It does this primarily by recognizing the presence of predefined procedure and function names and executing the packets of machine code they represent. A program—through a compiler—causes a computer to perform actions.

By using these standard machine-language building blocks and enforcing some simple rules of grammar, a compiler can effectively and efficiently convert a human-oriented, high-level language such as Pascal to machine-readable, executable code.

Language Components

Before you can begin the formal study of any language—whether it is a language you already know, such as English, or a foreign language such as French, German, or Farsi, or a computer language such as Pascal—you must define its components.

In a spoken language, the components consist of the ordinary parts of speech such as nouns, verbs, and prepositions. A computer language's "parts of speech" are reserved words, identifiers, tokens, separators, comments, numbers, symbols, characters, and strings.

Reserved Words

In Chapter 1, the FIRST program illustrated how Turbo Pascal's integrated environment can be used. You saw how the words `program`, `begin`, and `end` have special meaning in Pascal. These words belong to a family of *reserved words* that provide structure and context in a Pascal program.

6.0

The complete list of reserved words is as follows:

```
and            end              nil          shr
array          file             not          string
asm            for              object       then
begin          function         of           to
case           goto             or           type
const          if               packed       unit
constructor    implementation   procedure    until
destructor     in               program      uses
div            inline           record       var
do             interface        repeat       while
downto         label            set          with
else           mod              shl          xor
```

The following is a list of Turbo Pascal's standard directives. In versions prior to 6.0, these directives were reserved words (except `private`, which is introduced in Version 6.0). These standard directives differ from reserved keywords in the fact that you can redefine them, although this is highly unadvisable.

```
absolute       far              interrupt    private
assembler      forward          near         virtual
external
```

Note that `private` is a reserved word only in objects.

Each reserved word has a special meaning and cannot be used for any other purpose. Some, such as `begin` and `end`, you will use frequently. Others, unless you run the examples in this book, you will probably never see again.

Always remember that although *you* might be able to see the entire program on your screen, the compiler is "blind." You can probably determine the intent of a section of code just by looking at it, but the compiler must process your program one word at a time. Some of the most interesting error conditions (and error messages) appear when a reserved word is used incorrectly on one line, but the effect of the error is not seen until several lines later.

Identifiers

An *identifier* is any name you assign in your program. An identifier denotes the program name as well as any units, labels, constants, variables, procedures, or functions the program defines. Each identifier can have only one meaning in a program.

An identifier can consist of any number of continuous letters, digits, and underscores, but the first character must be a letter or an underscore. Uppercase and lowercase letters are considered identical; therefore, all of the following names are considered the same word:

```
PrintMessage
priNTmessaGE
printMessage
PRINTMESSAGE
```

Turbo Pascal uses only the first 63 characters. If, for example, you use an identifier with 100 characters, the last 37 are ignored. Alternatively, if the first 63 characters of one identifier match the first 63 characters of another, you get a duplicate identifier error.

Reserved words cannot be used as identifiers. If a reserved word is used inappropriately, strange error messages are likely to result.

Valid identifiers include the following:

```
X                    FlightNumber
Passenger_Name       Gate17
Seat4_Aisle8         Seven
```

Invalid identifiers include the following:

`2x4BoardFeet`	(Cannot begin with a digit)
`Type-3A_Conduit`	(Hyphen is an illegal character)
`Unit`	(Cannot use a reserved word)

Through your choice of identifiers you can develop highly readable, self-documenting programs. The two programs shown in listing 2.1 are functionally equivalent, but you can see for yourself which one is easier to understand:

Listing 2.1

```
program Q;                    program TestForRightTriangle;
var                           var
   x,                            SideA,
   y,                            SideB,
   z   : real;                   Hypotenuse : real;
```

continues

Listing 2.1 continued

<pre>begin
   x := 12.0;
   y := 5.0;
   z := 13.0;
   if z =
      Sqrt(x*x+ y*y) then
         writeln('Right');
end.</pre>
	<pre>begin
	   SideA := 12.0;
	   SideB := 5.0;
	   Hypotenuse := 13.0;
	   if Hypotenuse =
	      Sqrt(SideA*SideA+ SideB*SideB) then
	         writeln('Right');
	end.</pre>

Characters

A *character* is any one of the 256 standard and extended ASCII characters. You can enter a character in any of three ways:

1. You can simply type its normal symbol; for example, the letter *A*.
2. You can hold down the Alt key and enter the ASCII value of the character from the numeric keypad to the right of the keyboard. (A complete list of ASCII characters is in table 3.4.) If you have never done this before, give it a try. The letter *A* is ASCII 65; hold down the Alt key, enter **65** on the numeric keypad, and release the Alt key. The letter *A* will appear. This is the usual means for entering graphics and accent marks (sometimes called *extended* characters) that do not appear on your keyboard.
3. You can precede the ASCII value (an integer in the range 0 through 255) with the # symbol. Therefore, the letter *A* can be written as #65. This has limited appeal when you enter the normal symbols on a keyboard, but it greatly eases the difficulty of entering special (sometimes called *unprintable*) characters. For example, the character pair #7 represents the single character corresponding to the bell sound. Similarly, #10 is a line feed, #12 is a form feed, and #13 is a carriage return; all are treated by the compiler as single ASCII characters.

Strings

A *string* is a sequence of zero or more ASCII characters contained in a single program line and enclosed in apostrophes (single quotation marks). A string with no characters between the apostrophes is called a *null string*. If you want an apostrophe within a string, you must write it twice.

Examples of valid strings are

```
'Enter your selection: '
'File wasn''t found. Program terminated.'
'Didn''t receive valid response;  can''t continue!'
'The formula used was y = 4x + 7.'
```

Most of the time, strings consist of letters and numbers, but you may include any ASCII character. If you want to include one of the unprintable or extended characters, place it outside any apostrophes; if the control character is in the middle of a string, the string must be temporarily closed and then reopened.

Some character string examples follow:

```
'Hello, world.'
'This part of the string is above'#13#10'this part of
    the string'
'This is on the page before'#12'this page'
```

Remember that #13#10 is the ASCII code for a carriage return and line feed and that #12 is the ASCII code for a form feed.

Numbers

Numbers, as you might expect, consist of any valid combination of digits, plus and minus signs, and decimal points. Commas may not be used.

Numbers can be broadly grouped as real or integer. Quite simply, a real number contains a decimal point; an integer does not.

Any decimal point used in a real number must be preceded by a digit. If, for example, you wrote the number 0.6 as .6, the compiler may interpret the decimal point as a period and assume (prematurely) that you want the program to end. At best, Turbo will display an error message.

Real numbers may be written in scientific notation using the letter *E* (or *e*) to designate "times 10 to the power of." Table 2.1 shows the relationships.

Hexadecimal numbers are written with a leading dollar sign. Therefore, $10 equals 16 decimal, but 10 equals 10. The letters *A*, *B*, *C*, *D*, *E*, and *F* (or *a*, *b*, *c*, *d*, *e*, and *f*) designate decimal 10, 11, 12, 13, 14, and 15, respectively. For example, $C equals 12, $FF equals 255, and $a0 equals 160. Turbo Pascal limits the use of hexadecimal numbers to integers.

Table 2.1. Real-Number Formats in Turbo Pascal

In Turbo Pascal	*In scientific notation*	*In normal usage*
3.4E7	3.4×10^{7}	34,000,000
3.4E–7	3.4×10^{-7}	.00000034
–7.1E2	-7.1×10^{2}	–710

Symbols

Pascal uses special symbols in addition to letters and digits. The following symbols have special meanings:

`=`	Used in type and constant declarations
`( )`	Grouping symbols for complex expressions; used also for subroutine headings and calls and for declaring enumeration types
`$`	Used before a number to indicate that the number is hexadecimal
`#`	Used before a number to indicate that the number is to be interpreted as the ASCII value of the number
`;`	Used to separate statements and end declarations
`:=`	Assignment symbol
`:`	Used in variable declarations, labels, case statements, function headings, and formatting output
`'`	Single quotation mark—used with quoted and constant strings
`.`	Period—used as a decimal point to end programs and units and to access the fields of a record
`,`	Comma—used to separate identifiers and parameters
`..`	Double period—subrange; also used in array subscript declaration
`^`	Used to denote a pointer
`(. .)` or `[ ]`	Brackets for arrays or sets
`(* *)` or `{ }`	Comment delimiters

The following symbols are used as arithmetic operators. Their operation is discussed in greater detail in Chapter 4, "Expressions, Operands, and Operators."

*	Multiplication/set intersection
+	Addition/concatenation/set union
-	Subtraction/set difference/unary negate
/	Real division
<	Less than
<=	Less than or equal to/set inclusion
< >	Not equal to
=	Equal to
>	Greater than
>=	Greater than or equal to/set inclusion
@	Address

All other symbols, including foreign and graphics characters, are *undefined* and can appear in a Turbo Pascal program only in a string.

Tokens and Separators

Each sequence of characters that has a common meaning is called a *token*. For example, reserved words, numbers, strings, and symbols are all considered tokens. An individual token can be clearly identified because two adjacent tokens must be divided by at least one *separator*, which consists of a space or a comment. Note that as far as Pascal is concerned, each of the following is considered a space:

Space	(#32)
Carriage return	(#13)
Line feed	(#10)
Form feed	(#12)
Tab	(#09)

These are often referred to as *white space* characters.

Separators are required between tokens but may not occur within them. (Of course, within a string, a space is treated as the space character itself and not as a separator.) At least one separator must be between two tokens, but you may use any number of separators. In other words, any number of spaces is regarded by the compiler as a single separator.

With such a broad definition, the format of a Pascal program is quite flexible. For example, a carriage return is regarded as a separator, so statements and declarations may extend over several lines, and the spacing on a single line (indentations, for example) is left to the programmer. The FIRST program from the preceding chapter could have been written as:

```
program First; begin writeln( 'Hello, again!' ) end.
```

Viewed in this way, you can see how the program corresponds to the imperative sentence, *"Write 'Hello, Again!' on the screen!"* But you can see also how line spacing and indentation can play important roles in adding clarity to your work. You will be surprised at how quickly you adopt a legible style.

Comments

A *comment* is a special form of a separator that defines an area of text ignored by the compiler. Comments are principally used for program documentation. To separate each comment from the rest of the program, enclose the comment in braces:

```
{ This is a comment }
```

or in asterisk-parenthesis pairs:

```
(* This is a comment *)
```

The compiler treats the entire comment like a single space. A comment can appear anywhere in the program or not at all. Everything inside a comment is ignored unless a dollar sign ($) is placed in its first position. This special form of a comment is called a directive and is discussed in the "Compiler Directives" reference section.

One comment can appear in another comment (a process called *nesting*) only if each of the comments uses a different set of end symbols. For example, the following lines are a single comment:

```
(* Temporarily commenting out the next two lines
PageNumber := PageNumber + 1;    { Turn the page }
LineNumber := 0;                 { Start at first line }
*)
```

The `(*` opening symbol alerts the compiler to search for the `*)` closing symbol; the braces are ignored.

The Organization of a Pascal Program

A computer program consists fundamentally of action-oriented instructions, commonly called *code*, and the data manipulated by these instructions. Together, program data and code (declarations and statements) are commonly called the *program block*. Everything you need to express an idea in a computer language can be found in a block.

In fact, every action-oriented Pascal component (that is, every program, unit, procedure, and function) contains its own block. To keep them separate, you begin each block with a separate header.

Units, procedures, and functions are described in later chapters. For now, you will concentrate on the program itself.

Pascal's Parts of Speech

If you give someone the English language commands "Walk!" and "Lift!" the responses are likely to be "Where?" and "What?" A more complicated command such as "Travel!" is likely to be answered with "Where, when, and how?"

Even though a computer language is action oriented, action-oriented statements are not sufficient for communicating with a computer any more than verbs are sufficient for communicating in a spoken language. In English, people rely on nouns to serve as the subjects and the objects upon which the action of a verb is performed. In Pascal, you use data.

The analogy between English and Pascal is not as forced as you might think. Pascal was originally intended to be used primarily for teaching students how to program. Consequently, the original vision of Pascal was an elegantly simple set of English-like programming building blocks from which progressively more complicated programs could be constructed. The Pascal programming language is, in essence, a set of rules for writing imperative sentences.

The Parts of a Pascal Program

For a Pascal program, the *header* is the program declaration and the *block* is the program itself. Therefore, every Pascal program consists of the same three major components:

1. The *header*, consisting of the reserved word `program` followed by the program name.
2. The *data* to be manipulated by the instructions in the program, as defined in label, constant, type, and variable declarations. You place data immediately after the header but before the first program code statement.
3. Program *code* statements describing the actions to be performed. Any procedures or functions defined by the program are placed at the start of the code area. Code statements follow and are enclosed by the reserved words `begin` and `end`.

You end every program with a period.

General Format

The general format of a Pascal program is as follows:

```
program name;
   { Data declarations }
begin
   { Code statements }
end.
```

The header, data declarations, and code statements are optional. Because it is considered good programming style to include a header in your programs, however, all programs in this book follow that convention. The following three lines:

```
program Trivial;
begin
end.
```

form a legitimate (although incredibly boring) program. You can enter it into the compiler, and actually (yawn) run it. Nevertheless, it does demonstrate how three reserved words (`program`, `begin`, and `end`) separate the regions where data and code belong.

A Program Example

The following program, LAYOUT (listing 2.2), demonstrates the three-part structure of a program in greater detail.

Listing 2.2

```
{*** Header ***}    program Layout;
{**************}    label   Start;
{     Data     }    const   Secret = 'aardvark';
{ Declarations }    type    Format = string[ 8 ];
{**************}    var     Response : Format;
{**************}    begin
{              }       Start:   write( 'Make a guess: ' );
{     Code     }                readln( Response );
{  Statements  }                if Response <> Secret then goto Start;
{              }                writeln( 'Correct!!' );
{**************}    end.
```

The program asks the user to guess the name of an animal. (The correct answer is *aardvark*. Do not tell anyone.) The program continues until the user is successful. You can end the program early by pressing Ctrl-Break.

The header consists of the reserved word `program` followed by `Layout`, the program's name.

The data section consists of four declarations:

1. The label, `Start`, although it is used in the code section, just marks a location rather than performs an action or stores some information.

2. The constant, `Secret`, keeps the same value throughout the operation of the program.

3. The type, `Format`, defines the structure of variables. Here, the program defines an 8-character string.

4. The variable, `Response`, stores each guess and changes its contents every time a guess is entered. `Response` is defined to have the properties identified as `Format`. In other words, `Response` is defined to consist of an 8-character string.

The code section consists of four lines:

1. A `write` statement tells the user to make a guess. The label can be used to reference this line throughout the remainder of the program; other than that, `Start` has no effect on program execution.

2. A `readln` (pronounced "read line") statement accepts data input from the keyboard. Press the Enter key after each guess.

3. An `if...then` statement tests a condition and performs an action based on the result of that test. Here, the program tests whether the user answer, `Response`, is equal to the correct answer, `Secret`. If the two do not match (the `< >` stands for an inequality), the `goto Start` instruction redirects the flow of the program back to the line following the label `Start`.

4. A `writeln` (pronounced "write line") statement congratulates the user when the correct animal name is entered. Notice that because of the preceding `if...then` statement, the `writeln` statement is reached only if the user's answer, `Response`, matches the correct answer, `Secret`.

When a program runs, the computer reserves storage (memory space) according to the contents of the data declaration section. Then the program executes the first instruction following the `begin` statement. After that statement is finished executing, the statement on the next line is executed. After that statement is finished executing, the statement on the next line is executed, and so on. The program continues executing statements line-by-line until the final period is reached.

In the LAYOUT program, storage space is reserved for only two data items: `Secret` and `Response`. The label `Start` does not reside in memory; it simply marks a location in memory. This location is needed only by the compiler to generate the machine code to perform the `goto` statement; because the location is incorporated in the machine code itself, `Start` can be discarded when the program executes. Similarly, the `Format` type simply tells the compiler how to reserve space for the `Response` variable (as an 8-character string); after the compiler knows the style to use, `Format` is no longer needed.

After the program arranges storage for `Secret` and `Response`, control is passed to the statement following `begin`. The `Make a guess` message is displayed, the user's response is read, and the comparison is performed. Here, the flow of the program can be changed. If an incorrect guess is entered, the `if...then` test allows the `goto` statement to transfer program flow to the `Start` line. The flow of the program continues sequentially only when the correct response is entered.

Program Data Declarations

Although program declarations can occur in any sequence, they usually appear in the following order:

- Labels
- Constants
- Types
- Variables

The only restriction is that all identifiers must be defined before being used. This section discusses each of these declarations in more detail.

Label Declarations

In the BASIC language that came with your PC, every line in every program begins with a number. When you want to transfer control to another line (or when you want to bypass several lines), you jump to the new line using a `goto` statement.

Instead of a line number, Pascal uses a *label* to mark a location within a block of program code. Labels are declared with the reserved word `label` followed by the desired identifiers. In standard Pascal, each identifier may consist of a whole number in the range 0 through 9999.

Because the only practical application of labels is as the target of `goto` statements and because integers are less user friendly than ordinary alphanumeric identifiers, this restriction was supposed to be a deterrent to the use of `goto`. It did not work. The `goto` statement has remained (perhaps unfortunately) extremely popular. In fact, Turbo Pascal allows labels to be normal alphanumeric identifier names. If several labels are declared, each pair must be separated with a comma. The final label must be followed by a semicolon.

When a label is used in a program, the `label` identifier must be on the first line. Each label must be immediately followed by a colon.

In the LABELER program (listing 2.3), the label `Start` is used to mark the beginning of a loop.

Listing 2.3

```
program Labeler;
label
   Start;
var
   Counter : byte;
begin
            Counter := 0;
            Writeln( 'The loop is now beginning.' );
   Start:   Counter := Counter + 1;
            Writeln( 'This is line ', Counter );
            if Counter < 10 then Goto Start;
            Writeln( 'Done' );
end.
```

Labels may be inserted in your program also to provide additional comments.

Constant Definitions

A *constant* is an identifier that—once defined—has a single, unchangeable meaning.

The constant declaration section begins with the reserved word `const`. Each individual constant is declared as an identifier, followed by an equal sign, the value to be assigned to the identifier, and a semicolon.

In a program statement, constants and variables are treated equivalently, except constants cannot be redefined. Wherever the compiler detects a constant identifier, however, it treats the line exactly as if it were written with the value itself. For example, in the following:

```
const
   MinSize = 1;
   MaxSize = 20;
var
   Students : array [ MinSize..MaxSize ] of word;
   i : byte;
begin
   .
   .
   .
   for i := MinSize to MaxSize do
      Writeln( Students[ i ] );
```

the size of the array is interpreted by the compiler as `[ 1..20 ]` just as if the digits had appeared in place of the constant identifiers. In a similar way, the identifiers used in the `for...do` loop allow it to range from 1 through 20.

Constant Expressions

Turbo Pascal further allows *constant expressions* to be used in the place of a single constant. In the following lines:

```
const
   Radius        = 12;
   Diameter      = 2 * Radius;
   Circumference = 3.14159 * Diameter;
```

Turbo treats both the `Diameter` and `Circumference` identifiers as constants even though their values were derived from the value of `Radius`.

Remember that Turbo is a one-pass compiler. Anything appearing in a constant expression must be completely defined by the time the expression is encountered. Consequently, expressions cannot contain references to variables, typed constants, function calls, or the address operator (`@`). The following standard functions, however, may be used (these functions are defined in later chapters):

```
Abs       Lo       Ptr       Swap
Chr       Odd      Round     Trunc
Hi        Ord      SizeOf
Length    Pred     Succ
```

With the exception of these few restrictions, constant expressions operate just like the normal expressions described in Chapter 4, "Expressions, Operands, and Operators."

Several uses of constant expressions can be seen in the following extract of a report writing program:

```
const
   Title               = 'Turbo Programming Notes';
   TopLineOfPrint      = 6;
   BottomLineOfPrint   = 60;
   LeftMargin          = 10;
   RightMargin         = 75;
   PageLength          = BottomLineOfPrint - TopLineOfPrint + 1;
```

```
PageWidth          = RightMargin - LeftMargin + 1;
CharactersPerPage  = PageLength * PageWidth;
FormFeed           = Chr(12);
TopLine            = FormFeed + Title;
PositionOfTopLine  = ((PageWidth - Length(Title)) div 2) + LeftMargin;
```

Constant expressions are evaluated only once, when the program is first compiled. They do not detract from either the execution speed or the size of the final program. Yet, as you can see in the example, they can considerably simplify the process of program development.

Typed Constants

Turbo Pascal supports the use of *typed constants*, which enable you to assign to a variable not only an initial value, but also a type.

Typed constants are declared in the constant section. Despite this fact (and despite their unfortunate name), typed constants are really variables. Each typed constant is written in the form: identifier, colon, type, equal sign, and initial value.

The following demonstrates their use:

```
const
   NumberOfFlights : integer = 4;
   MatrixRows      : byte    = 6;
```

Both `NumberOfFlights` and `MatrixRows` can be redefined whenever you want.

Type Definitions

Type is the property of a Pascal variable that defines the size of the storage it requires, the range of values it can be assigned, and the operators that can act on it. After a type has been declared for a variable, the compiler will ensure that the variable is used appropriately; for example, you will not be allowed to assign a string to a variable defined as an integer.

A type declaration section begins with the reserved word `type`. Each individual type is written in the form of an identifier, followed by an equal sign, a description of the type, and a semicolon.

Table 2.2 lists Turbo Pascal's broad range of predefined data types that can be used on individual variables. The basic Pascal data types are numbers, which may be either real or integer; logical Boolean values, which may be either `True` or `False`; and ASCII characters, called *char* when used singly and *string* when multiple characters are used. More complicated data types, such as array, object, record, and set, are also available. Integer and real types are further divided into categories depending on the size and allowable range of the data.

***Table 2.2.** Turbo Pascal Standard Data Types*

Type	*Description*
`Boolean`	`True` or `False`
	Whole Numbers:
`byte`	0 . . . +255
`integer`	–32,768 . . . +32,767
`longint`	–2,147,483,648 . . . +2,147,483,647
`shortint`	–128 . . . +127
`word`	0 . . . +65,535
	Real Numbers:
`real`	2.9×10^{-39} . . . 1.7×10^{38}
`single`	1.5×10^{-45} . . . 3.4×10^{38}
`double`	5.0×10^{-324} . . . 1.7×10^{308}
`extended`	3.4×10^{-4932} . . . 1.1×10^{4932}
`comp`	$-2^{63}+1$ . . . $2^{63}-1$
`char`	Any one of the ASCII characters.
`string`	A sequence of up to 255 ASCII characters. If a size is not specified, a default of 255 is used.
`pointer`	A location in memory rather than the value itself.

The `Boolean`, `char`, and five whole-number types are referred to as *ordinal* types.

These predefined types are most often used in the variable declaration section when a simple variable is first defined. The type declaration section is used to define more complicated data structures based on the specific needs of the program. These user-defined types always use the standard types as building blocks.

Through the use of user-defined data types, shown in table 2.3, your Turbo Pascal programs can manipulate sophisticated data structures. For example, in the following section of code, the `StudentArray` type defines an array of records, one field of which consists of a user-defined set.

```
type
   Specialties   = ( Math, Physics, English, History );
   StudentData   = record
                      StudentName : string[ 20 ];
                      Major       : Specialties;
                      Graduation  : word;
                   end;
   StudentArray = array [ 1..25 ] of StudentData;
```

Table 2.3. Turbo Pascal User-Defined Data Types

Type	*Description*
enumerated	A set of values
subrange	A subset of another type
`array`	A repeating data structure
`set`	A collection of values
`file`	A data type that stores data on an auxiliary storage device
`record`	A combination of variables of other types

Data types are discussed in greater detail in Chapter 3, "Data and Data Types."

Variable Declarations

A variable declaration section begins with the reserved word `var`. Each individual variable is written in the form of an identifier, followed by a colon, the type of the variable, and a semicolon. A variable may be of any standard or user-defined type.

Examples of variable declarations include the following:

```
var
   i            : byte;
   ProductKey   : string[ 12 ];
   SalesHistory : array [ 1..12 ] of real;
```

Further illustrations of variable declarations can be found in other examples in this book.

Program Code Statements

Program code is defined by executable statements that specify the actions to be taken by the program. Statements are the active data movement and manipulation commands. From their content, the compiler determines the machine instructions to be generated. This section discusses Pascal statements in more detail.

Simple and Compound Statements

Wherever Pascal allows a statement to be used, it may be either simple or compound. A simple statement is a single command such as an assignment, `case`, `for...do`, or `repeat...until` statement. A compound statement consists of the reserved words `begin` and `end`, between which any number of other valid statements may be located. As far as the compiler is concerned, the `begin` and `end` pair define a single statement.

For example, the standard form of an `if...then...else` statement is as follows:

```
if <condition> then
   statement
else
   statement;
```

Through the use of the reserved words `begin` and `end`, you can perform several statements in the place of one, as shown in the following example:

```
if QuantitySold > 1000 then
   begin
      writeln( 'Great job!  You are getting a bonus!' );
      Commission := QuantitySold * 5.00;
```

```
    end
else
    begin
        writeln( 'You didn''t hit your quota. Try harder!' );
        Commission := 0;
    end;
```

The Assignment Statement

The assignment statement, the most fundamental statement in Pascal, replaces the contents of a variable. The identifier of the variable to be changed is stated first, followed by the assignment operator (:=), then followed by the new value. The new value can be either explicitly defined, as in:

```
Quantity := 45;                 { Assignment of a number }
Warning  := 'File not found';   { Assignment of a string }
SaveData := Y;                  { Assignment of a variable }
```

or stated as an expression (which may contain functions) from which the value can be derived, as in:

```
X := 45 div 9;                { Assignment of an expression }
Y := 3 * X = 6;               { Assignment of a Boolean }
Z := Sqrt( Sqr(X) + Sqr(Y) ); { Assignment of a function }
```

The *Case* Statement

A `case` statement selects one action out of several depending on the result of a single test. The expression to be tested is called the *selector* and each option is called a *case constant*. If the selector does not match any of the case constants, the statement identified with the word `else` is executed. You must end each `case` statement with an `end`. The `else` statement is optional; if it is not present and no case constant matches the selector, the compiler simply moves along to the first statement that follows the `end`.

If the selector expression is a number, it must evaluate to a non-negative ordinal value in the range 0 through +65,535. Real numbers and strings cannot be used as selectors, but `char`, `Boolean`, and `set` types are all valid selector options.

The `case` statements are among the most useful in Pascal. Their operation can be demonstrated with the following examples:

```
case Answer of
   'Y' : DoTheTask;
   'N' : CancelFutureWork;
   else  ShowHelpMessage;
end;
case Month of
   Jan..Mar : writeln( 'Winter' );
   Apr..Jun : writeln( 'Spring' );
   Jul..Sep : writeln( 'Summer' );
   Oct..Dec : writeln( 'Fall' );
end;
case MenuOption1 of
   1 : DoTask1;
   2 : DoTask2;
   3 : case MenuOption2 of
          1 : DoTask3A;
          2 : DoTask3B;
       end;
   4 : DoTask4;
 else   DemandRetype;
end;
```

The `case` statement is functionally equivalent to a long series of potentially confusing `if...then...else` statements.

The *For...To/Downto...Do* Statement

The `for` statement executes a statement a predetermined number of times. A control variable assumes a different sequential value during each pass.

A `for` statement is extremely efficient because—unlike a `while` or `repeat` loop—you do not need to perform a condition test on each pass, and the code that changes the control variable is highly optimized.

There are two forms of `for` statements. In the first, the control variable increases in its sequence. In the second, the control variable decreases with each pass. The reserved word `to` indicates an increase, and `downto` indicates a decrease, as follows:

```
for i := 'a' to 'z' do write( i );       { Outputs the alphabet }
for i := 'z' downto 'a' do write( i );  { Reverses the alphabet }
```

The control variable must be ordinal and must have been defined in the block in which the `for` statement is used.

The `for` statement is frequently the most convenient means of manipulating arrays. For example, the following code calculates the result of multiplying an $m \times n$ matrix `A` and an $n \times p$ matrix `B`. The product, `C`, is an $m \times p$ matrix.

```
for i := 1 to m do
    for j := 1 to p do begin
        C[i,j] := 0;
        for k := 1 to n do
            C[i,j] := C[i,j] + A[i,k]*B[k,j];
    end;
```

The initial and final values of the loop are determined as soon as the `for` statement begins. They cannot be affected by any actions ***within*** the statement being executed. Therefore, in the code:

```
j := 5;
for i := 1 to j do
    begin
        j := j + 8;
        writeln( i );
    end;
```

the `writeln` statement is executed only five times, even though the variable `j` changes with each pass.

The *Goto* Statement

A `goto` statement, written in the form

```
goto LabeledLine;
```

changes the flow of program execution by jumping to the statement immediately following the referenced label, which must be located in the same block as the `goto`.

The LABEL2 program (listing 2.4) shows how a label can be defined in an `if...then` statement. When executed, LABEL2 displays a single `Hello` message.

Listing 2.4

```
program Label2;
label
   Intrude;
var
   i : integer;
begin
            i := 23;
            if i = 0 then
   Intrude:     begin
                   write( 'Hello' );
                   i := 100;
                end;
            if i <> 100 then
               goto Intrude;
end.
```

The `goto` statement is deceptively simple to use. Nevertheless, you should avoid it. Other statements—most notably the `while...do` and `repeat...until` loops—can always be used instead and with greater reliability, readability, and control. The `goto` statement is not used in the remainder of this book.

The *If...Then...Else* Statement

The `if...then` statement tests a condition; if the condition is `True`, a statement is executed. For example:

```
if RecordCount > 100 then
   Write( 'It''s time to save your file!' );
```

If you want an action to occur when the condition is `True` and some other action to occur when the condition is `False`, you can use the `else` option to specify the alternate action, as in:

```
if FileExists then
   OpenTheFile
else
   CreateTheFile;
```

Some extremely useful (although extremely complicated) structures arise when the statement is itself another `if...then...else`. For example:

```
if Salary < 20000 then
   HourlyRate := HourlyRate + 0.75    { Flat rate }
else
   if Salary < 40000 then
      HourlyRate := HourlyRate * 1.08
   else
      HourlyRate := HourlyRate * 1.05;
```

The compiler assumes that each `else` is associated with the last unmatched `if`. You should indent your code to reflect the pairing.

The *Repeat...Until* Statement

A `repeat` statement defines the beginning of a series of statements that are executed at least once and continue to be executed `until` a certain condition is met.

For example, in the following code:

```
Counter := 10;
repeat
   writeln( 'Hello' );
   Counter := Counter - 1;
until Counter < 5;
```

the message `Hello` is displayed six times.

Because the statements between `repeat` and `until` must execute before the test is made, `repeat` loops are most useful to ensure that a certain sequence of code will continue to repeat until some condition is `True`.

```
repeat
   write( 'Enter the time: ' );
   readln( Hour );
until Hour in [ 0..24 ];
```

The *While...Do* Statement

The `while` statement executes another statement, identified by the prefix `do`, as long as a specified condition is `True`. Unlike the `repeat...until` loop, the `while` statement tests the condition *before* the loop is executed. Examples of the `while...do` loop include the following:

```
while not Eof( DataFile ) do begin  { Test for end of file }
   Statement1;
   Statement2;
   Statement3;
end;
while index > 0 do
   begin
      TargetString[ index ] := SourceString[ index ];
      index := index - 1;
   end;
```

The *With* Statement

A `with` statement can reference the fields of a record without specifying the record name every time. For example, given the following declarations:

```
type
   TravelData    = record
                      Name         : string;
                      Flight       : word;
                      TicketPrice  : real;
                   end;
var
   Passenger : TravelData;
```

the following sets of code are identical:

```
begin
   Passenger.Name        := 'Smith';
   Passenger.Flight      := 703;
   Passenger.TicketPrice := 324.65;
end;
```

```
with Passenger do
begin
   Name        := 'Smith';
   Flight      := 703;
   TicketPrice := 324.65;
end;
```

A `with` statement can also reference object fields and methods. This feature is discussed further in Chapter 20, "Object-Oriented Programming."

Procedures and Functions

A *procedure* is a subroutine that results in a series of actions directed toward a single purpose. A *function* is a subroutine specifically designed to return a single value; accordingly, functions are called only in expressions. Certain procedures and functions are of such widespread importance that they are provided as standard services in Pascal. As such, they need not be defined before they are invoked. For example, `writeln` and `readln` are standard procedures; `Sqr` and `Sqrt` are standard functions. The complete list of over 200 standard procedures and functions is in the *Library Reference*.

When these standard procedures and functions are not adequate for the task at hand, you can define a customized subroutine using a procedure declaration or a function declaration. The new subroutine can then be invoked in the same way that the standard routines are invoked.

These user-defined procedures and functions have the same basic structure as the program itself—a header followed by a block. Each procedure and function can have its own label, constant, type, and variable declarations. These are said to be *local* to the procedure. They remain active and can be accessed only in the procedure; they disappear when the procedure has finished executing.

Within a procedure or function, a block appears just as if it were a main program. It begins with the reserved word `begin`, contains a number of statements to be executed, and closes with the reserved word `end`. Procedures and functions, however, end with a semicolon rather than a period.

The PFDEMO program (listing 2.5) illustrates how a procedure and function can be used. The program produces a simple 5 × 5 addition table. The `DoHeadings` procedure prepares the table headings. The `Total` function performs the individual additions. `Total` and `DoHeadings` must be positioned after all the program data has been declared but before the first `begin` statement in the main body of the program.

Listing 2.5

```
program PFdemo;
var
   Value1, Value2 : byte;
function Total : byte;
begin
   Total := Value1 + Value2;
end;
```

```
procedure DoHeadings;
begin
   writeln( 'Addition Table' );
   writeln( '==============' );
   writeln;
   writeln( '         1    2    3    4    5' );
   writeln( '-------------------------------' );
end;
begin
   DoHeadings;
   for Value1 := 1 to 5 do begin
      write( '   ', Value1, '|' );
      for Value2 := 1 to 5 do
         write( '    ', Total );
      writeln;
   end;
end.
```

When PFDEMO executes, it produces the following addition table:

```
          1        2         3         4         5
--------------------------------------------------------
  1|      2        3         4         5         6
  2|      3        4         5         6         7
  3|      4        5         6         7         8
  4|      5        6         7         8         9
  5|      6        7         8         9        10
```

In the main body of the program, the `DoHeadings` procedure is treated just like a standard procedure, and the `Total` function is treated just like a standard function. A complete discussion of procedures and functions can be found in Chapter 5, "Procedures and Functions." For now, you need to be comfortable with only their basic structure.

Summary

In this chapter, you learned about the individual components of the Turbo Pascal language, and you saw how they combine to form a complete program:

- ❏ A reserved word has a unique and special meaning related to program structure and control.

- An identifier is any user-defined name.
- A character is any one of the ASCII characters.
- A string is a sequence of zero or more ASCII characters.
- A number consists of any valid combination of digits, plus and minus signs, and decimal points.
- A comment is an area of text that is completely ignored by the compiler.

You learned the meanings of the special symbols used by Turbo Pascal.

You learned that a Turbo Pascal program is structured in three major sections:

- The header consists of the reserved word `program` followed by the program name.
- Program data consists of the items of information that will be manipulated by the instructions in the program.
- Program code statements describe the actions to be performed.

You learned about the major categories of data:

- A label is used to mark a location in a program.
- A constant is an identifier that has a single, unchangeable meaning.
- Typed constants enable you to assign an initial value to a variable.
- A variable is information that can change during the course of the program.

You learned how to use the statements available in a Turbo Pascal program:

- The assignment statement replaces the value of a variable.
- `Case` selects one statement to be executed out of a list of many.
- `For` executes a statement repeatedly, and a sequence of values is assigned to a control variable.
- `Goto` transfers the flow of the program.
- `If` tests a condition and performs actions based on the result.
- `Repeat` repeats a series of statements one or more times.
- `While` repeats a series of statements zero or more times.

- `With` allows the fields of a record to be referenced without having to identify the record name with each use.

You learned that all statements appearing between the reserved words `begin` and `end` are treated as a single statement.

You learned that statements can be combined into units called procedures and functions.

- A procedure is a subroutine that results in series of actions directed toward a single purpose.
- A function is a subroutine specifically designed to return a single value.

CHAPTER 3

Data and Data Types

In everyday life, people tend (for better or worse) to assign categories for everything they see and every action they perform. These categories are what give the subject—be it an object or an event—its identity and character. The journalist's technique of "Who, What, Where, When, Why, and How" is an example of categories that can be used to gather, structure, and present information quickly, efficiently, and eloquently. People say that they have the facts about something when the most important categories have been objectively identified and accurately evaluated.

Data consists of the facts that you use to solve a specific problem. Data is usually expressed as numbers, characters, or conditions (true or false, for example). The different categories of data are called data *types*. Data items might include *red*, *42*, and *Ralph*; the corresponding data types might be *color*, *Hours_Worked*, and *First_Name*.

Knowing the data type helps you determine the validity of an individual data item. For example, hours worked is probably not a negative number, and a first name is probably something containing letters.

Similarly, the data type defines the set of actions that can be performed with the data. It makes no sense to take the square root of a first name, and it makes no sense to capitalize hours worked.

Perhaps not too surprisingly, this programming definition of a type—a valid range of data, plus a meaningful set of operations—is the same as the dictionary definition of the word *algebra*. Just as you use algebra to solve mathematical problems with pencil and paper, you use data types to solve programming problems with the PC.

The previous chapter briefly discussed the types supported by Turbo Pascal. This chapter describes those types in greater detail and shows how you can define new data types to better handle specific programming problems.

Integers

Turbo Pascal provides five data types for storing integer formats: `byte`, `shortint`, `integer`, `word`, and `longint`. Table 3.1 summarizes these types.

Table 3.1. *Data Types for Integer Formats*

Type	*Size*	*Ranges of allowed values*
`byte`	1 byte	0..255
`shortint`	1 byte	–128..+127
`integer`	2 bytes	–32,768..+32,767
`word`	2 bytes	0..65,535
`longint`	4 bytes	–2,147,483,648..+2,147,483,647

Note that `shortint` is the signed version of `byte`, and `integer` is the signed version of `word`. `Longint` is a data type you can use when you need to manipulate relatively large numbers accurately.

Notice that both `byte` and `shortint` occupy a single byte, and both `word` and `integer` occupy a single word. Each member of the pair interprets the bit patterns of a variable differently. If you are using *only* `bytes` or *only* `shortints`, for example, these differences will not matter. But if you mix the types (and this happens all the time), you might get some unexpected results. To understand this process better, you need to know something about how integer arithmetic works.

Clarification of Integer
Pascal groups the five data types `byte`, `shortint`, `integer`, `word`, and `longint` in the category called *integers*. Unfortunately, the word *integer* describes both the category and an individual type. A similar problem arises when Pascal users discuss *reals*. This situation came about because over the years, Borland has increasingly offered more features (the `shortint` and `longint` data types, for example) than most other compilers, so the single word *integer* used in most books and articles has come to be applied to a much broader range of types when used for Turbo Pascal. In this book, the intended meaning should always be clear from the context in which the word is used.

Integer Arithmetic

Human beings use addition and subtraction. Computers use two's complement arithmetic.

There is nothing more confusing than base 2 arithmetic, so forget about it for now. Consider instead the ordinary decimal (base 10) system. If a computer operated entirely on base 10 instead of just 0 and 1, you could use these digits:

0, 1, 2, 3, 4, 5, 6, 7, 8, and 9

Every number would be stored in a series of one or more bytes. Assume that you are using a decimal-system computer with each byte capable of holding the digits from 0 through 9. Further assume that you want to work with a decimal-word sized number of two bytes. Each decimal-word, therefore, can hold the following numbers:

00, 01, 02, 03, ..., 96, 97, 98, and 99

Because your decimal word is only two decimal-bytes long, any three-digit number (100 and above) is truncated back to two digits.

Given such a structure, most arithmetic operations are quite normal. After all,

$04 + 76 = 80$

$54 - 32 = 22$

$16 \times 03 = 48$

$72 \div 09 = 08$

Your decimal-system computer can handle results greater than 99 (that is, greater than can fit in a decimal-word) by simply truncating all the extra columns.

53 + 82 = 35 (135, truncated)

43 × 65 = 95 (2795, truncated)

But how does it answer questions such as

53 – 82 = ??

43 – 65 = ??

when negative numbers were not part of the definition? The answer is that you use numbers that "act like" negatives. The formal definition of a negative number is: Given a number X, its negative (–X) is the value that satisfies the equation:

X + (–X) = 0

You want to find the negatives of 82 and 65; thus, what numbers in your decimal computer could be added to 82 and 65 to produce zero (00)? The answer is 18 and 35. Remember that any total greater than 99 is simply truncated. As a result, any multiple of 100 is equal to 0, including 0, 00, 100, 500, 1000400, and 87623945300.

Of course, common sense tells you that 18 is not equal to (–82), and 35 is not equal to (–65), but when you use them in formulas where only the two right-hand columns of the result are significant, you quickly find that there is no other explanation for the answers you get.

Because 100 is the same as 0, you find that

(–82) = 0 – 82 = 100 – 82 = 18 so (–82) = 18

(–65) = 0 – 65 = 100 – 65 = 35 so (–65) = 35

Alternatively, you can do the math normally, then convert the answers.

53 – 82 = –29 and 100 – 29 = 71 so 53 – 82 = 71

43 – 65 = –22 and 100 – 22 = 78 so 43 – 65 = 78

When you also consider that

53 – 82 = 71 and 53 + 18 = 71

43 – 65 = 78 and 43 + 35 = 78

you see that (–82) does equal (+18) and (–65) does equal (+35).

Still not convinced? In an ordinary decimal system, the negative sign in a multiplication can float freely. Compare –(43 × 68) with (–43) × 68 and 43 × (–68).

–(43 × 68)	(–43) × 68	43 × (–68)
–(2924)	(+57) × 68	43 × (+32)
–(24)	3876	1376
76	76	76

So (–24) equals 76. Negative numbers in your decimal-word do not need the traditional format to act the same. You can find a positive number that is equivalent to any negative number within range. Therefore, your decimal-system computer has the following equalities:

–01 = +99

–02 = +98

–03 = +97

⋮

–47 = +53

–48 = +52

–49 = +51

–50 = +50

As a practical matter, *50* should not denote both a negative and positive amount, so you can arbitrarily say that *50* means (–50) and further say that (+50) is out of range.

Now slip back to binary, because the PC operates on base 2, not base 10. Instead of recycling to 0 at decimal 100, each byte returns to 0 with each multiple of 256. Hence, for a byte:

–1 = +255

–2 = +254

–3 = +253

⋮

–125 = +131

–126 = +130

–127 = +129

–128 = +128

Again, you do not want *128* to mean both a negative and positive amount, so you can say that *128* means (–128) and further say that (+128) is out of range. Notice however, that as a result of this definition, all binary negative numbers are in the range 128 through 255; in other words, all binary negative numbers have a 1 in their highest bit, and all binary positive numbers have a 0 in their highest bit.

Similarly, each word recycles to 0 with each multiple of 65,536. Therefore, for a word:

–1 = +65,535

–2 = +65,534

–3 = +65,533

⋮

–32,765 = +32,771

–32,766 = +32,770

–32,767 = +32,769

–32,768 = +32,768

Once more, *32,768* should not denote both a negative and positive amount, so you can say that *32,768* means (–32,768) and further say that (+32,768) is out of range. Notice that here again all negative numbers have a 1 in their highest bit, and all positive numbers have a 0 in their highest bit.

This discussion repeatedly states that (+65,534) "acts like" (–2). Obviously, however, it must also act like (+65,534). In other words, when you need a negative number, you now know how to obtain its functional equivalent. But when you need a positive number, you can use the positive number itself. So in the eight bits of a byte, you can have the values

–128, –127, ..., –2, –1, 0, +1, +2, ..., +126, +127

or

0, 1, 2, 3, ..., 253, 254, 255

depending upon whether or not you want negative numbers. You could, of course, have both +254 and –2 in the same byte, but to avoid confusion, do not let this happen. The N numbers that can be stored in a set of bytes are either

0, 1, 2, ..., N–2, N–1

or

–(N/2), –(N/2)+1, ..., –2, –1, 0, 1, 2, ..., (N/2)–2, (N/2)–1

Therefore, you represent positive and negative numbers in the same bytes just by shifting the range of values the bit patterns represent. When you use negatives, the numbers are *signed*, because the numbers have an implied positive or negative sign in the form of the highest bit; when the bit is 1, the number is negative, and when the bit is 0, the number is positive. When you use the full set of positives, the numbers are *unsigned*, and the highest bit has no special meaning.

Using Integer Types

The processor itself makes no distinction between signed and unsigned numbers. The choice is entirely dependent upon the programmer's intent; ensure that your program's instructions are used appropriately. An error is generated if you try to assign a value too large for the type of the specified variable.

To avoid undesirable results (truncating or rounding, for example) when you use integers of different types in the same expression, Turbo converts all of its terms into a *common type* before performing any operations. A common type is simply the smallest type that can hold all of the values. If the right side of the equation contains a `byte` and a `shortint`, the equation is evaluated as if all terms are `integers`. Similarly, a `byte` and a `word` are both evaluated as `words`. A `word` and an `integer` are evaluated as `longints`.

If the common type of an evaluated expression is larger than the assigned type of the variable on the left side of the equation, its contents may be truncated or converted, as necessary. For example:

```
{ 0..255 }      { 0..255 }      { -128..+127 }
ValueByte1  := ValueByte2  +  ValueShortInt;
```

If `ValueByte2` = (+99) and `ValueShortInt` = (–100), Turbo evaluates the sum as (–1), just as if both variables were `integer` types. When the result is assigned to `ValueByte1`, it is converted to (+255).

The format you select to represent an integer-type variable depends on its minimum and maximum bounds. To avoid unwanted surprises in your programs, always use integer types large enough to contain the full expected range comfortably.

Real Numbers

Unfortunately, only a narrow subset of all integer numbers can be handled by the PC. For example, integer types are too small to track the dollar value of a Fortune 500 company. They are also too inexact to contain the changes in thrust required by the space shuttle to attain orbit. Very large and very small numbers are handled by a different family of data types—the reals.

At the risk of oversimplifying the entire subject of number theory, mathematicians say that a number is *real* if it is either rational or irrational. A *rational* number is one that can be expressed as a fraction of whole numbers, such as 3/1, 13/19, and 1/2. A number is *irrational* if no whole number fraction can be found and it can be expressed only approximately, such as pi and the square root of 2. Real numbers are typically written as decimal values, such as 2.0, 3.14159, 1.414, and 0.5.

In Turbo Pascal, this definition is greatly simplified: a real number is any number that contains a decimal point. Table 3.2 lists Turbo's real-number data types, together with the size in bytes that they occupy, the range of values they can assume, and the number of significant digits they hold.

Table 3.2. *Real-Number Data Types*

Type	*Size*	*Range of allowed values*	*Significant digits*
Real	6 bytes	2.9×10^{-39} to 1.7×10^{38}	11–12
Single	4 bytes	1.5×10^{-45} to 3.4×10^{38}	7–8
Double	8 bytes	5.0×10^{-324} to 1.7×10^{308}	15–16
Extended	10 bytes	3.4×10^{-4932} to 1.1×10^{4932}	19–20
Comp	8 bytes	$-2^{63} + 1$ to $2^{63} - 1$	19–20

Single, double, extended, and comp data types can be used on an 8087 math coprocessor chip. This capacity is discussed more fully in Chapter 17, "The 8087 and External Devices," and in the reference section on compiler directives.

Real numbers, which are also called *floating-point* numbers, compress large values into a small number of bytes by using a format similar to that of scientific notation. Whereas scientific notation uses base 10, floating-point types store the binary representations of a sign (+ or –), an exponent, and a significand:

$$(+/-)\ \text{significand} \times 2^{\text{exponent}}$$

The actual bit layout does not really matter. Note, though, that both the significand and the exponent are stored as binary numbers; this is why the table of reals shows ranges that seem so unusual.

When you define a real number as a constant, Turbo Pascal stores the value in the smallest possible type. All of the numbers in the following example are stored as reals:

```
const
   NormalTemp     = 98.6;
   ExchangeRate   = 1.65;
   LifeSavings    = 43935.21;
   DiscountFactor = 0.76;
   NormalFactor   = 1.0;
```

Notice that the value of `DiscountFactor`, which is less than 1, is preceded by 0, whereas the value of `NormalFactor`, which is an integer, is written in decimal form. These concessions to style are required if Turbo Pascal is to understand the intended type; remember that a period not preceded by a number is treated as the final period of the program, and a number not written in decimal form is interpreted as a Turbo Pascal integer type.

Boolean Types

Boolean logic is named for George Boole, the English mathematician who studied the algebra of two elements. In Turbo Pascal, the two elements are `True` and `False`.

Actually, `Boolean` values are stored as numbers in a single byte. `False` is stored as 0. `True` is nonzero, but is typically stored as +1.

`Boolean` values are the most common method of controlling the flow of a program through their use in conditional and looping statements. When you assign a `Boolean` value to a variable, you effectively turn the variable into a condition. For example, given the following declaration:

```
var

   FirstParagraph : Boolean;

   DoneYet        : Boolean;
```

the Boolean variables can be assigned values of either True or False, as follows:

```
begin
    FirstParagraph := True;
    DoneYet        := False;
```

and can be used in Pascal statements just like conditions, as in the following:

```
if FirstParagraph then
    DoPageEjectAndTitle;
while not DoneYet do
    ProcessTheNextRecord;
```

Char Types

All information in the PC is managed in the fundamental unit, the *byte*, which may assume any one of 256 states. Turbo Pascal provides three data types for handling individual bytes: char, byte, and shortint. When a byte is used to represent the eight-bit number itself, the byte or shortint type is used. When a byte is used to represent one of the 256 extended ASCII characters, the char type is used. Even though all three data types are internally identical, a variable of type char cannot be used in an arithmetic expression.

The best way to understand the char type is to view every possible ASCII value. The values are listed in table 3.3.

As you can see, the digits from 0 through 9 are stored as ASCII 48 through ASCII 57; uppercase letters are stored as ASCII 65 through ASCII 90; and lowercase letters are stored as ASCII 97 through ASCII 122.

As strange as these patterns might seem, they have (or at least *had*) their uses. ASCII originated in the old teletype days. Originally, only the low 128 characters—called the *standard ASCII character set*—were used. Because each character could be represented with seven bits, the eighth bit was available to test the accuracy of the transmission. By setting or clearing the eighth bit, every byte could be transmitted with an odd number of bits (odd parity) or an even number of bits (even parity).

The low ASCII values—0 through 31—were used as control characters; the abbreviations have meanings like "enquiry" and "acknowledgment." (In other words, if the sixth and seventh bits were 0, for example, the byte contained a control character.)

Table 3.3. ASCII Values

Hex	*Dec*	*Screen*	*Hex*	*Dec*	*Screen*	*Hex*	*Dec*	*Screen*
00h	0		2Ch	44	,	58h	88	X
01h	1	☺	2Dh	45	-	59h	89	Y
02h	2	●	2Eh	46	.	5Ah	90	Z
03h	3	♥	2Fh	47	/	5Bh	91	[
04h	4	♦	30h	48	0	5Ch	92	\
05h	5	♣	31h	49	1	5Dh	93	]
06h	6	♠	32h	50	2	5Eh	94	^
07h	7	•	33h	51	3	5Fh	95	_
08h	8	◘	34h	52	4	60h	96	`
09h	9	○	35h	53	5	61h	97	a
0Ah	10	◙	36h	54	6	62h	98	b
0Bh	11	♂	37h	55	7	63h	99	c
0Ch	12	♀	38h	56	8	64h	100	d
0Dh	13	♪	39h	57	9	65h	101	e
0Eh	14	♫	3Ah	58	:	66h	102	f
0Fh	15	☼	3Bh	59	;	67h	103	g
10h	16	►	3Ch	60	<	68h	104	h
11h	17	◄	3Dh	61	=	69h	105	i
12h	18	↕	3Eh	62	>	6Ah	106	j
13h	19	‼	3Fh	63	?	6Bh	107	k
14h	20	¶	40h	64	@	6Ch	108	l
15h	21	§	41h	65	A	6Dh	109	m
16h	22	▬	42h	66	B	6Eh	110	n
17h	23	↨	43h	67	C	6Fh	111	o
18h	24	↑	44h	68	D	70h	112	p
19h	25	↓	45h	69	E	71h	113	q
1Ah	26	→	46h	70	F	72h	114	r
1Bh	27	←	47h	71	G	73h	115	s
1Ch	28	∟	48h	72	H	74h	116	t
1Dh	29	↔	49h	73	I	75h	117	u
1Eh	30	▲	4Ah	74	J	76h	118	v
1Fh	31	▼	4Bh	75	K	77h	119	w
20h	32		4Ch	76	L	78h	120	x
21h	33	!	4Dh	77	M	79h	121	y
22h	34	"	4Eh	78	N	7Ah	122	z
23h	35	#	4Fh	79	O	7Bh	123	{
24h	36	$	50h	80	P	7Ch	124	|
25h	37	%	51h	81	Q	7Dh	125	}
26h	38	&	52h	82	R	7Eh	126	~
27h	39	'	53h	83	S	7Fh	127	Δ
28h	40	(	54h	84	T	80h	128	Ç
29h	41	)	55h	85	U	81h	129	ü
2Ah	42	*	56h	86	V	82h	130	é
2Bh	43	+	57h	87	W	83h	131	â

continues

Table 3.3. continued

Hex	*Dec*	*Screen*	*Hex*	*Dec*	*Screen*	*Hex*	*Dec*	*Screen*
84h	132	ä	ADh	173	¡	D6h	214	╓
85h	133	à	AEh	174	«	D7h	215	╫
86h	134	å	AFh	175	»	D8h	216	╪
87h	135	ç	B0h	176	░	D9h	217	┘
88h	136	ê	B1h	177	▒	DAh	218	┌
89h	137	ë	B2h	178	▓	DBh	219	█
8Ah	138	è	B3h	179	│	DCh	220	▄
8Bh	139	ï	B4h	180	┤	DDh	221	▌
8Ch	140	î	B5h	181	╡	DEh	222	▐
8Dh	141	ì	B6h	182	╢	DFh	223	▀
8Eh	142	Ä	B7h	183	╖	E0h	224	α
8Fh	143	Å	B8h	184	╕	E1h	225	β
90h	144	É	B9h	185	╣	E2h	226	Γ
91h	145	æ	BAh	186	║	E3h	227	π
92h	146	Æ	BBh	187	╗	E4h	228	Σ
93h	147	ô	BCh	188	╝	E5h	229	σ
94h	148	ö	BDh	189	╜	E6h	230	μ
95h	149	ò	BEh	190	╛	E7h	231	τ
96h	150	û	BFh	191	┐	E8h	232	Φ
97h	151	ù	C0h	192	└	E9h	233	θ
98h	152	ÿ	C1h	193	┴	EAh	234	Ω
99h	153	Ö	C2h	194	┬	EBh	235	δ
9Ah	154	Ü	C3h	195	├	ECh	236	∞
9Bh	155	¢	C4h	196	─	EDh	237	φ
9Ch	156	£	C5h	197	┼	EEh	238	∈
9Dh	157	¥	C6h	198	╞	EFh	239	∩
9Eh	158	₧	C7h	199	╟	F0h	240	≡
9Fh	159	ƒ	C8h	200	╚	F1h	241	±
A0h	160	á	C9h	201	╔	F2h	242	≥
A1h	161	í	CAh	202	╩	F3h	243	≤
A2h	162	ó	CBh	203	╦	F4h	244	⌠
A3h	163	ú	CCh	204	╠	F5h	245	⌡
A4h	164	ñ	CDh	205	═	F6h	246	÷
A5h	165	Ñ	CEh	206	╬	F7h	247	≈
A6h	166	ª	CFh	207	╧	F8h	248	°
A7h	167	º	D0h	208	╨	F9h	249	•
A8h	168	¿	D1h	209	╤	FAh	250	·
A9h	169	⌐	D2h	210	╥	FBh	251	√
AAh	170	¬	D3h	211	╙	FCh	252	^{n}
ABh	171	½	D4h	212	╘	FDh	253	^{2}
ACh	172	¼	D5h	213	╒	FEh	254	■
						FFh	255	

Because uppercase letters begin at ASCII 65, if the seventh bit was set, the byte probably contained an alpha character. Also, uppercase and lowercase letters differ by 32 positions, so the setting of the sixth bit determined whether a letter was capitalized.

When IBM developed the PC, it decided the machine should perform parity testing with special circuits. Consequently, the eighth bit became available; as a result, an *additional* 128 characters could be introduced to handle foreign and graphics characters. The full 256 characters are commonly called the *extended ASCII character set*.

Except for special characters such as the form feed (12) and carriage return (13), you will almost always refer to a standard character by the symbol itself (for example, the letter *A* instead of 65). The characters shown in figure 3.1 are most frequently used for drawing boxes.

String Types

A `string` type consists of a series of ASCII characters. A string is declared with the following format:

```
var
   StrVar : string[ StringSize ];
```

The maximum StringSize is 255 characters. If the reserved word `string` appears *without* a size indicator, 255 is used as the default.

When stored in memory, each string occupies as many bytes as its maximum length plus 1. The zero byte contains the working length of the string, and the following bytes contain the individual characters of the string. For example, if the string `Name` is defined as follows:

```
var
   Name : string[ 30 ];
```

then `Name` requires 31 bytes of storage. The zero byte keeps track of the length of the most recently assigned string. The individual characters in a string can be accessed with subscripts; for example, `Name[5]` references the fifth character. If the following assignment is made:

```
Name := 'SHEILA';
```

then byte zero contains *6* (the length of the string), byte one contains *S*, byte two contains *H*, and so on. `Name` will be treated exactly as if it physically contains only six characters. For example, the statement:

```
writeln( 'Start of string +', Name, '+ End of string' );
```

produces:

```
Start of string +SHEILA+ End of string
```

Fig. 3.1. ASCII values of characters used to draw boxes.

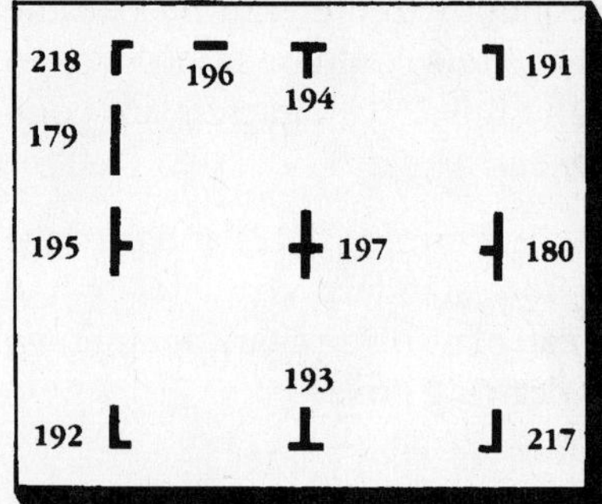

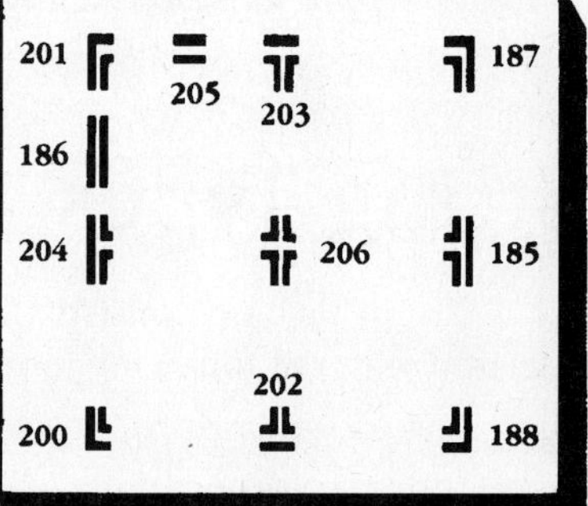

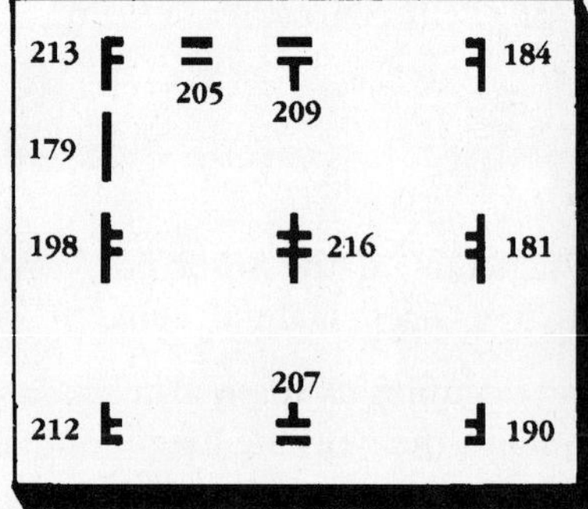

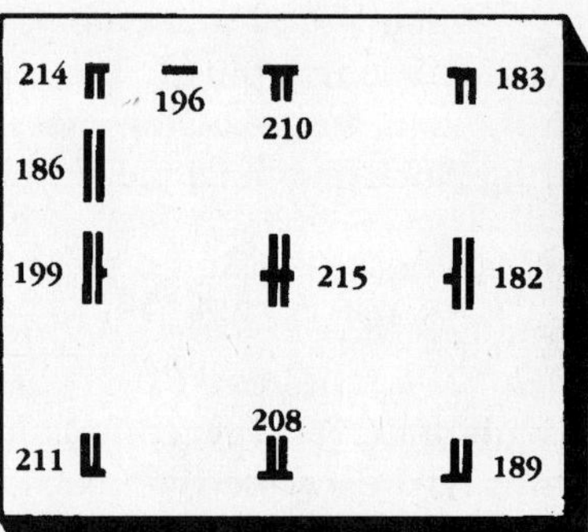

If Name is reassigned:

```
Name := 'ILANA';
```

then byte zero contains *5*, byte one contains *I*, byte two contains *L*, and so on. *Name* will be treated exactly as if it physically contains only five characters.

The STRING1 program (listing 3.1) demonstrates how the effective length of a string can vary.

Listing 3.1

```
program String1;
var
   TestString : string[ 15 ];
procedure ShowString;
var
   i : byte;
begin
   writeln( '  ***', TestString, '***' );
   for i := 0 to 15 do
      write( ord( TestString[i] ):4 );   {Allow 4 spaces}
   writeln;
   write( '    ' );   { 4 spaces, to bypass the size byte }
   for i := 1 to 15 do
      write( TestString[ i ]:4 );   {Allow 4 spaces}
   writeln;
   writeln;
end;
begin
   TestString := 'abcdefghijklmnopqrstuvwxyz';
   ShowString;
   TestString := 'ZYXWVUT';
   ShowString;
   TestString := '';
   ShowString;
   TestString := 'a1b2c3d4e5';
   ShowString;
end.
```

The *string* `TestString` is defined as being 15 characters long. Actually, the *variable* `TestString` is 16 bytes long; the first byte contains the length of the string. When you first initiate the string, its contents are undefined (in other words, the contents are meaningless), so begin by assigning it the alphabet:

```
TestString := 'abcdefghijklmnopqrstuvwxyz';
```

`TestString` was defined to be 15 characters long, so only the first 15 characters are captured. When the `ShowString` procedure is called, `TestString` turns out to contain the contents of figure 3.2.

Fig. 3.2. The contents of TestString with a 15-character assignment.

abcdefghijklmno															
Size Byte	String Contents														
15	97	98	99	100	101	102	103	104	105	106	107	108	109	110	111
	a	b	c	d	e	f	g	h	i	j	k	l	m	n	o

Next, `TestString` is assigned `ZYXWVUT`, which is only seven characters long. After `ShowString` is called, `TestString` contains the contents of figure 3.3.

Fig. 3.3. The contents of TestString with a 7-character assignment.

ZYXWVUT															
Size Byte	String Contents														
7	90	89	88	87	86	85	84	104	105	106	107	108	109	110	111
	Z	Y	X	W	V	U	T	h	i	j	k	l	m	n	o

As indicated by the size byte, only the first seven characters are significant, even though the eighth through fifteenth characters (here, *h* through *o*) are still in the string.

Next, `TestString` is assigned the null string (that is, a string of length zero). `ShowString` reveals the contents of figure 3.4.

Here, the size byte of 0 clearly indicates that the string is to be considered empty, even though no other changes have been made to the contents of the individual characters in `TestString`.

Finally, the string `a1b2c3d4e5` is assigned to `TestString`. As the `ShowString` procedure demonstrates, the size byte now contains 10, and only the first 10 characters in `TestString` have been overwritten (see fig. 3.5)

Fig. 3.4. The contents of TestString with a null string.

******															
Size Byte	String Contents														
0	90	89	88	87	86	85	84	104	105	106	107	108	109	110	111
	Z	Y	X	W	V	U	T	h	i	j	k	l	m	n	o

Fig. 3.5. The contents of TestString with the string a1b2c3d435.

a1b2c3d4e5															
Size Byte	String Contents														
10	97	49	98	50	99	51	100	52	101	53	107	108	109	110	111
	a	1	b	2	c	3	d	4	e	5	k	l	m	n	o

Using the default type `string` without a size indicator allocates 256 bytes of storage. You may be tempted to use such a type so that you do not have to worry about whether a string will fit, but you can quickly see how a great deal of storage can be consumed unnecessarily. For example, in the following definition:

```
var
   StrArray : array [ 1..100 ] of string;
```

the `StrArray` array consumes 100 × (255 + 1), or 25,600, bytes of storage.

At first, the dynamic nature of strings may seem wasteful, but fixed-length strings are relatively awkward to use. Collections of names, addresses, labels, and titles rarely have the same size. Conversely, "true" strings—strings that physically vary in length depending on the number of characters required—are extremely difficult to implement in a compiler.

Turbo Pascal provides a good compromise; it supports physically fixed-length strings, but the contents of the strings allow different sizes.

Enumerated Types

Suppose that your company is divided into four regions—North, South, East, and West—and that your program needs a variable, `Region`, to identify which geographic area it is currently processing. In many languages, you would be forced to use an integer to identify the choices, as follows:

```
var
   Region : byte;
   :
begin
   :
   for Region := 1 to 4 do
      case Region of
         1 : writeln( 'Northern Region' );
         2 : writeln( 'Southern Region' );
         3 : writeln( 'Eastern Region' );
         4 : writeln( 'Western Region' );
      end;
```

Using numbers to represent nonnumeric data is awkward at best, however, and can lead to confusion when reading a longer (or more complicated) program. Turbo Pascal provides the *enumerated* type for just such a purpose. The enumerated type is simply a list of *identifiers* enclosed in parentheses. The intention is to enable you to manipulate variables with understandable English descriptions instead of arbitrarily assigned integer values.

For example, with enumerated types the preceding program can be rewritten as shown in listing 3.2.

Listing 3.2

```
program Enum;
type
   RegionType = ( North, South, East, West );
var
   Region : RegionType;
begin
   for Region := North to West do
      case Region of
         North : writeln( 'Northern Region' );
         South : writeln( 'Southern Region' );
```

```
            East   : writeln( 'Eastern Region' );
            West   : writeln( 'Western Region' );
        end;
end.
```

When the ENUM program executes, it produces the following output:

```
Northern Region
Southern Region
Eastern Region
Western Region
```

Notice that the `for` loop cycles through the entire sequence: `North`, `South`, `East`, and `West`. Internally, Turbo Pascal stores each value in the enumeration as an integer—beginning with 0 and based on its sequence in the list—and automatically converts each identifier to its numeric equivalent. Enumeration provides a natural ordering that can be used by comparison operators. In the ENUM program, `North` is stored as 0, `South` is stored as 1, `East` is stored as 2, and `West` is stored as 3. The `Ord` function must be used to access the numeric value of the identifier; `Ord(North)` is 0, `Ord(South)` is 1, and so on.

Obviously, every identifier in the list must be individually enumerated. At first, this might seem to be something of a pain, but depending on the application, enumerated types can add immeasurably to the legibility of your programs. For example, if your program deals with the colors of the rainbow, you can define the enumerated type `Spectrum` and variables that use it as follows:

```
type
   Spectrum = ( Red, Orange, Yellow, Green, Blue, Indigo, Violet );
var
   Color : Spectrum;
   Tint  : array [ Red..Violet ] of integer;
```

The variables `Color` and `Tint` can take on any of the identifiers defined by `Spectrum`, such as

```
Color := Green;
Tint[ Orange ] := 7 * 4;
```

The compiler does not allow enumerated types to be input or output; your program can use them only internally. The statement

```
writeln( 'The color is ', Color );
```

will produce a compilation error.

Subrange Types

Frequently, you will want to limit the use of a variable to a range of values. Turbo Pascal provides the *subrange* type for such a purpose.

The subrange must be a subset of a previously defined type, called the *host* type. The range itself must be continuous. You define it by declaring the upper and lower bounds with two periods (..) separating them.

The compiler ensures that any variable of a subrange type remains within the specified range. An error results if you attempt an assignment outside that range. Subranges are particularly useful for guaranteeing that subscripts of arrays remain within predetermined bounds. For example, given the following subrange definitions:

```
const
   LowTeen  = 13;
   HighTeen = 19;
var
   Grade       : 0..100;
   Floor       : 1..5;
   UpperCase   : 'A'..'Z';
   WorkingAge  : 18..65;
   TeenYear    : LowTeen..HighTeen;
```

the following assignments are legal:

```
Grade := 96;
Floor := 3;
UpperCase := 'M';
WorkingAge := 43;
TeenYear := 17;
```

but each of the following assignments generates a range error:

```
Grade := 104;
Floor := 7;
UpperCase := 'm';
WorkingAge := 12;
TeenYear := 6;
```

A subrange of real numbers is not allowed, because an infinite number of floating-point numbers are between any two reals.

Set Types

A *set* is a finite collection of elements that share the same previously defined type, called the *base* type. A set variable is declared as:

```
var
   Bunch : set of BaseType;
```

The maximum number of elements in a set is 256. Further, the upper and lower bounds of the base type must have ordinal values that are themselves within the range 0 through 255. Consequently, the base type of a set cannot be `shortint`, `integer`, `longint`, or `word`. This is not a serious restriction. For example, sets can be defined as follows:

```
type
   Days      = ( Sun, Mon, Tue, Wed, Thu, Fri, Sat );
   LowerCase = 'a'..'z';
   Healthy   = ( Tofu, Sprouts, WheatGerm, PureWater );
   Parts     = ( Nuts, Bolts, Metal, Plastic, Cardboard );
var
   OneDay   : Days;
   WorkDays : set of Days;
   Vowels   : set of LowerCase;
   Spelling : set of char;
   InStock  : set of Parts;
   Menu     : set of Healthy;
```

When you assign a value to an enumerated type, such as `OneDay`, you do it directly, as follows:

```
OneDay := Wed;
```

But sets can contain several values. When you assign values to a set type, such as `WorkDays`, you place the identifiers within brackets, as follows:

```
WorkDays := [ Mon, Fri ];
```

Set operations are discussed in detail in Chapter 4, "Expressions, Operands, and Operators."

Pointers

Pointer variables contain the memory *address* of a data structure rather than the data structure itself. A `pointer` type is stored as a double word, with the offset part in the low word and the segment part in the high word.

A `pointer` variable can be defined in either of the following ways:

```
var
   Var1 : ^BaseType;
   Var2 : pointer;
```

`Var1` is a pointer to a variable of type `BaseType`. `BaseType` may be either a standard type—such as `byte` or `string`—or it may be a user-defined type that appeared in a previous type declaration statement. `Var1` can be used only to point to `BaseType` variables. `Var2` is a general pointer and can be used to point to a variable of any type.

Pointers are discussed in detail in Chapter 6, "Dynamic Data Structures."

Arrays

An *array* is a fixed number of variables that all have the same type. Each element of the array can be accessed by specifying its *index*.

An `array` type is declared with an array declaration, as follows:

```
var
   ArrayName : array [ IndexType ] of ArrayType;
```

`IndexType` is a subrange that specifies the array's dimensions. `ArrayType` may be any standard or user-defined data type. `ArrayType` may even be another array, in which case the declaration would appear as follows:

```
var
   Array1 : array [ 1..5 ] of array [ 1..10 ] of integer;
```

There is no restriction to the number of dimensions of an array. Multidimensional arrays can be defined also in the following manner:

```
var
   Array2 = array [ 1..5, 1..10 ] of integer;
```

Arrays are usually associated with mathematical and list processing, but any ordinal subrange is allowed with the exception of `Longint` and subranges of `Longint`.

```
type
   Months  = ( Jan, Feb, Nov, Dec );
   Days    = ( Sun, Mon, Fri, Sat );
var
   Calendar : array [ Jan..Dec, Sun..Sat ] of byte;
```

Records

A *record* is a data type that consists of any combination of *fields*, each of which is a variable of any data type. The `record` type enables you to reference any predetermined number of variables through a single identifier. Records are usually used with files and dynamic data structures.

An example of a `record` definition follows:

```
Passenger1 = record
                Name         : string;
                FlightNumber : word;
                Date         : array [ 1..3 ] of byte;
             end;
```

Each record can be composed of even smaller records, such as:

```
Passenger2 = record
                Name         : record
                                  First,
                                  Last    : string;
                               end;
                FlightNumber : word;
                Date         : record
                                  Month,
                                  Day,
                                  Year    : byte;
                               end;
             end;
```

Each field can be individually accessed in the form

```
RecordIdentifier.FieldName
```

For example, if a variable `Ticket` is defined as type `Passenger1`, then `Ticket.Name` references the passenger's name. If, instead, `Ticket` is defined as type `Passenger2`, then `Ticket.Name` still references the entire `Name` record, but `Ticket.Name.First` and `Ticket.Name.Last` are used to subdivide it. In both cases, `Ticket` references the entire record.

Occasionally, when you are considering what should be included in a record, you realize that some fields are never used at the same time, such as `MaidenName` and `WifesName`. At other times, you realize that entire sets of fields may be mutually exclusive. Rather than force you to list every field in every record, which rapidly consumes large blocks of memory that will never be accessed, Turbo Pascal enables you to use a variant record.

A *variant record* is, simply, a single record identifier that references physically different collections of fields. Some fields may be common to all records; the fields that differ form the *variant* part of the record.

A variant record is defined first by listing all common fields, then by using a `case` statement to identify the individual groups or variants. Each variant may be a different length but must be referenced with an ordinal constant. For example:

```
type
   Registers = record
                  case integer of
                     1 : ( AX, BX, CX, DX : word );
                     2 : ( AL, AH, BL, BH, CL, CH, DL
                           DH : byte );
               end;
var
   Settings : Registers;
```

The `Registers` record consists of either a record of four words or a record of eight bytes. If you make the following assignment:

```
                     { ---Hi----   ---Low---            }
Settings.CX := 256;  { 0000 0001   0000 0000 in binary }
```

then the following equalities are true:

`Settings.CL = 0` and `Settings.CH = 1`

because the `CL` and `CH` variables reside in the *same physical memory* as the `CX` variable. Therefore, a variant record helps you to access the same physical memory in several ways.

Frequently, you will need to keep track of which variant is in use. This can be accomplished by introducing an extra field, called a *tag field*, to identify the active variant. For example:

```
type
   FlightType = ( Domestic, Overseas );
   PassRec    = record
                   Name         : string;
                   FlightNumber : word;
                   Date         : array [ 1..3 ] of byte;
                   case Destination : FlightType of
                      Domestic   : ( DestCity,
                                     DestState    : string[ 30 ] );
                      Overseas   : ( OverseasTax : real;
                                     DestCountry : string[ 20 ] );
                end;
var
   Traveler : PassRec;
```

In the `PassRec` record, `Destination` is the tag field. `Destination` is actually stored as a separate field in the `PassRec` record. Its value can be either `Domestic` or `Overseas`, depending on the assignment you make, as follows:

```
Traveler.Destination := Domestic;
```

The presence of a tag field is a convenience for the programmer; no restrictions are placed on accessing variant fields. The tag field is used primarily when you retrieve an unknown record from an array or from a file; the tag field tells you which variant is being used and enables you to avoid inappropriate access of any data, which could cause a run-time error. For example, in the `PassRec` record, `DestCity` (a string) and `OverseasTax` (a real) reference some of the same memory locations; the `Destination` field can be tested to determine how the current record is being used.

File Types

A *file* is a *sequence* of components of the same type. A component may be a standard type, such as `byte` or `word`, or it may be a user-defined type, such as a `record`. There may be any number of components, but they may be accessed only one at a time.

A file can be declared in one of three ways:

```
var
   First  : File of PassRec;
   Second : Text;
   Third  : File;
```

The `First` file consists of records of the type `PassRec`. The `Second` file contains text characters organized into lines of (possibly) varying lengths. Notice that the format `File of` FileType is ideal for data files, and the `text` file type, as the name implies, is ideal for storing text. Both of these formats are called *typed* files. The `Third` file is *untyped*. An untyped file may contain data of many different types; when you use an untyped file, you must ensure that the individual data elements are handled correctly.

Files are discussed in greater detail in Chapter 13, "File Handling."

Procedure Types

With Turbo Pascal you assign a procedure or function to a variable declared as a `procedure` type. The `procedure` types are discussed in greater detail in Chapter 5, "Procedures and Functions."

Object Types

Beginning with version 5.5, Turbo Pascal supports object-oriented programming by allowing an identifier to be defined as an `object` type. A further discussion of `object` types can be found in Chapter 20, "Object-Oriented Programming."

Summary

In this chapter, you learned that a data type specifies a range of values and the set of operations that can be performed on those values.

You learned about the standard Turbo Pascal data types.

- The integer types `integer`, `shortint`, `longint`, `byte`, and `word` handle whole numbers.
- Five real data types are available for handling decimal numbers: `real`, `single`, `double`, `extended`, and `comp`.
- `Boolean` data types can be either `true` or `false`.
- The `char` data type defines single ASCII characters; a `string` is a series of ASCII characters.

- A `pointer` data type specifies the memory address of a data structure rather than the data structure itself.

You have learned how to define your own customized data types to solve a variety of specialized programming problems.

- An enumerated data type consists of a user-defined list of identifiers.
- A subrange is a continuous subset of a previously defined type.
- A set is a finite collection of elements that share the same previously defined type.
- An array is a fixed number of variables that all have the same type.
- A record allows you to reference any predetermined number of fields through a single identifier.
- A file is a sequence of components—all of the same type—that may be accessed only one at a time.
- A `procedure` data type is an advanced feature of Turbo Pascal that allows your program to handle a procedure or function as an ordinary data object.
- An `object` type declaration enables Turbo Pascal to support object-oriented programming.

CHAPTER 4

Expressions, Operands, and Operators

Most people associate computers with "number crunching"—processing extremely complex (or exceedingly tedious) mathematical problems accurately and rapidly. It is easy to understand how this impression arises. If you look back over the history of computing, the detail-oriented and number-intensive applications, such as payroll processing, were first able to economically justify commercial computer installations. Even today, most cost justifications begin by identifying which number-intensive applications can be performed better by the computer than by human hands. There are, after all, few ways to use a computer that do not demand some degree of numerical power.

Fortunately, almost every problem with a numeric origin can be reduced to one or more equations, which in turn can be expressed as the evaluation of a formula. In Turbo Pascal, expressions are the principal means of both defining and solving problems; everything from simple arithmetic through condition testing to trigonometry is phrased as an expression.

This chapter discusses how expressions are used in Turbo Pascal programs.

Overview of Operators and Operands

Simply put, an expression consists of an operation on one or more operands. To calculate the area of a rectangle, you use the expression `(height * width)`, where `height` and `width` are operands, and the multiplication symbol (*) is an operator.

Each operator has two basic properties: operand count and precedence. *Operand count* refers to the number of operands used by the operator. In Turbo Pascal, an operator is either *unary* (only one operand) or *binary* (two operands). The multiplication operator * is binary; it is used to obtain the product of two numbers. The minus sign can be used as either a unary operator (as, for example, in –4) or as a binary operator (as in 5 – 2) depending upon context.

Precedence refers to the priority Turbo Pascal assigns to the operation. For example, multiplication is generally regarded as having a higher priority than addition. When you see the equation

X = 2 + 4 * 3

your math classes taught you to evaluate the multiplication operator first, obtaining 2 + (4 * 3) = 14 rather than (2 + 4) * 3 = 18.

Parentheses can be used to force the processing sequence. If you had written the previous formula as

X = (2 + 4) * 3

you would have forced the addition to occur first and obtained 18 as the value for X. Parentheses are always evaluated outward from the innermost pair. Although precedence enables you to avoid excessive parentheses, you should still insert parentheses as often as necessary to clarify the processing order.

The order of operator precedence is given in table 4.1. Unless otherwise grouped by parentheses, all operators on the same line have equal precedence and are evaluated in the order they are written. When an operand is between two operators, it is assumed to belong to the operator with the higher precedence.

The readability of a Pascal program is considerably increased because there are only four operator precedence levels. In contrast, the C language has more than fifteen!

Table 4.1. *Operator Precedence*

Priority	*Operators*
1 (highest)	`@ NOT unary + -`
2	`* / DIV MOD AND SHL SHR`
3	`binary + - OR XOR`
4	`= <> < > <= >= IN`

Arithmetic Operators

Of all the operators supported by Turbo Pascal, the addition, subtraction, multiplication, and division operators are the easiest to understand. They perform just as their names imply (see table 4.2). However, different rules must be observed depending on whether the operators are applied to integer or real values.

Table 4.2. *Arithmetic Operators*

Operator	*Syntax*	*Meaning*
`+`	`+ expression`	Positive (unary)
`+`	`expression1 + expression2`	Addition (binary)
`-`	`- expression`	Negative (unary)
`-`	`expression1 - expression2`	Subtraction (binary)
`*`	`expression1 * expression2`	Multiplication
`/`	`expression1 / expression2`	Real division
`DIV`	`expression1 DIV expression2`	Integer division
`MOD`	`expression1 MOD expression2`	Remainder (modulus)

If an expression is assigned to an integer variable, every individual term must also be an integer type. Further, if division is performed, the integer division operator, `DIV`, must be used rather than the slash (`/`) operator, which denotes real division. Real terms can (and must) be converted to integers with the `Round` and `Trunc` functions.

Conversely, a real value is returned if *any* individual term is real. Further, a real value is returned whenever the slash real division operator is used, even if the dividend and divisor are both integers.

The DIV integer division operator cannot be used with real operands. It returns the integer portion of the quotient. The MOD operator (referring to *modular arithmetic*) returns the remainder. For example, the number 6 can be divided into 45 seven times, with a remainder of 3; hence:

45 DIV 6 = 7 and 45 MOD 6 = 3

The MATH1 program (listing 4.1) is a simple four-function calculator that creates an output similar to an adding machine tape.

Listing 4.1

```
program Math1;
uses Crt;
var
   LastOperator,
   LastEntry,
   Entry            : char;
   Operand1,
   Operand2         : LongInt;
begin
   Operand1 := 0;
   Operand2 := 0;
   Entry := '+';
   LastOperator := '+';
   repeat
      LastEntry := Entry;
      Entry := ReadKey;
      if (Entry = '+') and (Entry = LastEntry) then
         Operand1 := 0;     { Two + entries cause a zero }
      case Entry of
         '0'..'9' : begin
                       write( Entry );
                       Operand2 := Operand2*10 + (ord( Entry ) - 48);
                    end;
         '+',
         '-',
         '*',
         '/' : begin
                  case LastOperator of
                     '+' : Operand1 := Operand1 + Operand2;
```

```
                '-' : Operand1 := Operand1 - Operand2;
                '*' : Operand1 := Operand1 * Operand2;
                '/' : Operand1 := Operand1 div Operand2;
            end;
            Operand2 := 0;
            writeln;
            writeln( Operand1:10 );
            writeln( Entry );
            LastOperator := Entry;
         end;
    end;
  until not (Entry in [ '0'..'9', '+', '-', '*', '/' ]);
end.
```

Each integer is entered, followed by one of the keys +, –, *, or /. By storing and testing the `LastEntry` variable, two successive + keys will clear the total. The `LastOperator` variable is stored because the sequence

12345 + 23 –

adds and displays the total of 12345 and 23 only after you press the – key. The entry of an operator triggers the execution of the previous operator. The program ends when you enter any key other than a digit or an operator. (If you use the numeric keypad, be sure to set the NumLock key.)

Shift Operators

Figure 4.1 shows how the `SHL` (shift bits left) and `SHR` (shift bits right) operators are used to slide the bits in an integer left and right, respectively. Bits shifted off either end of the expression are lost. Bits on the right for `SHL` and on the left for `SHR` are zero-filled as their original contents are moved.

Fig. 4.1. The SHL and SHR operators.

```
                                7     6     5     4     3     2     1     0
SHL (Shift Left)   Lost <--   |<--  |<--  |<--  |<--  |<--  |<--  |<--  |<--  |  <-- 0

                                7     6     5     4     3     2     1     0
SHR (Shift Right)   0  -->    |-->  |-->  |-->  |-->  |-->  |-->  |-->  |-->  |  --> Lost
```

Shifting one bit to the left is equivalent to multiplying the expression by 2. Shifting one bit to the right is equivalent to dividing the expression by 2. You can take advantage of this to do fast multiplication and division by the powers of 2. Shifting left twice multiplies by 4, shifting left three times multiplies by 8, and so on.

When Turbo Pascal compiles a `SHR` or `SHL` operator, it produces a machine code shift instruction that is considerably faster than a functionally equivalent multiply or divide instruction. Because multiplying and dividing are among the slowest instructions on the 8086-family processors, using shifts can often speed operations by a factor of 10 or more.

The SHIFT2 program in listing 4.2 demonstrates the result of using the `SHR` and `SHL` operators. Each time the `ShowShifts` procedure is called it displays the results of different shift instructions. The `RevealBits` procedures illustrate the effect of the instructions on the bits themselves.

Listing 4.2

```
program Shift2;
var
   i : ShortInt;
procedure RevealBits( Subject : integer );
var
   j : byte;
   Compare : word;
begin
   Compare := 32768;    { In binary:  1000 0000 0000 0000 }
   write( '     ' );    { 5 spaces }
   for j := 15 downto 0 do begin
      if Compare and Subject <> 0 then write( '1' )
                                  else write( '0' );
      Compare := Compare div 2;
   end;
end;
procedure ShowShifts( Orig : ShortInt );
begin
   writeln( 'Shift  Left   Right            Left                   Right' );
   writeln( '-----  ----   -----            ----                   -----' );
   for i := 0 to 8 do begin
      write( i:3, (Orig shl i):8, (Orig shr i):8 );
      RevealBits( Orig shl i );
      RevealBits( Orig shr i );
```

```
      writeln;
    end;
    writeln;
  end;
begin
  ShowShifts( +53 );
  ShowShifts( -53 );
end.
```

The numbers +53 and –53 were chosen arbitrarily. When SHIFT2 executes, it produces the results shown in figure 4.2.

Fig. 4.2. *The output produced by the SHIFT2 program.*

```
Shift  Left  Right         Left                Right
-----  ----  -----         ----                -----
  0      53     53   0000000000110101   0000000000110101
  1     106     26   0000000001101010   0000000000011010
  2     212     13   0000000011010100   0000000000001101
  3     424      6   0000000110101000   0000000000000110
  4     848      3   0000001101010000   0000000000000011
  5    1696      1   0000011010100000   0000000000000001
  6    3392      0   0000110101000000   0000000000000000
  7    6784      0   0001101010000000   0000000000000000
  8   13568      0   0011010100000000   0000000000000000

Shift  Left  Right         Left                Right
-----  ----  -----         ----                -----
  0     -53    -53   1111111111001011   1111111111001011
  1    -106  32741   1111111110010110   0111111111100101
  2    -212  16370   1111111100101100   0011111111110010
  3    -424   8185   1111111001011000   0001111111111001
  4    -848   4092   1111110010110000   0000111111111100
  5   -1696   2046   1111100101100000   0000011111111110
  6   -3392   1023   1111001011000000   0000001111111111
  7   -6784    511   1110010110000000   0000000111111111
  8  -13568    255   1100101100000000   0000000011111111
```

Note that `SHR` can divide only positive numbers. Shifting –53 by one bit to the right produces +32741, not –26 as you might expect.

The `SHL` and `SHR` operators return 0 if the expression is shifted right or left by a number greater than or equal to the number of bits in the integer. For example, if `X` is a word-type variable, then

```
X shl 16
```

will always return 0, regardless of the current value of `X`.

Boolean Operators

The Boolean operators AND, NOT, OR, and XOR do double duty. They serve either as *logical* or *bitwise* operators. Table 4.3 summarizes what they do.

Table 4.3. *Boolean Operators*

Operator	*Syntax*	*Meaning*
NOT	NOT expression	Complement
AND	expression1 AND expression2	AND
OR	expression1 OR expression2	Inclusive OR
XOR	expression1 XOR expression2	Exclusive OR

The bitwise operators perform Boolean operations on each bit of an expression. The logical operators perform Boolean operations on the operands, each of which is itself considered either Boolean True or False. Turbo Pascal can tell the difference between the operator categories from context.

The logical and bitwise operators are shown in table 4.4, together with their meanings.

Table 4.4. *Logical and Bitwise Operators*

Values returned by bitwise operations for each bit pair						*Values returned by logical operations where X and Y are operands*					
X	Y	NOT X	X AND Y	X OR Y	Y XOR Y	X	Y	NOT X	X AND Y	X OR Y	Y XOR Y
1	1	0	1	1	0	T	T	F	T	T	F
1	0	0	0	1	1	T	F	F	F	T	T
0	1	1	0	1	1	F	T	T	F	T	T
0	0	1	0	0	0	F	F	T	F	F	F

Logical Operators

Logical operators perform Boolean manipulations that use entire operands. AND compares two operands and returns True only if both operands are True. OR compares two operands and returns True if either operand is True. XOR compares two operands and returns True only if the operands are different. NOT returns the opposite state of an operand.

By default, Turbo Pascal evaluates Boolean expressions only as far as necessary to determine the result of the entire expression. This feature, called *short-circuit evaluation*, results in extremely efficient program execution. For example, in the expression

```
if (A=4) OR (B>16) OR ((B*B-4*A*C)>0) then <statement>
```

if A is equal to 4, Turbo executes <statement> without bothering to test the second or third conditions. Similarly, if A does not equal 4, but B is greater than 16, Turbo executes <statement> without testing the third condition.

A similar process results when conditions are connected by AND operators. In the expression

```
if (A=4) AND (B>16) AND ((B*B-4*A*C)>0) then <statement>
```

if A does not equal 4, Turbo will not execute <statement>; the second and third conditions are never checked.

You can disable short-circuit evaluation by turning off the B compiler directive with {$B-}, which then forces every condition to be evaluated. This is desirable only when the conditions include function calls that also contain side effects. This topic is discussed in detail in the "Compiler Directives" reference section.

Bitwise Operators

The bitwise operators do Boolean manipulations on individual bits. Each bit of the result is determined by individually testing the corresponding bits in the operands. AND compares two bits and sets the result if both bits are set. OR compares two bits and sets the result if either bit is set. XOR compares two bits and sets the result if the bits are different. NOT reverses a single bit.

The AND instruction can clear the value of specific bits regardless of their current settings. To do this, AND the original value with a *mask* containing 0 for any bit positions you want to clear and 1 for any bit positions you want to remain unchanged. For example, to clear bits 4 through 6 of the byte variable X, you would use the following instruction:

```
X := X AND $8F;    { 1000 1111 to clear bits 4, 5, and 6 }
```

The OR instruction can set the value of specific bits regardless of their current settings. To do this, OR the original value with a mask containing 1 for any bit positions you want to set and 0 for any bit positions you want to remain unchanged. If you want to set bits 4 through 6 of the byte variable X, no matter what those bits contained previously, you could use the instruction:

```
X := X OR $70;    { 0111 0000 to set bits 4, 5, and 6 }
```

The XOR instruction can be used to toggle (reverse) the value of specific bits regardless of their current settings. To do this, XOR the original value with a mask containing 1 for any bit positions you want to toggle and 0 for any bit positions you want to remain unchanged. To change the setting of bit 4 in the byte variable X, the instruction would be:

```
X := X XOR $10;    { 0001 0000 to toggle bit 4 }
```

The unary NOT instruction is used to change the state of every bit in an integer. By itself, NOT is not a particularly useful arithmetic operator; you do not often need to know, for example, that for the byte values 70 and 213, NOT 70 equals 185, and NOT 213 equals 42. NOT is most commonly used in combination with the AND and OR operators. To set every bit *except* bits 4 through 6 of the byte variable X (that is, to set bits 0 through 3 and bit 7), no matter what those bits contained previously, you could use the instruction:

```
X := X OR NOT $70;    { 0111 0000 becomes 1000 1111 }
```

Relational Operators

The relational operators compare two expressions and return True if the condition specified by the operator is satisfied, or False if it is not. Relational operators are typically used with conditional directives. The operators and their return values are listed in table 4.5.

Relational tests can be used wherever Boolean expressions are allowed. This includes if...then, repeat...until, while...do, and case statements, as the BOOL1 program (listing 4.3) shows.

Table 4.5. Relational Operators

Operator	*Syntax*	*Returns* `True` *if:*
=	`expression1 = expression2`	`expression1` equals `expression2`
< >	`expression1 <> expression2`	`expression1` is not equal to `expression2`
<	`expression1 < expression2`	`expression1` is less than `expression2`
<=	`expression1 <= expression2`	`expression1` is less than or equal to `expression2`
>	`expression1 > expression2`	`expression1` is greater than `expression2`
>=	`expression1 >= expression2`	`expression1` is greater than or equal to `expression2`

Listing 4.3

```
program Bool1;
var
   i, j : integer;
begin
   writeln( 'Enter two integers: ' );
   write( 'First number:  ' );
   readln( i );
   write( 'Second number: ' );
   readln( j );
   case (i<j) of
      True  : writeln( i, ' is less than ', j );
      False : writeln( i, ' is not less than ', j );
   end;
end.
```

A typical session with BOOL1 follows:

```
Enter two integers:
First number:  2
Second number: 6
2 is less than 6
Enter two integers:
First number:  -5
Second number: -9
-5 is not less than -9
```

Each Boolean clause in a compound expression must be enclosed in parentheses, as in:

```
if (DinerCount >= RoomMax) OR (Expense > Profit) then
```

The `NOT` operator negates (that is, reverses) the state of a Boolean value. For example, if the expression `(X >= 3)` is `False`, `(NOT (X >= 3))` is `True`. Notice, though, that for each relational operator, you can use its functional opposite, for example, > for `NOT <=`, < for `NOT >=`, and <> for `NOT =`.

Notice in table 4.1 that `NOT` has a higher precedence than any relational operator. In the NEG1 program (listing 4.4), the first `writeln` procedure produces `True`, but the second `writeln` procedure produces `False`.

Listing 4.4

```
program Neg1;
var
   i, j : byte;
begin
   i := 100;
   j := 1;
   writeln( NOT i > j );
   writeln( NOT (i > j) );
end.
```

In the first `writeln` statement, the instruction `NOT i` is treated as `NOT 100` and results in 155 (the number 100 in binary is 01100100; its negation is 10011011, or 155), and when 155 is found to be greater than 1, the result is `True`. In the second `writeln` statement, 100 is found to be greater than 1, so its negation returns `False`. You can avoid such problems through the liberal use of parentheses.

Two strings are compared lexicographically. This is a fancy way of saying that the same rules that order dictionary entries are used when strings are being compared. Strings are sorted according to the ASCII value of each character. Therefore, `"CATS" < "DOG"` is `True`, even though `"CATS"` contains more characters. The defined size of a string is ignored; only the current contents matter.

For comparison, an operand of type `char` is treated as a `string` of length one.

Unfortunately, Boolean values can be compared other than for equality and inequality. In the BOOL2 program in listing 4.5, two Boolean variables are compared to test a "greater than" condition. `True` is stored as +1 and `False` is stored as 0, so `True` is greater than `False` and the message

```
VarI is greater than VarJ
```

is displayed. You should avoid such constructions whenever possible.

Listing 4.5

```
program Bool2;
var
   VarI, VarJ : Boolean;
begin
   VarI := True;
   VarJ := False;
   if VarI > VarJ then
      writeln( 'VarI is greater than VarJ' )
   else
      writeln( 'VarI is not greater than VarJ' );
end.
```

Set Operators

Sets are intended to bridge the gap between the esoteric, artificial world of the computer program and the hard, cold, concrete world of everyday existence. Because sets define collections of objects that represent the real world, it seems only fitting that the common logic of everyday life can be applied to their manipulation.

The relational set operators test either for equality or inclusion. The only consideration is the presence or absence of elements; neither the ordering of elements in a set operand nor the relative magnitude of individual elements has any bearing on the result of the test. Table 4.6 summarizes these operators.

Just as it does with arithmetic relation operators, the `NOT` operator negates (reverses) the state of a Boolean value. Therefore, if `Set1 = Set2` is `True`, `NOT (Set1 = Set2)` is `False`.

Table 4.6. Set Operators

Operator	*Syntax*	*Returns* `True` *if:*
=	`Set1 = Set2`	`Set1` and `Set2` are identical. Every element in `Set1` is contained in `Set2`, and every element in `Set2` is contained in `Set1`.
< >	`Set1 <> Set2`	One of the sets contains at least one element that is not in the other set.
<=	`Set1 <= Set2`	Every element in `Set1` is also in `Set2`.
<	`Set1 < Set2`	Every element in `Set1` is also in `Set2`. In addition, `Set2` contains at least one other element not found in `Set1`.
>=	`Set1 >= Set2`	Every element in `Set2` is also in `Set1`.
>	`Set1 > Set2`	Every element in `Set2` is also in `Set1`. In addition, `Set1` contains at least one other element not found in `Set2`.
IN	`elem IN Set1`	The element `elem` is found in `Set1`.

Three main operations can be performed on the elements of sets: union, difference, and intersection. The results of these operations conform to the ordinary rules of logic.

The union operator + produces a set that contains one of every element found in either operand. For example, the union

```
[ 1, 2, 3, 4, 5 ] + [ 3, 4, 5, 6, 7 ]
```

produces the set

```
[ 1, 2, 3, 4, 5, 6, 7 ]
```

which can also be written

```
[ 1..7 ]
```

The difference operator - (sometimes called the *complement* operator), produces a set that contains all elements of the first set that are not found in the second set. For example, the difference

```
[ 1, 2, 3, 4, 5 ] - [ 3, 4, 5, 6, 7 ]
```

produces the set

```
[ 1, 2 ]
```

The intersection operator * returns a set containing elements common to both set operands. For example, the intersection

```
[ 1, 2, 3, 4, 5 ] * [ 3, 4, 5, 6, 7 ]
```

produces the set

```
[ 3, 4, 5 ]
```

The union, difference, and intersection operators have their greatest value in defining new sets rather than in direct problem solving situations. For example, the SET2 program in listing 4.6 uses these operators to define sets.

Listing 4.6

```
program set2;
type
   Rainbow       = ( Red, Yellow, Orange, Blue, Green, Violet );
   DaysOfTheWeek = ( Sunday, Monday, Tuesday, Wednesday,
                     Thursday, Friday, Saturday );
   Months        = ( Jan, Feb, Mar, Apr, May, Jun,
                     Jul, Aug, Sep, Oct, Nov, Dec );
var
   Primaries, Composites, Crayons : set of Rainbow;
   FullWeek, WeekDays, WeekEnd    : set of DaysOfTheWeek;
   NoSchool, WarmEnough, Vacation : set of Months;
begin
   Primaries  := [ Red, Blue, Green ];
   Composites := [ Orange, Green, Violet ];
   Crayons    := Primaries + Composites;  { All colors in Rainbow }
   FullWeek   := [ Sunday..Saturday ];
   WeekEnd    := [ Saturday, Sunday ];
   WeekDays   := FullWeek - WeekEnd;     { Contains Monday..Friday }
   NoSchool   := [ May..Sep ];
   WarmEnough := [ Apr..Aug ];
   Vacation   := NoSchool * WarmEnough;   { Contains May..Aug }
   { Remainder of code follows }
end.
```

The address operator `@` returns the address of any variable, procedure, or function. It produces the same result as the `Addr` function, although much more efficiently. The `@` operator returns a value that is compatible with all pointer types.

The PTRFUNCT program (listing 4.7) defines the pointer variable `P2`, then uses the `@` operator to make it functionally equivalent to the byte variable `P1`.

Listing 4.7

```
program PtrFunct;
var
   P1 : byte;          { Defines a normal byte variable }
   P2 : ^byte;         { Defines a pointer to a byte }
begin
   P1 := 14;           { Assigns 14 to the byte variable }
   P2 := @ P1;         { Finds the address of P1 }
   writeln( P2^ );     { Outputs 14.  Notice the pointer symbol! }
end.
```

The Concatenation Operator

Most string and character operations are handled by functions or procedures. The one exception is the + operator, which is equivalent to the `Concat` function.

Using + on operands of `string` or `char` type returns a single string that is the concatenation of the two operands. The resulting string cannot exceed 255 characters; any excess characters are truncated on the right.

The new string consists of only the active portions of the operands. For example, in the code

```
var
   S1, S2, S3 : string[ 25 ];
begin
   S1 := 'abc';
   S2 := '12345678';
   S3 := S1 + S2;
```

the string `S3` has become `'abc12345678'` even though all three strings were defined to be 25 characters long.

Summary

In this chapter, you learned how to use expressions in Turbo Pascal. You learned the behavior of individual Turbo Pascal operators and that each operator is processed in order of precedence.

- ❑ The results of arithmetic operators depend on whether the operands are integer or real values.
- ❑ Shift operators "slide" the bits in an operand left or right.
- ❑ Logical operators perform Boolean operations on entire operands.
- ❑ Bitwise operators perform Boolean operations on the individual bits of an operand.
- ❑ Relational operators compare the magnitude of operands.
- ❑ Set operators test for equality or inclusion.
- ❑ The address operator returns the memory location of a data object.
- ❑ The concatenation operator combines two strings.

CHAPTER 5

Procedures and Functions

There is no one right way for a program to solve a given problem. In fact, the more complicated the programming task, the harder it is to ensure that *any* approach is correct. A variety of methods can help you simplify program design, however. Almost all involve breaking a problem down into smaller, more manageable tasks called *subroutines.* In Turbo Pascal, subroutines consist of procedures and functions.

Because of its extensive use of procedures and functions (actually, because of its almost total *reliance* on them), Turbo Pascal is considered a structured language. A *structured program* consists of subroutines that, when combined, create a working program. Most programs of any interest are broken up into subroutines.

This chapter discusses how you can use procedures and functions to write structured programs and offers guidance on how you can exploit the more advanced features of procedures and functions.

The Need for Structure

Many famous stories about software errors have been circulated. The original avionics software for the F-16 jet fighter contained a small bug that caused the plane to flip upside down whenever it crossed the equator. One of the early NASA space probes to Venus went off-course and was lost because of a software glitch. The Bank of New York lost millions of dollars in interest payments because a two-day computer crash prevented the bank from determining how much money it needed to repay the Federal Reserve Bank. In the PC world, almost every major software house has experienced some sort of delay in releasing a new product; many others have simply gone out of business because design errors made their products unmarketable.

These systems are a bit more complicated than the ones you are likely to develop with Turbo Pascal. Nevertheless, the same quality guidelines that now apply to the design of cruise missile guidance software can be applied also to the smallest programming chore.

Exhaustive Testing

Most introductory programming classes explain that one way to test your program is to trace its flow, keeping track of the contents of its variables as you go. Unfortunately, that technique has its limitations. For example, suppose that your program contains a loop with five sections that transfer control according to the diagram in figure 5.1.

Fig. 5.1. *A flowchart of a small program with only five sections.*

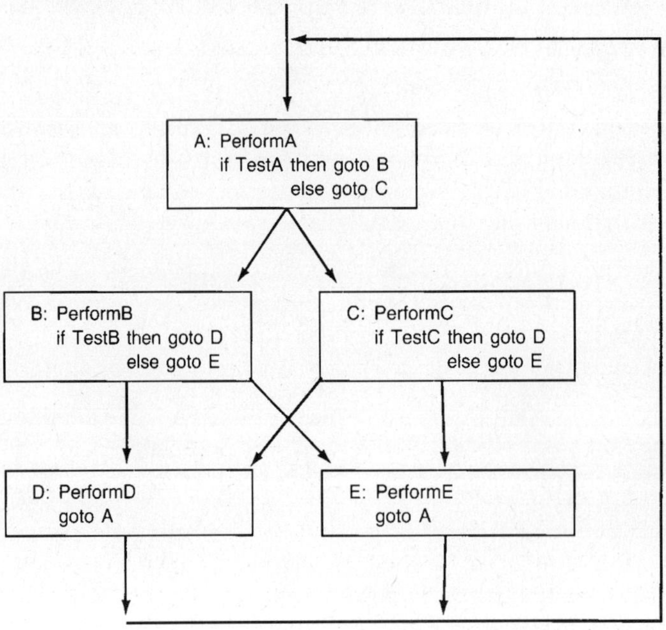

If every path is equally likely to be taken, there are four possible routes through the program. After 10 loops, there are 4^{10} (1,048,576) possible routes. Even if you needed only 1 second for each pass, your test would still take over 12 days. (After 20 passes, over 1 trillion combinations are possible. Your test would take about 35,000 years.)

Obviously, exhaustive testing is not the answer. But how else can you be sure that your program will work?

The solution is to test each of the components individually. If each component is itself formed from several other components, each of those must be tested as well. In other words, if a problem is too difficult or too complex, break it down into something more manageable.

In programming, this technique is commonly called *divide and conquer*. If the term sounds militaristic, it is because it was first used by Julius Caesar. It has been a successful tool ever since. You divide a difficult problem into a set of smaller, independent problems that are easier to understand and solve.

In Turbo Pascal, each subproblem is solved with a procedure or function.

The Use of Procedures and Functions

There are several advantages to using subroutines and structured design, including the following:

- Programs are more readable because subroutines identify the single purpose behind several lines of code.
- Programs are more efficient because every common action is defined (and stored) only once.
- Programs are more reliable because the underlying problem has been simplified as a result of being broken down into subroutines.
- Programs are easier to maintain because changing a single subroutine does not require modification of the entire program.
- Programs can be developed in less time because you do not need to develop new techniques for each new application.

In addition, structured programming imposes a discipline on the overall programming effort. That is not something you can quantify, but it is a very real advantage because it results in a final product of generally higher quality.

Procedure and Function Structure

Procedures and functions have the same basic structure as the program itself: a header followed by a block. They can be thought of as subprograms that will always be referenced and executed as a single unit.

A procedure is a subroutine that—like a statement—results in a series of actions directed toward a single purpose. A function is a subroutine specifically designed to return a value; accordingly, functions are called only in expressions. Certain procedures and functions are of such widespread importance that they are already defined by the compiler. These subroutines—such as `write`, `writeln`, and `readln`—are called *standard*. The complete list of over 200 standard procedures and functions can be found in the *Library Reference*.

When the standard subroutines are not adequate for the task at hand, the programmer may define a new subroutine through a procedure declaration or a function declaration. After the new subroutine is defined, it can be invoked by simply stating its name—the same way that the standard routines are invoked.

Procedures

A *procedure* consists of a collection of instructions that you want to execute as a single unit. A *parameter* is information (usually a variable) that is transferred between a procedure and a calling program. A procedure is executed simply by listing its name, together with any required parameters.

Components of a Procedure

Like a program, a procedure consists of three components:

- The *header*, consisting of the reserved word `procedure`, followed by the procedure name and any required parameters.
- The *data* that will be manipulated by the instructions in the procedure, as defined in label, constant, type, and variable declarations. Data is located immediately after the header but before the first procedure code statement.

- Program *code* statements describing the actions to be performed. Any procedures or functions defined by the procedure are placed at the start of the code area. Code statements follow, enclosed by the reserved words `begin` and `end`.

  Every procedure ends with a semicolon.

  The general format of a Pascal procedure is as follows:

```
procedure name( optional parameters );
   { Data declarations }
begin
   { Code statements }
end;
```

The header is always required, but both data and code are optional. For example, the following:

```
procedure Trivial;
begin
end;
```

defines a procedure that does absolutely nothing. If the `Trivial` procedure is called later in a program, its only effect would be to slow the execution of the program.

The rule in Pascal that says that a variable must be declared before it can be used applies to procedures and functions as well. After the procedure or function name is defined, however, it may be used just like other predefined procedure and function names. Through the act of creating your own subroutine, you temporarily extend the language.

A Procedure Example

The following procedure, `SayHello`, clears the screen and displays the `Hello` message.

```
procedure SayHello( Col, Row : byte );
begin;
   ClrScr;               { Clears the screen and positions the }
                         { cursor in the upper left corner }
   GotoXY( Col, Row ); { Moves the cursor to column Col of row Row }
   Write( "Hello" );     { Displays "Hello" on the screen }
end;
```

The `SayHello` procedure itself relies on three other procedures:

- `ClrScr` clears the screen and positions the cursor in the upper left corner of the screen.
- `GotoXY` positions the cursor at the X and Y coordinates specified as its parameters.
- `Write` displays a message, provided as a parameter, on the screen.

After the `SayHello` procedure is defined, it can be executed with a statement such as:

```
SayHello( 10, 5 ); { Places "Hello" in column 10 of row 5 }
```

There are only two differences between the `SayHello` procedure and an equivalent program:

1. The procedure ends with a semicolon, whereas a program ends with a period.
2. In the procedure, the variables `Col` and `Row` are undefined. Their values must come from an external source.

These are not big distinctions. A program, consisting of a header and a block, can invoke a procedure, which itself consists of a header and a block. Further, any given procedure can invoke other procedures and functions.

Functions

A *function* is similar to a procedure. It consists of a collection of instructions that you want to execute as a single unit. Its specific purpose, however, is to return a value.

Components of a Function

Like a procedure, a function consists of three components:

- The *header*, consisting of the reserved word `function`, followed by the function name and any required parameters. In addition, the function must itself be defined as a certain *type*.
- The *data* that will be manipulated by the instructions in the function, as defined in label, constant, type, and variable declarations. Data is located immediately after the header but before the first function code statement.

- Program *code* statements describing the actions to be performed. Any procedures or functions defined by the function are placed at the start of the code area. Code statements follow, enclosed by the reserved words `begin` and `end`.

  Every function ends with a semicolon.

  The general format of a Pascal function is as follows:

```
function name( optional parameters ) : functiontype;
   { Data declarations }
begin
   { Code statements }
end;
```

The header is always required, but both data and code are optional. However, a function generally contains at least one line of code that determines the value returned by the function. For example, the following:

```
function Trivial : integer;
begin
   Trivial := 0;
end;
```

defines a function called `Trivial` that is *functionally equivalent* to using 0. After `Trivial` is defined, the following codes are identical:

`X := 0;` and `X := Trivial;`

A Function Example

Two of the simplest standard functions are `Sqrt( x )`, which returns the square root of its parameter, and `Sqr( x )`, which returns the square of its parameter. The term *return* means that the entire function is equivalent to the variable it defines; hence it can be used wherever a single variable is allowed.

For example, the function `LongSide`, which returns the hypotenuse of a right triangle, is defined as follows:

```
function LongSide( A, B : real ) : real;
begin
   LongSide := Sqrt( Sqr(A) + Sqr(B) )
end;
```

A function is executed simply by listing its name, together with any required parameters. `LongSide` can be used wherever an ordinary variable can be used, such as in the following code:

```
if LongSide( 3.0, 4.0 ) = 5.0 then
   writeln( '3, 4, and 5 are Pythagorean triples!' );
```

Structured Programs and the Limits of Scope

In Turbo Pascal, subroutines may be *nested*. That is, each subroutine may contain another subroutine, which in turn may contain yet another subroutine, and so on.

Each nested subroutine can access the label, constant, type, and variable declarations of any of the parent subroutines that "surround" it. No parent subroutine, however, can access any of the label, constant, type, and variable declarations of a subroutine that nests in it. This limitation is called the *scope of an identifier*.

Similarly, a nested subroutine can be used only by the parent that defined it. This limitation is called the *scope of a subroutine*.

This section explains the effect of scope on program design and operation.

Global and Local Variables

All identifiers defined in any parent subroutines are called *global*, and all identifiers defined in a nested procedure or function are said to be *local* to the procedure or function.

In the SCOPE1 program (listing 5.1), the `First`, `Second`, and `Average` variables are global to the `CalculateAverage` procedure; therefore, they may be freely used within it. The `Total` variable is local to `CalculateAverage`; it cannot be used outside the procedure itself. Local variables are created by saving stack space for the variable at the start of the subroutine; this space is returned to the stack when the subroutine ends.

Listing 5.1

```
program Scope1;
var
   First, Second, Average : integer;
procedure CalculateAverage;
var
   Total : integer;
begin
   Total := First + Second;
   Average := Total div 2;
end;
begin
   First  := 12;
   Second := 38;
   CalculateAverage;
   Writeln( 'The average of ', First, ' and ', Second, ' is ', Average
    );
end.
```

Variable Definition

Clearly, the compiler is able to segregate identifiers according to the block in which they are defined. Whenever an identifier is used, the compiler looks to the declarations of the current block; if the identifier is not found, the compiler checks the next higher block, then the next, and so on, until a declaration is found.

After the declaration is located, no further searches are made. Consequently, each procedure and function can declare a local identifier that has the same name as a global identifier. In the SCOPE2 program (listing 5.2), the variable i is defined both globally in the program itself and locally in the ShowI procedure.

Listing 5.2

```
program Scope2;
var
   i : byte;
```

continues

Listing 5.2 continued

```
procedure ShowI;
var
   i : byte;
begin
   i := 48;
   writeln( 'Within the procedure, the value of "i" is ', i );
end;
begin
   i := 35;
   ShowI;
   writeln( 'Within the main program, the value of "i" is ', i );
end.
```

When SCOPE2 executes, it produces the following result:

```
Within the procedure, the value of "i" is 48
Within the main program, the value of "i" is 35
```

Notice that the global variable i is unaffected by either the declaration or assignment of the local variable with the same name.

Side Effects

Because of the rules of scope, variables can be created, stored, and used for as long as they are needed. Their life expectancy might be the duration of the entire program or the duration of a single subroutine. Although the tendency is to define every variable globally, a better approach is to reduce the life of a variable to as short a time as possible.

For example, if one subroutine needs to pass information to another subroutine, the information can be passed as a parameter. If the data is used only by the two routines, there is no need to define the data globally.

This is more than just good housekeeping. One of the most common programming errors is for procedures and functions to redefine (often unintentionally) the values of global variables. This process is known as the *side effect* of the subroutine, because it is rarely something that the programmer deliberately sets out to do.

Parameter Passing

The parameters specified in a procedure or function heading are called *formal parameters*. These parameters, like the variables defined in the subroutine itself, are *local* to the subroutine; no permanent space is reserved for them in memory. When the subroutine is called, the *actual parameters* to be sent to the subroutine are temporarily placed—in order—in a special area of memory called the *stack*. The subroutine reads this data—in order—from the stack. In other words, formal and actual parameters are transferred and matched by their order in the declaration, which becomes their order in the stack, not by name. The return value of a function is placed in one of the PC registers.

In the ACTFORM program (listing 5.3), `Factor1` and `Factor2` are formal parameters; `A` and `B` are actual parameters.

Listing 5.3

```
program ActForm;
var
   A, B : integer;
procedure Product( Factor1, Factor2 : integer );
begin
   writeln( Factor1, ' x ', Factor2, ' = ', Factor1*Factor2 );
end;
begin
   A := 12;
   B := 17;
   Product( A, B );
end.
```

By using the stack to transfer data, Turbo Pascal effectively isolates each procedure and function from the part of the program that calls it. Conceivably, each subroutine can process in total independence, without ever affecting the contents of any other program variable. For this reason, procedures and functions are commonly called *subprograms*.

Sometimes, however, you *want* a subroutine to access the variables in the main body of the program. When you want to replace the value of a single variable, you can use a function. But at other times, you need a subprogram to compute a number of results rather than just one (for example, to compute an array), or you need to both use and modify the same variable (as when you increment a page number). For these situations, a function is not appropriate; instead, a procedure is needed.

Finally, a third situation arises when you want a subroutine to ignore the type of a variable passed to it.

Turbo Pascal supports all of these situations by providing three ways to specify a parameter.

- A parameter not preceded by the reserved word `var`, but followed by a specific type, is called a *value parameter*.
- A parameter preceded by the reserved word `var` and followed by a specific type is called a *variable parameter*.
- A parameter preceded by the reserved word `var` and not followed by a specific type is called an *untyped variable parameter*.

Each of these methods is described fully in this section.

Value Parameters

When a parameter is passed by *value*, it is copied to the stack. Value parameters are completely local to the subroutine. Whenever the variable is used in the subroutine, the *copy* of the variable on the stack is read or modified; the *original* variable (the actual parameter) is never touched.

The types of the actual and formal parameters must be compatible; for example, you cannot send a string to a procedure that expects a number. But beyond that, the only restriction is that the actual parameter must represent data whose value *can* be copied to the stack. In other words, within the limits of the type constraint, any format of actual parameter is allowed: expression, function, variable name, constant name, number, or string.

Note that a `file` type does not directly contain data (you have to read the data from the file itself) and consequently cannot be placed on the stack. Therefore, neither a `file` type variable nor a structured type variable that contains a `file` type can be used as a value parameter.

In the VALUE1 program (listing 5.4), the variables `i` and `j` are passed as value parameters to the `AddUp` function. When the function is called, the program copies the contents of `i` and `j` to the stack. While the function executes, only the stack copies of the variables can be accessed. Although the function changes both the `Val1` and `Val2` parameters, only the stack is affected; the variables `i` and `j` were never touched and consequently retain their original values.

Listing 5.4

```
program Value1;
var
   i, j : word;
function AddUp( Val1, Val2 : word ) : word;
begin
   Val1 := Val1 + Val2;    { Deliberate use of Val1 }
   Val2 := 0;              { Deliberate use of Val2 }
   AddUp := Val1;
end;
begin
   i := 10;
   j := 5;
   writeln( AddUp( i, j ), ' is the total of ', i, ' and ', j );
end.
```

When VALUE1 executes, it produces the following result:

```
15 is the total of 10 and 5
```

Variable Parameters

A *variable parameter* is used when you want to directly access—and, presumably, modify—a variable defined outside the scope of the subroutine itself. A variable parameter is passed by *reference*. This means that instead of using the stack to store a copy of the variable, the compiler uses the stack to store a *pointer* to the memory location where the actual variable can be found.

While the subroutine executes, every reference to the variable parameter is passed—by the pointer—to the actual variable. Therefore, when you change a variable parameter, you are really changing the original variable.

The VAR1 program (listing 5.5) performs simple screen animation. A block character (ASCII 219) is moved across the screen, from left to right, on line 10. The horizontal position is determined by the action of the `MoveRight` procedure. When the block reaches column 80 (the right side of the screen), `MoveRight` returns to column 1. To do this, `MoveRight` needs to be able to both read and modify the current column number; Consequently, `MoveRight` is passed a variable parameter containing the current column. It moves the block character one position to the right until it reaches column 80, at which point it resets the block to the far left side.

Listing 5.5

```
program Var1;
uses Crt;
const
   Column : word = 1;    {Initialize Column to 1}
var
   i : word;
procedure MoveRight( var Xposition : word );
begin
   if Xposition = 80 then
      Xposition := 1
   else
      Inc( Xposition );
end;
procedure Horizontal;
begin
   GotoXY( Column, 10 );    writeln( ' ' );   {Erases the previous block}
   MoveRight( Column );
   GotoXY( Column, 10 );    write( #219 );
   Delay( 50 );
end;
begin
   ClrScr;
   for i := 1 to 160 do Horizontal
end.
```

VAR1 uses the `Delay` procedure to pause long enough for each position to be observable. The format of the procedure is `Delay( Msec )`, where Msec is the number of milliseconds you want to wait before the program proceeds to the next statement. `Delay` bases its actions on the system clock; this is superior to using a loop or other counting device, which varies in duration depending on the type of computer you are using.

One of the most common programming errors you will experience is forgetting the reserved word `var` in the subroutine header. In that case, the subroutine can access only a copy of the variable on the stack, leaving the original variable untouched. You can see the result of such an error in the VAR1 program. Delete the reserved word `var`, and rerun the program. With a variable parameter, the `MoveRight` procedure causes the block character to make two horizontal passes across the screen. With a value parameter, `MoveRight` has no effect on the `Column` variable; 160 lines are written, with the block remaining in the far left column.

A variable parameter puts a pointer on the stack instead of the data object itself. Thus, large data objects such as arrays can be more efficiently handled as variable parameters even if you do not intend to modify them.

Untyped Variable Parameters

When you define a subroutine with a value or variable parameter, you are implicitly telling the compiler that you want it to test for and ensure type compatibility between the formal and actual parameters.

Type compatibility is highly desirable while you are developing your program. If you transpose, omit, or otherwise bungle a subroutine call, it is a relief to know that Turbo Pascal will tell you about it immediately. However, you may want to allow a single subroutine to use parameters of different types.

In Turbo Pascal, you can bypass type checking through the use of *untyped variable parameters*. This is an advanced feature of the compiler, so use it carefully; debugging programs without type checking can be extremely painful. However, one useful result of untyped variables is that you can use the same subroutine to process *similar* structures. For example, with type checking in place, formal and actual array parameters must be both the same type and the same size. Untyped parameters are not so restrictive.

The UNTYPED program (listing 5.6) contains a procedure called `WriteArray`, which is defined with the untyped variable parameter `ArrType`. `WriteArray` is designed to display the contents of any integer array up to 100 elements long. `WriteArray` is called by providing it with the name of an array, together with the array's lower and upper bounds.

Listing 5.6

```
program Untyped;
var
   i      : word;
   Array1 : array [ 1..10 ] of integer;       { 10 elements }
   Array2 : array [ 5..9 ] of integer;        {  5 elements }
```

continues

Listing 5.6 continued

```
procedure WriteArray( var ArrType; Min, Max : word );
type
   GeneralArray = array [ 1..100 ] of integer;
var
   i : word;
   WorkArray : GeneralArray absolute ArrType;
begin
   writeln( '             Index   Value' );
   for i := 1 to ( Max - Min + 1 ) do
      writeln( i:8, ( Min + i - 1 ):8, WorkArray[ i ]:8 );
end;
begin
   for i := 1 to 10 do Array1[ i ] := i*i;
   for i := 5 to 9 do Array2[ i ] := i*i*i;
   writeln( 'Array1' );
   WriteArray( Array1, 1, 10 );
   writeln;
   writeln( 'Array2' );
   WriteArray( Array2, 5, 9 );
end.
```

When UNTYPED executes, it produces the following results:

```
Array1
             Index   Value
       1       1       1
       2       2       4
       3       3       9
       4       4      16
       5       5      25
       6       6      36
       7       7      49
       8       8      64
       9       9      81
      10      10     100
Array2
             Index   Value
       1       5     125
       2       6     216
       3       7     343
       4       8     512
       5       9     729
```

Exiting a Subroutine

The `Exit` procedure can be used to end the current procedure or function gracefully. Before you use `Exit`, be sure that any values returned by your procedure or function have already been assigned.

Suppose that you need to evaluate the roots of a quadratic equation:

$$Ax^2 + Bx + C = 0$$

You remember that the roots are those values of x for which the equation is true. For example, the equation:

$$x^2 - 5x + 6 = 0$$

has A equal to 1, B equal to –5, and C equal to 6. The equation only holds when x is equal to either 2 or 3. Sometimes no numbers can be found to solve the equation; in that case, the roots are called *imaginary*.

The roots can be found with the *quadratic formula*

$$x = \frac{-B \pm \sqrt{(B2 - 4AC)}}{2A}$$

Roots only exist if ($B^2 - 4AC$) is nonnegative. The `RealQuadraticRoots` procedure uses the quadratic formula to test whether the roots exist. If they do exist, the roots are returned; if they do not, the procedure ends early with a call to the `Exit` routine.

```
procedure RealQuadraticRoots( A, B, C : real; var Root1,
    Root2 : real );
var
   Hold : real;
begin
   Root1 := 0;
   Root2 := 0;
   Hold := Sqr(B)-4*A*C;
   if Hold < 0 then Exit;                { Imaginary roots! }
   Root1 := (-B - Sqrt(Hold))/(2*A);
   Root2 := (-B + Sqrt(Hold))/(2*A);
end;
```

The `SquareRoot` function returns the square root of a number to any desired degree of precision. It operates by making a series of guesses; each new guess is halfway between the two prior "best" guesses. Each guess is tested; if it is accurate to within a specified (user-defined) range, the function ends with the `Exit` procedure. (In fact, if it were not for the `EXIT` procedure, the repeat loop would never end!)

```
function SquareRoot( X : real ) : real;
var
   Top, Bottom, Guess : real;
begin
   Top := Abs(X);    { Note absolute value }
   Bottom := 0.0;
   repeat
      Guess := (Top + Bottom) / 2;
      SquareRoot := Guess;
      if abs(Sqr(Guess)-X) < 0.00001 then Exit;
      if Guess*Guess > X then Top    := Guess
                         else Bottom := Guess;
   until False;
end;
```

Although it might seem as if `SquareRoot` is nothing but trial and error, it actually converges quickly. The technique can be used to solve a variety of other numerical problems.

You can call the `Exit` procedure also in the main body of your program; if you do, it ends your program immediately. Note, though, that the preferred way to end your program early is with a call to the `Halt` procedure, discussed in Chapter 12 "Accessing DOS."

Recursion

A *recursive* subroutine is one that calls itself directly (that is, it uses its own name) or calls another subroutine that, in turn, calls the original. At first, this might seem unwise or downright illegal. But consider that in Turbo Pascal, every time a subroutine is called, storage space is allocated for a completely new set of local variables.

In most traditional languages—including BASIC, Cobol, and Fortran—if a subroutine calls itself, every one of its local variables is overwritten. If a Turbo Pascal subroutine calls itself, each use of the routine is independent.

The BACK program (listing 5.7) asks you to keep entering animal names until it detects a null string. Notice that the `writeln` statement can be executed only *after* the null string is entered; after that, the `Backwards` procedure ends, and control is returned to the line following the most recent procedure call. If the procedure was called by another copy of itself, control returns to that copy, and the `writeln` statement for the parent copy of the procedure is executed. This chain continues until the original procedure call in the main body of the program is reached.

Listing 5.7

```
program Back;
procedure Backwards;
var
   Animal : string[ 15 ];
begin
   write( 'Select an animal: ' );
   readln( Animal );
   if Animal <> '' then Backwards;
   writeln( Animal );
end;
begin
   Backwards
end.
```

The following is typical of the program's operation:

```
Select an animal: Antelope
Select an animal: Bear
Select an animal: Cat
Select an animal: Dog
Select an animal: Elephant
Select an animal: Fox
Select an animal: Giraffe
Select an animal: Hyena
Select an animal:
Hyena
Giraffe
Fox
Elephant
Dog
Cat
Bear
Antelope
```

Each `Select an animal` message was produced from a separate copy of the `Backwards` procedure. Each `writeln` was executed by those same copies as they end in reverse order.

This opens up some interesting possibilities. Clearly, Turbo Pascal can support the use of subroutines that are defined in terms of themselves, called *recursive subroutines*. Uses of recursive subroutines abound in mathematics, language theory, and artificial intelligence.

Factorials

If you have two objects, you can arrange them in only two ways (AB and BA). Three objects can be arranged in six ways (ABC, ACB, BAC, BCA, CAB, and CBA). In general, N objects can be arranged in N! ways. The exclamation mark is called a *factorial* sign. If N is a positive integer, the number N! (pronounced "N factorial") is defined to be equal to:

$$N \times (N-1) \times (N-2) \times (N-3) \times \ldots \times 4 \times 3 \times 2 \times 1$$

Therefore:

$$1! = 1$$

$$2! = 2 \times 1 = 2$$

$$3! = 3 \times 2 \times 1 = 6$$

$$4! = 4 \times 3 \times 2 \times 1 = 24$$

$$8! = 8 \times 7 \times 6 \times 5 \times 4 \times 3 \times 2 \times 1 = 40{,}320$$

Because of the availability of recursion in Turbo Pascal, *factorial* can be defined as follows:

if $N = 1$ then $N! = 1$ else $N! = N \times (N-1)!$

Such a definition is said to be *recursive*. You can apply it in the FACT1 program (listing 5.8), as follows.

Listing 5.8

```
program Fact1;
var
   number : longint;
function Fact( n : longint ) : longint;
begin
   if n = 1 then
      Fact := 1
   else
      Fact := n * Fact( n-1 );
```

```
end;
begin
   for number := 1 to 10 do
      writeln( number:2, '! = ', Fact( number ) );
end.
```

When FACT1 executes, it produces the following:

```
 1! = 1
 2! = 2
 3! = 6
 4! = 24
 5! = 120
 6! = 720
 7! = 5040
 8! = 40320
 9! = 362880
10! = 3628800
```

FACT1 operates by calling the `Fact` function n times; each time the `Fact` function calls itself, it uses the next lower integer as the parameter.

For something as simple as a factorial calculation, a nonrecursive solution is also possible, as shown in the FACT2 program (listing 5.9).

Listing 5.9

```
program Fact2;
var
   number : longint;
function fact( n : longint ) : longint;
var
   Index, Hold : longint;
begin
   Hold := 1;
   for Index := 1 to n do
      Hold := Hold * Index;
   fact := Hold;
end;
begin
   for number := 1 to 10 do
      writeln( number:2, '! = ', fact( number ) );
end.
```

At this level, it is difficult to determine which program is easier to define, understand, and use. Now it is time to add some complexity.

The Greatest Common Divisor

The *greatest common divisor (GCD)* of two integers is the largest whole number that can be evenly divided into both of them. The GCD of 12 and 18 is 6. The GCD of 18 and 36 is 18. The GCD of 17 and 53 is 1.

Program GCD1 (listing 5.10) uses a technique called *Euclid's method* to compute the GCD of two numbers. Essentially, Euclid's method states that the GCD of two numbers must equal the GCD of the smaller number of the original pair and the difference between the pair. By applying that observation repetitively, you can quickly arrive at the GCD of the original set.

Listing 5.10

```
program GCD1;
var
   First, Second, Answer : longint;
function GCD( a, b : longint ) : longint;
begin
   writeln( a:10, b:10 );
   if b = 0 then
      GCD := a
   else
      GCD := GCD( b, a mod b );
end;
begin
   write( 'Enter the first integer:  ' );
   readln( First );
   write( 'Enter the second integer: ' );
   readln( Second );
   Answer := GCD( First, Second );
   writeln( 'The greatest common denominator is: ', Answer );
end.
```

A sample execution of GCD1 is as follows:

```
Enter the first integer:  48
Enter the second integer: 36
```

```
         48         36
         36         12
         12          0
The greatest common denominator is: 12
Enter the first integer:  747346
Enter the second integer: 543469
     747346     543469
     543469     203877
     203877     135715
     135715      68162
      68162      67553
      67553        609
        609        563
        563         46
         46         11
         11          2
          2          1
          1          0
The greatest common denominator is: 1
```

Again, a nonrecursive approach can be taken, as demonstrated in the GCD2 program (listing 5.11). GCD2 uses an iterative technique to apply the same method.

Listing 5.11

```
program GCD2;
var
   First, Second, Answer : longint;
function GCD( a, b : longint ) : longint;
var
   c : longint;
begin
   writeln( a:10, b:10 );
   while b <> 0 do begin
      c := a mod b;
      a := b;
      b := c;
      writeln( a:10, b:10 );
   end;
   GCD := a;
end;
```

continues

Listing 5.11 continued

```
begin
   write( 'Enter the first integer:  ' );
   readln( First );
   write( 'Enter the second integer: ' );
   readln( Second );
   Answer := GCD( First, Second );
   writeln( 'The greatest common denominator is ', Answer );
end.
```

The Fibonacci Sequence

The Fibonacci sequence is the basis of most spiral designs. The sequence is defined by specifying the first two elements; every subsequent element is the sum of the previous pair. The FIB1 program (listing 5.12) includes a Fibonacci function that solves for the Nth element of the sequence by looping through every lower-order element. This approach is called *iteration*.

Listing 5.12

```
program Fib1;
var
   i : word;
function Fibonacci( Element : longint ) : longint;
var
   Index, Current, First, Second : longint;
begin
   First   := 1;
   Second  := 1;
   Current := 1;
   if Element > 2 then
      for Index := 1 to Element - 2 do begin
         Current := First + Second;
         Second  := First;
         First   := Current;
      end;
   Fibonacci := Current;
end;
```

```
begin
   for i := 1 to 10 do
      writeln( i:3, Fibonacci( i ):8 );
end.
```

The FIB2 program (listing 5.13) defines a Fibonacci function using a recursive approach. Intuitively, you can see that FIB2 is a bit simpler than FIB1.

Listing 5.13

```
program Fib2;
var
   i : word;
function Fibonacci( Element : longint ) : longint;
begin
   if Element <= 2 then
      Fibonacci := 1
   else
      Fibonacci := Fibonacci( Element - 1 ) + Fibonacci( Element - 2
   );
end;
begin
   for i := 1 to 10 do
      writeln( i:3, Fibonacci( i ):8 );
end.
```

When either of these programs is run, it produces the following output:

```
  1       1
  2       1
  3       2
  4       3
  5       5
  6       8
  7      13
  8      21
  9      34
 10      55
```

When To Use Recursion

Three major rules apply to the use of recursion.

Rule 1: In general, for every recursive technique you can devise, an iterative approach can also be found.

Rule 2: Each recursive call must apply to a simpler case than the previous one.

Rule 3: A means of easy escape must exist, so that the recursion is not infinite. It is called the *basis* of the recursive definition.

Unfortunately, no such hard and fast rules can be found to help determine when recursion *should* be used.

One of the most famous uses of recursion is to solve the puzzle of the *Towers of Hanoi*. This is a game consisting of three poles and a set of rings of different diameters. As the game opens, all the rings are on the left pole, arranged in order of their size; the smallest ring is on the top and the largest is on the bottom.

The object of the game is to move all the rings from the pole on the left to the pole on the right. A few restrictions make things interesting. First, you can move only one disk at a time. Each move consists of removing the topmost ring from one pole and placing it immediately on another pole. Second, you cannot place a larger ring on top of a smaller ring.

For two rings, you make three moves: move the small ring from the left to center, move the large ring from the left to the right, and finally move the small ring from the center to the right. For three rings, you need seven moves, as shown in figure 5.2.

With just a little thought, you can see that to move N disks from the left pole to the right pole, you do the following:

1. Move N –1 disks from the left pole to the center pole.

2. Move the largest disk from the left pole to the right pole.

3. Move the N –1 disks from the center pole to the right pole.

The HANOI1 program (listing 5.14) automates this strategy for any number of rings.

Fig. 5.2. Solving the Towers of Hanoi puzzle with three rings.

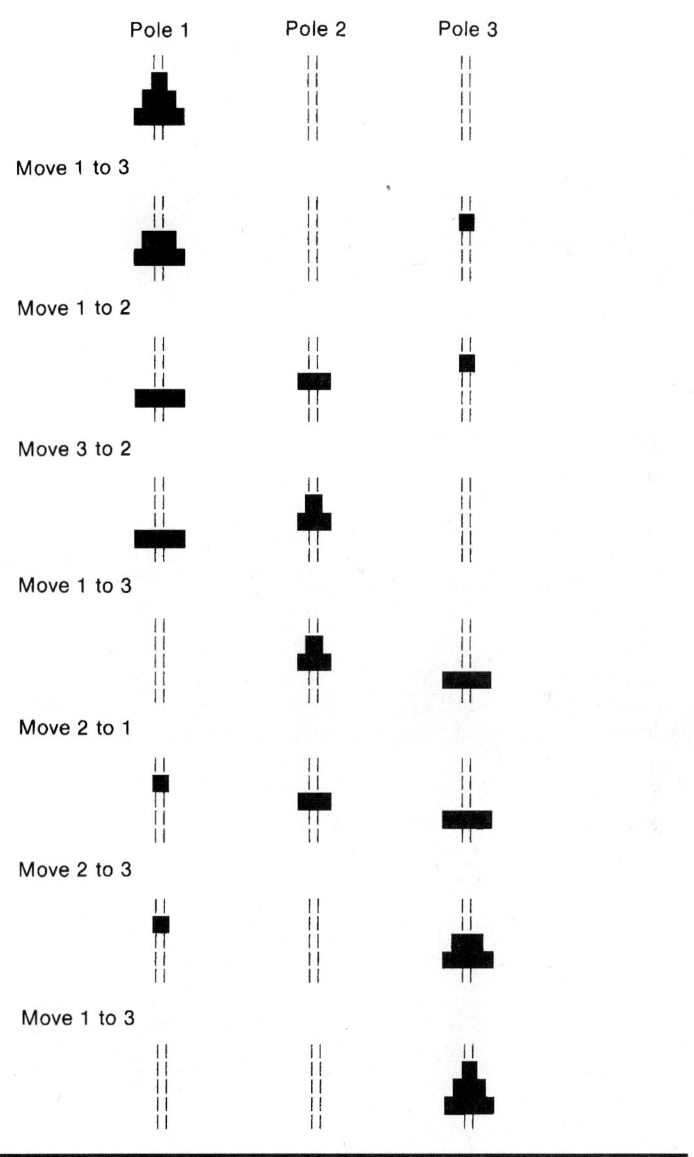

Listing 5.14

```
program Hanoi1;
var
   NumberOfDisks : integer;
procedure transfer( Disk, StartFrom, Target, StopOver : integer );
begin
   if Disk > 0 then begin
      transfer( Disk-1, StartFrom, StopOver, Target );
      writeln( 'Move ', StartFrom, ' to ', Target );
      transfer( Disk-1, StopOver, Target, StartFrom );
   end;
end;
begin
   write( 'Enter the number of disks: ' );
   readln( NumberOfDisks );
   transfer( NumberOfDisks, 1, 3, 2 );
end.
```

For three rings, HANOI1 provides the following advice:

```
Move 1 to 3
Move 1 to 2
Move 3 to 2
Move 1 to 3
Move 2 to 1
Move 2 to 3
Move 1 to 3
```

Of course, for anything larger, results presented in this manner could become boring quickly. Eight rings require 255 moves. Ten rings require 1,023 moves. The HANOI2 program (listing 5.15) animates the process by displaying the disks and the moves on the screen.

Listing 5.15

```
program Hanoi2;
uses Crt;
var
   i, j, NumberOfDisks : byte;
   GameBoard           : array[ 1..3, 1..10 ] of boolean;
procedure SetUp;
begin
   ClrScr;
```

```
   for i := 1 to 3 do                          { Clear the board }
      for j := 1 to 10 do
         GameBoard[ i, j ] := False;
   for i := 1 to NumberOfDisks do begin
      GameBoard[ 1, i ] := True;               { Put rings on left pole }
      GotoXY( 20-i, i );                       { Position for display }
      for j := 1 to 2*i do write( #219 );      { Write the block symbol }
   end;
end;
procedure transfer( Disk, StartFrom, Target, StopOver : integer );
procedure DisplayTheMove;
var
   k, k1 : byte;
begin
   k := 0;                                  { Find level of peg }
   repeat Inc(k) until GameBoard[ StartFrom, k ] = True;
   for k1 := 1 to abs(Target-StartFrom)*20 do begin
      if Target > StartFrom then begin      { Move disk left to right }
         GotoXY( StartFrom*20+k+k1-1, k );       write( #219 );
         GotoXY( StartFrom*20+k+k1-1-2*k, k );  write( ' ' );
      end else begin                        { Move disk right to left }
         GotoXY( StartFrom*20-k1-k, k );      write( #219 );
         GotoXY( StartFrom*20-k1-k+2*k, k);  write( ' ' );
      end;
      delay( 50 );                          { So movement is visible }
   end;
   GameBoard[ StartFrom, k ]  := False; { Remove from the old peg }
   GameBoard[ Target, k ] := True;      { Drop it on the new peg  }
   delay( 500 );                        { Wait between moves }
end;
begin
   if Disk > 0 then begin
      transfer( Disk-1, StartFrom, StopOver, Target );
      DisplayTheMove;
      transfer( Disk-1, StopOver, Target, StartFrom );
   end;
end;
begin
   write( 'Enter the number of Disks: ' );
   readln( NumberOfDisks );
   SetUp;
   transfer( NumberOfDisks, 1, 3, 2 );
end.
```

For the animation feature to work best, no more than ten disks should be specified when Hanoi2 is executed.

As an exercise, try to rewrite either of these programs without using recursion. It can be done (hint: use arrays to store intermediate results), but the resulting code quickly becomes complicated.

Recursion should be used whenever it is easier to use than iteration. In general, the more difficult the problem, the more likely that recursion will be the technique you prefer!

Forward Declarations

In the preceding section, a *recursive subroutine* was defined as one that calls itself either directly or indirectly. An example of an *indirect* call is when subroutine A calls subroutine B, and subroutine B calls subroutine A. When two or more subroutines call each other in such an indirect manner, they are said to exhibit *mutual recursion*.

But if A calls B, and B calls A, which one is defined first? After all, it was stated that every procedure and function has to be declared before it can be used. Take it one step further; how can *ordinary* recursion be allowed, because the subroutine obviously has not been totally defined before a call instruction is encountered?

The answer is that only the procedure or function header must be defined before the first call is made. Turbo Pascal needs to know the name of the subroutine (it must be able to recognize a call when it sees one), and it needs to know the parameter and function types, if any, to check the syntax of the call.

For two subroutines, each of which calls the other, one must obviously be listed second—*after* the first subroutine that needs to use it. But if you include a special *forward declaration* of its header prior to the first subroutine, the problem is solved.

The forward declaration is written exactly as the ordinary subroutine header, except it is followed by the reserved word `forward`. Later, when the actual subroutine is defined, you do not need to repeat any of the parameters.

You can use forward declarations for any subroutine, even those that are not used recursively. You will sometimes find programs in which, for documentation, every procedure or function is listed as a `forward` at the beginning of a program.

An *expression parser* is a program that can evaluate legal algebraic expressions. *Precedence* refers to the order in which each operation is evaluated. In Turbo Pascal, multiplication has a higher precedence than addition. Hence:

```
2 + 3 * 4
```

evaluates as 2+(3 * 4), or 14, rather than as (2+3) * 4, or 20. Parentheses are used to specify the parts of the expression that must be evaluated first. Hence, the statement:

```
(2 + 3) * 4
```

does evaluate to 20.

The EXPRESS program (listing 5.16) is a simple expression parser with the functions and levels of precedence shown in table 5.1.

***Table 5.1.** Precedence in the EXPRESS Program*

Precedence	*Operators*	*Name*
1 (highest)	( )	Parentheses
2	+-	Unary plus and minus
3	*/	Multiplication and division
4	+-	Binary plus and minus

Listing 5.16

```
program Express;
type
   TokenType = ( Number, Space, LParen, RParen,
                 Plus, Minus, Star, Slash, EndLine );
var
   Value,
   Result   : LongInt;
   Token    : TokenType;
   LinePos  : byte;
   Line     : string[ 80 ];
procedure DoBinaries( var Result : LongInt ); forward;
procedure Error( Message : string );
```

continues

Listing 5.16 continued

```
begin
   writeln( Message );
   Halt;
end;
procedure ScanLine;
begin
   if LinePos > Length( Line ) then
      Token := EndLine
   else begin
      case Line[ LinePos ] of
         '0'..'9' : begin
                        Token := Number;
                        Value := 0;
                        repeat
                           Value := 10*Value+Ord( Line[ LinePos ] )-48;
                           Inc( LinePos );
                        until ( LinePos > Length(Line) ) or
                              ( Line[ LinePos ] < '0' ) or
                              ( Line[ LinePos ] > '9' );
                     end;
              '(' : Token := LParen;
              ')' : Token := RParen;
              '+' : Token := Plus;
              '-' : Token := Minus;
              '*' : Token := Star;
              '/' : Token := Slash;
              ' ' : Token := Space;
            else    Error( 'Illegal characters on line' );
      end;
      if Token <> Number then Inc( LinePos );
   end;
   while Token = Space do ScanLine;
end;
procedure GetNextNumber( var Result : LongInt );
begin
   if Token = Number then begin
         Result := Result + Value;
         ScanLine;
      end else
         Error( 'Syntax error' );
end;
```

```
procedure DoParentheses( var Result : LongInt );    { Zero Level }
begin
   if Token = LParen then
      begin
         ScanLine;
         DoBinaries( Result );
         if Token = Rparen then ScanLine
                              else Error( 'Unbalanced parentheses' );
      end
   else
      GetNextNumber( Result );
end;
procedure DoUnaries( var Result : LongInt );    { First Level }
var
   Operation : TokenType;
begin
   Operation := Token;
   if (Token = Plus) or (Token = Minus) then
      ScanLine;
   DoParentheses( Result );
   if Operation = Minus then
      Result := -Result;
end;
procedure DoMultDiv( var Result : LongInt );    { Second Level }
var
   Next : LongInt;
   Operation : TokenType;
begin
   DoUnaries( Result );
   while (Token = Star) or (Token = Slash) do
      begin
         Operation := Token;
         ScanLine;
         Next := 0;
         DoUnaries( Next );
         case Operation of
            Star  : Result := Result * Next;
            Slash : if Next = 0 then Error( 'Division by 0' )
                                else Result := Result div Next;
         end;
      end;
end;
```

continues

Listing 5.16 continued

```
procedure DoBinaries{( var Result : LongInt )};   { Third Level }
var
   Next : LongInt;
   Operation : TokenType;
begin
   DoMultDiv( Result );
   while (Token = Plus) or (Token = Minus) do
      begin
         Operation := Token;
         ScanLine;
         Next := 0;
         DoMultDiv( Next );
         case Operation of
            Plus  : Result := Result + Next;
            Minus : Result := Result - Next;
         end;
      end;
end;
procedure Evaluate;    { Only process if something was entered }
begin
   if Length( Line ) <> 0 then begin
      LinePos := 1;
      ScanLine;
      Result := 0;
      DoBinaries( Result );
   end;
end;
begin
   repeat
      writeln;
      writeln( 'Enter your expression:' );
      readln( Line );
      Evaluate;
      if Length( Line ) > 0 then
         writeln( Result );
   until Length( Line ) = 0;
end.
```

When EXPRESS executes, it asks you to enter an equation:

```
Enter your expression:
12-4
8
Enter your expression:
 (  (12- 4) * (12  /4))
24
Enter your expression:
-40/+10
-4
Enter your expression:
(1+2)*(4*5)/(10*+1)
6
Enter your expression:
10 + (3*4
Unbalanced parentheses
```

In the EXPRESS program, the `DoParentheses`, `DoUnaries`, `DoMultDiv`, and `DoBinaries` procedures process each level of precedence separately. Each procedure is called in sequence to ensure that statement operators are evaluated in the proper order. Before any procedure can process operands at its own level, it must ensure that all higher-precedence operations have completed. Hence, `DoBinaries` calls `DoMultDiv`, `DoMultDiv` calls `DoUnaries`, and `DoUnaries` calls `DoParentheses`.

Consider, however, that if parentheses are detected, the expression in the parentheses must be evaluated independently; hence, the processing sequence must begin again at the lowest precedence level. Because `DoParentheses` must be able to call `DoBinaries` "out of order," the `DoBinaries` procedure must be declared forward.

The program ends with a null line or after any of these error conditions are detected:

- Illegal characters on line
- Syntax error
- Unbalanced parentheses
- Division by 0

Procedure Types

In Turbo Pascal, you can define a *procedure type* to enable a procedure or function to be treated just like an ordinary data object. This is an extremely clever method of allowing subroutines to be assigned to variables and passed as parameters, but it is also a technically complicated technique that you should use carefully.

A procedure-type declaration is designed to capture the `type` of the subroutine parameters and the `type` returned by a function. Therefore, it is declared like an ordinary procedure or function header but without the subroutine name, which is immaterial.

Sample procedure `type` declarations are as follows:

```
type
   Binary    = function ( First, Second : word ) : word;
   ProcHold  = procedure;
   SumProc   = procedure ( var X, Y; ActionProc : ProcHold );
   Rooter    = function ( RealPart, ImaginaryPart : real ):real;
```

Identifiers used in the declarations are similar to the formal parameters in an actual subroutine. The sequence is important, not the actual names you use. Any procedure or function having a *similar combination* of types defined in its header may be assigned to any variable defined as a compatible type.

Normally, when Turbo Pascal compiles a procedure or function call, it generates the most efficient machine code possible based on where the subroutine physically resides. Any subroutine you want to assign to a procedure-type variable must be compiled with the `{$ F+}` (force far calls) option in force. This directive is discussed in greater detail in the "Compiler Directives" reference section.

A Procedure-Type Example with Procedures

The PROC1 program (listing 5.17) is a password validation routine that uses procedure-type variables to determine the action to take when an unauthorized user tries to access the system.

Three sign-on attempts are allowed; the first two result in warning messages, and the third causes the program to end. Depending on the try, the `TestPassword` procedure is given the name of either the `Warning` or `Fatal` response procedure.

Listing 5.17

```
program Proc1;
const
   Attempt : byte = 0;
   GoodGuy : Boolean = False;
type
   String8    = string[ 8 ];
   ErrorLevel = procedure ( Try : byte );
var
   Response : String8;
F+}
procedure TestPassword( Answer : String8;  Severity : ErrorLevel );
const
   Secret   = 'Borland';
begin
   if Answer = Secret then
      GoodGuy := True
   else
      Severity( Attempt );
end;
procedure Warning( Try : byte );
begin
   writeln( #7'Incorrect response number ', Try );
   writeln( 'Please try again!' );
end;
procedure Fatal( Try : byte );
begin
   writeln( #7'After ', Try, ' tries, access is denied!' );
   Halt;
end;
{$ F-}
procedure UserSignOn;
begin
   repeat
      Inc( Attempt );
      write( 'Enter your password: ' );
      readln( Response );
      if Attempt < 3 then
         TestPassword( Response, Warning )
      else
```

continues

Listing 5.17 continued

```
        TestPassword( Response, Fatal );
    until GoodGuy;
    writeln( 'Welcome to the program' );
end;
begin
    UserSignOn;
{   program code goes here    }
end.
```

If the correct password is provided, the program executes normally:

```
Enter your password: Borland
Welcome to the program
```

If the correct password hasn't been entered after three attempts, an error message is generated and the program halts:

```
Enter your password: Fred
Incorrect response number 1
Please try again!
Enter your password: Bob
Incorrect response number 2
Please try again!
Enter your password: Rosebud
After 3 tries, access is denied!
```

A Procedure-Type Example with Functions

Procedure-type parameters can be applied also to functions. The FUNC1 program (listing 5.18) is a simple set of routines used to determine the maximum and minimum values of a function. A variation of FUNC1 could be used as part of a routine to determine the scale to be used in displaying a graph.

Listing 5.18

```
program Func1;
type
    Func = function ( Param : real ) : real;
```

```
var
   Minimum, Maximum : real;
{$ F+}
function Sine( X : real ) : real;
begin
   Sine := Sin( X );
end;
function Cosine( X : real ) : real;
begin
   Cosine := Cos( X );
end;
procedure FindMaxAndMin( CurrFunction : Func );
var
   i      : word;
   Param,
   Result : real;
begin
   Maximum := -10000.0;
   Minimum := +10000.0;
   for i := 1 to 100 do begin
      Param := i / 10;
      Result := CurrFunction( Param );
      if Result > Maximum then
         Maximum := Result;
      if Result < Minimum then
         Minimum := Result;
   end;
   writeln( 'Minimum= ', Minimum:0:6, ' Maximum= ', Maximum:0:6 );
end;
{$ F-}
begin
   write( 'For the Sine function:  ' );
   FindMaxAndMin( Sine );
   write( 'For the Cosine function:  ' );
   FindMaxAndMin( Cosine );
end.
```

When FUNC1 executes, it produces the following output:

```
For the Sine function:  Minimum= -0.999923 Maximum= 0.999574
For the Cosine function:  Minimum= -0.999693 Maximum= 0.999859
```

Summary

In this chapter, you learned how a complex programming problem can be broken down into subroutines. In Turbo Pascal, subroutines consist of procedures and functions.

You learned the differences between a procedure and a function, including how each is structured and called.

- A procedure consists of a collection of statements, possibly including other procedures, that operate as a group. A procedure is invoked by simply writing its name, just like an ordinary Pascal statement.
- A function is similar to a procedure except a function is designed to return a value of a specified type. A function can be used in any expression in which a variable of the same type would be permitted.

You have seen how the `Exit` procedure can end the processing in a subroutine.

You learned how a series of subroutines can be nested, and you learned the scope limits associated with the nesting process.

You learned how subroutines access information through parameters.

- Value parameters allow access to a copy of the original data.
- Variable parameters allow access to the original data itself.
- Untyped variable parameters allow subroutines to access data of different types.

You learned how subroutines can be called recursively, and thus mimic common recursive problem-solving techniques. You saw how forward declarations allow subroutines to be called before they are formally defined.

You learned that a special data object called a `procedure` type allows Turbo Pascal programs to pass procedures and functions as parameters to other procedures and functions.

CHAPTER 6

Dynamic Data Structures

Like most microprocessors, those in the 8086-family (the 8086, 80286, and 80386) have internal word-sized areas called *registers*. Some registers are specifically designed to hold memory addresses, whereas others are intended primarily for data storage and manipulation.

One common misconception is that for data to be used by a processor, it must first be placed in one of the registers. Although it is true that data in registers can be accessed much more quickly than data in memory, most microprocessor instructions (including arithmetic ones such as add and subtract) have options that allow for one or more operands to *remain* in memory. For example, the instruction that compares two 100-byte strings for equality requires only that the registers contain the strings' starting addresses and length—a considerable time savings over the brute force method of moving each pair of bytes to separate registers and comparing them individually.

A memory address is usually referenced by combining two words: a 16-bit segment and a 16-bit offset within the segment—the common syntax of the segment:offset format. Because any memory location can be completely specified by a four-byte address and most 8086 instructions allow memory addresses to be used in place of the actual data, program performance can be considerably enhanced using memory references wherever possible. Turbo Pascal provides a special data type called the `pointer` for just such a purpose.

This chapter discusses how PC memory is structured and accessed, then explains dynamic memory management in Turbo Pascal.

Referencing Memory

Most people believe that if their PC has 640K of memory, it must have 10 distinct physical segments of 64K each. In reality, segment boundaries and memory addressing are much more flexible.

The 8086-family processor has 20 address lines that control which byte of memory is accessed. There are 20 lines, so 2^{20} bytes (1,048,576 bytes or 1 megabyte) are accessible, even though DOS or hardware constraints limit *actual* memory to 640K on most machines.

Because a register is only 16 bits long, identifying a specific memory location requires the use of two registers, as follows:

- The first register (the *segment*) selects a paragraph that begins on—or just less than—the desired byte. All segments begin on paragraph boundaries. A *paragraph* is a 16-byte memory area; hence, a *paragraph boundary* is a memory location evenly divisible by 16. There are 64K paragraphs throughout the 1 megabyte of memory space. When DOS loads a program into the lowest available memory location, DOS is really selecting the next paragraph boundary above the last memory byte in current use.

- The second register (the *offset*) specifies the distance, or ***displacement***, between the desired byte and the starting byte of the referencing paragraph. This is why the size of a segment is generally considered to be 64K; after a segment is selected by having the index number of a paragraph loaded into a segment register, no 16-bit offset can access a memory location outside a 64K range.

Most programmers already know this, but in a slightly different form. Programming texts usually explain that the *true* address (called the ***absolute*** address) is found by shifting the segment word over one column to the left and adding the offset word. In hexadecimal, shifting one place to the left means multiplying by $10, which is 16 decimal. This is illustrated as follows:

Segment:	B800	(paragraph index)
Offset:	+ 0000	(distance from start of paragraph)
Absolute address:	B8000	(20-bit physical address)

The absolute address represents the actual memory location physically accessed by the 20-bit data bus.

Addresses within the current segment are termed *near*; those outside the current segment are termed *far*. Accessing a near address requires that only the offset register be changed. Accessing a far address requires changing both the segment and offset registers.

As a consequence of specifying addresses with two registers, any specific byte may be written and accessed in thousands of different ways. Consider the addresses B800:0000, B700:1000, and A8FF:F010. As shown in table 6.1, all three addresses point to the same physical byte in the PC's memory, despite the fact that they have unique segment and offset register values.

Table 6.1. Absolute Addresses of Three Memory Locations

	B800:0000	*B700:1000*	*A8FF:F010*
Segment register:	B800	B700	A8FF
Offset register:	+ 0000	+ 1000	+ F010
Absolute address:	B8000	B8000	B8000

So you can see that a 640K PC does not have 10 distinct *physical* 64K segments. Instead, the PC's memory consists of—potentially—40,960 overlapping *logical* segments. (640K equals 655,360 bytes, divided by 16 bytes per paragraph to give 40,960 paragraphs.) A logical segment takes up only as many 16-byte paragraphs as it needs. If one logical segment does not require the maximum 64K available space, DOS feels free to take the next free paragraph and use it as the start of the next logical segment.

Segment Usage

Data declaration (or data allocation) statements reserve and optionally initialize memory space for program variables and data. Instruction statements specify the machine instructions to be generated; they are the active, data movement, and manipulation commands (`add`, `move`, `compare`, and so on).

All program data and instructions are stored in memory. The 8086 has been physically designed in such a way that it expects the memory location of the instructions of its currently executing program to be specified with one unique combination of register pairs, the memory location of that program's data to be defined with a second register pair, and the memory area to be used as a stack to be defined with a third register pair. These areas are the code segment of memory, the data segment of memory, and the stack segment of memory, respectively. The locations of these memory areas are determined by the contents of the segment and offset register pairs shown in table 6.2.

Table 6.2. Segment and Offset Register Pairs

	Segment name	*Segment register*	*Offset register*	*Segment: Offset*
Program code	Code	CS	IP	CS:IP
Program data	Data	DS	SI	DS:SI
Stack	Stack	SS	SP	SS:SP

The Code Segment

The code segment (CS) register identifies the start of the program's instructions. The actual memory address of the next byte to be executed is found by locating the paragraph specified in the CS register, then adding the value in the instruction pointer (IP) register. To the 8086, running a program consists of starting at the first byte in a block of executable code and processing the instructions it finds there, one at a time.

The IP register always contains the address of the *next* instruction to be executed. Because alteration of this register will probably "crash" the program, the instruction pointer cannot be directly accessed or changed.

Although no direct way of learning the value of the IP register is available, the current value of the CS register can be found with the Turbo Pascal `CSeg` function.

The Data Segment

The data segment (DS) register identifies the start of the program's data. When the compiler encounters a data declaration, it reserves space in the data segment based on the size of the data item. If the data item is a typed constant, its initial value is inserted into memory; otherwise, the value of a data item consists of whatever was residing in the location prior to the start of the program.

The source index (SI) register is used for pointing to (indexing) a data item in the data segment. When an instruction requires data movement, the SI register points to the source data while another register, the destination index (DI) register, points to (indexes) the destination data.

The Turbo Pascal `DSeg` function returns the current value of the DS register. The SI and DI registers may be accessed indirectly, through an interrupt call, as explained in Chapter 16, "BIOS, DOS, and Assembly Language."

The Stack Segment

The stack segment (SS) register identifies the start of the program's stack. The stack pointer (SP) register always points to the current offset in the stack segment.

The *stack* is the area of memory used by your program as a scratch pad. Any data that must be temporarily stored is placed on the stack until it is needed. Although most programming texts explain a stack with the last in, first out analogy of a stack of cafeteria trays, in truth, every byte in the stack is directly accessible. The only reason that data is stored in the stack segment from left-to-right, for example, and read back right-to-left is to minimize memory use. Any other technique would create "holes" in the stack and result in an inefficient need for more memory.

The Turbo Pascal `SSeg` function returns the current value of the SS register. Similarly, the `SPtr` function returns the current value of the SP register.

Reading Segment and Offset Values

Turbo Pascal provides two functions, `Seg` and `Ofs`, to return the segment and offset, respectively, of any data object. The MEMORY1 program in listing 6.1 demonstrates how you access the various memory addresses with Turbo Pascal.

Listing 6.1

```
program Memory1;
uses Crt;
var
   StackLoc,
   SegWork,
   OfsWork  : word;
function HexByte( BinaryForm : byte ) : char;
```

continues

Listing 6.1 continued

```
const
   HexSymbols : array [ 0..15 ] of char = '0123456789ABCDEF';
begin
   HexByte := HexSymbols[ BinaryForm ];
end;
function HexWord( WordForm : word ) : string;
begin
   HexWord := '$' + HexByte( Hi( WordForm ) div 16 ) +
                    HexByte( Hi( WordForm ) mod 16 ) +
                    HexByte( Lo( WordForm ) div 16 ) +
                    HexByte( Lo( WordForm ) mod 16 );
end;
function SizeOfHexWord : longint;
begin
   SizeOfHexWord := Ofs( SizeOfHexWord ) - Ofs( HexWord );
end;
procedure ShowStackActivity( StartLoc : word );
begin
   writeln( (StartLoc - SPtr):3,
            ' bytes were used by the stack during this call ');
end;
begin
   ClrScr;
   writeln( 'Program segments begin as follows: ' );
   writeln;
   writeln( '       Code         ', CSeg:6, '  or  ', HexWord( CSeg ) );
   writeln( '       Data         ', DSeg:6, '  or  ', HexWord( DSeg ) );
   writeln( '       Stack        ', SSeg:6, '  or  ', HexWord( SSeg ) );
   writeln( '----------------------------------------------------------' );
   writeln( 'Segment:Offset of program code can be found at: ' );
   writeln;
   writeln( 'HexByte             ', Seg( HexByte ):6, Ofs( HexByte ):6 );
   writeln( 'HexWord             ', Seg( HexWord ):6, Ofs( HexWord ):6 );
   writeln( 'SizeOfHexWord       ', Seg( SizeOfHexWord ):6,
                                    Ofs( SizeOfHexWord ):6 );
   writeln( 'ShowStackActivity   ', Seg( ShowStackActivity ):6,
                                    Ofs( ShowStackActivity ):6 );
   writeln;
   writeln( 'The size of the HexWord function itself is ',
             SizeOfHexWord, ' or ',
             HexWord( SizeOfHexWord ), ' bytes' );
   writeln( '----------------------------------------------------------' );
```

```
    writeln( 'Segment:Offset of program data can be found at: ' );
    writeln;
    writeln( 'StackLoc              ', Seg( StackLoc ):6, Ofs( StackLoc ):6 );
    writeln( 'SegWork               ', Seg( SegWork  ):6, Ofs( SegWork  ):6 );
    writeln( 'OfsWork               ', Seg( OfsWork  ):6, Ofs( OfsWork  ):6 );
    writeln( '-------------------------------------------------------------' );
    writeln( 'A use of the stack is demonstrated by: ' );
    writeln;
    StackLoc := SPtr;
    ShowStackActivity( StackLoc );
end.
```

When MEMORY1 executes, the program produces an output similar to that of figure 6.1.

Fig. 6.1. The output produced by the MEMORY1 program.

```
Program segments begin as follows:

       Code            28604  or  $6FBC
       Data            28992  or  $7140
       Stack           29037  or  $716D
-------------------------------------------------------------
Segment:Offset of program code can be found at:

HexByte                28604     35
HexWord                28604     74
SizeOfHexWord          28604    255
ShowStackActivity      28604    345

The size of the HexWord function itself is 181 or $00B5 bytes
-------------------------------------------------------------
Segment:Offset of program data can be found at:

StackLoc               28992     84
SegWork                28992     86
OfsWork                28992     88
-------------------------------------------------------------
A use of the stack is demonstrated by:

 12 bytes were used by the stack during this call
```

The program will probably report different memory locations when it is executed on your PC. The actual values depend, among other things, on which memory-resident programs are currently running on your machine.

Notice that all global variables have a segment value equal to the contents of the DS register, and all functions and procedures have a segment value equal to the contents of the CS register. The offsets grow depending on the size required for each entry.

Ten bytes were used by the stack to execute the `ShowStackActivity` procedure. Two bytes were taken up by the `StartLoc` parameter. Eight other bytes were required to save the word-sized BP, SP, SS, and DS registers—an action performed whenever a procedure or function is called. By preserving these registers, the compiler can regain control of the program no matter what happens inside the subroutine itself.

A Note on COM and EXE Formats

In COM programs, such as those generated by Turbo Pascal Version 3.0 and prior versions, all segment registers contain the same value. Hence, the entire program must fit in a single 64K segment.

This format offers several advantages. Such a program compiles quickly, because no code needs to be generated for switching segment registers. A COM program also executes quickly, because segment registers do not need to be saved and restored while the program runs. The result is a highly efficient program—as long as the 64K limit is not a problem.

Sometimes, however, the 64K limit is simply too tight for developing programs. In these cases, programs need more than one 64K segment in which to store code or data. This is the advantage of the EXE file. Pascal programs resulting in EXE files can call subroutines and access data in any memory location (that is, both the segment and the offset registers are free to change).

If your code or data requires more than one *physical* 64K segment, it follows that you also need more than one *logical* segment to define it. In Pascal, this means that more than one program module—called a *unit*—is needed. Units are discussed further in Chapter 7, "Units."

Dynamic Memory Allocation

Each of the code, data, and stack segments can have a maximum size of only 64K, so there must be a considerable amount of memory remaining in the PC just waiting to be used. Turbo Pascal allows this memory area, called the *heap*, to be accessed and manipulated by pointer variables.

By default, the heap can be as large as the unused portion of memory in the PC. Its actual size, however, grows and shrinks dynamically, depending on the size required to hold the desired variables. No single variable, however, can exceed 64K.

An ordinary variable represents a value, and the space to hold this value is allocated in the data segment when the variable is declared. A fixed amount of memory is allocated by the compiler depending on the declared type and size of the particular variable, and that much memory is consumed regardless of the actual size of the variable at run time. A 100-element array of `char` consumes 100 bytes even if only the first 5 elements are used. Similarly, a 100-element array of records, each 20 bytes in length, consumes 2000 bytes even if only the first 2 records are used.

Pointers, on the other hand, are *dynamic* because the amount of allocated storage is controlled by the program during run time. A *pointer variable* contains the address of the first byte in memory where a data object is stored rather than the data object itself.

Storage for the object being referenced is allocated when the program is executed rather than when it is compiled. The data item being referenced can be any legal type, including a number, a string, a record, or even a procedure, a function, or another pointer. Pointer variables can be used anywhere ordinary variable names would be used.

A pointer is stored as a double word, with the offset part in the low word and the segment part in the high word.

Declaring Pointer Variables

To declare a pointer data type, simply insert a caret (the ^ symbol) followed by the name of the type being referenced. A few examples should serve to illustrate this method:

```
type
   Structure1 = array [ 1..100 ] of longint;
var
   Var1 : ^byte;
   Var2 : ^real;
   Var3 : ^Structure1;
```

Here, `Var1` is declared as a pointer to a byte, `Var2` is declared as a pointer to a real, and `Var3` is declared as a pointer to a 100-element array of `longint`.

The pointer is the only declaration that can define itself as something declared *later* in the same section. Technically, this is called a *forward pointer declaration*. The following set of declarations is legal and typical of those that appear in programs that use lists:

```
type
   DataArrow  = ^DataStuff;
   DataStuff  = record
                   Info1    : real;
                   Info2    : integer;
                   DataPtr  : DataArrow;
                end;
```

Although at first it looks like a dog chasing its tail, this declaration is nothing more than a clever device to enable you to create an entire series of `DataStuff` records, each of which contains a pointer to the *next* record in the chain.

Allocating Memory with *New*

Because a pointer variable contains a memory address, only four bytes of storage are allocated for it in the data segment when the program is compiled. Storage for the referenced memory area itself will not be created until the program runs and the `New` procedure is called, as follows:

```
New( VarName );
```

If `VarName` is declared as a pointer to the type `PointerType`, the `New` procedure sets aside (allocates) an area of memory large enough to contain a single variable of the size of `PointerType` and sets the `VarName` variable equal to the memory address where `PointerType` begins.

The area of memory now pointed to by `VarName` does not have its own name; it can be referred to—a process sometimes called *indirection*—only as

```
VarName^
```

Notice the caret appearing after the variable name; the *address* of the `PointerType` data is `VarName`, but the *value* of the `PointerType` data is `VarName^`.

This distinction is further demonstrated in the POINTER1 program in listing 6.2.

Listing 6.2

```
program Pointer1;
Type
   Message    = String[ 255 ];
   MsgPtr     = ^Message;
   IntPointer = ^Integer;
var
   Message1 : Message;
   Message2 : MsgPtr;
   VarX     : IntPointer;
   VarY     : Integer;
begin
   New( Message2 );
   Message1  := 'Message1 is stored in a string';
   Message2^ := 'Message2 is stored where Message2 points';
   writeln( Message1 );
   writeln( Message2^ );
   New( VarX );
   VarX^ := 12;
   VarY  := 3;
   writeln( 'The product of VarX and VarY is ', VarX^ * VarY );
   writeln( 'The size of Message1 is ',  SizeOf( Message1 ) );
   writeln( 'The size of Message2 is ',  SizeOf( Message2 ) );
   writeln( 'The size of Message2^ is ', SizeOf( Message2^ ) );
   writeln( 'The size of VarX is ',      SizeOf( VarX ) );
   writeln( 'The size of VarX^ is ',     SizeOf( VarX^ ) );
   writeln( 'The size of VarY is ',      SizeOf( VarY ) );
end.
```

When executed, POINTER1 generates the output shown in figure 6.2.

Notice the difference between the `Message1` and `Message2` variables, and between the `VarX` and `VarY` variables. Both `Message2` and `VarX` are 4-byte pointers, although `Message2^` and `VarX^` are treated as a 255-byte string and an integer, respectively, just like `Message1` and `VarY`. The contents of `Message1` and `Message2` differ considerably, but `Message1` and `Message2^` (with the caret) are ***absolutely equivalent*** from a functional standpoint.

Even though this memory-referencing technique seems to have tremendous flexibility, you must still obey some fundamental programming rules. Every pointer references a specific type; when a pointer is used, it must conform to the syntax of this type. For example, it is legal to multiply a constant by the pointer to an integer, but it is illegal to multiply a constant by the pointer to a string.

Fig. 6.2. Output produced by the POINTER1 program.

```
Message1 is stored in a string
Message2 is stored where Message2 points
The product of VarX and VarY is 36
The size of Message1 is 256
The size of Message2 is 4
The size of Message2^ is 256
The size of VarX is 4
The size of VarX^ is 2
The size of VarY is 2
```

Traditionally, `New` has been implemented only as a procedure. Beginning with Version 5.5 of Turbo Pascal, however, `New` can be used also as a function. Simply pass `New` an identifier for the type of variable you want to allocate, and `New` will return the memory location where space has been assigned in the heap.

For example, given the declarations:

```
type
   ByteType = ^byte;
var
   ByteVar : ByteType;
```

the following statements are equivalent:

```
New( ByteVar );                   { Procedure form }
ByteVar := New ( ByteType );   { Function form must use type identifier }
```

To maintain compatibilty with earlier versions, all remaining examples in this book use the procedure form of `New`.

Reusing Memory with the *Dispose* Procedure

The advantage of using dynamic variables is that memory is allocated only when needed and can also be deallocated after it is no longer required.

Memory can be returned to the heap for reuse through the `Dispose` procedure. The POINTER2 program in listing 6.3 demonstrates how this is done.

Listing 6.3

```
program Pointer2;
type
   RealPntr = ^real;
var
   index : byte;
   NumberList : array[ 1..20 ] of RealPntr;
begin
   for index := 1 to 20 do begin
      New( NumberList[ index ] );
      NumberList[ index ]^ := sqrt( index );
      writeln( index:3, NumberList[ index ]^:10:5 );
      Dispose( NumberList[ index ] );
   end;
end.
```

When POINTER2 executes, it allocates, uses, and deallocates 20 pointers in the `NumberList` array.

`Dispose` is not quite the inverse of `New`. With `New`, the pointer was automatically assigned the memory address of the allocated area of the heap. `Dispose` simply tells the compiler that the area is *available* for reuse; neither the contents of the heap nor the address in the pointer variable is changed.

Identifying an Unused Pointer

The predefined pointer constant `Nil` does not point to anything. (Actually, the value of `Nil` is equal to a double-word zero.) `Nil` may be assigned to a pointer variable of any type to indicate that the pointer no longer references an active memory location.

```
Dispose( Message2 );
Message2 := Nil;
Dispose( VarX );
VarX := Nil;
```

Note that you assign `Nil` to `Message2` and `VarX`, *not* to `Message2^` and `VarX^`.

When you get into the habit of using `Nil` as the default value for all of your program's pointers, you can be sure that a pointer is active before you try to use it, as follows:

```
if VarX = Nil then
   New( VarX );
VarX^ := 17;
```

Allocating Memory with the *Mark* and *Release* Procedures

`Dispose` deallocates space for one pointer-type variable at a time. If many pointer variables have been created, `Dispose` can be highly inefficient, because an individual procedure call must be done for each item to be deallocated. For this reason, Turbo Pascal provides the `Mark` and `Release` procedures.

The compiler always allocates space in the heap sequentially. If a long series of data is to be defined by a succession of `New` procedure calls, `Mark` can be used to flag the position in the heap *prior* to the start of the allocations. When space for the pointer variables is no longer needed, `Release` can deallocate all the space allocated *since* the `Mark` procedure was executed. In this way, large amounts of memory can be freed with a single procedure call.

`Mark` is called with one pointer argument. In effect, it sets the pointer equal to the memory location at the current top of the heap.

`Release` is called with the same pointer argument used in the `Mark` procedure. `Release` resets the top of the heap to the memory location referenced by the pointer.

Just as with `Dispose`, the `Release` procedure frees the heap of unwanted variables but does not affect either the contents of the heap or the contents of the individual pointers.

The POINTER3 program in listing 6.4 demonstrates how you can use `Mark` and `Release`.

Listing 6.4

```
program Pointer3;
type
   RealPntr = ^real;
var
   index : byte;
   HeapMarker : ^pointer;
   NumberList : array[ 1..20 ] of RealPntr;
begin
   Mark( HeapMarker );
   for index := 1 to 20 do begin
      New( NumberList[ index ] );
      NumberList[ index ]^ := sqrt( index );
      writeln( index:3, NumberList[ index ]^:10:5 );
   end;
   Release( HeapMarker );
end.
```

When POINTER3 executes, the `Mark` procedure saves a pointer to the current top of the heap in `HeapMarker`. The program then allocates and uses heap memory equal in size to 20 real numbers. After the program finishes with this space, the `Release` procedure resets the top of the heap to the position stored in `HeapMarker`.

The choice of whether to use `Dispose` or `Mark` and `Release` depends principally on two issues:

- No memory deallocation is necessary unless a memory constraint is reached. For short programs such as POINTER5 and POINTER6 (listings 6.6 and 6.7), there is no need to bother; for a spreadsheet or database program, frequent deallocation may be required.
- `Mark` and `Release` free entire *blocks* of heap memory. If your program creates even a single pointer reference between the two procedure calls you might need to use later, you will have to use the `Dispose` procedure to return heap memory selectively.

Allocating Memory with the *GetMem* and *FreeMem* Procedures

When you allocate variables with the `New` procedure, one byte of heap space is used for each byte of the data structure being referenced.

One method of dynamic memory allocation unique to Turbo Pascal is the combination of the `GetMem` and `FreeMem` procedures. They are similar to `New` and `Dispose` in that they allocate and deallocate memory one variable at a time, but they differ in that with `GetMem` and `FreeMem` you can specify how much memory in the heap you want to control, regardless of the size implied by the pointer type.

The POINTER4 program in listing 6.5 demonstrates how `GetMem` and `FreeMem` procedures are used.

Listing 6.5

```
program Pointer4;
type
   SqrPntr = ^Squares;
   Squares = array[ 1..100 ] of integer;
var
   index   : byte;
   Array1,
   Array2  : SqrPntr;
   Message : ^string;
begin
   GetMem( Array1, 10 );
   GetMem( Array2, 20 );
   New( Message );
   Message^ := 'This is the start of the program.';
   writeln( Message^ );
   Message^ := 'This is the terminating message line.  Good-bye.';
   writeln( 'The size of Array1 is ', SizeOf( Array1^ ) );
   writeln( 'The size of Array2 is ', SizeOf( Array2^ ) );
   for index := 1 to 20 do Array1^[ index ] := index * index;
   for index := 1 to 20 do Array2^[ index ] := index * index;
   for index := 1 to 15 do
      writeln( index:6, Array1^[ index ]:8 );
   writeln( Message^ );
   Dispose( Message );
   FreeMem( Array1, 10 );
   FreeMem( Array2, 20 );
end.
```

When POINTER4 executes, it generates the output shown in figure 6.3.

Fig. 6.3. *Output produced by the POINTER4 program.*

```
This is the start of the program.
The size of Array1 is 200
The size of Array2 is 200
     1         1
     2         4
     3         9
     4        16
     5        25
     6        36
     7        49
     8        64
     9         1
    10         4
    11         9
    12        16
    13        25
    14        36
    15        49
 - β  ☺!☺D☺i☺É☺minating message line.  Good-bye.earned
                                                              Zå ♠<n☺7q12<n☺7q
88987q7q7q ☻2↨☻ 7qk♦+♠Épn☺7q♣♠┌>n☺╜on☺7qⁿ?♪╜oⁿ>♣$00B5through text files. You hav
e see
```

The garbage appears in the final message because memory sizes were not properly tested. The `GetMem` allocation procedures

```
GetMem( Array1, 10 );
GetMem( Array2, 20 );
```

reserved 10 bytes and 20 bytes, respectively, for `Array1` and `Array2`. Because both of these variables consist of arrays of integers, and integers are each two bytes in length, `Array1` was effectively set to a size large enough to hold 5 integers, whereas `Array2` was slightly larger, with a 10-integer capacity.

When the first 20 integers in `Array1` were initialized to the squares of the index, the first 5 elements fit comfortably in the memory area allocated for `Array1` in the heap, while the last 15 overflowed this area and began to fill the heap memory area set aside for `Array2`. Then, when the first 20 integers in `Array2` were initialized to the squares of the index, the first 10 elements fit in the memory area allocated in the heap for `Array2`, while the last 10 overflowed this area and began to fill the heap memory area set aside for the message.

The compiler never generated an error, because its syntax-checking logic believed that the arrays were each 100 integers (200 bytes) long. Obviously, there is some danger in using `GetMem` and `FreeMem`, but there is also one major advantage. As long as you are willing to assume responsibility for range checking in the body of your program, you have complete control over the size of your data objects.

When memory is deallocated with the `FreeMem` procedure, the number of bytes specified must exactly match the number of bytes originally allocated with the `GetMem` call. Otherwise, the wrong amount of memory will be returned to the heap for reuse, and the other pointers declared in your program will become fair game.

Pointer Operations

The only operations directly allowed on pointer variables are assignments and comparisons. Assignments can take place only between pointers of compatible type. This can be accomplished by executing another `New` procedure, assigning the `Nil` value to the pointer, or setting the pointer equal to the address of another pointer of the same type.

Similarly, the equality and inequality operators (= and < >) can be used only on compatible pointer-type operands. When Turbo Pascal compares two pointers, it compares the segment and offset parts individually. (It is much more efficient for the compiler to test two word-sized pairs than to first compute and then compare two four-byte numbers.)

Because two logically different pointers can point to the same physical memory location, pointers returned by the `New` and `GetMem` procedures are always normalized. *Normalized* means that the compiler returns a segment value that is as large as possible to make the offset value 15 bytes or less, regardless of the actual content of the segment register that controls the address.

Linked Lists

Pointers offer several unique advantages over other data types. For example, the `array` structure has several limitations when used for list processing:

- ❏ The array has a fixed size regardless of the actual number of elements used and regardless of whether your program even needs the full size at any given time.
- ❏ The full size of the array consumes space in the data section of the program, regardless of how many elements are actually used and whether your program needs to use the array at any given time.

- When an item is inserted in the middle of an array, every entry after the insertion point must be moved down toward the end of the array to make room for the new entry.
- When an entry is removed, every element after the removal point must be moved over toward the beginning of the array to fill the open space.

The linked list, one of the most common uses of pointers, sidesteps these limitations. If one of the fields of a record is a pointer to another record of the same type, several records can be linked together into a list, the size of which can be changed as records are added and deleted. You start with a pointer to the first record in the list; the pointer in the last record is set to `Nil`.

Setting the final pointer to `Nil` allows each record to be tested before it is processed. For example, given the following definitions:

```
type
  PtrType    = ^DataRecord;
  DataRecord = record
                 DataStuff : integer; { or real, or whatever }
                 NextPtr   : PtrType;
               end;
```

the list can be written when the pointer to the first record is passed to the following procedure:

```
procedure WriteList( FirstPtr : PtrType );
var
   Scooter : PtrType;
begin
   Scooter := FirstPtr;
   while Scooter <> Nil do begin
      writeln( Scooter^.DataStuff );
      Scooter := Scooter^.NextPtr;
   end;
end;
```

A linked list is actually an advanced data type and, as such, is not used during the remainder of this book. The following example, however, introduces you to a simple but typical linked-list application. The POINTER5 program in listing 6.6 clears the screen and lists the names of the files in the current subdirectory that have the PAS extension. Essentially, POINTER5 produces an unsorted directory listing, similar to the sequence produced by the DOS `DIR` command.

Listing 6.6

```
program Pointer5;
uses Dos, Crt;
var
   FileInfo : SearchRec;
begin
   ClrScr;
   FindFirst( '*.PAS', AnyFile, FileInfo );
   while DosError = 0 do
      begin
         writeln( FileInfo.Name );
         FindNext( FileInfo );
      end;
end.
```

The `FindFirst` and `FindNext` procedures are discussed in more detail in Chapter 14, "Directory Handling."

The POINTER6 program in listing 6.7 begins with this same file-retrieval mechanism. However, as each file is read, the program maintains a linked list in which each new record is inserted into the list based on the alphabetical sequence of the file names.

Listing 6.7

```
program Pointer6;
uses Dos, Crt;
type
   HeapRecordPtr = ^HeapRecord;
   HeapRecord = record
                   NextOne   : HeapRecordPtr;
                   DirRecord : SearchRec;
                end;
var
   FileInfo : SearchRec;
   Trace,
   First,
   Fresh,
   Prior    : HeapRecordPtr;
begin
   ClrScr;
   FindFirst( '*.pas', AnyFile, FileInfo );
```

```
   New( Fresh );                 { Create the last record               }
   Fresh^.NextOne := Nil;        { There's no record after the last one  }
   First := Fresh;               { "First" points to the first record in }
                                 {    the list--namely, the last record  }
   while DosError = 0 do
      begin
         Trace := First;        { Start search in first record in chain  }
         Prior := Trace;        { Next record will be inserted           }
                                {    between Prior and Trace             }
         while (Trace^.NextOne <> Nil) and
               (Trace^.DirRecord.Name < FileInfo.Name) do
            begin
               Prior := Trace;               { Move Prior over one       }
               Trace := Trace^.NextOne;      { Now move Trace over one }
            end;
         New( Fresh );                { Reserve memory for the new record }
         if First = Trace then        { First record in list              }
            First := Fresh
         else                         { Insert between Prior and Trace    }
            Prior^.NextOne := Fresh;
         Fresh^.NextOne := Trace;          { Set new pointer field        }
         Fresh^.DirRecord := FileInfo;     { Set new data field           }
         writeln( FileInfo.Name );      { Write each record as it's read }
         FindNext( FileInfo );          { Retrieve the next record        }
      end;
   writeln( '-----------------------------' );
   Trace := First;
   while Trace^.NextOne <> Nil do            { Write out the linked list }
      begin                                  {    in alphabetical order  }
         writeln( trace^.DirRecord.Name );
         First := Trace;
         Trace := Trace^.NextOne;
      end;
end.
```

When POINTER6 executes, it displays the names of all Turbo Pascal source files (actually, all files with the PAS extension). The names are displayed twice. The first time, the names are in random order, in the same sequence as a DIR command. The second time, the names appear in alphabetical order.

The *Addr* Function and the @ Operator

Both the `Addr` function and the `@` operator return the memory address of any data object, including variables, procedures, and functions. Like `Nil`, both `Addr` and `@` are compatible with all pointer-type variables.

> **Preference of the @ Operator**
> The `@` operator is functionally equivalent to the `Addr` function, but because of its greater economy, the `@` form is preferred. The only advantage of the `Addr` function is in maintaining compatibility with other Pascal compilers. If you plan to transfer your programs to another compiler—a process called *porting*—and the compiler does not recognize the `@` operator, you can continue to use the `Addr` function. For the remainder of this book, however, only the `@` operator is shown.

When the `@` operator is applied to a procedure, function, or global variable (or when it is applied to a local variable inside a procedure or function), the results are straightforward: `@` returns a pointer to the memory address where the data item is stored.

The `@` operator can be applied also to a parameter passed to a procedure or function. The mechanics are slightly different depending on whether the parameter is passed as a value parameter, as in:

```
procedure SampleProc1( Param1  : Anytype v );
```

or as a variable parameter, as in:

```
procedure SampleProc2( var Param2  : Anytype );
```

Value parameters are copied onto the stack. Variable parameters have only their addresses placed on the stack. The application of the `@` operator to a parameter follows similar rules. Applying `@` to a value parameter results in a pointer to the stack location containing the copy of the value. Applying `@` to a variable parameter results in a pointer to the actual variable.

The PARMPASS program in listing 6.8 uses the `TypicalProc` procedure to demonstrate this difference. `TypicalProc` is declared with one variable parameter and one value parameter; the memory locations of these parameters are displayed when the procedure is invoked.

Listing 6.8

```
program ParmPass;
uses Crt;
var
   Var1,
   Var2  : byte;
procedure TypicalProc( var Param1 : byte;  Param2 : byte );
begin
   writeln( 'Param1 is at          ', Seg( Param1 ):8, Ofs( Param1 ):8 );
   writeln( 'Param2 is at          ', Seg( Param2 ):8, Ofs( Param2 ):8 );
end;
begin
   ClrScr;
   Var1 := 100;
   Var2 := 100;
   writeln( 'Code segment is at  ', CSeg:8 );
   writeln( 'Data segment is at  ', DSeg:8 );
   writeln( 'Stack segment is at ', SSeg:8 );
   writeln;
   writeln( 'Var1 is at            ', Seg( Var1 ):8, Ofs( Var1 ):8 );
   writeln( 'Var2 is at            ', Seg( Var2 ):8, Ofs( Var2 ):8 );
   TypicalProc( Var1, Var2 );
end.
```

When PARMPASS is executed, it produces the results shown in figure 6.4. Both global variables reside in the data segment. Notice how the memory location of the variable parameter is identical to the original global variable itself; the memory address of the value parameter, however, is somewhere in the stack segment.

Selecting Addresses

So far, whenever you have used a pointer, you have not needed to worry about the area of memory it referenced. It is enough to know that the Turbo Pascal compiler always selects a safe place for the pointer in the heap. Every time you request another area of memory with `New` or `GetMem`, you can be sure that the new region will not overlap any other areas of memory allocated previously.

Fig. 6.4. Output produced by the PARMPASS program.

```
Code segment is at      28604
Data segment is at      28881
Stack segment is at     28925

Var1 is at              28881       68
Var2 is at              28881       69
Param1 is at            28881       68
Param2 is at            28925    16374
```

Sometimes, however, you need to be able to read from (or write to) a *specific* area of memory. In this section, you learn how to select and use specific memory regions.

Creating Absolute Pointers

The `Ptr` function can be used to *create* a pointer to any desired memory location. `Ptr` accepts two parameters: the first specifies the segment, and the second specifies the offset in the segment. No specific data type is associated with the `Ptr` function, so you can use it with any pointer variable.

Every IBM-compatible PC uses certain memory regions for system control. This is one of the reasons that DOS is able to run successfully on computers from different manufacturers. For example, the word beginning at $0040:$0013 contains the size of the PC's internal memory, in 1K blocks. This value, which is reset whenever the PC boots, is freely available to any program that needs to know how much memory is installed in the machine.

You can read this value using the `Ptr` function, as demonstrated in the ABSO program in listing 6.9.

Listing 6.9

```
program Abs0;
var
   MemorySize : ^word;
begin
   MemorySize := Ptr( $0040, $0013 );
   writeln( 'This PC has ', MemorySize^, 'K bytes of internal memory.' );
end.
```

Here, `MemorySize` is a variable, defined as a pointer to a word. Of course, the memory *location* of the variable should never change. `MemorySize` was intended to reference only one memory address, even though you could freely reassign it.

Overlaying Absolute Variables

You can restrict a variable to a specific memory address by declaring it with the reserved word `absolute`. Program ABS1 in listing 6.10 "freezes" the first byte of `MemorySize` at the `absolute` location $0040:$0013.

Listing 6.10

```
program Abs1;
var
   MemorySize : word absolute $0040:$0013;
begin
   writeln( 'This PC has ', MemorySize, 'K bytes of internal memory.' );
end.
```

In the ABS1 program, `MemorySize` is *not* a pointer. Rather, it is an ordinary word-sized variable that happens to be located at $0040:$0013 instead of somewhere in the data segment. No restrictions are placed on its use. Consequently, if you change its contents with an ordinary assignment statement, such as:

```
MemorySize := 64;
```

then the next program that needs to know how much memory is in your PC will assume that 64K bytes are installed—regardless of the actual size. Obviously, the `absolute` clause and the `Ptr` function should be used only with extreme care.

Both the absolute clause and the Ptr function require you to know the exact segment and offset of the memory you want to reference. Absolute demands that you explicitly identify the location at compile time, whereas Ptr allows the location to be derived during execution. Absolute is used most often when you want to access the specific memory addresses used by the PC or DOS itself, as you did in the ABS1 program. Ptr is used most often when you want a single variable to access several different memory locations while a program is executing.

A third (and more common) situation arises when you want to reference the same program data item by two different names. The simplest solution is often to use a variant record, as demonstrated in the ABS2A program (listing 6.11).

Listing 6.11

```
program Abs2A;
type
   Combined = record
                 case integer of
                    1 : ( ByteForm : byte );
                    2 : ( CharForm : char )
              end;
var
   BC : Combined;
begin
   BC.ByteForm := $41;
   writeln( BC.ByteForm:5, BC.CharForm:5 );
end.
```

ABS2A defines its single variable, BC, as a variant record of the type Combined. The two components of Combined—ByteForm and CharForm—are both one byte long, and both refer to the same memory location. When the ByteForm field is used, the data item is treated as a simple number, from 0 through 255. When the CharForm field is used, the data item is treated as one of the 256 ASCII characters.

ABS2A begins by assigning the hexadecimal value $41 to the BC.ByteForm field. When the writeln procedure executes, ByteForm interprets $41 as the decimal value 65, whereas CharForm interprets $41 as the capital letter *A*.

In a similar way, Turbo allows a modified version of the absolute statement that accepts the name of a previously declared variable rather than a specific address. Program ABS2B in listing 6.12 shows how you can use this form of the `absolute` directive.

Listing 6.12

```
program Abs2B;
var
   ByteForm : byte;
   CharForm : char  absolute ByteForm;
begin
   for ByteForm := 65 to 77 do
      write( ByteForm:5 );
   writeln;
   for ByteForm := 65 to 77 do
      write( CharForm:5 );
   writeln;
   writeln;
   writeln;
   for ByteForm := 78 to 90 do
      write( ByteForm:5 );
   writeln;
   for ByteForm := 78 to 90 do
      write( CharForm:5 );
   writeln;
end.
```

Because `CharForm` is declared as being `absolute` to `ByteForm`, both variables begin at the same memory location, but both regard the data as having different types. When ABS2B executes, it produces the table of ASCII values shown in figure 6.5.

Variable Names as Memory References
Remember that to the Turbo Pascal compiler, every variable name is itself a memory reference. For example, when you write a statement such as

```
A := B + C;
```

the compiler adds the value stored at memory location B to the value stored at memory location C, and moves the sum to memory location A.

Fig. 6.5. Output produced by the ABS2B program.

```
 65   66   67   68   69   70   71   72   73   74   75   76   77
  A    B    C    D    E    F    G    H    I    J    K    L    M

 78   79   80   81   82   83   84   85   86   87   88   89   90
  N    O    P    Q    R    S    T    U    V    W    X    Y    Z
```

Accessing Memory as an Array

All of the memory referencing techniques you have seen here thus far allow access to only a single segment and offset address. Although these techniques are useful, many applications require free access to large blocks of memory.

Turbo Pascal provides a powerful method of memory management in the form of the predefined arrays `Mem`, `MemW`, and `MemL`. Each of these arrays treats the entire one megabyte internal memory of the PC as a single array. `Mem` is an array of bytes, `MemW` is an array of words, and `MemL` is an array of `LongInts`.

All three arrays are one-dimensional, but each takes an index in segment:offset form—that is, a word-sized value representing a segment, followed by a colon, followed by another word-sized value representing the offset in the segment.

The ABS3 program in listing 6.13 uses the `Mem` array to access the byte at $0040:$0049, which contains information on the type of display adapter installed in your PC. If the byte contains the number 7, the display is monochrome. Every other value represents one of the possible color adapters.

Listing 6.13

```
program Abs3;
function ScreenIsInColorMode : Boolean;
begin
   if Mem[ $0040 : $0049 ] = 7 then
      ScreenIsInColorMode := False
   else
      ScreenIsInColorMode := True;
end;
begin
   case ScreenIsInColorMode of
      True  : writeln( 'Color Adapter Card Installed' );
      False : writeln( 'Monochrome Display Adapter Installed' );
   end;
end.
```

The ABS3 program might detect a color adapter card even if you have only a monochrome screen. Most COMPAQ® portables, for example, are equipped with screens that display individual colors as different shades of green.

Throughout this book, the `Mem` array is used extensively to develop powerful system-level applications. A short example can be found in the ABS4 program in listing 6.14.

Listing 6.14

```
program Abs4;
uses Printer;
var
   Row, Column,
   SegmentNumber : word;
function VideoSegment : word;
begin
   if Mem[ $0040 : $0049 ] = 7 then
      VideoSegment := $B000
   else
      VideoSegment := $B800;
end;
begin
   SegmentNumber := VideoSegment;
```

continues

Listing 6.14 continued

```
    for Row := 0 to 24 do begin
       for Column := 0 to 79 do
          write( Lst, chr( Mem[ SegmentNumber : 2*Column + 160*Row ] ) );
       writeln( Lst );
    end;
    write( Lst, #12 );
end.
```

The operation of ABS4 is similar to the hardware Print Screen function on your PC. When you press Shift-PrtSc, the current screen image is listed on your system printer. When you execute ABS4, the program prints the screen image. The program first tests the memory location at $0040:$0049 to determine whether a monochrome or color graphics display adapter is installed. Monochrome adapters store data in segment $B000, whereas color adapters use segment $B800. After the video memory segment is known, ABS4 outputs its contents to the system printer.

A complete discussion of video memory can be found in Chapter 10, "Text Display." For now, it is enough to accept many of the features of the ABS4 program on faith.

Memory Use

This section discusses the major components of memory. The final two subsections in this section, "Determining the Size of the Heap" and "The Heap Error Function," are advanced topics presented as reference material only. Feel free to skip these sections.

The memory map of a Turbo Pascal program is shown in figure 6.6.

The Program Segment Prefix

The program segment prefix (PSP) is a 256-byte area established by MS-DOS when the EXE file is loaded. It contains information needed by the operating system to transfer control of the computer to the program in order for it to run, and it contains information needed to return control to the operating system after the program finishes. The segment address of the PSP is stored in the predeclared word `PrefixSeg`. The program segment prefix is discussed in greater detail in Chapter 12, "Accessing DOS."

Fig. 6.6. The memory map of a Turbo Pascal program.

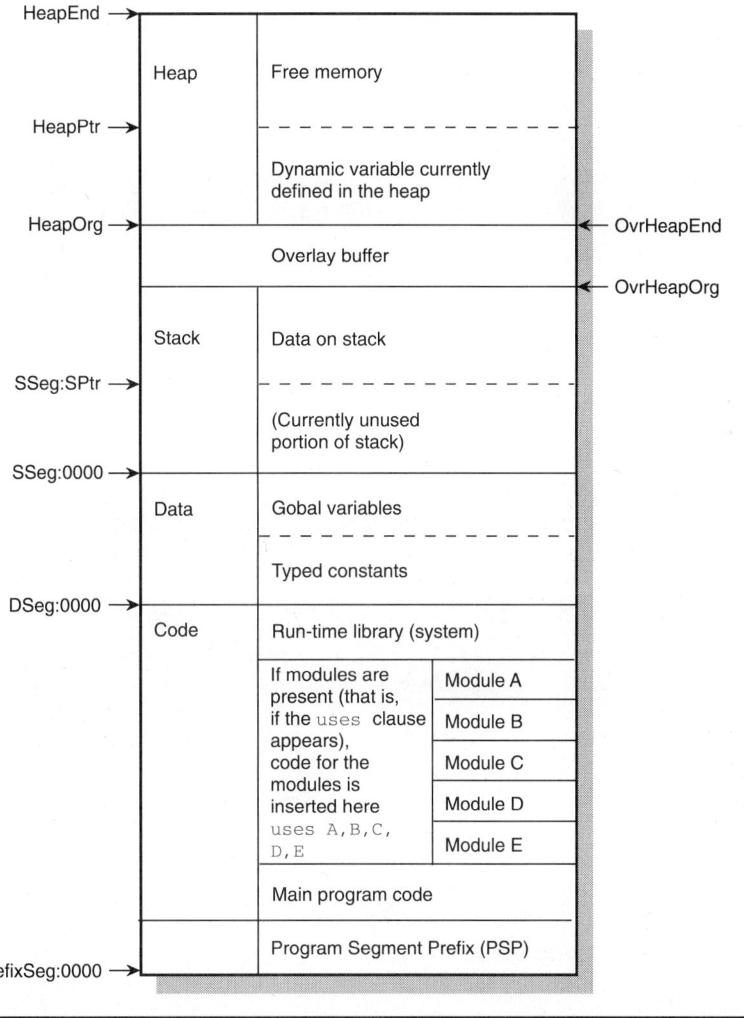

The Code Region

The instructions in each Turbo Pascal unit are placed in separate code segments. In other words, the CS register is changed depending on whether the currently executing code is from the main program or from one of the separate units. (Units are discussed in greater detail in Chapter 7, "Units.")

The individual code segments are placed in sequence: the main program occupies the first segment, and the code segments that follow it are occupied by the individual unit code in reverse order from how they are listed in the `uses` clause of the main program. The last code segment is occupied by the run-time library—that is, the System unit.

Any number of code segments may exist (up to the available memory of the system) but the size of an individual code segment cannot exceed 64K. Note that even when separate modules are not used (that is, when no `uses` clause exists), the program incorporates at least two code segments.

The Data Region

Although program code may occupy as many segments as necessary, program data (consisting of all typed constants followed by all global variables) must reside completely in a single segment; the DS register is never changed during program execution. Hence, programs that require more than the maximum 64K data area must rely on dynamically allocated memory in the heap.

The Stack Region

Like the data area, the stack segment also cannot exceed 64K; the SS register is never changed during program execution. When the program begins, the stack segment (SS) register and the stack pointer (SP) are loaded so that SS:SP points to the first byte past the stack segment. The stack grows downward, meaning that as a new variable is placed on the stack, the SP register points to lower and lower memory locations depending on the variable's size.

The Heap Region

The heap is the area of memory set aside for dynamic variable allocation. It can conceivably use all the memory remaining in the PC after the program is loaded.

The heap is also the region of memory where the overlay buffer, discussed in Chapter 15, and the graphics buffer, discussed in Chapter 11, reside.

Although the size requirements for the code and data segments are known during compilation, the size of the stack and heap can be determined only approximately, because they depend upon the exact use of the program. Consequently, *ranges* of memory can be specified with the `{$M}` compiler directive. The default stack size is 16K. By default, the heap will occupy all remaining memory.

The pointer to the bottom of the heap is stored in the variable `HeapOrg`, which stays unchanged during program execution. The pointer to the top of the heap is stored in the variable `HeapPtr`, which moves upward by the size of each dynamic variable allocated by the `New` or `GetMem` procedures.

The Free List

When the `Dispose` or `FreeMem` procedure is used to free up a dynamic variable other than the last one allocated, gaps of free memory are created in the heap, causing *memory fragmentation*. The first eight bytes of each free block store the address of the next free block and the size of the current free block. This *free list* has a `FreeList` variable in the System unit that points to the first free block.

If any deallocation frees up an area bordering on another unassigned region, the free list entry for the unassigned region is modified to encompass the complete free zone. Each block of free heap space is defined by a single free list entry.

Whenever a dynamic variable is allocated, the free list is checked before the heap is expanded. If the compiler finds a large enough block of free memory, it gets used before any new space is apportioned.

The `Release` procedure clears all memory between the address of its pointer argument and the address pointed to by `HeapPtr`. Because this process destroys the free list, it is never a good idea to mix calls to `Mark` and `Release` with calls to `Dispose` and `FreeMem`.

Determining the Size of the Heap

To find the true memory availability of the heap, Turbo provides the `MaxAvail` and `MemAvail` functions. `MaxAvail` returns a value equal to the largest *single* free block of space in the heap. `MemAvail` returns a value equal to the *sum* of all free blocks in the heap.

Of course, if you never deallocated heap space, or if you deallocated memory only at the top of the heap, `MaxAvail` and `MemAvail` return the same value. Conversely, after you `Dispose` of memory in the middle of the heap, `MemAvail` may not represent a meaningful value, especially if you are using pointers to data objects of different sizes.

This is demonstrated by the POINTER7 program (listing 6.15).

Listing 6.15

```
program Pointer7;
type
   WastedArray = array[ 1..101 ] of real;
var
   index : byte;
   NumberList : array[ 1..10 ] of ^WastedArray;
   OriginalMemAvail : longint;
   OriginalMaxAvail : longint;
begin
   OriginalMemAvail := MemAvail;
   OriginalMaxAvail := MaxAvail;
   writeln( 'Allocating...' );
   for index := 1 to 10 do begin
      New( NumberList[ index ] );
      writeln( index:3,
               MemAvail:10, MaxAvail:10,
               (OriginalMemAvail - MemAvail):10,
               (OriginalMaxAvail - MaxAvail):10 );
   end;
   writeln( 'Deallocating...' );
   for index := 2 to 9 do begin
{
      if index mod 3 = 0 then
}
         Dispose( NumberList[ index ] );
      writeln( index:3,
               MemAvail:10, MaxAvail:10,
               (OriginalMemAvail - MemAvail):10,
               (OriginalMaxAvail - MaxAvail):10 );
   end;
   writeln( 'Final results:' );
   writeln( '   MemAvail is ', MemAvail );
   writeln( '   MaxAvail is ', MaxAvail );
end.
```

The results of the execution of POINTER7 are shown in figure 6.7.

Fig. 6.7. Output produced by the POINTER7 program, with only one memory "hole."

```
Allocating...
  1     174488     174488        600        600
  2     173888     173888       1200       1200
  3     173288     173288       1800       1800
  4     172688     172688       2400       2400
  5     172088     172088       3000       3000
  6     171488     171488       3600       3600
  7     170888     170888       4200       4200
  8     170288     170288       4800       4800
  9     169688     169688       5400       5400
 10     169088     169088       6000       6000
Deallocating...
  2     169688     169088       5400       6000
  3     170288     169088       4800       6000
  4     170888     169088       4200       6000
  5     171488     169088       3600       6000
  6     172088     169088       3000       6000
  7     172688     169088       2400       6000
  8     173288     169088       1800       6000
  9     173888     169088       1200       6000
Final results:
   MemAvail is 173888
   MaxAvail is 169088
```

First, the available heap space decreases as ten new arrays are allocated. Next, the middle eight arrays are returned to the heap, leaving a "hole" of increasing size as more memory frees up. There are, in effect, two blocks of memory available, separated by a single array.

The eight-byte discrepancy between the two sets of numbers is caused by the free-list record defining the boundaries of the available gap. The eight bytes consist of two four-byte pointers: one for the top of the block and one for the bottom. To illustrate, if you remove the commenting braces around the statement

```
if index mod 3 = 0 then
```

the program produces the results shown in figure 6.8. Notice that every time a free block is created, Turbo adds another eight-byte free record to the heap.

The Heap Error Function

It is far better to retain control of a program than for it to end with a run-time error. For example, in a spreadsheet program in which the value of each cell is dynamically allocated, the typical user would prefer to see an

`Insufficient Memory` message and have the opportunity to save the current file rather than to watch helplessly while the program ends with a Turbo system message and the consequent loss of several hours of work.

Fig. 6.8. Output produced by the POINTER7 program, with three memory "holes."

```
Allocating...
  1     174472    174472      600       600
  2     173872    173872     1200      1200
  3     173272    173272     1800      1800
  4     172672    172672     2400      2400
  5     172072    172072     3000      3000
  6     171472    171472     3600      3600
  7     170872    170872     4200      4200
  8     170272    170272     4800      4800
  9     169672    169672     5400      5400
 10     169072    169072     6000      6000
Deallocating...
  2     169072    169072     6000      6000
  3     169672    169072     5400      6000
  4     169672    169072     5400      6000
  5     169672    169072     5400      6000
  6     170272    169072     4800      6000
  7     170272    169072     4800      6000
  8     170272    169072     4800      6000
  9     170872    169072     4200      6000
Final results:
   MemAvail is 170872
   MaxAvail is 169072
```

When `New` or `GetMem` encounters any memory allocation problem, the procedure immediately calls the Turbo Pascal heap error function. If the heap error function is unable to resolve the problem, `New` or `GetMem` simply ends the program with a run-time error.

You can install your own customized version of the heap error function by assigning its address to the predefined `HeapError` pointer variable, as follows:

```
HeapError := @ HeapFunc;
```

The syntax of the default heap error function is as follows:

```
{$F+}    function HeapFunc( Size : word ) : integer;    {$F-}
```

Your `HeapError` function must obey the same structure. Remember that the default heap error function resides in the Turbo Pascal System unit—a different code segment than the one that contains your program. Consequently, the `{$F+}` compiler directive forces `HeapError` to use the far call model, which creates the proper pointer format.

The `Size` parameter contains the size of the allocation request that generated the error. The default Turbo Pascal heap error function would try to find `Size` bytes of free memory. Your function should be less ambitious and settle for providing a means to end the program gracefully without causing it to abort uncontrollably.

Both `New` and `GetMem` expect one of the following return values from the heap error function:

0 Failure. A run-time error occurs immediately.

1 Failure. No run-time error is generated; rather, the `New` or `GetMem` procedure is forced to return a `Nil` pointer.

2 Success. The originating `New` or `GetMem` procedure is tried once again. Note, however, that another call to the heap error function could result, so some code must be provided to prevent the program from locking up.

The standard heap error function always returns 0, which triggers a run-time error. If, instead, your customized heap error function always returns a value of 1, your program can test the results of every call to `New` and `GetMem` to see if `Nil` is returned. If so, you know that the allocation was unsuccessful, and you can provide a harmless way for the program to end.

The MEMORY2 program (listing 6.16) demonstrates how this works.

Listing 6.16

```
program Memory2;
uses Crt;
type
   BigArray = array[ 1..10000 ] of integer;
var
   Pntr : ^BigArray;
   Counter : word;
{$F+}
function HeapFunc( Size : word ) : Integer;
begin
   if size > 0
      then begin
              writeln( 'Error in attempt to allocate ',Size, ' bytes on the heap ' );
              HeapFunc := 1;
           end;
end;
{$F-}
begin
```

continues

Listing 6.16 continued

```
   ClrScr;
   HeapError := @HeapFunc;
   Counter := 0;
   repeat
      New( Pntr );
      Counter := Counter + 1;
      writeln( 'Allocation number ', Counter );
   until Pntr = Nil;
   writeln( 'Ending program' );
end.
```

When MEMORY2 executes, it generates the results shown in figure 6.9.

Fig. 6.9. Output produced by the MEMORY2 program.

```
Allocation number 1
Allocation number 2
Allocation number 3
Allocation number 4
Allocation number 5
Allocation number 6
Allocation number 7
Allocation number 8
Error in attempt to allocate 20000 bytes on the heap
Allocation number 9
Ending program
```

Note that the failure of the `New` procedure triggered the call to `HeapError`, but after it executed, the program returned control to the statement following `New`.

Summary

In this chapter, you learned the general structure and operation of PC memory, and you saw the specific memory-management tools available in Turbo Pascal.

You learned how the segment registers allow the CPU to simultaneously access different memory regions. You saw how to identify the segment and offset of any Turbo Pascal data object, and you learned how to position variables in any desired memory location.

You learned how the unused portion of PC memory, called the heap, is available for your program to use for data storage. You learned how Turbo Pascal manages heap memory, and you saw how to recover from heap errors. You learned how heap memory can be allocated and deallocated and how it can be accessed with pointers.

CHAPTER 7

Units

A *program* is the main module of Turbo Pascal source code that you write and execute. A *unit* is simply a collection of subroutines that the program can invoke; but the unit is compiled, stored, loaded into memory, and accessed independently of the program itself.

Prior to the release of Version 4.0, Turbo Pascal required all program code to fit in a single 64K segment. Programs consisting of many small, relatively independent components could circumvent this restriction by being developed as chain files or overlays. However, many other programs—generally, the more sophisticated applications—simply could not be conveniently designed in such a format.

Units broke the 64K barrier. Because there is no limit to the number of units your program uses, and because each unit is loaded into its own memory segment, your applications are limited only by the size of memory in your machine.

And as if this is not enough, units offer several other administrative advantages:

- Units allow each program component to be developed, tested, and debugged independently.
- Programs incorporating units do not always need to be completely recompiled every time they are used or modified.
- Units enable you to build a library of precompiled, tested code that you can easily incorporate in any program.

This chapter explains what a unit is and how units are used. It also discusses the standard units available in Turbo Pascal. Finally, it discusses how you can develop and manage your own units.

Standard Units

Turbo Pascal supports over 200 procedures and functions, together with dozens of lower-level instructions, such as addition and set membership. Instead of including the machine code for every one of these operations in every program you compile, Turbo stores the subroutines in eight *standard units*.

The eight standard units are as follows:

Crt	Display and keyboard support
Dos	Use general DOS functions
Graph	Use graphics support
Graph3	Implement Turbo Pascal 3.0 Turtlegraphics
Overlay	Implement the overlay manager
Printer	Access the printer
System	Use Turbo Pascal's run-time library
Turbo3	Maintain compatibility with Turbo Pascal 3.0

The Graph unit resides in the GRAPH.TPU file. The Turbo3 and Graph3 units reside in the TURBO3.TPU and GRAPH3.TPU files, respectively. All other standard units reside in the TURBO.TPL library file. Each unit in a library can be extracted selectively by the compiler and merged, or *linked*, with your program as needed. Whenever you compile a program, Turbo automatically accesses the TURBO.TPL file and pulls out the routines it requires. This is why the installation procedures in Chapter 1 told you to place the TURBO.TPL file in the same directory as the compiler.

Crt and Dos versus CRT and DOS
Crt and Dos (with only the first letter capitalized) refer to the Crt and Dos standard units. CRT and DOS (with all capital letters) refer to cathode-ray tube and disk operating system, respectively.

Using a Standard Unit

Even though five of the standard units (System, Crt, Dos, Printer, and Overlay) physically reside in the same library file (TURBO.TPL), Turbo Pascal treats each unit as a unique entity and, except for the System unit, accesses each unit only when you specifically direct the program to do so. For example, if your program uses a routine in the Crt unit, you *must* include a `uses` clause immediately after the program header, as follows:

```
uses Crt;
```

If you want to access data objects in more than one unit, name each one in the `uses` clause. Separate each name with a comma, and end the final name with a semicolon. For example, if you need both the Crt and Dos units, the clause should appear as follows:

```
uses Crt, Dos;
```

The System unit is the only exception. The compiler *always* accesses the System unit because it contains the most frequently used data objects required by every program you write.

The standard units may be an efficient way to store Turbo Pascal code and data, but standard units are not automatically accessed. Remember that it is *your* responsibility to tell the compiler which units to use. Turbo's first assumption is that every data object used in your program is defined in the System unit or the program. Failure to include the proper `uses` clause usually results in an `Unknown identifier` error.

To help you avoid such problems, your Turbo Pascal distribution disks contain a documentation file (with the INT extension) for each standard unit. Every procedure and function header, and every global type, constant, and variable are listed. You may want to print these files and keep them nearby for ready reference. (They are in the default subdirectory, TP\DOC.) In addition, each procedure and function description in the Turbo Pascal *Library Reference* (and in the reference section at the end of this book) indicates the unit that contains it.

The System Unit

The *System unit* contains Turbo Pascal's run-time library, which includes every one of Turbo's standard built-in procedures and functions. Essentially, the System unit contains everything needed to support every *standard* procedure, function, or operation. In other words, whatever the compiler needs to produce a basic, no-frills program can be found there.

Because the System unit is required by every application you write, it need not be directly declared in your program. The System unit is automatically linked with your code during compilation.

The Dos Unit

The *Dos unit* provides excellent system-level support for the most commonly used DOS functions. These include routines for the system date and time, searching directories, and handling files. The Dos unit contains the majority of the Turbo Pascal product enhancements; in fact, none of its procedures or functions is considered part of standard Pascal.

The VERSION program (listing 7.1) demonstrates how the Dos unit can be used. `DosVersion` is a function in the Dos unit that returns a word containing the version number of the operating system currently running on your machine. The major number (for example, the 2 in 2.10) is returned in the low byte, and the minor number (the 10 in 2.10) is in the high byte.

Listing 7.1

```
program Version;
uses Dos;                        { Accesses the Dos unit }
var
   Level : word;                 { Defines a word-sized work variable }
begin
   Level := DosVersion;          { Gets the current version number }
   writeln( _Your machine is currently running DOS Version _,
            Lo( Level ),         { Low byte contains the major number }
            _. ,
            Hi( Level ) )        { High byte contains the minor number }
end.
```

The following is typical of the output of the VERSION program:

```
Your machine is currently running DOS Version 2.10
```

The Crt Unit

The *Crt unit* includes sophisticated screen and keyboard management functions. Normally, Turbo Pascal programs use standard DOS routines for all input and output operations. Although this ensures that your programs can run successfully on PCs from almost every manufacturer, the reliance on DOS adds considerable system overhead. Use of the Crt unit enables your program to bypass DOS and directly access the low-level BIOS routines and video memory in your machine. Use of the Crt unit must be restricted to programs that run on IBM PCs, ATs, PS/2s, and true compatibles.

The CRTOUT program (listing 7.2) demonstrates the use of the Crt unit. It clears the screen, positions the cursor in the center of the display, then writes the `Hello, world!` message.

Listing 7.2

```
program CrtOut;
uses Crt;                          { Accesses the Crt unit }
begin
   ClrScr;                         { Clears the screen }
   GotoXY( 34, 12 );               { Positions the cursor }
   write( _Hello, world!  )        { Displays the Hello message }
end.
```

The Printer Unit

The *Printer unit* has only one purpose: it defines the `Lst` file and assigns it to your system printer. Well, technically, it assigns the file to your LPT1 device, which is most likely your system printer. Therefore, a program that `uses` this unit allows `write` and `writeln` statements specifying the `Lst` file to output directly to the printer.

The PRINTOUT program (listing 7.3) demonstrates the use of the Printer unit. It prints the `Hello, world!` message followed by a form feed.

Listing 7.3

```
program PrintOut;
uses Printer;                          { Accesses the Printer unit }
begin
   write( Lst, _Hello, world! #12 )    { Prints the message and }
                                       { triggers a form feed (#12) }
end.
```

The Overlay Unit

The *Overlay unit* contains the code to support the use of Turbo Pascal's overlay management system. Overlays are sections of a single program that execute at different times and consequently can occupy, or *overlay*, the same physical memory area when they run. With overlays, a large program can utilize the smallest possible internal memory.

The ADDUP2 and USEADD2 programs (listings 7.4 and 7.5) demonstrate the use of the overlay unit. ADDUP2 is the component being overlaid. ADDUP2 is stored in a separate file and is compiled independently to the disk. USEADD2 is the calling program. Overlays are discussed in greater detail in Chapter 15.

Listing 7.4

```
unit AddUp2;
{$O+,F+}
interface
   function WastefulAdd( Var1, Var2 : word ) : word;
implementation
   function WastefulAdd;
   begin
      WastefulAdd := Var1 + Var2
   end;
end.
```

Listing 7.5

```
program UseAdd2;
{$F+}
uses Overlay, AddUp2;
{$O AddUp2}
begin
   OvrInit( _UseAdd2.OVR  );
   writeln( WastefulAdd( 5, 6 ) )
end.
```

The Graph Unit

The *Graph unit* is a sophisticated library of over 50 separate graphics routines that can be run on a wide variety of machines. Because of the size and complexity of its procedures and functions, the Graph unit has its own file, GRAPH.TPU, separate from the other standard units. When Turbo compiles a graphics program, it accesses both TURBO.TPL and GRAPH.TPU, as well as one of the graphics driver files, that is, one of the files with the BGI extension. In addition, if special display fonts are required, one or more CHR files must also be accessible.

The BALLOON program (listing 7.6) demonstrates how you can use the Graph unit. The program draws circles of increasing diameter, giving the illusion of an inflating balloon. When you run it in the integrated environment, you even experience a "pop" when the program ends. (Note that the `InitGraph` procedure assumes that your graphics files are in the C:\TP directory; you may need to modify this parameter based on your own configuration.)

Listing 7.6

```
program Balloon;
uses Graph;                              { Accesses the Graph unit }
var
   Driver,                               { Graphics driver type }
   Mode    : integer;                    { Graphics mode type }
   i       : word;
begin
   Driver := Detect;                     { Identify the graphics driver }
   InitGraph( Driver, Mode, _C:\TP ˉ );  { Initiate graphics }
   for i := 1 to 100 do
      Circle( 250, 100, i );             { Blow up the balloon }
   CloseGraph;
end.
```

Graphics routines are discussed in greater detail in Chapter 11, "Graphics Display."

Compatibility with Earlier Versions of Turbo Pascal

Borland has substantially enhanced Turbo Pascal since Version 3.0 was first introduced. Version 5.0, for example, is an order of magnitude more sophisticated than its grandfather product. As a result of these improvements, a program written with an earlier version of the compiler may not be completely compatible with the latest release.

The Turbo3 and Graph3 units are included to improve *downward compatibility* with the earlier code. If you have any problems compiling a program written with an earlier version of Turbo Pascal, you might be able to use the Turbo3 and Graph3 units to avoid rewriting major portions of the code.

The Turbo3 Unit

The *Turbo3 unit* includes variables and procedures that have ceased to be supported or have been substantially modified since Version 3.0 was introduced. The procedures included in the Turbo3 unit principally involve keyboard handling, screen display, and some minor I/O routines.

If you have trouble compiling a program written in an earlier version of Turbo Pascal, add the following line after the program header:

```
uses Turbo3;
```

Note that some program modifications may still be necessary. Consult the Turbo Pascal *User's Guide* for further details.

The Graph3 Unit

The *Graph3 unit* implements the full set of Turbo Pascal Version 3.0 graphics, including Turtlegraphics.

If you have trouble compiling a graphics program written in an earlier version of Turbo Pascal, follow these steps:

1. Remove the `{$I GRAPH.P}` compiler directive in the older code.

2. If only the graphics routines are causing the compile-time or run-time errors, add the following line after the program header:

```
uses Graph3;
```

3. If other procedures have also changed, use the following line instead:

```
uses Turbo3, Graph3;
```

Remember: Use only the Graph unit—not the Graph3 unit—in future programs.

The Structure of a Unit

Each unit has four components—header, interface, implementation, and initialization—arranged as shown here:

```
unit  identifier;
interface
uses  list-of-units;    { Optional }
   { Public declarations of constants, types, and variables  }
   { intended to be accessible to the user of the unit, plus }
   { the headings of all public subroutines.                 }
implementation
uses   list-of-units;    { Optional }
   { Private declarations of constants, types, and variables }
   { intended to be inaccessible to the user of the unit,    }
   { including all private procedures and functions in their }
   { entirety, and the bodies of all subroutines declared in }
   { the interface section.                                  }
begin
   { Optional initialization statements                      }
end.
```

Let us consider each section individually.

The Heading

Every unit begins with a *unit header* similar in format to a program header. As an example, the first line of a unit named Trig would appear as follows:

```
unit Trig;
```

The presence of the reserved word `unit` tells the compiler two things:

1. The file is a unit, so it contains `interface` and `implementation` sections.
2. When the unit is compiled, its output file should have the TPU extension rather than the EXE extension.

The Interface

The `interface` section declares every data object—that is, every constant, type, variable, procedure, and function—that you want the unit to share with any program or unit that calls it. Labels cannot be declared because the target label of a `goto` statement must be in the same block as the `goto` statement itself.

Only the headers of procedures and functions need to be declared. Other programs need to know the types of the parameters and functions but not their innermost details. The bodies of the subroutines are defined later in the `implementation` section.

If the unit needs to use another unit and you want the other unit also to be available to the calling program, declare that other unit in a `uses` clause at the beginning of the `interface` section.

The Implementation

The `implementation` section is the meat of the unit. It contains all of the procedures and functions that make the unit useful, including the bodies of the subroutines whose headings were previously declared in the `interface` section.

Any constant, type, or variable declared in the `interface` section is automatically available to the code in the `implementation` section. Additional private declarations can be made in the `implementation` section, but they will be local to the unit.

If the unit needs to use another unit and you do not want the other unit to be available automatically to the calling program, declare that other unit in a `uses` clause at the beginning of the `implementation` section.

The Initialization

Most units are passive; they store procedures and functions and wait to be called by the host program. Some units, however, require variables to be initialized or require some code to be executed (such as code to open a file) before the unit can be used.

Turbo Pascal provides a means for a unit to execute an opening set of instructions, called *initialization code*, before the first statement in the main program is executed. Simply place all initialization code at the end of the `implementation` section and preface the statements with the reserved word `begin`.

Initialization code is optional. The presence of the word `begin` tells the compiler to perform an initialization; if no `begin` statement is present, no initialization occurs.

If the main program `uses` several units, each unit is initialized in the order in which it is declared in the `uses` clause.

Developing Your Own Units

Now that you have seen the components of an individual unit, it is time to see how units and programs work together.

A program uses the subroutines in a unit in the same manner that it uses a forward procedure or function. The program does not care where the subroutine resides or when it is defined as long as the header is declared.

Suppose that you create a simple addition function called `Adder`, as follows:

```
function Adder( Var1, Var2 : word ) : word;
begin
   Adder := Var1 + Var2
end;
```

Suppose further that because of its general usefulness, you decide to turn it into a unit called ADDUP (listing 7.7).

Listing 7.7

```
unit AddUp;
interface
   function Adder( Var1, Var2 : word ) : word;
implementation
   function Adder;
   begin
      Adder := Var1 + Var2
   end;
end.
```

After the ADDUP unit is compiled to disk, the `Adder` function becomes available to any program that calls for it. One such program is USEADDER (listing 7.8).

Listing 7.8

```
program UseAdder;
uses AddUp;
begin
   writeln( Adder( 5, 6 ) )
end.
```

Because USEADDER includes the `uses AddUp` directive, the `Adder` function is available just as if it had been declared in the USEADDER program.

Conceptually, a unit and its calling program fit together like a lock and key. Figure 7.1 shows the combination of the USEADDER program and the ADDUP unit.

The following sections discuss the rules for creating and using your own units.

Using a Unit

You can use a custom unit in the same way you use the predefined ones—by declaring it in a `uses` clause in the main program. If several units are to be accessed, separate each name in the `uses` clause with a comma. You end the final unit with a semicolon.

Fig. 7.1. The combination of the USEADDER program and the ADDUP unit.

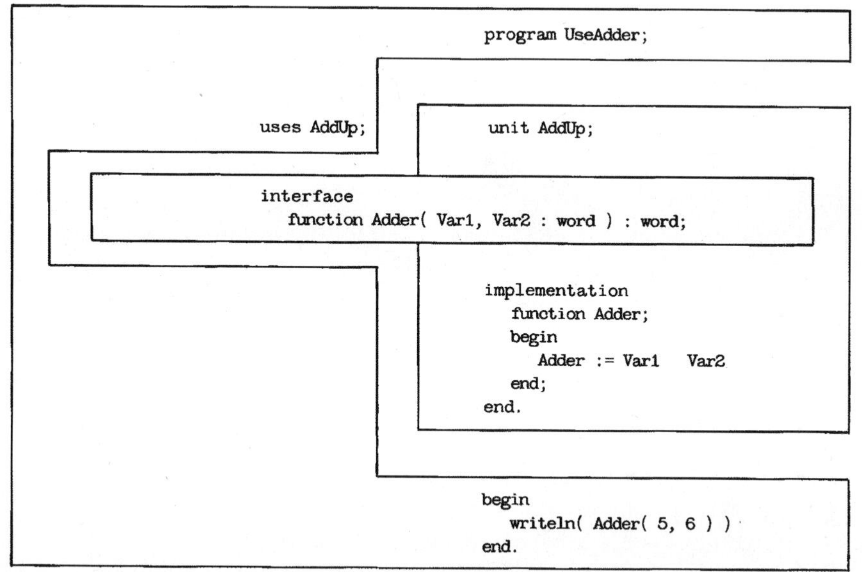
program UseAdder;
uses AddUp;
unit AddUp;
interface
function Adder(Var1, Var2 : word) : word;
implementation
function Adder;
begin
Adder := Var1 Var2
end;
end.
begin
writeln(Adder(5, 6))
end.

When the main program is compiled, Turbo looks for every unit named in the `uses` clause. It assumes that the name of the unit file is the same as the name of the specified unit but with the TPU extension. Suppose that the compiler sees the following declaration in the main program:

```
uses FileA, FileB;
```

Turbo Pascal assumes that the code for the units is in the FileA.TPU and FileB.TPU files, respectively.

Writing Units

Although capable of doing almost anything a regular program can do, a unit is primarily used to hold general-purpose procedures and functions that you want to access from several different programs. Alternatively, a large program may use units to collect related code segments that—as units—operate independently.

Believe it or not, because of the similarities that a unit shares with a program, creating a unit is a simple, almost mechanical process. To prove this point, here is a set of rules for you to follow.

1. Begin with the unit skeleton presented earlier. The unit header (the reserved word `unit` followed by an identifier) is placed in the first line.

2. Identify all public data objects—all global constants, types, variables, procedures, and functions—in the unit and declare them in the `interface` section. If any global data objects require the use of another unit, that other unit must be named in a `uses` statement at the beginning of the `interface` section.

3. Identify all private data objects—all local constants, types, variables, procedures, and functions—and include them in the `implementation` section. In addition, include the code for the global procedures and functions you declared in the `interface` section. If any local data objects require the use of a unit not already identified in the `interface` section, that other unit must be named in a `uses` statement at the beginning of the `implementation` section.

4. If the unit contains any initialization code (most units will not have any), place the initialization code just before the final `end` statement in the file, then segregate the code from the rest of the `implementation` section by placing a `begin` statement before its first line.

5. Save the unit to disk.

6. Compile the unit to disk. Even though a unit is entered, debugged, and compiled just like a program, it cannot be directly run. Instead, the unit must be made available to other programs by being compiled to disk with the `Compile/Destination disk` option discussed in Chapter 1. Turbo Pascal automatically assigns the TPU extension to the file name of a compiled unit.

Unfortunately, describing how to create a unit is a bit like describing a spiral staircase without using your hands; it is much easier to point to an example.

Example 1: Trigonometric Functions

The only trigonometric functions defined by Turbo Pascal are `Sin`, `Cos`, and `ArcTan`. Fortunately, these functions can be combined to derive any other trigonometric value.

For example, the `Trigs` unit contains derived tangent, secant, cosecant, and cotangent functions. As you read the following steps to create the unit, refer to its final form in listing 7.9.

1. Begin the unit with the header:

   ```
   unit Trigs;
   ```

2. Because the `tan`, `sec`, `csc`, and `cot` functions are public, insert their headers into the `interface` section, as shown in listing 7.9. No other data objects are global, and no other units are required, so you do not need to make additional entries.
3. Insert the bodies of the four functions into the `implementation` section. Because their complete headers appeared in the `interface` section, you do not need to declare their parameters and return types. However, you can include the information here as comments to improve overall program documentation.
4. No initialization code is required, so the unit is complete.
5. Save the unit as TRIGS.PAS.
6. Compile the unit to disk, as shown in figure 7.2.

Listing 7.9

```
unit Trigs;
interface
   function tan( Radians : real ) : real;     { tangent }
   function sec( Radians : real ) : real;     { secant }
   function csc( Radians : real ) : real;     { cosecant }
   function cot( Radians : real ) : real;     { cotangent }
implementation
   function tan { ( Radians : real ) : real };    { tangent }
   var
      cosine : real;
   begin
      cosine := cos( Radians );
      if abs( cosine ) <= 0.001 then
         tan := 99999.999999
      else
         tan := sin( Radians ) / cosine;
   end;
   function sec { ( Radians : real ) : real };    { secant }
   var
      cosine : real;
   begin
      cosine := cos( Radians );
```

continues

Listing 7.9 continued

```
    if abs( cosine ) <= 0.001 then
       sec := 99999.999999
    else
       sec := 1.0 / cosine;
 end;
 function csc { ( Radians : real ) : real };    { cosecant }
 var
    sine : real;
 begin
    sine := sin( Radians );
    if abs( sine ) <= 0.001 then
       csc := 99999.999999
    else
       csc := 1.0 / sine;
 end;
 function cot { ( Radians : real ) : real };    { cotangent }
 var
    sine : real;
 begin
    sine := sin( Radians );
    if abs( sine ) <= 0.001 then
       cot := 99999.999999
    else
       cot := cos( Radians ) / sine;
 end;
end.
```

The USETRIGS program (listing 7.10) demonstrates how simple it is to use the `Trigs` unit. USETRIGS contains a `uses` clause similar in format to one you would use to access a standard unit. No other special conditions apply. The output of USETRIGS is shown in figure 7.3. Notice how the number 99999.999999 is used to avoid division by zero.

Listing 7.10

```
program UseTrigs;
uses Trigs;
var
   Degrees : word;
   Radians : real;
```

```
begin
   writeln( _Degs          Sin          Cos          Tan ,
          _          Sec          Csc          Cot  );
   writeln;
   for Degrees := 0 to 20 do begin
      Radians := (5*Degrees) * Pi / 180.0;
      writeln( (5*Degrees):4, _  _,
               sin( Radians ):12:6,
               cos( Radians ):12:6,
               tan( Radians ):12:6,
               sec( Radians ):12:6,
               csc( Radians ):12:6,
               cot( Radians ):12:6 );
   end;
end.
```

Fig. 7.2. *Compile the TRIGS.PAS unit to disk.*

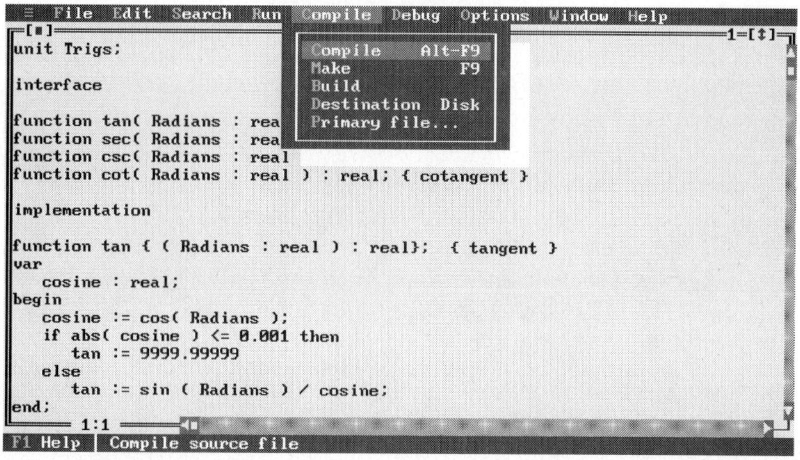

```
 ≡  File  Edit  Search  Run  Compile  Debug  Options  Window  Help
╔═[■]═══════════════════════════════════════════════════════1═[↕]═╗
unit Trigs;                   Compile     Alt-F9
                              Make            F9
interface                     Build
                              Destination  Disk
function tan( Radians : rea   Primary file...
function sec( Radians : rea
function csc( Radians : real
function cot( Radians : real ) : real; { cotangent }

implementation

function tan { ( Radians : real ) : real};  { tangent }
var
   cosine : real;
begin
   cosine := cos( Radians );
   if abs( cosine ) <= 0.001 then
      tan := 9999.99999
   else
      tan := sin ( Radians ) / cosine;
end;
════ 1:1 ═════
 F1 Help │ Compile source file
```

Example 2: Hexadecimal Conversion

The `Hexes` unit contains useful hexadecimal conversion functions. As you read the following steps to create the unit, refer to its final form in listing 7.11.

Fig. 7.3. Output produced by the USETRIGS program.

Degs	Sin	Cos	Tan	Sec	Csc	Cot
0	0.000000	1.000000	0.000000	1.000000	99999.999999	99999.999999
5	0.087156	0.996195	0.087489	1.003820	11.473713	11.430052
10	0.173648	0.984808	0.176327	1.015427	5.758770	5.671282
15	0.258819	0.965926	0.267949	1.035276	3.863703	3.732051
20	0.342020	0.939693	0.363970	1.064178	2.923804	2.747477
25	0.422618	0.906308	0.466308	1.103378	2.366202	2.144507
30	0.500000	0.866025	0.577350	1.154701	2.000000	1.732051
35	0.573576	0.819152	0.700208	1.220775	1.743447	1.428148
40	0.642788	0.766044	0.839100	1.305407	1.555724	1.191754
45	0.707107	0.707107	1.000000	1.414214	1.414214	1.000000
50	0.766044	0.642788	1.191754	1.555724	1.305407	0.839100
55	0.819152	0.573576	1.428148	1.743447	1.220775	0.700208
60	0.866025	0.500000	1.732051	2.000000	1.154701	0.577350
65	0.906308	0.422618	2.144507	2.366202	1.103378	0.466308
70	0.939693	0.342020	2.747477	2.923804	1.064178	0.363970
75	0.965926	0.258819	3.732051	3.863703	1.035276	0.267949
80	0.984808	0.173648	5.671282	5.758770	1.015427	0.176327
85	0.996195	0.087156	11.430052	11.473713	1.003820	0.087489
90	1.000000	0.000000	99999.999999	99999.999999	1.000000	0.000000
95	0.996195	-0.087156	-11.430052	-11.473713	1.003820	-0.087489
100	0.984808	-0.173648	-5.671282	-5.758770	1.015427	-0.176327

1. Begin the unit with the header:

   ```
   unit Hexes;
   ```

2. The `HexNybble`, `HexByte`, and `HexWord` functions are public, so you insert their headers into the `interface` section, as shown in listing 7.11. Notice that the return type for `HexByte` is a two-character string type named `String2`, and the return type for `HexWord` is a four-character string type named `String4`. Neither of these types is standard, so both must be declared in the `interface` section prior to the function headers. No other data objects are global, and no other units are required, so no other entries need to be made.

3. Insert the bodies of the three functions into the `implementation` section. Because their complete headers appeared in the `interface` section, their parameters and return types do not need to be redeclared. However, you can include information as comments to improve overall program documentation.

4. No initialization code is required, so the unit is complete.

5. Save the unit as HEXES.PAS.

6. Compile the unit to disk, as shown in figure 7.4.

Listing 7.11

```
unit Hexes;
interface
   type
      String2 = string[ 2 ];
      String4 = string[ 4 ];
   function HexNybble( Number : byte ) : char;
   function HexByte( Number : byte ) : String2;
   function HexWord( Number : word ) : String4;
implementation
   function HexNybble { ( Number : byte ) : char };
   begin
      if Number < 10 then HexNybble := Chr( 48+ Number )
                     else HexNybble := Chr( 55+ Number );
   end;
   function HexByte { ( Number : byte ) : String2 };
   begin
      HexByte := HexNybble( Number div 16 ) + HexNybble( Number mod 16 );
   end;
   function HexWord { ( Number : word ) : String4 };
   begin
      HexWord := HexByte( Hi(Number) ) + HexByte( Lo(Number) );
   end;
end.
```

The USEHEX program (listing 7.12) demonstrates how simple it is to use the `Hexes` unit. USEHEX contains a `uses` clause similar in format to one you would use to access a standard unit. No other special conditions apply.

Listing 7.12

```
program UseHex;
uses Hexes;
var
   i : byte;
   j : word;
begin
   for i := 14 to 18 do writeln( i:8, HexByte( i ):6 );
   writeln;
   for j := 32765 to 32770 do writeln( j:8, HexWord( j ):6 )
end.
```

Fig. 7.4. Compile the HEXES.PAS unit to disk.

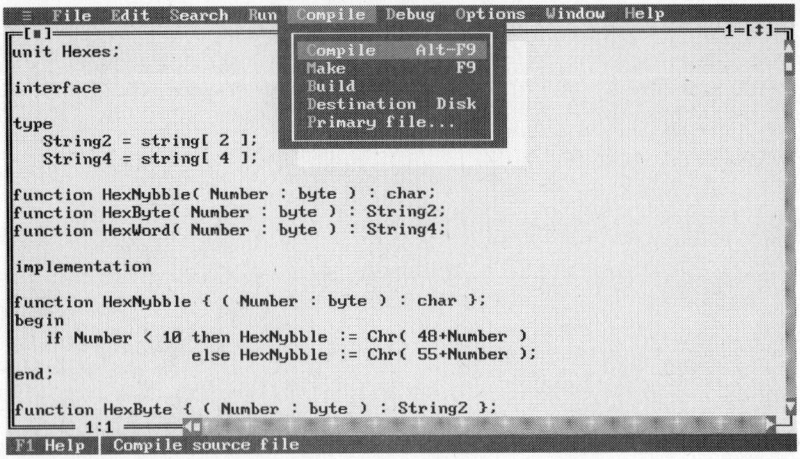

```
 ≡  File  Edit  Search  Run  Compile  Debug  Options  Window  Help
[■]                                                          1=[↕]
unit Hexes;                   Compile     Alt-F9
                              Make            F9
interface                     Build
                              Destination   Disk
type                          Primary file...
   String2 = string[ 2 ];
   String4 = string[ 4 ];

function HexNybble( Number : byte ) : char;
function HexByte( Number : byte ) : String2;
function HexWord( Number : byte ) : String4;

implementation

function HexNybble { ( Number : byte ) : char };
begin
   if Number < 10 then HexNybble := Chr( 48+Number )
                  else HexNybble := Chr( 55+Number );
end;

function HexByte { ( Number : byte ) : String2 };
       1:1
F1 Help | Compile source file
```

When executed, USEHEX produces the output shown in figure 7.5.

Fig. 7.5. Output produced by the USEHEX program.

```
   14    0E
   15    0F
   16    10
   17    11
   18    12

32765  7FFD
32766  7FFE
32767  7FFF
32768  8000
32769  8001
32770  8002
```

Using the TPUMOVER Unit Mover Program

Every program that `uses` a unit must be able to access that unit's TPU file. If, as frequently happens, the TPU file is in a different directory than the program you are developing, you need to help the compiler find it. There are two ways to do this:

1. Copy the TPU file into the current directory. This is the simplest technique, but you can end up with multiple versions of your unit program scattered throughout your disks.
2. Tell the integrated environment where the TPU file resides by appending the unit's path to the current `Unit directories` entry, located in the Options/Directories menu, as shown in figure 7.6.

Fig. 7.6. The Directories menu.

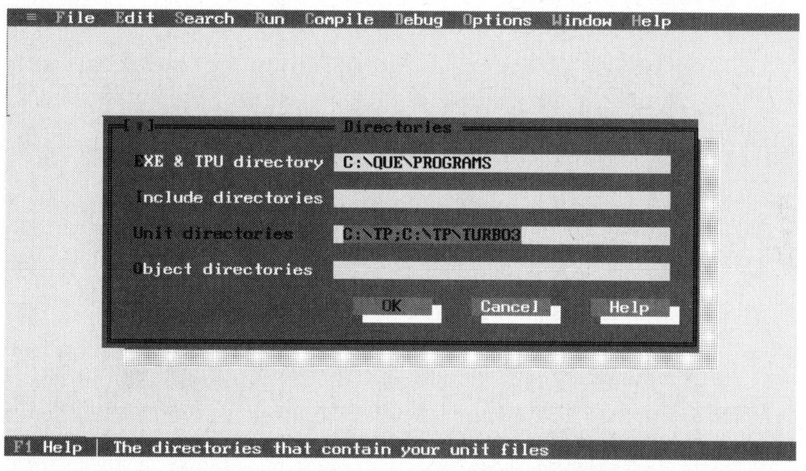

Both of these methods can become tiresome or impractical when several units in other directories must be accessed by the same program. As the number of units proliferate, the mundane housekeeping chores (listing directories, copying units, keeping track of current unit versions, and so on) will make you wonder why you started using units in the first place.

Fortunately, Turbo Pascal provides an answer. Although an individual unit is stored in its own TPU file, you can combine several units into a single

TPL library file similar to the way the TURBO.TPL library stores the standard units. To the compiler, reading a unit from a library is functionally equivalent to reading it from the disk and also provides several practical advantages.

1. Because one library can store several units, you do not need individual TPU files cluttering up your directories.

2. Program reliability is increased, because having one "official" unit library ensures that you always use the latest version of a unit.

3. Libraries simplify code sharing. It is much easier to copy or erase one TPL library file than a dozen TPU files.

4. It takes less disk space to store one TPL library than to store its component TPU units individually.

5. Libraries reduce compile times by minimizing disk access.

TPUMOVER.EXE is the library management program for Turbo Pascal units. You run it to create and maintain your own library files and even to manage the standard TURBO.TPL library. TPUMOVER.EXE is frequently called the *mover utility* because it is used principally to move units into and out of libraries. Specifically, its most common application is to ensure ease of access to your custom units by adding them to the TURBO.TPL library itself.

Protect Your Library File
Modifying the TURBO.TPL library is serious, but not hazardous. Nevertheless, you should make a backup copy of the file before you begin.

Let us assume that you want to add the `Hexes` and `Trigs` units to the TURBO.TPL library. You can do this with the TPUMOVER.EXE program from the DOS command line. If you have been using Turbo Pascal Versions 4.0 through 5.5, you will notice that the interactive version of TPUMOVER.EXE is not available in Version 6.0.

The following discussion assumes that your DOS path contains C:\TP\UTILS, the directory where TPUMOVER.EXE resides. It also assumes that both the HEXES.TPU and TRIGS.TPU files are in the current directory and that the TURBO.TPL library is in the \TP directory. Be sure that you specify the complete path names when necessary.

Like all Turbo products, TPUMOVER.EXE is extremely user friendly. To see for yourself, enter the following command:

```
TPUMOVER
```

Typing no command-line arguments after TPUMOVER tells the program that you want it to display help messages. TPUMOVER.EXE responds by listing the complete command-line syntax, as shown in figure 7.7.

Fig.* 7.7. *The help screen from the TPUMOVER.EXE utility.

```
C:\>tpumover
TPU Mover  Version 6.00  Copyright (c) 1987,90 Borland International

Syntax: TPUMOVER filename operations

Where filename is a library file name (default extension .TPL) and
operations is an optional list one or more of the following commands:

+unitname    Add a unit to the library.
-unitname    Delete a unit from the library.
*unitname    Extract a unit from the library.

If no operations are specified, TPUMOVER outputs a list of the units
in the library file.

C:\>
```

To see the current contents of the TURBO.TPL library, use the following command. (Note that this feature is available in Version 5.5, but not in Version 6.0.)

```
TPUMOVER \TP\TURBO.TPL
```

TPUMOVER.EXE responds by displaying a list of the units, their code sizes, their data sizes, and the units they use, as shown in figure 7.8.

Refer to the command-line syntax in figure 7.7 as you add the Hexes and Trigs units to the TURBO.TPL library with the command:

```
TPUMOVER \TP\TURBO.TPL +HEXES +TRIGS
```

If the process is successful, the only message is the program header:

```
TPU Mover  Version 6.0  Copyright (c) 1987,1990 Borland International
```

Fig. 7.8. The units in TURBO.TPL.

```
C>tpumover \tp\turbo.tpl
TPU Mover  Version 6.00  Copyright (c) 1987,90 Borland International

Unit            Code  Data  Uses
SYSTEM         21585   676
OVERLAY         1855    26  SYSTEM
CRT             1556    20  SYSTEM
DOS             1594     6  SYSTEM
PRINTER           54   256  SYSTEM

C>
```

The default file extension is TPU, so you must specify the TPL extension as part of the library name. If you do not, TPUMOVER.EXE assumes that you want to create a *new* library named TURBO.TPU instead of add the units to TURBO.TPL, as you intended. No status or error message is produced in either case.

Let us view the updated contents of TURBO.TPL by typing the command:

```
TPUMOVER \TP\TURBO.TPL
```

Figure 7.9 shows the response of TPUMOVER.EXE, confirming that `Trigs` and `Hexes` library units are now part of the TURBO.TPL library.

To extract a unit, specify the subdirectory where you want the unit copied. For example, to extract HEXES and copy HEXES.TPU to the \TPU subdirectory, you would enter the following

```
TPUMOVER \TP\TURBO.TPL \TPU\HEXES
```

When you want to add a unit, specify only the unit name to be deleted. Do not include directory information. For example, to delete HEXES from TURBO.TPL, you would enter the following command:

```
TPUMOVER \TP\TURBO.TPL -HEXES
```

Fig. 7.9. The updated contents of TURBO.TPL.

```
C>tpumover \tp\turbo.tpl
TPU Mover  Version 6.00  Copyright (c) 1987,90 Borland International

Unit              Code  Data  Uses
SYSTEM           21585   676
OVERLAY           1855    26  SYSTEM
CRT               1556    20  SYSTEM
DOS               1594     6  SYSTEM
PRINTER             54   256  SYSTEM
HEXES              226     0  SYSTEM
TRIGS              522     0  SYSTEM

C>
```

Summary

This chapter began by introducing you to the standard Turbo Pascal units:

- ❑ The System unit contains the code that supports Turbo's built-in subroutines.
- ❑ The Dos unit supports the most commonly used DOS functions.
- ❑ The Crt unit provides screen and keyboard services.
- ❑ The Printer unit helps you use your system printer.
- ❑ The Overlay unit supports Turbo's overlay management system.
- ❑ The Graph unit is a library of graphics routines.
- ❑ The Turbo3 and Graph3 units provide compatibility with earlier Turbo Pascal versions.

You also saw how several individual units can be combined to form a single library.

Next, the major components of a unit—heading, interface, implementation, and initialization—were explained. You then learned how to develop units of your own design. Rules were presented for writing and using custom units. Two examples were presented; the first contained common trigonometric functions, and the second provided hex conversion routines.

Finally, you saw how to use the TPUMOVER library management program.

CHAPTER

8

Debugging Your Programs

Almost all programs contain errors sometime during their development. In fact, as soon as you think your program is perfect, give it to someone else to run. Suddenly, the strangest things start to happen! Printers jam, disks fill up, and power fails. The smallest task exhausts every byte of internal memory. Impatient users type ahead in the program, only to find that they have made a mistake and cannot undo the effect of their responses. All at once, your "perfect" program is riddled with holes.

Errors—both large and small—are a fact of programming life. Strangely enough, the big errors are usually the easiest to correct. Sometimes, it is difficult even to be sure that a small error is present—until the program crashes, of course. When you ask programmers how they learned the process of debugging, you are likely to get a single word in response: experience.

Fortunately, programming in Turbo Pascal is different. Turbo provides a powerful, built-in debugger that helps you look inside a program while it is running. With the debugger, you can trace the complete flow of the program, and you can see how each variable changes every step of the way. In this chapter, you learn how to use the debugger to solve even the most troublesome programming challenges.

Categories of Errors

There are three major categories of errors: compile-time errors, run-time errors, and logic errors.

Compile-Time Errors

A compile-time error is generally the result of lexical or syntactic mistakes. A lexical error occurs when an individual word, number, or program symbol is illegal, such as writing the hexadecimal value $23 as 23h. A syntactic error happens when you break one of the formal rules of Turbo Pascal, such as specifying the wrong number of parameters in a subroutine or forgetting a semicolon. Turbo will not let your program run until all compile-time errors are repaired.

Most compile-time errors are obvious and easy to correct. When Turbo detects one, it halts compilation, moves the cursor (and scrolls the screen, if necessary) to the offending line of code, and displays both an error number and a brief English-language error message.

Run-Time Errors

A run-time, or semantic, error arises when perfectly valid Turbo Pascal statements are combined illegally. Examples include trying to write to files not opened for output, range errors, memory overflows, and division by zero—in short, any of the numerous things that Turbo Pascal can detect while the program is running.

Run-time errors end the program and cause an error number and a message to be displayed. If the program was running in the integrated environment, Turbo returns to the editor and moves the cursor to the line of code that triggered the problem. Run-time errors can be a nuisance, but because you know which line of code was running when the error occurred, it is usually a simple matter to analyze and repair the problem.

Logic Errors

A logic error is generated when the program does something you do not want or does not do something you expect. A logic error is a design fault in the program. Logic errors are the most difficult to isolate. After all, Turbo "believes" that it is running a good program.

Sometimes a logic error is obvious. If the first page number on a report is 38, for example, you probably forgot to initialize your page-counter variable. At other times, depending on the complexity of your program's design, you might not even know which part of the program contains the error. The most complicated and time-consuming problems are usually caused by the combination of two or more individually trivial mistakes.

The debugger is designed to detect logic errors.

A Debugging Example

Now run the TURBO.EXE editor and enter the BAD1 program in listing 8.1. After you have proofread your typing, press F2 and save the program to disk. Do *not*—repeat, do *not*—run the program. BAD1 contains an example of the most difficult species of bug to find, the kind that hangs the machine.

Listing 8.1

```
program Bad1;
var
   i : integer;
   X : array [ 1..3 ] of integer;
begin
   i := 0;
   while i <> 3 do begin
      X[i] := i*i + 5;
      Inc( i );
   end;
   for i := 1 to 3 do
      writeln( X[i] );
end.
```

From a quick glance, BAD1 appears to be designed to calculate, store, and display values using the following formula:

```
X[i] := i*i + 5;
```

Even without a computer, you can determine that the contents of the first three elements of the `X` array will be 6, 9, and 14.

However, BAD1 contains a fatal flaw. Because the variable `i` is initially set to 0, the first formula computed by the program is the one for array element 0, as follows:

```
X[0] := 0*0 + 5;
```

Even though the `X` array is declared only for elements 1 through 3, the compiler dutifully calculates the position of element 0 to be the two bytes *immediately in front of* the `X` array. In other words, the compiler believes that `X[0]` occupies the same memory location as the index variable `i` itself. Consequently, the assignment

```
X[0] := 5;
```

is the same as

```
i := 5;
```

In the next program statement, the `Inc` procedure increases `i` to 6; therefore, the second pass through the `while` loop assigns `X[6]`. Similarly, the third pass assigns `X[7]`, the fourth pass assigns `X[8]`, and so on. Just as the compiler used the location of the `X` array to calculate where `X[0]` must reside, it also derives the locations for `X[6]`, `X[7]`, and `X[8]`.

Because the value of `i` will never be 3, the `while` loop will never end. The program will continue until the value of `i` is large enough that array element `X[i]` overwrites a critical memory location. If you actually run the BAD1 program, you will probably find that you have to reboot your PC. In fact, if you disregarded the warning and ran the program, you should probably reboot even if you do not find any problems with your PC.

If the `{$R+}` range-checking option had been enabled, this error would have been discovered fairly quickly. This discussion assumes that range checking remains at its default setting of `{$R-}`.

Traditional Debugging Techniques

If you did not already know what was wrong with BAD1, you would probably begin your debugging effort by inserting `writeln` statements at key points throughout the program, as follows:

```
      begin
         i := 0;
         while i <> 3 do begin
{* 1 *}     WRITELN( 'Now at statement 1:', I:5, X[I]:5 );
            X[i] := i*i + 5;
```

```
{* 2 *}      WRITELN( 'Now at statement 2:', I:5, X[I]:5 );
             Inc( i );
{* 3 *}      WRITELN( 'Now at statement 3:', I:5, X[I]:5 );
          end;
{* 4 *}      WRITELN( 'Now at statement 4:', I:5, X[I]:5 );
          for i := 1 to 3 do
             writeln( X[i] );
       end.
```

Next, you would save the program to disk under a different name, then compile and run it. Using this technique, the results of the first seven passes through the `while` loop are shown in figure 8.1.

***Fig. 8.1.** The initial output produced by the modified BAD1 program.*

```
Now at statement 1:    0    0
Now at statement 2:    5    0
Now at statement 3:    6 8195
Now at statement 1:    6 8195
Now at statement 2:    6   41
Now at statement 3:    7 3738
Now at statement 1:    7 3738
Now at statement 2:    7   54
Now at statement 3:    812304
Now at statement 1:    812304
Now at statement 2:    8   69
Now at statement 3:    9  432
Now at statement 1:    9  432
Now at statement 2:    9   86
Now at statement 3:   10    0
Now at statement 1:   10    0
Now at statement 2:   10  105
Now at statement 3:   11 1026
Now at statement 1:   11 1026
Now at statement 2:   11  126
Now at statement 3:   12 3745
```

The value of `i` changes immediately from 0 to 5 between the first and second lines, so it is obvious that the execution of the assignment statement

```
X[i] := i*i + 5;
```

changed the value of `i`. It is also clear that the PC hangs and needs to be rebooted because assignments are being made to nonexistent elements of the `X` array—a process that is likely to adversely affect control of the operating system itself.

Using the Integrated Debugger

Now try to perform the same analysis using the Turbo Pascal integrated debugger.

6.0

To use the debugger, both the `{$D}` and the `{$L}` options must be enabled. The default settings are `{$D+}` and `{$L+}`. To enable `{$D}` and `{$L}` in the IDE, select Options/Compiler. Then tab to the Debugging check box. To enable `{$D}`, select `Debug information`. To enable `{$L}`, select `Local symbols`. (Press the space bar to make your selection.) Make sure that the `X` symbol is in the check box of both options, or simply include the following as the first line of your program:

```
{$D+,L+}
```

To the debugger, keeping track of a variable throughout the execution of a program is called *watching*. Specifying which variable to track is called *adding a watch*. The following steps explain how to watch the `i` and the `X` variables:

1. Load the original BAD1.PAS program.

2. Choose the `Add watch` option from the Debug/Watches menu selection. (Note that pressing Ctrl-F7 selects the option directly.) An Add Watch dialog box appears in the center of the screen, as shown in figure 8.2.

   By default, the dialog box contains the word currently being referenced by the cursor, so the word `program` has no significance here. After you become comfortable with the debugger and its features, you will get in the habit of positioning the cursor and pressing Ctrl-F7. For now, add your first watch expression by entering **i** and then pressing the Enter key. The Watches window appears at the bottom of the screen. It contains the variable `i`, together with the phrase `Unknown identifier`.

3. To add the variable `X` to the Watches window (and while this window is still the active one), press the Enter key. The Add Watch dialog box reappears. Type **X** and press Enter. The variable `X` appears in the Watches window, as shown in figure 8.3.

Fig. 8.2. The Add Watch window.

```
≡ File Edit Search Run Compile Debug Options Window Help
[■] BAD1.PAS 1=[↕]
program Bad1;
var
  i : integer;
  X : array[ 1..3 ] of integer;
begin
  i := 0;
  while i      [■] Add Watch
     X[i]
     Inc(      Watch expression
  end;          program
  for i :=
    writel           OK    Cancel    Help
end.

1:1
F1 Help | Enter expression to add as watch
```

Fig. 8.3. The BAD1 program, with i and X selected as watch variables.

```
≡ File Edit Search Run Compile Debug Options Window Help
BAD1.PAS 1
program Bad1;
var
  i : integer;
  X : array[ 1..3 ] of integer;
begin
  i := 0;
  while i <> 3 do begin
     X[i] := i*i + 5;
     Inc( i );
  end;
  for i := 1 to 3 do
    writeln( X[i] );
end.
[■] Watches 2=[↑]
  X: Unknown identifier
  i: Unknown identifier
F1 Help  F7 Trace  F8 Step  ←┘ Edit  Ins Add  Del Delete  F10 Menu
```

Now start running the program. Notice the bottom line of the display; the F7 function key is marked `Trace`. *Tracing* is the process of stepping through a program one executable statement at a time.

1. Press the F7 key to begin the trace. Three things immediately happen. First, Turbo compiles the program. Second, because of the compilation, `i` and `X` are no longer unknown identifiers but known numeric variables; hence, the Watch window now shows that `i` and `X` contain numbers. Third, the first executable line in the program (the `begin` statement in front of the main body) is highlighted. The resulting screen is shown in figure 8.4.

Fig. 8.4. *The initial contents of the i and X variables.*

```
≡ File  Edit  Search  Run  Compile  Debug  Options  Window  Help
                           BAD1.PAS                              1
program Bad1;
var
  i : integer;
  X : array[ 1..3 ] of integer;
begin
  i := 0;
  while i <> 3 do begin
     X[i] := i*i + 5;
     Inc( i );
  end;
  for i := 1 to 3 do
     writeln( X[i] );
end.
[■]                        Watches                              2
 X: (-23947,68,-16742)
 i: 12554

F1 Help  F7 Trace  F8 Step  ◄┘ Edit  Ins Add  Del Delete  F10 Menu
```

Throughout the tracing process, Turbo highlights the line containing the *next* instruction to be executed.

2. Continue to press the F7 key to advance the trace. With each keystroke, another executable statement is processed. Check the Watch window as you go. When the highlighted line passes the assignment statement—that is, immediately after the assignment statement is processed—the variable `i` changes its value to 5, as shown in figure 8.5.

3. Press the F7 key again. The `Inc` statement changes the value of `i` to 6. Keep pressing F7 until you have cycled through the `while` loop a second time. The value of `i` changes to 7, as shown in figure 8.6, but the values in the `X` array remain unchanged.

Just as with the earlier `writeln` method, the integrated debugger enables you to conclude that the assignment statement is what changed the value of `i`.

Fig. 8.5. The value of the variable i is set to 5.

```
 ≡  File  Edit  Search  Run  Compile  Debug  Options  Window  Help
                                 BAD1.PAS                        1
program Bad1;
var
  i : integer;
  X : array[ 1..3 ] of integer;
begin
  i := 0;
  while i <> 3 do begin
     X[i] := i*i + 5;
     Inc( i );
  end;
  for i := 1 to 3 do
    writeln( X[i] );
end.
[■]                              Watches                     2=[↑]
  X: (-23947,68,-16742)
  i: 5
F1 Help  F7 Trace  F8 Step  ←┘ Edit  Ins Add  Del Delete  F10 Menu
```

Fig. 8.6. The value of i has changed; the contents of X remain the same.

```
 ≡  File  Edit  Search  Run  Compile  Debug  Options  Window  Help
                                 BAD1.PAS                        1
program Bad1;
var
  i : integer;
  X : array[ 1..3 ] of integer;
begin
  i := 0;
  while i <> 3 do begin
     X[i] := i*i + 5;
     Inc( i );
  end;
  for i := 1 to 3 do
    writeln( X[i] );
end.
[■]                              Watches                     2=[↑]
  X: (-23947,68,-16742)
  i: 7
F1 Help  F7 Trace  F8 Step  ←┘ Edit  Ins Add  Del Delete  F10 Menu
```

6.0 The Debugging Commands

Now that you have gotten a taste of what the built-in debugger can do, it is time to examine more fully the debugging features of the integrated

6.0

environment. Figure 8.7 shows the Debug menu option. Note that the entire set of debugging commands is not concentrated in the Debug option; some debugging commands are in the System, Search, Run, Options, and Window options.

Fig. 8.7. The Debug menu.

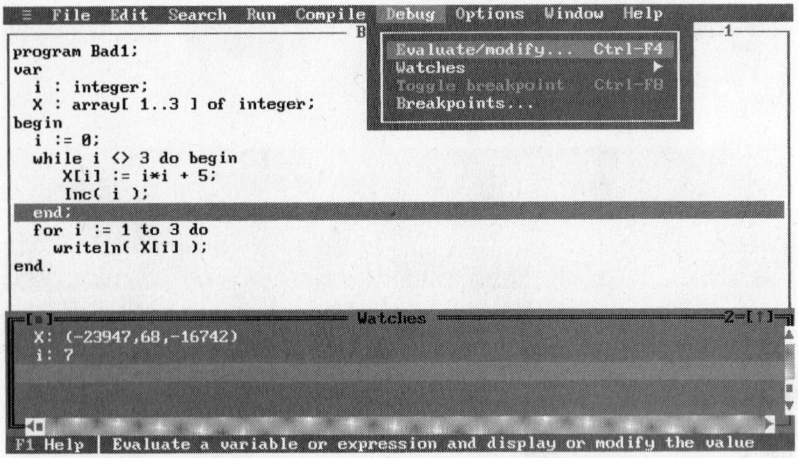

```
 ≡  File  Edit  Search  Run  Compile  Debug  Options  Window  Help
                                       Evaluate/modify...   Ctrl-F4
program Bad1;                          Watches                    ►
var                                    Toggle breakpoint    Ctrl-F8
  i : integer;                         Breakpoints...
  X : array[ 1..3 ] of integer;
begin
  i := 0;
  while i <> 3 do begin
     X[i] := i*i + 5;
     Inc( i );
  end;
  for i := 1 to 3 do
     writeln( X[i] );
end.
                                  Watches
  X: (-23947,68,-16742)
  i: 7
F1 Help | Evaluate a variable or expression and display or modify the value
```

Evaluate/Modify (Ctrl-F4)

During a debugging session, the Evaluate/modify command enables you to test the value of an expression or variable. In addition, it helps you change the value of any variable.

To see how the Evaluate/modify command helps debug your program, pick up the debugging session from where you left off (figure 8.6). Recall that by cycling through the `while` loop, you determined that the value of `i` was out of bounds and the `X` array was not receiving any assignments.

Now, in the debugging session, modify the value of `i` by choosing the Evaluate/modify option from the Debug menu. (The equivalent hot key is Ctrl-F4.) The compiler displays a dialog box containing three long horizontal boxes and four buttons. The boxes are labeled Expression, Result, and New value. Enter the character **i** in the Expression box, then press the Enter key. The current value of `i`, the number 7, appears immediately in the Result box. Now use the Tab key to move the cursor to the New value box. Enter the number **1**, then press the Enter key. The Result box changes to reflect the new value. Note that the value of `i` shown in the Watches window has been updated to 1, as shown in figure 8.8.

Fig. 8.8. *The Evaluate option from the Debug menu.*

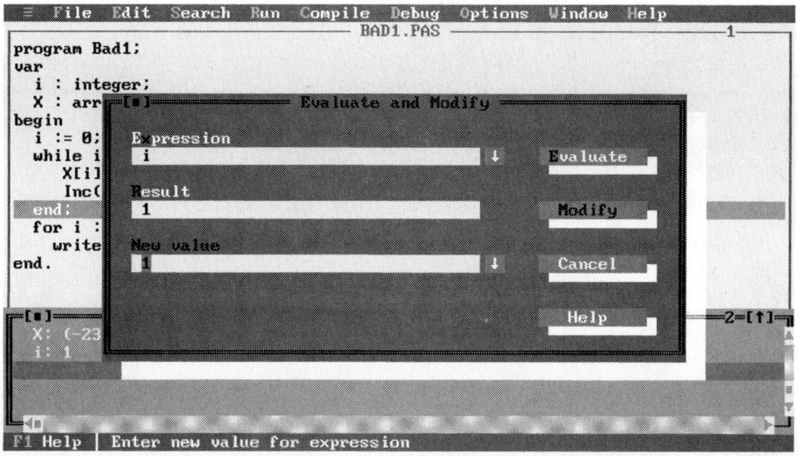

Now press the Esc key to return to the debugging session. The value of `i` in the Watch box changes to 1, indicating that your new value has been accepted.

Press F7 several times to cycle through the `while` loop. Notice that the debugger uses your new value of `i` just as if it had been assigned in the program. As you cycle through the `while` loop, you will also notice the values in the `X` array changing. After the second loop, when `i` is equal to 3, the highlighted line drops down to the `for` loop. The screen now appears as shown in figure 8.9.

Clearly, the condition in the `while` statement prevented the value of `X[3]` from being modified by the assignment statement.

Now it is time to correct the program. Move the cursor and change the line

```
i := 0;
```

to

```
i := 1;
```

and also change the line

```
while i <> 3 do begin
```

to

```
while i < 4 do begin
```

Press F7 to continue the debugging session. As figure 8.10 shows, a verification window appears, asking if you want these changes to be reflected in the compiled code. Respond with **Y** for yes. Turbo recompiles the program. The new version of the program can be saved by pressing F2.

***Fig. 8.9.** The values of the i and X variables immediately after completion of the while loop.*

```
 ≡  File  Edit  Search  Run  Compile  Debug  Options  Window  Help
                              BAD1.PAS                              1
program Bad1;
var
  i : integer;
  X : array[ 1..3 ] of integer;
begin
  i := 0;
  while i <> 3 do begin
     X[i] := i*i + 5;
     Inc( i );
  end;
  for i := 1 to 3 do
    writeln( X[i] );
end.
[■]                           Watches                              2=[↑]
  X: (6,9,-16742)
  i: 3
F1 Help  F7 Trace  F8 Step  ←┘ Edit  Ins Add  Del Delete  F10 Menu
```

***Fig. 8.10.** The Verify box.*

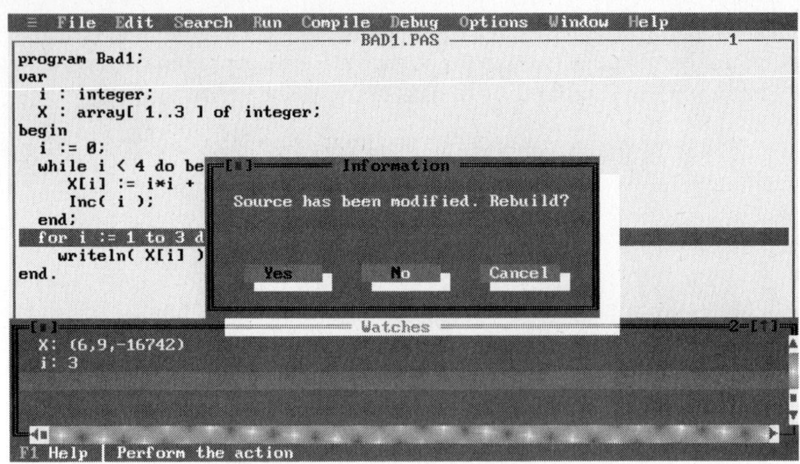

Using the Evaluate Box as a Calculator
Whenever you want, you can use the Evaluate box as a calculator—whether or not a debugging session is in progress. Just enter any arithmetic expression, press Enter, and the result appears in the Result box.

Call Stack (Ctrl-F3)

During a debugging session, you can use the `Call stack` command to display—in sequence—the list of currently executing procedure and function calls together with their parameters. By examining this list, you can quickly learn your program's flow of control.

To see how the `Call stack` command works, follow these steps:

1. Enter the Turbo Pascal editor, and load the HANOI1 program (listing 5.15 in Chapter 5).

2. Place the cursor on the `end` statement that ends the `transfer` procedure.

3. Execute the `Go to cursor` option of the Run menu. (This is equivalent to pressing the F4 function key.) Turbo compiles the program and runs it until it reaches the marked line. One of the program's first actions is to ask you for the desired number of disks; enter 4 at the prompt. At this point, the screen looks like figure 8.11.

6.0

4. Now invoke the `Call stack` option by selecting the Window/Call stack menu selection. (Ctrl-F3 is its equivalent hot key.) The Call stack window appears at the bottom portion of the screen, as shown in figure 8.12.

The *call stack* is a LIFO (last in, first out) list showing which procedures and functions are currently open. The HANOI1 program itself called the `transfer` procedure with the parameters (4,1,3,2). The `transfer` procedure then called itself recursively, using the parameters (3,1,2,3). The `transfer` procedure was called three more times, the final time with the parameters (0,1,3,2).

Use the cursor keys to select any one of the entries in the list, then press the Enter key. The cursor immediately moves to the line that invoked the procedure or function call.

Fig. 8.11. The HANOI1 program after the first completion of the transfer procedure.

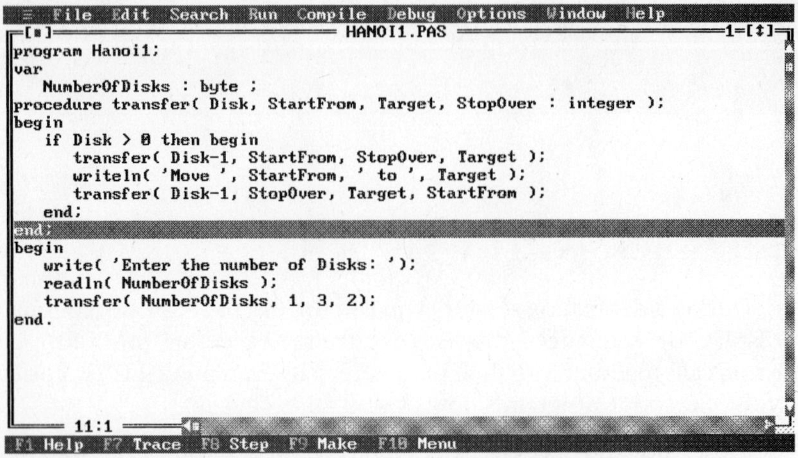

```
 ≡  File  Edit  Search  Run  Compile  Debug  Options  Window  Help
[■]                       HANOI1.PAS                          1=[↕]
program Hanoi1;
var
   NumberOfDisks : byte ;
procedure transfer( Disk, StartFrom, Target, StopOver : integer );
begin
   if Disk > 0 then begin
      transfer( Disk-1, StartFrom, StopOver, Target );
      writeln( 'Move ', StartFrom, ' to ', Target );
      transfer( Disk-1, StopOver, Target, StartFrom );
   end;
end;
begin
   write( 'Enter the number of Disks: ');
   readln( NumberOfDisks );
   transfer( NumberOfDisks, 1, 3, 2);
end.

      11:1
F1 Help  F7 Trace  F8 Step  F9 Make  F10 Menu
```

Fig. 8.12. The contents of the Call Stack window.

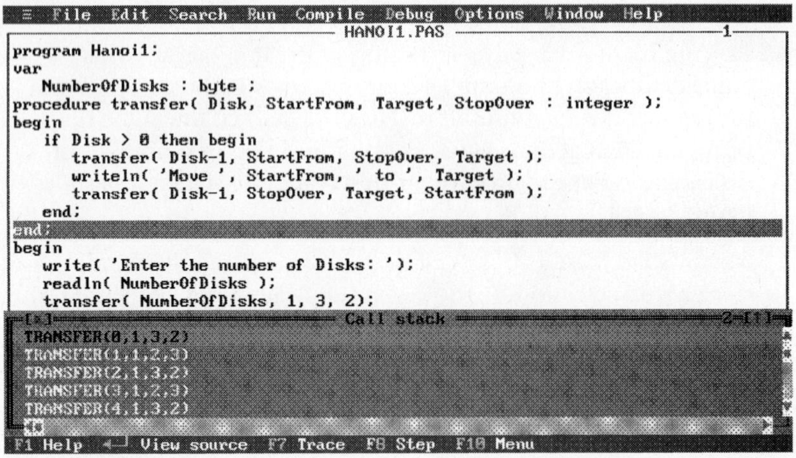

```
 ≡  File  Edit  Search  Run  Compile  Debug  Options  Window  Help
                          HANOI1.PAS                          1
program Hanoi1;
var
   NumberOfDisks : byte ;
procedure transfer( Disk, StartFrom, Target, StopOver : integer );
begin
   if Disk > 0 then begin
      transfer( Disk-1, StartFrom, StopOver, Target );
      writeln( 'Move ', StartFrom, ' to ', Target );
      transfer( Disk-1, StopOver, Target, StartFrom );
   end;
end;
begin
   write( 'Enter the number of Disks: ');
   readln( NumberOfDisks );
   transfer( NumberOfDisks, 1, 3, 2);
[■]                       Call stack                          2=[↕]
 TRANSFER(0,1,3,2)
 TRANSFER(1,1,2,3)
 TRANSFER(2,1,3,2)
 TRANSFER(3,1,2,3)
 TRANSFER(4,1,3,2)

F1 Help  ←┘ View source  F7 Trace  F8 Step  F10 Menu
```

Find Procedure

Although the `Find procedure` command is part of the Search menu option, it is intended for debugging. You invoke it using the Search/Find procedure menu option. The `Find procedure` command prompts you for the name of one of these routines, locates it, and moves the cursor to its first line.

Integrated Debugging (On)

The Options/Debugger menu selection provides you with a check box that enables you to turn the integrated debugging switch on or off. This switch controls whether Turbo Pascal maintains the tables and performs the extra routines required to support interactive debugging.

By default, Turbo's debugging features are ready for use. If you plan to compile a program to disk, interactive debugging is not needed; in these cases, you can save internal memory space by turning the option off.

Standalone Debugging (Off)

The Options/Debugger menu selection provides another check box; this one enables you to turn the standalone debugging switch on or off. This switch should be turned on when you want to use Borland's Turbo Debugger product on a program that you compile to disk.

When the option is turned on, the compiler stores all of its debugging tables in a separate section of the EXE file. Although the EXE file is larger because of it, program execution speed is not affected.

The standalone Turbo Debugger product is available as a separate software package. Although it is an excellent tool for developing large programming applications, you will probably find that Turbo Pascal's built-in debugger offers more than enough power and performance for most purposes.

Display Swapping (Smart)

The Options/Debugger menu selection provides you with a radio button that enables you to select the setting for display swapping. The value

6.0

for this setting affects the way Turbo handles screen displays during debugging sessions. There are three available options:

- `Smart`. Temporarily displays the output screen whenever your program performs an output operation. The swapping is fast, but noticeable; you can press the Alt-F5 key to examine your output more leisurely.
- `Always`. Temporarily displays the output screen after every program statement.
- `None`. Superimposes the output and editor screens. Use this setting only for programs that do not do any screen output. Otherwise, the display can become muddled. The `Refresh display` command can be used to restore the screen's appearance.

The default setting is `Smart`.

Refresh Display

The `Refresh display` command is in the (system)/Refresh display menu selection. This command provides a convenient way to restore the screen after your program—debugged when the `Display swapping` switch was set to `None`—overwrites the display.

Add Watch (Ctrl-F7)

The `Add watch` command is invoked from the Debug/Watches/Add watch menu (the equivalent hot key is Ctrl-F7), as shown in figure 8.13. With this command, you can add a variable or an expression to the top of the Watches window. Note that adding a new variable does not automatically display the Watches window if it is blocked by other windows. You must invoke the Window/Watch menu option for that purpose.

While the Watches window is visible, the watched variables remain until you invoke the `Remove all watches` command from the Debug/Watches menu. The value of each watched variable is displayed beside its name. You can resize the Watches window to view fewer or more variables. You can also move the Watch window, if needed.

Fig. 8.13. The Debug/Watches/Add watch menu.

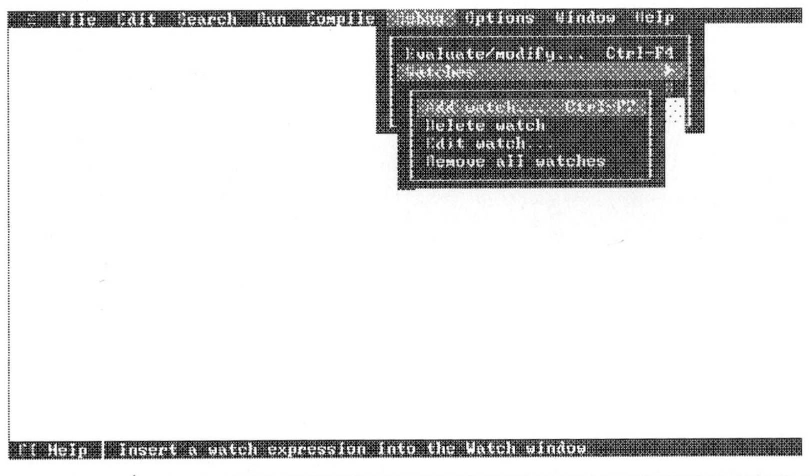

Delete Watch

The `Delete watch` command is invoked from the Debug/Watches/Delete watch menu selection. This option deletes the current watch item. The current item is highlighted by having a green display background and a small bullet to its left. To change the current item, make the Watches window active, then use the up and down arrow keys to choose other items in the window. While the Watches window is active you can delete the current item by using the Del key.

Edit Watch

`The Edit watch` command is invoked from the Debug/Watches/Edit watch menu selection. This command copies the current watch expression to a special Edit Watch dialog box. You can use the standard Turbo Pascal editing keys to modify the expression in the dialog box. Press Enter to install the changes, or press Esc to cancel the changes.

When the Watches window is active, you can select the current item for editing more easily by simply pressing the Enter key.

Remove All Watches

The `Remove all watches` command is invoked from the Debug/Watches/Remove all watches menu selection. With this command, you can empty the contents of the Watches window in one swoop. However, the `Remove all watches` command does not close the Watches window.

Toggle Breakpoint (Ctrl-F8)

The `Toggle breakpoint` command is invoked from the Debug/Toggle breakpoint menu selection. This command selects the line containing the cursor as a breakpoint (the cursor must be at an executable statement for the breakpoint to be valid during program debugging). Every selected line is highlighted. If the line is already a breakpoint, the `Toggle breakpoint` command cancels the selection.

Breakpoint

The `Breakpoint` command is invoked from the Debug/Breakpoint menu selection. This command displays a dialog box containing a breakpoint-list scrollable window and a number of control buttons, as shown in figure 8.14. The window contains a list (by file name) of each breakpoint, its line number, and its condition. The control buttons enable you to edit, delete, view, and clear all breakpoints.

Run (Ctrl-F9)

The `Run` command is invoked from the Run/Run menu selection. (The equivalent hot key is Ctrl-F9.) The `Run` command initiates program execution. If necessary, Turbo automatically compiles the program before the execution occurs. If you have changed the program since its last compilation, Turbo asks if it should recompile the code before it proceeds.

If you are in the middle of a debugging session, you can use the `Run` command to resume program execution from the point at which it was last interrupted.

Fig. 8.14. The Breakpoint list.

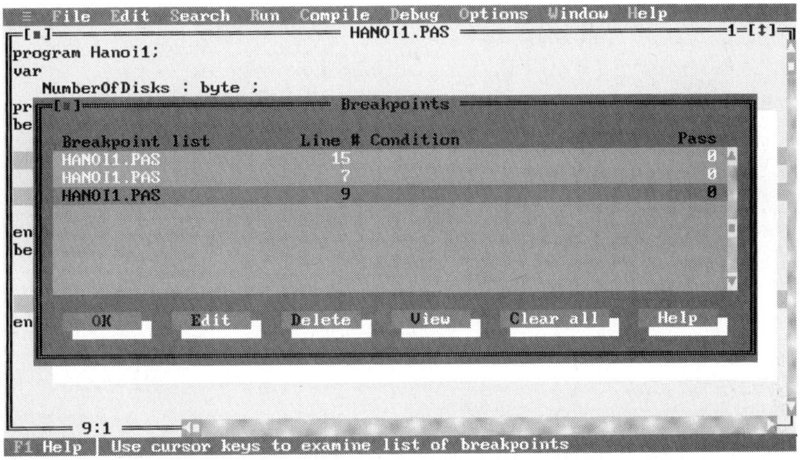

```
 ≡  File  Edit  Search  Run  Compile  Debug  Options  Window  Help
=[■]=========================== HANOI1.PAS ==========================1=[↕]=
program Hanoi1;
var
   NumberOfDisks : byte ;
pr =[■]================= Breakpoints ====================
be
    Breakpoint list          Line # Condition                     Pass
    HANOI1.PAS                  15                                   0
    HANOI1.PAS                   7                                   0
    HANOI1.PAS                   9                                   0
en
be
en     OK        Edit      Delete      View      Clear all      Help
======== 9:1 ========
 F1 Help | Use cursor keys to examine list of breakpoints
```

Program Reset (Ctrl-F2)

The `Program reset` command is invoked from the Run/Program reset menu selection. It tells the compiler to end the current debugging run. Any dynamic memory allocated by the program is released. Any open files are closed. Typed constants are reset, but any variables are left untouched. The next line to be executed will be the first executable line of the program.

Breakpoint and watch expressions are unaffected by this command. If you want to completely end the debugging and run the program normally, you will need to remove all watches and breakpoints.

Go to Cursor (F4)

The `Go to cursor` command is invoked from the Run/Go to cursor menu selection. (The equivalent hot key is F4.) The `Go to cursor` command executes all program statements until it reaches the line containing the cursor. With this command, you can bypass large blocks of program code without first establishing a breakpoint.

If you are already in the middle of a debugging session, the `Go to cursor` command starts its run with the line immediately following the last line executed. If the program has not yet run or you have just issued a `Program reset` command, the program starts running its first executable line. If necessary, Turbo will first compile the program.

Trace Into (F7)

The `Trace into` command is invoked from the Run/Trace into menu selection. (The equivalent hot key is F7.) The `Trace into` command executes the next program statement. By repeatedly using the `Trace into` command, you can run your program one line at a time. If the next line is a procedure or function call, the procedure or function itself is also executed a line at a time. If the next executable line happens to reside in another unit or in an include file, the debugger automatically loads that file before proceeding.

Step Over (F8)

The `Step over` command is invoked from the Run/Step over menu selection. (The equivalent hot key is F8.) The `Step over` command is similar to the `Trace into` command, except that if the next line is a procedure or function call, the procedure or function is executed in a *single* step. The debugger then moves the highlighted line to the first statement following the subroutine call.

User Screen (Alt-F5)

The `User screen` command is invoked from the Window/User screen menu selection. (The equivalent hot key is Alt-F5.) This command enables you to view the output screen.

Summary

In this chapter, you learned how to use Turbo Pascal's built-in debugger to identify and correct logic errors in your programs. Through a simple case study, you saw that the process of debugging consists primarily of observing and controlling the contents of selected variables during the execution of small sections of a program or the program as a whole.

This process of observing is called tracing. The specific variables to be traced are called watch variables.

The Turbo Pascal integrated environment has the following options, scattered in various menus:

- `Add watch` adds a variable or an expression to the Watch window.
- `Breakpoint` lists, edits, deletes, views, and clears breakpoints.
- `Call stack` displays a list of the currently executing procedure and function calls together with their parameters.
- `Delete watch` deletes the current watch item.
- `Display swapping` selects screen display options.
- `Edit watch` allows you to edit the current watch expression.
- `Evaluate/modify` tests and modifies the value of a variable or expression.
- `Find procedure` moves the cursor to the first line of any specified procedure or function.
- `Go to cursor` executes all statements before the line containing the cursor.
- `Integrated debugging` controls whether or not to support interactive debugging.
- `Program reset` ends the current debugging run.
- `Refresh display` restores the screen.
- `Remove all watches` clears all items from the Watch window.
- `Run` initiates program execution.
- `Standalone debugging` prepares a program for later processing by Borland's Turbo Debugger product.
- `Step over` is similar to `Trace into` but executes procedures and functions in a single step.
- `Toggle breakpoint` either creates or cancels a breakpoint.
- `Trace into` executes the next statement.
- `User screen` displays the output screen.

Part II

Programming

CHAPTER 9

Keyboard Input

Buried somewhere in the documentation of almost every software product—from word processors to Turbo Pascal—is the inevitable phrase that assures the reader that the keyboard acts "just like a typewriter."

And—for the most part—it is true. The keyboard and screen are electronically connected; when you press a key on the keyboard, you know from experience that the character appears immediately on the screen. You can position the cursor, remove mistakes with the Backspace or Del key, and enter uppercase letters when the Shift key is pressed. To borrow the slogan of desktop publishing packages: "What you see is what you get."

But what appears at first to be a single event is actually the combination of three distinct activities: keyboard entry, screen display, and editing. Most of the time they occur together so quickly that you do not notice (or appreciate) the complexity of each component. Turbo Pascal, however, *does* make the distinction, and in the process offers the programmer the means to develop powerful data entry tools.

This chapter introduces the techniques your programs can use to acquire information from the keyboard. It does this by discussing how the keyboard operates, how (and where) the information is stored, and how you can use the tools provided by Turbo Pascal to access and manipulate keyboard data. By understanding the flow of data, you will be better able to exploit the full power of Turbo Pascal.

Command-Line Parameters

A Turbo Pascal program can get data from the keyboard at two distinct times: in the program itself (that is, while the program is running, as with the `read` and `readln` routines) and as part of the command line. Perhaps not surprisingly, two distinct methods are involved.

Programs frequently allow or expect command-line parameters, for example:

```
COPY infile,outfile
DUMP details.obj
PAYABLES july
```

Within a program, you can work interactively with the user. Prompting messages can appear (`File name:`), input editing code can be used (`That number was out of range. Please retype.`), and validations can be obtained (`Are you sure?`). In short, you develop a dialog. When you enter information as part of the command line, this flexibility does not usually exist. The prime objective is simply to capture the data.

Turbo Pascal provides two functions for just that purpose. `ParamCount` returns the number of parameters on the command line. `ParamStr` is an array of strings, each element of which contains a single parameter. For example, `ParamStr(3)` returns the third parameter from the command line. (Beginning with DOS 3.0, `ParamStr (0)` returns the path and file name of the executing program.)

These functions can be demonstrated with the CLINE program (listing 9.1), which simply returns each command-line parameter on a separate line.

Listing 9.1

```
program CLINE;
var
   i : byte;
begin
   if ParamCount < 1 then
      writeln( 'Please try again with some command-line parameters.' )
   else
      for i := 1 to ParamCount do
         writeln( 'Parameter', i:2, ': ', ParamStr( i ) );
end.
```

To run CLINE from the DOS prompt, you would enter the following:

```
C>CLINE infile.pas outfile.lst
Parameter 1: infile.pas
Parameter 2: outfile.lst
```

```
C>CLINE opt1 opt2 opt3
Parameter 1: opt1
Parameter 2: opt2
Parameter 3: opt3
```

Parameters are assumed to be separated by spaces or tabs. Commas, slashes, and semicolons are all treated as ordinary characters—*not* as separators. This can create some problems, especially if you (or your users) expect to employ traditional separators, as demonstrated by the following examples. Try the following entries:

```
C>CLINE opt1,opt2,opt3
Parameter 1: opt1,opt2,opt3
```

```
C>CLINE file1/opt3; suboption2
Parameter 1: file1/opt3; suboption2
```

```
C>CLINE city='Los Angeles'
Parameter 1: city='Los
Parameter 2: Angeles'
```

It may be easier to access the entire command line as a single string and process it on a character-by-character basis. As you will see in Chapter 12, "Accessing DOS," the contents of the command line can be found at a memory location stored 128 bytes into the program segment prefix. The CLINE2 program in listing 9.2 demonstrates how the command line can be accessed.

Listing 9.2

```
program CLINE2;
type
   CmdLineArray = string[ 127 ];
var
   CmdLine : ^CmdLineArray;
begin
   CmdLine := Ptr( PrefixSeg, $80 );
   if Length( CmdLine^ ) < 1 then
      writeln( 'Please try again with some command-line parameters.' )
   else
      write( Length( CmdLine^ ), ' characters: ', CmdLine^ );
end.
```

The command-line string—no matter how complicated—is captured and returned in its entirety.

```
C>CLINE2 opt1,opt2,opt3/sub4; a,b..c
28 characters: opt1,opt2,opt3/sub4; a,b..c
```

The program segment prefix is described in greater detail in Chapter 12.

Keyboard Operation

The keyboard is more than a collection of simple switches and wires. It contains (and is controlled by) its own microprocessor, an Intel 8048 (or an Intel 8042 for the AT), which is also called the ***keyboard controller***.

Each of the 83 keys on the keyboard is numbered—arbitrarily—from 1 through 83. This number, called a *scan code*, was assigned by the PC's designers based on the key's physical location; it has no relationship to either the meaning of the key or the ASCII value of the character being typed. (A table of scan codes can be found in the Turbo Pascal handbook.) Each time you press one of the keys, you send its scan code to the 8048. When you release the key, another scan code gets sent to the 8048, but this time with a value 128 higher than the first. In other words, the eighth bit of the scan code is 0 when the key is pressed and 1 when it is released. The AT is slightly different; it sends the same scan code each time, but precedes the release signal with the $F0 byte.

Chapter 3, "Data and Data Types," discussed how each ASCII character can be defined by a single eight-bit byte. The standard ASCII character set consists of 128 values (the eighth bit is 0) and includes upper- and lowercase letters, numbers, and punctuation. IBM introduced an extended version of ASCII that defines an additional 128 values (the eighth bit is set) and includes line drawing symbols, foreign character sets, and technical symbols. Yet nowhere is a key such as Function Key 1 or Alt-A defined. Such keys are called *specials* and further increase the number of usable characters.

Obviously, there are fewer keys on the keyboard than potential symbols; by separately recognizing the press and release (or make and break) scan codes, special key combinations (such as shift-, alternate-, and control-key prefixes) can be captured. For example, the four actions:

1. Pressing the Shift key
2. Pressing the Q key
3. Releasing the Q key
4. Releasing the Shift key

must together be identifiable as the single character known as an uppercase *Q*.

The keyboard controller makes no attempt to evaluate the meaning of any scan code signals. Instead, it simply alerts the 8086 to the availability of keyboard input. The CPU converts the scan code sequences into useful data. Every recognized character is stored in one word of data. The high byte is called the *ASCII byte*, and the low byte is called the *extended byte*.

If the character is one of the 256 standard ASCII characters, its ASCII code is stored in the high byte of the word and the extended byte is undefined (but generally it is the scan code of the chosen key). For the uppercase *Q* example, the ASCII byte will contain 81 (the ASCII code for *Q*).

If the character is a special key, the ASCII byte contains a 0, and the extended byte contains an extended key code. Pressing the PgUp key, for example, results in a 0 in the ASCII byte and 73 in the extended byte.

To summarize, *every single* character entered on the keyboard produces *two* bytes. Either the first byte is the ASCII value of the character and the second byte can be ignored, or the first byte is 0 and the second byte has a special (non-ASCII) meaning called an extended code.

Reading Data from the Keyboard

In most of your programs, you will want to input ASCII characters with either `read` or `readln`, just as all the examples have done up to now. Remember that neither procedure is directly connected to the keyboard; both get their data indirectly, by accessing the buffer.

Information from the keyboard is input one line at a time and stored—in its entirety—in the internal buffer. When variables are read, this buffer is used as the input source.

The *Read* and *Readln* Procedures

Both the `read` and the `readln` procedures read data items into variables. The difference between them is that wherever a `read` procedure is positioned when it ends, the next `read` or `readln` procedure begins; but when a `readln` procedure ends, the remainder of the line (including the carriage return and line feed) is ignored.

This difference is best illustrated with an example. The READER1 and READER2 programs (listings 9.3 and 9.4) are identical except that the `YorN` variable is input with a `read` procedure in READER1 and a `readln` procedure in READER2.

Listing 9.3

```
program Reader1;
var
   YorN : char;
   Name : string;
begin
   write( 'Should we continue? (Y)es or (N)o: ' );
   read( YorN );
   writeln( 'Your answer was ', UpCase( YorN ) );
   write( 'What is your name? ' );
   readln( Name );
   writeln( 'Hello, ', Name );
end.
```

Listing 9.4

```
program Reader2;
var
   YorN : char;
   Name : string;
begin
   write( 'Should we continue? (Y)es or (N)o: ' );
   readln( YorN );
   writeln( 'Your answer was ', UpCase( YorN ) );
   write( 'What is your name? ' );
   readln( Name );
   writeln( 'Hello, ', Name );
end.
```

Both programs accept one char variable followed by one string variable. Run the READER1 program, but do not cooperate—instead of a single character, enter five: **abcde**, followed by a carriage return. The `read` procedure assigns the letter *a* to `YorN` but will not advance the position in the buffer. Consequently, the remaining characters, *bcde*, plus the carriage return, will be read without a pause by the `readln` procedure.

```
Should we continue? (Y)es or (N)o: abcde
Your answer was A
What is your name? Hello, bcde
```

In READER2, the `readln` procedure assigns the letter *a* to the variable `YorN`, then advances the buffer position. The remaining characters, *bcde*, plus the carriage return, will be completely ignored.

```
Should we continue? (Y)es or (N)o: abcde
Your answer was A
What is your name? Fred
Hello, Fred
```

The `read` procedure is used primarily for file input. You should always use the `readln` procedure for keyboard entry and, further, you should try to use a single `readln` procedure for each variable.

Line Input

By temporarily storing data in the buffer, `read` and `readln` help you to edit your work as you go along. The following editing commands are available:

Backspace	Deletes the last character entered
Escape	Deletes the entire input line
Enter	Terminates the input line and stores the end-of-line marker (the carriage return/line feed combination of #13#10) in the buffer

You have probably already used these keys, but if you have not, enter the LINEIN0 program (listing 9.5) and try them. Note that you must press Ctrl-C to end the program.

Listing 9.5

```
program LineIn0;
var
   Str : string;
begin
   writeln( 'Please enter some lines.' );
   repeat
```

continues

Listing 9.5 continued

```
      readln( Str );
      writeln( Str );
   until False;
end.
```

If you include the Crt unit in your program with the statement

```
uses Crt;
```

several additional editing features become available:

Ctrl-A	Same as Escape; deletes the entire input line
Ctrl-D	Recalls one character from the last input line
Ctrl-F	Recalls the remainder of the last input line
Ctrl-S	Same as Backspace; deletes the last character entered

The LINEIN1 program (listing 9.6) illustrates the inclusion of the Crt unit. Execute the program, and try the new editing commands. Except for the `uses` clause, no other change to the program has been made. If you run LINEIN1 from the IDE, press Ctrl-Break twice to exit; if you run the program from DOS, press Ctrl-Break once to exit. (In either case, Ctrl-C has no effect.)

Listing 9.6

```
program LineIn1;
uses Crt;
var
   Str : string;
begin
   writeln( 'Please enter some lines.' );
   repeat
      readln( Str );
      writeln( Str );
   until False;
end.
```

Ctrl-Z and the End of the File

When you include the Crt unit in your program, you transform the keyboard from a simple input device into the functional equivalent of a text file. As a consequence, you have the option of testing for an end-of-file (EOF) condition.

The predefined Boolean variable `CheckEof` is used by the Crt unit to determine whether end-of-file testing is allowed. Normally, `CheckEof` is `False` and the test is disallowed. If you set `CheckEof` to `True`, however, entering Ctrl-Z during the execution of a `read` or `readln` statement sets `Eof` (the end-of-file flag) to `True`. After this happens, no further input is allowed unless the procedure

```
Reset( input );
```

is executed, which resets `Eof` to `False`. In essence, the `Reset` procedure reopens the keyboard for input.

The LINEIN2 program in listing 9.7 demonstrates the end-of-file test. The program continues to ask for lines to display until you enter a Ctrl-Break or Ctrl-Z. Ctrl-Break ends the program. If you run LINEIN2 from the IDE, press Ctrl-Break twice; if you run the program from DOS, press Ctrl-Break once. Ctrl-Z is interpreted as an end of file; `Eof` is set to `True`, and the `No more data can be entered` message is displayed.

Listing 9.7

```
program LineIn2;
uses Crt;
var
   Str : string;
begin
   CheckEof := True;
   writeln( 'Please enter some lines.' );
   repeat
      readln( Str );
      writeln( Str );
   until Eof;
   writeln( 'No more data can be entered' );
end.
```

Note that entering Ctrl-Z during the execution of the `readln` procedure causes a null string to be assigned to the `Str` variable. If `readln` had a numeric variable as its parameter, the variable would have been assigned a 0.

Text files are discussed in greater detail in Chapter 13, "File Handling."

Reading a Single Character

The Turbo Pascal function `ReadKey` can be used to identify a single keystroke. If the entry is one of the ASCII characters, `ReadKey` returns its ASCII value. If the entry is a special character, `ReadKey` returns a null value (that is, an ASCII 0). In the latter case, `ReadKey` must be executed a second time to pick up the extended code of the entry.

The KEY1 program in listing 9.8 displays the values returned by `ReadKey`. To end the program, enter a lowercase *z*.

Listing 9.8

```
program Key1;
uses Crt;
var
   Selection : char;
begin
   repeat
      Selection := ReadKey;
      if Selection = chr( 0 ) then
         writeln( '    0 and ', ord( ReadKey ) )
      else
         writeln( Selection, '  ', ord( Selection ) );
   until Selection = 'z';
end.
```

When KEY1 is executing, entering *a*, *b*, *c*, *Q*, *R*, *S*, Function 1, Function 2, Home, and Alt-H results in the following:

```
a  97
b  98
c  99
Q  81
R  82
```

```
S  83
   0 and 59
   0 and 60
   0 and 71
   0 and 35
```

The numbers 97, 98, 99, 81, 82, and 83 correspond to the ASCII values of the letters that were entered. The numbers 59, 60, 71, and 35 correspond to the extended key codes for the special characters.

Reading without Echoing

Sometimes you want to prevent the display of keyboard input on the screen. The best example of this situation is when you ask for a password.

The PASS1 program (listing 9.9) reads each keystroke and, instead of displaying the character, displays an asterisk. PASS1 allows two attempts at guessing the password before ending.

Listing 9.9

```
program Pass1;
uses Crt;
const
   Secret = 'BLAISE';
type
   String8 = string[ 8 ];
function Password : String8;
var
   Count : byte;
   WorkString : String8;
   Entry : char;
begin
   Count := 0;
   WorkString := '';
   Entry := ' ';
   repeat
      if KeyPressed then begin
         Entry := UpCase( ReadKey );
         write( '*' );
         if ord(Entry) <> 13 then
```

continues

Listing 9.9 continued

```
            WorkString := WorkString + Entry;
         Inc( Count );
      end;
   until (Count = 8) or (ord(Entry) = 13);
   Password := WorkString;
end;
begin
   ClrScr;
   gotoXY( 1, 5 );
   write( 'Please enter your password: ' );
   if Password <> Secret then begin
      writeln;
      write( 'One more try: ' );
      if Password <> Secret then begin
         writeln;
         writeln( 'Sorry.  Please obtain authorization.' );
         Exit;
      end;
   end;
   writeln;
   writeln( 'Welcome to the program!' );
end.
```

One interesting consideration of this program is that the password variable `Secret` may have contained *any* eight characters. Most people think of a password as being alphanumeric; the PASS1 program allows it to contain, for example, function keys and backspaces. Some of the most secure passwords consist of unprintable characters. For example, to change the password to include a backspace after the `A`, change the definition of `Secret` to `'BLA' #8'ISE'` (#8 is the code for backspace). Similarly, you can define `Secret` as `'BLA' #0#68'ISE'` to use the F10 function key.

Esc, Ctrl-Break, and Ctrl-C

If you have been entering and running the examples in this book, you have probably had more than one occasion to use Ctrl-Break to end a contrary program. Further, if you have any experience with PCs, you have probably pressed the Escape key fairly often.

These keystrokes have advantageous results during program development, but they are often undesirable during the execution of a real-world application. Imagine the user of one of your programs who finishes an hour or more of boring but important data entry, then—for whatever reason—presses Ctrl-Break. The following worst-case events transpire immediately:

1. The program ends.
2. No files will have been closed, so all the data is lost.
3. The diskette requires repair with the CHKDSK utility.
4. You get a phone call.

Fortunately, Turbo Pascal provides a way to disable early termination. The Crt unit uses the Boolean variable `CheckBreak` to enable and disable the action of Ctrl-Break. When `CheckBreak` is `True`—the default state—pressing Ctrl-Break will cause the program to abort when it next writes to the display. But when `CheckBreak` is `False`, pressing Ctrl-Break has no effect.

The CHECKCB program (listing 9.10) disables the Ctrl-Break key, then displays English equivalents for several of the special keys. Compile it to disk and run it outside the integrated environment. To end the program, press Escape, Ctrl-Break, or Ctrl-C.

Listing 9.10

```
program CheckCB;
uses Crt;
const
   EndLoop : Boolean = False;
var
   ch, Answer : char;
procedure TerminateRoutines;
begin
   EndLoop := True;
   { Any other file closings, screen displays, etc. }
   { required for smooth program termination }
end;
begin
   CheckBreak := False;
   ClrScr;
   writeln( 'Enter special keys.' );
```

continues

Listing 9.10 continued

```
writeln( 'Terminate with Escape, Ctrl-C, or Ctrl-Break.' );
repeat
   if KeyPressed then begin
      ch := ReadKey;
      if (ord( ch ) = 3) or                  { Ctrl-C or Ctrl-Break? }
         (ord( ch ) = 27) then begin         { Escape key?           }
         repeat
            write( 'Are you sure you want to stop? (Y/N) ' );
            readln( Answer );
         until UpCase( Answer ) in [ 'Y', 'N' ];
         if UpCase( Answer ) = 'Y' then
            TerminateRoutines;
      end;
      if ch = chr(0) then begin
         ch := ReadKey;
         case ord(ch) of
                 71 : writeln( 'Home' );
                 72 : writeln( 'Up arrow' );
                 73 : writeln( 'PgUp' );
                 75 : writeln( 'Left arrow' );
                 77 : writeln( 'Right arrow' );
                 79 : writeln( 'End' );
                 80 : writeln( 'Down arrow' );
                 81 : writeln( 'PgDn' );
                 82 : writeln( 'Ins' );
                 83 : writeln( 'Del' );
                114 : writeln( 'Ctrl-PrtSc' );
                115 : writeln( 'Ctrl-Left Arrow' );
                116 : writeln( 'Ctrl-Right Arrow' );
                117 : writeln( 'Ctrl-End' );
                118 : writeln( 'Ctrl-PgDn' );
                119 : writeln( 'Ctrl-Home' );
           120..128 : writeln( 'Alt-', ord(ch)-119 );
                                 { Alt + digits 1..9 }
                129 : writeln( 'Alt-0' );
                130 : writeln( 'Alt-Minus' );
                131 : writeln( 'Alt-Equal' );
                132 : writeln( 'Ctrl-PgUp' );
             59..68 : writeln( 'F', ord(ch)-58 );
                                 { Function keys 1..10 }
             84..93 : writeln( 'Shift-F', ord(ch)- 83 );
                                 { Shift + Function keys 1..10 }
```

```
              94..103 : writeln( 'Ctrl-F', ord(ch)- 93 );
                                   { Ctrl + Function keys 1..10 }
             104..113 : writeln( 'Alt-F', ord(ch)-103 );
                                   { Alt + Function keys 1..10 }
          end;
       end;
    end;
  until EndLoop;
end.
```

Disabling Ctrl-Break works only for a program compiled to disk. Ctrl-Break always ends a program run in the integrated environment because the integrated environment—not your program—senses the key.

Changing the State of Ctrl-Break Checking

If, when `CheckBreak` is `True`, you want Ctrl-Break to end the program immediately rather than wait for the next screen output, use the `SetCBreak` procedure to change the current state of Ctrl-Break checking. The syntax is as follows:

```
SetCBreak( BreakTest : Boolean );
Executing the statement
SetCBreak( True );
```

This causes DOS to test for Ctrl-Break during *every* system call, not just during I/O routines. You can return to the default setting by executing

```
SetCBreak( False );
```

The `GetCBreak` procedure returns a variable that tells you the current state of Ctrl-Break checking:

```
GetCBreak( var BreakTest : Boolean );
```

The Keyboard Buffer

The ASCII and extended byte pairs generated by each keystroke are placed in a 16-word (32-byte) circular buffer in the main memory of the PC. Any program requesting keyboard input reads data from this buffer one word (two bytes) at a time.

A circular buffer is like a queue. Characters are stored in a first-come, first-served basis. The only difference is that there is no clearly defined beginning or end in a circular buffer. Characters from the keyboard simply fill up the spaces in sequence. The start of the queue is called the ***head*** of the buffer. The *tail* of the buffer points to the next open slot. When a character fills the highest memory location in the buffer, the tail wraps around and is reset to the lowest memory location, where it awaits the next character to be entered.

When the head and tail both point to the same location, the buffer is empty. After 15 characters have been entered, the tail cannot advance further, because no open slots remain. Hence, the buffer can hold only 15 characters; trying to enter another one generates the familiar beep sound that indicates the buffer is full.

Figure 9.1 shows how the command

```
DIR *.*
```

(which is executed when you press the Enter key) can be inserted in a circular buffer. Note that the starting point is arbitrary.

Data entered in the keyboard buffer is not really erased; new keystrokes simply overwrite the old. The actual starting location of the buffer can be found in the main memory of the PC at $0040:$001E. The head is located at $0040:$001A, and the tail is located at $0040:$001C. The bytes in the head and tail positions contain values from $1E through $3C, indicating the offsets of the locations they reference.

The memory locations for the head and tail are not part of the buffer itself. The head and tail could have been placed anywhere in memory, but for convenience, DOS puts them just before the start of the buffer. After the entry of the `DIR *.*` command, the buffer and pointers might look like the diagram in figure 9.2. Again, the head location is arbitrary.

The best way to understand how the buffer works is to see it in action. The SHOWBUFF program in listing 9.11 continuously displays the contents of the buffer on the screen, together with the head and tail locations. The program ends after 500 displays or after you press Ctrl-C.

*Fig. 9.1. Processing the DIR *.* command in the keyboard buffer.*

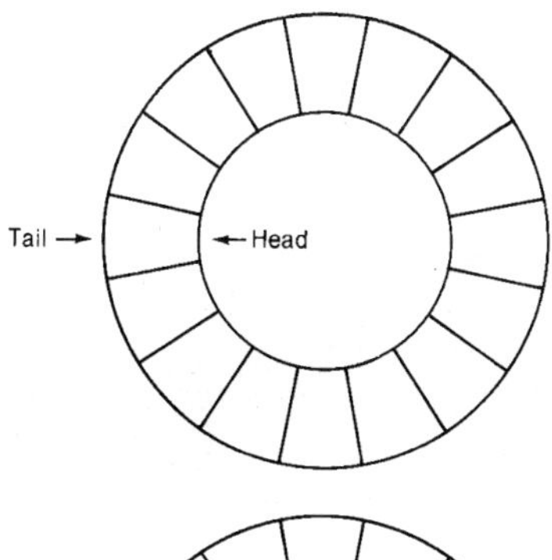

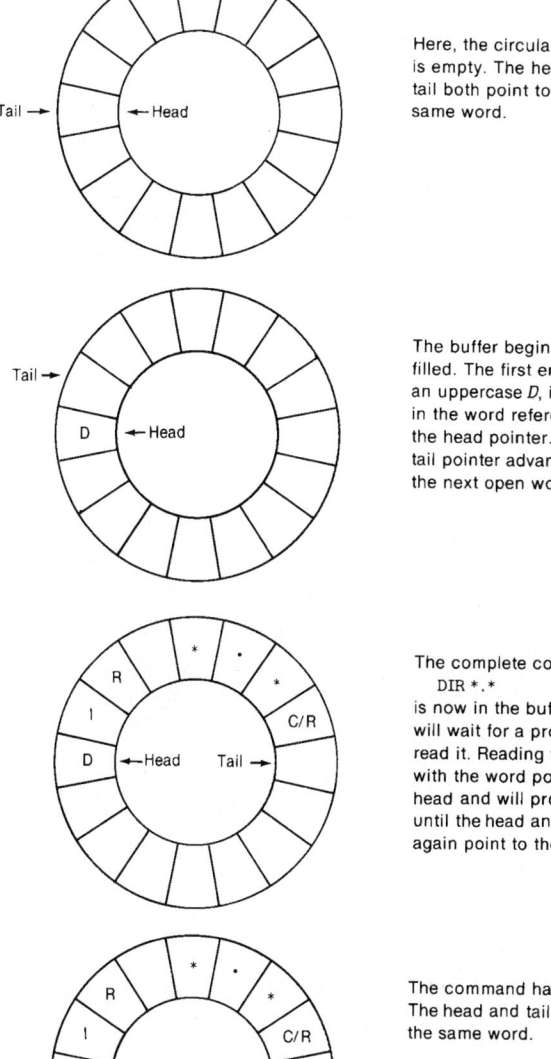

Here, the circular buffer is empty. The head and tail both point to the same word.

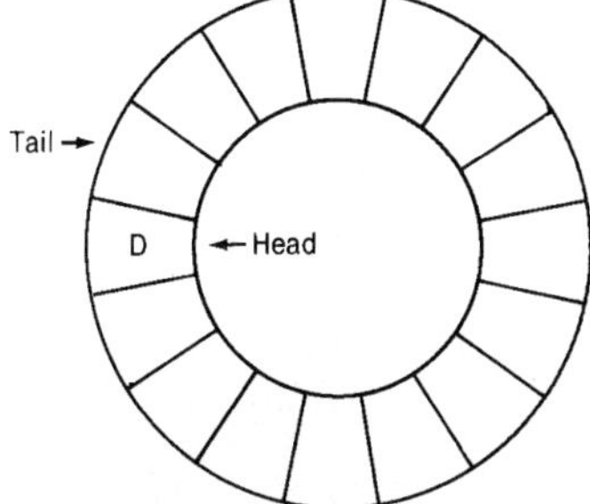

The buffer begins to be filled. The first entry, an uppercase *D*, is placed in the word referenced by the head pointer. The tail pointer advances to the next open word.

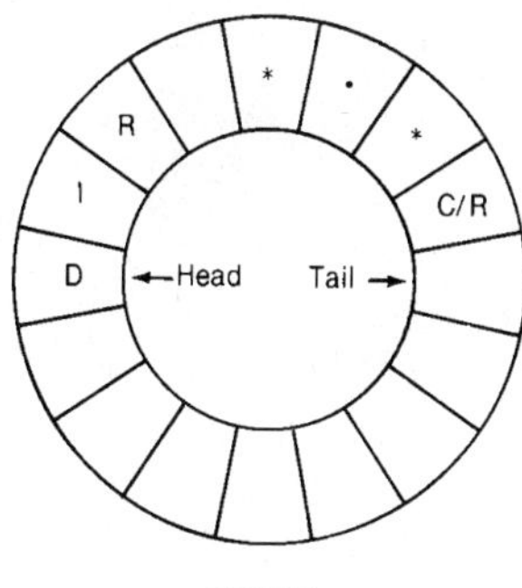

The complete command:

```
DIR *.*
```

is now in the buffer and will wait for a program to read it. Reading will begin with the word pointed to by head and will proceed until the head and tail once again point to the same word.

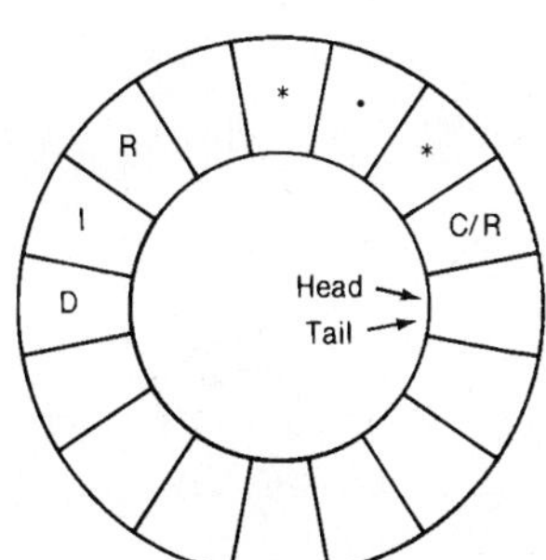

The command has been read. The head and tail again point to the same word.

The buffer is now awaiting a new entry, which will begin where the head now points. The original command remains in the buffer and will be overwritten with the next set of keystrokes.

*Fig. 9.2. An example of how the DIR *.* command might be entered in the keyboard buffer.*

	Address	ASCII Code		Extended Code	Address
	0040:003C				0040:003D
	0040:003A				0040:003B
	0040:0038				0040:0039
Tail →	0040:0036				0040:0037
	0040:0034	13	C/R	28	0040:0035
	0040:0032	42	*	9	0040:0033
	0040:0030	46	.	52	0040:0031
	0040:002E	42	*	9	0040:002F
	0040:002C	32		57	0040:002D
	0040:002A	82	R	19	0040:002B
	0040:0028	73	I	23	0040:0029
Head →	0040:0026	68	D	32	0040:0027
	0040:0024				0040:0024
	0040:0022				0040:0023
	0040:0020				0040:0021
	0040:001E				0040:001F

	Address			Address
(Tail)	0040:001C	$36		0040:001D
(Head)	0040:001A	$26		0040:001B

Listing 9.11

```
program ShowBuff;
uses Crt;
var
   i, Pass, Row : byte;
   BlankRow,
   HeadRow,
   TailRow      : byte;
   KeyBuffer    : array[ 1..32 ] of byte absolute $0040:$001E;
```

```
    HeadPointer   : byte                    absolute $0040:$001A;
    TailPointer   : byte                    absolute $0040:$001C;
begin
    Pass := 0;          { Track how many times the buffer is displayed }
    BlankRow := 10;
    ClrScr;
    GotoXY( 31, 1 ); write( 'The Keyboard Buffer' );
    GotoXY( 33, 3 ); write( 'ASCII  Extended' );
    repeat
       Pass := Pass + 1;
       Row := 5;
       for i := 16 downto 1 do begin
          GotoXY( 32, Row );
          write( KeyBuffer[i*2-1]:4, chr( KeyBuffer[i*2-1] ):3 );
          GotoXY( 41, Row );
          writeln( KeyBuffer[i*2]:4 );
          Row := Row + 1;
       end;
       TailRow := 35 - ( TailPointer div 2 );
       HeadRow := 35 - ( HeadPointer div 2 );
       GotoXY( 20, TailRow );
       write( '(', TailPointer:2, ') Tail->' );
       if BlankRow <> TailRow then begin
          GotoXY( 20, BlankRow );
          write( '           ' );   { 11 spaces }
          BlankRow := TailRow;
       end;
       GotoXY( 47, HeadRow );
       write( '<-Head (', HeadPointer:2, ')' );
    until Pass > 500;   { Stop after 500 passes }
end.
```

For example, the program might begin as shown in figure 9.3. The head and tail point to the same word, so the buffer is empty. The characters currently in the buffer will be overwritten. The first character in the command (the `D`) is entered where the tail was pointing. After entry, the tail advances to the next slot to be filled, as shown in figure 9.4.

The next character (the `I`) is placed where the tail had been pointing. This position is the highest location in the buffer, so the tail must now wrap around and point to the lowest location, as shown in figure 9.5.

Fig. 9.3. An empty keyboard buffer.

	ASCII Code		Extended Code	
	32		32	
(58) Tail →	32		32	← Head (58)
	32		32	
	32		32	
	32		32	
	32		32	
	32		32	
	32		32	
	32		32	
	32		32	
	32		32	
	32		32	
	32		32	
	32		32	
	32		32	
	32		32	

Fig. 9.4. The keyboard buffer after an uppercase D *is entered.*

	ASCII Code		Extended Code	
(60) Tail →	32		32	
	68	D	32	← Head (58)
	32		32	
	32		32	
	32		32	
	32		32	
	32		32	
	32		32	
	32		32	
	32		32	
	32		32	
	32		32	
	32		32	
	32		32	
	32		32	
	32		32	

Fig. 9.5. The keyboard buffer after an uppercase I *is entered.*

	ASCII Code		Extended Code	
	73	I	23	
	68	D	32	← Head (58)
	32		32	
	32		32	
	32		32	
	32		32	
	32		32	
	32		32	
	32		32	
	32		32	
	32		32	
	32		32	
	32		32	
	32		32	
	32		32	
(30) Tail →	32		32	

The third character (the R) is entered in the normal manner. The buffer now appears as shown in figure 9.6.

Fig. 9.6. The keyboard buffer after an uppercase R *is entered.*

	ASCII Code		Extended Code	
	73	I	23	
	68	D	32	← Head (58)
	32		32	
	32		32	
	32		32	
	32		32	
	32		32	
	32		32	
	32		32	
	32		32	
	32		32	
	32		32	
	32		32	
	32		32	
(32) Tail →	32		32	
	32	R	32	

After the rest of the characters are entered, including the Enter key (an ASCII 13), the buffer appears as shown in figure 9.7.

*Fig. 9.7. The keyboard buffer after the DIR *.* command has been entered.*

	ASCII Code		Extended Code	
	73	I	23	
	68	D	32	← Head (58)
	32		32	
	32		32	
	32		32	
	32		32	
	32		32	
	32		32	
(42) Tail →	32		32	
	13		28	
	42	*	9	
	46	.	52	
	42	*	9	
	32		57	
	82	R	19	

After the `DIR *.*` command is processed, the buffer appears as shown in figure 9.8.

The head advanced as characters were read from the buffer. Because the head and tail now point to the same byte, the buffer is "empty." The current contents of the buffer will be overwritten when more keys are pressed.

Note that when you run the SHOWBUFF program, you will probably find that the buffer contains characters. Even so, because the head and tail begin by pointing to the same byte, DOS treats the buffer as being empty.

Remapping Scan Codes

All of this may seem unnecessarily complicated at first. For example, why even bother using scan codes when the ASCII characters are available?

The answer is that scan codes give you the flexibility to redefine the keyboard. Different countries, for example, have different standard keyboard layouts. (These are described in greater detail in your operating system manual.) Similarly, the `ECHO` command in DOS can be used to redefine keys to any desired string. Your CONFIG.SYS file must include the statement `DEVICE=ANSI.SYS` for key reconfiguration to work on your machine.

*Fig. 9.8. The keyboard buffer after the DIR *.* command has been processed.*

	ASCII Code		Extended Code	
	73	I	23	
	68	D	32	
	32		32	
	32		32	
	32		32	
	32		32	
	32		32	
	32		32	
	32		32	
(42) Tail →	32		32	← Head (42)
	13		28	
	42	*	9	
	46	.	52	
	42	*	9	
	32		57	
	82	R	19	

The REDEF1 program in listing 9.12, for example, redefines all lowercase letters to their uppercase equivalents. Run the program, then exit Turbo and type a command at the DOS prompt. No matter what you do (short of another redefinition) you will not be able to make lowercase letters appear.

Listing 9.12

```
program Redef1;
var
   letter : char;
begin
   for letter := 'a' to 'z' do    { Redefine lowercase to uppercase }
      writeln( 'echo ', chr(27), '[', ord(letter), ';', ord(letter)-32, 'p' );
end.
```

To solve this slight annoyance, you can either reboot your machine or run the REDEF2 program (listing 9.13) to map lowercase scan codes to their default lowercase letters.

Listing 9.13

```
program Redef2;
var
   letter : char;
begin
   for letter := 'a' to 'z' do   { Redefine lowercase back to lowercase }
      writeln( 'echo ', chr(27), '[', ord(letter), ';', ord(letter), 'p' );
end.
```

On a more practical level, the REDEF3 program (listing 9.14) redefines the F10 function key to the instruction pair:

```
CD\TP
TURBO
```

Run the REDEF3 program, then exit the compiler. You can now begin Turbo Pascal from any directory simply by pressing F10.

Listing 9.14

```
program Redef3;
begin
   writeln( 'echo ', chr(27),'[0;68;"CD\TP";13;"TURBO";13p' );
end.
```

Entering Data into the Buffer

You can insert characters into the buffer and have your program chain to another program upon completion. The ADDBUFF program (listing 9.15) introduces the `NextCommand` procedure, which places any desired string in the buffer, just as if the characters were entered through the keyboard. When ADDBUFF finishes its run, the `DIR *.*` command is executed.

Listing 9.15

```
program AddBuff;
procedure NextCommand( Command : string );
type
   KeyArray = array[ $1E..$3D ] of byte;
```

```
var
   i : byte;
   CmdSize : byte;
   HeadPointer : byte absolute $0040:$001A;
   TailPointer : byte absolute $0040:$001C;
   KeyBuffer : ^KeyArray;
begin
   KeyBuffer := Ptr( $0040, $001E );
   TailPointer := $1E;
   HeadPointer := TailPointer;
   CmdSize := Length( Command );
   for i := 1 to CmdSize do begin
      KeyBuffer^[ TailPointer ] := ord( Command[ i ] );
      write( command[ i ] );
      TailPointer := TailPointer + 2;
   end;
   KeyBuffer^[ TailPointer ] := 13;
   KeyBuffer^[ TailPointer + 1 ] := 28;
   TailPointer := TailPointer + 2;
end;
begin
   NextCommand( 'DIR *.*' );
end.
```

Testing the Buffer

The Turbo Pascal `KeyPressed` function returns `True` if an entry is available to be read from the keyboard. `KeyPressed` is handy when you want to provide for input, but you do not want to stop processing if no input is available. In a game program, for example, animation should continue, although the keyboard should be periodically tested for new commands.

In the KEY1A program (listing 9.16), all letters of the alphabet are displayed continuously at the same cursor position. To move the cursor (and create a chain of random letters), you can use the Up Arrow, Down Arrow, Right Arrow, and Left Arrow keys. The program ends when you press the End key.

Listing 9.16

```
program Key1A;
uses Crt;
const
   Row       : byte = 12;
   Column    : byte = 40;
   GameOver  : Boolean = False;
   OutSpot   : word = 0;
begin
   ClrScr;
   repeat
      if KeyPressed then
         if ReadKey = chr(0) then    { Special character }
            case ord(ReadKey) of
               72 : Row      := Row - 1;       { Up Arrow }
               75 : Column   := Column - 1;    { Left Arrow }
               77 : Column   := Column + 1;    { Right Arrow }
               80 : Row      := Row + 1;       { Down Arrow }
               79 : GameOver := True;          { End key }
            end;
      if not (Row in [ 1..25 ]) then Row := 1;
      if not (Column in [ 1..80 ]) then Column := 1;
      gotoXY( Column, Row );
      OutSpot := (OutSpot mod 26) + 1;
      write( chr(OutSpot + 64) );
   until GameOver;
end.
```

Note that the Pascal code

```
if KeyPressed then ...
```

is equivalent to

```
if Mem[$0040:$001A] <> Mem[$0040:$001C] then ...
```

Frequently, the opposite situation arises. You want to read characters from the keyboard, but you do not want to pick up any characters that may have been typed ahead and are idly sitting in the buffer. The most familiar example is the DOS `ERASE` command. If you enter the command `ERASE *.*`, you must *wait* for the `Are you sure?` message before you can answer Y or N.

Two versions of a `FlushBuffer` procedure follow. Version 1 reads the contents of the buffer, if any, into the dummy variable `Empty`. A `uses Crt;` statement is required at the beginning of the module.

```
procedure FlushBuffer;  { Version 1 }
var
   Empty : char;
begin
   while KeyPressed do Empty := ReadKey;    { Requires "uses Crt;" }
end;
```

Version 2 simply sets the location referenced by the head pointer equal to the location referenced by the tail pointer. The two pointers are now equal, so the buffer is considered to be empty.

```
< procedure FlushBuffer;  { Version 2 }
begin
   Mem[$0040:$001A] := Mem[$0040:$001C];  { HeadPointer := TailPointer }
end;
```

Shift and Toggle Keys

Some keys are never (or rarely) used alone, and consequently they leave no trace in the keyboard buffer. For example, knowing that the Shift key has been pressed is of little value by itself. Turbo programs operate quite comfortably by directly processing the upper- or lowercase form of a letter; they would bog down quickly if each letter had to be tested for the presence of a preceding Shift or CapsLock.

When you press one of the ***shift keys*** (that is, a Shift, Ctrl, or Alt), the keyboard interrupt routines modify the next character to be entered before placing it in the keyboard buffer. Similarly, the interrupt routines examine the current state of each of the ***toggle keys*** (CapsLock, NumLock, ScrollLock, and Ins).

Each shift and toggle key is mapped to at least one bit in the pair of bytes at memory locations $0040:$0017 and $0040:$0018.

In the byte at $0040:$0017, the upper four bits indicate the status of the four toggle keys. If CapsLock is on, for example, bit 6 is set and continues to be set until CapsLock is pressed again. The lower four bits indicate whether the Alt, Ctrl, or Shift keys are down. Notice in figure 9.9 that the left and right Shift keys are treated as having separate meanings. These bits are set only while the key is pressed.

Fig. 9.9. The keyboard status byte at $0040:$0017.

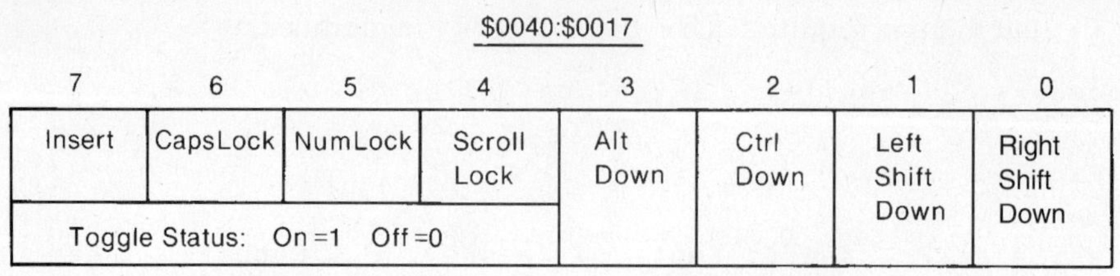

In the byte at $0040:$0018, the upper four bits indicate whether the four toggle keys are pressed. If CapsLock is pressed, for example, bit 6 will be set only until CapsLock is released. Bit 3 indicates that the Ctrl-NumLock combination (which temporarily suspends program execution) is currently in force. As figure 9.10 shows, the lowest three bits are undefined. (On the PC*jr*, bit 2 controls whether the keyboard click is on or off.)

Fig. 9.10. The keyboard status byte at $0040:$0018.

$0040:$0018

7	6	5	4	3	2	1	0
Insert Down	CapsLock Down	NumLock Down	Scroll Lock Down	Ctrl-NumLock On			
Key Status: Down = 1 Up = 0							

These bits are updated automatically whenever one of the toggle or shift keys is pressed or released. The Ins key is the only one of these keys that also creates an entry in the keyboard buffer; specifically, it produces 0 for the ASCII byte and 82 for the extended byte.

Because the keyboard interrupt routine checks the contents of the keyboard status bytes before determining the final entry to make to the keyboard buffer, changing these bytes has the same effect as the key action indicated by the values of the bits.

The SHOWKEY program (listing 9.17) reveals how these bits change with various character entries. The program ends when you enter a lowercase *z*. Notice in figure 9.11 that the combination of CapsLock and Shift, for example, cancels out and produces a lowercase *a*.

Listing 9.17

```
program SHOWKEY;
uses Crt;
var
   Selection : char;
   KeyFlag1  : byte absolute $0040:$0017;
   KeyFlag2  : byte absolute $0040:$0018;
procedure ShowBits( Specimen : byte );
var
   i,
   Compare : byte;
begin
   Compare := 128;
   for i := 7 downto 0 do begin
      if Specimen and Compare = 0 then write( '0' )
                                  else write( '1' );
      Compare := Compare shr 1;
   end;
end;
begin
   repeat
      Selection := ReadKey;
      write( Selection, '  ', ord( Selection ):4, '  ' );
      ShowBits( KeyFlag1 );
      write( '  ' );
      ShowBits( KeyFlag2 );
      writeln;
   until Selection = 'z';
end.
```

The KEYSET program (listing 9.18) alternately clears and sets the CapsLock toggle bit to force a change in the default of the case of any letters being entered. Notice how the constants are defined.

Listing 9.18

```
program KEYSET;
uses Crt;
const
   InsertOn        = $80;   { Key Flag at 0040:0017 }
```

continues

Listing 9.18 continued

```
    CapsLockOn      = $40;
    NumLockOn       = $20;
    ScrollLockOn    = $10;
    AltKeyDown      = $08;
    CtrlKeyDown     = $04;
    LeftShiftDown   = $02;
    RightShiftDown  = $01;
    InsertKeyDown   = $80;    { Key Flag at 0040:0018 }
    CapsLockDown    = $40;
    NumLockDown     = $20;
    ScrollLockDown  = $10;
    CtrlNumLockOn   = $08;
var
    TypedItem : char;
    KeyFlag1 : byte absolute $0040:$0017;
    KeyFlag2 : byte absolute $0040:$0018;
begin
    ClrScr;
    KeyFlag1 := KeyFlag1 and (not CapsLockOn);   { Turns caps off }
    writeln( 'CapsLock isn''t on' );
    repeat
       TypedItem := ReadKey;
       write( TypedItem );
    until TypedItem = 'z';
    writeln; writeln;
    KeyFlag1 := KeyFlag1 or CapsLockOn;    { Turns caps on }
    writeln( 'CapsLock is on' );
    repeat
       TypedItem := ReadKey;
       write( TypedItem );
    until TypedItem = 'Z';
end.
```

The KEYSET program first clears the CapsLock setting so all characters can be entered normally. When a lowercase *z* is typed, KEYSET turns the CapsLock bit on, just as if the CapsLock key had been pressed on the keyboard. The program ends when an uppercase *Z* is typed. The output from the program looks like the following:

```
CapsLock isn't on
iuwrye fdgvvkjhgoeiwrty eryowytw dkjhgfkz
CapsLock is on
REWOIUYTOIEYKDFHGKLSHACDJHFO YEWRQ 2396Z
```

Fig. 9.11. Sample output produced by the SHOWKEY program.

SHOWKEY Program Output			Key Entered
a	97	00000000 00000000	Lowercase *a*
A	65	00000010 00000000	Left-Shift *a*
A	65	00000001 00000000	Right-Shift *a*
	1	00000100 00000000	Ctrl-*a*
	0	00001000 00000000	Alt-*a*
▲	30	00001000 00000000	Alt-*a*
			CapsLock key pressed
A	65	01000000 00000000	Lowercase *a*
a	97	01000010 00000000	Left-Shift *a*

After the program is finished, the CapsLock setting remains enabled until it is reset from the keyboard.

It is common to run programs that affect—or are affected by—the settings of the toggle keys. The KEYSTAT program (listing 9.19) can be executed from the DOS prompt or included in a batch file to establish specific toggle key states.

Listing 9.19

```
program KEYSTAT;
const
   InsertOn      = $80;   { Key Flag at 0040:0017 }
   CapsLockOn    = $40;
   NumLockOn     = $20;
   ScrollLockOn  = $10;
var
   i, j         : byte;
   UpperString  : string[ 10 ];
   KeyFlag1     : byte absolute $0040:$0017;
procedure DisplayHelp;
begin
   writeln;
   writeln( 'Syntax:' );
   writeln( 'keys condition(s)' );
   writeln;
   writeln( 'where "condition" is one or more of the following, in any' );
```

continues

Listing 9.19 continued

```
   writeln( 'order, separated by spaces:' );
   writeln;
   writeln( '    ion = Insert mode on    ioff = Insert mode off' );
   writeln( '    con = CapsLock on       coff = CapsLock off' );
   writeln( '    non = NumLock on        noff = NumLock off' );
   writeln( '    son = ScrollLock on     soff = ScrollLock off' );
   writeln;
   writeln( 'Letters may be either upper- or lowercase.' );
end;
begin
   if ParamCount < 1 then
      DisplayHelp
   else
      for i := 1 to ParamCount do begin
         UpperString := ParamStr( i );
         for j := 1 to length( UpperString ) do
            UpperString[ j ] := UpCase( UpperString[ j ] );
         if UpperString = 'ION' then
            KeyFlag1 := KeyFlag1 or InsertOn
         else if UpperString = 'IOFF' then
            KeyFlag1 := KeyFlag1 and (not InsertOn)
         else if UpperString = 'CON' then
            KeyFlag1 := KeyFlag1 or CapsLockOn
         else if UpperString = 'COFF' then
            KeyFlag1 := KeyFlag1 and (not CapsLockOn)
         else if UpperString = 'NON' then
            KeyFlag1 := KeyFlag1 or NumLockOn
         else if UpperString = 'NOFF' then
            KeyFlag1 := KeyFlag1 and (not NumLockOn)
         else if UpperString = 'SON' then
            KeyFlag1 := KeyFlag1 or ScrollLockOn
         else if UpperString = 'SOFF' then
            KeyFlag1 := KeyFlag1 and (not ScrollLockOn)
         else begin
            DisplayHelp;
            Halt;
         end;
      end;
end.
```

The program accepts parameters that specify desired toggle key states. For example, to ensure that all toggle keys are disabled, enter:

```
KEYSTAT ioff coff noff soff
```

Similarly, to enable the CapsLock state, enter

```
KEYSTAT con
```

Summary

In this chapter, you learned how your programs can read and process information entered through the keyboard. You learned how to read data from the command line, and you learned several techniques for editing data entered with the `read` and `readln` procedures.

You learned that every keystroke produces two bytes of information. Either the first byte is the ASCII value of the character and the second byte can be ignored, or the first byte is 0 and the second byte has a special (non-ASCII) meaning called an extended code.

You learned that these bytes are placed in a special keyboard buffer that your program uses as its source of input. The `ReadKey` function can be used to identify a single keystroke and process extended keystrokes. You learned how the `KeyPressed` function can be used to test if a character is available to be read from the keyboard buffer. You saw that you can insert characters into the buffer and have your program execute a DOS command upon completion.

You learned how to prevent input from appearing on the screen, and you learned how to handle the Esc, Ctrl-Break, and Ctrl-C keystrokes.

You learned how you can use the `ECHO` command to redefine the meaning of keystrokes entered from DOS.

You learned how to control the settings of the shift keys (Shift, Ctrl, and Alt) and the toggle keys (CapsLock, NumLock, ScrollLock, and Ins) by accessing the keyboard status bytes at memory locations $0040:$0017 and $0040:$0018.

CHAPTER 10

Text Display

Suppose that you have sweated endless hours developing the world's most sophisticated spreadsheet program. It manipulates n-dimensional data structures, performs marvelously fast data retrieval, and achieves miraculously fast internal processing. It also displays all its data in the lower left corner of the screen and scrolls up one line per cell, just like an adding machine tape. Your program is brilliant, but no one wants to use it.

This happens more often than you might think.

Screen layouts, together with keyboard entry routines, constitute the *user interface*. Through the user interface a program communicates with the outside world; consequently, the user interface establishes the program's character and identity. If a program has a personality, it can be read on the screen. In less fanciful terms, the images on the screen help determine how user-friendly your program is. To improve the quality of your program, you need to improve the quality of the screens that your program displays.

This chapter discusses screen management techniques using the Monochrome Display Adapter (MDA) and the text display modes of the various color and graphics adapter boards. Graphics routines are discussed in Chapter 11, "Graphics Display."

Screen Memory

Even though only 640K of memory is available to your program, the 8086-family processor can—and does—physically access the full 1M of address space. For example, if your PC has color capability, the memory beginning at $B800:0000 (which is B80000h or 753,664 decimal) is where the PC places its screen images. This area is referred to as *screen memory*, or *video memory*. If your PC has a monochrome display, screen memory begins at $B000:0000.

The 8086 never writes "to the screen"; instead, it writes to this particular memory area. Manufacturers of monitors and color adapter boards design their products to read these memory locations continuously and move their contents to specific cursor positions on the screen. In other words, the chore of writing "to the screen" is the responsibility of specially designed hardware circuits over which the CPU has no control.

Contents of Video Memory

A 25-line by 80-column screen has 2000 possible cursor positions. The 2000 words that begin at memory location $B800:0000 (or $B000:0000 if your machine is monochrome) define the current screen image. The first byte of each word is the ASCII character to be displayed, and the second byte is the *attribute* of the display, which controls such characteristics as color and whether the character should blink.

Therefore, beginning at memory location $B800:0000 (or $B000:0000 in a monochrome system), the PC stores an image of whatever it wants to display on the screen. The first word in this memory region represents the upper left corner of the screen. Each successive word in memory defines cursor positions to the right of the previous character. The 81st word in memory defines the first character on the second line of the screen. The 2000th word defines what appears on the lower right corner of the screen.

Writing to Video Memory

Because anything in this memory area is automatically displayed, it follows that you can directly control the contents of the screen by writing directly to this area of memory, as demonstrated by the SCR1 program (listing 10.1).

Listing 10.1

```
program Scr1;
var
   i, Slider, Disp : word;
   Attrib          : byte;
begin
   Attrib := 0;
   for Slider := 0 to 255 do begin
      Disp := 0;
      for i := 0 to ( (23 * 80) - 1 ) do begin
         Mem[ $B800 : 2*i ]     := Lo( Disp );
         Inc( Disp );
         Mem[ $B800 : 2*i + 1 ] := Attrib;
         if Attrib = 255 then Attrib := Slider else Inc( Attrib );
      end;
   end;
end.
```

Remember that the segment address $B800 must be changed to $B000 in a monochrome system.

By simply changing the contents of the memory array, the SCR1 program cycles through and displays every combination of ASCII character and attribute bytes. Running the program results in an explosion of colors and styles, only one phase of which is illustrated in figure 10.1.

Fig. 10.1. *Output produced by the SCR1 program.*

Screen Coordinates

If you use the standard (X,Y) coordinate system to define a cursor position on the screen, with the upper left corner at (1,1) and the lower right corner at (80,25), with a little algebra you can see that the offset value for a cursor position can be found at:

Words: $80 \times (\text{Row} - 1) + (\text{Column} - 1)$

or

Bytes: $160 \times (\text{Row} - 1) + 2 \times (\text{Column} - 1)$

If you want to display a box of asterisks in the center of your screen (for example, rows 10 through 15 and columns 20 through 60), you can simply determine the appropriate offsets, as shown in the SCR1A program (listing 10.2).

Listing 10.2

```
program Scr1A;
var
   Row,
   Column : byte;
begin
   for Row := 10 to 15 do
      for Column := 20 to 60 do begin
         Mem[ $B800 : 160*(Row-1)+2*(Column-1) ]  := ord( '*' );
         Mem[ $B800 : 160*(Row-1)+2*(Column-1) + 1 ] := 4;  { Red }
      end;
end.
```

Figure 10.2 shows the output from the program displayed against the image generated by the SCR1 program. SCR1A uses the byte form of the displacement. By setting each attribute to 4, the program ensures that the asterisks are all red. (Colors are covered in more detail shortly.)

A more practical application is found in the rapid display of messages. The `WriteString` procedure in the SCR1B program (listing 10.3) outputs a string directly to video memory.

Fig. 10.2. Output produced by the SCR1A program.

Listing 10.3

```
program Scr1B;
var
   Message : string;
procedure WriteString( OutString : string; Column, Row : byte );
var
   X : byte;
begin
   X := 1;
   while ( X <= Length( OutString ) ) do begin
      Mem[ $B800 : 2*(80*(Row-1)+Column+X-2) ] := ord( OutString[ X ] );
      Mem[ $B800 : 2*(80*(Row-1)+Column+X-2)+1 ] := 4;    { Red }
      X := X + 1;
   end;
end;
begin
   Message := 'Hello.  Special program now beginning...';
   WriteString( Message, 20, 10 );
end.
```

Screen Output

Normally, programs that write "to the screen" do not go to all this trouble. DOS itself offers a complete line of screen management services. One DOS call displays a character, another erases the screen, still another scrolls the screen, and so on. (Consider the code you would otherwise have to develop to scroll the screen by one line!) Nevertheless, for simply displaying blocks of characters, direct screen addressing (that is, direct screen *memory* addressing) is the fastest technique available.

Using the Crt Unit

Like most programs, Turbo Pascal normally relies on the DOS and BIOS functions when it generates screen output. When the Crt unit is included with a program, however, Turbo automatically performs its screen output with the faster direct memory method. Each use of a `write` or `writeln` bypasses the slower DOS routines in favor of directly positioning the output strings in the appropriate memory locations, which are then directly transferred to the screen. Therefore, the Crt unit allows screen displays to be as fast as memory access times. If your program performs screen writing extensively, it should include a `uses Crt;` line even if no other procedures or functions from the Crt unit are needed.

Because the standard output file (the screen) is bypassing the normal DOS control code, one side effect of using the Crt unit is that output from `write` and `writeln` statements cannot be redirected or piped with the | or > character on the command line. For example, in the CRTR1 program (listing 10.4), two `writeln` statements use the standard output device, and two others use a defined file. (Files are discussed in more detail in Chapter 13, "File Handling.")

Listing 10.4

```
program Crtr1;
uses Crt;
var
   AnyFile : Text;
begin
   writeln( 'Line 1:  This text is sent to the standard output device.' );
   writeln( 'Line 2:  It bypasses DOS and can''t be redirected.' );
   Assign( AnyFile, '' );
```

```
    Rewrite( AnyFile );
    writeln( AnyFile, 'Line 3:  This text is sent to a different file. It' );
    writeln( AnyFile, 'Line 4:  uses DOS services, so it can be redirected.' );
end.
```

All four lines are displayed when CRTR1 executes from the command line.

```
Line 1:    This text is sent to the standard output device.
Line 2:    It bypasses DOS and can't be redirected.
Line 3:    This text is sent to a different file. It
Line 4:    uses DOS services, so it can be redirected.
```

If you try to redirect its output to the printer, however, only the lines that use DOS procedures are captured. Lines 1 and 2 bypass DOS, so they continue to be displayed on the screen.

```
Line 1:    This text is sent to the standard output device.
Line 2:    It bypasses DOS and can't be redirected.
```

This is not a problem for most applications. A program that optionally allows CRT or printer output usually offers the user a choice at the beginning of its run, when the file parameter is assigned to either the printer or a null file. This technique allows the program to use only a single set of `write` and `writeln` procedures. For example, in lines 3 and 4 of the CRTR1 program, the `AnyFile` parameter could have been assigned to either `PRN` or `null` depending on the user's selection. Unfortunately, this means that the direct memory output routines would be sacrificed.

Using the *AssignCrt* Procedure

To assign the file parameter to the CRT while not abandoning direct memory optimizations, Turbo Pascal offers the `AssignCrt` procedure. It operates just like an ordinary `Assign`, except you do not need to specify a file name. The CRTR2 program in listing 10.5 demonstrates how the output mechanism can be selected. Again, because `AssignCrt` uses direct memory output and bypasses DOS, `write` and `writeln` procedures directed to the CRT cannot be redirected.

Listing 10.5

```
program Crtr2;
uses Crt;
var
   AnyFile : Text;
   Choice  : char;
begin
   repeat
      write( '(P)rinter or (C)rt : ' );
      Choice := ReadKey;
   until UpCase(Choice) in [ 'P', 'C' ];
   writeln( Choice );
   case UpCase(Choice) of
      'P' : Assign( AnyFile, 'PRN' );
      'C' : AssignCRT( AnyFile );
   end;
   Rewrite( AnyFile );
   writeln( AnyFile, 'Line 1:   This text is sent to the CRT or to' );
   writeln( AnyFile, 'Line 2:   the printer.  It cannot be redirected.' );
end.
```

Disabling Direct Video Output

Inevitably, the situation arises in which you need a procedure or function in the Crt unit, but you do not want Turbo Pascal to use the direct memory writes. In this case, you can either assign the output to a null file, as listing 10.4 did for lines 3 and 4 of the CRTR1 program, or simply switch off the optimized routines by setting the predefined Boolean variable `DirectVideo` to `False`.

Note that the `TextMode` procedure, discussed later in this chapter, resets `DirectVideo` to `True` whenever it is called.

Contending with Snow

The monochrome screen uses 720 horizontal and 350 vertical dots, or *pixels*, for its display. Therefore, each of its 80 × 25 characters takes a 9 × 14 image. Color Graphics Adapters (CGAs) use 640 horizontal and 200 vertical pixels. Therefore, each CGA character takes up an 8 × 8 pattern.

There are two differences between a monochrome display and a CGA display. First, a monochrome display always displays crisper and cleaner text images than a CGA display. Second, a monochrome display is faster than a CGA display.

Because a CGA display is slower, an *older* CGA sometimes has trouble with interference—lines or spots commonly called *snow*—when the adapter writes directly to video memory. Snow is produced when the CGA board is trying to display both the regular screen image and your new video memory input. The distortion is caused when the CGA board tries to jump between them.

To compensate for this, the Crt unit includes special code that ensures that CGA video memory writes occur only during the nondisplaying horizontal retrace intervals. This code is enabled or disabled by the value of the predefined Boolean variable `CheckSnow`, which is set to `True` when the program first runs and after each execution of the `TextMode` procedure.

If your PC has a newer CGA, you can disable this snow-checking logic by setting `CheckSnow` to `False`. This should result in significantly faster displays.

Snow generally is not a problem when you are working with monochrome displays, Extended Graphics Adapters (EGAs), Video Graphics Adapters (VGAs), or the newer CGAs. And, of course, snow is not a problem if you disable direct video by setting `DirectVideo` to `False`. (More advanced snow-handling techniques are discussed in Chapter 17, "The 8087 and External Devices.")

The Attribute Byte

Each character on the screen consists of a rectangular cursor block of a certain color over which an ASCII character (also of a certain color) is superimposed. Associated with each screen position is a word-size memory value. The first byte in the word defines the ASCII character, and the second byte—the *attribute byte*—defines the color pattern to use in the display.

Attribute Bit Settings

The eight bits in the attribute byte are used in the manner shown in figure 10.3.

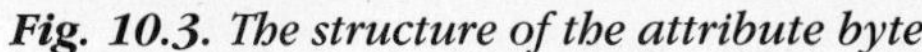

Fig. 10.3. The structure of the attribute byte.

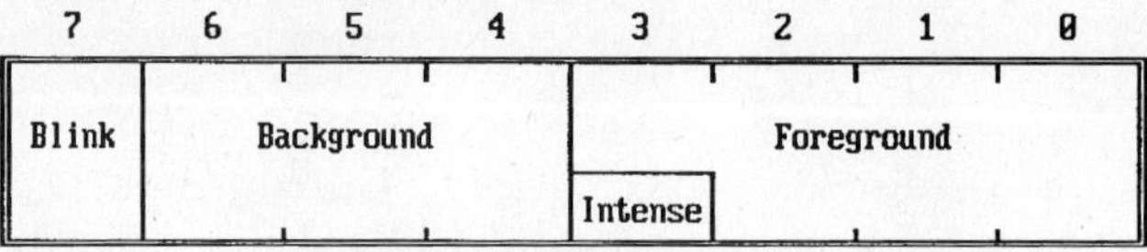

The color of the background rectangle is determined by the setting of the *Background* bits. The color of the character itself is controlled by the *Foreground* bits. The Foreground field is generally considered as being four bits long, but functionally it consists of a three-bit color selector and a one-bit *intensifier*. If the character is to be displayed in high-intensity form, the Intense bit is set. Finally, if you want the character to blink, the Blink bit is set. The Blink and Intense bits affect only the character and not the background.

Choosing Colors

To help select color combinations, Turbo Pascal predefines several color constants. The values 0 through 7 correspond to the colors black through light gray. Both the background rectangle and the character itself (in the foreground) can have any combination of these colors.

Foreground and Background	*Value*
Black	0
Blue	1
Green	2
Cyan	3
Red	4
Magenta	5
Brown	6
LightGray	7

When the intensity bit is set, the Foreground field can assume eight new values. Do not be confused by the *Light* prefixes in the following. Light colors are simply less dark and therefore significantly brighter.

Foreground	*Value*
DarkGray	8
LightBlue	9
LightGreen	10
LightCyan	11
LightRed	12
LightMagenta	13
Yellow	14
White	15

Finally, to enable blinking, just add the `Blink` constant:

Blinking	*Value*
Blink	128

Using Colors

To display a blinking red asterisk on a blue background at a general cursor position (column, row), you could use the following lines of code:

```
Mem[ $B800 : 160*(Row-1)+2*(Column-1) ] := ord( '*' );
Mem[ $B800 : 160*(Row-1)+2*(Column-1) + 1 ] :=
   Blink + (Blue Shl 4) + Red;
```

Fortunately, Turbo Pascal offers a simpler technique. The `TextColor` procedure selects the color of the foreground character, and the `TextBackground` procedure selects the background color. Adding the `Blink` constant to the parameter of either function enables the blinking process. Therefore, to display the asterisk, all you need do is

```
GotoXY( Column, Row );
TextColor( Red + Blink );
TextBackground( Blue );
write( '*' );
```

Turbo Pascal uses a default attribute byte called `TextAttr`. After its value is adjusted with the `TextColor` and `TextBackground` procedures, the colors (and the blinking) become the new defaults for all subsequent write and writeln procedures. You can adjust the TextAttr variable directly, but executing the TextColor and TextBackground procedures is easier and provides better program documentation. Although Turbo provides no procedures to directly identify the current color scheme, you can obtain this information by testing the bits of the TextAttr variable.

To display the complete set of color combinations for your hardware, execute the ATTR2 program (listing 10.6). Each background and foreground pair is presented, with and without blinking enabled. The background number is shown first, followed by the foreground value (in hexadecimal, so that the values will fit on the screen). Sample output is shown in figure 10.4. (Remember, however, that in the actual program, the right side of the screen will be blinking.)

Listing 10.6

```
program Attr2;
uses Crt;
var
   Blinker,
   Color,
   Background : byte;
begin
   ClrScr;
   writeln( 'Background/Foreground Combinations with Blinking' );
   for Color := 0 to 15 do begin
      for Blinker := 0 to 1 do begin
         TextColor( Color + 128*Blinker );
         for Background := 0 to 7 do begin
            TextBackground( Background );
            write( Background:2 );
            if Color > 9 then write( chr(55+Color):2 )
                         else write( Color:2 );
         end;
         TextBackground( Black );                { Reset }
         if Blinker = 0 then write( '       ' );  { 7 spaces }
      end;
      writeln;
   end;
end.
```

Fig. 10.4. Output produced by the ATTR2 program.

```
Background/Foreground Combinations with Blinking
 0 0 1 0 2 0 3 0 4 0 5 0 6 0 7 0          0 0 1 0 2 0 3 0 4 0 5 0 6 0 7 0
 0 1 1 1 2 1 3 1 4 1 5 1 6 1 7 1          0 1 1 1 2 1 3 1 4 1 5 1 6 1 7 1
 0 2 1 2 2 2 3 2 4 2 5 2 6 2 7 2          0 2 1 2 2 2 3 2 4 2 5 2 6 2 7 2
 0 3 1 3 2 3 3 3 4 3 5 3 6 3 7 3          0 3 1 3 2 3 3 3 4 3 5 3 6 3 7 3
 0 4 1 4 2 4 3 4 4 4 5 4 6 4 7 4          0 4 1 4 2 4 3 4 4 4 5 4 6 4 7 4
 0 5 1 5 2 5 3 5 4 5 5 5 6 5 7 5          0 5 1 5 2 5 3 5 4 5 5 5 6 5 7 5
 0 6 1 6 2 6 3 6 4 6 5 6 6 6 7 6          0 6 1 6 2 6 3 6 4 6 5 6 6 6 7 6
 0 7 1 7 2 7 3 7 4 7 5 7 6 7 7 7          0 7 1 7 2 7 3 7 4 7 5 7 6 7 7 7
 0 8 1 8 2 8 3 8 4 8 5 8 6 8 7 8          0 8 1 8 2 8 3 8 4 8 5 8 6 8 7 8
 0 9 1 9 2 9 3 9 4 9 5 9 6 9 7 9          0 9 1 9 2 9 3 9 4 9 5 9 6 9 7 9
 0 A 1 A 2 A 3 A 4 A 5 A 6 A 7 A          0 A 1 A 2 A 3 A 4 A 5 A 6 A 7 A
 0 B 1 B 2 B 3 B 4 B 5 B 6 B 7 B          0 B 1 B 2 B 3 B 4 B 5 B 6 B 7 B
 0 C 1 C 2 C 3 C 4 C 5 C 6 C 7 C          0 C 1 C 2 C 3 C 4 C 5 C 6 C 7 C
 0 D 1 D 2 D 3 D 4 D 5 D 6 D 7 D          0 D 1 D 2 D 3 D 4 D 5 D 6 D 7 D
 0 E 1 E 2 E 3 E 4 E 5 E 6 E 7 E          0 E 1 E 2 E 3 E 4 E 5 E 6 E 7 E
 0 F 1 F 2 F 3 F 4 F 5 F 6 F 7 F          0 F 1 F 2 F 3 F 4 F 5 F 6 F 7 F
```

Not too surprisingly, characters disappear when the foreground and background colors are the same. Obviously, colors will be displayed only if your PC is equipped with color capability. On a monochrome system, the attribute byte can display only five formats: hidden, normal, highlighted, underlined, and reverse video. Hidden text corresponds to Black characters on a Black background. Reverse video is a Black foreground on a LightGray (white) background. Underlined characters appear when the foreground color is set to Blue. Normal and highlighted states are the same as those in a color system.

Modifying Intensity

Although listed as two distinct colors, pairs such as Red and LightRed appear to the eye as two different intensities of the same color.

Turbo Pascal provides three procedures to change the Intense bit of the `TextAttr` default attribute. `LowVideo` clears the Intense bit, and `HighVideo` sets it. The `NormVideo` procedure sets the entire `TextAttr` byte to the value it had when the program started.

As the INTENSE1 program in listing 10.7 executes, the color of the display changes from Red (for low intensity) to LightRed (for high intensity) back to the default color contained in `TextAttr` when the program began. Again, the only action taken by the `LowVideo` and `HighVideo` procedures is to clear and set the default Intense bit. Executing `TextColor( Red )` followed by `HighVideo` has the same effect as executing `TextColor ( LightRed )`. Consequently, both lines display the same color characteristics.

Listing 10.7

```
program Intense1;
uses Crt;
begin
   TextColor( Red );    { As an example }
   LowVideo;    write( 'Low Low Low...' );
   HighVideo;   write( 'High High High...' );
   NormVideo;   write( 'Norm Norm Norm' );
   writeln;
   TextColor( LightRed );
   LowVideo;    write( 'Low Low Low...' );
   HighVideo;   write( 'High High High...' );
   NormVideo;   write( 'Norm Norm Norm' );
   writeln;
end.
```

Although the intensity procedures do not add any more colors to the set you already have, they can be used quite effectively for highlighting screen messages. A partial set of choices can be displayed by executing the INTENSE2 program (listing 10.8).

Listing 10.8

```
program Intense2;
uses Crt;
var
   Cycle : byte;
begin
   ClrScr;
   for Cycle := 1 to 24 do begin
      TextColor( Random( 15 ) + 1 );
      TextBackground( Random( 8 ) + 1 );   write( 'Color Color Color....' );
      LowVideo;                            write( 'Low Low Low....' );
      HighVideo;                           write( 'High High High....' );
      NormVideo;                           write( 'Normal Normal Normal' );
      writeln;
   end;
end.
```

Each level of intensity is displayed, together with the color number, as shown in figure 10.5.

Fig. 10.5. Output produced by INTENSE2 program.

```
Color Color Color....Low Low Low....High High High....Normal Normal Normal
Color Color Color....Low Low Low....High High High....Normal Normal Normal
Color Color Color....Low Low Low....High High High....Normal Normal Normal
Color Color Color....Low Low Low....High High High....Normal Normal Normal
Color Color Color....Low Low Low....High High High....Normal Normal Normal
Color Color Color....Low Low Low....High High High....Normal Normal Normal
Color Color Color....Low Low Low....High High High....Normal Normal Normal
Color Color Color....Low Low Low....High High High....Normal Normal Normal
Color Color Color....Low Low Low....High High High....Normal Normal Normal
Color Color Color....Low Low Low....High High High....Normal Normal Normal
Color Color Color....Low Low Low....High High High....Normal Normal Normal
Color Color Color....Low Low Low....High High High....Normal Normal Normal
Color Color Color....Low Low Low....High High High....Normal Normal Normal
Color Color Color....Low Low Low....High High High....Normal Normal Normal
Color Color Color....Low Low Low....High High High....Normal Normal Normal
Color Color Color....Low Low Low....High High High....Normal Normal Normal
Color Color Color....Low Low Low....High High High....Normal Normal Normal
Color Color Color....Low Low Low....High High High....Normal Normal Normal
Color Color Color....Low Low Low....High High High....Normal Normal Normal
Color Color Color....Low Low Low....High High High....Normal Normal Normal
Color Color Color....Low Low Low....High High High....Normal Normal Normal
Color Color Color....Low Low Low....High High High....Normal Normal Normal
Color Color Color....Low Low Low....High High High....Normal Normal Normal
Color Color Color....Low Low Low....High High High....Normal Normal Normal
```

Text Mode

A text screen can be either 40 or 80 columns wide and 25, 43, or 50 lines long. It can display either color characters or a single color (usually green or amber) with shading to simulate colors. Together, size and color define the *mode* of a screen.

Programs that use 80 columns do not work well on 40-column screens. Similarly, some programs deliberately display only 40 columns on a screen capable of displaying 80 to show larger character sizes. If you develop a program with a color monitor, you may want to switch to a black-and-white mode to see how it looks when executing on a monochrome display. If your system has EGA or VGA capability, you may want to display 43 or 50 lines on your screen instead of the default of 25 lines.

Turbo Pascal predefines several constants that can be used to identify the mode of the screen, as shown in table 10.1.

To set a specific mode, call the `TextMode` procedure with one of the predefined constants as a parameter. Note that `TextMode` always clears the screen before resetting it. `TextMode` is demonstrated in the MODE2 program (listing 10.9), which switches through all available screen options.

Table 10.1. *Screen Mode Constants*

Mode	*Value*	*Meaning*
BW40	0	40 × 25 black-and-white on Color Adapter
CO40	1	40 × 25 color on Color Adapter
BW80	2	80 × 25 black-and-white on Color Adapter
CO80	3	80 × 25 color on Color Adapter
Mono	7	80 × 25 on Monochrome Adapter
Font8×8	256	Add-on for ROM font

Listing 10.9

```
program Mode2;
uses Crt;
begin
   TextMode( BW40 );
   writeln( '40x25 Black & White on a Color Adapter' );
   readln;
   TextMode( CO40 );
   writeln( '40x25 Color on a Color Adapter' );
   readln;
   TextMode( BW80 );
   writeln( '80x25 Black & White on a Color Adapter' );
   readln;
   TextMode( CO80 );
   writeln( '80x25 Color on a Color Adapter' );
   readln;
   TextMode( Mono );
   writeln( '80x25 on a Monochrome Adapter' );
   readln;
   { ============================================== }
   TextMode( CO80 + Font8x8 );
   writeln( '80x25 Color on a Color Adapter' );
   writeln( 'with Add-in ROM Font' );
   readln;
end.
```

The `Font8x8` constant is added to `CO80` to activate the compressed EGA or VGA mode. EGA compressed text is 80 columns by 43 lines. VGA compressed text is 80 columns by 50 lines. If these special adapters are not available, the use of the `Font8x8` constant has no effect.

When you run MODE2, you will probably notice that several of the messages appear identical. That is to be expected. After all, changing the mode of your screen does not change its capabilities. You may, for example, disable color generation on a color system, but the color video adapter card is still present in your PC and video memory remains in the $B800 segment. On a color system, the call

```
TextMode( Mono );
```

is equivalent to

```
TextMode( BW80 );
```

Similarly, on a monochrome system, the mode cannot be changed to color.

To keep track of the mode, Turbo Pascal provides the predefined word-sized variable `LastMode`. In spite of its confusing name, `LastMode` actually contains the *current* video mode. To learn how your PC is configured, your program can examine this variable, as demonstrated by the MODE1 program in listing 10.10.

Listing 10.10

```
program Mode1;
uses Crt;
begin
   case Lo( LastMode ) of
      BW40 : writeln( 'Mode is 40 x 25 B/W on Color Adapter' );
      CO40 : writeln( 'Mode is 40 x 25 Color on Color Adapter' );
      BW80 : writeln( 'Mode is 80 x 25 B/W on Color Adapter' );
      CO80 : writeln( 'Mode is 80 x 25 Color on Color Adapter' )
      Mono : writeln( 'Mode is 80 x 25 on Monochrome Adapter' );
      else   writeln( 'Non-standard mode' );
   end;
   if Lastmode and 256 <> 0 then
      writeln( 'Extended display enabled' );
end.
```

`LastMode` can be tested to determine which segment ($B800 or $B000) contains the video memory for your PC. The MODE1A program (listing 10.11) performs such a test.

Listing 10.11

```
program Mode1A;
uses Crt;
var
   VideoSegment : word;
procedure SetVideoSegment;
begin
   if LastMode = 7 { Mono } then
      VideoSegment := $B000
   else
      VideoSegment := $B800;
end;
begin
   SetVideoSegment;
   :
   :  { Continue }
   :
end.
```

The `VideoSegment` variable can now be used as the segment value when you are using video memory.

Generally, one mode is selected and used throughout the entire program. Occasionally, however, a program operates in more than one mode; in this case, `LastMode` should be saved prior to the mode change.

```
var
  StoredMode : word;
.
.
.
begin
.
.
.
   StoredMode := LastMode;
   TextMode( BW40 );          { Switch to 40-column black & white mode }
.
.
.
   TextMode( StoredMode );    { Return to original mode }
.
.
.
end;
```

Cursor Positioning and Screen Control

Turbo Pascal provides several screen positioning and line control routines. Many of them, such as `GotoXY`, you have already used. This section increases your familiarity with these tools and introduces a few new ones.

Setting Cursor Position

The `GotoXY` routine enables you to place the cursor at any desired position on the screen. Through the repeated use of `GotoXY` and `write`, you can "paint the screen."

The GOTO3 program (listing 10.12) displays a screen, shown in figure 10.6, designed to capture the entries for a mailing list. Each individual field (`Name`, `Address`, `City`, `State`, and `Zip`) is read as a string and edited to remove leading blanks. All letters are capitalized, and within each field, multiple blanks are transformed to single blanks. For example, the field:

```
"     LoS    aNgeLeS"
```

becomes

```
"LOS ANGELES"
```

Each field is redisplayed after each entry and edit.

Listing 10.12

```
program Goto3;
uses Crt;
var
   Name    : string[ 20 ];
   Address : string[ 30 ];
   City    : string[ 25 ];
   State   : string[ 2 ];
   Zip     : string[ 5 ];
function EditedStr( Column, Row, StrLength : byte ) : string;
var
   BlankTest, i : byte;
```

continues

Listing 10.12 continued

```
    StrEntry,
    StrExit : string;
    InChar : char;
begin
    repeat
        GotoXY( Column, Row );
        for i := 1 to StrLength do write( '_' );
        GotoXY( Column, Row );
        StrEntry[ 0 ] := chr( 0 );    { Length of "StrEntry" now equals zero }
        repeat
            InChar := ReadKey;
            if InChar <> chr( 13 ) then
                StrEntry := StrEntry + InChar;
            write( InChar );
        until (InChar = chr( 13 )) or (Length( StrEntry ) = StrLength);
        StrExit[ 0 ] := chr( 0 );    { Length of "StrExit" now equals zero }
        if Length( StrEntry ) > 0 then begin
            { Strip leading blanks }
            BlankTest := 1;
            while (StrEntry[ BlankTest ] = ' ') and
                    (BlankTest <= Length( StrEntry )) do
                Inc( BlankTest );
            { Convert to uppercase and disallow multiple blanks }
            if Length( StrEntry ) >= BlankTest then
                for i := BlankTest to Length( StrEntry ) do
                    if not ((StrEntry[ i ] = ' ') and (StrEntry[ i-1 ] = ' ')) then
                        StrExit := StrExit + UpCase( StrEntry[ i ] );
        end;
    until Length( StrExit ) > 0;
    GotoXY( Column, Row ); for i := 1 to StrLength do write( ' ' );
    GotoXY( Column, Row ); write( StrExit );
    EditedStr := StrExit;
end;
begin
    ClrScr;
    GotoXY( 10,  8 );   write( 'Name: ____________________' );
    GotoXY(  7, 10 );   write( 'Address: ______________________________' );
    GotoXY( 10, 12 );   write( 'City: ___________________________' );
    GotoXY(  9, 14 );   write( 'State: __' );
    GotoXY( 11, 16 );   write( 'Zip: _____' );
```

```
    Name    := EditedStr( 16,  8, 20 );
    Address := EditedStr( 16, 10, 30 );
    City    := EditedStr( 16, 12, 25 );
    State   := EditedStr( 16, 14,  2 );
    Zip     := EditedStr( 16, 16,  5 );
end.
```

Fig. 10.6. Output produced by the GOTO3 program.

```
   Name: ____________________
Address: ______________________________
   City: _________________________
  State: __
    Zip: _____
```

Line Control

The ClrScr procedure was called at the beginning of the GOTO3 program. ClrScr, one of several screen-management procedures offered by Turbo Pascal, erases the screen and positions the cursor in the upper left corner. The ClrEol procedure erases all characters on the current line to the right of the cursor. The position of the cursor remains unchanged.

The DelLine procedure deletes the line containing the cursor. All lines below the current line scroll up. The relative position of the cursor remains unchanged. The InsLine procedure inserts an empty line in the same line as the cursor. All lines below the current line scroll down. The relative position of the cursor remains unchanged.

The actions of the ClrScr, ClrEol, DelLine, and InsLine procedures can be explored in the WHERE1 program (listing 10.13). It fills the screen with characters, positions the cursor in a random location, and enables you to call one of the four procedures. It begins with the screen shown in figure 10.7.

Listing 10.13

```
program Where1;
uses Crt;
const
   Width  : byte = 80;
   Bottom : byte = 24;
var
   Row, Column,
   RowCode        : byte;
   Choice         : char;
begin
   ClrScr;
   Randomize;
   for Column := 1 to 80 do
      for Row := 1 to 23 do begin
         RowCode := Row mod 10;
         GotoXY( Column, Row );
         TextColor( Random( 6 ) + 1 );
         write( RowCode );
      end;
   repeat
      NormVideo;
      GotoXY( 1, 25 );
      write( '(1)ClrEol  (2)DelLine  (3)InsLine  (4)ClrScr  (5)End' );
      Row    := Random( Bottom ) + 1;
      Column := Random( Width ) + 1;
      GotoXY( Column, Row );
      TextColor( Red + Blink );
      write( '+' );
      repeat
         Choice := ReadKey;
      until Choice in [ '1'..'5' ];
      GotoXY( 1, 25 );  ClrEol;
      GotoXY( Column, Row );   TextColor( White );   write( '+' );
      case Choice of
         '1' : ClrEol;
         '2' : begin
                  DelLine;
                  Dec( Bottom );
               end;
         '3' : begin
                  InsLine;
```

```
            Inc( Bottom );
         end;
      else  ClrScr;
    end;
  until Choice = '5';
end.
```

Fig. 10.7. Output produced by the WHERE1 program.

```
11111111111111111111111111111111111111111111111111111111111111111111111111111111
22222222222222222222222222222222222222222222222222222222222222222222222222222222
33333333333333333333333333333333333333333333333333333333333333333333333333333333
44444444444444444444444444444444444444444444444444444444444444444444444444444444
55555555555555555555555555555555555555555555555555555555555555555555555555555555
66666666666666666666666666666666666666666666666666666666666666666666666666666666
77777777777777777777777777777777777777777777777777777777777777777777777777777777
88888888888888888888888888888888888888888888888888888888888888888888888888888888
99999999999999999999999999999999999999999999999999999999999999999999999999999999
00000000000000000000000000000000000000000000000000000000000000000000000000000000
11111111111111111111111111111111111111111111111111111111111111111111111111111111
22222222222222222222222222222222222222222222222222222222222222222222222222222222
3333333333333333333333333333333333333333333333333333+333333333333333333333333333
44444444444444444444444444444444444444444444444444444444444444444444444444444444
55555555555555555555555555555555555555555555555555555555555555555555555555555555
66666666666666666666666666666666666666666666666666666666666666666666666666666666
77777777777777777777777777777777777777777777777777777777777777777777777777777777
88888888888888888888888888888888888888888888888888888888888888888888888888888888
99999999999999999999999999999999999999999999999999999999999999999999999999999999
00000000000000000000000000000000000000000000000000000000000000000000000000000000
11111111111111111111111111111111111111111111111111111111111111111111111111111111
22222222222222222222222222222222222222222222222222222222222222222222222222222222
33333333333333333333333333333333333333333333333333333333333333333333333333333333

(1)ClrEol  (2)DelLine  (3)InsLine  (4)ClrScr  (5)End
```

Locating the Cursor Position

The WHERE1 program has one major advantage: Even though the target cursor location is assigned randomly, you always know where the cursor is located. Most programs that allow the cursor to roam freely still keep track of its location in special variables. The variables are passed as parameters to any procedure dependent upon cursor location. For example, in the Turbo Editor, the cursor row and column positions are always displayed; if auto-indent is turned off, pressing the Enter key repositions the cursor to the first column of the next row.

Sometimes it is simply not convenient to keep track of the cursor's position. In an operational version of the GOTO3 program, cursor location would be precisely controlled. Yet the user might be in the process of entering data in a field before he or she presses a Help key. That action would trigger the display of a help message, then reposition the cursor on the same spot where the help feature was invoked. Without using much imagination, you can see that maintaining fields with cursor position in a form-entry program is more trouble than it might be worth.

Turbo Pascal provides a simple alternative. The `WhereX` and `WhereY` functions return the X-coordinate and Y-coordinate, respectively, of the cursor at any time. A procedure that needs to know the current cursor location can simply call these functions, as demonstrated in the WHERE2 program (listing 10.14).

Listing 10.14

```
program Where2;
uses Crt;
var
   Row, Column, RowCode : byte;
procedure ClearEndScreen;
var
   CurrentX, CurrentY, RowWork, MaxRows : byte;
begin
   CurrentX := WhereX;                 { Locate current X-coordinate }
   CurrentY := WhereY;                 { Locate current Y-coordinate }
   ClrEol;                             { First, clear the current line }
   MaxRows := Hi( WindMax ) + 1;       { Number of rows in current window }
   if MaxRows > CurrentY then
      for RowWork := CurrentY + 1 to MaxRows do begin
         GotoXY( 1, RowWork );         { Go to start of each successive line }
         ClrEol;                       { Clear each successive line }
      end;
   GotoXY( CurrentX, CurrentY );       { Return to the original spot }
end;
begin
   ClrScr;
   Randomize;
   for Column := 1 to 80 do
      for Row := 1 to 23 do begin
         RowCode := Row mod 10;
         GotoXY( Column, Row );
         TextColor( Random( 6 ) + 1 );
         write( RowCode );
```

```
      end;
   GotoXY( Random( 80 ) + 1, Random( 24 ) + 1 );
   TextColor( Red + Blink );
   write( '+' );
   Delay( 2000 );
   ClearEndScreen;
   GotoXY( 1, 25 );
   NormVideo;
   write( 'Hit enter to end...' );
   readln;
end.
```

The WHERE2 program fills the screen with characters, then randomly positions the cursor. After a short delay, it calls the `ClearEndScreen` procedure, which clears all characters to the right of the cursor and all characters on all lines below the cursor.

Using the `WhereX` and `WhereY` functions, `ClearEndScreen` can determine its starting point without having been passed separate position parameters. Notice, in fact, that the main body of the program does not even bother storing the cursor's coordinates.

The predefined variable `WindMax` was used by `ClearEndScreen` to determine the number of rows to erase. `WindMax` is discussed in greater detail in the next section.

Managing Windows

The SCR1A program presented in listing 10.1 at the beginning of the chapter displayed characters in a small rectangular area of the screen. Such a region, commonly called a *window*, can be managed easily in Turbo Pascal.

Windows are used most frequently to display information or interact with the user without destroying or obscuring most of the original screen. In the Turbo Pascal interactive environment, for example, pull-down menus appear and disappear in windows as needed, leaving the bulk of the screen intact.

The Turbo Pascal `Window` procedure is called with four byte-sized location parameters as follows:

```
Window( left, top, right, bottom );
```

Window changes the default screen into a rectangle with an upper left position of (`left, top`) and a lower right position of (`right, bottom`).

After `Window` executes, all standard screen display instructions (such as `GotoXY`, `ClrScr`, and `writeln`) will be processed relative to the new window, not to the original screen. One exception is another `Window` instruction, which always uses absolute references. The original screen size is restored by the call:

```
Window( 1, 1, 80, 25 );
```

The minimum window size is 1 column by 1 row. The maximum window size is the original system default of 25 rows by 80 columns, assuming a 25-line display. For an EGA, a display can show 43 lines—the maximum window size is `WINDOW(1,1,80,43)`. For a VGA, a display can show 50 lines—the maximum window size is `WINDOW(1,1,80,50)`.

Identifying the Current Window

The coordinates of the upper left corner of the current window can be found in the predefined variable `WindMin`. Similarly, `WindMax` contains the coordinates of the lower right corner. `WindMin` and `WindMax` are word-sized variables, with the upper byte holding the Y-coordinate and the lower byte holding the X-coordinate. Unlike every other screen procedure, `WindMin` and `WindMax` assume that screen coordinates range from (0,0) to (79,24). These variables can be used as follows:

```
Left    := Lo( WindMin ) + 1;    { Upper left X-coordinate  }
Top     := Hi( WindMin ) + 1;    { Upper left Y-coordinate  }
Right   := Lo( WindMax ) + 1;    { Lower right X-coordinate }
Down    := Hi( WindMax ) + 1;    { Lower right Y-coordinate }
Width   := Right - Left + 1;
Height  := Bottom - Top + 1;
Area    := Width * Height;
```

Using a Single Window

The SCR3 program (listing 10.15) fills the screen with asterisks, opens a window in the center of the screen, then displays the attention-getting message `ERROR` in blinking red letters, as shown in figure 10.8.

Listing 10.15

```
program Scr3;
uses Crt;
var
   Row, Column : byte;
begin
   ClrScr;
   for Column := 1 to 80 do
      for Row := 1 to 23 do begin
         GotoXY( Column, Row );
         TextColor( Random( 6 ) + 1 );
         write( '*' );
      end;
   Window( 25, 8, 55, 16 );
   ClrScr;
   GotoXY( 13, 5 );
   TextColor( Red + Blink );
   write( 'ERROR' );
end.
```

Fig. 10.8. *Output produced by the SCR3 program.*

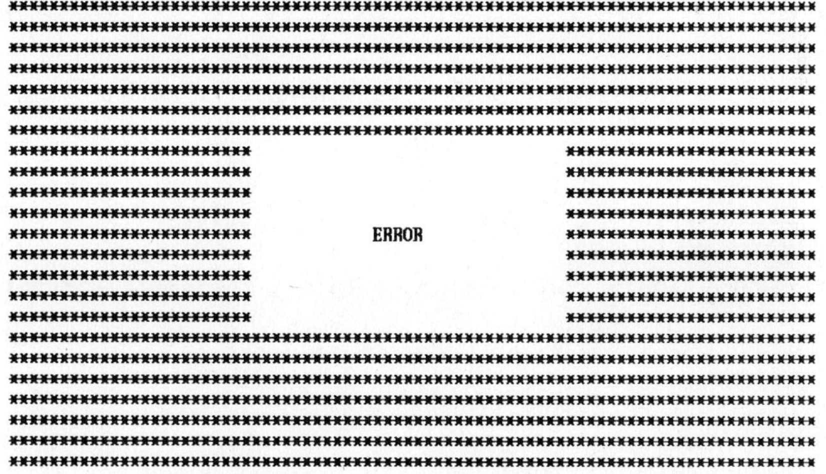

Notice that the second `ClrScr` and `GotoXY` calls affect only the current window, not the entire screen. The window itself effectively becomes the new screen.

Saving and Restoring Multiple Windows

In most windowing applications, a window appears, characters are displayed, input is received, and the window closes, leaving no trace of its presence. Turbo Pascal makes generating and using a window easy. It does not, however, provide a direct way to save the contents of a screen before a window is called, nor does it offer an easy way to restore the screen to its original image after the window is no longer needed.

The WIND2 program in listing 10.16 introduces the `OpenWindow` and `CloseWindow` procedures. `OpenWindow` saves the original screen image before it executes the call to the `Window` procedure. `CloseWindow` closes the most recently opened window and restores the prior screen image. `OpenWindow` and `CloseWindow` allow up to ten windows to be opened at the same time.

Listing 10.16

```
program Wind2;
uses Crt;
type
   ScreenImage   = array [ 0..1999 ] of word;
   FrameRec      = record
               UpperLeft,
               LowerRight    : word;
               ScreenMemory  : ScreenImage;
            end;
var
   SnapShot      : ^ScreenImage;
   FrameStore    : array [ 1..10 ] of ^FrameRec;
   WindowNumber  : byte;
procedure OpenWindow( UpLeftX, UpLeftY, LoRightX, LoRightY : byte );
begin
   WindowNumber := WindowNumber + 1;
   New( FrameStore[ WindowNumber ] );
   with FrameStore[ WindowNumber ]^ do begin
      ScreenMemory := SnapShot^;
      UpperLeft    := WindMin;
      LowerRight   := WindMax;
   end;
```

```
   Window( UpLeftX, UpLeftY, LoRightX, LoRightY );
end;
procedure CloseWindow;
begin
   with FrameStore[ WindowNumber ]^ do begin
      SnapShot^ := ScreenMemory;
      Window( (Lo(UpperLeft)+1),  (Hi(UpperLeft)+1),
           (Lo(LowerRight)+1), (Hi(LowerRight)+1) );
   end;
   Dispose( FrameStore[ WindowNumber ] );
   WindowNumber := WindowNumber - 1;
end;
procedure FillScreen( Filler : byte );
var
   Row, Column : byte;
begin
   ClrScr;
   if Odd( Filler ) then begin
      TextBackground( White );
      TextColor( Black );
   end;
   for Column := 0 to Lo( WindMax ) - Lo( WindMin ) do
      for Row := 0 to Hi( WindMax ) - Hi( WindMin ) do
      write( Filler );
   NormVideo;
end;
begin
   SnapShot := Ptr( $B800, $0000 );    { Set to $B000 if monochrome }
   WindowNumber := 0;
   OpenWindow( 30, 5, 50, 18 );
   FillScreen( 2 );
   OpenWindow( 10, 10, 65, 15 );
   FillScreen( 3 );
   OpenWindow( 15, 12, 35, 22 );
   FillScreen( 4 );
   GotoXY( 1, 1 ); write( 'Hit enter... ' ); Readln;
   CloseWindow;
   GotoXY( 1, 1 ); write( 'Hit enter... ' ); Readln;
   CloseWindow;
   GotoXY( 1, 1 ); write( 'Hit enter... ' ); Readln;
   CloseWindow;
end.
```

The `FillScreen` procedure shows the location and shape of each window by filling it with a number, as shown in figure 10.9.

Fig. 10.9. Output produced by the WIND2 program.

The `OpenWindow` procedure dynamically stores a record containing the current screen image and the current `WindMin` and `WindMax` variables. `CloseWindow` retrieves that record, restores the screen, then uses `WindMin` and `WindMax` to call `Window` and reset the screen size. More efficiently written procedures might save and restore only the area of the window.

Notice that the first line in the main body of the program identifies the start of video memory. Incorporating a procedure such as `SetVideoSegment` (shown in the MODE1A program in listing 10.11) would enable WIND2 to work on all PC types. Instead of the command

```
SnapShot := Ptr( $B800, $0000 );    { Set to $B000 if monochrome }
```

you could use

```
SnapShot := Ptr( VideoSegment, $0000 );
```

Summary

In this chapter, you learned how Turbo Pascal programs can manage the Monochrome Display Adapter (MDA) and the text display modes of the various color and graphics adapter boards.

You learned about the screen memory of your PC, and you saw how any data moved to this region is automatically displayed on the screen. You learned that each cursor position is defined by a word of memory. The first byte of this word is the ASCII character to be displayed, and the second byte is the attribute of the display. Individual bits in the attribute byte determine the foreground and background colors, the intensity, and whether the character will blink. You learned about the Turbo Pascal procedures that control color and intensity.

You learned that when the Crt standard unit is included with a program, Turbo automatically performs its screen output with the faster direct memory method. You learned how to disable direct output to video memory, and you learned how to control "snow."

You learned how to use screen positioning and line control routines, and how to locate the X- and Y-coordinates of the cursor.

You learned how to use windows, and you saw how multiple windows can be managed in Turbo Pascal.

CHAPTER 11

Graphics Display

No matter how many rows and columns of numbers your programs produce, numeric amounts always tend to be regarded as *data*. It is not until patterns emerge and relationships are perceived that data becomes *information*.

Probably the most powerful visual method of projecting information is graphics. A single graphic image can provide more information in one glance than entire libraries of data. Scientists and engineers use graphics to understand the meaning of their experiments. Business people use graphics to gain quick insight into financial trends. Magazine publishers and network news programs use graphics to compress long stories into succinct facts. A well-designed graph has impact, and the message it conveys is remembered because of it.

This chapter provides you with a solid foundation in the use of Turbo Pascal graphics routines.

The Graphics Screen

The default text screen consists of a rectangle of 25 rows of 80 characters. If you stare closely at one of the characters, you will notice that it consists of its own rectangular pattern of dots. Each of these dots is called a *pixel*, short for picture element. The monochrome screen contains 252,000 pixels, densely packed in 350 lines of 720 columns.

In text mode, these pixels can be used in only 2000 discrete blocks, 9 pixels wide by 14 pixels high. Each block contains one of the 256 ASCII characters. The pattern is controlled by PC hardware that automatically turns each pixel on or off depending on the ASCII value in the corresponding screen memory address. Other characteristics, such as color and intensity, are also determined for the entire block.

In graphics mode, each pixel can be individually traced, or *bit mapped*, to its own unique memory location and consequently can be directly controlled by your program.

The Borland Graphics Interface

In text mode, you can write ASCII characters directly to screen memory. If you try that in graphics mode, you are likely to get bizarre (but interesting) results. Special software is required to convert the images you want to display into the appropriate dots on the screen. This software is the Borland Graphics Interface, or BGI. Different graphics board manufacturers use various mapping techniques, so a different interface—provided in a file with the BGI extension—is used for your specific configuration.

Graphics Adapters

The BGI files available in Turbo Pascal are listed in table 11.1. Before you try to run any of the graphics routines in this book, make sure that the correct interface file for your graphics adapter is available to the Turbo Pascal compiler.

Table 11.1. *Graphics Adapter Driver Files*

Name	*Driver*
Color Graphics Adapter	CGA.BGI
MultiColor Graphics Array	CGA.BGI
Enhanced Graphics Adapter	EGAVGA.BGI
Video Graphics Array	EGAVGA.BGI
Hercules Monochrome Graphics	HERC.BGI
AT&T 400 Line Graphics	ATT.BGI
IBM PC 3270 Graphics	PC3270.BGI
IBM 8514 Graphics	IBM8514.BGI

A BGI file is commonly called a *driver*, because it is, technically, a device driver for the graphics display. Each vendor's product is driven by a different set of software signals. A device driver converts Turbo Pascal commands into instructions that can be understood by the graphics hardware.

Graphics Resolution and Modes

The *resolution* of a screen is determined by the number of pixels it contains. The greater the resolution, the cleaner and crisper the display. You see a consequence of poor resolution every day: newspaper photographs are notoriously "grainy" compared to the pictures you take with your own camera. It is natural, then, that computer users demand new, higher resolution graphics adapters.

The PC needs only 4000 bytes to define the contents of a text screen completely—one character byte and one attribute byte for each of the 2000 possible cursor positions. Graphics screens, because of their greater need for detail, are allocated 16K bytes of memory. Even this fourfold increase provides only about 130,000 bits, considerably fewer than the 252,000 pixels available in text mode.

Your PC sidesteps this problem in three ways:

1. Most graphics adapters use fewer pixels than a monochrome screen. For example, one of the most popular graphics adapters (and the only one supported by the earlier versions of Turbo Pascal) is the Color Graphics Adapter (CGA). Normally, CGA offers 200 rows of pixels, with each row consisting of only 320 columns of pixels. A quick calculation reveals that such a screen contains 64,000 pixels—only a quarter of those in text mode. Even in high-resolution mode, a CGA screen is arranged in a 640 × 200 pattern—still only half the number of a text display.

2. Graphics adapters contain memory, which reduces the burden on the PC. But it also makes it impossible to write directly to video memory—one of the functions of the Borland Graphics Interface.

3. Most graphics adapters offer fewer colors than the 16 found in text mode. For example, the high-resolution CGA screen can draw in only 2 colors.

The resolution of a screen together with the number of available colors and memory pages (defined later) are described by the *mode* of the graphics adapter. Graphics modes for each driver are compared in table 11.2.

Table 11.2. Turbo Pascal Graphics Drivers and Modes

Graphics adapter	*Graphics driver*	*Mode name*	*Value*	*Resolution (column × row)*	*Palette*	*Pages*
CGA	CGA.BGI	CGAC0	0	320 × 200	C0	1
		CGAC1	1	320 × 200	C1	1
		CGAC2	2	320 × 200	C2	1
		CGAC3	3	320 × 200	C3	1
		CGAHi	4	640 × 200	2 colors	1
MCGA	CGA.BGI	MCGAC0	0	320 × 200	C0	1
		MCGAC1	1	320 × 200	C1	1
		MCGAC2	2	320 × 200	C2	1
		MCGAC3	3	320 × 200	C3	1
		MCGAMed	4	640 × 200	2 colors	1
		MCGAHi	5	640 × 480	2 colors	1
EGA	EGAVGA.BGI	EGALo	0	640 × 200	16 colors	4
		EGAHi	1	640 × 350	16 colors	2
		EGA64Lo	0	640 × 200	16 colors	1
		EGA64Hi	1	640 × 350	4 colors	1
		EGAMonoHi	3	640 × 350	2 colors	1*
		EGAMonoHi	3	640 × 350	2 colors	2†
Hercules	HERC.BGI	HercMonoHi	0	720 × 348	2 colors	2
AT&T	ATT.BGI	ATT400C0	0	320 × 200	C0	1
		ATT400C1	1	320 × 200	C1	1
		ATT400C2	2	320 × 200	C2	1
		ATT400C3	3	320 × 200	C3	1
		ATT400Med	4	640 × 200	2 colors	1
		ATT400Hi	5	640 × 400	2 colors	1
VGA	EGAVGA.BGI	VGALo	0	640 × 200	16 colors	4
		VGAMed	1	640 × 350	16 colors	2
		VGAHi	2	640 × 480	16 colors	1
3270 PC	PC3270.BGI	PC3270Hi	0	720 × 350	2 colors	1
IBM 8514	IBM8514.BGI	IBM8514LO	0	640 × 480	256 colors	1
		IBM8514HI	1	1024 × 768	256 colors	1

* 1 page if the graphics board contains 64K of memory.
† 2 pages if the graphics board contains 256K of memory.

The Palette column identifies the colors available in each mode. Each entry in the column is either a specified number of colors or a *C* followed by an integer in the range 0 through 3. These integers identify a palette—a set of three colors, plus the background color. The colors in each palette are listed in table 11.3.

Table 11.3. *Turbo Pascal CGA, MCGA, and AT&T Graphics Palettes*

Palette	*Color 0*	*Color 1*	*Color 2*	*Color 3*
C0	Background	LightGreen	LightRed	Yellow
C1	Background	LightCyan	LightMagenta	White
C2	Background	Green	Red	Brown
C3	Background	Cyan	Magenta	LightGray

Using the background color is like writing with an empty pen; whatever you draw is invisible. Note that the background color is always included in every total. As a result, each entry described as *2 colors* is really monochrome.

A Note on Mode
Unfortunately, the word *mode* is a bit overused. For the remainder of this chapter, unless I specifically refer to text mode or graphics mode, the word *mode* is used solely to indicate a resolution, color, and page count option of a graphics adapter. For example, the CGA offers five modes. Each mode can be referenced by an integer in the range 0 through 4 or by one of the predefined constants CGAC0, CGAC1, CGAC2, CGAC3, or CGAHi.

The Coordinate System

Just as in text mode, every pixel on the graphics screen is referenced with an (X, Y) coordinate system. The upper left corner's coordinates are (0, 0), and the lower right corner's coordinates can be obtained from the screen resolution. For example, a CGA in mode CGAC0 has (319, 199) for its lower right corner. The center of the same screen would be addressed as (160, 100).

The Current Pointer

In text mode, the cursor is always visible. Unless changed with a `GotoXY` statement, the cursor always comes to rest one space to the right of the last position written. If the last write was in column 80, the cursor would advance to the first position of the following line. If the last referenced position was the 80th column of the 25th line, the entire screen would scroll up one line, and the cursor would appear in the first column of the 25th line.

Both the cursor's appearance and its tendency to wrap around characters from the end of a line to the next line are directly controlled by DOS or, alternatively, by the software routines that emulate DOS in the Crt unit. Graphics mode is different. Because the screen image is under control of the circuitry on the graphics board itself, DOS rules do not apply.

The cursor on the text screen references the entire 9 × 14 pixel block. In graphics mode, only a single pixel is referenced at any one time. The location of this pixel is called the *current pointer*, or *CP*. Its position is directly over the last referenced character, not one space beyond as it is in text mode. Because a blinking CP would distort the graphics image, the CP is not visible on the screen.

Entering and Exiting Graphics

When you include the Crt unit in your program, all `Write` and `Writeln` statements automatically bypass DOS and use the faster direct video memory routines. The Graph unit operates differently. Even if you include the Graph unit in your program, Turbo Pascal still assumes that the default mode is text rather than graphics.

There is a good reason for this. Although you can write programs specifically to display graphics images, most applications use graphics as a supplement rather than as an end in itself. Spreadsheets and database managers, for example, may switch to graphics mode temporarily, but the majority of their efforts rely on text displays. In general, most interactive user interfaces are programmed in text mode.

In addition, graphics displays tend to be considerably slower than text displays. On some systems, the delay is hardly noticeable, but on others, the delay can irritate even the most patient user. You can avoid this problem by switching back to text mode when you do not use graphics.

Initializing Graphics Mode

You enter graphics mode by calling the InitGraph procedure:

```
procedure InitGraph( var GraphDriver   : integer;
                     var GraphMode     : integer;
                         PathToDriver  : String );
```

The GraphDriver and GraphMode parameters identify the graphics driver and mode, respectively. PathToDriver holds the name of the subdirectory that contains the graphics drivers; simply use a null string if the files are in the current directory.

There are two ways to use InitGraph:

1. If you set GraphDriver to 0 before calling InitGraph, Turbo Pascal will initialize graphics using the defaults for your machine.

   ```
   GraphDriver := Detect;
   InitGraph( GraphDriver, GraphMode, 'C:\TP' );
   ```

   The predefined constant Detect (which is equal to 0) is used as the starting value for GraphDriver when InitGraph is first called. Because GraphDriver is a variable parameter, it cannot directly accept a constant parameter.

   After InitGraph ends, GraphDriver contains a value corresponding to the graphics adapter Turbo detected, and GraphMode contains a value corresponding to what Turbo believes is the adapter's optimal mode. The values returned in the GraphDriver parameter can be compared to the predefined constants in table 11.4. The values for GraphMode are the same as those in table 11.2. For example, if your PC is equipped with the Color Graphics Adapter, GraphDriver will be equal to CGA, and GraphMode may equal CGAHi.

2. It is highly unlikely that your PC contains more than one graphics adapter, but some PCs and some adapters may not be properly detected. To initialize graphics using a specific driver and mode, choose a valid combination of values for the GraphDriver and GraphMode parameters before you call InitGraph.

   ```
   GraphDriver := CGA;
   GraphMode := CGAHi;
   InitGraph( GraphDriver, GraphMode, 'C:\TP' );
   ```

   If InitGraph is successful, it loads the BGI driver file into heap memory, enters graphics mode, initializes all graphics settings to their defaults, and clears the screen.

Table 11.4. Graphics Drivers

Driver	*Value*
Detect	0
CGA	1
MCG	2
EGA	3
EGA64	4
EGAMono	5
IBM8514	6
HercMono	7
ATT400	8
VGA	9
PC3270	10

These examples, as well as all other examples in this book, assume that the graphics files reside in the C:\TP\BGI directory.

Detecting Graphics Hardware

If you are curious about the configuration of your PC, you can call `InitGraph` to learn which graphics adapter is installed and which mode Turbo Pascal believes is optimal. Unfortunately, one of the effects of `InitGraph` is to convert the PC to graphics mode. A more direct approach is to use the `DetectGraph` procedure:

```
procedure DetectGraph( var GraphDriver, GraphMode : integer );
```

`DetectGraph` is the procedure `InitGraph` uses when you call it with a `GraphDriver` parameter of 0. By calling `DetectGraph` directly, you are assured of obtaining the same values. The `DetectGraph` procedure is demonstrated in the GRAFINFO program in listing 11.1.

Listing 11.1

```
program GrafInfo;
uses Graph;
var
   GraphDriver, GraphMode : integer;
begin
   DetectGraph( GraphDriver, GraphMode );
   writeln( GraphDriver:8, GraphMode:8 )
end.
```

If you run the GRAFINFO program on a COMPAQ PLUS, it reveals a driver of 1 and a mode of 4. Table 11.4 shows that the graphics adapter is a CGA. Table 11.2 reveals that CGA mode 4 (CGAHi) is high resolution, with a 640 × 200 pixel screen.

If `DetectGraph` does not find a graphics adapter, `GraphDriver` returns a value of –2.

Detecting Graphics Modes

As you have seen, graphics adapters usually offer more than one mode. Although the `DetectGraph` procedure recommends an optimal mode, several other Turbo Pascal subroutines help you learn about other modes available for your adapter.

```
function GetDriverName : string;
function GetGraphMode : integer;
function GetMaxMode : integer;
function GetModeName( GraphMode : integer ) : string;
procedure GetModeRange( GraphDriver : integer;
                        var LoMode, HiMode : integer);
```

The `GetDriverName` function returns the name of the current driver. This function was not used in the GRAFINFO program because `GetDriverName` operates by accessing the currently loaded BGI file; therefore, it can run only when the graphics system is active.

`GetGraphMode` returns the number of the current mode, as given in table 11.2. It can be used as the parameter for `GetModeName`, which returns the name of a given mode.

Except for EGAMono, the currently loaded graphics driver has mode numbers ranging from 0 through `GetMaxMode`. The `GetModeRange` procedure returns the lowest and highest graphics modes for any given driver.

The GRFINFO2 program in listing 11.2 combines all of these routines into a display that could be used as a help screen or as part of a menu.

Listing 11.2

```
program GrfInfo2;
uses Graph;
var
   GraphDriver, GraphMode, Low, High, Driver : integer;
begin
   GraphDriver := Detect;
   InitGraph( GraphDriver, GraphMode, 'C:\TP' );
   GetModeRange( GraphDriver, Low, High );
   writeln( 'Currently using the ', GetDriverName, ' driver ',
            'in mode ', GetModeName( GetGraphMode ) );
   writeln;
   writeln( '   Lowest mode is  ', Low );
   writeln( '   Highest mode is ', High );
   writeln;
   writeln;
   writeln( 'Other modes supported by the ', GetDriverName,
            ' driver are:' );
   writeln;
   for Driver := 0 to GetMaxMode do
      writeln( '    ', GetModeName( Driver ) );
   readln;          { Press Enter to continue }
   CloseGraph;
end.
```

When GRFINFO2 executes on a COMPAQ PLUS, it produces the output shown in figure 11.1.

The Run/User Command (Alt-F5)
You can use the Run/User screen menu command (the Alt-F5 hot key) to examine output in text mode only. Graphics images are cleared by the `CloseGraph` procedure when graphics mode ends and text mode is restored. Consequently, most of the programs in this chapter use the `readln` procedure to retain the graphics display while waiting for the Enter key to be pressed.

Fig. 11.1. Output produced by the GRFINFO2 program.

```
Currently using the CGA driver in mode 640 x 200 CGA

   Lowest mode is  0
   Highest mode is 4

Other modes supported by the CGA driver are:

   320 x 200 CGA C0
   320 x 200 CGA C1
   320 x 200 CGA C2
   320 x 200 CGA C3
   640 x 200 CGA
```

Detecting the Size of the Screen

Unless you can guarantee that your programs will always run in a specific mode on a specific graphics adapter, you should avoid writing code that assumes a constant resolution. Of course, you could maintain a table of graphics drivers, modes, and screen sizes—and continue to update it as new products are developed—but Turbo Pascal provides a simpler method:

```
function  GetMaxX : integer;
function  GetMaxY : integer;
```

The `GetMaxX` and `GetMaxY` functions return the number of the pixel in the extreme right column and bottom row, respectively. For example, on a COMPAQ PLUS, which has a high-resolution 640 × 200 CGA, `GetMaxX` returns 639 and `GetMaxY` returns 199.

Because the upper left corner of the display is (0, 0) and the bottom right corner is (`GetMaxX`, `GetMaxY`), the code that locates the center of any screen is given by the coordinates:

```
Xmidpoint := GetMaxX div 2;
Ymidpoint := GetMaxY div 2;
```

Using this technique, the BALLOON program from Chapter 7 can be rewritten as shown in listing 11.3.

Listing 11.3

```
program Balloon2;
uses Graph;
var
   Driver, Mode : integer;
   Xmidpoint, Ymidpoint, Radius : word;
begin
   Driver := Detect;
   InitGraph( Driver, Mode, 'C:\TP' );
   Xmidpoint := GetMaxX div 2;
   Ymidpoint := GetMaxY div 2;
   for Radius := 1 to GetMaxY div 4 do
      Circle( 250, 100, Radius );
   CloseGraph
end.
```

Note that even the maximum radius of the circle can be expressed in terms of `GetMaxY`.

Locating the Pointer Position on the Graphics Screen

Any time during a graphics session, you can locate the current pointer (CP) by using the `GetX` and `GetY` functions:

```
function  GetX : integer;
function  GetY : integer;
```

`GetX` and `GetY` return the X-coordinate and Y-coordinate, respectively. These functions are particularly useful because the CP in graphics mode is invisible, unlike the cursor in text mode.

Ending the Graphics Session

The `CloseGraph` procedure ends the graphics session. It frees the heap of the graphics driver and any buffers used by the graphics routines, and restores the screen to its original mode. If the screen was in text mode when `InitGraph` was called, the screen returns to text mode after `CloseGraph` is finished.

If you do not call `CloseGraph`, your program will still end normally, but your screen will remain in graphics mode. You will have to restore the text mode yourself, either by executing a DOS `MODE` command or by rebooting the PC.

Switching between Text and Graphics Modes

You will often develop programs that switch between text and graphics modes. Turbo Pascal provides the following routines to help you do this smoothly:

```
procedure RestoreCrtMode;
procedure SetGraphMode( Mode : integer );
```

`RestoreCrtMode` exits the graphics mode and restores the screen to its mode when `InitGraph` was invoked. The `SetGraphMode` procedure returns the system to graphics mode, resets all graphics settings to their defaults, and clears the screen. `SetGraphMode` can be used also while you are in a graphics session to change to a new mode.

Using `RestoreCrtMode` and `SetGraphMode` is preferable to using a combination of `CloseGraph` and `InitGraph`. `RestoreCrtMode` does not clear the BGI driver from memory; therefore, you can avoid the disk file loading process performed by `InitGraph`.

The SWITCH program in listing 11.4 demonstrates how you can use `RestoreCrtMode` and `SetGraphMode`.

Listing 11.4

```
program Switch;
uses Crt, Graph;
var
   Driver, Mode : integer;
   Radius, CenterX, CenterY : word;
```

continues

Listing 11.4 continued

```
begin
   ClrScr;
   write( 'Press ENTER to see a hole' );
   readln;
   Driver := Detect;
   InitGraph( Driver, Mode, 'C:\TP' );
   CenterX := GetMaxX div 2;
   CenterY := GetMaxY div 2;
   Circle( CenterX, CenterY, CenterY );
   OutText( 'Press ENTER' );
   readln;
   RestoreCrtMode;
   write( 'Press ENTER to see it close' );
   readln;
   SetGraphMode( Mode );
   for Radius := CenterY downto 1 do
      Circle( CenterX, CenterY, Radius );
   OutText( 'Press ENTER to end the program' );
   readln;
   CloseGraph;
end.
```

SWITCH alternates modes—from text to graphics, from graphics to text, and finally from text to graphics. You might want to experiment by replacing `RestoreCrtMode` and `SetGraphMode` with `CloseGraph` and `InitGraph`; if you do, you may notice a reduction in performance.

Handling Graphics Errors

Graphics are usually a supporting portion of an application, so Turbo Pascal does not allow run-time graphics errors to end a program. Instead, a subroutine simply fails to perform; it sets an internal variable to a value that indicates the nature of the error, but otherwise the program proceeds normally.

This internal value can be examined with the `GraphResult` function:

```
function  GraphResult : integer;
```

You can interpret the error codes returned by `GraphResult` according to the values in table 11.5. Note that the error code is reset to 0 after the call.

Table 11.5. GraphResult Error Codes

Constant name	*Error code*	*Error**
`grOk`	0	No error
`grNoInitGraph`	–1	(BGI) graphics not installed
`grNotDetected`	–2	Graphics hardware not detected
`grFileNotFound`	–3	Device driver file not found ( )
`grInvalidDriver`	–4	Invalid device driver file ( )
`grNoLoadMem`	–5	Not enough memory to load driver
`grNoScanMem`	–6	Out of memory in scan fill
`grNoFloodMem`	–7	Out of memory in flood fill
`grFontNotFound`	–8	Font file not found ( )
`grNoFontMem`	–9	Not enough memory to load font
`grInvalidMode`	–10	Invalid graphics mode for selected driver
`grError`	–11	Graphics error
`grIOerror`	–12	Graphics I/O error
`grInvalidFont`	–13	Invalid font file ( )
`grInvalidFontNum`	–14	Invalid font number

*In the actual error message, the name of the file that provoked the error appears in the parentheses.

The Constant name column in the table contains the names of predefined constants provided by Turbo Pascal. A typical use of `GraphResult` follows:

```
InitGraph( GraphDriver, GraphMode, 'C:\TP' );
if GraphResult <> grOK then
   Halt( 1 );
```

For each valid `ErrorCode`, the `GraphErrorMsg` function

```
function  GraphErrorMsg( ErrorCode : integer ) : String;
```

returns an English error message corresponding to that in table 11.5. (In a real error message, the parentheses shown in the table would hold the name of the file that provoked the error.) With `GraphErrorMsg`, you can include more informative error messages.

```
InitGraph( GraphDriver, GraphMode, 'C:\TP' );
GraphError := GraphResult; { Save the value, because }
                           { GraphResult resets to zero }
                           { after each call }
if GraphError <> grOK then begin
   writeln ( GraphErrorMsg( GraphError ));
   Halt( 1 );
end;
```

You can list all graphics error descriptions by using the GRAPHERR program in listing 11.5.

Listing 11.5

```
program GraphErr;
uses Graph;
var
   ErrorNumber : integer;
begin
   for ErrorNumber := 0 downto -14 do
      writeln( ErrorNumber:8, '     ', GraphErrorMsg( ErrorNumber ) );
end.
```

Calling *GraphResult*

You can call `GraphResult` after using any of the following routines: `Bar`, `Bar3D`, `ClearViewPort`, `CloseGraph`, `DetectGraph`, `DrawPoly`, `Fill-Poly`, `FloodFill`, `GetGraphMode`, `ImageSize`, `InitGraph`, `InstallUserDriver`, `InstallUserFont`, `PieSlice`, `RegisterBGIdriver`, `RegisterBGIfont`, `SetAllPalette`, `SetFillPattern`, `SetFillStyle`, `SetGraphBufSize`, `SetGraphMode`, `SetLineStyle`, `SetPalette`, `SetTextJustify`, and `SetTextStyle`. The examples in this book do not test for errors in order to present cleaner code, but your programs should check `GraphResult` after every critical command.

Plotting Individual Points

The most direct way of drawing graphics characters on the screen is to access individual pixels. Turbo Pascal provides the `PutPixel` and `GetPixel` subroutines for that purpose.

```
procedure PutPixel( X, Y : integer; Pixel : word );
function  GetPixel( X, Y : integer ) : word;
```

The `PutPixel` procedure paints the single pixel located at (X, Y) with the color specified by the `Pixel` parameter. The `GetPixel` function gets the color of the pixel located at (X, Y).

Colors are discussed in more detail later. For now, think of the colors as the same set of predefined constants and values discussed in the last chapter, repeated here in table 11.6.

Table 11.6. *Predefined Color Constants*

Name	*Value*
Black	0
Blue	1
Green	2
Cyan	3
Red	4
Magenta	5
Brown	6
LightGray	7
DarkGray	8
LightBlue	9
LightGreen	10
LightCyan	11
LightRed	12
LightMagenta	13
Yellow	14
White	15

PutPixel and GetPixel are demonstrated in the DNAHELIX program in listing 11.6.

Listing 11.6

```
program DNAhelix;
uses Graph;
var
   grDriver, grMode, Swing : integer;
   Width, Crest, Ypos, i : word;
begin
   grDriver := Detect;
   InitGraph( grDriver, grMode, 'C:\TP' );
   Ypos := GetMaxY div 2;
   Crest := GetMaxY div 8;
   Width := GetMaxX;
   for i := 0 to Width do begin
      Swing := Round( Crest * Sin( 10*Pi*i / Width ) );
      PutPixel( i, Ypos + Swing, i mod 15 );
      PutPixel( i, Ypos - Swing, (GetPixel( i, Ypos + Swing ) + 8 ) mod 15 );
   end;
   readln;
   CloseGraph;
end.
```

When DNAHELIX executes, it uses PutPixel to produce a string of multicolored pixels in the shape of a sine wave. As the sine wave moves across the screen, a second PutPixel call accesses the color of the pixel in the first wave by a call to GetPixel, then produces a mirror image shape in a different color, as shown in figure 11.2.

Line Routines

You could draw every graphics image by using a (rather large) number of PutPixel instructions. Fortunately, Turbo Pascal includes most fundamental shapes as standard features. This section discusses the various ways you can generate lines.

Fig. 11.2. Output produced by the DNAHELIX program.

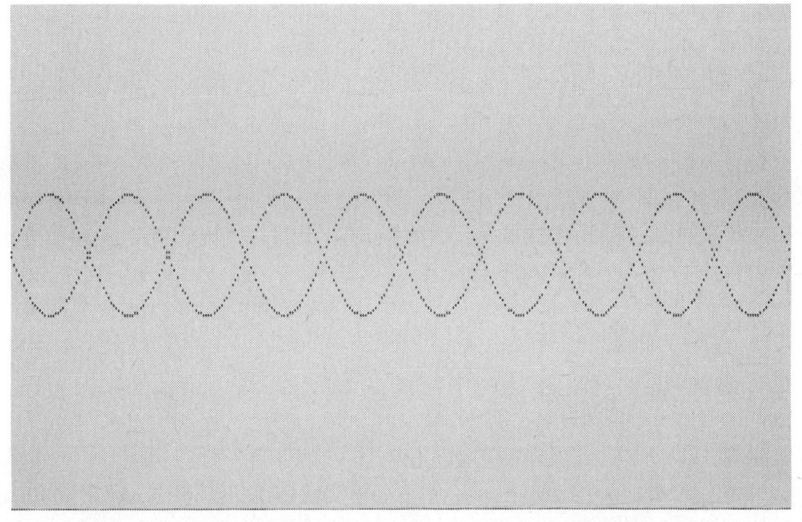

Drawing a Straight Line

Next to turning on a single pixel, drawing a line is the most intuitive process in graphics:

```
procedure Line( X1, Y1, X2, Y2 : integer );
```

The `Line` procedure draws a straight line from (X1, Y1) to (X2, Y2).

The TANLINES program in listing 11.7 uses a combination of `Line` instructions to draw four sets of tangents in a box.

Listing 11.7

```
program TanLines;
uses Graph;
var
   grDriver, grMode : integer;
   y, Ymax, Ymid : word;
```

continues

Listing 11.7 continued

```
begin
   grDriver := Detect;
   InitGraph( grDriver, grMode, 'C:\TP' );
   Ymax := GetMaxY;
   Ymid := Ymax div 2;
   for y := 1 to Ymid do begin
      Line( Ymid - Y, 0, 0, Y );               { Upper left }
      Line( Ymid + Y, 0, Ymax, Y );            { Upper right }
      Line( 0, Ymid + Y, Y, Ymax );            { Lower left }
      Line( Ymid + Y, Ymax, Ymax, Ymax - Y );  { Lower right }
   end;
   readln;
   CloseGraph;
end.
```

When TANLINES executes, it creates the illusion of an oval in silhouette, as shown in figure 11.3.

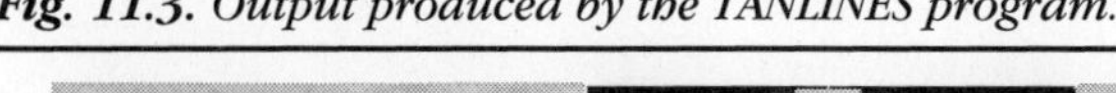

***Fig. 11.3.** Output produced by the TANLINES program.*

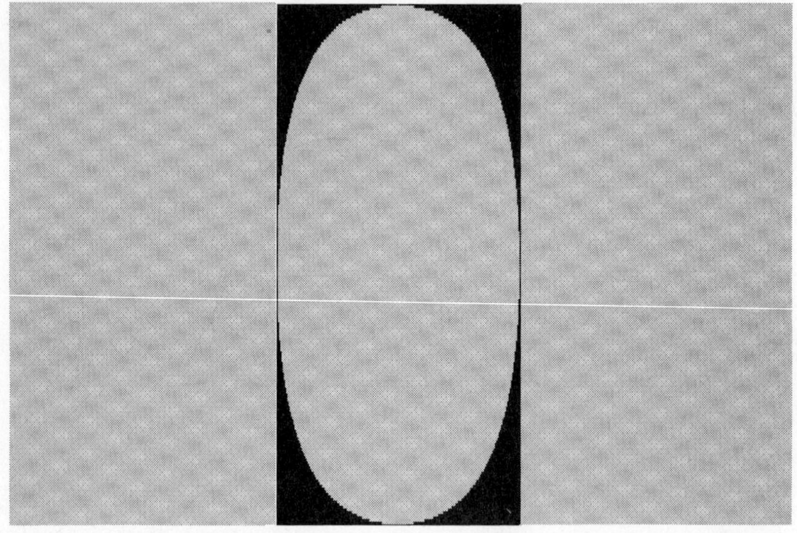

After you execute the procedure

```
Line( X1, Y1, X2, Y2 );
```

the current pointer is repositioned to the pixel at (X2, Y2). Now suppose that you want to draw a second line, as follows:

```
Line( X2, Y2, X3, Y3 );
```

Instead of having to specify the current pointer explicitly as the start of the line, you could use the simpler procedure

```
procedure LineTo( X, Y : integer );
```

`LineTo` draws a straight line from the current pointer to the pixel at (X, Y) and resets the current pointer to (X, Y). Therefore, the pairs of instructions

```
Line( X1, Y1, X2, Y2 );
Line( X2, Y2, X3, Y3 );
```

and

```
Line( X1, Y1, X2,  Y2 );
LineTo( X3, Y3 );
```

are equivalent, but the second pair operates slightly faster.

You can move the current pointer to any desired pixel with the following:

```
procedure MoveTo( X, Y : integer );
```

`MoveTo` moves the CP to (X, Y), but it has no visible impact on the screen. Consequently, the instructions:

```
Line( X1, Y1, X2, Y2 );
```

and

```
MoveTo( X1, Y1 );
LineTo( X2, Y2 );
```

are equivalent. This is demonstrated in the TANLINE2 program in listing 11.8, which is functionally identical to TANLINES.

Listing 11.8

```
program TanLine2;
uses Graph;
var
   grDriver, grMode : integer;
   Y, Ymax, Ymid : word;
```

continues

Listing 11.8 continued

```
begin
   grDriver := Detect;
   InitGraph( grDriver, grMode, 'C:\TP' );
   Ymax := GetMaxY;
   Ymid := Ymax div 2;
   for y := 1 to Ymid do begin
      MoveTo( Ymid - Y, 0 );      LineTo( 0, Y );              { Upper left  }
      MoveTo( Ymid + Y, 0 );      LineTo( Ymax, Y );           { Upper right }
      MoveTo( 0, Ymid + Y );      LineTo( Y, Ymax );           { Lower left  }
      MoveTo( Ymid + Y, Ymax );   LineTo( Ymax, Ymax - Y );    { Lower right }
   end;
   readln;
   CloseGraph;
end.
```

Drawing Relative Lines

The `MoveTo`, `Line`, and `LineTo` procedures are useful only when you know specific coordinates in advance. Frequently, it is easier to move or draw a line a *relative distance* from the current pointer.

```
procedure MoveRel( DX, DY : integer );
procedure LineRel( DX, DY : integer );
```

Remember that `GetX` and `GetY` return the X- and Y-coordinates of the current pointer, respectively. `MoveRel( DX, DY )` is equivalent to

```
MoveTo( GetX + DX, GetY + DY );
```

and

```
LineRel( DX, DY )
```

is equivalent to

```
LineTo( GetX + DX, GetY + DY );
```

The `LineRel` procedure is particularly useful for drawing shapes. For example, given a specific coordinate for one of the corners of a square, a hexagon, and an octagon, what are the coordinates of the remaining corners? The square is easy, but the other figures take some thought. Consider, though, that instead of identifying the *specific* coordinate of each corner, it might be easier to determine the *relative* coordinate. The SHAPES program in listing 11.9 uses relative movements to display a rectangle, a hexagon, and an octagon.

Listing 11.9

```
program Shapes;
uses Graph;
const
   S2 = 1.414;    { Square root of 2 }
   S3 = 1.732;    { Square root of 3 }
   DeltaX0 : array[ 1..4 ] of real = ( 2, 0, -2, 0 );
   DeltaY0 : array[ 1..4 ] of real = ( 0, 1, 0, -1 );
   DeltaX1 : array[ 1..6 ] of real = ( 2, 1, -1, -2, -1, 1 );
   DeltaY1 : array[ 1..6 ] of real = ( 0, S3/2, S3/2, 0, -S3/2, -S3/2 );
   DeltaX2 : array[ 1..8 ] of real = ( 2, S2, 0, -S2, -2, -S2, 0, S2 );
   DeltaY2 : array[ 1..8 ] of real = ( 0, S2/2, 1, S2/2, 0, -S2/2, -1, -S2/2 );
   Factor : integer = 30;    { Scaling factor }
var
   Height, Width : word;
   grDriver, grMode : integer;
   i : byte;
begin
   grDriver := Detect;
   InitGraph( grDriver, grMode, 'C:\TP' );
   Height := GetMaxY div 5;
   Width := GetMaxX div 7;
     {Display a rectangle}
   MoveTo( Width, Height );
   for i := 1 to 4 do
      LineRel( Round( Factor*DeltaX0[ i ] ), Round( Factor*DeltaY0[ i ] ) );
     {Display a hexagon}
   MoveTo( 3*Width, Height );
   for i := 1 to 6 do
      LineRel( Round( Factor*DeltaX1[ i ] ), Round( Factor*DeltaY1[ i ] ) );
     {Display an octagon}
   MoveTo( 5*Width, Height );
   for i := 1 to 8 do
      LineRel( Round( Factor*DeltaX2[ i ] ), Round( Factor*DeltaY2[ i ] ) );
   readln;
   CloseGraph;
end.
```

When SHAPES executes, it uses the values in the typed constant arrays to draw relative lines. Three figures are produced: a rectangle, a hexagon, and an octagon, as shown in figure 11.4.

***Fig. 11.4.** Output produced by the SHAPES program.*

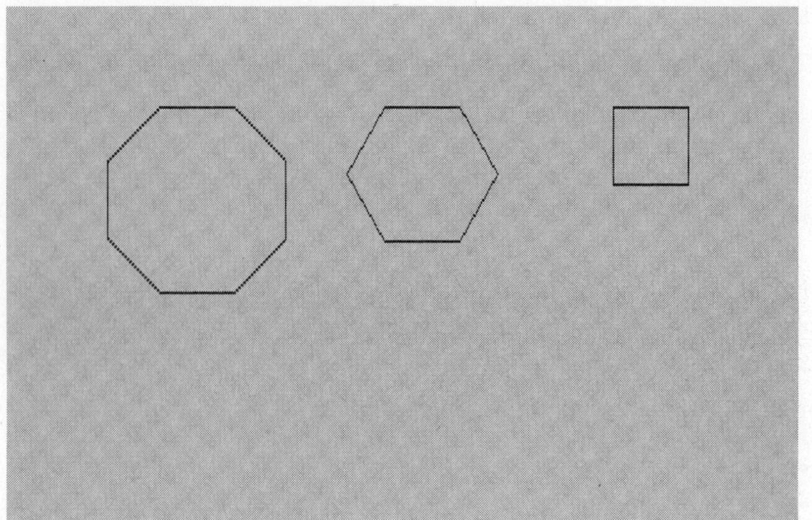

The figures (such as fig. 11.4) might not appear symmetrical on your screen. Unfortunately, the pixels on the typical graphics screen are not distributed in a perfect square. You will learn how to compensate for this deficiency later when the aspect ratio is discussed.

Line Styles

Having a choice of line style and thickness is especially useful when you want to identify or even emphasize one small feature of a larger image. This is the same technique employed in architectural drawings, in which a thick line indicates an outer wall, a thin line indicates an inner wall, and a dotted line shows the location of hidden pipes or wiring.

So far, all of our drawings have used solid lines. We can change that with the following routine:

```
procedure SetLineStyle( LineStyle : word;
                        Pattern   : word;
                        Thickness : word );
```

`SetLineStyle` enables you to modify both the width and style of your lines. The `LineStyle` parameter can have any one of the following values:

```
SolidLn    = 0;
DottedLn   = 1;
CenterLn   = 2;
DashedLn   = 3;
```

As the names of the constants imply, you can choose from solid, dotted, center-dotted, and dashed lines. The `Thickness` parameter enables you to draw each line with a normal or thick width.

```
NormWidth  = 1;
ThickWidth = 3;
```

If you are using one of the four standard `LineStyle` options, set `Pattern` equal to zero.

The GRID program in listing 11.10 shows every combination of style and width.

Listing 11.10

```
program Grid;
uses Graph;
var
   GraphDriver, GraphMode : integer;
   Swath, Xjump, Yjump, Thickness : word;
begin
   GraphDriver := Detect;
   InitGraph( GraphDriver, GraphMode, 'C:\TP' );
   Xjump := GetMaxX div 11;
   Yjump := GetMaxY div 11;
   for Swath := 0 to 10 do begin
      if Odd( Swath ) then Thickness := 1
                      else Thickness := 3;
      SetLineStyle( Swath mod 4, 0, Thickness );
      Line( Swath*Xjump, 0, Swath*Xjump, 10*Yjump );
      Line( 0, Swath*Yjump, 10*Xjump, Swath*Yjump );
   end;
   readln;
   CloseGraph;
end.
```

When GRID executes, it produces the display shown in figure 11.5.

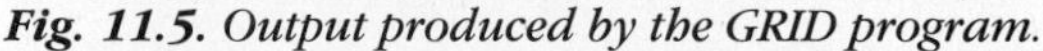

Fig. 11.5. Output produced by the GRID program.

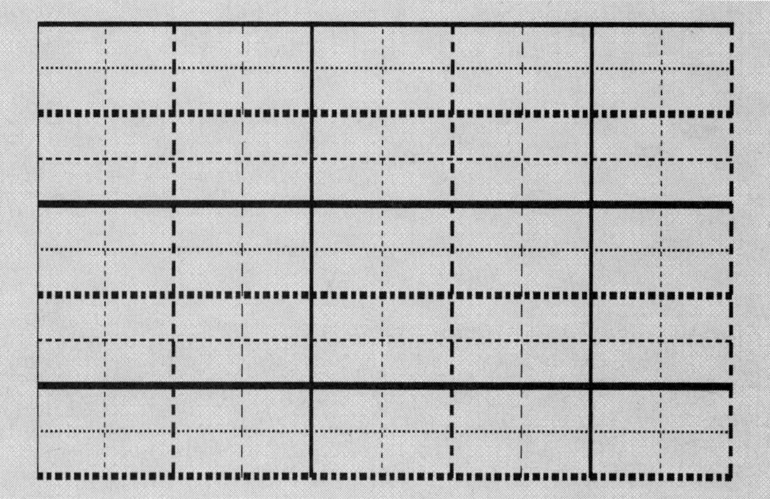

To increase your available options even more, you can define your own customized line styles. Just set the `LineStyle` parameter equal to the predefined constant `UserBitLn`, which equals 4, and select the pattern you want with the word-sized `Pattern` parameter. Think of the `Pattern` parameter as a series of 16 bits; a 1 indicates that the pixel is on, and a 0 indicates that the pixel is off, as follows:

```
Solid       1111111111111111   $FFFF
Dotted      1010101010101010   $AAAA
Big dashes  1111111100000000   $FF00
Empty       1000000000000001   $F001
```

Hence, if `LineStyle` has been set to the value of `UserBitLn`, setting `Pattern` to `$AAAA` results in dotted lines, and setting `Pattern` to `$FFFF` results in solid lines.

This feature is demonstrated in the GRID2 program in listing 11.11.

Listing 11.11

```
program Grid2;
uses Graph;
var
```

```
   GraphDriver, GraphMode : integer;
   Swath, Xmax, Yjump : word;
begin
   GraphDriver := Detect;
   InitGraph( GraphDriver, GraphMode, 'C:\TP' );
   Xmax  := GetMaxX;
   Yjump := GetMaxY div 17;
   for Swath := 1 to 16 do begin
      SetLineStyle( UserBitLn, ( 1 Shl Swath)-1, ThickWidth );
      Line( 0, Swath*Yjump, Xmax, Swath*Yjump );
   end;
   readln;
   CloseGraph;
end.
```

When GRID2 executes, it produces the image shown in figure 11.6.

Fig. 11.6. *Output produced by the GRID2 program.*

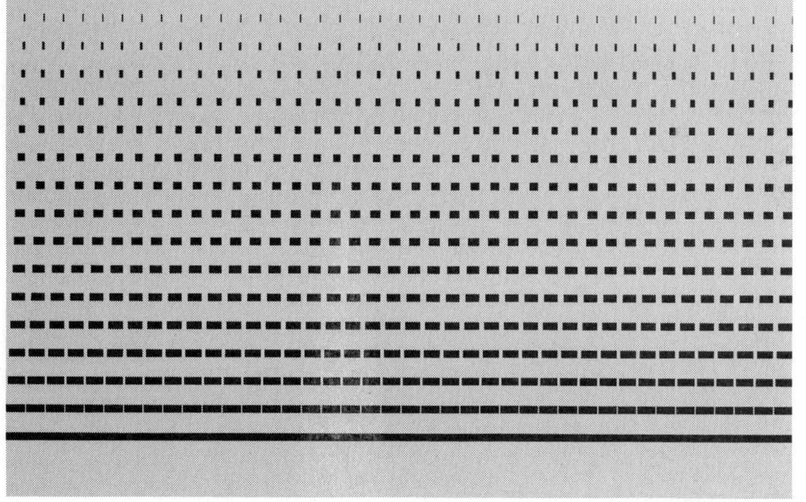

The `Pattern` parameter used by GRID2 takes the form:

```
( 1 Shl Swath )-1
```

which is equivalent to the expression:

$2^{swath} - 1$

As `Swath` varies from 1 to 16, the `SetLineStyle` procedure changes the value of the `Pattern` parameter by increasing the number of set bits, as follows:

$2^1 - 1 = 1$: 0000000000000001
$2^2 - 1 = 3$: 0000000000000011
$2^3 - 1 = 7$: 0000000000000111
.
.
.
$2^{16} - 1 = 65{,}535$: 1111111111111111

Consequently, the length of each dash increases as the lines go lower on the screen.

Saving and Restoring Line Styles

If you need to switch frequently between two line styles, it is useful to be able to save and restore the current line settings. You can do this with the `GetLineSettings` procedure:

```
procedure GetLineSettings( var LineInfo : LineSettingsType );
```

`GetLineSettings` returns the current line style, pattern, and thickness in the fields of the `LineInfo` record. `LineInfo` is declared as being of the predefined type `LineSettingsType`, as follows:

```
LineSettingsType = record
                       LineStyle : word;
                       Pattern   : word;
                       Thickness : word;
                   end;
```

Call `GetLineSettings` when you want to save the current line style, pattern, and thickness. Later, you can restore these settings with the call

```
with LineInfo do
   SetLineStyle( LineStyle, Pattern, Thickness );
```

Lines and Solids

With the `SetLineStyle` procedure, you can increase the contrast among a set of lines by varying their width and style. But what happens if a line is drawn over a solid? Normally, the two images merge, and the line is invisible until (and unless) it exits the solid at the other end. You can change this with the following procedure:

```
procedure SetWriteMode( WriteMode : integer );
```

`SetWriteMode` sets the writing mode for drawing lines. The writing mode, determined by the `WriteMode` parameter, determines how a line is physically displayed. `WriteMode` can assume either of the values:

```
CopyPut        = 0;
XORPut         = 1;
```

When `WriteMode` is set to `CopyPut`, the line is copied to the screen, the images blend together, and the line disappears. When `WriteMode` is set to `XORPut`, overlapping images are displayed by blanking the affected pixels; the line appears black against the background and can be distinguished easily.

`SetWriteMode` is best illustrated with an example. The LINETYPE program in listing 11.12 draws two lines through a solid rectangle—first with `WriteMode` set to `CopyPut`, and then with `WriteMode` set to `XORPut`.

Listing 11.12

```
program LineType;
uses Graph;
var
   Width, Height : word;
   GraphDriver, GraphMode : integer;
begin
   GraphDriver := Detect;
   InitGraph( GraphDriver, GraphMode, 'C:\TP' );
   Width := GetMaxX div 3;
   Height := GetMaxY div 4;
   Bar( 0, Height, GetMaxX, Height * 3 );
   SetWriteMode( CopyPut );
   Line( Width, 0, Width, GetMaxY );
   SetWriteMode( XORPut );
   Line( Width*2, 0, Width*2, GetMaxY );
   readln;
   CloseGraph;
end.
```

> **The *Bar* Procedure**
> You will be formally introduced to the `Bar` procedure shortly. For now, you have probably already figured out that its four parameters follow the (X1, Y1, X2, Y2) format. But instead of drawing a diagonal line, `Bar` uses the coordinates as the upper left and lower right corners of a solid rectangle.

When LINETYPE executes, it produces the drawing shown in figure 11.7. When `WriteMode` was set to `CopyPut`, the line wrote over whatever was on the screen. When `WriteMode` was set to `XORPut`, the screen was blank where the two shapes overlapped.

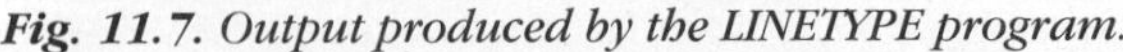

***Fig. 11.7.** Output produced by the LINETYPE program.*

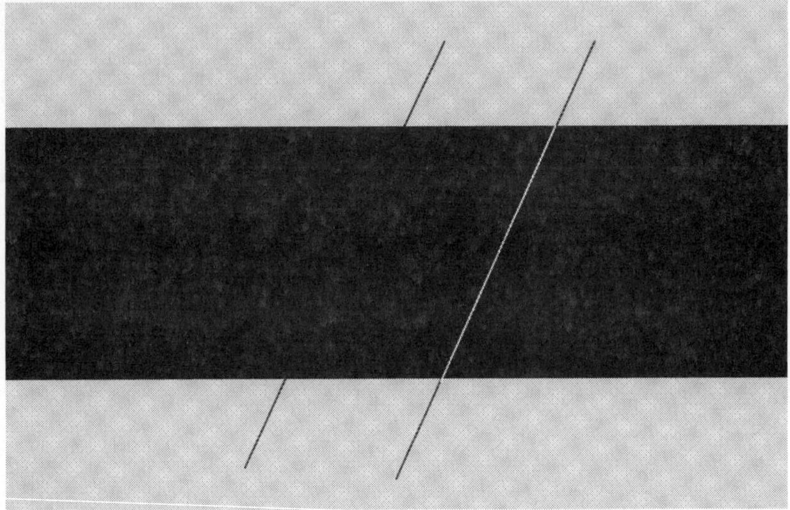

Viewports

In text mode, you could use the `Window` procedure to segregate a small region of the screen. Every subsequent screen instruction—except for another call to Window—was made relative to that region. Graphics mode has something similar: the viewport. This section discusses how to create—and manipulate—viewports.

Creating the Viewport

A graphics viewport is created with the `SetViewPort` procedure:

```
procedure SetViewPort( X1, Y1, X2, Y2 : integer; Clip : boolean );
```

The upper left corner is given by (X1, Y1) and the lower right corner by (X2, Y2). The X1-coordinate must be greater than or equal to 0 and less than or equal to X2. Similarly, the Y1-coordinate must be greater than or equal to 0 and less than or equal to Y2.

If the `Clip` parameter is set to `True`, you can output only to the area inside the viewport. This restriction is called *clipping*. If the `Clip` parameter is set to `False`, no such restriction applies; you can output anywhere on the screen. Instead of using `True` or `False` for the `Clip` parameter, Turbo Pascal provides the following predefined constants:

```
ClipOn  = True;
ClipOff = False;
```

After `SetViewPort` establishes a viewport, the upper left corner of the viewport becomes the new coordinate (0, 0), as shown in figure 11.8.

All graphics screen commands—except for another call to `SetViewPort`—are relative to the viewport itself. The VIEWER program in listing 11.13 demonstrates this feature.

Listing 11.13

```
program Viewer;
uses Graph;
var
   GraphDriver, GraphMode : integer;
begin
   GraphDriver := Detect;
   InitGraph( GraphDriver, GraphMode, 'C:\TP' );
   SetViewPort( GetMaxX div 2,  { These lines reset the upper left of }
                GetMaxY div 2,  { the viewport to the center of the screen }
                GetMaxX, GetMaxY, ClipOff );
   Circle( 0, 0, GetMaxY div 4 );  { This circle will appear in }
                                   { the center of the screen   }
   readln;
   CloseGraph;
end.
```

Fig. 11.8. Viewport coordinates before and after a call to `SetViewPort`.

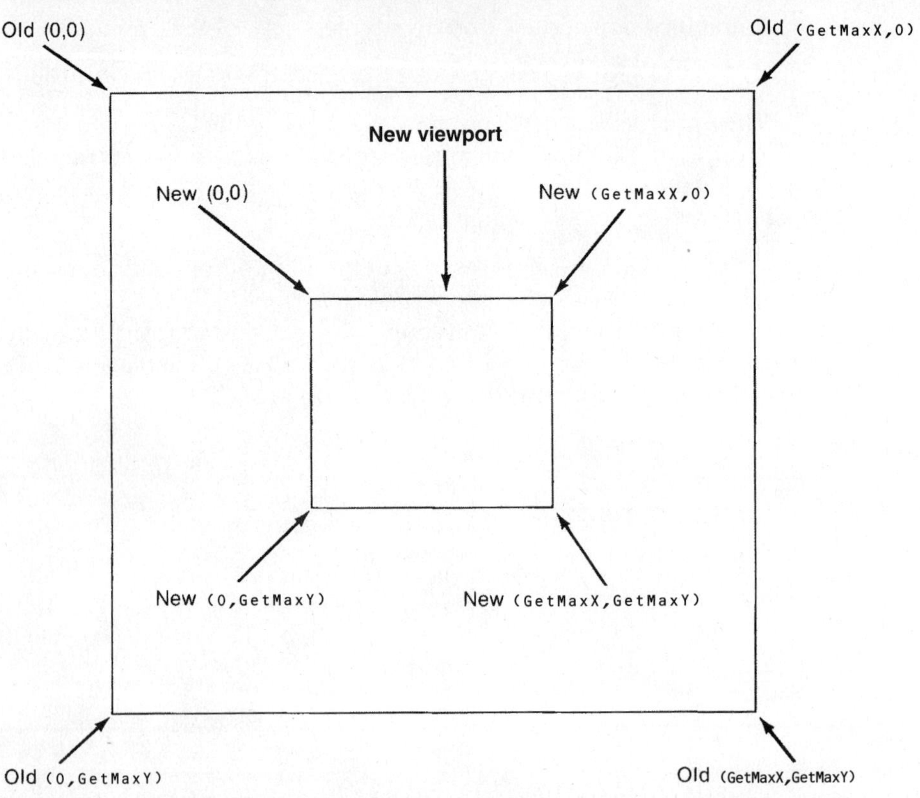

VIEWER resets the viewport to the lower right corner of the screen. As a result, the (0, 0) coordinate is repositioned to the center of the display. When the `Circle` procedure is called, the circle—centered on (0, 0)—appears in the middle of the screen.

The effect of clipping can be seen in the CLIP program in listing 11.14.

Listing 11.14

```
program Clip;
uses Graph;
var
   Height, Width : word;
   GraphDriver, GraphMode : integer;
begin
```

```
   GraphDriver := Detect;
   InitGraph( GraphDriver, GraphMode, 'C:\TP' );
   Height := GetMaxY div 5;
   Width := GetMaxX div 5;
   Rectangle( Width, Height, Width*2, Height*3 );
   SetViewPort( Width, Height, Width*2, Height*3, ClipOn );
   Line( 0, Height, GetMaxX, 0 );
   SetViewPort( 0, 0, GetMaxX, GetMaxY, ClipOff );   { Resets the screen }
   Rectangle( Width*3, Height, Width*4, Height*3 );
   SetViewPort( Width*3, Height, Width*4, Height*3, ClipOff );
   Line( 0, Height, GetMaxX, 0 );
   SetViewPort( 0, 0, GetMaxX, GetMaxY, ClipOff );   { Resets the screen }
   OutTextXY( Width, Height*4, 'CLIPPING IS ON' );
   OutTextXY( Width*3, Height*4, 'CLIPPING IS OFF' );
   readln;
   CloseGraph;
end.
```

When CLIP executes, it creates two viewports and draws two lines, producing the diagram shown in figure 11.9. Both lines start within a viewport and end outside it. When clipping is on, the line is confined to the viewport. When clipping is off, no such restriction applies. Note that the calls to `SetViewPort` use coordinates relative to the entire screen, while the coordinates passed to `Line` are relative to the viewport.

Fig. 11.9. Output produced by the CLIP program.

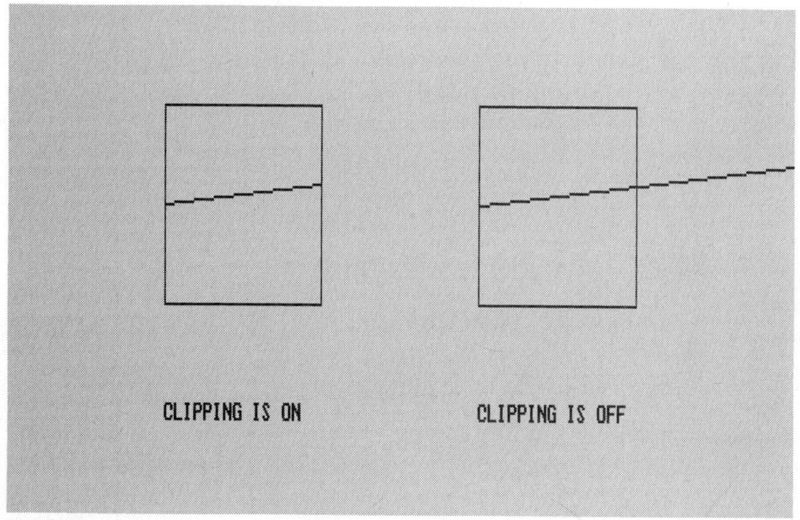

The *Rectangle* Procedure

The `Rectangle` procedure is similar to `Bar`, except `Rectangle` draws an empty shape. In this case, `Rectangle` draws a box around each viewport. The `OutTextXY` procedure positions—and then writes—a text message at the (X, Y) coordinates specified by its first two parameters.

Saving and Restoring Viewport Settings

If you need to switch between two graphics windows, it is useful to be able to save and restore each viewport setting quickly. You can do this with the `GetViewSettings` procedure:

```
procedure GetViewSettings( var ViewPort : ViewPortType );
```

`GetViewSettings` returns the current coordinates and clipping status in the fields of the `ViewPort` record. `ViewPort` is declared as being of the predefined type `ViewPortType`, as follows:

```
ViewPortType = record
                  X1, Y1, X2, Y2 : integer;
                  Clip           : boolean;
               end;
```

After you have used `SetViewPort` to create the first viewport—and before you use it again to create the second viewport—call `GetViewSettings` to save the current coordinates and clipping status. Later, you can restore these settings with the statement:

```
with ViewPort do
   SetViewPort( X1, Y1, X2, Y2, Clip );
```

Clearing the Viewport

There are two ways to erase the screen:

```
procedure ClearViewPort;
procedure ClearDevice;
```

`ClearViewPort` clears only the current viewport. `ClearDevice` clears the entire screen. Both procedures reset the current pointer to (0, 0), but neither affects the current viewport location.

The effects of `ClearViewPort` and `ClearDevice` can be seen in the CLEARVUE program in listing 11.15.

Listing 11.15

```
program ClearVue;
uses Graph;
var
   Radius : word;
   GraphDriver, GraphMode : integer;
begin
   GraphDriver := Detect;
   InitGraph( GraphDriver, GraphMode, 'C:\TP' );
   SetViewPort( GetMaxX div 2, GetMaxY div 2, GetMaxX, GetMaxY, ClipOff );
   for Radius := 1 to GetMaxY div 2 do
      Circle( 0, 0, Radius );
   readln;
   ClearViewPort;
   readln;
   ClearDevice;
   readln;
   for Radius := 1 to GetMaxY div 2 do
      Circle( 0, 0, Radius );
   CloseGraph;
end.
```

When CLEARVUE executes, it creates a viewport in the lower right quarter of the screen. As a result, the origin—the (0,0) coordinate—is in the center of the screen. Next, circles are drawn around the origin. Because clipping is turned off, the circles appear mostly outside the viewport. After you press the Enter key, the `ClearViewPort` command clears the viewport and in the process erases the lower right quarter of the circle. At this point, the screen appears as shown in figure 11.10. After you press Enter again, `ClearDevice` clears the entire screen. Press the Enter key a final time, and the circle is redrawn once again—in the middle of the screen—proving that viewport settings were unchanged.

Fig. 11.10. Output produced by the CLEARVUE program.

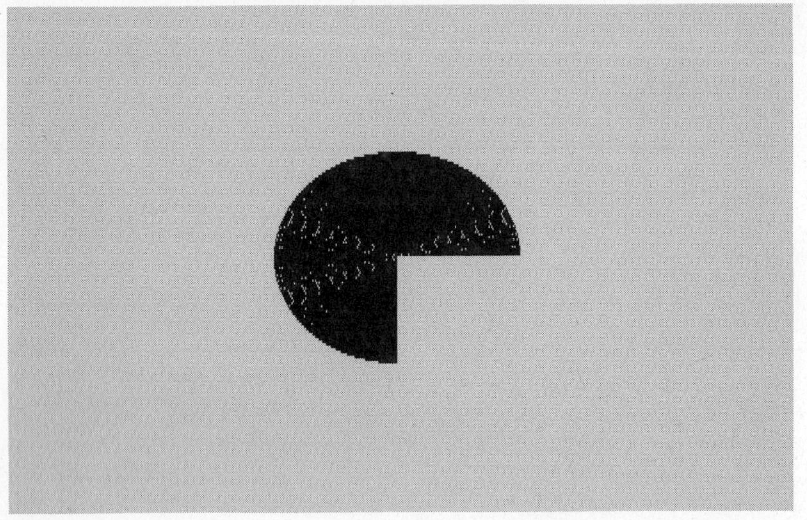

Page Swapping Routines

By now you have noticed the time it takes to draw each graphics image. For most applications, the delay is noticeable, but acceptable. But some applications—animation, game, and training programs, for example—are more effective if they can immediately display a completed graphics screen, just as if the user was turning a page in a book.

In graphics terms, a *page* is an area of memory large enough to hold a single graphics screen. Ideally, if your program could access two graphics pages, it could display the contents of one page while drawing graphics images on the second (invisible) page. Then your program could quickly switch the two pages, giving the impression that the images were drawn instantaneously.

EGA, VGA, and Hercules graphics cards all contain enough memory for more than one page; the exact number is given in the Pages column in table 11.2. If your PC uses a different graphics adapter (such as CGA), your machine has only a single page available and, consequently, page swapping is not available.

You can access the individual pages with the following routines:

```
procedure SetVisualPage( Page : word );
procedure SetActivePage (Page : word );
```

All graphics output is directed to the page selected by `SetActivePage`. The screen displays the contents of the page selected by `SetVisualPage`. If your PC does not support multiple pages, calling `SetActivePage` and `SetVisualPage` will have no effect on your program.

Paging routines are demonstrated by the ANIMATOR program in listing 11.16.

Listing 11.16

```
program Animator;    { EGA, VGA, or Hercules only }
uses Graph;
var
   Xmid, Ymid, Radius : word;
   GraphDriver, GraphMode : integer;
begin
   GraphDriver := Detect;
   InitGraph( GraphDriver, GraphMode, 'C:\TP' );
   Xmid := GetMaxX div 2; qqqqqqq
   Ymid := GetMaxY div 2;
   SetVisualPage( 0 );
   SetActivePage( 1 );
   for Radius := 1 to GetMaxY div 2 do
      Circle( Xmid, Ymid, Radius );
   SetVisualPage( 1 );
   readln;
   CloseGraph;
end.
```

ANIMATOR begins by setting the visual page to 0 and setting the active page to 1. This means that while the screen is displaying the (empty) contents of page 0, all of the circles are drawn on page 1. When the final circle has been completed, the screen is switched to page 1, immediately displaying all of the circles at once. (This is a trick used by demonstration programs in computer stores to make the graphics displays appear to change instantaneously.)

The ANIMATE2 program in listing 11.17 shows a simple technique that you can include in your programs to take advantage of multiple pages whenever they are available. Calling the `TurnThePages` procedure at the beginning of the program and before each display makes the graphics images appear more dramatic.

Listing 11.17

```
program Animate2;    { EGA, VGA, or Hercules only }
uses Graph;
const
   PageCounter : word = 0;
var
   Xmid, Ymid, Radius : word;
   GraphDriver, GraphMode : integer;
procedure TurnThePages;
begin
   Inc( PageCounter );
   if Odd( PageCounter ) then
      begin
         SetVisualPage( 1 );
         SetActivePage( 0 );
      end
   else
      begin
         SetVisualPage( 0 );
         SetActivePage( 1 );
      end;
end;
begin
   GraphDriver := Detect;
   InitGraph( GraphDriver, GraphMode, 'C:\TP' );
   Xmid := GetMaxX div 2;
   Ymid := GetMaxY div 2;
   TurnThePages;
   for Radius := 1 to GetMaxY div 2 do
      Circle( Xmid, Ymid, Radius );
   TurnThePages;
   readln;
   CloseGraph;
end.
```

Colors

The paint-by-number drawing sets that you find in toy stores include a collection of drawings and a set of paints. Each of the drawings is marked in such a way that every area on the page contains a number corresponding to a specific color of paint. Every part of every drawing that is supposed to be green might be marked, for example, with the 2, and every part of every drawing that is supposed to be red might be marked with the 4. The set of paints, naturally enough, is marked the same way; the second paint is green, and the fourth paint is red. Match them and you have an attractive picture. Child's play!

Turbo Pascal works the same way. A *palette* is the set of available colors for your screen. Instead of globs of pigment, however, Turbo Pascal stores a palette as an array of numbers. The *index* of each element of the array corresponds to the reference on the paint-by-number diagram, and the value of the element corresponds to the color of the paint.

In other words, each pixel on the screen has a numeric color value associated with it. Turbo chooses the color of the pixel by using its color value as an index into the palette array.

Obviously, understanding the palette is as important for mastering the art of painting colors on the screen as it is for painting colors on the canvas. The remainder of this section explores the Turbo Pascal color routines.

Identifying Colors

Two procedures read the contents of the palette array:

```
procedure GetDefaultPalette( var Palette : PaletteType );
procedure GetPalette( var Palette : PaletteType );
```

`GetDefaultPalette` returns a copy of the original contents of the palette, just as it was immediately after `InitGraph` initialized the graphics system. `GetPalette` returns the current palette.

Both `GetDefaultPalette` and `GetPalette` take a single parameter consisting of a record of type `PaletteType`, which is predefined as follows:

```
const
   MaxColors = 15;
type
```

```
PaletteType = record
                Size   : byte;
                Colors : array[0..MaxColors] of shortint;
              end;
```

The `Size` field is not extremely important for now. It tells you how many entries are in the `Colors` array. Because Turbo Pascal supports 16 colors (numbered 0 through 15), `MaxColors` is declared as a constant of 15; consequently, you already know that `Size` is 16.

Of greater concern is the *effective* size of the palette—that is, how many colors can actually be displayed for your graphics driver and mode. You can learn the effective palette size with the `GetPaletteSize` function. On a CGA in mode C1, `GetPaletteSize` returns 3; consequently, although 16 array elements are defined, you can use only elements 0 through 3.

A Special Note on CGA, MCGA, and AT&T Graphics

If your PC is equipped with a CGA, an MCGA, or an AT&T adapter, you should be aware of some special restrictions that apply to the use of colors on your machine.

Refer back to table 11.2 for a summary of the palette associated with each mode. In the low-resolution modes C0 through C3, each pixel is represented in memory by two bits. These bits can take on the binary values for 0, 1, 2, or 3. In other words, each pixel can assume at most one of four colors. The first four elements of the `Colors` array correspond to the colors in table 11.3. Mode C0 (actually, mode CGAC0, MCGAC0, or ATT400C0) initializes `Colors` to palette C0; mode C1 (actually, mode CGAC1, MCGAC1, or ATT400C1) initializes `Colors` to palette C1; and so on. Only four colors can be used, so only the first four elements of the `Colors` array have any meaning.

In high-resolution mode, each pixel is controlled by a single bit; hence, its color can be either 0 (the background) or 1 (the drawing color). Notice that in table 11.2, high-resolution mode was shown to have a palette of two colors.

Figure 11.1 showed the output produced when the GRFINFO2 program (listing 11.2) is run on a PC with a CGA board. Notice how the default mode is the two-color 640 × 200 pixel high-resolution mode. In other words, if your PC uses a CGA, an MCGA, or an AT&T adapter, and you want to display the full four-color palette on your screen, you must select a specific mode. For example, instead of using the default code:

```
GraphDriver := Detect;
InitGraph( GraphDriver, GraphMode, 'C:\TP' );
```

you might use:

```
GraphDriver := CGA;
   { Assuming you have a CGA }
GraphMode := CGAC0;
   { Palette 0 (LightGreen, LightRed, Yellow) }
InitGraph( GraphDriver, GraphMode, 'C:\TP' );
```

Of course, programs that do not use colors can continue to be run in one of the high-resolution modes.

Selecting a Drawing Color

You can select the current drawing color with the `SetColor` procedure. For example, `SetColor(2)` selects the second palette color for the current drawing color. The color you choose may range from 0 through the maximum allowed for your adapter and the current mode. This maximum can be determined by calling the `GetMaxColor` function. For example, on a PC equipped with a CGA and running in a low-resolution mode such as CGAC0, `GetMaxColor` returns 3.

At any point in the program, you can use the `GetColor` function to learn the current drawing color.

Selecting a Background Color

In the `Palette.Colors` array, the first entry (element number 0) is the background color. You can select the current background color with the `SetBkColor` procedure. For example, `SetBkColor(2)` selects the second palette color for the current background color. Just as with the `SetColor` procedure, the color you choose must be in the range from 0 through `GetMaxColor`.

You can use the `GetBkColor` function to identify the current drawing color.

Changing Individual Palette Colors

To change the colors in your palette, use the following procedure:

```
procedure SetPalette( ColorNum : word; Color : shortint );
```

`SetPalette` changes palette color `ColorNum` to the color specified by `Color`. To change color 2 to cyan, simply call

```
SetPalette( 2, Cyan );
```

There are a few restrictions to remember when you change palette colors. First, a CGA card will change only color 0 (the background). All other colors must remain as indicated in table 11.3. Second, `SetPalette` cannot be used on an IBM 8514. For that machine, you need to use the `SetRGBPalette` procedure.

Changing the Entire Palette

You can change every color of the EGA and VGA palettes with the routine:

```
procedure SetAllPalette( var Palette );
```

`SetAllPalette` takes a `PaletteType` variable as its parameter. `SetAllPalette` is best explained with an example. Suppose that you want to change the first palette color to red and the third palette color to green. When you call `SetAllPalette`, the first `Palette.Size` colors will be affected. Prepare the `Palette` variable as follows:

```
Palette.Size := 3;
Palette.Colors[ 1 ] := Red;
Palette.Colors[ 3 ] := Green;
```

To leave a particular palette color unchanged, set its value to –1. Finish the preparation of the `Palette` variable as follows:

```
Palette.Colors[ 0 ] := -1;
Palette.Colors[ 2 ] := -1;
```

Finally, call

```
SetAllPalette( Palette );
```

After `SetAllPalette` executes, every pixel on the screen that was painted with palette colors 1 and 3 is immediately changed. Note, however, that unless you plan on changing several colors frequently, `SetPalette` is almost always simpler and faster than `SetAllPalette`.

Again, remember the restrictions: CGA cards can change only color 0 (the background), and `SetAllPalette` cannot be used on an IBM 8514.

Changing Colors on the VGA and the IBM 8514

A color television picture tube and a color PC display have one thing in common: both use only three primary colors (red, green, and blue) to produce every color, shade, and hue on the screen. In other words, every nuance of color is some combination of intensities of the three primaries.

To modify a palette entry for a VGA card or for an IBM 8514, you specify the relative intensities of red, green, and blue.

```
procedure SetRGBPalette( ColorNum,
              RedValue, GreenValue, BlueValue : integer );
```

You will find a complete list of colors in the adapter's technical manual. For a partial list, you can use the values in table 11.7.

Hence, the command to change palette color number 7 to green is

```
SetRGBPalette( 7, $24, $FC, $24 );
```

Filling a Drawing

Line drawings are similar to stick figures of people: they get the idea across, but they do not offer any substance in the process. Quite simply, line drawings need to be "fleshed out" to increase their appeal. In this section, you learn how to fill shapes with patterns and colors and in the process considerably increase the power and impact of your graphics displays.

Filling Solids

Normally when you use the `FillPoly`, `Bar`, `Bar3D`, and `PieSlice` procedures, the figures produced are solid and are painted with the maximum color of the palette (that is, `Palette.Colors[GetMaxColor]`). To change these defaults, use the routine:

```
procedure SetFillStyle( Pattern : word; Color : word );
```

Table 11.7. VGA Color Hues

Color	*Red*	*Green*	*Blue*
Black	$00	$00	$00
Blue	$00	$00	$FC
Green	$24	$FC	$24
Cyan	$00	$FC	$FC
Red	$FC	$14	$14
Magenta	$B0	$00	$FC
Brown	$70	$48	$00
White	$C4	$C4	$C4
Gray	$34	$34	$34
Light Blue	$00	$00	$70
Light Green	$00	$70	$00
Light Cyan	$00	$70	$70
Light Red	$70	$00	$00
Light Magenta	$70	$00	$70
Yellow	$FC	$FC	$24
Bright White	$FC	$FC	$FC

`SetFillStyle` takes two parameters: a `Color` value that you can obtain from table 11.6 and a `Pattern` that you can obtain from table 11.8.

User-Defined Fill Styles

When you pass `SetFillStyle` a `Pattern` parameter equal to `UserFill`, you are telling Turbo to customize the fill pattern. You can do this with the procedure:

```
procedure SetFillPattern( Pattern : FillPatternType; Color : word );
```

`SetFillPattern` takes two parameters: a word-sized `Color` specification and a parameter of type `FillPatternType`, which defines the pattern you want. `FillPatternType` is a predefined `array of byte`:

Table 11.8. Fill patterns for `GetFillSettings` *and* `SetFillStyle`

Constant	*Value*	*Pattern*
`EmptyFill`	0	The background color
`SolidFill`	1	A solid color
`LineFill`	2	Hyphens (- - -)
`LtSlashFill`	3	Thin slashes (///)
`SlashFill`	4	Thick slashes
`BkSlashFill`	5	Thick backslashes
`LtBkSlashFill`	6	Thin backslashes (\\\)
`HatchFill`	7	Light crosshatch marks
`XHatchFill`	8	Heavy crosshatch marks
`InterleaveFill`	9	Interleaved lines
`WideDotFill`	10	Widely spaced dots
`CloseDotFill`	11	Closely spaced dots
`UserFill`	12	User-defined

```
FillPatternType = array[1..8] of byte;
```

Recall that the default character size is an 8 × 8 matrix of pixels. Each byte of the `FillPatternType` array defines one row—top to bottom—in a custom character. The bits in each byte define the columns.

The use of `SetFillPattern` is demonstrated by the USERFILL program in listing 11.18.

Listing 11.18

```
program UserFill;
uses Graph;
const
   Shape : FillPatternType = ( $08,   { 00001000 }
                               $1C,   { 00011100 }
                               $3E,   { 00111110 }
                               $7F,   { 01111111 }
```

continues

Listing 11.18 continued

```
                                 $3E,    { 00111110 }
                                 $1C,    { 00011100 }
                                 $08,    { 00001000 }
                                 $00     { 00000000 } );
var
   GraphDriver, GraphMode : integer;
   Height : word;
begin
   GraphDriver := Detect;
   InitGraph( GraphDriver, GraphMode, 'C:\TP' );
   Height := GetMaxY div 3;
   SetFillPattern( Shape, 1 );
   Bar( 0, Height, GetMaxX, Height*2 );
   readln;
   CloseGraph;
end.
```

When USERFILL executes, `SetFillPattern` changes the default color to `Colors [1]` and the default fill pattern to the one defined by the `Shape` array. Notice how the bits of the `Shape` array are arranged to form a diamond. The effect is visible in figure 11.11.

***Fig. 11.11.** Output produced by the USERFILL program.*

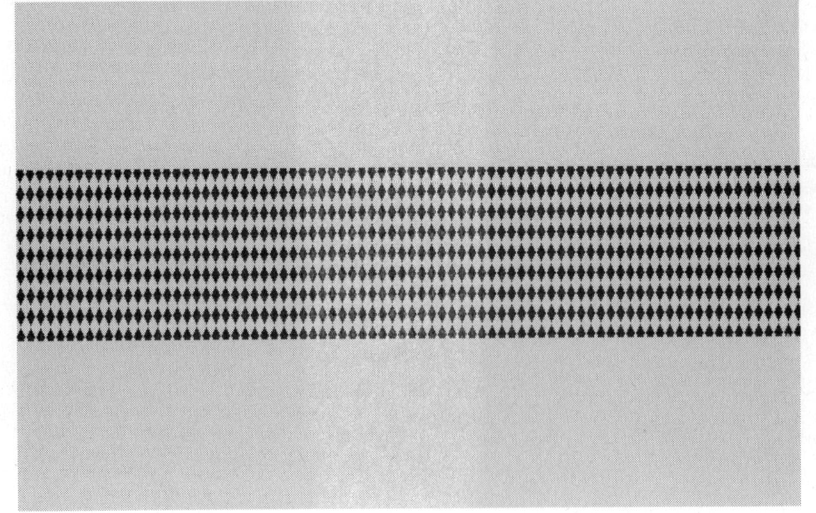

Determining Patterns and Colors

With the `GetFillSettings` procedure, you can obtain a copy of the current fill pattern and color as set by `SetFillStyle` or `SetFillPattern`.

```
procedure GetFillSettings( var FillInfo : FillSettingsType );
```

The `FillSettingsType` record is predefined as follows:

```
FillSettingsType = record
                     Pattern : word;
                     Color   : word;
                   end;
```

If the `Pattern` parameter is equal to `UserFill`, you can obtain a copy of the custom character with the routine:

```
procedure GetFillPattern( var FillPattern : FillPatternType );
```

Using `GetFillSettings` and `GetFillPattern`, you can rapidly save information about the current fill pattern and color.

Flood Filling

You can use `SetFillStyle` and `SetFillPattern` with only the `FillPoly`, `Bar`, `Bar3D`, and `PieSlice` procedures. Other shapes require a different routine:

```
procedure FloodFill( X, Y : integer; Border : word );
```

`FloodFill` fills a bounded region with the current fill pattern determined by the most recent call to `SetFillStyle` or `SetFillPattern`. The coordinates (X, Y) must specify a point in an enclosed region that you want to fill. The boundaries must be lines of the color `Border`. If the position of (X, Y) lies outside the region, the exterior is filled.

The `FloodFill` procedure can be demonstrated with the GRID3 program in listing 11.19.

Listing 11.19

```
program Grid3;
uses Graph;
const
```

continues

Listing 11.19 continued

```
   Color : word = Green;
var
   GraphDriver, Graphmode : integer;
   Row, Column, Style,
   Swath, Xjump, Yjump, Xcenter, Ycenter : word;
begin
   GraphDriver := Detect;
   InitGraph( GraphDriver, Graphmode, 'C:\TP' );
   Xjump := GetMaxX div 10;
   Yjump := GetMaxY div 10;
   SetColor( Color );
   for Swath := 0 to 10 do begin
      SetLineStyle( SolidLn, 0, ThickWidth );
      Line( Swath*Xjump, 0, Swath*Xjump, 10*Yjump );
      Line( 0, Swath*Yjump, 10*Xjump, Swath*Yjump );
   end;
   for Row := 0 to 9 do
      for Column := 0 to 9 do begin
         Style := ( 10*Row+Column ) mod 12;
         Xcenter := Column*Xjump + ( Xjump div 2 );
         Ycenter := Row*Yjump + ( Yjump div 2 );
         SetFillStyle( Style, Color );
         FloodFill( Xcenter, Ycenter, Color );
      end;
   readln;
   CloseGraph;
end.
```

GRID3 draws 100 rectangles and "flood fills" them with changing patterns. The results of the GRID3 program can be seen in figure 11.12.

Increasing Buffer Size

Flood filling relies on the presence of a 4K buffer in the heap, allocated as part of the `InitGraph` initialization process. In rare cases, you may need to increase the buffer slightly to avoid overflows. You can do this with the routine:

```
procedure SetGraphBufSize( BufSize : word );
```

Here, `BufSize` is the number of bytes you want to reserve.

> An alternative use of the `SetGraphBufSize` procedure is to reduce the size of the buffer to free space on the heap. In that case, call `SetGraphBufSize` with a value less than 4K.
>
> Note that `SetGraphBufSize` must be called before `InitGraph`.

Fig. 11.12. *Output produced by the GRID3 program.*

Drawing Shapes

This section discusses how to draw complete figures: rectangles, bars, and polygons.

Rectangles and Bars

You have already used the `Rectangle` and `Bar` procedures described earlier in this chapter.

```
procedure Rectangle( X1, Y1, X2, Y2 : integer );
procedure Bar( X1, Y1, X2, Y2 : integer );
```

Both procedures draw from the upper left corner at (X1, Y1) to the lower right corner at (X2, Y2). The only functional difference is that `Rectangle` draws a hollow figure, whereas `Bar` draws a solid one.

One use of the `Bar` procedure is to draw a business-type bar graph. You can achieve a three-dimensional effect with the procedure:

```
procedure Bar3D( X1, Y1, X2, Y2 : integer; Depth : word; Top : boolean );
```

The `Depth` parameter specifies the perceived depth of the bar. The `Top` parameter is a Boolean value that determines whether or not the bar has a top. You can use `True` or `False`, or the more understandable predefined constants:

```
TopOn  = True;
TopOff = False;
```

Use `TopOff` when you want to stack another bar on top of the current one.

Rectangles and bars are demonstrated with the BARS program in listing 11.20. BARS draws four shapes: a rectangle around the entire screen, a bar image, a three-dimensional bar with a top, and a three-dimensional bar without a top.

Listing 11.20

```
program Bars;
uses Graph;
var
   Width, Height : word;
   GraphDriver, GraphMode : integer;
begin
   GraphDriver := Detect;
   InitGraph( GraphDriver, GraphMode, 'C:\TP' );
   Rectangle( 0, 0, GetMaxX, GetMaxY );
   Width  := GetMaxX div 8;
   Height := GetMaxY div 4;
   Bar( Width, Height, Width*2, Height*3 );
   Bar3D( Width*3, Height, Width*4, Height*3, Width div 4, TopOn );
   Bar3D( Width*5, Height, Width*6, Height*3, Width div 4, TopOff );
   readln;
   CloseGraph;
end.
```

The output of the BARS program is shown in figure 11.13.

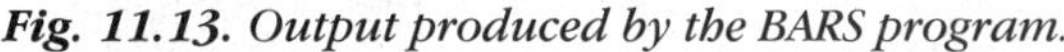

Fig. 11.13. Output produced by the BARS program.

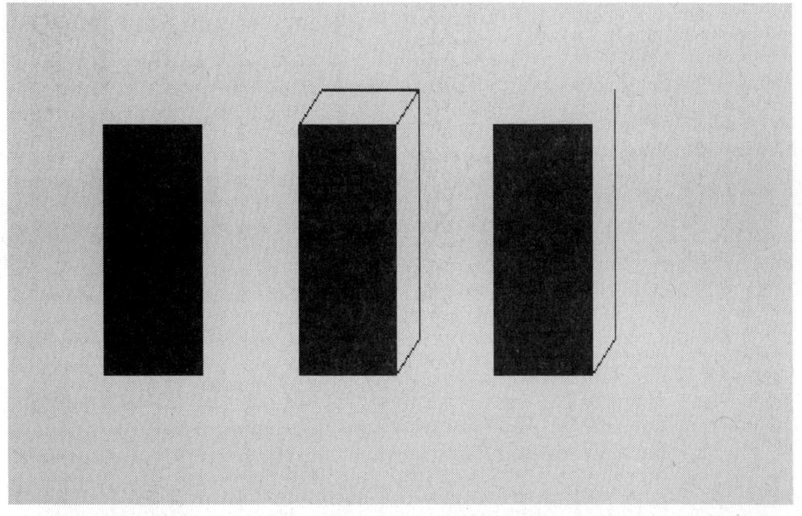

Polygons

A *polygon* is any enclosed shape drawn with straight lines. The sides of a polygon need not all be the same length, but they are not allowed to cross one another. Triangles, squares, pentagons, and hexagons are examples of polygons.

To draw a polygon, specify its corners with the `DrawPoly` and `FillPoly` procedures.

```
procedure DrawPoly( NumPoints : word; var PolyPoints );
procedure FillPoly( NumPoints : word; var PolyPoints );
```

`DrawPoly` "connects the dots" and draws the outline of the polygon using the color selected by `SetColor`. `FillPoly` first draws the outline, then fills it in using the pattern and color determined by `SetFillStyle`.

`PolyPoints` is an untyped parameter that contains an array of the (X, Y) coordinates of the corners. Each coordinate consists of a record of the predefined type `PointType`, as follows:

```
PointType = record
              X, Y : integer;
            end;
```

For the `DrawPoly` procedure, `NumPoints` is the number of corners in the polygon plus 1. Both the beginning and ending corners must be specified; therefore, for a polygon with *N* corners, `PolyPoints[1]` must equal `PolyPoints[N+1]`.

The `FillPoly` procedure does not need this repetition. `NumPoints` is simply the number of corners in the polygon, and `PolyPoints` contains only one element for each corner. Strangely, however, `FillPoly` will work correctly if the first and last elements of the `PolyPoints` array are repeated.

`DrawPoly` and `FillPoly` are demonstrated in the POLY program in listing 11.21. You will notice from the value of some of the X-coordinates that POLY is intended to run in a high-resolution mode.

Listing 11.21

```
program Poly;
uses Graph;
const
   StopSign1 : array [ 1..7 ] of PointType =
      (    ( X :  50;    Y :  50 ),
           ( X : 150;    Y :  50 ),
           ( X : 200;    Y :  93 ),
           ( X : 150;    Y : 136 ),
           ( X :  50;    Y : 136 ),
           ( X :   0;    Y :  93 ),
           ( X :  50;    Y :  50 )    );
   StopSign2 : array [ 1..6 ] of PointType =
      (    ( X : 450;    Y :  50 ),
           ( X : 550;    Y :  50 ),
           ( X : 600;    Y :  93 ),
           ( X : 550;    Y : 136 ),
           ( X : 450;    Y : 136 ),
           ( X : 400;    Y :  93 )    );
var
   GraphDriver, Graph Mode : integer;
begin
   GraphDriver := Detect;
   InitGraph( GraphDriver, Graph Mode, 'C:\TP' );
   SetColor( Red );
   DrawPoly( 7, StopSign1 );
   SetColor( Green {Black} );
   SetFillStyle( CloseDotFill, Red );
```

```
    FillPoly( 6, StopSign2 );
    readln;
    CloseGraph;
end.
```

The output from the program is shown in figure 11.14.

Fig. 11.14. Output produced by the POLY program.

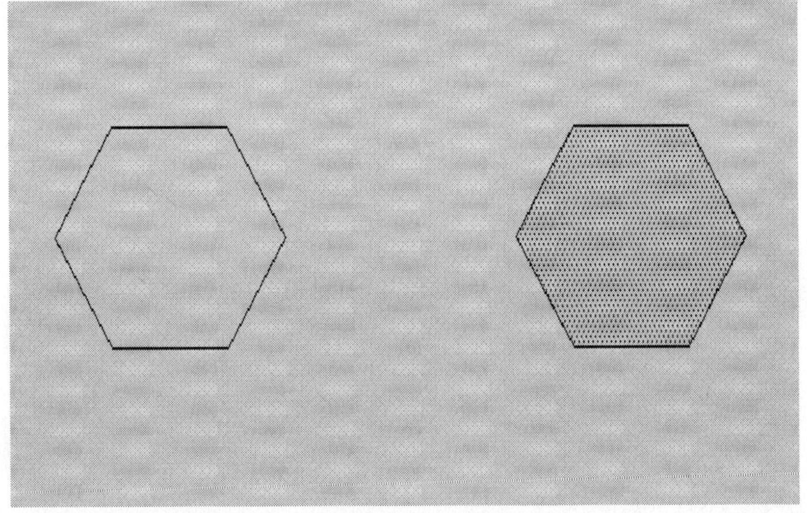

POLY uses the `DrawPoly` procedure to draw a stop sign (well, actually a hexagon) on the left side of the screen. On EGA and VAG adapters, the hexagon appears in red. POLY also uses the `FillPoly` procedure to draw a similar hexagon on the right side of the screen, but this time with a `CloseDotFill` interior.

To emphasize the difference between the border and the interior of the hexagon on the right, green was used for the boundary and red was used for the center. If you do not want a boundary line to appear, you can call `SetColor` with black.

Note how `DrawPoly` is passed seven coordinates, whereas `FillPoly` receives only six. You may want to experiment with the number of corners. For example, if you omit the last coordinate when you call `DrawPoly`, the hexagon is drawn with one open side. You should also notice that if `Shapes` is an array of `PointType`, the statements

```
DrawPoly( SizeOf( Shapes ) div SizeOf( PointType ), Shapes );
```

and

```
FillPoly( SizeOf( Shapes ) div SizeOf( PointType ), Shapes );
```

enable you to vary the number of corners in the `Shapes` array, without worrying about modifying code in the body of the program.

Parameters with *DrawPoly* and *FillPoly*
Before you continue to the next section, consider for a moment how cleverly the `DrawPoly` and `FillPoly` procedures handled parameters. With few exceptions (such as `write` and `writeln`), Turbo Pascal does not allow procedures or functions to have a variable number of parameters. (Certainly no user-defined procedure or function is allowed such a luxury!)

Because polygons can have any number of sides, the `DrawPoly` and `FillPoly` procedures could not be written with a fixed number of parameters. By defining a `PointType` parameter and letting `PointType` be user-defined, this restriction was circumvented. You might find this trick useful in your programs.

Curves

This section discusses the Turbo Pascal routines for generating curved images.

The Aspect Ratio

At the beginning of the chapter, it was mentioned that the monochrome screen is 350 pixels high by 750 pixels wide. If you take a quick glance at your screen, it probably seems relatively square. It is reasonable to assume, then, that pixels are packed together more closely in the horizontal direction.

The *aspect ratio* is a measure of the relative height and width of a pixel, as follows:

(display width) ÷ (display height)

On a screen with an aspect ratio of 0.5, each pixel is half as wide as it is tall. Consequently, 100 horizontal pixels are exactly as long as 50 vertical pixels.

You can determine the aspect ratio for your screen with the routine:

```
procedure GetAspectRatio( var Xasp, Yasp : word );
```

`GetAspectRatio` returns two word-type variables from which the aspect ratio can be computed. If you call `GetAspectRatio` on a COMPAQ PLUS in high-resolution CGA 640 × 350 mode, you get:

```
Xasp =   4167
Yasp =  10000
```

This gives an aspect ratio of 0.4167, indicating that the width of a pixel is only 41.67 percent of its height.

Turbo Pascal uses the aspect ratio to compensate for the shape of a screen when your program draws circles, arcs, and pie slices. If you are not satisfied with the default, you can change the aspect ratio of your screen with the `SetAspectRatio` procedure.

```
procedure SetAspectRatio( Xasp, Yasp : word );
```

The use of `SetAspectRatio` is demonstrated in the ASPECT program in listing 11.22.

Listing 11.22

```
program Aspect;
uses Graph;
var
   Height, Width, Radius : word;
   Xasp, Yasp : word;
   GraphDriver, GraphMode : integer;
begin
   GraphDriver := Detect;
   InitGraph( GraphDriver, GraphMode, 'C:\TP' );
   Height := GetMaxY div 2;
   Width := GetMaxX div 3;
   Radius := GetMaxY div 4;
   Circle( Width, Height, Radius );       { Good circle }
   GetAspectRatio( Xasp, Yasp );
   SetAspectRatio( 4*Xasp, Yasp );
   Circle( Width*2, Height, Radius );     { Distorted circle }
   readln;
   CloseGraph;
end.
```

The ASPECT program draws two circles, as shown in figure 11.15. The circle on the left uses the default aspect ratio and appears acceptably round. The circle on the right uses an aspect ratio in which the default `Xasp` parameter is increased by a factor of four. The compiler now thinks the width is four times larger than it really is, and tries to compensate by increasing the circle's vertical size, resulting in an extremely tall ellipse.

Fig. 11.15. Output produced by the ASPECT program.

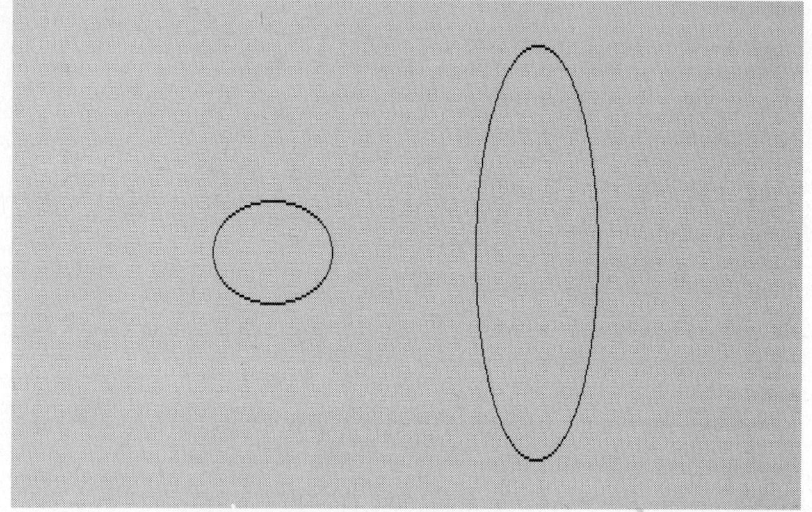

Because Turbo corrects only the circle, arc, and pie slice procedures, other figures must be adjusted manually. In general, you can do this by dividing the X-coordinate of your drawings by the aspect ratio, as shown in the TANLINE3 program in listing 11.23.

Listing 11.23

```
program TanLine3;
uses Graph;
var
   Xasp, Yasp : word;
   GraphDriver, GraphMode : integer;
   Y, Ymax : word;
   Ratio : real;
begin
   GraphDriver := Detect;
```

```
   InitGraph( GraphDriver, GraphMode, 'C:\TP' );
   YMax := GetMaxY;
   GetAspectRatio( Xasp, Yasp );
   Ratio := Yasp / Xasp;  { inverse aspect ratio }
   for y := 1 to YMax do
      Line( Max-y, 0, 0, y );
   SetViewPort( Ymax, 0, GetMaxX, GetMaxY, ClipOn );
   for Y := 1 to Ymax do
      Line( Round( Ratio * ( Ymax - Y ) ), 0, 0, Y );
   readln;
   CloseGraph;
end.
```

TANLINE3 is a modification of the TANLINES program, in which tangents are drawn to give the illusion of a circle. The output of TANLINE3 is shown in figure 11.16. Two separate arcs are displayed. The drawing on the right compensates for the screen's aspect ratio. Notice how TANLINE3 uses the `SetViewPort` procedure to change the screen coordinates.

***Fig. 11.16.** Output produced by the TANLINE3 program.*

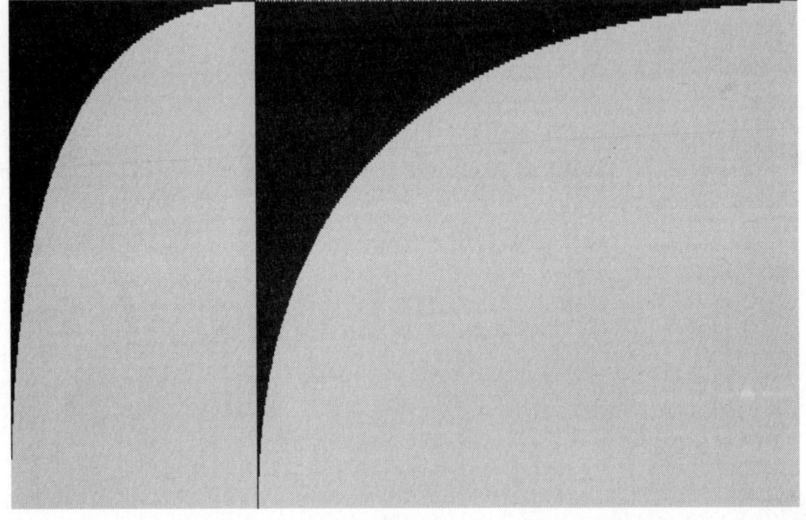

Circles and Ellipses

You have seen the `Circle` procedure several times in this chapter.

```
procedure Circle( X, Y : integer; Radius : word );
```

`Circle` draws a complete circle centered at (X, Y) with a radius of `Radius`. The interior of the circle is left untouched.

In the last section, you saw how to distort the aspect ratio to force the `Circle` procedure to draw an ellipse. There is, fortunately, an easier way to accomplish the same thing using the `Ellipse` and `FillEllipse` procedures.

An *ellipse* is any oval shape—including a circle—whose width and height can be controlled independently.

```
procedure Ellipse( X, Y : integer;
                   StAngle, EndAngle : word;
                   XRadius, YRadius  : word );
```

Ellipse draws an elliptical arc, centered at (X,Y), from the starting angle `StAngle` to the ending angle `EndAngle`. `XRadius` and `YRadius` are the horizontal and vertical axes, respectively. Figure 11.17 explains these parameters graphically. Notice that angles are measured counterclockwise, in degrees, with 0 degrees in the three o'clock position.

Just as with the `Circle` procedure, `Ellipse` draws only the arc; the center of the ellipse is unaffected. However, unlike the `Circle` procedure, `Ellipse` does not adjust its shape to compensate for the aspect ratio of your screen. Hence, even if `XRadius` and `YRadius` are equal, the ellipse still appears to be oval.

To draw a filled ellipse or a filled circle, use the `FillEllipse` procedure.

```
procedure FillEllipse( X, Y : integer;
                       XRadius, YRadius  : word );
```

`FillEllipse` draws an ellipse centered at (X, Y). `XRadius` and `YRadius` are the horizontal and vertical axes, respectively.

The `FillEllipse` procedure is demonstrated in the BUG program in listing 11.24.

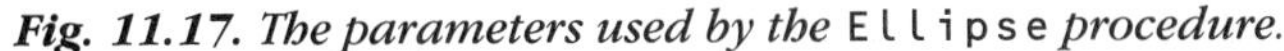

Fig. 11.17. The parameters used by the `Ellipse` *procedure.*

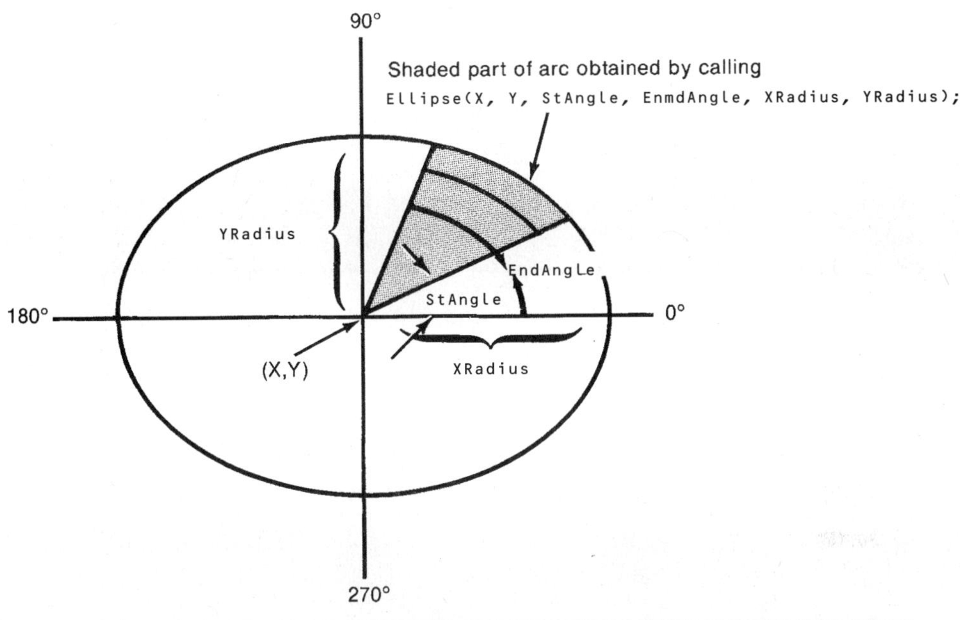

Listing 11.24

```
program Bug;
uses Graph;
var
   Xpos, Ypos, Xinc, grDriver, grMode : integer;
   Width, Height, Xradius, Yradius, i : word;
begin
   grDriver := Detect;
   InitGraph( grDriver, grMode, 'C:\TP' );
   GetAspectRatio( Width, Height );
   Ypos := GetMaxY div 2;
   Xinc := GetMaxX div 20;
   Xradius := Xinc div 2;
   Yradius := Round( Xradius * Width / Height );
   for i := 2 to 18 do begin
      SetColor( Random( GetMaxColor - 1 ) + 1 );   { Never set to background }
      SetFillStyle( ( i - 2 ) mod 13, i - 2 );
```

continues

Listing 11.24 continued

```
      FillEllipse( Xinc * i, Ypos, Xradius, Yradius );
      if i < 18 then OutTextXY( Xinc * i, Ypos + Yradius, 'L' );
   end;
   OutTextXY( Xinc * 18, Ypos - 2*Yradius, 'V' );
   write( 'The Turbo Bug' );
   readln;
   CloseGraph;
end.
```

The results of the BUG program are shown in figure 11.18. The caterpillar is created by several calls to the `FillEllipse` procedure. Notice how BUG uses the aspect ratio to force each ellipse into a circle.

***Fig. 11.18.** Output produced by the BUG program.*

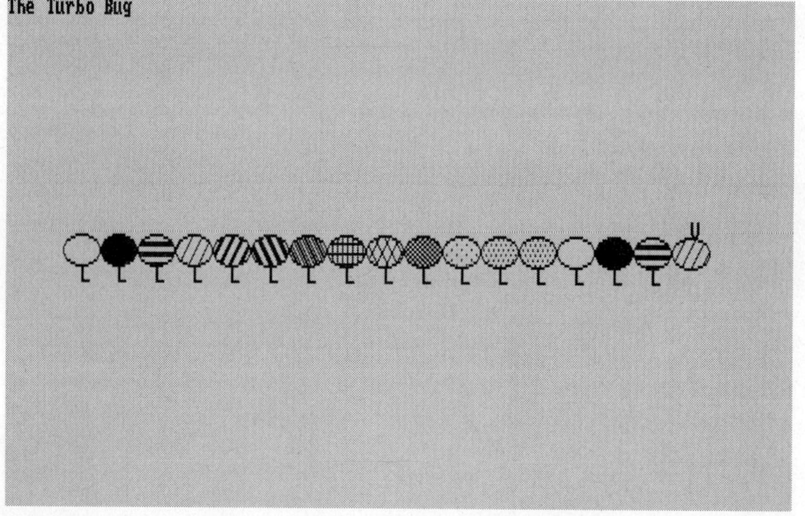

Arcs

An *arc* is a portion of a circle.

```
procedure Arc( X, Y : integer; StAngle, EndAngle, Radius : word );
```

The `Arc` procedure is similar to `Circle`, except it draws only from the starting angle, `StAngle`, to the ending angle, `EndAngle`. Angles are measured counterclockwise, in degrees, with 0 degrees in the three o'clock position.

With most graphics routines, if you know the coordinates of the current pointer prior to calling the routine, you can calculate the location of the CP after the routine finishes. The same is true for the `Arc` procedure, but the trigonometry can be involved, especially because the compiler compensates for the aspect ratio of your screen. To simplify the effort, Turbo Pascal offers the following procedure:

```
procedure GetArcCoords( var ArcCoords : ArcCoordsType );
```

`GetArcCoords` returns the coordinates of the last `Arc` command in a record of the predefined type `ArcCoordsType`, defined as follows:

```
ArcCoordsType = record
                  X, Y             : integer;
                  Xstart, Ystart : integer;
                  Xend, Yend       : integer;
                end;
```

The `ArcCoords` record returns the coordinates of the center point of the arc (`X, Y`), plus the coordinates of its starting point (`Xstart, Ystart`) and ending point (`Xend, Yend`).

Pie Slices and Sectors

You can draw partially filled circles and ellipses with the `PieSlice` and `Sector` procedures.

```
procedure PieSlice( X, Y : integer; StAngle, EndAngle, Radius : word );
procedure Sector( X, Y : Integer;
          StAngle, EndAngle,
          XRadius, YRadius : word );
```

The `PieSlice` procedure draws and fills a pie slice; it uses (`X, Y`) as its center point and `Radius` as its radius, and draws from starting angle `StAngle` to ending angle `EndAngle`. The `Sector` procedure draws and fills an elliptical sector. `Sector` has the same parameters as `PieSlice`, except the width and height are controlled individually by `XRadius` and `YRadius`, respectively. Angles are measured counterclockwise, in degrees, with 0 degrees in the three o'clock position.

The WEDGE program in listing 11.25 demonstrates how `PieSlice` and `Sector` are used.

Listing 11.25

```
program Wedge;
uses Graph;
var
   Xmid, Ymid : word;
   GraphDriver, GraphMode : integer;
begin
   GraphDriver := Detect;
   InitGraph( GraphDriver, GraphMode, 'C:\TP' );
   Xmid := GetMaxX div 4;
   Ymid := GetMaxY div 2;
   Arc( Xmid, Ymid, 55, 350, Xmid div 2 );
   PieSlice( Xmid, Ymid, 0, 45, Xmid );
   Sector( Xmid*3, Ymid, 90, 360, Xmid div 2, Ymid );
   readln;
   CloseGraph;
end.
```

The results of the WEDGE program are shown in figure 11.19. Notice that both the `Arc` and `PieSlice` figures have automatically been adjusted for the aspect ratio of the screen.

Saving and Restoring Graphics Screens

Chapter 10 discussed how to save and restore text windows. Recall that to save the display, you copy the 2000-word video memory to a special buffer. To restore the screen, you copy the buffer back to video memory.

Admittedly, manipulating an entire text screen is a brute-force approach, especially because most of the time you want to save only a small portion of the display. The technique is simple to code, however, and it is not difficult to find space on the heap for 2000 words.

On the other hand, a single graphics screen can take up to 16K of the PC's internal memory plus additional memory on the graphics adapter board. Saving one or more complete graphics screens rapidly consumes space on the heap. For practical reasons, you have to limit yourself to dealing with only a small portion of a screen at one time.

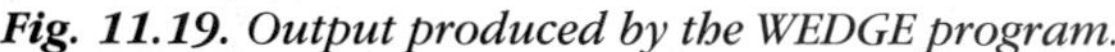

Fig. 11.19. Output produced by the WEDGE program.

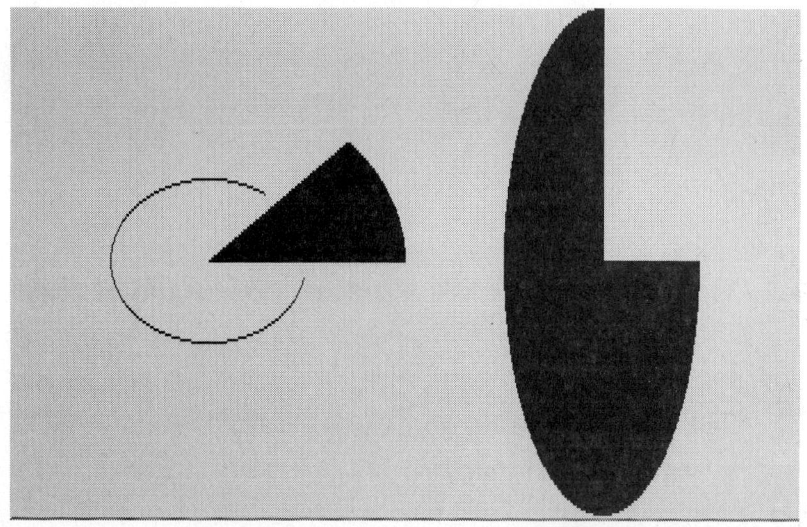

Turbo Pascal provides the `ImageSize` function, the `GetImage` function, and the `PutImage` procedure to simplify this task.

```
function ImageSize( X1, Y1, X2, Y2 : integer ) : word;
procedure GetImage( X1, Y1, X2, Y2 : integer; var BitMap );
procedure PutImage( X, Y : integer; var BitMap; BitBlt : word );
```

The `GetImage` procedure saves an area of the screen—the rectangle defined by the upper left coordinates of (X1, Y1) and lower right coordinates of (X2, Y2)—by locating its video memory and copying it into a buffer identified by the untyped variable `BitMap`. The width and height of the rectangle are also saved. Use the `GetMem` procedure to allocate the buffer and `FreeMem` to return it to the heap when you are done. The `ImageSize` function calculates the number of bytes you need to reserve.

The `PutImage` procedure returns the contents of the buffer to the screen. Because `GetImage` stored the dimensions of the rectangle as part of the `BitMap` buffer, `PutImage` needs only the upper left starting coordinates.

The `BitBlt` parameter enables you to choose how `PutImage` redisplays the rectangle. Turbo Pascal defines the following five constants for you to use as options:

- ❑ `CopyPut 0 { MOV }`
- ❑ `XORPut 1 { XOR }`
- ❑ `OrPut 2 { OR }`
- ❑ `AndPut 3 { AND }`
- ❑ `NotPut 4 { NOT }`

`CopyPut` indicates a complete replacement; the buffer image writes over whatever was on the screen. `NotPut` returns the inverse image. The remaining options determine the final display by logically comparing each pixel on the screen with the corresponding pixel in the buffer: `XORPut` performs a logical exclusive OR; `OrPut` performs a logical inclusive OR; and `AndPut` performs a logical AND.

These techniques are demonstrated in the BITGRAPH program, shown in listing 11.26.

Listing 11.26

```
program BitGraph;
uses Graph;
var
   Image                         : pointer;
   i, Width, Height, Storage : word;
   GraphDriver, GraphMode        : integer;
begin
   GraphDriver := Detect;
   InitGraph( GraphDriver, GraphMode, 'C:\TP' );
   Width := GetMaxX div 5;
   Height := GetMaxY div 4;
   for i := 1 to 100 do begin
      SetColor( Random( GetMaxColor ) + 1 );
      Circle( Random( Width ), Random( GetMaxY ), Random( Width div 4 ) );
   end;
   Storage := ImageSize( 0, 0, Width, GetMaxY );
   GetMem( Image, Storage );
   GetImage( 0, 0, Width, GetMaxY, Image^ );
   readln;
   ClearDevice;
   Bar( 0, Height, GetMaxX, Height * 3 );
```

```
   readln;
   for i := 0 to 4 do
      PutImage( i*Width, 0, Image^, i );
   FreeMem( Image, Storage );
   readln;
   CloseGraph;
end.
```

BITGRAPH divides the screen into five vertical sections. It begins by randomly displaying 100 circles in the section on the far left, as shown in figure 11.20.

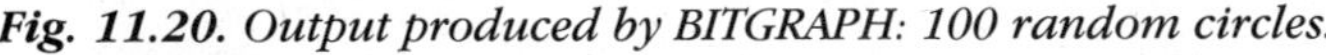

Fig. 11.20. Output produced by BITGRAPH: 100 random circles.

After you press the Enter key, BITGRAPH stores the left section in a buffer named `Image^`. Then it displays a large rectangle, horizontally across the middle of the screen, as shown in figure 11.21.

After you press Enter again, BITGRAPH returns the original image to the screen in each of the five sections, using a different `BitBlt` option each time. Figure 11.22 compares the effects of using `CopyPut`, `XORPut`, `OrPut`, `AndPut`, and `NotPut`.

Fig. 11.21. Output produced by BITGRAPH: a solid rectangle.

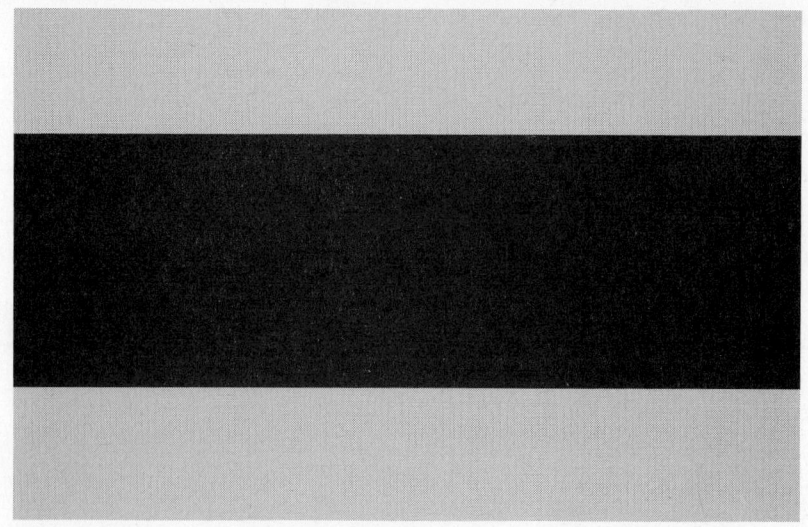

Fig. 11.22. Output produced by BITGRAPH: five display options.

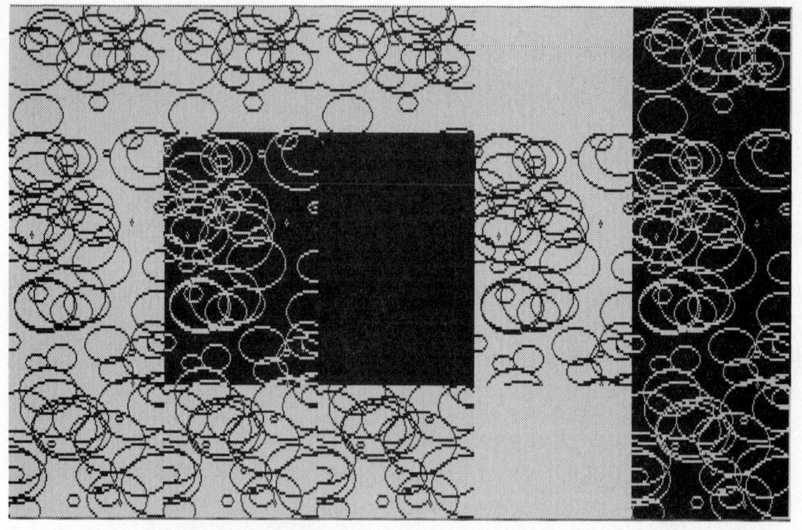

Displaying Text

The `write` and `writeln` statements operate the same in graphics mode as they do in text mode. Unfortunately, the Graph unit does not include a way to freely position `write` and `writeln` output. No matter where the current pointer is located, the first occurrence of `write` or `writeln` appears in the upper left corner of the screen. Every subsequent occurrence begins immediately to the right of the previous message or, if the previous call was to a `writeln`, in the first position of the next line.

A Note about Using the Crt Unit
If you use the Crt unit in your program, `write` and `writeln` switch to the special display routines that output directly to text video memory. To redirect `write` and `writeln` to the graphics screen, set the `DirectVideo` variable to `False`, as follows:

```
DirectVideo := False;
```

This enables you to use the other features of the Crt unit without losing the use of `write` and `writeln` in the process.

The Graph unit provides its own means of displaying text:

```
procedure OutText( TextString : string );
procedure OutTextXY( X, Y : integer; TextString : string );
```

The `OutText` procedure displays a string beginning at the current pointer. After `OutText` is finished, the CP is moved to the first position after the last string character. The `OutTextXY` procedure displays a string at `(X, Y)`. The CP remains at `(X, Y)` after `OutTextXY` is run.

Text Style

The default graphics character set is called a *bit-mapped font*. The shape of each of the 256 standard ASCII characters is stored as an 8 × 8 matrix of pixels. When a bit-mapped character is enlarged, it appears jagged, and its block-like structure is clearly evident.

In addition, Turbo Pascal provides four stroked fonts: Triplex, Small, Sans Serif, and Gothic. With a *stroked font*, each character is defined by a set of reference points similar to those you used earlier in the chapter to draw polygons. Consequently, a stroked font can retain its appearance as the character is enlarged or compressed.

You can select the font you want with the `SetTextStyle` procedure.

```
procedure SetTextStyle( Font, Direction : word; CharSize : word );
```

`SetTextStyle` controls not only the text font but also the direction (horizontal or vertical) in which the text should be written and the size of the characters.

Select the text font by specifying a value from 0 through 4 or by using one of the predefined constants shown in table 11.9.

Table 11.9. *Text Fonts*

Constant	*Value*	*File*
`DefaultFont`	0	GRAPH.TPU
`TriplexFont`	1	TRIP.CHR
`SmallFont`	2	LITT.CHR
`SansSerifFont`	3	SANS.CHR
`GothicFont`	4	GOTH.CHR

`DefaultFont` is the default 8 × 8 bit-mapped font. All others are stroked fonts. Each stroked font is stored in a separate file with a CHR extension. To use a stroked font, be sure its file resides in the same directory as the one you specified in the `InitGraph` procedure.

The `Direction` parameter enables you to choose between displaying text horizontally (left to right) or vertically (bottom to top). You can use the values 0 or 1, respectively, or one of the predefined constants:

```
HorizDir   = 0;
VertDir    = 1;
```

Unlike text mode, the graphics mode features of Turbo Pascal help you scale the character fonts to any size. The `CharSize` parameter is a word value containing the multiplication factor. A value of 1 indicates normal-sized characters, 2 indicates characters twice the normal size, and so on.

The use of `SetTextStyle` is demonstrated in the EYECHART program in listing 11.27.

Listing 11.27

```
program EyeChart;
uses Graph;
var
   Alphabet : byte;
   Height, Width, FontType, FontSize : word;
   GraphDriver, GraphMode : integer;
begin
   GraphDriver := Detect;
   InitGraph( GraphDriver, GraphMode, 'C:\TP' );
   Height := GetMaxY div 5;
   Width := GetMaxX div 10;
   for FontType := 0 to 4 do begin
      writeln( 'Font ', FontType );
      Alphabet := 84;
      MoveTo( GetMaxX div 5, FontType*Height );
      for FontSize := 1 to 6 do begin
         SetTextStyle( FontType, HorizDir, FontSize );
         Inc( Alphabet );
         OutText( Chr( Alphabet ) );
         MoveRel( Width, 0 );
      end;
   end;
   readln;
   CloseGraph;
end.
```

When EYECHART executes, it produces the output shown in figure 11.23.

Vertical text is demonstrated in the CHART2 program in listing 11.28.

Listing 11.28

```
program Chart2;
uses Graph;
var
   Width, Height, FontType, Letter : word;
   GraphDriver, GraphMode : integer;
```

continues

Listing 11.28 continued

```
begin
   GraphDriver := Detect;
   InitGraph( GraphDriver, GraphMode, 'C:\TP';
   Width := GetMaxX div 6;
   Height := GetMaxY div 5;
   for FontType := 0 to 4 do begin
      MoveTo( Width*( FontType+1 ), 0 );
      SetTextStyle( FontType, VertDir, 8 );
      OutText( 'abcdefghijklmnopqrstuvwxyz' );
   end;
   readln;
   CloseGraph;
end.
```

Fig. 11.23. *Output produced by the EYECHART program.*

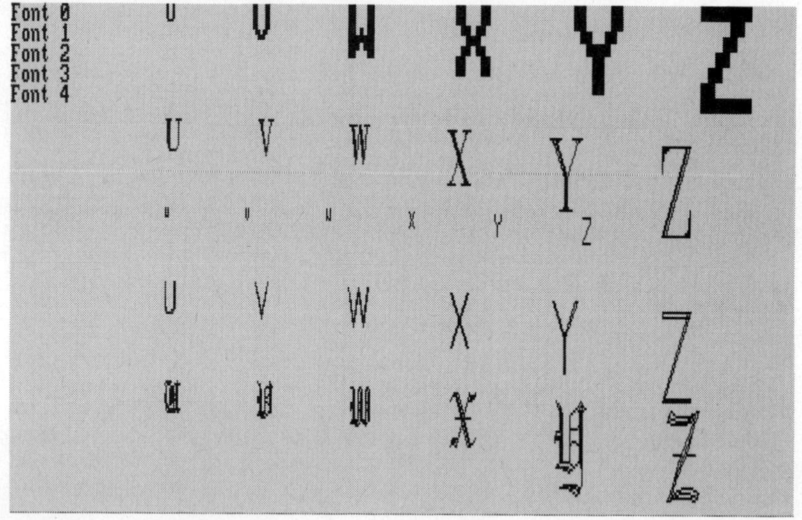

CHART2 produces the output shown in figure 11.24. Notice that the end of the string in the `OutText` procedure is positioned at the top of the screen.

Fig. 11.24. Output produced by the CHART2 program.

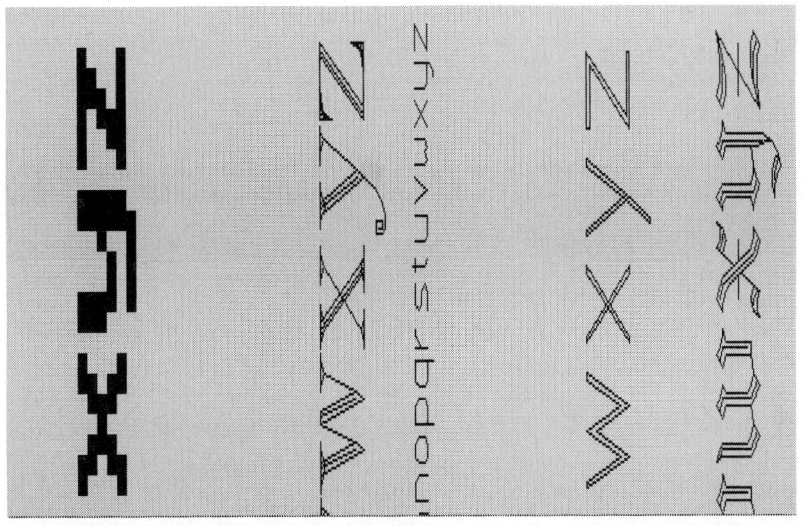

Text Justification

In figures 11.23 and 11.24, you probably noticed that even though the programs attempted to position the characters evenly, their locations appeared somewhat haphazard. The `SetTextJustify` procedure helps you to justify the characters—horizontally and vertically—relative to the current pointer.

```
procedure SetTextJustify( Horiz, Vert : word );
```

For the `Horiz(ontal)` parameter, use one of the constants:

```
LeftText   =    0;

CenterText =    1;

RightText  =    2;
```

For the `Vert(ical)` parameter, use one of the constants:

```
BottomText =    0;

CenterText =    1;

TopText    =    2;
```

The JUSTTEXT program in listing 11.29 demonstrates how the `SetTextJustify` procedure operates.

Listing 11.29

```
program JustText;
uses Graph;
var
   i, Height, Width,
   Horizontal, Vertical : word;
   GraphDriver, GraphMode : integer;
begin
   GraphDriver := Detect;
   InitGraph( GraphDriver, GraphMode, 'C:\TP' );
   Height := GetMaxY div 4;
   Width := GetMaxX div 4;
   SetTextStyle( DefaultFont, HorizDir, 6 );
   for i := 1 to 3 do begin
      Line( 0, Height*i, GetMaxX, Height*i );
      Line( Width*i, 0, Width*i, GetMaxY );
   end;
   for Horizontal := 0 to 2 do
      for Vertical := 0 to 2 do begin
         MoveTo( ( Horizontal+1 )*Width, ( Vertical+1 )*Height );
         SetTextJustify( Horizontal, Vertical );
         OutText( 'O' );
      end;
   readln;
   CloseGraph;
end.
```

When JUSTTEXT executes, it produces the results shown in figure 11.25. All nine possible combinations are presented. The vertical justification options are shown top to bottom, whereas the horizontal justification options are shown left to right.

Determining Text Settings

If your program switches between two or more text character styles, you can use the `GetTextSettings` procedure to obtain and store the current text font, direction, size, and justification:

Fig. 11.25. Output produced by the JUSTTEXT program.

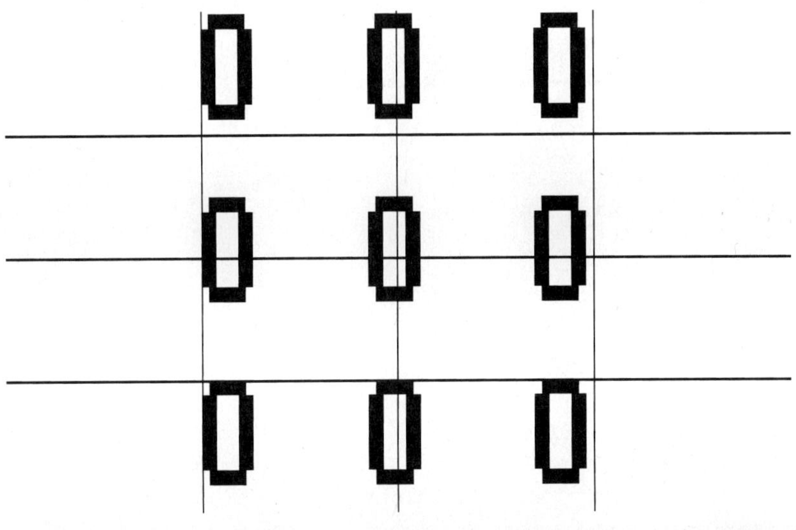

```
procedure GetTextSettings( var TextInfo : TextSettingsType );
```

`GetTextSettings` uses a single variable parameter of type `TextSettingsType`, which is defined as follows:

```
TextSettingsType = record
                      Font      : word;
                      Direction : word;
                      CharSize  : word;
                      Horiz     : word;
                      Vert      : word;
                   end;
```

Assuming that you defined a variable `TextInfo` as type `TextSettingsType`, you can retrieve the current settings with the call

```
GetTextSettings( TextInfo );
```

Later, to return to the original settings, use the contents of `TextInfo` as inputs to `SetTextStyle` and `SetTextJustify`.

```
with TextInfo do begin
   SetTextStyle( Font, Direction, CharSize );
   SetTextJustify( Horiz, Vert );
end;
```

Controlling Text Size

The `SetTextStyle` procedure restricts you to integral multiples of the standard font sizes. If you want to shrink the size of a stroked font or change its proportions, you can use the `SetUserCharSize` procedure.

```
procedure SetUserCharSize( MultX, DivX, MultY, DivY : word );
```

The width and height of any stroked font used after `SetUserCharSize` is called will be adjusted by factors of:

$$\frac{\text{MultY}}{\text{DivX}} \quad \text{and} \quad \frac{\text{MultX}}{\text{DivY}}$$

respectively. To use `SetUserCharSize`, you must first call the `SetTextStyle` procedure with the following for its `CharSize` parameter:

```
UserCharSize = 0;
```

Using the predefined constant `UserCharSize` tells the compiler that you want to modify the proportions of a stroked font. Next, call `SetUserCharSize`.

This technique is demonstrated in the TEXTSIZE program in listing 11.30.

Listing 11.30

```
program TextSize;
uses Graph;
var
   GraphDriver, GraphMode : integer;
   Width, Height : word;
begin
   GraphDriver := Detect;
   InitGraph( GraphDriver, GraphMode, 'C:\TP' );
   Width := GetMaxX div 2;
   Height := GetMaxY div 4;
   SetTextJustify( CenterText, CenterText );
   SetUserCharSize( 4, 1, 2, 1 );
   SetTextStyle( SansSerifFont, HorizDir, UserCharSize );
   OutTextXY( Width, Height, 'CONTRACT' );
```

```
    SetUserCharSize( 1, 1, 1, 1 );
    SetTextStyle( SansSerifFont, HorizDir, UserCharSize );
    OutTextXY( Width, 2*Height, 'THIS IS THE BODY OF THE AGREEMENT...' );
    SetUserCharSize( 1, 2, 1, 2 );
    SetTextStyle( SansSerifFont, HorizDir, UserCharSize );
    OutTextXY( Width, 3*Height, 'THIS IS THE FINE PRINT...' );
    readln;
    CloseGraph;
end.
```

When TEXTSIZE executes, it produces the results shown in figure 11.26. Note that the `SetUserCharSize` procedure allowed TEXTSIZE to independently vary the character width and height.

Fig. 11.26. *Output produced by the TEXTSIZE program.*

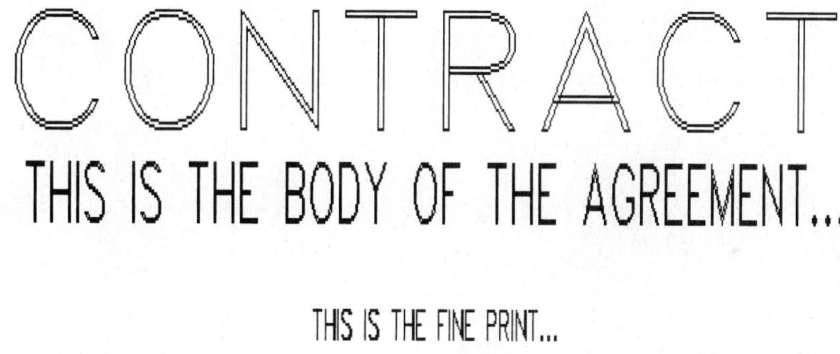

CONTRACT

THIS IS THE BODY OF THE AGREEMENT...

THIS IS THE FINE PRINT...

Determining Text Size

On a text screen, the size of a string is easy to determine. Its height is 1/25 (four percent) of the size of the screen, and its length can be found with the `Length` function.

The size of a string on a graphics screen is more difficult to ascertain, especially after selecting and scaling a font. Fortunately, Turbo Pascal provides two functions that return the height and width of a graphics string:

```
function  TextHeight( TextString : string ) : word;
function  TextWidth (TextString : string ) : word;
```

The `TextHeight` function returns the height of a string in pixels. The `TextWidth` function returns the width of a string in pixels.

The TEXTRING program in listing 11.31 uses `TextHeight` and `TextWidth` to determine the size of a string, then calculates the radius of a circle to enclose it.

Listing 11.31

```
program TextRing;
uses Graph;
var
   GraphDriver, GraphMode : integer;
   StartX, StartY, Radius : word;
   Height, Width : LongInt;
   Message : string[ 20 ];
begin
   GraphDriver := Detect;
   InitGraph( GraphDriver, GraphMode, 'C:\TP' );
   Message := 'Press the ENTER key.';
   SetTextJustify( CenterText, CenterText );
   SetTextStyle( SansSerifFont, HorizDir, 4 );
   StartX := GetMaxX div 2;
   StartY := GetMaxY div 2;
   OutTextXY( StartX, StartY, Message );
   Height := TextHeight( Message );
   Width := TextWidth( Message );
   Radius := Round( 1.1*( Sqrt( Height*Height + Width*Width ) / 2 ) );
   Circle( StartX, StartY, Radius );
   readln;
   CloseGraph;
end.
```

When TEXTRING executes, it produces the results shown in figure 11.27. You can experiment with different font sizes and string lengths; the circle produced will adapt as needed.

Fig. 11.27. Output produced by the TEXTTRING program.

Graphics Defaults

The `GraphDefaults` procedure resets the graphics parameters to the values they had immediately after the graphics system was initialized with `InitGraph`:

```
procedure GraphDefaults;
```

`GraphDefaults` resets all system default values, as follows:

- ❏ The current pointer is moved to the upper left corner of the screen.
- ❏ The viewport is returned to the full screen.
- ❏ The palette, drawing, and background colors are returned to the defaults.
- ❏ The line style and pattern are restored.
- ❏ The fill style, color, and pattern are restored.
- ❏ The active font, text style and justification, and user character size are restored.

Interestingly, though, `GraphDefaults` does not clear the screen. If you want that done as well, follow the call to `GraphDefaults` with a call to `ClearDevice`.

Including Drivers and Fonts with Your Programs

Generally, it is not inconvenient to have the BGI device driver files and the CHR stroked character font files reside somewhere on your disk. After all, your program loads and runs successfully as long as you can reference the location of the files when you initialize the graphics system, as follows:

```
GraphDriver := Detect;
InitGraph( GraphDriver, GraphMode, 'C:\TP' );
```

Now suppose that you like your graphics program so much that you want to give a copy to a friend. Or you have developed a business graphics application at work and need to run it on five other PCs. Or you want to make your program available through public domain groups—or even sell it commercially.

Suddenly, you have a problem. Unless every machine that runs your program has a directory named C:\TP that contains the appropriate BGI device driver and CHR character font files, your program will not operate.

The immediate solution is to change the path in the `InitGraph` call to a null string (indicating the current directory) and include all of the BGI and CHR files when you distribute your program. But even this is only temporary relief. If your program has any value at all, people will want to run it outside the directory in which it is stored by including its location as part of their PC's `PATH` command. Again, your program will not operate, because the BGI and CHR files are not where `InitGraph` searches. So, you include a line in your documentation: "These files must always reside in the current directory." It works, of course, but it does not seem professional.

A different problem arises when you use several stroked fonts. By default, your program keeps only one character set in its memory at a time. Consequently, if you switch between two (or more) character fonts, your program must reload each font from the disk every time it is used. It does not take long before even your more patient users complain about the performance delays and the grinding noises during disk access.

The answer to all these troubles is to include the BGI and CHR files in your program itself. In other words, if all of the device drivers and fonts you need could be compiled along with your program, you would not need to worry about their physical location on disk, nor would your users experience noticeable delays when switching among several character fonts.

In this section, you learn how this can be done.

Loading Drivers and Fonts

There are two ways to combine drivers and fonts with your programs.

1. *The heap memory method.* Normally, `InitGraph` places the selected driver and font on the heap. You can do this directly. Read all the BGI and CHR files you want, place them on the heap, and give their locations to `InitGraph` so that it can bypass the loading process.

2. *The external procedure method.* Convert the BGI and CHR files into object files with the BINOBJ.EXE program, then link the object files into your program. Tell `InitGraph` that the code for the drivers and fonts can be found in procedures in the program.

Both approaches work, but the first method suffers from the same drawback discussed before, namely that the BGI and CHR files must accompany your program and must reside in a predetermined directory. The Turbo Pascal *Programmer's Guide* describes how this technique can be implemented.

The second technique is cleaner and more efficient. It is the one described here. No matter which method you use, you are registering the drivers and fonts with `InitGraph` when you specify their memory locations. (In this context, *registering* means "signing up," as in registering to vote, registering for school, or registering for the draft.) Registering is performed with the following functions:

```
function  RegisterBGIdriver( Driver : pointer ) : integer;
function  RegisterBGIfont( Font : pointer ) : integer;
```

`RegisterBGIdriver` and `RegisterBGIfont` register a driver file and a font, respectively, with the graphics system. Both take a pointer as their single parameter. If you use the heap memory method, the pointer points to the starting location of the driver or font on the heap. If you use the external procedure method, the pointer points to the linked-in procedure.

Creating Object Files with BINOBJ.EXE

Locate the BINOBJ.EXE program that was supplied with your Turbo Pascal distribution disks. If you have installed Turbo on a hard drive, you will probably find the program in the C:\TP subdirectory, next to the compiler.

The BINOBJ.EXE program converts the binary versions of the CHR character file and the BGI driver file to object file format. A *binary file* is nothing other than data. An *object file* contains either code or data that a Turbo Pascal program can use. An object file, which has OBJ as its extension, can be linked with your program by using the `{$L}` compiler directive.

BINOBJ.EXE takes three parameters, as follows:

```
BINOBJ   <source[.BIN]>   <destination[.OBJ]>   <publicname>
```

The source file is the binary file you want to convert. It assumes .BIN as its default extension. The destination file is the OBJ file you want to produce. The public name is the name of the procedure you will use in your program.

Before you proceed, remember: you are about to create new object files based on the BGI and CHR files; the original drivers and fonts will not be modified in any way.

The easiest way to usc BINOBJ.EXE is in the form of a batch file. The PORTABLE.BAT file in listing 11.32 contains batch instructions that create object files for every driver and font.

Listing 11.32

```
C:\TP\UTILS\BINOBJ  C:\TP\BGI\GOTH.CHR  GOTH     GOTHfont
C:\TP\UTILS\BINOBJ  C:\TP\LITT.CHR      LITT     LITTfont
C:\TP\UTILS\BINOBJ  C:\TP\SANS.CHR      SANS     SANSfont
C:\TP\UTILS\BINOBJ  C:\TP\TRIP.CHR      TRIP     TRIPfont
C:\TP\UTILS\BINOBJ  C:\TP\ATT.BGI       ATT      ATTDriver
C:\TP\UTILS\BINOBJ  C:\TP\CGA.BGI       CGA      CGADriver
C:\TP\UTILS\BINOBJ  C:\TP\EGAVGA.BGI    EGAVGA   EGAVGADriver
C:\TP\UTILS\BINOBJ  C:\TP\HERC.BGI      HERC     HerculesDriver
C:\TP\UTILS\BINOBJ  C:\TP\IBM8514.BGI   IBM8514  IBM8514Driver
C:\TP\UTILS\BINOBJ  C:\TP\PC3270.BGI    PC3270   PC3270Driver
```

To use the file, simply enter the following command from the DOS prompt:

```
PORTABLE
```

DOS responds by running the BINOBJ.EXE program for every driver and font. (You could have typed in each line individually, but the odds are fairly high that you will want to use this technique again some time.) You can confirm that the batch file operated correctly by verifying the presence of the object files with the command:

```
DIR * .OBJ
```

DOS responds with a listing of the ten files:

```
GOTH.OBJ
LITT.OBJ
SANS.OBJ
TRIP.OBJ
ATT.OBJ
CGA.OBJ
EGAVGA.OBJ
HERC.OBJ
IBM8514.OBJ
PC3270.OBJ
```

Each instruction in the batch file performed a similar conversion for every driver and font. For example, the command:

```
C:\TP\UTILS\BINOBJ   C:\TP\BGI\GOTH.CHR   GOTH   GOTHfont
```

took the binary data file GOTH.CHR residing in the C:\TP\BGI subdirectory and created an object file version, GOTH.OBJ, in the current subdirectory. This object file can now be referenced as a procedure in a Turbo Pascal program using the name GOTHfont. Although it is declared as a procedure, GOTHfont does not contain any executable code. Fortunately, `InitGraph` does not care; it expects data, so it will treat GOTHfont as data.

Incorporating Drivers and Fonts in Your Programs

The process of linking an object file into your program is demonstrated in the ALLSTUFF program, shown in listing 11.33. The drivers and character fonts are declared as external procedures. Each procedure name corresponds to the third parameter in the BINOBJ.EXE command: the public name. By declaring a procedure as external, you are simply telling the compiler that its contents can be found in another file—specifically, the one you name with the `{$L}` compiler directive. During compilation, Turbo reads each external file and physically includes it with the main program. The OBJ files will not be needed after the compilation is completed, but you will probably want to keep them around for next time.

Listing 11.33

```
program AllStuff;
uses Graph;
var
   FontStyle, Height : word;
   GraphDriver, GraphMode : integer;
procedure GOTHfont;          external;    {$L GOTH.OBJ }
procedure LITTfont;          external;    {$L LITT.OBJ }
procedure SANSfont;          external;    {$L SANS.OBJ }
procedure TRIPfont;          external;    {$L TRIP.OBJ }
procedure ATTDriver;         external;    {$L ATT.OBJ }
procedure CGADriver;         external;    {$L CGA.OBJ }
procedure EGAVGADriver;      external;    {$L EGAVGA.OBJ }
procedure HerculesDriver;    external;    {$L HERC.OBJ }
procedure IBM8514Driver;     external;    {$L IBM8514.OBJ }
procedure PC3270Driver;      external;    {$L PC3270.OBJ }
procedure LoadTheFont( ProcedurePointer : pointer );
begin
   if RegisterBGIfont( ProcedurePointer ) < 0 then begin
      writeln( 'Error registering font: ', GraphErrorMsg( GraphResult ) );
      Halt( 1 );
   end;
end;
procedure PrepareTheFonts;
begin
   LoadTheFont( @GOTHfont );
   LoadTheFont( @LITTfont );
   LoadTheFont( @SANSfont );
   LoadTheFont( @TRIPfont );
end;
procedure LoadTheDriver( ProcedurePointer : pointer );
begin
   if RegisterBGIdriver( ProcedurePointer ) < 0 then begin
      writeln( 'Error registering driver: ', GraphErrorMsg( GraphResult ) );
```

```
      Halt( 1 );
    end;
end;
procedure PrepareTheDrivers;
begin
    LoadTheDriver( @ATTDriver );
    LoadTheDriver( @CGADriver );
    LoadTheDriver( @EGAVGADriver );
    LoadTheDriver( @HerculesDriver );
    LoadTheDriver( @IBM8514Driver );
    LoadTheDriver( @PC3270Driver );
end;
begin
    PrepareTheFonts;
    PrepareTheDrivers;
    GraphDriver := Detect;
    InitGraph( GraphDriver, GraphMode, '' );
    Height := GetMaxY div 6;
    SetTextJustify( CenterText, CenterText );
    for  FontStyle := DefaultFont to GothicFont do begin
        SetTextStyle( FontStyle, HorizDir, 4 );
        OutTextXY( GetMaxX div 2, Height*( FontStyle+1 ), 'Greetings!' );
    end;
    readln;
    CloseGraph;
end.
```

The `RegisterBGIdriver` and `RegisterBGIfont` functions register each of the external files with the GRAPH.TPU unit as a potential driver or font. `InitGraph`, which is called here with a null string for its search path, looks first to the GRAPH.TPU internal driver and font tables, locates the names of the procedures, and looks no further. All drivers and fonts are already available in the program, so no disk access is required.

When ALLSTUFF executes, it produces five `Greetings!` messages, as shown in figure 11.28.

Admittedly, ALLSTUFF is not a fancy program, but consider: It can run on any graphics adapter on any PC that supports Turbo Pascal, and it runs without the need for separate BGI or CHR files! You can use ALLSTUFF as a template for making your applications independent of separate drivers and fonts.

Fig. 11.28. Output produced by the ALLSTUFF program.

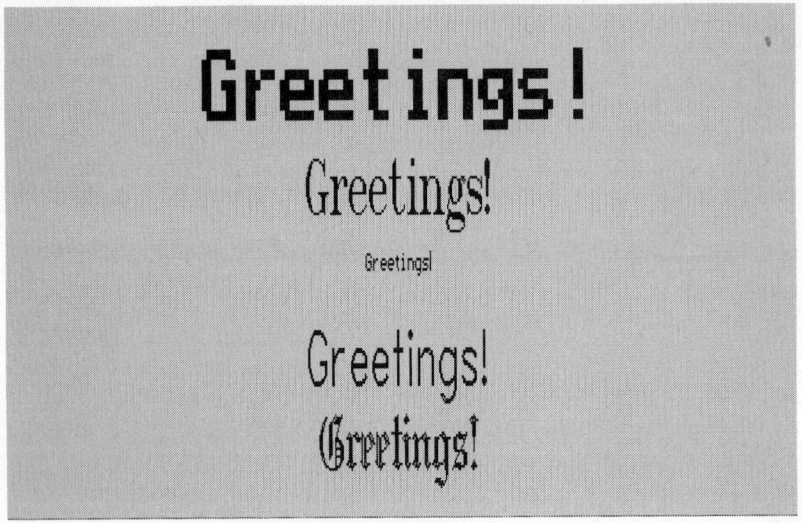

Of course, ALLSTUFF is the "full-size" version. In your program, you should remove all references to unused fonts. Similarly, if you know your program will not need to run on a PC equipped with a specific graphics adapter, you should eliminate unnecessary driver references as well. The difference between an EXE file that runs on all graphics cards with all fonts and an EXE file that uses one font on one card is about 45,000 bytes.

Installing New Fonts and Drivers

It is quite likely that software firms and public domain groups will soon begin to offer additional CHR character font files. It is even more likely that if a new graphics adapter board is introduced to the market, it will come complete with its own BGI (or comparable) driver file. In both cases, installation instructions will probably be provided with the product. However, just in case, you should know that there are two ways to incorporate new font and driver files in your programs:

- ❑ Convert the new font or driver file to object format with the BINOBJ.EXE program and link the object file to your program. This method was demonstrated earlier.

- ❑ Use two special functions: `InstallUserFont` and `InstallUserDriver`.

Now you will see how to use `InstallUserFont` and `InstallUserDriver` to install new fonts and drivers.

Installing a New Font

To install a new stroked character font, use the procedure:

```
function InstallUserFont( FontFileName : string ) : integer;
```

`InstallUserFont` takes the name of the font file as its single parameter, loads the font into heap memory, and returns an identification number that can be used by `SetTextStyle` to reference the font.

Assuming that you have defined an integer variable `NewFont`, perform the installation with the command:

```
NewFont := InstallUserFont( 'FontFile.CHR' );
```

You should call `GraphResult` immediately afterward to test for an error. If the font table was full when you called `InstallUserFont`, `NewFont` will have a value of 0. Otherwise, `NewFont` contains a positive integer that can be used to reference the new font, as follows:

```
SetTextStyle( NewFont, HorizDir, 1 );
```

All subsequent `OutText` and `OutTextXY` statements use the new font design.

Additional information on installing character fonts is in the Turbo Pascal *Library Reference*.

Installing a New Driver

When you open the box of your new graphics board, you will probably find three items:

1. The board.
2. An instruction manual.
3. A diskette, containing a BGI device driver file and (optionally) code for a Turbo Pascal autodetection function that returns `True` if it determines that the new board is installed and `False` if the board is not present.

Autodetection is what enables you to call

```
GraphDriver := Detect;
InitGraph( GraphDriver, GraphMode, '' );
```

and trust that `InitGraph` will correctly identify the graphics card in your machine and install the appropriate driver.

To add the new device driver to the BGI device driver table, use the procedure:

```
function InstallUserDriver( DriverFileName : string;
                            AutoDetectPtr : pointer ) : integer;
```

`InstallUserDriver` takes two parameters. `DriverNameFile` is the name of the file containing the new device driver. `AutoDetectPtr` is a pointer to the autodetection function. If no function was included, `AutoDetectPtr` is set to `Nil`.

Assuming that you have defined an integer variable `NewDriver`, perform the installation with the command:

```
NewDriver := InstallUserDriver( 'DrvFile.BGI', Nil );
```

or

```
NewDriver := InstallUserDriver( 'DrvFile.BGI', @AutoDetect );
```

You should call `GraphResult` immediately afterward to test for an error. If the internal driver table is full, `NewDriver` will have a value of 0. Otherwise, `NewDriver` can serve as an identifier to reference the new driver. For example, if no autodetection function was included, you can initiate graphics as follows:

```
GraphDriver := NewDriver;
GraphMode := ???;                              { Read the handbook! }
InitGraph( GraphDriver, GraphMode, '' );
```

Of course, if the autodetection function was included, you could initiate graphics more traditionally:

```
GraphDriver := Detect;
InitGraph( GraphDriver, GraphMode, '' );
```

Additional information on installing device drivers is in the Turbo Pascal *Library Reference*.

A Note on Autodetection
Autodetection is not always possible. Remember that the IBM 8514 graphics adapter appears to the `DetectGraph` procedure just like a VGA card.

Advanced Topic: User Heap Management

The Graph unit includes two internal heap management routines: the `GraphGetMem` procedure allocates heap memory for graphics, and the `GraphFreeMem` procedure frees the heap after graphics is shut down.

Neither `GraphGetMem` nor `GraphFreeMem` are directly accessible to your program. However, Turbo Pascal provides two predefined procedure pointer variables.

- The `GraphGetMemPtr` variable points to the `GraphGetMem` procedure. You can use `GraphGetMemPtr` to point to your own heap allocation procedure.
- The `GraphFreeMemPtr` variable points to the `GraphFreeMem` procedure. You can use `GraphFreeMemPtr` to point to your own heap deallocation procedure.

The Turbo Pascal *Programmer's Reference* contains specifics on how to use `GraphGetMemPtr` and `GraphFreeMemPtr` to develop your own heap management routines. However, in almost every application, the Turbo Pascal defaults are more than adequate.

Summary

In this chapter, you learned how to use Turbo Pascal's graphics procedures and functions. You learned the performance characteristics of the most common graphics adapters, and you learned how individual drivers (in the form of BGI files) and fonts (in the form of CHR files) are used by your programs.

You saw how Turbo Pascal can automatically select an optimal graphics mode based on the equipment installed in your PC. You learned how to initiate and end a graphics session, how to switch between text and graphics modes, and how to handle errors in graphics operations.

You learned about the graphics window, called a viewport, and you saw how viewports can be created, saved, restored, and cleared.

You learned how color palettes are used in Turbo Pascal, and you learned how individual colors are selected and changed.

You learned how to plot an individual point, called a pixel. You learned how to draw lines in a variety of styles and widths. You learned how to draw a variety of polygons, arcs, circles, and ellipses in both outline and solid form.

You learned how to combine text with your graphics displays, and you saw how to control text size, justification, and direction.

You learned how to incorporate BGI and CHR files in your programs, and you saw how new drivers and fonts can be added to those already available.

CHAPTER 12

Accessing DOS

A common statement in microcomputer literature is "Programs run under the control of DOS." On a practical level, this is not strictly true. The 8086-family processor can perform only one task at a time. When a program is executing, the program itself tells the CPU what to do next; the operating system is sitting idly by in another part of memory. Nevertheless, linkages or potential linkages exist between the program and the operating system.

Your program interacts with DOS in three ways. First, all DOS services and functions remain—on an individual basis—available for use throughout program execution. Second, when DOS initiates a program, it stores useful information in an accessible area of memory known as the program segment prefix (PSP). Third, when a program ends, it triggers a sequence of DOS calls that can be affected by the program.

This chapter discusses some of the various Turbo Pascal procedures and functions that allow direct interaction with DOS operations.

System Date and Time

The system date and time can be accessed with the Turbo Pascal procedures `GetDate` and `GetTime`, respectively. The opposite procedures, `SetDate` and `SetTime`, enable you to reset the system date and time to any legal settings.

These procedures access the DOS software system clock and calendar. If your machine has an internal hardware clock (such as AST's SixPak Plus), the clock can be changed only with the routines provided by the manufacturer.

The date and time procedures are called in the following format:

```
GetDate( Year, Month, Day, DayofWeek );
GetTime( Hour, Minute, Second, Sec100 );
SetDate( Year, Month, Day );
SetTime( Hour, Minute, Second, Sec100 );
```

`Year` may be any year from 1980 through 2099. `Hour` is expressed in military fashion (24-hour clock format) from 0 through 23. `Minute` and `Second` must be in the range 0 through 59. `Sec100`, which represents hundredths of a second and ranges from 0 through 99, is inaccurate and should not be trusted for critical time calculations. `DayofWeek` ranges from 0 through 6, corresponding to Sunday through Saturday.

Retrieving the Date and Time

The DATE1 program (listing 12.1) demonstrates how to use `GetDate` and `GetTime` to create strings that can be included as part of your screen and printer headings.

Listing 12.1

```
program Date1;
uses Dos;
const
   DayNames : array [ 0..6 ] of string[ 4 ] =
              ( 'Sun ', 'Mon ', 'Tue ', 'Wed ', 'Thu ', 'Fri ', 'Sat ' );
   MonNames : array [ 1..12 ] of string[ 4 ] =
              ( 'Jan ', 'Feb ', 'Mar ', 'Apr ', 'May ', 'Jun ',
                'Jul ', 'Aug ', 'Sep ', 'Oct ', 'Nov ', 'Dec ' );
type
   String2  = string[ 2 ];
   String4  = string[ 4 ];
   String8  = string[ 8 ];
   String16 = string[ 16 ];
var
   Year,          { 1980..2099 }
   Month,         { 1..12 }
```

```
    Day,           { 1..31 }
    DayofWeek,     { 0 (Sunday) .. 6 (Saturday) }
    Hour,          { 0..23 }
    Minute,        { 0..59 }
    Second,        { 0..59 }
    Sec100         { 0..99 }
                              : word;
    DateString     : String16;  { DayofWeek Mon Day Year }
    TimeString1,                { Hour:Minute:Second }
    TimeString2    : String8;   { Hour:Minute AM/PM }
function DString2( DateIn : word ) : String2;
begin
    DString2 := chr( 48 + DateIn div 10 ) + chr( 48 + DateIn mod 10 );
end;
function DString4( YearIn : word ) : String4;
begin
    DString4 := DString2( YearIn div 100 ) + DString2( YearIn mod 100 );
end;
begin
    GetDate( Year, Month, Day, DayofWeek );
    DateString := DayNames[ DayofWeek ] +
                  MonNames[ Month ] +
                  DString2( Day ) + ', ' +
                  DString4( Year );
    writeln( DateString );
    GetTime( Hour, Minute, Second, Sec100 );
    TimeString1 := DString2( Hour ) + ':' +
                   DString2( Minute ) + ':' +
                   DString2( Second );
    writeln( TimeString1 );
    TimeString2 := DString2( Hour mod 12 ) + ':' +
                   DString2( Minute ) + ' ' +
                   chr( ord( 'A' ) + 15*( Hour div 12 ) ) + 'M';
    writeln( TimeString2 );
end
```

When the program is executed, it produces one standard date and two standard time formats:

```
Mon Aug 01, 1988
22:17:09
10:17 PM
```

Changing the Date

When you use `SetDate` and `GetDate` together, you can have DOS calculate which day of the week a certain date falls on. The DATE2 program (listing 12.2) exploits this feature by creating a calendar for any given month and year.

Listing 12.2

```
program Date2;
uses Dos;
var
   OldYear,        Year,          { 1980..2099 }
   OldMonth,       Month,         { 1..12 }
   OldDay,         Day,           { 1..31 }
   OldDayofWeek,   DayofWeek      { 0 (Sunday) .. 6 (Saturday) }
                 : word;
   DayCount      : byte;
   i             : byte;
begin
   repeat
      write( 'Enter month, year: ' );
      readln( Month, Year );
   until (Year>1979) and (Year< 2100) and (Month in [ 1..12 ]);
   Day := 1;
   GetDate( OldYear, OldMonth, OldDay, OldDayofWeek );
   SetDate( Year, Month, Day );
   GetDate( Year, Month, Day, DayofWeek );
   SetDate( OldYear, OldMonth, OldDay );
   case Month of      { How many days are in the month? }
      1, 3, 5, 7, 8, 10, 12 : DayCount := 31;
      4, 6, 9, 11 : DayCount := 30;
      2 : if Year mod 4 = 0 then DayCount := 29 else DayCount := 28;
   end;
   writeln;
   writeln( ' Sun Mon Tue Wed Thu Fri Sat' );
   for i := 1 to DayCount + DayofWeek do begin
      if i mod 7 = 1 then writeln;
      if i <= DayofWeek then write( '    ' ) else write( (i - DayofWeek):4 );
   end;
   writeln;
end.
```

If you run the program for February 1988 and January 2000, the program produces the following output:

```
Enter month, year: 2 1988
 Sun Mon Tue Wed Thu Fri Sat
       1   2   3   4   5   6
   7   8   9  10  11  12  13
  14  15  16  17  18  19  20
  21  22  23  24  25  26  27
  28  29
Enter month, year: 1 2000
 Sun Mon Tue Wed Thu Fri Sat
                           1
   2   3   4   5   6   7   8
   9  10  11  12  13  14  15
  16  17  18  19  20  21  22
  23  24  25  26  27  28  29
  30  31
```

Essentially, the program calculates how far to shift over before beginning to write the days of the month. Note that the original system date is restored as soon as possible. If `SetDate` is called with invalid parameters, no action results.

Timing Program Operations

`SetTime` can be used to determine the duration of execution. The DATE3 program (listing 12.3) compares the execution speed of half a million `repeat` loops with the same number of `for` loops. At the beginning of each process, `SetTime` resets the system clock to all zeros; at the end, `GetTime` directly obtains the amount of time passed.

Listing 12.3

```
program Date3;
uses Dos;
var
   Hour,      { 0..23 }
   Minute,    { 0..59 }
   Second,    { 0..59 }
   Sec100     { 0..99 }
```

continues

Listing 12.3 continued

```
              : word;
   i          : longint;
procedure StartTheTimer( Message : string );
begin
   writeln;
   writeln( Message );
   SetTime( 0, 0, 0, 0 );
end;
procedure EndTheTimer;
begin
   GetTime( Hour, Minute, Second, Sec100 );
   writeln( 'Time elapsed:' );
   writeln( Hour:5,    ' hours' );
   writeln( Minute:5, ' minutes' );
   writeln( Second:5, ' seconds' );
   writeln;
end;
begin
   StartTheTimer( 'The "repeat" loop' );
      i := 0;
      repeat
         i := i + 1;
      until i = 500000;
   EndTheTimer;
   StartTheTimer( 'The "for" loop' );
      for i := 1 to 500000 do begin end;
   EndTheTimer;
end.
```

Not surprisingly, the comparison reveals that the `for` loop is slightly faster than the `repeat` loop:

```
The "repeat" loop
Time elapsed:
    0 hours
    0 minutes
   18 seconds
The "for" loop
Time elapsed:
    0 hours
    0 minutes
   14 seconds
```

The problem with this method, however, is that the system clock now must be reset. A better method of calculating duration is to compare the parameters from two successive `GetTime` calls, as shown in the DATE4 program (listing 12.4).

Listing 12.4

```
program Date4;
uses Dos;
var
   Hour,          OldHour,      { 0..23 }
   Minute,        OldMinute,    { 0..59 }
   Second,        OldSecond,    { 0..59 }
   Sec100,        OldSec100     { 0..99 }
                                : word;
   HoursPassed,
   MinutesPassed,
   SecondsPassed                : integer;
   i : longint;
procedure StartTheTimer( Message : string );
begin
   writeln;
   writeln( Message );
   GetTime( OldHour, OldMinute, OldSecond, OldSec100 );
end;
procedure EndTheTimer;
begin
   GetTime( Hour, Minute, Second, Sec100 );
   HoursPassed   := Hour - OldHour;
   MinutesPassed := Minute - OldMinute;
   SecondsPassed := Second - OldSecond;
   if Hour < OldHour then
      HoursPassed := HoursPassed + 24;
   if Minute < OldMinute then begin
      MinutesPassed := MinutesPassed + 60;
      HoursPassed   := HoursPassed - 1;
   end;
   if Second < OldSecond then begin
      SecondsPassed := SecondsPassed + 60;
      MinutesPassed := MinutesPassed - 1;
   end;
   writeln( 'Time elapsed:' );
```

continues

Listing 12.4 continued

```
    writeln( HoursPassed:5,    ' hours' );
    writeln( MinutesPassed:5, ' minutes' );
    writeln( SecondsPassed:5, ' seconds' );
    writeln;
end;
begin
    StartTheTimer( 'The "repeat" loop' );
        i := 0;
        repeat
            i := i + 1;
        until i = 500000;
    EndTheTimer;
    StartTheTimer( 'The "for" loop' );
        for i := 1 to 500000 do begin end;
    EndTheTimer;
end.
```

The same output is obtained, but the system clock has not been corrupted.

By the way, the following offers proof that you should use the increment function whenever possible. If you change the code in the `repeat` loop from

```
i := i + 1;
```

to

```
Inc( i );
```

you will see a significant improvement in performance.

Creating Tones

Every programmer with more than two minutes of experience is familiar with the beep sound produced by the PC. Although a few particularly obnoxious programs beep every time a key is pressed, most applications properly use the sound as part of a warning or an error message.

Sound generation is not limited to warning beeps; sound capabilities are part of the tool kit you have available to develop user interfaces. The same hardware that produces the beep can be used to produce a far wider range of tones.

The beep is nothing more than ASCII character 7. To generate it, all you need do is write the following:

```
program Sound1;
begin
   writeln( chr( 7 ));    { or writeln( #7 ); }
end.
```

When used sparingly, beeps are an excellent way of getting the user's attention. When used excessively, they detract from the quality of a program.

The Turbo Pascal procedure `Sound` causes the speaker to emit a tone that continues until disabled with the `NoSound` procedure. `Sound` is called with a single word-sized parameter specifying the desired frequency in hertz (cycles per second).

If `Sound` is immediately followed by `NoSound`, the speaker in your PC will not be able to respond fast enough to generate any noise. The `Delay` procedure is usually used to allow the speaker enough time to react. `Delay` takes a single word-sized parameter that specifies the delay in milliseconds (1000 milliseconds equals 1 second).

By selecting the right combination of frequencies and delays, you can produce a pleasant set of musical tones. In the SOUND2 program (listing 12.5), the numbers 1 through 7 correspond to the notes of an electronic organ. The program ends when any other key is pressed.

Listing 12.5

```
program Sound2;
uses Crt;
const
   C = 523;
   D = 587;
   E = 659;
   F = 699;
   G = 784;
   A = 880;
   B = 988;
var
   Key : char;
   OffBoard : boolean;
   Note : word;
```

continues

Listing 12.5 continued

```
begin
   OffBoard := False;
   repeat
      Key := ReadKey;
      case Key of
         '1' : Note := C;
         '2' : Note := D;
         '3' : Note := E;
         '4' : Note := F;
         '5' : Note := G;
         '6' : Note := A;
         '7' : Note := B;
         else  OffBoard := True;
      end;
      if not OffBoard then begin
         write( Key:2 );    { Displays each note }
         Sound( Note );
         Delay( 100 );      { 100 milliseconds = 0.1 second }
         NoSound;
      end;
   until OffBoard = True;
   writeln;
end.
```

The DOS Environment Table

The *environment* is a collection of strings that programs can locate and use as a reference. Each string is established with the DOS `SET` instruction and stored by the operating system. Most environment variables are established as part of the AUTOEXEC.BAT start-up file.

Each string is in the form

```
EnvironmentVariable = EnvironmentString
```

The most common environment variables are `COMSPEC`, which is usually set to the location of the COMMAND.COM program, and `PATH`, which defines the preferred sequence of directories to search when you look for a file that is not completely defined. Environment strings are stored in an area of memory called the *environment table*, which can be as large as 32K.

Using the Environment Table

To examine the contents of your environment table, execute the DOS SET command—without parameters—as follows:

```
C>set
COMSPEC=C:\COMMAND.COM
PATH=C:\DOS;C:\WORD;C:\TURBOC;C:\TP
```

Although some variables, such as COMSPEC and PATH, have clearly defined uses, any variable name and assignment is allowed. For example, the favorite_show variable can be defined as follows:

```
C>set favorite_show= "My Fair Lady"
```

The new entry can be confirmed by inspecting the environment table again:

```
C>set
COMSPEC=C:\COMMAND.COM
PATH=C:\DOS;C:\WORD;C:\TURBOC;C:\TP
FAVORITE_SHOW="My Fair Lady"
```

If you now want to remove this variable, simply set it to "nothing," and test the results, as follows:

```
C>set favorite_show=
C>set
COMSPEC=C:\COMMAND.COM
PATH=C:\DOS;C:\WORD;C:\TURBOC;C:\TP
```

There is no magic about the use of environment variables. Although some DOS functions expect certain names to have certain meanings, you can use any convenient environment name to reference any data you want.

For example, suppose that you work in an office that has PCs in several departments. Each PC could be configured with a unique AUTOEXEC.BAT file, which might include lines like the following:

```
set pc_id=004
set dept=Finance
```

This PC now includes two unique environment entries.

```
C>set
COMSPEC=C:\COMMAND.COM
PATH=C:\DOS;C:\WORD;C:\TURBOC;C:\TP
PC_ID=004
DEPT=Finance
```

If programs running on this PC could access this information, department-specific and user-specific applications could be developed without the hassle of recompiling software for each machine.

> **Changing the Environment Table**
> Changes to the environment table must be made directly from DOS, not from the File/DOS shell option of the Turbo Pascal integrated environment.

Accessing Environment Strings

`EnvCount` returns the number of strings in the DOS environment table. The `EnvStr` function returns the entire string, whereas `GetEnv` returns the value of a specified environment variable. The ENV1A program (listing 12.6) lists the contents of the environment table.

Listing 12.6

```
program Env1A;
uses Dos;
var
   i : byte;
begin
   for i := 1 to EnvCount do
      writeln( EnvStr(i) );
end.
```

When executed, ENV1A might produce the following:

```
COMSPEC=C:\COMMAND.COM
PATH=C:\DOS;C:\WORD;C:\TURBOC;C:\TP
PC_ID=004
DEPT=Finance
```

Normally, to find the contents of the `PC_ID` variable, you would have to read through the environment table until you found `PC_ID` in the first five characters of a string, then extract the seventh through the last character in the string. With the `GetEnv` function you can do this directly. The ENV1B program (listing 12.7) demonstrates `GetEnv`.

Listing 12.7

```
program Env1B;
uses Dos;
begin
   writeln( GetEnv( 'pc_id' ) );
end.
```

When the ENV1B program executes, it displays the single line:

```
004
```

The `Val` procedure could be used to convert the string to numeric format. Notice that the `GetEnv` function ignores case and treats `pc_id` and `PC_ID` identically.

The Program Segment Prefix

Before DOS loads an EXE file for execution, it creates and loads a 256-byte area called the program segment prefix (PSP). The PSP is where DOS stores the information it needs to regain control of the PC when the program ends.

Some of the more useful fields in the PSP are listed in table 12.1. Areas marked *Reserved* contain data useful only to the operating system. Although these fields are freely accessible to your program, under no circumstances should you attempt to modify any of them. The following sections discuss how these PSP fields can be accessed and used.

Accessing the Program Segment Prefix

You can access any field in the PSP by using pointers. The segment address of the PSP is given by the predeclared variable `PrefixSeg`. The PSP1 program (listing 12.8) demonstrates how you can obtain the top-of-memory information.

Table 12.1. Contents of the Program Segment Prefix

Offset			
Hex	*Decimal*	*Length*	*Contents*
$00	0	2	Reserved
$02	2	2	Top of memory (that is, the last paragraph allocated to the program)
$04	4	6	Reserved
$0A	10	2	Offset, previous contents of the termination handler
$0C	12	2	Segment, interrupt vector (Int $22)
$0E	14	2	Offset, previous contents of Ctrl-C/ Ctrl-Break
$10	16	2	Segment, interrupt vector (Int $23)
$12	18	2	Offset, previous contents of the critical-error handler
$14	20	2	Segment, interrupt vector (Int $24)
$16	22	22	Reserved
$2C	44	2	Segment address of the environment table
$2E	46	82	Reserved
$80	128	128	Buffer for both the command line and the disk transfer area (DTA)

Listing 12.8

```
program PSP1;
var
   TopOfMemory : ^word;
   LongTopOfMemory,
   Bytes,
   KBytes : longint;
begin
   TopOfMemory := Ptr( PrefixSeg, 2 );     { Access top of memory info }
   LongTopOfMemory := TopOfMemory^ + 1;    { Reference starts at zero   }
```

```
    Bytes := 16 * LongTopOfMemory;          { Size is in paragraphs     }
    KBytes := Bytes div 1024;
    writeln( 'System memory is as follows:' );
    writeln( LongTopOfMemory:10, ' paragraphs' );
    writeln( Bytes:10, ' bytes' );
    writeln( KBytes:9, 'K bytes' );
end.
```

The top-of-memory field in the PSP contains the number of the highest paragraph used by the program. By default, Turbo allocates all remaining internal memory, so the top-of-memory for the program is the same as the top-of-memory paragraph for the PC. Executing this program gives the following:

```
System memory is as follows:
     40960 paragraphs
    655360 bytes
      640K bytes
```

Note, though, that the program obtains this result through trickery. If the program's memory use had been reduced with the `{$M}` compiler directive, the program would have obtained a lower number. Either way, the PSP contains the highest memory location used by the program.

Interrupt Vectors

Three addresses, called *interrupt vectors*, begin at offset $0A (10 decimal). The first one, the termination handler, contains the memory address to go to when the current program ends execution. Typically, this address would contain the start of the code DOS needs to regain control of the PC from the spent program.

The second address points to the location of the code that executes if, during the running of the program, an operator presses the Ctrl-C or Ctrl-Break combination. Without the availability of this address, the CPU might know to suspend program execution, but it would not know what to do next.

The third address, the critical-error handler, is the start of the code the CPU executes if an unrecoverable run-time error is encountered.

By placing these addresses in a convenient location, the operating system creates a safety net the CPU can use to return control to DOS if a program experiences an "exception" condition.

All three addresses contain the previous (that is, original) memory locations. Nothing stops your program from establishing its own error-handling or interrupt-handling routines, but DOS needs to be restored to the condition it was in prior to the program's run. These addresses, then, represent a scratch pad for DOS to use to keep track of information it needs.

The Environment Table Address

The PSP contains the segment address of the environment table. The table consists of ASCIIZ strings terminated by a null character (that is, a byte set to 0). An *ASCIIZ string* consists of a series of characters followed by a null character.

The ENV1 program (listing 12.9) displays the contents of the environment table.

Listing 12.9

```
program Env1;
var
   i,j,
   EnvSegment : word;
   EnvString  : string[ 80 ];
begin
   EnvSegment := MemW[ PrefixSeg : $2C ];  { Get segment from PSP     }
   i := 0;                                 { The offset begins at 0   }
   repeat                                  { For the entire table     }
      j := 0;
      repeat                               { Just the current entry   }
         j := j + 1;
         EnvString[ j ] := chr( Mem[ EnvSegment : i ] );
         i := i + 1;
      until EnvString[ j ] = chr( 0 );     { Test for null character }
      EnvString[ 0 ] := chr( j - 1 );      { Chop null from string    }
      writeln( EnvString );                { Write the Env string     }
   until Mem[ EnvSegment : i ] = 0;        { Stop if two nulls found }
   writeln;
   writeln( 'End' );
end.
```

When executed, ENV1 produces the following:

```
COMSPEC=C:\COMMAND.COM
PATH=C:\DOS;C:\WORD;C:\TURBOC;C:\TP
PC_ID=004
DEPT=Finance
End
```

Fortunately, as you saw earlier in the chapter, Turbo Pascal provides the `EnvCount`, `EnvStr`, and `GetEnv` functions to simplify the use of environment strings.

Accessing the Command Line

A string containing a copy of the command line is stored in the PSP beginning at offset $80. This string has the same format as an ordinary Turbo Pascal string. Byte $80 contains its dynamic length, and byte $81 contains its first character.

To access the command line in your program, simply define a string pointer variable such as the following:

```
type
   CmdArray = string[ 127 ];
var
   CmdLine : ^CmdArray;
```

Next, in the body of the program, assign the address of the PSP command-line string to the pointer variable:

```
CmdLine := Ptr( PrefixSeg, $80 );
```

The contents of the command line can now be accessed with the `CmdLine^` variable. An example of this technique is found in the EXEC2 program (listing 12.13) later in this chapter.

Note that this area of the PSP doubles as a buffer for any file input or output. Consequently, if your program needs to process the command-line field, it should do so before any disk I/O is performed.

Program Termination

For all the good words and posturing about writing only structured code, programmers sometimes want to end a program *immediately*.

Suppose a program needs four files to be successfully opened before it can begin its main processing; in pure, structured form, its skeleton might look like the following:

```
begin
   OpenFileA;
   if A_WasOpenedWithoutIncident then begin
      OpenFileB;
      if B_WasOpenedWithoutIncident then begin
         OpenFileC;
         if C_WasOpenedWithoutIncident then begin
            OpenFileD;
            if D_WasOpenedWithoutIncident then begin
               GoAheadAndRunTheProgram;
            end;
         end;
      end;
   end;
end;
```

By the time the programmer has included the `else` statements to display error messages, he or she begins to feel that the religion of structure has found its first martyr.

As the example shows, testing for fatal error conditions usually requires a disproportionate amount of code. Fortunately, Turbo Pascal provides the `Halt` procedure to safely end execution at any point in a program.

Termination with *Halt*

The `Halt` procedure terminates a program no matter where the procedure is located. For example, a program could be designed to terminate if either of two parameters is invalid:

```
case Opt1 of
    1 : Opt1is1;
    2 : Opt1is2;
    3 : Opt1is3;
   else begin
           writeln( 'Option 1 is invalid' );
           Halt;
        end;
end;
```

```
case Opt2 of
    1 : Opt2is1;
    2 : Opt2is2;
    3 : Opt2is3;
   else begin
           writeln( 'Option 2 is invalid' );
           Halt;
        end;
end;
```

It might not be structured, but it is efficient. Using the `Halt` procedure unquestionably saves you from writing and debugging many longer lines of code.

Termination in a Batch File

Presumably, when your programs encounter an error, they will do everything possible to end the program smoothly (close files, display messages, ask for help, and so on). Sometimes, you also have to worry about the bigger picture. If you terminate a program that is being run within a batch file, you should let the batch file know what happened.

To provide this feature, `Halt` can optionally accept a word-sized parameter (for example, `Halt(5);`) and pass that parameter to the program or batch file that called the terminated program. `Halt` without a parameter is equivalent to `Halt(0)`.

The HALT1 program (listing 12.10) terminates with a `Halt` procedure call when the user tries to calculate the square root of a negative number.

Listing 12.10

```
program Halt1;
var
   Selection : real;
begin
   repeat
      write( 'Enter a number: ' );
      readln( Selection );
      if Selection > 0 then
         writeln( 'The square root of ', Selection:1:1,
                  ' is ', Sqrt( Selection ):1:5 )
```

continues

Listing 12.10 continued

```
        else
            if Selection < 0 then begin
                writeln( 'I can''t handle negative numbers!' );
                Halt( 1 );
            end;
    until Selection = 0;
    writeln( 'Good-bye' );
end.
```

This program is designed to be executed under the control of the BATCH1.BAT batch file:

```
echo off
echo BATCH1.BAT:  Executing the HALT1.EXE program.
halt1
if errorlevel 1 goto problems
goto finished
:problems
echo The program terminated with an error.
:finished
```

Admittedly, an interactive square root program is not the type of application you ordinarily design to run within a batch file, but it does enable you to directly control whether the program ends normally or with an error.

Within a batch file, an `if errorlevel n` test is true if the actual error level (the parameter passed by the `Halt` procedure) is greater than or equal to `n`.

Compare the following two runs of BATCH1.

```
C>batch1
C>echo off
BATCH1.BAT:  Executing the HALT1.EXE program.
Enter a number: 234
The square root of 234.0 is 15.29706
Enter a number: 23.9
The square root of 23.9 is 4.88876
Enter a number: 0
Good-bye
```

```
C>batch1
C>echo off
BATCH1.BAT:   Executing the HALT1.EXE program.
Enter a number: 234
The square root of 234.0 is 15.29706
Enter a number: 23.9
The square root of 23.9 is 4.88876
Enter a number: -5
I can't handle negative numbers!
The program terminated with an error.
```

The first run terminated normally with the `Good-bye` sign-off message. The default value of 0 was passed to the batch file. During the second run, the entry of a negative number triggered the `Halt` procedure to pass an error code of 1 to the batch file. Both the program and the batch file generated error messages.

Using *Halt* To Pass Parameters

Programs frequently use different error codes to indicate the type of error encountered. For example, the `DosError` variable uses the following codes:

0	No error
2	File not found
3	Path not found
5	Access denied
6	Invalid handle
8	Not enough memory
10	Invalid environment
11	Invalid format
18	No more files

Instead of treating the parameter as an error code, some programs use the parameter to indicate a *condition* that can be tested in the batch file. For example, the HALT2 program (listing 12.11) deliberately passes a 1, 2, or 3 *condition code* to its controlling batch file.

Listing 12.11

```
program Halt2;
var
   Selection : word;
begin
   repeat
      write( 'Choose an application: ' );
      readln( Selection );
   until Selection in [ 1, 2, 3 ];
   Halt( Selection );
end.
```

The parameter could be read by the DOS variable `errorlevel` to select a specific application, as in the BATCH2.BAT file.

```
echo off
echo BATCH2.BAT:  Executing the HALT2.EXE program.
halt2
if errorlevel 3 goto menu3
if errorlevel 2 goto menu2
if errorlevel 1 goto menu1
:menu1
echo Menu1 program goes here
goto finished
:menu2
echo Menu2 program goes here
goto finished
:menu3
echo Menu3 program goes here
:finished
```

Together, these files patiently await a valid user response, as illustrated here:

```
C>batch2
C>echo off
BATCH2.BAT:  Executing the HALT2.EXE program.
Choose an application: 9
Choose an application: -45
Choose an application: 78
Choose an application: 2
Menu2 program goes here
```

Forcing a Run-Time Error

Using the `Halt` procedure, a program can terminate without causing a run-time error. If you want to generate a run-time error, Turbo Pascal offers the `RunError` procedure. For example, to terminate the program with a run-time error of 152, `Drive not ready`, the command is

```
RunError( 152 );
```

If no parameter is given, `RunError(0)` is assumed.

Running a Program within Another Program

Although batch files are useful for segmenting large applications into smaller units, it is sometimes more convenient to have one program call another program directly.

In Turbo Pascal, this is accomplished with the `Exec` procedure. One program (the *parent*) can call another program (the *child*). After the child program is finished, control returns to the parent. This action is usually referred to as *process handling*.

Running the *Exec* Procedure

The `Exec` procedure takes two parameters, as follows:

```
Exec( FileName, CommandTail : string );
```

`FileName` is the complete file name of the program you want to execute, including the extension. If the program is not in the current directory, the complete path name must also be specified. The `CommandTail` is a string containing command-line parameters (if any) required to run the child program. Any problems in using the procedure can be identified by accessing the `DosError` variable.

Any program can be executed in this manner, running just as if it were the program originally invoked. DOS even creates a separate PSP for it.

The memory directive `{$M}` should be used to minimize the memory consumed by the parent. In the absence of this directive, the parent would be allocated all available memory, leaving no room for the child program to run. Because you cannot adjust the memory already assigned to the TURBO.EXE integrated environment, always compile `Exec` programs to disk and run them from the DOS prompt.

To better isolate the parent and child processes, the `SwapVectors` procedure should be called immediately before and after the `Exec` procedure. In so doing, `SwapVectors` alternately stores and restores important contents of the interrupt vector table, discussed in Chapter 18, "Interrupt Service Routines."

The EXEC1 program (listing 12.12) calls EXEC2.EXE (listing 12.13), which happens to be in the same directory. EXEC2 does nothing more than display command-line parameters, which here consist of three arbitrarily chosen file names.

Listing 12.12

```
program Exec1;
{$M 1024,0,0  Sets all memory usage to minimum levels}
uses Dos;
begin
   writeln( 'You are in the parent program.' );
   SwapVectors;
   Exec( 'Exec2.exe', 'file1.pas file2.pas file3.pas' );
   SwapVectors;
   writeln( 'You are in the parent program.' );
end.
```

Listing 12.13

```
program Exec2;
type
   CmdArray = string[ 127 ];
var
   CmdLine : ^CmdArray;
begin
   CmdLine := Ptr( PrefixSeg, $80 );
   writeln( 'You are in the child program.' );
   writeln( 'The command tail is: ', CmdLine^ );
end.
```

When you run EXEC1, it generates the following results:

```
C>exec1
You are in the parent program.
You are in the child program.
The command tail is: file1.pas file2.pas file3.pas
You are in the parent program.
```

Accessing the Termination Parameter

If the child program terminates with the `Halt` procedure, the parent can access the exit code with the `DosExitCode` function. `DosExitCode` returns a word-sized value; its low byte is the low byte of the exit code, and its high byte indicates the cause of the termination, as summarized in table 12.2.

Table 12.2. *Causes of Program Termination Given by DosExitCode*

High byte of DosExitCode	*Reason the child program terminated*
0	Normal termination
1	Ctrl-C
2	Device error
3	Keep procedure executed

After `DosExitCode` is called, the error/condition code is reset to 0. The EXEC3 and EXEC4 programs (listings 12.14 and 12.15) demonstrate its use.

Listing 12.14

```
program Exec3;
{$M 1024,0,0 }
uses Dos;
var
   Message : word;
begin
```

continues

Listing 12.14 continued

```
   writeln( 'You are in the parent program.' );
   SwapVectors;
   Exec( 'Exec4.exe', '' );
   SwapVectors;
   Message := DosExitCode;
   write( 'The child terminated ' );
   case Hi( Message ) of
      0 : writeln( 'normally.' );
      1 : writeln( 'by Ctrl-C.' );
      2 : writeln( 'because of a device error.' );
      3 : writeln( 'by the Keep procedure.' );
   end;
   writeln( 'The child wants the parent to know: ', Lo( Message ) );
end.
```

Listing 12.15

```
program Exec4;
var
   ConditionCode : word;
begin
   writeln( 'You are in the child program.' );
   repeat
      write( 'What do you want to tell the parent? ' );
      readln( ConditionCode );
   until ConditionCode in [ 0..255 ];
   writeln( 'We need to tell the parent: ', ConditionCode );
   Halt( ConditionCode );
end.
```

Executing the EXEC3 program—and selecting 173 as the message to be passed—results in the following output:

```
C>exec3
You are in the parent program.
You are in the child program.
What do you want to tell the parent? 173
We need to tell the parent: 173
The child terminated normally.
The child wants the parent to know: 173
```

When EXEC3 called the `DosExitCode` function, it obtained the value $00AD. The high byte ($00) indicated normal termination while the low byte ($AD or 173) contained the message itself.

Executing DOS Utilities

Although any program can be executed with the `Exec` procedure, some care must be taken when using it to run DOS utilities.

Only a few DOS commands (such as `FORMAT` and `SORT`) are stand-alone programs. Most of the common instructions (including `DIR` and `COPY`) are options of the COMMAND.COM program. When you type a file name at the DOS prompt, it is COMMAND.COM that executes, checking first to see if one of its intrinsic functions (such as `DIR`) is being requested. If the name is not recognized, COMMAND.COM assumes that you want to execute a stand-alone program.

The EXEC5 program (listing 12.16) demonstrates how to list a directory from a Turbo Pascal program. Note that the COMMAND.COM file is assumed to reside in the root directory.

Listing 12.16

```
program Exec5;
{$M 1024,0,0}
uses Dos;
procedure RunDirectory;
begin
   SwapVectors;
   Exec( 'c:\command.com', '/c dir *.*' );
   SwapVectors;
end;
begin
   writeln( 'The directory follows:' );
   RunDirectory;
   writeln( 'End of directory' );
end.
```

Just as in the previous uses of the `Exec` procedure, Turbo Pascal is being directed to run a program with certain specified options. In this case, however, the desired program is a copy of COMMAND.COM. The `/C` code is an option of COMMAND.COM; in DOS versions before 3.3, `/C` is used to indicate that the remainder of the line (`dir *.*`) is an *intrinsic* option.

Of course, you may not know where the COMMAND.COM file resides on your disk. Further, different PCs are configured differently. Instead of assuming that COMMAND.COM is always in the root directory, you could use the `GetEnv` function to locate it automatically, as follows:

```
Exec( GetEnv( 'comspec' ), '/c dir *.*' );
```

If you want to run a stand-alone DOS program such as the CHKDSK utility, COMMAND.COM is not needed. The procedure call would simply be

```
Exec( 'c:\dos\chkdsk.com', 'c:' );
```

If your program does not need command-line parameters, the second string in `Exec` can be null. For example, to run CHKDSK on the current drive, all you need is:

```
Exec( 'c:\dos\chkdsk.com', '' );
```

Note that in later versions of DOS, the CHKDSK utility is an EXE file.

Exit Procedures

So far you have seen that when a program terminates, DOS restores the value of the major interrupt vectors by copying the addresses from the PSP, and passes along any generated error/condition code to the calling program.

Turbo provides a few additional program termination services. For example, it closes the standard input and output files, and if the program ended because of a run-time error, it displays a run-time error message.

These concluding routines are called *exit* procedures. They represent a well-defined sequence of procedure calls—both in Turbo and in DOS—triggered by any program termination event. Normal termination, a Ctrl-C break, and run-time errors all cause the program to jump to the first procedure in the chain, the address of which is stored in the pointer variable `ExitProc`.

Developing Custom Exit Procedures

Although it is not a good idea to affect the internal flow of these calls, with Turbo Pascal you can create your own exit procedures and insert them on the *top* of the chain. To do this, set the ExitProc pointer to the address of your exit procedure, then restore ExitProc to its original value after your procedure finishes.

Customized exit procedures offer you a means to control—but not prevent—program termination. If your program uses a printer, the final page eject command could be issued. In a communications program, you can ensure that you sign off and hang up the phone. In a word processing or spreadsheet program, you can save the current work file.

The basic technique is demonstrated in the EXIT1 program (listing 12.17).

Listing 12.17

```
program Exit1;
var
   ExitAddress : pointer;
{$F+}
procedure CustomizedExit;
{$F-}
begin
   { Any user-defined termination code could go here }
   writeln( 'Program is terminating...' );
   ExitProc := ExitAddress;         { Restore original exit routine }
end;
begin
   ExitAddress := ExitProc;         { Save original exit address }
   ExitProc := @CustomizedExit;     { New exit is "CustomizedExit" }
   { The rest of the program is written normally }
end.
```

The global ExitAddress variable is used to save the value of ExitProc, which contains the address of the first default exit procedure. ExitProc is then set to the address of your own exit procedure, called CustomizedExit in this program. At the end of CustomizedExit, ExitProc is reset to its original value, beginning the default termination sequence.

Although CustomizedExit is not explicitly called, it is the first logical procedure invoked when the program terminates. Running the program results in the following display:

```
Program is terminating...
```

Notice that the force far calls directive {$F} was used to force Turbo to treat CustomizedExit as a far procedure. This is because the code for the default exit procedure chain resides in the run-time library, which sits in a different code segment from the main program (as explained in Chapter 6). Consequently, saving, modifying, and restoring the `ExitProc` pointer require accessing both the segment and offset address components.

Determining the Cause of Program Termination

Table 12.3 shows how the `ExitCode` and `ErrorAddr` variables can be used to determine what caused your program to terminate.

***Table 12.3.** Contents of Variables*

Termination type	*ExitCode*	*ErrorAddr*
Normal	0	`Nil`
`Halt( n );`	n	`Nil`
Run-time error	Error code	The address of the statement causing the error

If the program terminated normally, `ExitCode` is 0, and `ErrorAddr` is `Nil`. If termination resulted from the execution of the `Halt` procedure, `ExitCode` contains the value of the `Halt` parameter and `ErrorAddr` is `Nil`. Remember that `Halt` without a parameter is equivalent to `Halt(0)`.

If program termination resulted from a run-time error, `ExitCode` contains the number of the error. `ErrorAddr` points to the code generating the error. `ErrorAddr` is the variable that Turbo tests to determine if a run-time error message should be displayed. When `ErrorAddr` is set to `Nil`, no message appears.

By testing the `ExitCode` and `ErrorAddr` variables, your customized exit procedures can appropriately react to both normal and abnormal termination, as demonstrated in the EXIT2 program (listing 12.18).

Listing 12.18

```
Program Exit2;
var
   ExitAddress : pointer;
   Selection : longint;
```

```
{$F+}
procedure CustomizedExit;
{$F-}
begin
   if ErrorAddr <> Nil then begin
      writeln;
      writeln( 'This program is terminating as a result ' );
      writeln( 'of run-time error number ', ExitCode:3, '.  It was' );
      writeln( 'encountered at:' );
      writeln;
      writeln( '    Segment: ', seg( ErrorAddr ):5 );
      writeln( '    Offset:  ', ofs( ErrorAddr ):5 );
      writeln;
      ErrorAddr := Nil;            { Prevents Turbo from generating }
                                   { another error message }
   end;
   ExitProc := ExitAddress;        { Restore original exit routine }
end;
begin
   ExitAddress := ExitProc;        { Save original exit address }
   ExitProc := @CustomizedExit;    { New exit is "CustomizedExit" }
   repeat
      write( 'Please enter an integer: ' );
      readln( Selection );
      writeln( 'The square of ', Selection, ' is ', Sqr( Selection ) );
   until Selection = 0;
end.
```

This program is designed to calculate integer squares. It ends when the user enters 0. The `CustomizedExit` procedure is always executed; if the program terminates normally, however, `ErrorAddr` is `Nil`, and no error message is produced.

```
Please enter an integer: 43
The square of 43 is 1849
Please enter an integer: 11
The square of 11 is 121
Please enter an integer: 0
The square of 0 is 0
```

If a nonintegral entry is made, the customized error message is displayed.

```
Please enter an integer: 4
The square of 4 is 16
```

```
Please enter an integer: 76
The square of 76 is 5776
Please enter an integer: 2.3
This program is terminating as a result
of run-time error number 106.  It was
encountered at:
   Segment: 27815
   Offset:    546
```

Note that the segment and offset values will probably differ on your machine. The 106 error code corresponds to the `Invalid numeric format` run-time error. You will probably agree that this message is much more polite than the standard run-time error. In a professionally written program, you might also include a brief apology and the name and phone number of the customer support person to be contacted.

Customized Exit Procedures for Units

In addition to the main program, each module can have a customized exit procedure. Procedures on the exit chain are executed in the reverse order from the one in which they were installed. Therefore, if the code establishing a customized exit procedure is placed in the initialization section of each unit, the exit procedures will be executed in the reverse order in which the units are declared in the `uses` clause. Turbo continues to call exit procedures until the `ExitProc` pointer becomes `Nil`. Because `ExitProc` is set to `Nil` every time it is called, you must ensure that the pointer is properly restored after each use. Otherwise, the default routines will not execute, and the program will terminate abnormally.

The next example illustrates how customized exit code can be used in a unit. In the event of an abnormal termination, the EXIT3 module (listing 12.19) displays the system variables defined in the System unit.

Listing 12.19

```
unit Exit3;
interface
implementation
type
   HexFormat = string[ 5 ];   { $xxxx }
var
   ExitAddress : pointer;
function Hex( HexWord : word ) : HexFormat;
```

```
const
   HexDigits : array[ 0..15 ] of char = '0123456789ABCDEF';
begin
   Hex := '$' + HexDigits[ hi( HexWord ) div 16 ] +
            HexDigits[ hi( HexWord ) mod 16 ] +
            HexDigits[ lo( HexWord ) div 16 ] +
            HexDigits[ lo( HexWord ) mod 16 ];
end;
procedure writeWord( Wname : word );
begin
   write( Hex( Wname ), '          ' );
   writeln( Wname );
end;
procedure writePntr( Pname : pointer );
begin
   write( Hex( seg( Pname ) ), ':', Hex( ofs( Pname ) ) );
   write( '     ' );
   writeln( seg( Pname ):5, ':', ofs( Pname ):5 );
end;
{$F+}
procedure TerminationData;
{$F-}
begin
   write( 'Program segment prefix  ' );   writeWord( PrefixSeg );
   write( 'Stack pointer low limit ' );   writeWord( StackLimit );
   write( 'Overlay buffer origin   ' );   writeWord( OvrHeapOrg );
   write( 'Overlay buffer pointer  ' );   writeWord( OvrHeapPtr );
   write( 'Overlay buffer end      ' );   writeWord( OvrHeapEnd );
   write( 'Heap origin             ' );   writePntr( HeapOrg );
   write( 'Heap pointer            ' );   writePntr( HeapPtr );
   write( 'Free list pointer       ' );   writePntr( FreePtr );
   write( 'Minimum free list size  ' );   writeWord( FreeMin );
   write( 'Heap error function     ' );   writePntr( HeapError );
   write( 'Exit procedure          ' );   writePntr( ExitAddress ); {!}
   write( 'Exit code               ' );   writeln( ExitCode );
   write( 'Runtime error address   ' );   writePntr( ErrorAddr );
   write( 'Random seed             ' );   writeln( RandSeed );
   write( 'File open mode          ' );   writeln( FileMode );
   write( '8087 test result        ' );   writeln( Test8087 );
   ExitProc := ExitAddress;
end;
begin
   ExitAddress := ExitProc;
   ExitProc := @TerminationData;
end.
```

The EXIT4 program (listing 12.20) demonstrates how easy it is to use this mini-debugger unit. The only required modification is the addition of a `uses Exit3;` clause.

Listing 12.20

```
program Exit4;
uses Exit3;   { The mini-debugger }
var
   Selection : longint;
begin
   repeat
      write( 'Please enter an integer: ' );
      readln( Selection );
      writeln( 'The square of ', Selection, ' is ', Sqr( Selection ) );
   until Selection = 0;
end.
```

Any run-time error immediately triggers the execution of the termination procedure from the EXIT3 unit.

```
Please enter an integer: 12
The square of 12 is 144
Please enter an integer: 17
The square of 17 is 289
Please enter an integer: CAT
Program segment prefix   $3A08            14856
Stack pointer low limit  $0000            0
Overlay buffer origin    $3FC0            16320
Overlay buffer pointer   $3FC0            16320
Overlay buffer end       $3FC0            16320
Overlay buffer end       $3FC0            16320
Heap origin              $3BC0:$3FF4      15296:16372
Heap pointer             $3BC0:$3FF4      15296:16372
Free list pointer        $3BC0:$3FF4      15296:16372
Minimum free list size   $0000            0
Heap error function      $3BC0:$3FF4      15296:16372
Exit procedure           $3BC0:$3FF4      15296:16372
Exit code                106
Runtime error address    $3BC0:$3FF4      15296:16372
Random seed              0
File open mode           2
8087 test result         0
Runtime error 106 at 0000:0082.
```

Note that the segment and offset values will probably differ on your machine.

Additional debugging information can be included, if desired. For example, by adding the following lines:

```
write( 'Code segment          ' );    writeWord( CSeg );
write( 'Data segment          ' );    writeWord( DSeg );
write( 'Stack segment         ' );    writeWord( SSeg );
write( 'Stack pointer         ' );    writeWord( SPtr );
```

you can display segment information.

Summary

In this chapter, you learned about the various Turbo Pascal procedures and functions that allow direct interaction with DOS operations.

You learned how your programs can read and set the system date and time. You saw—and heard—how to produce the common beep effect and how to produce tones of any desired frequency.

You learned about the DOS environment table, how environment strings can be added or removed from it, and how the strings can be accessed by your programs.

You learned about the program segment prefix (PSP) and the useful information DOS stores in it.

You learned how to control the termination of a Turbo Pascal program, and how to pass parameters between programs. You saw how your programs can be run within batch files. You learned how your programs can activate and control the execution of a second program and how your programs can execute DOS utilities. You learned how to write customized exit routines for programs and units.

You can utilize the topics presented in this chapter in a wide variety of programming applications. They are powerful tools that will help you solve many frequently encountered problems.

CHAPTER 13

File Handling

The electronics in your PC make it incredibly fast. The reaction times of the individual logic circuits in the CPU are measured in nanoseconds; that's *billionths* of a second. To try to grasp how fast that is, consider that electricity travels at the speed of light. In one second, a beam of light travels 186,000 miles—more than seven times around the equator of the Earth. Yet in one nanosecond that same beam of light moves *less than 12 inches*! (You can see why the early room-full-of-vacuum-tubes computers could not offer anywhere near the speed of the machine that now fits comfortably on top of your desk.)

On the flip side, disk drives are incredibly slow. Few PC users have not complained about the time "wasted" as they waited for the drive's grinding noises to stop and the red light to go out.

Yet disk drives—and the files they contain—are critical to program development. The file is Turbo Pascal's principal means of communicating with data outside the main memory of the PC. Programming applications often need to store large volumes of data. Further, because files are independent of any one program, they provide an excellent means of sharing common data among several programs.

In this chapter, you learn about the three different types of files supported by Turbo Pascal, and you learn about the procedures and functions that allow files to be used in your program.

File Handling in Turbo Pascal

There has always been a (mostly) friendly battle between hardware and software enthusiasts. Hardware people delight in cramming more bits into smaller amounts of silicon, installing more memory capacity in their PCs, and acquiring the latest in graphics displays and laser printers. Software people like nothing better than developing an elegant algorithm and generally making their programs faster, larger, and more sophisticated.

Fortunately, these preferences are compatible. A computer does, after all, consist of a blend of hardware and software technologies. Some concepts, such as a file, overlap the two worlds.

In the hardware arena, a file is a *physical device* on which you store and retrieve information. The Turbo Pascal distribution disks that contain the compiler and its supporting programs and files are either 5 1/4-inch or 3 1/2-inch floppy disks. Your PC may have a hard disk that can hold 5, 10, 20, 40, or more megabytes. Storage media range from the primitive, such as cassette tapes, to the advanced, such as optical disks.

Turbo Pascal regards all of these physical forms of file storage to be identical. In fact, when you first learn about files, it is better to ignore their physical form. Instead, think of a file as having two components:

- A name, which may or may not include a physical drive or directory reference or both
- A continuous stream of characters containing data

A file contains data, so a *logical file* is simply another data type, just like byte, integer, record, and array. Turbo Pascal hides the underlying complexity.

File names in Pascal, as in DOS, are up to eight characters long, optionally followed by a period and an extension of up to three characters. Both DOS and Turbo Pascal make assumptions about the contents of a file based on its extension. For example, PAS is assumed to be a Turbo Pascal source program, and EXE is assumed to be an executable file.

The only impact the physical medium has on your programming is that your file name should help the system find the file. When you reference a file that does not reside in the current drive and directory (or may not reside there the next time you run the program), include the drive and directory as part of the file's name. For example, the full name of the EDITOR.PAS file on drive C in subdirectory \TURBO\SOURCE is

```
C:\TURBO\SOURCE\EDITOR.PAS
```

Otherwise, all Turbo Pascal file programming is the same, regardless of where or how a file is stored.

File Variable Types

Although there is only one type of physical disk file, the Turbo Pascal compiler supports three types of logical files, named for the syntax of their declarations: text, typed, and untyped.

```
var
   FileName1 : file of DataRecord;     { Typed file   }
   FileName2 : file;                   { Untyped file }
   FileName3 : Text;                   { Text file    }
```

A *typed file* contains data of only the one particular type named in the declaration. An *untyped file* is unstructured. It may contain any data in any format in any length. The most common reason to declare a file as untyped is to manipulate its contents in large blocks, not as individual characters.

Unfortunately, the names *typed* and *untyped* imply complete definition. But a third file type also exists. A *text file* contains lines of characters (that is, data of type `char`) terminated by a carriage return (#13) and, usually, a line feed (#10). Lines may vary in length. Note that a text file is *not* the same as a file of type `char`.

Text Files

A text file is the most commonly used file type. Even if Turbo Pascal is the first software package you have ever used, you have already been using text files extensively—perhaps without realizing it. All Turbo Pascal source code is stored in text files that have PAS as their extension. Therefore, if you have tried any of the examples that accompany this text, you used text files to store the program code.

In addition, all of the unit header files on the Turbo Pascal distribution disks (such as SYSTEM.INT, GRAPH.INT, and DOS.INT) are text files. You can list them on your printer using a word processor or simply by entering a DOS command such as the following:

```
TYPE SYSTEM.DOC > PRN
```

In general, whenever you use a file that contains *lines* of ASCII characters, you should declare a file as type `text`.

Comparison to Other File Types

Turbo Pascal treats each text file as if it contains a series of lines. Each line is composed of a sequence of characters terminated by an end-of-line marker, which consists of either a carriage return (#13) or a carriage-return and line-feed combination (#13#10). Text files offer special subroutines for detecting and manipulating end-of-line markers. A line may have any number of characters, including no characters at all.

It is natural to envision a text file as something that holds letter and number patterns that form English language phrases. After all, when you hear a file described as "text" and you are presented with examples that include program source code and documentation, you expect a text file to contain—well, to contain text.

In practice, the reason that a text file is so frequently used is that *any* file can be declared as `Text`—including a file such as TURBO.EXE, which contains nothing but illegible, unreadable, and unpronounceable hexadecimal!

Remember the original definition of a file: a data structure that consists of a sequence of ASCII characters. Suppose that you find a strange file on your disk. (Actually, this happens more often than most programmers like to admit.) Suppose further that you want to examine it with Turbo Pascal. Your first consideration is how the file should be declared. Your reasoning would proceed as follows:

1. Because you do not know what data types the file might contain, you would not consider declaring it as a typed file. Of course, you could declare it as a `file of byte`, but that assumes that the file contains only numbers. (For example, the three hexadecimal characters $44, $6F, and $67 would be interpreted as the decimal values 68, 111, and 103—not as the intended character string `Dog`.) Similarly, a `file of char` assumes that the file holds nothing but characters, and gives no special importance to the end-of-line markers.

2. You could declare the file as untyped, but untyped files, as you will see, typically deal in large groups of bytes called *blocks*. Untyped files do not offer an easy way to process their contents on a character-by-character basis.

3. Therefore, you have no other alternative; you are forced to treat the file in the most general way possible—as type `Text`.

Of course, after you have determined what the file contains, you may decide to go back and declare it as a typed or an untyped file.

Declaring a Text File

The first step in using a text file is to declare an identifier as type `Text`, as follows:

```
var
   InFile         : Text;
   OutputDetails  : Text;
   WorkFile       : Text;
```

Note that the format of a text file declaration is identical to that of any other declaration. A text file is considered its own data type.

Identifying the Physical File

To relate the internal file data structure with the external physical data file, you use the `Assign` procedure. In the following example, the `OutputDetails` identifier, previously declared as a text file, is defined to refer to the DOS file DATAFILE.TXT in the current drive and directory:

```
Assign( OutputDetails, 'DATAFILE.TXT' );
```

The DOS drive and path may be included as part of the file name. The `Assign` procedure must be called before any other file-related procedure or function that uses the `OutputDetails` identifier. The `Assign` procedure is the only time your program calls a file by its DOS name; all future references to DATAFILE.TXT will be made by the `OutputDetails` identifier.

Opening a Text File

After you use `Assign` for an identifier to an external file, the next step is to physically open it with one of these procedures: `Reset`, `Rewrite`, or `Append`.

The `Reset` procedure opens an existing text file for input, starting at the beginning of the file. The syntax is

```
Reset( TextFileIdentifier );
```

If the file specified in the `Assign` procedure does not exist, a run-time error is generated. If the file is already open (the result of a previous `Reset`, `Rewrite`, or `Append` operation), `Reset` first closes the file and moves the file pointer back to its beginning and then reopens the file so that the next input command will read its first record. (The `Close` procedure is discussed in the next section.)

The `Rewrite` procedure opens a text file for output. The syntax is

```
Rewrite( TextFileIdentifier );
```

The `Rewrite` procedure first searches for the DOS file specified in the `Assign` procedure. If the file already exists, `Rewrite` deletes it. If the file does not exist, `Rewrite` creates it. This ensures that the file is always empty and that output starts at the beginning of the file.

The `Append` procedure opens an existing text file for output, starting at the end of the file. The syntax is

```
Append( TextFileIdentifier );
```

The `Append` procedure first searches for the DOS file specified in the `Assign` procedure. A run-time error is generated if the file cannot be found. Note that if the file does not already exist, you must use `Rewrite` to create it.

A text file can be opened for either input or output, but not for both. You can, however, switch between input and output modes simply by issuing a new `Reset`, `Rewrite`, or `Append` procedure whenever you want. You need not call the `Assign` procedure more than once, however. For example, the body of a program that creates a file, reads information from it, then adds new data to the file would have the following form:

```
Assign( WorkFile, 'Data.DAT' );
Rewrite( WorkFile );
.
.
.
    { Statements that create new records }

Reset( WorkFile );
.
.
.
    { Statements that read the new records }
.
.
.
Append( WorkFile );
.
.
.
    { Statements that write new records after the end of the file }
```

Closing a File

Every file must be closed when your program finishes using it. The syntax is

```
Close( TextFileIdentifier );
```

If, in this example, the `TextFileIdentifier` file had been opened for output with `Rewrite` or `Append`, then `Close` would write out any data that might still remain in the buffer. (Buffers are discussed in more detail later in this chapter.) Therefore, failure to `Close` an output file may result in lost data! In addition, `Close` updates an output file's DOS disk directory entry to reflect the new size and the last date and time the file was modified.

Closed files must be reopened with `Reset`, `Rewrite`, or `Append` before further input or output operations can take place. However, because Turbo Pascal does not forget the relationship between the logical and physical file names, it is not necessary to issue another `Assign` procedure.

Now, the truth is that Turbo Pascal automatically closes all files when your program terminates. Consequently, it is not really necessary to explicitly `Close` a file, but you should do so for the following reasons:

- DOS allows only 15 Turbo Pascal files to be opened at one time. It is not difficult for some file-intensive programs with sloppy housekeeping to exceed that number.
- The `Close` procedure deallocates any memory buffer space assigned to the file. Therefore, `Close` frees memory.
- Keeping a file open longer than necessary increases the chance (however slight) of accidental file damage or loss. For example, if a power failure strikes, the data in the buffer of an open output file may not have been saved. In addition, because the DOS directory entry has not been updated, the disk may need to be repaired with the CHKDSK utility.
- Other Pascal compilers probably do not offer such a feature, so your program's "portability" is reduced.
- Future versions of Turbo Pascal may not be so forgiving.
- It is simply good, professional practice.

Reading from a Text File

If you have been reading this book from the beginning, you have already seen several dozen examples of programs that use `read` and `readln` for keyboard input. Except for the addition of a text file identifier as their first parameter, the two procedures operate similarly when they are applied to text files.

The `read` procedure:

```
read( TextFile, Var1 { , Var2, Var3, ... } );
```

inputs data items from `TextFile` and assigns them to the variables listed as parameters. The file pointer is then set so that the next `read` will begin with the data item that follows on the same line.

The `readln` procedure:

```
readln( TextFile, Var1 { , Var2, Var3, ... } );
```

inputs data just like a `read`, except it then advances the file pointer to the beginning of the *next* line in the file. In other words, `readln` *skips* any remaining characters in the current line through the end-of-line marker.

For both `read` and `readln`, the data items input from the file must be compatible with the types of the corresponding variables. Each data item can be read only once.

The properties of the `read` and `readln` procedures can best be illustrated with an example. The text file you will use—NUMARRAY.DAT, shown in listing 13.1—consists of 10 rows of digits enclosed in brackets and separated by periods. Each row is terminated with a carriage return and line feed (#13#10).

Listing 13.1

```
[01].[02].[03].[04].[05].[06].[07].[08].[09]
[11].[12].[13].[14].[15].[16].[17].[18].[19]
[21].[22].[23].[24].[25].[26].[27].[28].[29]
[31].[32].[33].[34].[35].[36].[37].[38].[39]
[41].[42].[43].[44].[45].[46].[47].[48].[49]
[51].[52].[53].[54].[55].[56].[57].[58].[59]
[61].[62].[63].[64].[65].[66].[67].[68].[69]
[71].[72].[73].[74].[75].[76].[77].[78].[79]
[81].[82].[83].[84].[85].[86].[87].[88].[89]
[91].[92].[93].[94].[95].[96].[97].[98].[99]
```

The READSTR program in listing 13.2 inputs the NUMARRAY.DAT text file twice: the first time with `read` and, after the file is `reset`, the second time with `readln`.

Listing 13.2

```
program ReadStr;
uses Crt;
var
   StrChars : Text;
   Str5A,    Str5B,    Str5C,   Str5D   : string[ 5 ];
   Str15A,   Str15B,   Str15C,  Str15D  : string[ 15 ];
   Str100A,  Str100B,  Str100C          : string[ 100 ];
begin
   ClrScr;
   Assign( StrChars, 'NumArray.DAT' );
   writeln;
   writeln( '=====================================================' );
   writeln( 'Using Read:' );
   writeln;
   Reset( StrChars );
   Read( StrChars, Str5A, Str5B, Str5C, Str5D );
   writeln( Str5A, '*', Str5B, '*', Str5C, '*', Str5D, '*' );
   Read( StrChars, Str15A, Str15B, Str15C, Str15D );
   writeln( Str15A, '*', Str15B, '*', Str15C, '*', Str15D, '*' );
   Read( StrChars, Str100A, Str100B, Str100C );
   writeln( Str100A, '*', Str100B, '*', Str100C, '*' );
   writeln;
   writeln( '=====================================================' );
   writeln( 'Using Readln:' );
   writeln;
   Reset( StrChars );
   Readln( StrChars, Str5A, Str5B, Str5C, Str5D );
   writeln( Str5A, '*', Str5B, '*', Str5C, '*', Str5D, '*' );
   Readln( StrChars, Str15A, Str15B, Str15C, Str15D );
   writeln( Str15A, '*', Str15B, '*', Str15C, '*', Str15D, '*' );
   Readln( StrChars, Str100A, Str100B, Str100C );
   writeln( Str100A, '*', Str100B, '*', Str100C, '*' );
   writeln;
   writeln( '=====================================================' );
   writeln;
   Close( StrChars );
end.
```

Figure 13.1 contains the output from the READSTR program. The results of the input with `read` are displayed at the top. The `readln` results are at the bottom. READSTR outputs an asterisk after each variable to show it more easily.

Fig. 13.1. The output produced by the READSTR program.

```
=======================================================
Using Read:

[01].*[02].*[03].*[04].*
[05].[06].[07].*[08].[09]***
***

=======================================================
Using Readln:

[01].*[02].*[03].*[04].*
[11].[12].[13].*[14].[15].[16].*[17].[18].[19]**
[21].[22].[23].[24].[25].[26].[27].[28].[29]***

=======================================================
```

The `read` procedure fills each variable with the maximum number of characters until it reaches the end-of-line marker. No `read` can proceed past the end-of-line marker in the first line; all subsequent `read` attempts return only empty strings.

Like `read`, each `readln` procedure assigns characters until it reaches an end-of-line marker, and thereafter returns only empty strings. But unlike `read`, after each `readln` finishes, the file pointer is advanced to the first character of the next line.

Clearly, you need a means to both detect and bypass the end-of-line markers in a text file.

Detecting the End of a File and the End of a Line

Turbo Pascal provides two Boolean functions, `Eof` and `Eoln`, that smooth the process of reading data from files.

Eof returns True when the end of the file has been reached. Eoln also returns True when no more data items remain and the character about to be input is an end-of-line marker.

Eof and Eoln are demonstrated in the READSTR1 program in listing 13.3.

Listing 13.3

```
program ReadStr1;
uses Crt;
var
   StrChars : Text;
   Str5A    : string[ 5 ];
begin
   ClrScr;
   Assign( StrChars, 'NumArray.DAT' );
   writeln;
   writeln( '====================================================' );
   writeln( 'Using Eoln:' );
   writeln;
   Reset( StrChars );
   while not Eoln( StrChars ) do begin
      Read( StrChars, Str5A );
      Write( Str5A, '*' );
   end;
   writeln;
   writeln;
   writeln( '====================================================' );
   writeln( 'Using Eof:' );
   writeln;
   Reset( StrChars );
   while not Eof( StrChars ) do begin
      Read( StrChars, Str5A );
      Write( Str5A, '*' );
   end;
   writeln;
   writeln( '====================================================' );
   writeln;
   Close( StrChars );
end.
```

READSTR1 produces the output shown in figure 13.2. Note that after `Eoln` correctly detects the first end-of-line marker, the first `while` loop concludes, the text file is `Reset`, and the program proceeds to the test for `Eof`.

Fig. 13.2. *Output produced by the READSTR1 program.*

```
=====================================================
Using Eoln:

[01].*[02].*[03].*[04].*[05].*[06].*[07].*[08].*[09]*

=====================================================
Using Eof:

[01].*[02].*[03].*[04].*[05].*[06].*[07].*[08].*[09]****************************
********************************************************************************
********************************************************************************
********************************************************************************
********************************************************************************
********************************************************************************
********************************************************************************
********************************************************************************
********************************************************************************
********************************************************************************
********************************************************************************
********************************************************************************
********************************************************************************
********************************************************************************
********************************************************************************
********************************************************************************
*********************************************
```

The only way READSTR1 can end is by interrupting it with Ctrl-Break. Because the `read` procedure cannot proceed beyond the end-of-line marker, the `while` loop will never encounter the end-of-file. As READSTR1 is currently written, `Eof` can never return `True`.

You can use `Eof` and `Eoln` in combination if you do not know how many data items are in a line or how many lines are in a file. The process is as follows:

1. Use `read` for data items until `Eoln` returns `True`.

2. Use `readln` to bypass the end-of-line marker and move the file pointer to the beginning of the next line. This also has the effect of resetting `Eoln` to `False`.

3. Repeat steps 1 and 2 until `Eof` returns `True`.

This technique is demonstrated in the READSTR2 program in listing 13.4.

Listing 13.4

```
program ReadStr2;
   uses CRT;
var
   StrChars : Text;
   Str5A    : string[ 5 ];
begin
   ClrScr;
   Assign( StrChars, 'NumArray.DAT' );
   Reset( StrChars );
   while not Eof( StrChars ) do begin
      while not Eoln( StrChars ) do begin
         read( StrChars, Str5A );
         write( Str5A, '*' );
      end;
      readln( StrChars );
      writeln;
   end;
   Close( StrChars );
end.
```

READSTR2 produces the output shown in figure 13.3.

Fig. 13.3. *Output produced by the READSTR2 program.*

```
[01].*[02].*[03].*[04].*[05].*[06].*[07].*[08].*[09]*
[11].*[12].*[13].*[14].*[15].*[16].*[17].*[18].*[19]*
[21].*[22].*[23].*[24].*[25].*[26].*[27].*[28].*[29]*
[31].*[32].*[33].*[34].*[35].*[36].*[37].*[38].*[39]*
[41].*[42].*[43].*[44].*[45].*[46].*[47].*[48].*[49]*
[51].*[52].*[53].*[54].*[55].*[56].*[57].*[58].*[59]*
[61].*[62].*[63].*[64].*[65].*[66].*[67].*[68].*[69]*
[71].*[72].*[73].*[74].*[75].*[76].*[77].*[78].*[79]*
[81].*[82].*[83].*[84].*[85].*[86].*[87].*[88].*[89]*
[91].*[92].*[93].*[94].*[95].*[96].*[97].*[98].*[99]*
```

Notice the similarity between the output of READSTR2 and the NUMARRAY.DAT text file. This resemblance is deliberate. If you remove the single `writeln` procedure, READSTR2 correctly returns all the data in the text file in a single, continuous stream.

SeekEof and *SeekEoln*

You can use the `Eof` and `Eoln` functions to determine if the *current* position of the file pointer is at the end of a line or the end of a file. Two other text file procedures, `SeekEof` and `SeekEoln`, can be used to detect if the *next* input will result in `Eof` and `Eoln` being `True`.

`SeekEof` acts just like `Eof`, except it looks ahead, skipping all blanks, tabs, line feeds, and carriage returns before it returns the end-of-file status. Using `SeekEof` to search for the next significant character enables you to ignore blank lines.

`SeekEoln` is similar to `SeekEof` except it skips all blanks and tabs while it searches for the next end-of-line marker. Using `SeekEoln` enables you to ignore blanks at the end of a line.

The READSTR3 program in listing 13.5 uses `SeekEof` to read the NUMARRAY.DAT file.

Listing 13.5

```
program ReadStr3;
   uses CRT;
var
   StrChars : Text;
   Str5A    : string[ 5 ];
begin
   ClrScr;
   Assign( StrChars, 'NumArray.DAT' );
   Reset( StrChars );
   while not seekEof( StrChars ) do begin
      read( StrChars, Str5A );
      write( Str5A, '*' );
   end;
   Close( StrChars );
end.
```

The output from READSTR3 is shown in figure 13.4. Notice how `SeekEof` ignored the line feeds and carriage returns, making it unnecessary to perform a separate end-of-line test. Using `SeekEof` enables you to avoid the more complicated logic of the earlier READSTR2 program.

Fig. 13.4. *Output produced by the READSTR3 program.*

```
[01].*[02].*[03].*[04].*[05].*[06].*[07].*[08].*[09]*[11].*[12].*[13].*[14].*[15
].*[16].*[17].*[18].*[19]*[21].*[22].*[23].*[24].*[25].*[26].*[27].*[28].*[29]*[
31].*[32].*[33].*[34].*[35].*[36].*[37].*[38].*[39]*[41].*[42].*[43].*[44].*[45]
.*[46].*[47].*[48].*[49]*[51].*[52].*[53].*[54].*[55].*[56].*[57].*[58].*[59]*[6
1].*[62].*[63].*[64].*[65].*[66].*[67].*[68].*[69]*[71].*[72].*[73].*[74].*[75].
*[76].*[77].*[78].*[79]*[81].*[82].*[83].*[84].*[85].*[86].*[87].*[88].*[89]*[91
].*[92].*[93].*[94].*[95].*[96].*[97].*[98].*[99]*
```

Because `SeekEof` and `SeekEoln` ignore blanks and tabs, they are ideal for extracting information from text files. This can be demonstrated with the LINEDATA.DAT data file, shown in figure 13.5. The dots represent blank spaces. As you can see, LINEDATA.DAT contains frequent occurrences of leading and trailing blank characters. Lines 4, 6, 16, 19, and 23 contain only blanks. Lines 12, 13, and 22 are completely empty. In short, LINEDATA.DAT is not the type of file you would normally want to encounter.

The LINECNT program in listing 13.6 reads and displays the LINEDATA.DAT file three times. First, LINECNT uses `Eof` to test for the end of the file, displaying each line as it goes. Second, LINECNT repeats the process with `SeekEof`. Finally, LINECNT uses a combination of `SeekEof` and `SeekEoln`. Note that LINECNT processes each line in its entirety as a single string.

Fig. 13.5. *The contents of the LINEDATA.DAT file.*

```
1    ·1··2···3····4·····5······
2    ··2···4····6·····8·····10······
3    ···3····6·····9·····12······15
4    ························
5    ····4·····8·····12······16·······20
6    ··························································
7    ·····5·····10······15·······20··25·······
8    ······6······12·······18··24···30····
9    ·······7·······14··21···28····35·····
10   ··8··16···24····32·····40······
11   ···9···18···27·····36······45··
12
13
14   ···10····20···30······40·······50··
15   ····11·····22···33·······44··55·······
16   ·
17   ·····12······24···36··48···60·······
18   ······13·······26··39···52····65··········
19   ·······
20   ·······14··28···42····56·····70·······
21   ··15···30····45·····60······75··········
22
23   ·····
```

Listing 13.6

```
program LineCnt;
uses Crt;
var
   InFile   : Text;
   Contents : string;
   LineNo   : word;
begin
   Assign( InFile, 'LineData.DAT' );
   ClrScr;
   Reset( InFile );
   LineNo := 0;
   while not Eof( InFile ) do begin
      readln( InFile, Contents );
      Inc( LineNo );
      writeln( LineNo:6, '   ', Contents, '*' );
   end;
   readln;
   ClrScr;
   Reset( InFile );
   LineNo := 0;
   while not SeekEof( InFile ) do begin
      readln( InFile, Contents );
      Inc( LineNo );
```

```
        writeln( LineNo:6, '    ', Contents, '*' );
    end;
    readln;
    ClrScr;
    Reset( InFile );
    LineNo := 0;
    while not SeekEof( Infile ) do begin
        while not SeekEoln( InFile ) do begin
            readln( InFile, Contents );
            Inc( LineNo );
            writeln( LineNo:6, '    ', Contents, '*' );
        end;
    end;
    readln;
    Close( InFile );
end.
```

The results of LINECNT's first pass of the file are shown in figure 13.6. The LINEDATA.DAT file is displayed in its entirety. Asterisks mark the end of each line. The second and third passes produce identical results, shown in figure 13.7.

***Fig. 13.6.** Output produced by the first part of the LINECNT program.*

```
     1    1  2   3    4     5      *
     2     2   4    6     8       10    *
     3      3    6     9     12       15*
     4                         *
     5       4     8     12      16       20*
     6                                                       *
     7        5     10      15       20  25       *
     8         6      12       18  24   30    *
     9          7       14  21   28    35     *
    10     8  16   24    32     40      *
    11      9   18   27     36      45  *
    12   *
    13   *
    14      10    20   30      40       50  *
    15       11     22   33       44  55       *
    16    *
    17        12      24   36  48   60       *
    18         13       26  39   52    65          *
    19         *
    20          14  28   42    56     70       *
    21     15  30     45     60      75          *
    22   *
    23        *
```

In processing the text file as a series of strings, `SeekEof` and `SeekEoln` eliminated all blank lines, empty lines, and even leading blanks. If, instead, you process the text file as a series of individual variables of type `char`, you can eliminate *every* unnecessary character. The LINECNT1 program (listing 13.7) does just that.

Fig. 13.7. Output produced by both the second and third parts of the LINECNT program.

```
 1   1  2   3    4      5       *
 2   2   4    6      8     10       *
 3   3    6     9      12      15*
 4   4     8     12      16       20*
 5   5     10      15      20  25       *
 6   6      12       18  24   30     *
 7   7       14  21   28    35     *
 8   8  16   24    32     40       *
 9   9   18   27     36     45  *
10  10     20   30      40       50  *
11  11      22   33      44  55       *
12  12       24   36  48   60        *
13  13        26  39   52   65          *
14  14  28   42    56     70        *
15  15   30    45     60       75          *
```

Listing 13.7

```
program LineCnt1;
   uses CRT;
var
   InFile   : Text;
   LineNo   : word;
   AlphaNum : char;
begin
   ClrScr;
   Assign( InFile, 'LineData.DAT' );
   Reset( InFile );
   LineNo := 0;
   while not SeekEof( Infile ) do begin
      Inc( LineNo );
      write( LineNo:6, '   ' );
      while not SeekEoln( InFile ) do begin
         read( InFile, AlphaNum );
         write( AlphaNum );
      end;
```

```
      writeln;
   end;
   Close( InFile );
end.
```

The output from LINECNT1 is shown in figure 13.8. All of the blank spaces have been eliminated.

Fig. 13.8. Output produced by the LINECNT1 program.

```
  1    12345
  2    246810
  3    3691215
  4    48121620
  5    510152025
  6    612182430
  7    714212835
  8    816243240
  9    918273645
 10    1020304050
 11    1122334455
 12    1224364860
 13    1326395265
 14    1428425670
 15    1530456075
```

Because `SeekEof` and `SeekEoln` ignore major portions of a text file while searching for significant characters, they have limited appeal when you use them to input character or string data. However, `SeekEof` and `SeekEoln` are ideal for processing the *numeric* contents of a text file.

The LINECNT2 program, shown in listing 13.8, is designed to extract the numbers in the LINEDATA.DAT text file.

Listing 13.8

```
program LineCnt2;
uses Crt;
var
   InFile     : Text;
   i, LineNo  : word;
begin
```

continues

Listing 13.8 continued

```
   Assign( InFile, 'LineData.DAT' );
   ClrScr;
   Reset( InFile );
   while not Eof( InFile ) do begin
      while not Eoln( InFile ) do begin
         read( InFile, i );
         write( i:3 );
      end;
      readln( InFile );
      writeln;
   end;
   readln;
   ClrScr;
   Reset( InFile );
   LineNo := 0;
   while not SeekEof( Infile ) do begin
      Inc( LineNo );
      write( LineNo:6, '   ' );
      while not SeekEoln( InFile ) do begin
         read( InFile, i );
         write( i:3 );
      end;
      writeln;
   end;
   readln;
   Close( InFile );
end.
```

LINECNT2 processes the text file twice, the first time with `Eof` and `Eoln` (see fig. 13.9), and the second time with `SeekEof` and `SeekEoln` (see fig. 13.10).

As you can see in figure 13.9, `Eof` and `Eoln` are not capable of directly handling blank lines. In fact, notice how the trailing blank line was actually input as a zero! `SeekEof` and `SeekEoln` are far cleaner, because they jump over every non-numeric character.

Fig. 13.9. Output produced by the first part of the LINECNT2 program.

```
 1  2  3  4  5  2  4  6  8 10  3  6  9 12 15
 4  8 12 16 20
 5 10 15 20 25  6 12 18 24 30  7 14 21 28 35  8 16 24 32 40  9 18 27 36 45 10 2
0 30 40 50 11 22 33 44 55 12 24 36 48 60 13 26 39 52 65 14 28 42 56 70 15 30 45
60 75  0
```

Fig. 13.10. Output produced by the second part of the LINECNT2 program.

```
 1       1  2  3  4  5
 2       2  4  6  8 10
 3       3  6  9 12 15
 4       4  8 12 16 20
 5       5 10 15 20 25
 6       6 12 18 24 30
 7       7 14 21 28 35
 8       8 16 24 32 40
 9       9 18 27 36 45
10      10 20 30 40 50
11      11 22 33 44 55
12      12 24 36 48 60
13      13 26 39 52 65
14      14 28 42 56 70
15      15 30 45 60 75
```

A Note on *SeekEof* and *SeekEoln*

Strictly speaking, `SeekEof` and `SeekEoln` skip more than just blanks and tabs.

`SeekEof` bypasses all characters from ASCII 0 through ASCII 32 (#0 through #32), with the exception of #26. This range includes blanks (#32) and ASCII control characters such as tabs (#9), line feeds (#10), and carriage returns (#13). The single exception, #26, is also called Ctrl-Z; `SeekEof` cannot ignore it because it is the character Turbo Pascal uses to indicate the presence of an end-of-file.

`SeekEoln` is identical to `SeekEof` except, of course, it also cannot ignore the line feed (#10) and carriage return (#13).

Writing Data

You can output to a text file after opening it with `Rewrite` or `Append`, as discussed earlier in the chapter. The `write` and `writeln` procedures perform the data transfer.

Except for the addition of a text file identifier as their first parameter, `write` and `writeln` operate the same way with text files as they do when outputting to the screen. Both procedures accept any number of parameters.

The syntax of `write` and `writeln` is as follows:

```
write( TextFile, Var1 { , Var2, Var3, ... } );
writeln( TextFile, Var1 { , Var2, Var3, ... } );
```

After you call a `write` procedure, the next `write` or `writeln` begins its output wherever the original `write` procedure ended. After you call a `writeln`, the next `write` or `writeln` begins its output on a new line. In other words, `writeln` always terminates with an end-of-line marker (#13#10). You can generate a blank line in the file by using a `writeln` with no data item parameters.

Formatting Text File Output

When you output a string to a text file, the field width equals the number of bytes actually in the string, not the size of the string itself. No leading or trailing spaces are generated. All numeric data is written as a continuous sequence of digits, broken only by an occasional decimal point or plus or minus sign. Real numbers are output in scientific notation.

In short, text file output can easily appear cluttered. You can see this in the UNFORMED program in listing 13.9.

Listing 13.9

```
program Unformed;
var
   i : LongInt;
   r : real;
   s : string[ 100 ];
   c : char;
   F : Text;
begin
   Assign( F, 'DataForm.DAT' );
   Rewrite( F );
   s := 'abc';
   c := 'X';
   for i := 1 to 5 do
      write( F, i );
   for i := 1 to 5 do begin
      r := Sqrt( i );
      write( F, r );
   end;
   for i := 1 to 5 do
      write( F, s );
   for i := 1 to 5 do
      write( F, c );
   Close( F );
end.
```

When it executes, UNFORMED creates the DATAFORM.DAT file. To see what it contains, you have to use a special program such as your Turbo Pascal editor or the DOS `TYPE` utility.

You can also use the DUMP program, which is discussed in greater detail at the end of this chapter. When DUMP is used on DATAFORM.DAT, it produces the display shown in figure 13.11.

DUMP displays the contents of a file in both hexadecimal and character form. The entries in the first six columns each contain four hexadecimal values. The corresponding 24 characters are in the column on the far right.

Fig. 13.11. A dump of the DATAFORM.DAT file, produced by the UNFORMED program.

```
dataforn.dat                  Page 1 of 1                    140 bytes

31323334 3520312E 30303030 30303030 30303030 3030452B 12345 1.00000000000000E+
30303030 20312E34 31343231 33353632 33373333 33452B30 0000 1.41421356237333E+0
30303020 312E3733 32303530 38303735 36383136 452B3030 000 1.73205080756816E+00
30302032 2E303030 30303030 30303030 30303045 2B303030 00 2.00000000000000E+000
3020322E 32333630 36373937 37353031 3038452B 30303030 0 2.23606797750108E+0000
61626361 62636162 63616263 61626358 58585858          abcabcabcabcabcXXXXX
```

Notice how all the data items output by UNFORMED run together. The only spaces represent the positive signs of the five real numbers.

Data stored in this form is difficult to process. Fortunately, there is a simple solution. If, within a `write` or `writeln` procedure, you follow a data item with a colon and a positive number, Turbo Pascal will interpret the number as the minimum desired width of the data item. This number can be written as a constant, a variable, or an expression.

The complete format for a real number is a bit more complicated: a colon followed by a positive number specifying the field width, followed by another colon and another positive number specifying the number of characters to follow the decimal point. If necessary, the compiler automatically rounds the number.

If the specified field width is larger than the data item, the data item is right-justified and given one or more leading spaces. On the other hand, if the data item is larger than the specified width, the compiler will automatically expand the width of the field; the data item will not be truncated.

The FORMED program (listing 13.10) outputs the same data items as the UNFORMED program. This time, however, the `write` procedures use the formatting techniques just described.

Listing 13.10

```
program Formed;
var
   i : LongInt;
   r : real;
   s : string[ 100 ];
   c : char;
   F : Text;
begin
   Assign( F, 'DataForm.DAT' );
   Rewrite( F );
   s := 'abc';
   c := 'X';
   for i := 1 to 5 do
      write( F, i:3 );
   for i := 1 to 5 do begin
      r := Sqrt( i );
      write( F, r:8:4 );
   end;
   for i := 1 to 5 do
      write( F, s:5 );
   for i := 1 to 5 do
      write( F, c:3 );
   Close( F );
end.
```

Once again, you can use the DUMP program to see what FORMED output to the DATAFORM.DAT file. DUMP produces the display shown in figure 13.12.

Disk Files and Buffers

Now you are ready to take a quick tour through a diskette. Let us focus on a 5 1/4-inch double-sided double-density (DSDD) floppy diskette, because it is the most common type. This floppy diskette is so common that it is probably the format of your Turbo Pascal distribution diskettes. Other diskettes have different physical characteristics, but the principles are the same.

Fig. 13.12. A dump of the DATAFORM.DAT file, produced by the FORMED program.

```
dataforn.dat                        Page 1 of 1                        95 bytes

20203120 20322020 33202034 20203520 20312E30 30303020   1  2  3  4  5  1.0000
20312E34 31343220 20312E37 33323120 20322E30 30303020  1.4142  1.7321  2.0000
20322E32 33363120 20616263 20206162 63202061 62632020  2.2361  abc  abc  abc
61626320 20616263 20205820 20582020 58202058 202058   abc  abc  X  X  X  X  X
```

A diskette stores data in concentric rings centered on its hub. A *double-sided* diskette has ring patterns on both sides. A *double-density* diskette has 40 such rings on each side. Each ring is called a *track*. Track 0, which contains DOS booting information, is on the outside, and Track 39 is closest to the center. Each track consists of 9 *sectors* of 512 bytes. The sector is the smallest amount of data that DOS allows the computer to read at one time.

With a little arithmetic, you can calculate the storage capacity of a double-sided double-density diskette as follows:

$$2 \text{ sides} \times 40 \text{ tracks/side} \times 9 \text{ sectors/track} \times 512 \text{ bytes/sector}$$

This equation yields 368,640 bytes.

DOS groups pairs of sectors into *clusters*. Cluster 0 is Sector 0 and Sector 1, Cluster 1 is Sector 2 and Sector 3, and so on. Rather than keep track of all 720 individual sectors, DOS chooses instead to keep track of the 360 clusters. Therefore, file space is always allocated in multiples of 1024-byte clusters. This is why erasing a file that contains a single byte adds 1024 bytes of available space to your disk, and why the number of free bytes returned by the `DIR` command is always a multiple of 1024.

To understand why a disk drive is so slow, you have to remember that two actions must be taken before data transfer is complete:

1. The disk head (the electronic read-write device) must be positioned to the correct track. The time it takes for this physical movement is usually measured in milliseconds.
2. Once over the correct track, the spinning action of the diskette moves every byte in the track under the disk head every few hundredths of a second.

If a file is larger than 1024 bytes, its next cluster may be located on another track, which means that these two steps must be repeated. Large files are only rarely stored in contiguous clusters. As a diskette fills up, its available clusters can become widely scattered. You have probably noticed that even the DOS `COPY` utility seems to take forever on a well-used diskette. Clearly, minimizing disk head movement could save a great deal of time.

Controlling Buffer Size

So what does all this have to do with Turbo Pascal? Well, suppose that you have an array of bytes, as follows:

```
var
   ByteArray : array [ 1..1000 ];
```

Further suppose that you want to input data into `ByteArray` from a text file. You would probably use code like the following:

```
for i := 1 to 1000 do
   read( TextFileId, ByteArray[ i ] );
```

From the previous discussion, you know that 1000 separate diskette accesses would need to be performed—a process requiring several seconds at best.

Fortunately, Turbo Pascal automatically provides a text file *buffer* of 128 bytes. When your program processes the first `read` procedure, it stores 128 bytes (one quarter of a sector) in this buffer. Every subsequent `read` procedure gets its data electronically from the buffer, not mechanically from the disk. The next physical diskette access occurs only when all the bytes in the buffer have been assigned.

The compiler always uses a buffer when it processes a text file. Because DOS transfers data in complete sectors of 512 bytes, storing 128 of them is far from wasteful or time-consuming. After all, even if you wanted to input only a single byte, DOS would still try to send you 512!

The buffer size was set at 128 bytes because of historical reasons relating to early versions of DOS. However, it turns out that 128 bytes is an excellent compromise for most file processing operations.

Of course, if your program needs to manipulate larger chunks of data (such as when reading a word processing file or a spreadsheet data file into memory), the default size of 128 bytes is far smaller than you would really like. It would be helpful, for example, to reduce disk head movement by storing an entire 1024-byte cluster in the buffer, because you know that your program will need to use it shortly anyway.

Turbo Pascal provides the `SetTextBuf` procedure for just such a situation. The syntax is as follows:

```
SetTextBuf( var TextFileIdentifier : Text;  BufferVar   { ; Size : word } );
```

`TextFileIdentifier` is the text file variable. `BufferVar` is the name of the variable that you want to use as the new buffer. The optional `Size` field determines the size of the buffer. If `Size` is omitted, `SizeOf(BufferVar)` will be used.

You should call `SetTextBuf` after you have performed the file `Assign` but before you have opened it with `Reset`, `Rewrite`, or `Append`.

The NEWTYPE program (listing 13.11) demonstrates how `SetTextBuf` is used. NEWTYPE operates just like the DOS `TYPE` utility, except that while `TYPE` continuously scrolls the screen, NEWTYPE pauses after each screen is filled and waits for you to press the Enter key. This enables you to examine a file one page at a time.

Listing 13.11

```
program NewType;
uses Crt;
var
   TextFile            : Text;
   IndividualCharacter : char;
   Buffer              : array [ 1..1024 ] of char;   { A full cluster }
begin
   if ParamCount = 1 then begin
      Assign( TextFile, ParamStr( 1 ) );
      SetTextBuf( TextFile, Buffer );      { Assumes all 1024 characters }
      Reset( TextFile );
      while not Eof( TextFile ) do begin
         ClrScr;
         while (WhereY <> 24) and (not Eof( TextFile )) do begin
```

```
            read( TextFile, IndividualCharacter );
            write( IndividualCharacter );
         end;
         readln;
      end;
   end;
end.
```

Flushing a File

So far, you have seen how Turbo Pascal uses the buffer to store data being input *from* a text file. In a similar fashion, `write` and `writeln` procedures transfer program data *to* the buffer. The buffer is physically output to the disk only when it becomes full.

Earlier, the chapter stressed how important it is to close a file as soon as your program finishes with it. Unfortunately, some programs, such as word processors and spreadsheets, do not have this luxury. They must keep a file open until the user closes it—often after a long time has passed.

To minimize the risk of lost data, you can *flush* the text file's buffer—causing whatever data is in the buffer to be immediately saved to disk—by using the Turbo Pascal `Flush` procedure. The syntax is simply:

```
Flush( TextFileIdentifier );
```

Although you can call `Flush` whenever you want, the best time to use it is just before input in an interactive program. Waiting for a user response is frequently the longest period of program inactivity.

I/O Error Checking

Normally, Turbo Pascal treats all run-time errors as fatal. It believes that it is doing you a favor by aborting the program immediately whenever an error is encountered.

Sometimes, however, Turbo's well-intentioned desire to protect you can prove more bothersome than benevolent. For example, suppose that you want to append data to a text file. If the file already exists, it should be opened with `Append`. If it does not exist, it should be opened with `Rewrite`.

Unfortunately, if you begin with `Append`, your program will generate a fatal run-time error if the file cannot be found. Similarly, if you begin with `Rewrite`, the current contents of the file will be lost.

Turbo Pascal helps you avoid problems like this. You can disable I/O error checking with the `{$I-}` compiler directive. I/O error checking can later be turned back on by using the `{$I+}` directive.

While I/O error checking is off, no I/O error will fatally abort the program. Instead, your program must test the success or failure of every critical I/O operation with the `IOResult` function. In fact, until you do call `IOResult`, every subsequent I/O procedure or function call will be ignored!

`IOResult` returns zero for a successful operation; a nonzero value indicates an error has occurred. The possible return codes are given in table 13.1.

Your DOS programmer's reference manual and Appendix A of the Turbo Pascal *Programmer's Guide* contain more information on the causes of these errors. But do not despair. Unless you are trying to detect a specific type of error, it is usually enough to test for a nonzero value. For example, to append to an existing file or, alternatively, to create a new file, you can use the following code:

```
      Assign( InfoFile, FileName );
{$I-} Append( InfoFile ); {$I+}
      if IOResult <> 0 then
         Rewrite( InfoFile );
```

Here, any error that results from a failure of the `Append` procedure is most likely a nonexistent file. Of course, if the file does exist but is write protected, the `Rewrite` procedure will generate a fatal run-time error. Similarly, if you perform I/O checking after both the `Append` and the `Rewrite` procedures but do not test each subsequent `write` or `writeln`, a fatal run-time error will result from using up all remaining space on the disk.

Note that after `IOResult` is called, the error code is reset to 0. If you need to use the same value of `IOResult` in more than one place, you should first assign it to an integer variable, as follows:

```
ErrorCode := IOResult;
if ErrorCode = 2 then
   writeln( 'File not found.' )
else if ErrorCode = 3 then
   writeln( 'Path not found.' );
```

Table 13.1. *Possible Return Codes of* `IOResult`

Category	*Value*	*Meaning*
DOS Errors	0	No error
	2	File not found
	3	Path not found
	4	Too many open files
	5	File access denied
	6	Invalid file handle
	12	Invalid file access code
	15	Invalid drive number
	16	Cannot remove current directory
	17	Cannot rename across drives
I/O Errors	100	Disk read error
	101	Disk write error
	102	File not assigned
	103	File not open
	104	File not open for input
	105	File not open for output
	106	Invalid numeric format
Critical Errors	150	Disk is write-protected
	151	Unknown unit
	152	Drive not ready
	153	Unknown command
	154	CRC error in data
	155	Bad drive request structure length
	156	Disk seek error
	157	Unknown media type
	158	Sector not found
	159	Printer out of paper
	160	Device write fault
	161	Device read fault
	162	Hardware failure

The most common use of `IOResult` is simply to ensure that a file is successfully opened. The NEWTYPE2 program in listing 13.12 slightly modifies the NEWTYPE program to terminate gracefully if the specified file cannot be found.

Listing 13.12

```
program NewType2;
uses Crt;
var
   TextFile              : Text;
   IndividualCharacter : char;
   Buffer               : array [ 1..1024 ] of char;    { A full cluster }
begin
   if ParamCount = 1 then begin
      Assign( TextFile, ParamStr( 1 ) );
      SetTextBuf( TextFile, Buffer );      { Assumes all 1024 characters }
{$I-}
      Reset( TextFile );
{$I+}
      if IOResult <> 0 then
         writeln( ParamStr( 1 ), ' wasn''t found.' )
      else begin
         while not Eof( TextFile ) do begin
            ClrScr;
            while (WhereY <> 24) and (not Eof( TextFile )) do begin
               read( TextFile, IndividualCharacter );
               write( IndividualCharacter );
            end;
            readln;
         end;
      end;
   end;
end.
```

The *IOResult* Function

Notice from the contents of table 13.1 that `IOResult` can detect more than just file errors. The function is described more extensively in the next chapter, which discusses directory operations.

To save space, most of the programs in this book do not use I/O checking. However, `IOResult` could be used in any program that contains input or output. See the discussion of the `{$I}` compiler directive in the "Reference" section for further examples.

Typed Files

A typed file contains data of the type named in the file declaration. In the following example, the files F1, F2, F3, and F4 are all declared as typed files.

```
type
   CustomerRecord = record
                       Name         : string[ 30 ];
                       AcctNumber   : longint;
                       CreditLimit  : real;
                    end;
var
   F1 : file of byte;
   F2 : file of CustomerRecord;
   F3 : file of char;
   F4 : file of real;
```

Accessing a typed file is extremely fast because the compiler can assume that its contents consist entirely of data of the declared type. Specifically, Turbo Pascal assumes that all data items in a typed file are stored in exactly the same format as when they are stored in RAM.

Reading from Typed Files

The data elements in a typed file are not stored with any separating end-of-line characters. Consequently, the `readln` and `writeln` procedures, which require end-of-line characters to separate each line, cannot be used; `read` and `write` must be used exclusively. This is an example of how a `Text` file differs from a `file of char`.

Writing to Typed Files

The best way to see the difference between text and typed files is with examples. The FILECMP program in listing 13.13 writes a single word to both a text file and a typed file.

Listing 13.13

```
program FileCmp;
var
   TextFile  : text;
   TypedFile : file of word;
   Value     : word;
begin
   Assign( TextFile, 'File1.txt' );
   Rewrite( TextFile );
   Assign( TypedFile, 'File1.typ' );
   Rewrite( TypedFile );
   Value := $9AE5;
   write( Value );
   write( TextFile, Value );
   write( TypedFile, Value );
   Close( TextFile );
   Close( TypedFile );
end.
```

The hex characters $9AE5 translate to 39,653 in decimal. If, after FILECMP executes, you use the DUMP program to view the contents of the FILE1.TXT file, you see the display shown in figure 13.13. In a text file, the number is stored as the five ASCII characters for 3, 9, 6, 5, and 3—that is, bytes $33, $39, $36, $35, and $33.

***Fig. 13.13.** A dump of the FILE1.TXT file, produced by the FILECMP program.*

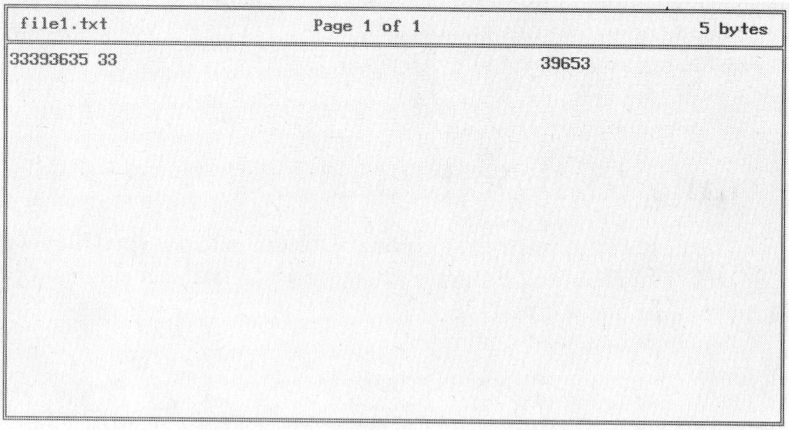

```
file1.txt                    Page 1 of 1                    5 bytes
33393635 33                                 39653
```

Next, if you apply the DUMP program to view the contents of the FILE1.TYP file, you obtain the display in figure 13.14. (Remember that DOS swaps the high and low bytes in a word.)

Fig. 13.14. A dump of the FILE1.TYP file, produced by the FILECMP program.

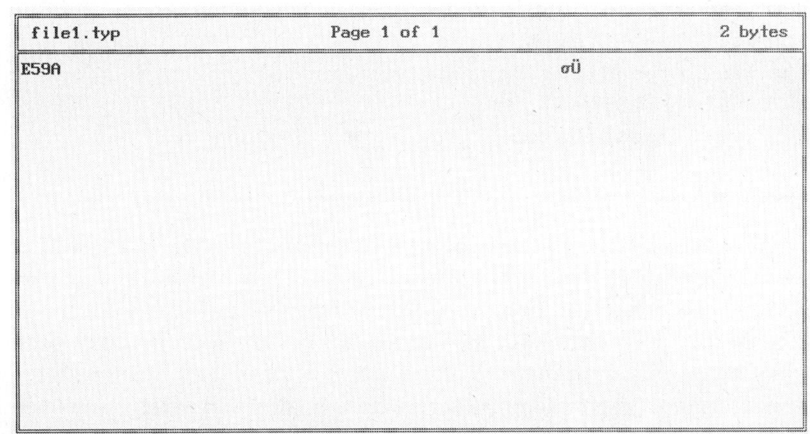

A time-consuming conversion process must take place before data items can be exchanged between text files and internal memory. Data from typed files avoids this time and effort.

If you are familiar with the BASIC programming language, you can follow this comparison: Pascal's text files correspond to BASIC's ASCII files, and Pascal's typed files correspond to BASIC's binary files.

Now look at what happens with string variables. The FILECMP1 program in listing 13.14 compares string output in text and typed files.

Listing 13.14

```
program FileCmp1;
var
   TextFile  : text;
   TypedFile : file of string;
   Message   : string;
begin
   Assign( TextFile, 'File1.txt' );
```

continues

Listing 13.14 continued

```
    Rewrite( TextFile );
    Assign( TypedFile, 'File1.typ' );
    Rewrite( TypedFile );
    Message := 'This message is 35 characters long.';
    write( Message );
    write( TextFile, Message );
    write( TypedFile, Message );
    Close( TextFile );
    Close( TypedFile );
end.
```

After FILECMP1 executes, the new contents of the FILE1.TXT file can be examined with DUMP. As shown in figure 13.15, the text file contains only the 35 characters representing the *contents* of the string. The new FILE1.TYP file is shown in figure 13.16. The typed file holds the *entire* string: the leading byte containing the size of the active portion (hexadecimal $23 is decimal 35); the 35-character message; and, finally, 220 bytes of garbage.

***Fig. 13.15.** A dump of the FILE1.TXT file, produced by the FILECMP1 program.*

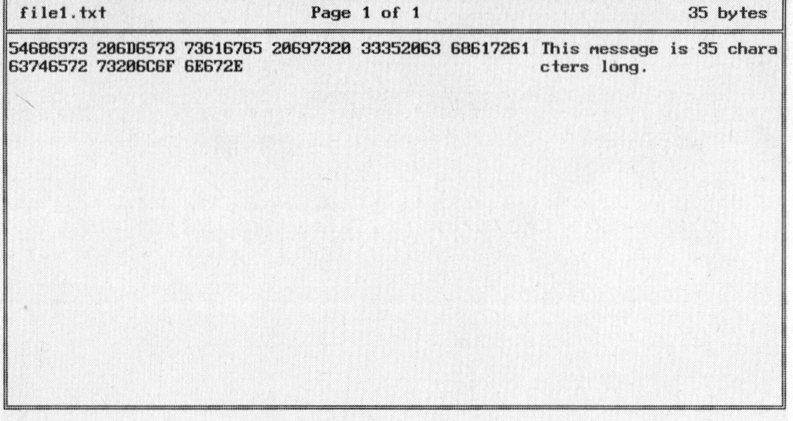

Fig. 13.16. A dump of the FILE1.TYP file, produced by the FILECMP1 program.

```
file1.typ                        Page 1 of 1                            256 bytes

23546869 73206D65 73736167 65206973 20333520 63686172 #This message is 35 char
61637465 7273206C 6F6E672E 0B30B001 0000B500 0B30D801 acters long.
0000BA00 00900000 0001BF00 00900000 8001C400 0B30E001
0000C900 00900000 0000D100 0B304002 0000D600 00900000
0001DB00 0B306002 0000E000 0B301800 0000E800 8001041E
04570206 31C00450 0200F100 00FF0004 9A0E0B30 B0010000
0204BF0E 0B900000 0001061E 57000501 049A0E0B 30D80100
0002120C 00001501 0204BF0E 00900000 0000041E 04570204
BF0E0090 00008001 041E0457 020631C0 04500200 43010051
01049A0E 0B30B001 00000200 35010057 01049A0E 0B30D801
00000212 0D000067 010204BF 0E009000
```

Untyped Files

You declare a file as untyped when you do not care about its contents. Data from an untyped file can be input directly into any variable of any type. Similarly, you can output to an untyped file from any variable of any type.

It might seem initially as though an untyped file has the same properties as a text file, but there are three major differences:

- The text file input and output procedures `read`, `readln`, `write`, and `writeln` cannot be used on untyped files. Instead, two new procedures—`BlockRead` and `BlockWrite`, discussed in the next section—must be used.
- By default, text files use a 128-byte buffer for transferring data between main memory and disk. If you use the `SetTextBuf` procedure, you can specify your own buffer area. Untyped files do not use any buffers. All data transfers are made directly between the disk and a specified memory area. This saves memory space, as well as the time it takes to move data to and from the buffer.
- When writing data from memory to a text file, data items are converted from binary to ASCII format. Similarly, when reading data from a text file to memory, data items are converted from

ASCII format to binary. No such conversion process is performed on an untyped file. In fact, no type checking of any kind is performed.

Declaring and Opening an Untyped File

An untyped file is declared with the reserved word `File` and nothing more. For example:

```
var
   UnTypedFile : File;
```

Untyped files can be opened with only `Reset` or `Rewrite`.

Blocking Data

The `BlockRead` and `BlockWrite` procedures are designed to transfer data in large chunks, more properly called *blocks*. A block can be any size, but the default size is 128 bytes. The syntax of `BlockRead` and `BlockWrite` is as follows:

```
BlockRead( var F: file; var Buffer; Count: word; [; var Result: word] );
BlockWrite( var F: file; var Buffer; Count: word; [; var Result: word] );
```

`BlockRead` inputs `Count` blocks from the untyped file `F`. The data is assigned to the variable specified by `Buffer`. The actual number of blocks read is returned in the optional parameter `Result`.

`BlockWrite` outputs `Count` blocks to the untyped file `F`. The data is read from the variable specified by `Buffer`. The actual number of blocks output is returned in the optional parameter `Result`.

If `Result` is not specified, the compiler generates an I/O error if the actual number of blocks transferred was less than `Count`. Therefore, if `Result` is equal to `Count`, all of the blocks were processed successfully.

Setting the Size of a Block

`BlockRead` and `BlockWrite` can handle only *complete* blocks. Partially filled blocks will not be transferred. Consequently, it is important to choose a block size that divides evenly into the size of the data you are working with.

Because few files are obliging enough to contain exact multiples of the default block size of 128 bytes, it would be helpful to reset the block size to something more general, such as 1. Fortunately, the `Reset` and `Rewrite` procedures offer a record size parameter that enables you to choose the length of a block in an untyped file.

The syntax for untyped files is

```
Reset( UntypedFileIdentifier, RecSize );
Rewrite( UntypedFileIdentifier, RecSize );
```

`RecSize` can be any value from 1 up through 65,535, but using 1 is the safest choice for most applications.

Block versus Record

For untyped files, the terms *block* and *record* are sometimes used interchangeably. *Block* is more precise, because it refers to a chunk of a file without regard for its content. *Record* implies that the data has the same structure as found in a Pascal `Record` type. Unfortunately, *record* is one of those words with multiple meanings. Computer people have always referred to any group of bytes read from or written to a file at the same time as a *logical record*.

The QUIKCOPY program in listing 13.15 demonstrates how `BlockRead` and `BlockWrite` are used. QUIKCOPY is a simpler version of the DOS `COPY` utility. Two file names are read from the command line; the contents of the first file are copied to the second.

Listing 13.15

```
program QuikCopy;
var
   InFile, OutFile : file;
   Buffer          : array [ 1..512 ] of char;
   NumberRead, NumberWritten : word;
begin
   if ParamCount <> 2 then Halt( 1 );
   Assign( InFile, ParamStr( 1 ) );
   Reset( InFile, 1 );
```

continues

Listing 13.15 continued

```
    Assign( OutFile, ParamStr( 2 ) );
    Rewrite( OutFile, 1 );
    repeat
       BlockRead( InFile, Buffer, SizeOf( Buffer ), NumberRead );
       BlockWrite( OutFile, Buffer, NumberRead, NumberWritten );
    until (NumberRead = 0) or (NumberRead <> NumberWritten);
    Close( InFile );
    Close( OutFile );
end.
```

Notice how both the `Reset` and `Rewrite` procedures open files with a block size equal to 1 byte. The test:

```
until (NumberRead = 0) or (NumberRead <> NumberWritten);
```

serves several purposes. After the first loop, `NumberRead` is equal to 0 only if no block had been successfully read—a situation that could occur only if the input file was empty. Similarly, later in the program, `NumberRead` equals 0 when no more records remain—that is, when the file is empty. The second condition, `NumberRead <> NumberWritten`, can be true only if a disk write error occurred.

Moving Data to Internal Memory

One of the most common uses of the block transfer commands is to move data rapidly between internal memory and the disk. Here are two programs that demonstrate how this is done.

The SEE program in listing 13.16 uses `BlockRead` to transfer a selected file onto the heap. Once there, its contents can be scanned conveniently and displayed to the screen a page at a time. Unlike the NEWTYPE and NEWTYPE2 programs presented earlier in the chapter, SEE enables you to page backward and to return directly to the first page.

Listing 13.16

```
program See;
uses Crt, Dos;
const
    EndProg   : Boolean = False;
```

```
   PageIndex : word = 1;
var
   InFile                     : file;
   FileArea                   : pointer;
   Size, Result, MemSeg, i    : word;
   Pages                      : array[ 1..200 ] of word;
   ch                         : char;
begin
   if ParamCount = 0 then Halt( 1 );
   Assign( InFile, ParamStr( 1 ) );
   Reset( InFile, 1 );
   Size := FileSize( InFile );
   GetMem( FileArea, Size );
   MemSeg := Seg( FileArea^ );
   BlockRead( InFile, FileArea^, Size, Result );
   FillChar( Pages, SizeOf( Pages ), 0 );
   repeat
      ClrScr;
      i := Pages[ PageIndex ];
      repeat
         write( Chr( Mem[ MemSeg:i ] ) );
         Inc( i );
      until (i = Size) or (WhereY = 25);
      repeat
         ch := ReadKey;
         if ch = #27 then
            EndProg := True
         else if ch = #0 then
            case ReadKey of
               #71 : PageIndex := 1;          { Home }
               #73 : if PageIndex > 1 then    { PgUp }
                        Dec( PageIndex );
               #81 : if i < Size then begin   { PgDn }
                        Inc( PageIndex );
                        Pages[ PageIndex ] := i;
                     end;
               else ch := #255;
            end;
      until (ch = #0) or EndProg;
   until EndProg;
   Close( InFile );
end.
```

The `FileSize` function (discussed in greater detail in the next chapter) returns the number of bytes in the input file. Knowing this, SEE is able to reserve a suitable area on the heap. After the file is transferred, its first page is displayed on the screen. The Home, PgUp, and PgDn keys control the next screen to be displayed. You can end the program by pressing the Esc key.

SEE is designed principally for viewing text files such as program source code. Lines longer than 80 characters are wrapped to the next line. Because of this feature, SEE does not know in advance how many lines of text will fill a screen; consequently, the `WhereY = 25` test determines page breaks.

The DUMP program in listing 13.17 expands these ideas. DUMP is the program used earlier in the chapter to view the contents of both text and binary files. The program displays data in both hexadecimal and character format.

Listing 13.17

```
program Dump;
uses Crt, Dos;
const
   EndProg   : Boolean = False;
   PageIndex : word = 1;
   Displayed : word = 456;
var
   InFile                          : file;
   FileArea                        : pointer;
   Size, Result, MemSeg, i, j,
   DisplaySize, LineSize,
   MaxPages                        : word;
   Pages                           : array[ 1..200 ] of word;
   ch                              : char;
   FileName                        : string;
   DisplayLine                     : array [ 1..24 ] of byte;
function CreateHex( binary_form : byte ) : char;
begin
   case binary_form of
      0..9 : CreateHex := chr( binary_form + 48 );
      10..15 : CreateHex := chr( binary_form + 55 );
   end;
end;
```

```
procedure horizon( left, right : char );
begin
   write( left );
   for i := 1 to 78 do write( #205 );
   write( right );
end;
procedure MakeBorder;
begin
   ClrScr;
   horizon( #201, #187 );
   write( #186, ' ' );
   write( FileName );
   GotoXY( 67, 2 ); write( Size:6, ' bytes' );
   GotoXY( 80, 2 ); write( #186 );
   horizon( #204, #185 );
   for i := 4 to 23 do begin
      GotoXY( 1, i ); write( #186 );
      GotoXY( 80, i ); write( #186 );
   end;
   GotoXY( 1, 24 );
   horizon( #200, #188 );
end;
begin
   if ParamCount = 0 then Halt( 1 );
   FileName := ParamStr( 1 );
   Assign( InFile, FileName );
   Reset( InFile, 1 );
   Size := FileSize( InFile );
   MakeBorder;
   GetMem( FileArea, Size );
   MemSeg := Seg( FileArea^ );
   BlockRead( InFile, FileArea^, Size, Result );
   MaxPages := (Size div Displayed) + 1;
   for i := 1 to MaxPages do
      Pages[ i ] := (i - 1) * Displayed;
   GotoXY( 33, 2 );
   write( 'Page 1 of ', MaxPages );
   Window( 2, 4, 79, 23 );
   repeat
      ClrScr;
      i := Pages[ PageIndex ];
      repeat
```

continues

Listing 13.17 continued

```
      LineSize := 0;
      repeat
         Inc( LineSize );
         DisplayLine[ LineSize ] :=Mem[ MemSeg:i ];
         Inc( i );
      until (LineSize = 24) or (i = Size);
      for j := 1 to LineSize do begin
         write( CreateHex( DisplayLine[ j ] div 16 ),
                CreateHex( DisplayLine[ j ] mod 16 )   );
         if j mod 4 = 0 then write( ' ' );
      end;
      for j := LineSize + 1 to 24 do begin
         write( '  ' );
         DisplayLine[ j ] := ord( ' ' );
         if j mod 4 = 0 then write( ' ' );
      end;
      for j := 1 to 24 do
         if DisplayLine[ j ] in [ 7, 8, 10, 13 ] then
            write( ' ' )
         else
            write( chr( DisplayLine[ j ] ) );
   until (i=Size) or (i >= Pages[ PageIndex + 1 ]);
   repeat
      ch := ReadKey;
      if ch = #27 then
         EndProg := True
      else if ch = #0 then
         case ReadKey of
            #71 : PageIndex := 1;           { Home }
            #73 : if PageIndex > 1 then     { PgUp }
                     Dec( PageIndex );
            #81 : if i < Size then          { PgDn }
                     Inc( PageIndex );
            #79 : PageIndex := MaxPages;    { End }
            else ch := #255;
         end;
         Window( 1, 1, 80, 25 );
         GotoXY( 37, 2 );
         write( PageIndex:3 );
```

```
            Window( 2, 4, 79, 23 );
        until (ch = #0) or EndProg;
    until EndProg;
    Window( 1, 1, 80, 25 );
    GotoXY( 1, 25 );
end.
```

Here again, `BlockRead` is used to copy a file to the heap. But this time, the program displays the contents continuously, without starting new lines after each carriage return. You know at once how many screens will be needed. Consequently, in addition to the Home, PgUp, and PgDn keys, the End key is also available. You can end the program by pressing the Esc key.

Using DUMP on its own source file, with the command:

```
DUMP DUMP.PAS
```

produces the screen shown in figure 13.17. Both SEE and DUMP are extremely useful programming utilities.

Fig. 13.17. A dump of the DUMP program.

```
dump.pas                           Page 1 of 10                          4511 bytes

70726F67 72616D20 44756D70 3B0D0A20 20757365 73204372 program Dump;    uses Cr
742C2044 6F733B0D 0A202063 6F6E7374 0D0A2020 20202045 t, Dos;    const       E
6E645072 6F672020 203A2042 6F6F6C65 616E203D 2046616C ndProg   : Boolean = Fal
73653B0D 0A202020 20205061 6765496E 64657820 3A20776F se;      PageIndex : wo
7264203D 20313B0D 0A202020 20204469 73706C61 79656420 rd = 1;      Displayed
3A20776F 7264203D 20343536 3B0D0A20 20766172 0D0A2020 : word = 456;    var
20202049 6E46696C 65202020 20202020 20202020 20202020    InFile
20202020 2020203A 2066696C 653B0D0A 20202020 2046696C          : file;      Fil
65417265 61202020 20202020 20202020 20202020 20202020 eArea
203A2070 6F696E74 65723B0D 0A202020 20205369 7A652C20  : pointer;       Size,
52657375 6C742C20 4D656D53 65672C20 692C206A 2C0D0A20 Result, MemSeg, i, j,
20202020 44697370 6C617953 697A652C 204C696E 6553697A     DisplaySize, LineSiz
652C0D0A 20202020 204D6178 50616765 73202020 20202020 e,      MaxPages
20202020 20202020 20202020 203A2077 6F72643B 0D0A2020               : word;
20202050 61676573 20202020 20202020 20202020 20202020    Pages
20202020 2020203A 20617272 61795B20 312E2E32 3030205D          : array[ 1..200 ]
206F6620 776F7264 3B0D0A20 20202020 63682020 20202020  of word;       ch
20202020 20202020 20202020 20202020 20202020 3A206368                       : ch
61723B0D 0A202020 20204669 6C654E61 6D652020 20202020 ar;      FileName
```

Random Access Files

Files can be processed either sequentially or randomly. In a *sequential* file, you can start to read characters only from the beginning of the file, and you can write characters only after the current position of the file pointer. In a *random* file, each record may be read from or written to without regard for its position in the file.

Sequential files are used when their data will always be processed in a specific order or when (as with SEE and DUMP) the file needs to be manipulated in its entirety. However, random processing is essential when information must be rapidly retrieved from or stored to the middle of a large file; sequential processing would simply take too much time.

Text files are strictly sequential. Because each line in a text file may be a different length, you could not guarantee that a new line written to the middle of the file would have exactly the same length as the line it replaced. If the new line was longer, the overlap would corrupt other lines around it. If the new line was shorter, part of the original line would be unaffected.

On the other hand, typed and untyped files always process identically sized records. By positioning the file pointer to any desired record, you can read from or write to the file in any order you want.

Typed files and untyped files can always be both read and written to regardless of whether they were opened with `Reset` or `Rewrite`.

Accessing Records Randomly

The `Seek` procedure is used to position the file pointer to a specific record. This procedure accepts as a parameter the desired record number. The first record number in the file is 0. (You can use the `FilePos` function to learn the record number of the current file position.)

The MAKERAND program (listing 13.18) demonstrates how random file accessing works.

Listing 13.18

```
program MakeRand;
uses Crt;
type
   String20 = string[ 20 ];
   PassengerRecord = record
                        LastName  : String20;
                        FlightNo  : word;
                        AirFare   : real;
                     end;
```

```
var
   Passenger    : PassengerRecord;
   PassFile     : file of PassengerRecord;
   Who, Change : char;
procedure ClearBottomLines;
begin
   GotoXY( 1, 23 );   ClrEol;
   GotoXY( 1, 24 );   ClrEol;
   GotoXY( 1, 25 );   ClrEol;
   GotoXY( 1, 24 );
end;
procedure MakeReservation( LastNameIn : String20;
                           FlightNoIn : word;
                           AirFareIn  : real );
begin
   with Passenger do begin
      LastName := LastNameIn;
      FlightNo := FlightNoIn;
      AirFare  := AirFareIn;
      write( PassFile, Passenger );
   end;
end;
procedure ConfirmReservation;
begin
   ClrScr;
   Seek( PassFile, Ord( UpCase( Who ) ) - 65 );
   read( PassFile, Passenger );
   with Passenger do begin
      GotoXY( 20, 10 );   write( '    Last Name : ', LastName );
      GotoXY( 20, 12 );   write( 'Flight Number : ', FlightNo );
      GotoXY( 20, 14 );   write( '     Air Fare : ', AirFare:0:2 );
   end;
   ClearBottomLines;
end;
procedure ChangeReservation;
var
   Modifier : byte;
begin
   ClearBottomLines;
   write( 'Change:  (1) Flight Number   (2) AirFare   (3) No change   ' );
   readln( Modifier );
   with Passenger do begin
```

continues

Listing 13.18 continued

```
      case Modifier of
         1 : begin
                GotoXY( 36, 12 );
                readln( FlightNo );
             end;
         2 : begin
                GotoXY( 36, 14 );
                readln( AirFare );
             end;
      end;
      if Modifier - 1 < 2 then begin
         Seek( PassFile, Ord( UpCase( Who ) ) - 65 );
         write( PassFile, Passenger );
         ConfirmReservation;
      end;
   end;
   ClearBottomLines;
end;
begin
   Assign( PassFile, 'PassData.Dat' );
   Rewrite( PassFile );
   MakeReservation( 'Adams',   174,  456.72 );
   MakeReservation( 'Baker',   392,  893.21 );
   MakeReservation( 'Charles', 263,  765.38 );
   MakeReservation( 'Dover',   551, 1298.43 );
   MakeReservation( 'Edwards', 290,   99.99 );
   MakeReservation( 'Finch',   327,  223.64 );
   Reset( PassFile );
   ClrScr;
   repeat
      repeat
         GotoXY( 1, 1 );
         writeln(  'Enter the first letter of the last name' );
         write( 'or enter ''X'' to exit the program: ' );
         readln( Who );
      until UpCase( Who ) in [ 'A'..'F', 'X' ];
      if UpCase( Who ) <> 'X' then begin
         ConfirmReservation;
         repeat
            write( 'Change (Y/N)? ' );
            readln( Change );
```

```
        ClearBottomLines;
      until UpCase( Change ) in [ 'Y', 'N' ];
      if UpCase( Change ) = 'Y' then
        ChangeReservation;
    end;
  until UpCase( Who ) = 'X';
end.
```

MAKERAND uses the `MakeReservation` procedure to create a typed file containing airline reservation records. The six people supported conveniently have last names starting with unique letters of the alphabet. The `ChangeReservation` procedure can retrieve a record at random, change its contents, and replace the new record back in the file. Notice how the `Seek` procedure uses the last name of the passenger to automatically determine which record to access.

The opening screen is shown in figure 13.18. Requesting `B` (for Baker) results in the display shown in figure 13.19. The contents of the record can be changed at will, then recalled to confirm that the modification took place.

***Fig. 13.18.** The opening screen of the MAKERAND program.*

```
Enter the first letter of the last name
or enter 'X' to exit the program:
```

Although MAKERAND uses a typed file of records, other useful applications can be created, for example, from files of bytes, reals, and Booleans.

Fig. 13.19. The contents of the second record in the PASSDATA.DAT file as displayed by the MAKERAND program.

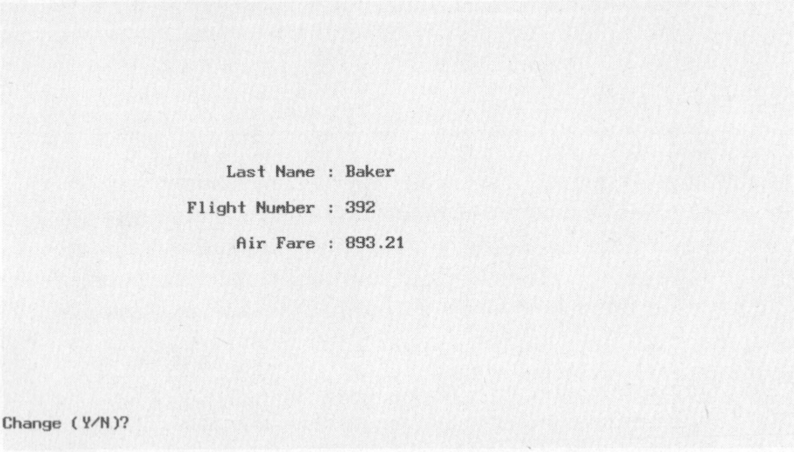

```
                Last Name  : Baker

            Flight Number  : 392

                 Air Fare  : 893.21




Change (Y/N)?
```

Appending and Truncating Typed and Untyped Files

Although typed and untyped files opened with `Reset` or `Rewrite` can be read from or written to at your discretion, they cannot be opened for `Append`. Instead, a small trick is required.

The command

```
Seek( FileID, FileSize( FileID ) );
```

positions the file pointer one record *beyond* the end of the file. Using this line causes all subsequent `write` or `BlockWrite` procedures to append their data to the existing file.

You can use the `Truncate` procedure to truncate a typed or an untyped file past the current position of the file pointer.

Summary

Table 13.2 contains the procedures and functions presented in this chapter together with a summary of the file types with which the subroutines can be used. This chapter presented many of these subroutines in the form of utilities that you will find yourself using throughout the remainder of the book.

Table 13.2. *Turbo Pascal File Subroutines*

Category	*Subroutine*	*Text*	*Typed*	*Untyped*
File Opening	`Append`	Yes	No	No
	`Assign`	Yes	Yes	Yes
	`Reset`	Yes	Yes	Yes
	`Rewrite`	Yes	Yes	Yes
	`Close`	Yes	Yes	Yes
File Input	`BlockRead`	No	No	Yes
	`Read`	Yes	Yes	No
	`Readln`	Yes	No	No
File Output	`BlockWrite`	No	No	Yes
	`Write`	Yes	Yes	No
	`Writeln`	Yes	No	No
Location Tests	`Eof`	Yes	Yes	Yes
	`Eoln`	Yes	No	No
	`SeekEof`	Yes	No	No
	`SeekEoln`	Yes	No	No
Random Access	`FilePos`	No	Yes	Yes
	`FileSize`	No	Yes	Yes
	`Seek`	No	Yes	Yes
	`Truncate`	No	Yes	Yes

In this chapter, you learned that the Turbo Pascal compiler supports three logical file types, named for the syntax of their declarations: text, typed, and untyped.

- A text file contains lines of characters terminated by a carriage return and a line feed.
- A typed file contains only data of the one particular type named in its declaration.

- An untyped file is completely unstructured and may contain any data in any format in any length.

You saw examples of how each of these three file types is used.

You learned how to relate a logical file in your program with a physical file on disk. You saw how to open a file for input or output and how to close a file when your program is finished with it. You learned a variety of ways to exchange formatted and unformatted data between your program and the disk. You learned how to bypass separators in text files, and you saw how records in typed and untyped files can be processed randomly.

You learned how to test for I/O errors and how to recover from them.

CHAPTER 14

Directory Handling

Many problems can arise when you work with files. A program and its data file can be stored in different directories or on different drives; both need to be located, no matter where they are. Programs can crash when you run out of disk space. Files might need to be created in or erased from a particular subdirectory. You may want to create new file names automatically.

In the last chapter, you saw how to use files to store and retrieve information. This chapter approaches files from the other direction—as residents of disk drives and directories.

Disk Drive Specifications

The `DiskSize` function returns the total number of bytes that can be stored on the specified drive. The disk may be any type, from a microfloppy through a mammoth hard disk. `DiskFree` returns the free space (that is, the number of unused bytes available for use).

Both functions take a single, byte-sized parameter to indicate the drive: 1 for drive A, 2 for drive B, and so on. The default drive is specified by setting the parameter to 0.

The DISK1 program (listing 14.1) describes space usage on the default drive.

Listing 14.1

```
program Disk1;
uses Dos;
var
   BytesFree,
   TotalSize,
   Utilization : longint;
begin
   BytesFree := DiskFree( 0 );
   TotalSize := DiskSize( 0 );
   Utilization := 100 - (BytesFree * 100 div TotalSize);
   writeln( 'The default drive has ',
            BytesFree, ' bytes free out of ',
            TotalSize, ' for ',
            Utilization, '% utilization.' );
end.
```

If the specified drive is invalid (if you specify drive 45, for example) or unavailable (such as when drive 1 is specified, but no floppy is inserted), the functions return –1. Program DISK2 (listing 14.2) uses this property to develop a simple drive availability function.

Listing 14.2

```
program Disk2;
uses Dos;
function DriveInUse( DriveNumber : byte ) : boolean;
begin
   DriveInUse := DiskSize( DriveNumber ) > 0;
end;
begin
   if DriveInUse( 1 ) then
      writeln( 'Begin processing.' )
   else
      writeln( 'Please insert a formatted floppy disk.' );
end.
```

Directories

It is common for programs to access files on other drives and directories. For example, a program may reside in a utility directory accessed through your system path, whereas your data files are in the current directory. Conversely, you may restrict an application to execute in only one directory or to direct all its output to a single directory. Turbo Pascal provides several directory management functions to control directory access.

Determining the Current Directory

You use the Turbo Pascal `GetDir` procedure to determine the currently active directory for any drive. `GetDir` accepts two parameters: the drive number (again, 0 for the default, 1 for drive A, 2 for drive B, and so on) and a string to contain the directory name when the procedure is finished. Because an I/O error can result if `GetDir` is unsuccessful, `IOResult` should be tested. The WHEREAMI program (listing 14.3) returns the name of the active directory on the disk drive specified in the command line. Compile the program to disk and execute it from DOS.

Listing 14.3

```
program WhereAmI;
{$I- I/O error checking is now disabled }
var
   CurrentDirectory : string;
   Drive : byte;
   CmdCode : integer;
begin
   if ParamCount = 0 then
      Drive := 0
   else
      Val( ParamStr( 1 ), Drive, CmdCode );
   if CmdCode <> 0 then
      writeln( 'A drive number must be specified' )
   else begin
      GetDir( Drive, CurrentDirectory );
      if IOResult = 0 then
```

continues

Listing 14.3 continued

```
        writeln( 'The current directory is ', CurrentDirectory )
      else
        writeln( 'Directory not found' );
   end;
end.
```

When executed, WHEREAMI may return the following:

```
The current directory is C:\payroll\data
```

Notice that the letter of the drive is always included as the first character of the path name. As a consequence, you can identify the current drive by calling `GetDir` for drive 0.

Changing the Current Directory

When a program is executing, it resides entirely in internal memory, independent of the current drive or directory. Consequently, a program can change both the default drive and directory without adversely affecting its execution. In Turbo Pascal, this is accomplished with the `ChDir` procedure.

`ChDir` is called with a string containing the complete name of the new path. The letter of the drive must be included. Because an I/O error results if `ChDir` is unsuccessful, `IOResult` should be used to test that the change has occurred.

The CLIMBUP program (listing 14.4) is a useful routine that uses `GetDir` to determine the current directory, then changes the default to the directory one level up.

Listing 14.4

```
program ClimbUp;
var
   CurrentDirectory : string;
   i : byte;
begin
   GetDir( 0, CurrentDirectory );
   writeln( 'The current directory is ', CurrentDirectory );
   i := Length( CurrentDirectory );
   while CurrentDirectory[ i ] <> '\' do i := i - 1;
```

```
    if i > 3 then
       begin
          CurrentDirectory[ 0 ] := chr( i - 1 );
          ChDir( CurrentDirectory );
          writeln( 'The new directory is ', CurrentDirectory );
       end
    else
       writeln( 'Already at root directory!' );
end.
```

For example, the directory may change as follows:

```
The current directory is C:\finance\payroll\data
The new directory is C:\finance\payroll
```

Because you knew that the requested directory existed, you did not bother to perform the `IOResult` test.

Creating a New Directory

Sometimes, however, a directory does not already exist and must be created. The `MkDir` procedure can solve this problem. `MkDir` is called with a string containing the complete path name of the directory to be made, including the letter of the drive. An I/O error results if the procedure is unsuccessful. You can test `IOResult` to see if the new directory has been successfully created, and you can use the `ChDir` procedure to enter it.

The MAKETEMP program (listing 14.5) creates and then enters a temporary directory one level lower than the current directory. If such a directory already exists, an error message is produced.

Listing 14.5

```
program MakeTemp;
{$I- I/O checking is disabled}
var
   CurrentDirectory : string;
begin
   GetDir( 0, CurrentDirectory );
   writeln( 'The current directory is ', CurrentDirectory );
   CurrentDirectory := CurrentDirectory + '\TEMP';
```

continues

Listing 14.5 continued

```
   MkDir( CurrentDirectory );
   if IOResult <> 0 then
      writeln( CurrentDirectory, ' already exists.' )
   else begin
      ChDir( CurrentDirectory );
      writeln( 'The new directory is ', CurrentDirectory );
   end;
end.
```

For example, executing MAKETEMP in the C:\FINANCE\PAYROLL directory results in the following:

```
The current directory is C:\FINANCE\PAYROLL
The new directory is C:\FINANCE\PAYROLL\TEMP
```

Removing a Directory

The Turbo Pascal `RmDir` procedure can remove the temporary directory after you are finished with it. (Actually, you may want to remove several levels of temporary directories, depending on how many times you ran MAKETEMP.)

Just like its DOS equivalent, `RmDir` requires that the directory be empty, with no files or subordinate directories. Also, the directory to be removed cannot be the current directory. `RmDir` is called with a string containing the complete path name and, like `ChDir` and `MkDir`, can result in an I/O error if unsuccessful.

You can use the SCRUBDIR program (listing 14.6) to bump up your current directory by one level and to remove the original directory, provided it does not contain any files.

Listing 14.6

```
program ScrubDir;
{$I- I/O checking is disabled}
var
   OldDirectory,
   CurrentDirectory : string;
   i : byte;
```

```
begin
   GetDir( 0, CurrentDirectory );
   writeln( 'The current directory is ', CurrentDirectory );
   i := Length( CurrentDirectory );
   if i = 3 then    { Only remove if not the root directory }
      writeln( 'Can''t remove root directory!' )
   else begin
      OldDirectory := CurrentDirectory;
      while CurrentDirectory[ i ] <> '\' do i := i - 1;
      CurrentDirectory[ 0 ] := chr( i - 1 );
      ChDir( CurrentDirectory );
      RmDir( OldDirectory );
      if IOResult = 0 then
         writeln( 'The new directory is ', CurrentDirectory )
      else begin
         writeln( 'Directory not empty!' );
         ChDir( OldDirectory );
      end;
   end;
end.
```

Accessing File Information

Programmers tend to be spoiled by the efficiency of Turbo Pascal. For each use of a file management procedure such as `Reset` or `Rewrite`, Turbo must generate instructions to locate the file, reserve buffer space for the file, establish pointers, and so on. One Pascal procedure can trigger a dozen tasks.

These detailed file access instructions are so common at the DOS level that whenever a program looks up an entry in the disk directory, a special record is automatically created in internal memory. This record—called a *file control block (FCB)*—contains such file information as the file's name, total size, time and date of creation, and attribute (discussed later in this chapter).

The file control block has been slightly restructured by Turbo Pascal into the predefined record `SearchRec`, which allows access to several useful fields:

```
SearchRec = record
              Fill: array[1..21] of Byte;
              Attr: Byte;
              Time: Longint;
              Size: Longint;
              Name: string[12];
            end;
```

The 21-byte filler contains technical details needed by DOS; *never* allow your programs to modify it. You will learn about each of the other fields in detail.

Accessing a Directory Entry

The FCB is a record created by DOS and placed as a *reference* in internal memory to provide easy access to directory data. Changing a field in the FCB has no effect on the characteristics of the underlying file, but the change may sufficiently confuse DOS to provoke a run-time error. To modify any file characteristics (that is, to change a file's name, attribute, or time stamp) you need special procedures, which are discussed in the next section. Reading from or writing to an individual file still requires the use of the `Assign`, `Reset`, and `Rewrite` procedures.

Turbo Pascal provides the `FindFirst` and `FindNext` procedures to access the information contained in the FCB. The primary purpose of these procedures is to quickly scan an entire directory and identify files with certain characteristics.

`FindFirst` takes three parameters: a target file name, the desired attribute, and the output record of type `SearchRec`. The target file name is in the same format you would use in a DOS directory call, with wild-card characters permitted. For example, to find all Pascal source files in the current directory, the target file string `*.PAS` is used. The attribute field is discussed in greater detail in the next section; for now, specify the predefined constant `AnyFile`.

`FindNext` uses the output record from the most recent `FindFirst` call to search for the next FCB entry that matches the name and attribute.

Accessing the Name and Size of a File

In the `SearchRec` record, the `Name` field is the DOS file name and extension, separated by a period, without the path or drive designator. The `Size` field is the size of the file in bytes.

To see how these fields are used, retrieve a set of file control blocks using the `FindFirst` and `FindNext` procedures, as demonstrated in the BASICDIR program (listing 14.7).

Listing 14.7

```
program BasicDir;
uses Dos;
var
   FileInfo : SearchRec;
begin
   FindFirst( 'DIR*.PAS', AnyFile, FileInfo );
   while DosError = 0 do
      begin
         with FileInfo do writeln( Name:14, Size:8 );
         FindNext( FileInfo );
      end;
end.
```

When executed, BASICDIR produces a primitive directory listing similar to the following:

```
DIR1.PAS      541
DIR5.PAS      254
DIR2.PAS      514
DIR4.PAS      804
DIR6.PAS      537
DIR7.PAS      913
DIR8.PAS     1044
DIR9.PAS      376
```

Notice that the `FileInfo` record of type `SearchRec` is used to provide, store, and pass information. It should not be modified in any way.

Accessing the Attribute Byte

Files come in several flavors. A *read-only* file, as the name implies, can only be read; you cannot write to it or erase it. A *hidden* file is skipped in a normal directory search (that is, a search that does not specifically request that hidden files be included). A *system* file, like a hidden file, is used by DOS and is also skipped in a normal directory search. A file name may be the *volume* name of the disk on which it resides, or it may be the name of a *subdirectory*.

The *attribute byte* describes the type of file and how it can be processed. Each of its bits corresponds to a particular characteristic. More than one of the bits can be set at the same time. The structure of the attribute byte is shown in figure 14.1.

Fig. 14.1. ***The structure of the file attribute byte.***

7	6	5	4	3	2	1	0
Reserved for System Use		Archive	Directory Name	Volume Label	System File	Hidden File	Read Only

In addition to identifying file types, the attribute byte also tracks a file's archival status. Whenever a file is created or modified, the *archive* bit is set. The bit is set to 0 only after a DOS `BACKUP` operation is performed. Therefore, subsequent `BACKUP` operations can ignore unmodified files.

To help with the process of testing, setting, and clearing the file attribute byte, Turbo predefines several constants that reflect the various bit patterns. Table 14.1 summarizes the constants and their patterns.

For example, to learn the names of all subordinate directories in the current directory, you simply read every FCB and test for the presence of a 1 in bit four (starting from bit zero) of the attribute byte. In other words, you test if the attribute byte is equal to the predefined variable `Directory`, as shown in the FINDDIRS program (listing 14.8).

Listing 14.8

```
program FindDirs;
uses Dos;
var
   level     : byte;
```

```
procedure GetFileData( Path : string );
var
   Path2    : string;
   FileInfo : SearchRec;
   i        : byte;
begin
   level := level + 1;
   FindFirst( Path + '\*.*', Directory, FileInfo );
   while DosError = 0 do
      begin
         if (FileInfo.Attr = Directory ) and
            (FileInfo.Name[ 1 ] <> '.') then begin
            for i := 1 to 12*(level - 1) do write( ' ' );
            writeln( FileInfo.Name );
            Path2 := Path + '\' + FileInfo.Name;
            GetFileData( Path2 );
         end;
         FindNext( FileInfo );
       end;
   level := level - 1;
end;
begin
   level := 0;
   GetFileData( 'c:' );
end.
```

Table 14.1. *File Attribute Constants*

Predefined constant	*Value (hex)*	*Bit pattern*
`ReadOnly`	$01	0000 0001
`Hidden`	$02	0000 0010
`SysFile`	$04	0000 0100
`VolumeID`	$08	0000 1000
`Directory`	$10	0001 0000
`Archive`	$20	0010 0000
`AnyFile`	$3F	0011 1111

The FINDDIRS program uses recursion to produce an indented tree diagram of all directories on drive C (see fig. 14.2).

Fig. 14.2. Sample output produced by FINDDIRS.

```
123
TP
            DOC
            EXAMPLES
            TURBO3
TURBOC
            LIB
            LIBRARY
                        INCLUDE
                        CLIB
                        MATH
                        EMU
QUE
            TEXT
                        PIX
            PROGRAMS
WORD
            SAVE

C>
```

When doing comparisons, the Turbo procedures `FindFirst` and `FindNext` test whether the logical `AND` of the attribute byte and the predefined constant are nonzero; in other words, the constants are additive. Therefore, to test for *either* a hidden file *or* an archive file, the parameter you pass is `( Hidden + Archive )`. Similarly, if you want every entry except a directory name, you can use `( AnyFile - Directory )`.

Accessing the Time Field

The long integer `Time` contains the packed format of the time and date of the last write operation on the file. The high-order word is the *date stamp*, which is stored in the format shown in figure 14.3. The parameters of the date stamp are listed in table 14.2.

***Table 14.2.** Date Stamp Parameters*

Code	*Bits*	*Contents*	*Value*
D	0–4	Day of month	1 to 31
M	5–8	Month	1 to 12
Y	9–15	Year	1980, for example

Fig. 14.3. The structure of the date stamp word.

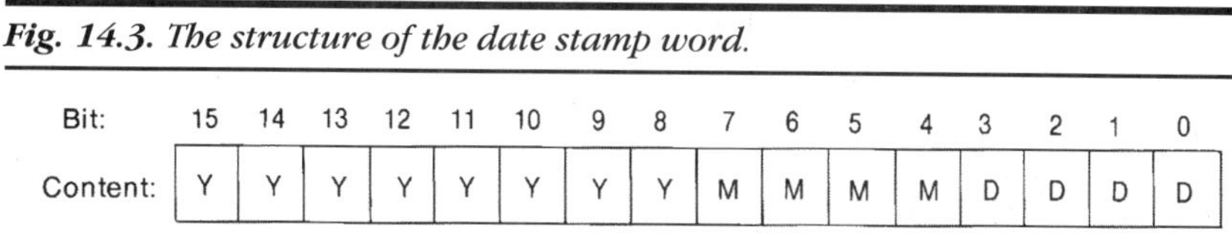

The low-order word is the *time stamp,* which is stored in the format shown in figure 14.4. The parameters of the time stamp are listed in table 14.3.

Fig. 14.4. The structure of the time stamp word.

Bit:	15	14	13	12	11	10	9	8	7	6	5	4	3	2	1	0
Content:	H	H	H	H	H	M	M	M	M	M	M	S	S	S	S	S

***Table 14.3.** Time Stamp Parameters*

Code	*Bits*	*Contents*	*Value*
S	0–4	Number of 2-second increments	0 to 29
M	5–10	Minutes	0 to 59
H	11–15	Hours	0 to 23

Notice that the data is stored in the order of significance. Even without unpacking the fields, two `Time` variables can be directly compared to determine chronological sequence.

In addition to the `FindFirst` and `FindNext` procedures, the time field of a file can be accessed with the `GetFTime` procedure. Similarly, it can be reset with the `SetFTime` procedure. Both `GetFTime` and `SetFTime` are discussed later in this chapter.

Fortunately, Turbo provides the `PackTime` procedure to create the packed date and time format from ordinary word-sized variables. Similarly, the packed format can be converted to more manageable word-sized variables with the `UnpackTime` procedure. `PackTime` and `UnpackTime` both expect one long integer parameter and one parameter of the predefined record type `DateTime`.

```
DateTime = record
             Year,Month,Day,Hour,Min,Sec: Word;
           end;
```

By adding the `GetFTime` and `UnpackTime` procedures to the BASICDIR program to create TODAY (listing 14.9), you can test each returned FCB record to find the files created only today. Note that the program assumes that the COMMAND.COM file is in the root directory on drive C.

Listing 14.9

```
program Today;
{$M 1024,0,0     Minimum memory so Exec can work }
uses Dos;
var
   Year,
   Month,
   Day,
   DayofWeek : word;
   FileInfo  : SearchRec;
   FileDate  : DateTime;
   CmdString : string;
begin
   GetDate( Year, Month, Day, DayofWeek );
   FindFirst( '*.*', Archive, FileInfo );
   while DosError = 0 do
      begin
         UnpackTime( FileInfo.Time, FileDate );
         if ( FileDate.Year = Year ) and
            ( FileDate.Month = Month ) and
            ( FileDate.Day = Day ) then
            begin
               writeln( 'Now copying ', FileInfo.Name );
               CmdString := '/C copy ' + FileInfo.Name + ', a:';
               exec( 'C:\command.com', CmdString );
            end;
         FindNext( FileInfo );
      end;
end.
```

TODAY is a backup program designed to identify the files created today and copy them to a diskette for safekeeping. When it executes, it copies each file to drive A and displays progress messages as follows:

```
Now copying DIR10.PAS
        1 File(s) copied
Now copying DISK2.PAS
        1 File(s) copied
Now copying DIR3.EXE
        1 File(s) copied
Now copying DIR3.PAS
        1 File(s) copied
Now copying DIR5.BAK
        1 File(s) copied
Now copying DIR5.PAS
        1 File(s) copied
Now copying DIR6.PAS
        1 File(s) copied
```

Managing Individual Files

In the discussion of the date and time stamps, you saw how the `FindFirst` and `FindNext` procedures use the file control block to scan a directory and quickly obtain information about several major file characteristics.

Although `FindFirst` and `FindNext` are extremely useful for locating a set of files, they are not intended for manipulating individual files. Again, information in the FCB is only a reference copy; directory data can be accessed, but none of it can be changed. Furthermore, because you usually know the name of the file you want to modify, `FindFirst` and `FindNext` are unnecessary.

The fields in the FCB were copied from the *disk directory*, the official source of all disk data. The disk directory contains the file's name and extension, attribute, date-and-time stamp, and size. In addition, it contains the technical data DOS needs to physically find the file on the disk.

This section discusses the procedures Turbo Pascal provides to modify the key file characteristics (name, attribute, and date-and-time stamp) found in the disk directory.

Modifying the Time Field

By maintaining the time and date of the last `write` operation on a file, DOS provides one of the most useful pieces of identifying information next to the file name itself. There is, consequently, only one good reason to change a file's time and date fields: when another program will produce an undesirable result unless the time and date have been modified.

The TODAY backup program presented in listing 14.9 uses the date of the file to determine whether the file should be saved on a floppy disk. To save even more files (and increase your peace of mind), it would be useful to be able to reset the date stamp of selected files to today's date so that TODAY can capture them as well.

The CPYSINCE program uses `PackTime` and `SetFTime` to do just that. First, a comparison date of one month ago is stored in the `FileTimeCutoff` variable. As each file name is read, its date is tested. If the file was created in the last month, its date and time are reset.

Compile CPYSINCE (listing 14.10) to disk and execute it directly from DOS. Entering the command

```
CPYSINCE dir*.pas
```

ensures that all files created in the last month that match the template `dir*.pas` will have their date-and-time stamp reset to the current PC clock setting.

Listing 14.10

```
program CpySince;
uses Dos;
var
   Year, Month, Day, DayofWeek   : word;    { GetDate }
   Hour, Minute, Second, Sec100 : word;    { GetTime }
   FileInfo          : SearchRec;
   TimeNow           : DateTime;
   FileTimeThen,
   FileTimeCutoff,
   FileTimeNow       : longint;
   FileReference     : file;
begin
   if ParamCount <> 1 then
      writeln( 'Improper file format' )
   else begin
      GetDate( Year, Month, Day, DayofWeek );
      GetTime( Hour, Minute, Second, Sec100 );
      TimeNow.Year := Year;
```

```
        TimeNow.Month := Month;
        TimeNow.Day := Day;
        TimeNow.Hour := Hour;
        TimeNow.Min := Minute;
        TimeNow.Sec := Second;
        PackTime( TimeNow, FileTimeNow );
        if Month = 1 then
           TimeNow.Month := 12
        else
           TimeNow.Month := Month - 1;
        PackTime( TimeNow, FileTimeCutoff );
        FindFirst( ParamStr( 1 ), AnyFile, FileInfo );
        while DosError = 0 do
           begin
              Assign( FileReference, FileInfo.Name );
              Reset( FileReference );
              GetFTime( FileReference, FileTimeThen );
              if FileTimeCutoff < FileTimeThen then begin
                 SetFTime( FileReference, FileTimeNow );
                 writeln( FileInfo.Name:12, ' being modified' );
              end;
              Close( FileReference );
              FindNext( FileInfo );
           end;
     end;
end.
```

Although `FindFirst` and `FindNext` were used to identify the desired files, each file had to be individually opened (assigned and reset) before `GetFTime` and `SetFTime` could be used. `FindFirst` and `FindNext` access the file control block, which is copied from the disk directory; `GetFTime` and `SetFTime` access the disk directory.

The `PackTime` and `UnpackTime` procedures do not perform a range check on the dates you supply them. Similarly, `GetFTime` and `SetFTime` do not test the validity of their time-and-date parameters. This means that if you do not care about the details of when a file was created, you have four extra bytes to use at your discretion. For example, suppose you have a budgeting application in which several departments send you data for consolidation. Each file on each diskette could have the same name, but you could use the two bytes of the time field to track the number of the originating PC.

Erasing and Renaming a File

Two Turbo Pascal procedures operate directly on the file name field in the disk directory: `Rename` and `Erase`. As their names imply, `Rename` changes the name of a file, and `Erase` deletes it. A file can be renamed or erased only if the read-only bit of its attribute byte is not set. `Rename` and `Erase` have no effect on directory names.

Renaming is straightforward. If the new name is not already assigned to a file in the directory, DOS writes over the original name field.

Erasing is more subtle. A file is erased when the first byte of its name in the directory entry is changed to the special character $E5. Figure 14.5 shows how the name of the PAYROLL.DAT file changes when the file is erased.

Fig. 14.5. The effect on the directory entry after deleting the PAYROLL.DAT file.

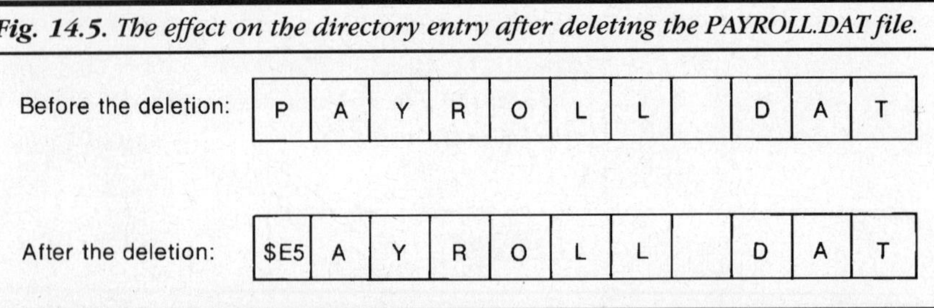

In addition, the file allocation table (FAT) is told that the clusters used by the file are now available for reassignment.

Erasing a File

The Turbo Pascal `Erase` procedure requires that a file be assigned but does not allow it to be opened at the time the erase occurs. You can call `Erase` in a `FindFirst/FindNext` loop without affecting the search. The NOBACKS program (listing 14.11) erases—perhaps unwisely—all backup files in the current directory.

Listing 14.11

```
program NoBacks;
uses Dos;
const
```

```
   FileCounter    : word = 0;
var
   FileInfo       : SearchRec;
   FileReference : file;
begin
   FindFirst( '*.BAK', (AnyFile - Directory), FileInfo );
   while DosError = 0 do
      begin
         writeln( 'Erasing ', FileInfo.Name );
         Assign( FileReference, FileInfo.Name );
         Erase( FileReference );
         Inc( FileCounter );
         FindNext( FileInfo );
      end;
   if FileCounter = 0 then
      writeln( 'No backup files were found.' )
   else
      writeln( FileCounter, ' backup file(s) erased.' );
end.
```

Wiping a File Clean

When DOS scans the disk directory and encounters a file name with $E5 in the first position, it simply ignores it. "Undelete" programs (most notably, the undelete feature of the Norton Utilities™ package) access the disk directory and identify file names with $E5 in their first byte. The file is restored by replacing the first byte with a valid character and telling the FAT that the clusters are again in use.

Therefore, when a file is erased, its contents become *available* for reuse; but until they *are* reused, the contents remain untouched. If the file contains confidential, sensitive, or embarrassing information, it should first be overwritten, then erased. The WIPEOUT program (listing 14.12) performs such a service. WIPEOUT takes the complete file name as its only parameter, reads the file byte-by-byte to determine its size, overwrites the file with asterisks, and only then erases it.

Listing 14.12

```
program WipeOut;
{$I- Disable I/O checking}
uses Dos;
var
   FileReference : file of byte;
   DummyByte     : byte;
   i,
   NumberOfBytes : longint;
   Attribute     : word;
begin
   if ParamCount = 0 then
      writeln( 'No file specified' )
   else begin
      Assign( FileReference, ParamStr( 1 ) );
      Reset( FileReference );
      if IOResult <> 0 then
         writeln( 'File not found' )
      else begin
         GetFAttr( FileReference, Attribute );
         if Attribute and ReadOnly <> 0 then
            writeln( 'File is read only.  Cannot erase.' )
         else begin
            NumberOfBytes := 0;
            while not eof( FileReference ) do begin
               NumberOfBytes := NumberOfBytes + 1;
               read( FileReference, DummyByte );
            end;
            Close( FileReference );
            if NumberOfBytes > 0 then begin
               Rewrite( FileReference );
               DummyByte := ord( '*' );
               for i := 1 to NumberOfBytes do
                  write( FileReference, DummyByte );
               writeln( NumberOfBytes, ' bytes were overwritten' );
               Close( FileReference );
            end;
            Erase( FileReference );
            writeln( 'The file has been erased' );
         end;
      end;
   end;
end.
```

Renaming a File

The Turbo Pascal `Rename` procedure has restrictions similar to `Erase`: The file must be assigned but unopened. In addition, it is the programmer's responsibility to test whether the new file name already exists in the directory. The NEWNAME program (listing 14.13) demonstrates how you can use `Rename` to modify a single file.

Listing 14.13

```
program NewName;
uses Dos;
var
   OldFileName,
   NewFileName      : string;
   FileReference,
   FileReference2   : file;
begin
   write( 'Old file name: ' );
   readln( OldFileName );
   Assign( FileReference, OldFileName );
{$I-}
   Reset( FileReference );
{$I+}
   if IOResult <> 0 then
      writeln( 'Old file not found.  Request ignored.' )
   else begin
      write( 'New file name: ' );
      readln( NewFileName );
      Assign( FileReference2, NewFileName );
{$I-}
      Reset( FileReference2 );
{$I+}
      if IOResult = 0 then
         writeln( 'New file in use.  Request ignored.' )
      else
         Rename( FileReference, NewFileName );
   end;
end.
```

Notice that the program checks for the existence of *both* the original file and the new file.

Determining the Size of a File

The WIPEOUT program in listing 14.12 reads a file one byte at a time to learn the total file size. A separate file-size field is included as part of the FCB record, but unless the file was originally accessed with `FindFirst` and `FindNext`, that information is not readily available. To remedy this deficiency, Turbo Pascal provides the `FileSize` procedure, which returns the number of records in a file.

Record size is measured from the perspective of the operating system. If the file was created as a file of a specific type (for example, `file of InfoRecord` or `file of longint`), the record size is the size of the typed field. Untyped files and text files are assumed to have record sizes equal to the default buffer size of 128 bytes.

You can circumvent this problem by declaring a file to be a `file of byte` and in the process force the record size to be one byte long. In so doing, you make the number of records equal to the size of the file. The SIZER program (listing 14.14) demonstrates this trick by determining its own length.

Listing 14.14

```
program Sizer;
var
   FileName      : string;
   FileReference : file of byte;
begin
   FileName := 'Sizer.pas';
   Assign( FileReference, FileName );
   Reset( FileReference );
   writeln( FileName, ' is ', FileSize( FileReference ), ' bytes long' );
end.
```

When executed, you see the following:

```
Sizer.pas is 268 bytes long
```

Sometimes you need to know not only whether a file exists but also whether it contains data. You could obtain this information directly by opening the file and seeing if the first `read` operation results in an end of file. Alternatively, you can use the `FileSize` function, as shown in program HOWBIG (listing 14.15).

Listing 14.15

```
program HowBig;
var
   FileToCheck : string;
function FileHasContent( FileName : string ) : boolean;
var
   FileReference : file of byte;
begin
   Assign( FileReference, FileName );
{$I- Disable I/O checking}
   Reset( FileReference );
{$I+ Reinstate I/O checking}
   if IOResult <> 0 then
      FileHasContent := False
   else
      FileHasContent := FileSize( FileReference ) > 0;
end;
begin
   FileToCheck := 'HowBig.pas';
   if FileHasContent( FileToCheck ) then
      writeln( FileToCheck, ' exists!' )
   else
      writeln( FileToCheck, ' wasn''t found' );
end.
```

Applying `FileSize` to yet another directory list, you obtain the closest program yet to the DOS utility `DIR`. The NEWDIR program (listing 14.16) demonstrates its use. Again, the file variable is defined as a `file of byte`, so `FileSize` will directly return the correct result.

Listing 14.16

```
program NewDir;
uses Dos;
var
   FileInfo      : SearchRec;
   TimeNow       : DateTime;
   FileTimeStamp : longint;
   FileReference : file of byte;
   StartString   : string;
```

continues

Listing 14.16 continued

```
begin
   if ParamCount <> 1 then
      StartString := '*.*'
   else
      StartString := ParamStr( 1 );
   FindFirst( StartString, (AnyFile - Directory), FileInfo );
   while DosError = 0 do
      begin
         Assign( FileReference, FileInfo.Name );
         Reset( FileReference );
         GetFTime( FileReference, FileTimeStamp );
         UnpackTime( FileTimeStamp, TimeNow );
         write( FileInfo.Name:12, FileSize( FileReference ):9 );
         with TimeNow do writeln( Month:4, '-', Day:2, '-', Year:2,
                                  Hour:4, ':', Min:2, ':', Sec:2 );
         Close( FileReference );
         FindNext( FileInfo );
      end;
end.
```

Executing the program with the command

```
NEWDIR ex*.pas
```

results in the following:

```
EXEC2.PAS      242   7-29-1988  16:48: 0
EXEC5.PAS      234   7-29-1988  20:29:44
EXEC1.PAS      216   7-29-1988  16:53:44
EXEC3.PAS      499   7-29-1988  17:48:48
EXIT2.PAS     1032   7-30-1988  16:51:56
EXEC4.PAS      334   7-29-1988  17:43:14
EXIT4.PAS      277   7-30-1988  17:19:58
EXEC6.PAS      234   7-29-1988  20:31:22
EXIT1.PAS      474   7-27-1988  12:25: 2
EXIT3.PAS     3455   7-30-1988  17:22: 6
EXEC7.PAS       93   7-29-1988  21:24: 2
```

Modifying the Attribute Byte

You have already seen how useful a file's attribute byte can be. Not only does it identify the basic nature of a disk directory entry, but it can also serve to provide added security by preventing a file from being deleted. For example, it is not uncommon for a program to remove the read-only status on an important file at the beginning of its run and to reinstate read-only status upon program termination.

The `GetFAttr` and `SetFAttr` procedures can be used to retrieve and reset the attribute byte, respectively. Both procedures take two parameters: an assigned but unopened file name and a word-sized variable representing the attribute itself.

The FEATURES program (listing 14.17) offers a means of changing the settings of the attribute byte in a group of files. It is executed with the following command:

```
FEATURES <file-spec> <original> <new>
```

The `<file-spec>` parameter may include wild-card characters. The `<original>` and `<new>` parameters represent the archive, hidden, and read-only bits. In the following sample command line and in listing 14.17, the uppercase letters `A`, `H`, and `R` represent set bits; the lowercase letters `a`, `h`, and `r` indicate cleared bits. For example, to set the read-only bit in all files of the form `dir*.pas`, enter the command

```
FEATURES dir*.pas r R
```

The bits can later be cleared with the command:

```
FEATURES dir*.pas R r
```

Notice that to test whether a bit is set, the attribute byte is logically `AND`ed with one of the predefined constants `Archive`, `Hidden`, or `ReadOnly`. The result is zero when the bit is set and nonzero otherwise. Bits are turned on by logically `OR`ing the attribute byte with one of the predefined constants; they are cleared by `AND`ing the attribute byte with another byte (the logical `NOT` of a predefined constant) in which every bit is set except for the one you want to switch off.

Listing 14.17

```
program Features;
uses Dos;
var
   FileInfo       : SearchRec;
   Match          : boolean;
   OldAttr,
   NewAttr        : word;
```

continues

Listing 14.7 continued

```
    Old,
    New           : string;
    FileReference : file;
begin
    if ParamCount <> 3 then
       writeln( 'Improper parameters' )
    else begin
       Old := ParamStr( 2 );
       New := ParamStr( 3 );
       if (Old[ 1 ] in [ 'a', 'A', 'h', 'H', 'r', 'R' ]) and
          (New[ 1 ] in [ 'a', 'A', 'h', 'H', 'r', 'R' ]) then begin
          FindFirst( ParamStr( 1 ), (AnyFile - Directory), FileInfo );
          while DosError = 0 do
             begin
                Assign( FileReference, FileInfo.Name );
                GetFAttr( FileReference, OldAttr );
                case Old[ 1 ] of
                   'a' : Match := (OldAttr and Archive )  = 0;
                   'A' : Match := (OldAttr and Archive ) <> 0;
                   'h' : Match := (OldAttr and Hidden  )  = 0;
                   'H' : Match := (OldAttr and Hidden  ) <> 0;
                   'r' : Match := (OldAttr and ReadOnly)  = 0;
                   'R' : Match := (OldAttr and ReadOnly) <> 0;
                   else  Match := False;
                end;
                if Match then begin
                   case New[ 1 ] of
                      'a' : NewAttr := OldAttr and $DF;   { Not Archive  }
                      'A' : NewAttr := OldAttr or $20;    { Archive      }
                      'h' : NewAttr := OldAttr and $FD;   { Not Hidden   }
                      'H' : NewAttr := OldAttr or $02;    { Hidden       }
                      'r' : NewAttr := OldAttr and $FE;   { Not ReadOnly }
                      'R' : NewAttr := OldAttr or $01;    { ReadOnly     }
                      else  NewAttr := OldAttr;
                   end;
                   SetFAttr( FileReference, NewAttr );
                   writeln( FileInfo.Name, ' has been modified' );
                end else
                   writeln( FileInfo.Name, ' hasn''t been modified' );
                FindNext( FileInfo );
             end;
```

```
      end else
         writeln( 'Improper attribute selections' );
   end;
end.
```

Examining File Names

If a file does not reside in the current directory, Turbo Pascal procedures such as `Assign` require a complete file path. For example, a file identified as WORKFILE.DAT is assumed to belong to the current drive and directory. If the file is not found, an error is generated; no attempt is made to locate it elsewhere. To avoid this problem, the file must be referenced in its complete form, for example, C:\PASCAL\CODE\WORKFILE.DAT. This complete specification is called the *fully qualified file name*.

Turbo Pascal never modifies the name, drive, or directory of a declared file. Every file name is passed to the operating system precisely as it is defined in the program. However, a well-designed program should be able to find a required file wherever it is saved or, alternatively, should help the user to find the file.

This section discusses the procedures offered by Turbo Pascal to create, modify, and locate fully qualified files.

Expanding the File Name

The Turbo Pascal function `FExpand` will create a fully qualified file name using the current drive and directory as defaults. The FEXP1 program (listing 14.18) demonstrates its use.

Listing 14.18

```
program FExp1;
uses Dos;
var
   FileString : string;
begin
   repeat
```

continues

Lisitng 14.18 continued

```
        readln( FileString );
        writeln( FExpand( FileString ) );
        writeln;
    until Length( FileString ) = 0;
end.
```

FEXP1 enables you to experiment with `FExpand`. When the function is applied to a fully qualified file name, it simply returns the parameter itself. When the function is applied to any other file name, it uses the currently active drive and directory as a basis for creating a fully qualified file name. The following is an example of output from FEXP1:

```
fexp1.pas
C:\QUE\PROGRAMS\FEXP1.PAS
fexp1.pas
C:\QUE\PROGRAMS\FEXP1.PAS
fexp1.*
C:\QUE\PROGRAMS\FEXP1.*
.\progdata.dat
C:\QUE\PROGRAMS\PROGDATA.DAT
..\progdata.dat
C:\QUE\PROGDATA.DAT
c:\turbo\code\progdata.dat
C:\TURBO\CODE\PROGDATA.DAT
a:*.*
A:\*.*
```

FExpand is not needed if your program uses only the current directory. However, if you access more than one directory (especially if you call the `ChDir` procedure), the `FExpand` function enables you to preserve the original drive and directory names.

Searching Several Directories

Usually, the search for a file can be narrowed to a few directories. You are probably using a `PATH` environment variable in your PC for just such a purpose. If you enter the name of a program that does not reside in the current directory, DOS automatically searches for the program in each of the directories specified by the `PATH` variable.

Similarly, in Turbo Pascal, the `FSearch` function can be used to search for a file in a given set of directories. `FSearch` takes two parameters: the name of the file you want to find and a string containing the directories to search. If it finds the file in one of the directories, `FSearch` returns the fully qualified file name; otherwise, it returns a null string.

You will probably want to limit your search to the same directories you identified in the `PATH` entry of your PC's environment table. For example, if your PC is configured with the following environment table entry:

```
PATH=C:\DOS;C:\WORD;C:\TURBOC;C:\TP
```

the FEXP2 program (listing 14.19) will search for the TURBO.EXE file in the current directory of the current drive. If unsuccessful, the program will continue the search in C:\DOS, then C:\WORD, then C:\TURBOC, and then C:\TP.

Listing 14.19

```
program FExp2;
uses Dos;
var
   FileName,
   FileString : string;
begin
   FileName := 'turbo.exe';
   FileString := FSearch( FileName, GetEnv( 'path' ) );
   if Length( FileString ) = 0 then
      writeln( FileName, ' not found' )
   else
      writeln( FExpand( FileString ) );
end.
```

When the file is found (in the C:\TP directory), the following string is displayed:

```
C:\TP\TURBO.EXE
```

Creating a New File Name

Frequently, you will encounter the opposite situation. You may have an application that requires you to develop a variation of the original file name.

For example, suppose that you want to create a listing file for a Pascal source program. You would begin by prompting for the name of the original file, with .PAS as its default extension. Your output file might be the same name but would have .LST as its default extension.

In Turbo Pascal, the `FSplit` procedure can break a fully qualified file name into its three main components: the directory, name, and extension. In the FEXP3 program (listing 14.20), the user is prompted first for the name of a Pascal program, then for the names of the object and listing files. The default extensions of the object and listing files are .OBJ and .LST, respectively. The name may also be changed if the user wants to change it.

Listing 14.20

```
program FExp3;
uses Dos;
var
   FileSource, FileObject, FileList : string;
   PathName      : PathStr;
   Directory0,
   Directory     : DirStr;
   FileName0,
   FileName      : NameStr;
   Extension     : ExtStr;
   FileString    : string;
begin
   Repeat
      write( 'Source file name (*.pas): ' );
      readln( FileString );
      FSplit( FileString, Directory0, FileName0, Extension );
      if Extension = '' then    { Default extension requested }
         FileString := Directory0 + FileName0 + '.pas';
      PathName := FSearch( FileString, GetEnv( 'path' ) );
      FSplit( PathName, Directory0, FileName0, Extension );
   until PathName <> '';  { Source file must exist }
   FileSource := PathName;
   write( 'Object file name (', FileName0, '.obj): ' );
   readln( FileString );
   FSplit( FileString, Directory, FileName, Extension );
   if Directory = '' then Directory := Directory0;
   if FileName  = '' then FileName  := FileName0;
   if Extension = '' then Extension := '.obj';
   FileObject := Directory + FileName + Extension;
```

```
    write( 'Listing file name (', FileName0, '.lst): ' );
    readln( FileString );
    FSplit( FileString, Directory, FileName, Extension );
    if Directory = '' then Directory := Directory0;
    if FileName  = '' then FileName  := FileName0;
    if Extension = '' then Extension := '.lst';
    FileList := Directory + FileName + Extension;
    writeln;
    writeln( 'Source:  ', FileSource );
    writeln( 'Object:  ', FileObject );
    writeln( 'Listing: ', FileList );
end.
```

Note that some duplication could have been avoided using a procedure or a function, but presented in this manner the code more clearly demonstrates the program flow.

In the following output example, WORKPROG.PAS was identified as the source file. The default object and listing file names were then displayed; only the changes had to be entered.

```
Source file name (*.pas): workprog
Object file name (workprog.obj): .ob2
Listing file name (workprog.lst): w2
Source:  workprog.pas
Object:  workprog.ob2
Listing: w2.lst
```

Summary

In this chapter, you learned how to use the Turbo Pascal procedures and functions that manage files and directories.

You learned how to obtain the total size of any disk, and you saw how to determine the amount of free space it contains.

You learned how your programs can determine the current directory, change to a different directory, create a new directory, and remove an empty directory.

You learned how to access the information kept by the disk directory itself. For each file, this information includes the file name, size, attribute byte, and date-and-time stamp. You learned that the bits in the attribute byte describe the type of file and how it can be processed. You saw how to rename or completely erase a file, how to modify the date-and-time stamp, and how to modify the attribute byte.

Several directory programs were presented, including utilities you can use to search the disk for files that have common, user-specified characteristics. You learned how to search for a file in several directories, including the directory specified by the DOS system path.

You also learned several useful routines to expand the name of a file into its component parts and to create a new file name.

Part III

Advanced Programming

CHAPTER 15

Overlays

In the early days of mainframe computers, memory size was a serious constraint. 4K, 8K, and 16K memories were considered huge! What little memory was available had to be used sparingly.

Few applications—then or now—could fit entirely in such a small space, so programs were written in modules that could be called into memory for only as long as they were needed, then exchanged for another module containing code for a different, independent purpose. A payroll report program, for example, might have one module to print the headings on each page and another module to print the lines of data. Only the code controlling the running totals (subtotals and totals of wages and withholdings, page numbers, and so on) remained in memory at all times.

In the 1960s, the COBOL programming language gained immense popularity in business circles because it simplified the development of these overlaying modules (or more simply, *overlays*). COBOL forced programmers to write data and procedures in separate sections and encouraged programmers to construct collections of subroutines rather than one big program.

The early days of personal computers were not much different. Although today programmers tend to think of 64K as one row of chips on a board, originally 64K was the upper limit of memory in most machines. However, having learned the lessons of history, programmers knew that if they were able to set aside a section of memory and overlay it with independent code modules, the effective size of a program would be unlimited. The Pascal language, which combined the best elements of COBOL with greater ease of use, emerged as the most convenient tool for that purpose.

As PC memory became less expensive, it became less of a programming restriction. Version 4.0 of Turbo Pascal enabled programs to use units and consequently to break the 64K barrier; the support of overlays was temporarily discontinued. However, two problems remained. On one end, the absence of overlays meant that smaller machines (and there are still lots of them around) no longer had a way to support larger programs. On the other end, programs could be large, but their effective size was now limited by the size of the machine on which they ran.

In Version 5.0, Turbo Pascal reintroduced overlays. Their availability, coupled with the capability of executable programs to exceed the 64K size limit, now provides almost unlimited memory management power.

This chapter introduces five rules to follow when creating overlays and demonstrates those rules through a simple programming exercise. In the process, the chapter discusses what overlays are, how to use them, and what situations you should avoid.

What Is an Overlay?

Overlays are parts of a program (really, collections of subroutines) that can share the same physical memory. In Turbo Pascal, the smallest collection of overlay subroutines is the unit. Each unit, in its entirety, is swapped into the common memory area before a routine is called within the unit.

When an overlay program is compiled, Turbo creates two files. The executable (EXE) file contains that portion of the code that remains in memory throughout program execution. In addition, Turbo places all the overlay units into a separate OVR file, where they remain available for the resident program to access. The OVR file either remains in a convenient location on disk or can be loaded into expanded memory for faster access.

Through overlays, Turbo ensures that a program uses the minimum amount of internal memory. The total size of a program that uses overlays consists of a resident section that remains in memory throughout the execution of the program and a buffer big enough to accommodate the largest of the overlay units.

Figure 15.1 illustrates the memory map of a program using the four overlays A, B, C, and D. As long as the units can be called independently, only one unit needs to reside in the overlay buffer at any time. Because C is the largest unit, the total amount of memory required is equal to the size of the main program body (shown as a solid color) plus a buffer area large enough to hold unit C. Without the capability to create overlays, all four units would have been placed in memory simultaneously.

Fig. 15.1. Memory map of a program using overlays.

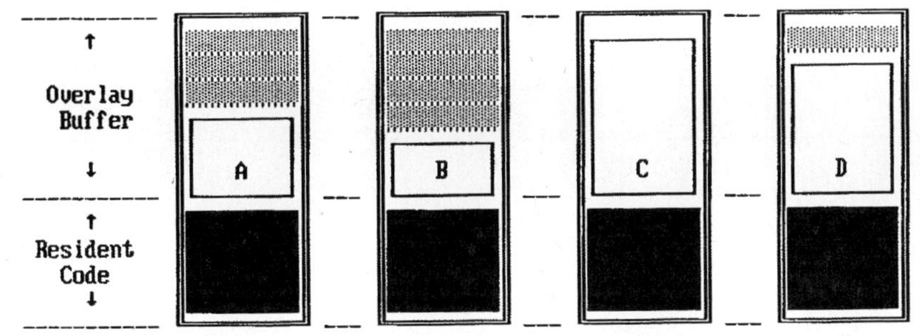

A Programming Example

To see how Turbo Pascal uses overlays, we will use the OVRMST1 program, which is designed to produce a billing summary for a small law office. The four attorneys (Fred, Wilma, Barney, and Betty) commonly handle five types of cases (divorce, criminal, bankruptcy, corporate, and probate). OVRMST1 summarizes the total billings by lawyer and by specialty. The firm's billings are shown in table 15.1.

Table 15.1. *Billings Used for OVRMST1*

	Divorce	*Criminal*	*Bnkrptcy*	*Corp*	*Probate*	*Total*
Fred	8000	1000	500	0	0	9500
Wilma	0	25000	250	0	0	25250
Barney	0	0	0	0	12000	12000
Betty	1000	0	0	25000	250	26250
Total	9000	26000	750	25000	12250	73000

The OVRMST1 program consists principally of a two-dimensional array and two independent addition routines.

Developing the Program

The OVRMST1 program (listing 15.1) is fairly straightforward. Ordinarily, the raw billing data would be read from a separate file, but to make the operation of the program easier to follow, you can enter the data directly in the form of a typed constant array.

Listing 15.1

```
program OvrMst1;
type
   Attorneys = ( Fred, Wilma, Barney, Betty );
   Cases     = ( Divorce, Criminal, Bankruptcy, Corporate, Probate );
   Billings  = array [ Attorneys ] of array [ Cases ] of real;
const
                                   {  Div    Crim  Bkrp   Corp   Prob }
   Revenue : Billings = ( { Fred }   ( 8000,  1000,  500,     0,     0 ),
                          { Wilma }  (    0, 25000,  250,     0,     0 ),
                          { Barney } (    0,     0,    0,     0, 12000 ),
                          { Betty }  ( 1000,     0,    0, 25000,   250 ) );
   Names   : array [ Fred..Betty ] of string[ 8 ] =
           ( 'Fred    ', 'Wilma   ', 'Barney  ', 'Betty   ' );
   Source  : array [ Divorce..Probate ] of string[ 6 ] =
           ( '   Div', '  Crim', '  Bkrp', '  Corp', '  Prob' );
var
   Lawyer    : Attorneys;
   Specialty : Cases;
   Tally     : real;
   Total     : real;
begin
   writeln( 'This section is where you would read data from a file.' );
   Total := 0.0;
   for Lawyer := Fred to Betty do begin
      write( Names[ Lawyer ] );
      Tally := 0.0;
      for Specialty := Divorce to Probate do
         Tally := Tally + Revenue[ Lawyer, Specialty ];
      writeln( Tally:8:0 );
      Total := Total + Tally;
   end;
   writeln( Total:16:0 );
   writeln;
   Total := 0.0;
```

```
   for Specialty := Divorce to Probate do begin
      write( Source[ Specialty ] );
      Tally := 0.0;
      for Lawyer := Fred to Betty do
         Tally := Tally + Revenue[ Lawyer, Specialty ];
      writeln( Tally:10:0 );
      Total := Total + Tally;
   end;
   writeln( Total:16:0 );
   writeln;
end.
```

Accountants use the term *foot* to mean the calculation of totals for each column. Similarly, the term *crossfoot* means the calculation of totals for each line. To *foot and crossfoot* a report means to independently add the numbers down and across; if the totals do not match, an error was made.

The OVRMST1 program foots and crossfoots the billing report. When run, it produces the following:

```
This section is where you would read data from a file.
Fred          9500
Wilma        25250
Barney       12000
Betty        26250
             73000

   Div        9000
  Crim       26000
  Bkrp         750
  Corp       25000
  Prob       12250
             73000
```

The message is included to indicate the normal sequence of events. Again, the revenue array would normally be read from a file, not entered as a typed constant, as in this example.

Converting to Units

Now you can modify the program by creating units: one for the footing calculation and another for the crossfooting calculation.

Because both the footing and crossfooting units require access to the global data, a third unit, `OvrSub0`, is created as shown in listing 15.2.

Listing 15.2

```
unit OvrSub0;
interface
type
   Attorneys = ( Fred, Wilma, Barney, Betty );
   Cases     = ( Divorce, Criminal, Bankruptcy, Corporate, Probate );
   Billings  = array [ Attorneys ] of array [ Cases ] of real;
const
                                        {  Div   Crim  Bkrp   Corp    Prob }
   Revenue : Billings = ( { Fred }      ( 8000,  1000,  500,      0,      0 ),
                          { Wilma }     (    0, 25000,  250,      0,      0 ),
                          { Barney }    (    0,     0,    0,      0, 12000 ),
                          { Betty }     ( 1000,     0,    0, 25000,    250 ) );
   Names   : array [ Fred..Betty ] of string[ 8 ] =
           ( 'Fred    ', 'Wilma   ', 'Barney  ', 'Betty    ' );
   Source  : array [ Divorce..Probate ] of string[ 6 ] =
           ( '   Div', '  Crim', '  Bkrp', '  Corp', '  Prob' );
var
   Lawyer    : Attorneys;
   Specialty : Cases;
   Tally     : real;
implementation
end.
```

The crossfooting unit, `OvrSub1`, and the footing unit, `OvrSub2`, are defined in listing 15.3.

Listing 15.3

```
unit OvrSub1;
interface
uses OvrSub0;
   procedure CrossFoot;
implementation
   procedure CrossFoot;
   var
      Total : real;
   begin
```

```
      Total := 0.0;
      for Lawyer := Fred to Betty do begin
         write( Names[ Lawyer ] );
         Tally := 0.0;
         for Specialty := Divorce to Probate do
            Tally := Tally + Revenue[ Lawyer, Specialty ];
         writeln( Tally:8:0 );
         Total := Total + Tally;
      end;
      writeln( Total:16:0 );
      writeln;
   end;
end.
unit OvrSub2;
interface
uses OvrSub0;
   procedure Foot;
implementation
   procedure Foot;
   var
      Total : real;
   begin
      Total := 0.0;
      for Specialty := Divorce to Probate do begin
         write( Source[ Specialty ] );
         Tally := 0.0;
         for Lawyer := Fred to Betty do
            Tally := Tally + Revenue[ Lawyer, Specialty ];
         writeln( Tally:10:0 );
         Total := Total + Tally;
      end;
      writeln( Total:16:0 );
      writeln;
   end;
end.
```

Almost all of the data and code are now contained in the three units, so the OVRMST2 program (listing 15.4) can be fairly short.

Listing 15.4

```
program OvrMst2;
uses OvrSub1, OvrSub2;
begin
   writeln( 'This section is where you would read data from a file.' );
   CrossFoot;
   Foot;
end.
```

The `OvrSub0` module is compiled to disk first, followed by `OvrSub1`, `OvrSub2`, and finally the main OVRMST2 program. When OVRMST2 is executed, it produces results identical to OVRMST1.

Creating Overlays from the Units

It is probably fairly obvious that your PC contains enough internal memory to run OVRMST2 without any trouble. Assume, however, that you now want to turn `OvrSub1` and `OvrSub2` into overlays.

Preparing Each Unit

Because a unit must operate differently when it becomes an overlay, you should alert the compiler to your intentions as soon as possible.

Rule 1: Turbo Pascal must know immediately whether you intend to use a unit as an overlay. Therefore, every overlay unit must be compiled with the `{$O+}` directive.

The presence of `{$O+}` at the beginning of a unit does not force the unit to be used as an overlay. This directive just ensures that the units *can* be used as overlays, if so desired. If you develop units you plan to use in overlay as well as nonoverlay applications, compiling them with `{$O+}` ensures that you can do both with just one version of the unit.

Using Far Calls

When overlays are not used, Turbo Pascal places the main program and each unit in its own memory segment. Therefore, all subroutine calls across segments require far calls (that is, calls that specify both the segment and offset). Similarly, when parameters are passed across segments, far pointers must be used. The compiler handles this automatically.

For example, suppose that UnitA contains the following procedure:

```
procedure DisplayProgress( Message : string );
begin
   GotoXY( 1, 25 );
   write( Message );
end;
```

and UnitB contains the following call:

```
DisplayProgress( 'Now sorting file. Please wait.' );
```

Turbo Pascal places the constant string `'Now sorting file. Please wait.'` in UnitB's code segment, passes a far pointer to its location to the `DisplayProgress` procedure in UnitA, and invokes `DisplayProgress` from UnitB with a far call.

Now suppose that UnitA and UnitB are overlays. Both the message and the procedure that displays it will reside in the same segment (although at different times), so the compiler no longer regards a far procedure call as necessary. In addition, the compiler passes the message string with a near pointer.

This cannot be allowed. Somehow, you must tell the compiler that even though the two units are in the same physical segment, they are really overlays. Otherwise, the compiler will not be able to differentiate between the unit that contains the string and the unit that contains the procedure and will not know which unit to place in memory. To complicate the situation further, when UnitB calls the `DisplayProgress` procedure in UnitA, then UnitA is moved into memory, overwriting the memory location where the constant string was stored!

Turbo Pascal solves these problems in a simple and clever way.

Rule 2: Every subroutine and every pointer used by a program containing overlays should be far, with both the segment and offset specified. Therefore, every unit (in addition to the main program itself) should be compiled with the force far calls directive, `{$F+}`.

Note that the easiest way to satisfy the far call requirement is to place the `{$F+}` directive at the beginning of the main program and each unit. Alternatively, you can change the default `{$F-}` setting to `{$F+}` using a `/$F+` command-line directive for the TPC.EXE command-line compiler, or you can change the /O/C/Force Far Calls menu command in the interactive environment.

Technically, only a near pointer is required, but compiling the program with the force far calls directive enables the compiler to use the segment half of each pointer to identify the desired overlay unit. Whenever Turbo Pascal detects a call from one unit compiled with `{$O+}` to another unit compiled with `{$O+}`, the compiler is certain to copy parameters to the stack before passing pointers to them. Next, Turbo determines whether the unit being called is currently in memory. If the unit resides in memory, the call proceeds normally; if it does not, the required unit is first brought into memory, then the call proceeds.

Turbo makes no other changes to the code generated by the overlay unit. In fact, overlays are so similar to units, you do not have to make any other modifications to a unit when you use it as an overlay.

Creating the Overlay Units

You can combine the first two rules into a single modification: add the `{$O+,F+}` directive pair immediately after the `unit` declaration. The `{$O+}` directive tells the compiler to treat the units as overlays. The `{$F+}` directive ensures that all procedures, functions, and pointers will be called with the far calling model.

The revised files `OvrSub1A` and `OvrSub2A` (listings 15.5 and 15.6, respectively) now appear as follows.

Listing 15.5

```
unit OvrSub1A;
{$O+,F+}
interface
uses OvrSub0;
   procedure CrossFoot;
implementation
   procedure CrossFoot;
   var
      Total : real;
```

```
   begin
      Total := 0.0;
      for Lawyer := Fred to Betty do begin
         write( Names[ Lawyer ] );
         Tally := 0.0;
         for Specialty := Divorce to Probate do
            Tally := Tally + Revenue[ Lawyer, Specialty ];
         writeln( Tally:8:0 );
         Total := Total + Tally;
      end;
      writeln( Total:16:0 );
      writeln;
   end;
end.
```

Listing 15.6

```
unit OvrSub2A;
{$O+,F+}
interface
uses OvrSub0;
   procedure Foot;
implementation
   procedure Foot;
   var
      Total : real;
   begin
      Total := 0.0;
      for Specialty := Divorce to Probate do begin
         write( Source[ Specialty ] );
         Tally := 0.0;
         for Lawyer := Fred to Betty do
            Tally := Tally + Revenue[ Lawyer, Specialty ];
         writeln( Tally:10:0 );
         Total := Total + Tally;
      end;
      writeln( Total:16:0 );
      writeln;
   end;
end.
```

No change is made to the `OvrSub0` unit containing the global declarations. Only the units being transformed to overlays are affected.

A Note on Initialization Sections in Overlay Units

Whenever any subroutine in an overlay unit is called, the entire unit is brought into memory. If each unit contains initialization code, that code is also moved, even though it was designed to be executed only once.

Depending on the size of the initialization code and the number of times the overlay unit is swapped into memory, you may note some performance degradation. Further, because the overlay buffer must be large enough to accommodate the largest unit, the presence of initialization code may increase the buffer size.

To avoid these situations, try to combine all initialization code into a single, small overlay unit. You may even have a separate overlay unit containing nothing but initialization code. This should reduce the size of the other individual units, decrease the time it takes to move them in memory, and decrease the size of the overlay buffer.

Modifying the Main Program

You saw from Rule 2 that the main program must be recompiled with the force far calls directive. A few other changes must also be made. The main program controls overall execution, so the OVRMST2 program will undergo more modifications than the units.

Including Run-Time Code Support

When the `{$O+}` directive was included in the overlay units, Turbo Pascal was being informed that the compilation process (at least for those units) would be different from normal. However, as you might expect, the overlay process itself requires additional run-time support.

Rule 3: The main program must include the `Overlay` unit in the *first* position of the `uses` statement.

The `uses` statement in the main program will be modified as follows:

```
uses Overlay, OvrSub1A, OvrSub2A;
```

Including the `Overlay` unit ensures that run-time support is made available to the compiled code.

Identifying the Overlays

A program may use both overlay and nonoverlay units. Therefore, the overlay units must be specifically identified.

Rule 4: Turbo Pascal must know immediately which units are to be treated as overlays. Thus, the main program must specify every overlay unit with the `{$O filename}` directive.

The `{$O filename}` directive tells the compiler which of the units in the `uses` clause are to be treated as overlays; consequently, the directive must appear *after* the units are named.

```
uses Overlay, OvrSub1A, OvrSub2A;
{$O OvrSub1A }
{$O OvrSub2A }
```

Remember that the `{$O+}` directive in the individual units alerted the compiler only to the *possibility* that they would be used as overlays; the `{$O filename}` directive in the main program makes the formal request.

Initializing Run-Time Support

The `Overlay` standard unit is declared first in the `uses` statement, so any initialization code it contains will be run before the initialization code of any other unit and before the main program begins. However, this also means that the `Overlay` unit initialization code is executed before you identify which other units are to be treated as overlays. Therefore, the remaining run-time overlay support must be initialized in the main program through a call to the `OvrInit` procedure.

Rule 5: The run-time overlay support must be initialized before its use. Therefore, the `OvrInit` overlay initiation procedure must be executed before any procedure or function calls are made to subroutines defined in the overlay units.

The `OvrInit` procedure ideally should be called as early as possible. `OvrInit` initializes the overlay manager and opens the OVR (overlay) file. If the `filename` parameter does not specify a drive or a subdirectory, the overlay manager searches for the file in the current directory, in the directory that contains the EXE file (if running under DOS Version 3.x), and in the directories specified by the DOS `PATH` environment variable.

Final Version of the Main Program

Incorporating these rules, the new main program is structured as shown in listing 15.7.

Listing 15.7

```
program OvrMst3;
{$F+ Forces a Far call for all procedures and functions }
uses Overlay, OvrSub1A, OvrSub2A;
{$O OvrSub1A }
{$O OvrSub2A }
begin
   OvrInit( 'OvrMst3.OVR' );
   writeln( 'This section is where you would read data from a file.' );
   CrossFoot;
   Foot;
end.
```

After `OvrSub1A`, `OvrSub2A`, and OVRMST3 are compiled, the new program produces the same output as the original program. Footing and crossfooting produce the same totals by different means, so the two units are able to compute the same totals independently.

This should not be too surprising, because the code has not really undergone much of a change. Three new directives and one new procedure call were added, and one line of code was modified.

With just a few exceptions, the five rules that have been presented are sufficient to convert any unit to overlay form.

Using Overlay Routines

The `Overlay` standard unit defines the procedures `OvrInit`, `OvrInitEMS`, `OvrSetRetry`, `OvrSetBuf`, and `OvrClearBuf`, and the functions `OvrGetBuf` and `OvrGetRetry`. Any errors occurring from executing these routines may cause your program to terminate with a run-time error.

You can test the result of each subroutine call by examining the predefined integer variable `OvrResult`. Any nonzero value indicates an error and requires immediate remedy. Table 15.2 shows the possible return values, together with several predefined constants you can use to make the test of `OvrResult` easier to understand.

***Table 15.2.** Results Returned by OvrResult*

Predefined constant	*Value*	*Typical error messages*
`ovrOk`	0	No error
`ovrError`	–1	No overlays/Buffer too small/Heap not empty
`ovrNotFound`	–2	OVR file was not found
`ovrNoMemory`	–3	Not enough available heap space
`ovrIOError`	–4	I/O error reading overlay file
`ovrNoEMSDriver`	–5	EMS driver not installed
`ovrNoEMSMemory`	–6	Not enough free EMS memory

Your programs can use `OvrResult` to recover from almost any situation. Use of the constants is discussed in greater detail throughout the rest of the chapter.

Initiating the Overlay Manager

As stated in Rule 5, the initialization code must be placed before the first call to an overlay routine. The following code initialized the overlay manager:

```
OvrInit( 'OvrMst3.OVR' );
```

Essentially, the `OvrInit` procedure either works or does not. If unsuccessful, the first call to any routine in an overlay unit aborts the program and produces run-time error 208, `Overlay manager not installed.`

This is the basis for the advice that `OvrInit` should be called as soon as possible after the program begins. Imagine the disgruntled user who works with your program (for example, a spreadsheet) for several hours, only to have it abort before the session can be saved to disk!

Nothing can be done within the program to recover from the error. However, you can include the following code immediately after the `OvrInit` call to help the user understand its cause:

```
if OvrResult <> ovrOk then begin
   case OvrResult of
      ovrError    { -1 } : writeln( 'Program doesn''t have overlays' );
      ovrNotFound { -2 } : writeln( '.OVR file wasn''t found' );
   end;
   Halt( 1 );
end;
```

Placing Overlays in EXE Files

You have probably noticed that most commercially available software applications consist of a single, large EXE file. Usually no separate OVR file can be found. You may have noticed also that the sizes of some EXE files exceed the available memory of the PCs on which they run, yet the applications somehow manage to execute successfully.

The secret of these large programs is that overlays do not automatically need to reside in independent OVR files. Instead, overlays can be appended to the EXE file, taking the space normally reserved for debugging information.

To use this feature, the Options/Debugger/Standalone debugging option must be disabled (that is, set to off) when the program is compiled. Next, use the DOS `COPY` command with the `/B` option to merge the two files, as follows:

```
COPY /B PROGNAME.EXE + PROGNAME.OVR
```

Finally, tell the compiler to read the overlays from the EXE file by specifying the program name when you call the `OvrInit` procedure:

```
OvrInit( 'PROGNAME.EXE' );
```

Remember that beginning with DOS 3.0, `ParamStr(0)` returns the directory and file name of the executing program. Hence, the procedure call

```
OvrInit( ParamStr(0) );
```

may also be used.

Using Expanded Memory

If EMS, named for the Lotus-Intel-Microsoft Expanded Memory Specification, is available on your PC and if an EMS driver is detected, a call to the `OvrInitEMS` procedure loads the OVR file into memory and closes the OVR file on disk. Storing the OVR file in memory significantly reduces the time required to access each overlay.

If `OvrInitEMS` is not successful, the program continues to use the disk-based OVR file. Consequently, unless you know that your program will never run on a machine with EMS, including a call to `OvrInitEMS` offers a considerable potential increase in execution speed with little increase in the size of the executable file.

`OvrInitEMS` should be called immediately after `OvrInit`, as follows:

```
OvrInit( 'OvrMst3.ovr' );
OvrInitEMS;
```

After `OvrInitEMS` is called, `OvrResult` can be tested as follows:

```
if OvrResult <> ovrOk then
   case OvrResult of
      ovrIOError      { -4 } : writeln( 'I/O error reading overlay file' );
      ovrNoEMSDriver { -5 } : writeln( 'EMS driver not installed' );
      ovrNoEMSMemory { -6 } : writeln( 'Not enough free EMS memory' );
   end;
```

Changing the Size of the Overlay Buffer

When the `OvrInit` procedure is called, the size of the overlay buffer is initialized to the size of the largest overlay plus a small allowance for some interfacing information. At any time during the execution of the program, you can use the `OvrGetBuf` function to obtain the current size of the overlay buffer. For example:

```
writeln( 'The overlay buffer now contains ', OvrGetBuf, ' bytes' );
```

Although the default size of the overlay buffer is adequate for most applications, sometimes you might find a larger buffer useful. For example, suppose that your program needs frequent access to two different overlay units. If the combined size of the units exceeds the current size of the buffer, both units cannot be available at the same time. You can remedy this by using the `OvrSetBuf` procedure to increase the size of the overlay buffer to contain both overlay units.

The overlay buffer physically resides at the bottom of heap memory. Therefore, the single parameter of `OvrSetBuf`, a long integer containing the desired size, must be greater than or equal to the initial size of the overlay buffer and less than or equal to `(MemAvail+ OvrGetBuf)`. Any additional buffer allocation is obtained from the beginning of the heap. If `OvrSetBuf` decreases the size of the buffer, the extra space becomes available to the heap.

The size of the heap can be adjusted only when it is empty. Consequently, `OvrSetBuf` must be executed *before* any dynamic variables are allocated with `New` or `GetMem` and *before* the `InitGraph` procedure allocates heap space for any graphics operations. Further, if you need to increase the size of the overlay buffer, you should first use the `{$M}` compiler directive to increase the minimum size of the heap (listing 15.8).

Listing 15.8

```
{$M 16384,65536,655360  Increase HeapMin from 0 to 64K! }
uses Overlay,...
const
   OvrExtra = 8192;   { 8K }
begin
   OvrInit( 'OvrMst3.ovr' );
   OvrInitEMS;
   OvrSetBuf( OvrGetBuf + OvrExtra );   { Bump up by 8K }
   :
   :
end;
```

The success or failure of the call to `OvrSetBuf` can be tested as shown in listing 15.9.

Listing 15.9

```
if OvrResult <> ovrOk then begin
   case OvrResult of
      ovrError    { -1 } :
         writeln( 'Requested buffer size too small or heap not empty' );
      ovrNotFound { -2 } : writeln( '.OVR file wasn''t found' );
      ovrNoMemory { -3 } : writeln( 'Not enough available heap space' );
   end;
   Halt( 1 );
end;
```

The overlay manager continues to function if `OvrSetBuf` returns an error, but the size of the overlay buffer remains unchanged.

Loading Units into the Buffer

Whenever a subroutine in one of the overlay units is called, Turbo checks to see if the unit is already in the buffer. If it is not, the entire overlay unit is loaded. If you use EMS memory for the buffer, or if you increase the size of the buffer with `OvrSetBuf`, all or almost all of the overlays may reside in the buffer at the same time.

The overlay buffer acts like a ring; that is, individual overlays are loaded on top of one another. If it becomes necessary to load a unit that cannot fit in the remaining space, the compiler "slides" all of the units toward the end of the buffer, effectively moving the free space to the bottom of its memory. The new unit is then placed at the beginning of the buffer, consuming this free space and overwriting as many of the earliest units as it needs.

This process is illustrated in figure 15.2. In this example, the size of the buffer has been increased substantially but not enough to contain all four units simultaneously. The first overlay to be loaded, unit A, is placed at the bottom of the buffer. Unit B and unit C can fit in the available space above it. When it comes time to load unit D, however, not enough memory is remaining. Consequently, units A, B, and C are moved against the top of the buffer. Unit D is then loaded at the bottom of the buffer, where it consumes all of the open space and proceeds to overwrite a portion of the memory occupied by unit A. Because units are only usable in their entirety, the remainder of unit A's memory is considered to be available for the next overlay to be loaded.

If, after loading unit D, one of unit A's subroutines is called, unit A will be loaded into the buffer on top of unit D, overwriting unit B in the process.

Fig. 15.2. Loading units into the overlay buffer.

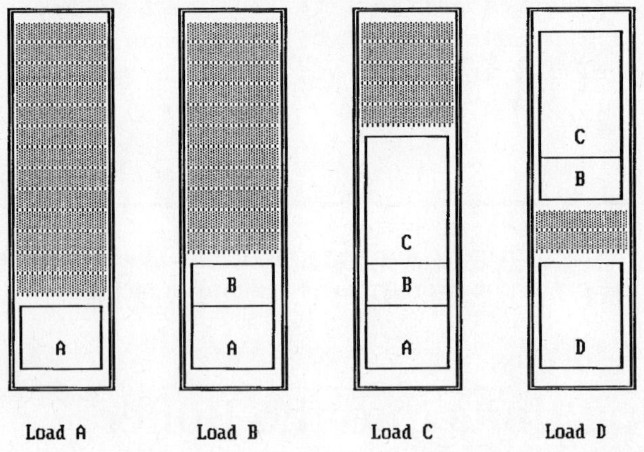

Placing Units on Probation

The ring design of the overlay buffer assumes that most subroutine calls are made to the most recently loaded units. This is reasonable because the majority of your overlays are probably needed only once. Often, however, one or two of your units contain the most frequently accessed code. Ideally, these frequently called overlays should remain in the buffer as long as possible.

Turbo Pascal solves this problem by allowing you to designate a region at the end of the buffer as a "probation area." If any calls are made to the unit while it is in this region, the unit will remain in the buffer; instead of being overwritten, the unit is simply returned to the bottom of the buffer and takes another turn through the ring. However, if no calls are made to the unit while it is in the probation area, the unit is overwritten in the normal manner.

The `OvrSetRetry` procedure sets the size of the probation area. The `OvrGetRetry` function returns the current setting. The default setting is 0, meaning that no probation area is automatically reserved. Some experimenting may be required to determine the best size for your particular application, but a good rule of thumb is to begin with a probation area between 1/3 and 1/2 the size of the overlay buffer.

The `OvrClearBuf` procedure completely clears the overlay buffer. Any subsequent call to a routine in an overlay unit causes that unit to be reloaded.

The overlay manager never requires you to call `OvrClearBuf`; in fact, doing so considerably decreases your application's performance.

Summary

In this chapter, you learned that overlays can be used to minimize the internal memory required to execute a Turbo Pascal program, and you saw how any user-written unit can be converted to overlay format. Specifically, you learned five rules to follow to transform normal units into overlays:

- ❑ Every overlay unit must be compiled with the `{$O+}` directive.
- ❑ Every overlay unit and the main program should be compiled with the `{$F+}` directive.
- ❑ The main program must include the `Overlay` standard unit in the first position of the `uses` statement.
- ❑ The main program must specify every overlay unit with the `{$O filename}` directive.
- ❑ The main program must execute the `OvrInit` overlay initiation procedure as soon as possible.

You learned how to apply these rules by working with a simple case study. In the process, you saw how the main program and the individual units are prepared, and you learned how the run-time support for the Turbo Pascal overlay manager is initialized.

Finally, you learned some advanced overlay features, such as the use of expanded memory, how to change the size of the overlay buffer, and how the overlay buffer can be cleared.

CHAPTER 16

BIOS, DOS, and Assembly Language

Programmers are traditionally concerned with only the final success or failure of their efforts. In fact, most judge the quality of software by its transparency; that is, the degree to which the product hides its inner workings and the details of its output. As a result, programming languages strive to be "user friendly." Turbo Pascal is probably the greatest such success story. It gracefully balances the need to protect the user from the complexities of the PC with the need to protect the microprocessor from poor coding practices.

One consequence of this benevolent protection is that programmers do not often need to get close to the CPU. Most of the time, this is more of a blessing than a problem. Yet, both fortunately and unfortunately, the programmer can realize the potential and flexibility of the PC only by understanding what software choices are available and when each choice is the most appropriate.

Every microprocessor has its own set of low-level subroutines that can be accessed to perform certain basic input and output functions. These subroutines are hard-coded in ROM (read-only memory) and can be accessed immediately by any program. Collectively, they are called the Basic Input/Output System (BIOS). They primarily serve as the interface between the operating system and the hardware of the PC.

DOS itself relies on BIOS services. BIOS routines are custom designed for the specific hardware configuration of a PC. COMPAQ portables, IBM ATs, the PC*jr*, and the latest laptops may all have different hardware internals, yet the BIOS routines they contain can all understand and appropriately react to the same DOS commands. When referring to the *operating system* of the PC, a programmer is usually talking about the way DOS and BIOS services are teamed.

BIOS and DOS services are prewritten, pretested subroutines that together form one of the most powerful languages available on the PC. When a Turbo Pascal program executes, it runs on top of—not in place of—the operating system. As a consequence, the full power of the PC is immediately available—just one layer down.

Turbo Pascal provides several tools to bring DOS and BIOS services within reach. Because these routines are the most fundamental commands available on your PC, accessing these services is useful for applications requiring special hardware access, increased speed, or smaller code size. By taking advantage of these tools, your programs can often obtain more than a tenfold improvement in speed—about the difference between a fast car and a jet.

This chapter demonstrates how you can use Turbo Pascal to directly access BIOS and DOS services as easily as you would access a standard procedure or function. In addition, for those infrequent occasions when you need even greater processing speed, you will see how Turbo Pascal enables you to directly incorporate assembly language in your programs.

Communicating with BIOS and DOS Services

In most ways, BIOS and DOS services behave just like ordinary Turbo Pascal procedures. A routine is called, it performs its tasks, and it returns control to the calling program when it finishes.

In Chapter 6, you saw how the CPU uses its segment and pointer registers to manipulate information stored in internal memory. Although most of the individual processor instructions have options that allow operations directly on data in memory, you can achieve even greater speed by placing the data in one of four general-purpose registers.

The only functional difference between BIOS and DOS routines and ordinary Turbo Pascal procedures is in how parameters are passed. A Turbo Pascal program uses internal memory (specifically, the stack) to exchange information with its subroutines. BIOS and DOS routines, on the other hand, pass parameters in the registers.

Using the Registers

Whenever you call a BIOS or DOS routine, you pass a set of variable parameters that correspond to the contents of the most frequently used registers. To simplify this process, Turbo Pascal predefines a variant record type, as follows:

```
Registers = record
         case Integer of
            0 : (AX, BX, CX, DX, BP, SI, DI, DS, ES, Flags : Word);
            1 : (AL, AH, BL, BH, CL, CH, DL, DH : Byte);
    end;
```

The AX, BX, CX, and DX registers are word-sized, *general-purpose* registers. Each one can be accessed either as two 8-bit registers or as a single 16-bit register. The AH, BH, CH, and DH registers represent the high-order bytes of the corresponding registers. Similarly, the AL, BL, CL, and DL registers represent the low-order bytes.

The BP, SI, and DI registers are the base pointer, source index, and destination index registers, respectively. The BP register contains the current working offset of the stack segment. The SI and DI registers hold the offsets of items in the data segment. For example, when a string is copied from memory location *A* to memory location *B*, SI holds the offset of *A* and DI holds the offset of *B*. Unless you write code that relies heavily on assembly language, you will have little or no practical interest in the contents of the BP, SI, and DI registers.

The flags register consists of 16 bits, each of which indicates a characteristic or result of an arithmetic or logical operation.

The general-purpose registers most often pass parameters between your program and the BIOS and DOS services. The success or failure of the service can usually be determined by examining the contents of the flags register. Because these are the registers used most frequently, we will examine each of them in more detail.

The General-Purpose Registers

The general-purpose registers are the workhorses of the CPU. All of them can be used to store temporary data. However, to increase processing speed even further, each general-purpose register is designed with its own set of specialties.

The AX (accumulator) register is the primary accumulator register. Most arithmetic instructions are optimized to work slightly faster (and require less code) when using it. As you will see shortly, the accumulator register is used also to hold the specific *function* of the BIOS or DOS service you want to execute.

The BX (base) register is the only general-purpose register that can be used as a memory pointer. Ultrafast memory operations store addresses here.

The CX (count) register holds the count for several of the instructions that do looping or other repeated operations, such as the shift and rotate instructions. Other constants, such as the row and column numbers of a screen, are also often stored here.

The DX (data) register is most often used for storing data. Whereas the BX register is often used to store a pointer to some data item, the DX register stores the value itself.

Table 16.1 summarizes the most common uses of the general-purpose registers.

Table 16.1. *Typical Register Uses*

Register	*Typical operation*
AX	Word multiply, divide, I/O
AL	Byte multiply, divide, I/O, translate, decimal arithmetic
AH	Byte multiply, divide
BX	Translation and data area addressing
CX	String operations, loops, and repeats
CL	Shift and rotate counts
DX	Word multiply, divide, indirect I/O

The Flags Register

The flags register consists of 16 bits that either control various conditions or reflect the current status of the processor. A diagram of the flags register is shown in figure 16.1. All of these bits indicate the results of an operation. Changing their settings before a service is called has no effect.

Fig. 16.1. *The contents of the flags register.*

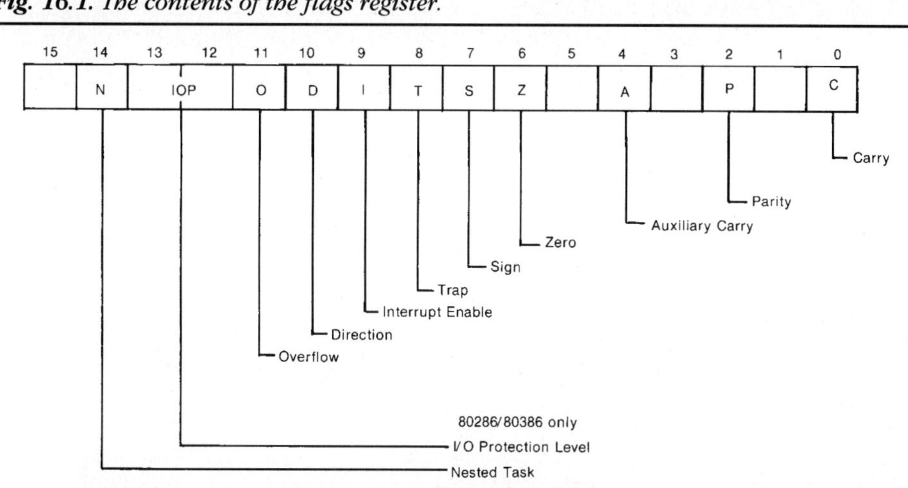

The individual bits have the following meanings:

- Carry. The *carry* flag is set if an operation between two 16-bit numbers generates a carry as a result of an addition, or a borrow as a result of a subtraction.
- Parity. The *parity* flag is set if the low-order byte of the result of an operation contains an even number of set (one) bits. This flag is used primarily for data communication programs.
- Auxiliary Carry. The *auxiliary carry* flag is set if the low-order four bits of an operation generate a carry as a result of an addition or a borrow as a result of a subtraction. This flag is used primarily for binary-coded decimal (BCD) arithmetic.
- Zero. The *zero* flag is set if the result of an operation is 0.
- Sign. The *sign* flag is equal to the high-order bit of the result of an operation (0 is positive, and 1 is negative). This flag is useful only in the context of a signed arithmetic operation.

- Trap. If the *trap* flag is set, the processor pauses between each individual operation. Debuggers use this feature to execute a program one instruction at a time.
- Interrupt Enable. If the *interrupt enable* flag is set, BIOS and DOS services (interrupts) are permitted. If the flag is clear, interrupt processing is temporarily disabled.
- Direction. If the *direction* flag is set, string operations process down from high addresses to low addresses. If clear, string operations process up from low addresses to high addresses.
- Overflow. The *overflow* flag is set if an arithmetic operation results in a value too large to fit in the destination operand or too small (technically, this is called an *underflow*) if the operation used signed numbers.

The *I/O protection level* and *nested task* flags are used for systems programming functions not described in this book.

Table 16.2 contains several predefined constants that you can use to test the settings of the various flags. For example, if you use a `Registers` variable named `Regs` and you want to determine if the parity flag is set, simply test whether (`Regs.Flags` and `FParity`) is nonzero.

Table 16.2. *Bit Settings in the Flags Register*

Constant	*Value*
`FCarry`	$0001
`FParity`	$0004
`FAuxiliary1`	$0010
`FZero`	$0040
`FSign`	$0080
`FOverflow`	$0800

Calling BIOS Services

The `Intr` procedure can be used to call any of the BIOS services.

```
Intr( IntNo : byte;  var Regs : Registers )
```

`IntNo` is the number of the BIOS service, and `Regs` is a variable parameter of the type `Registers`.

Unlike Turbo Pascal, in which all standard procedures and functions have specific names, BIOS services are always referenced by number. Theoretically, 256 BIOS services are available (numbered from 0 through 255). But on a practical level, most of these slots are not used, and of the ones that are taken, only about 10 are useful for Pascal programming.

The word *service* recurs in discussions of BIOS operations because each BIOS number can represent a collection of individual subroutines called *functions*. This is similar to the way a single Turbo Pascal unit can contain dozens of procedures and functions. For example, to move the cursor to a specific screen location, your Turbo Pascal program includes the statement `uses Crt` and you execute a `GotoXY` operation; to do the same thing with BIOS code, you execute BIOS service number $10, function number $02. (The individual services and functions are identified shortly.) The function number is always placed in the AH register prior to executing the `Intr` procedure.

Calling DOS Services

A DOS service is called with the `MsDos` procedure.

```
MsDos( var Regs : Registers )
```

Here again, `Regs` is a variable parameter of the type `Registers`.

The similarity between the syntax of the `Intr` and `MsDos` procedures is not accidental. Like the BIOS services, DOS services are also referenced only by number. But unlike the BIOS services, only one DOS service is useful to Pascal programmers: number $21. Because DOS uses some of the available BIOS slots to store its code in the PC's memory, DOS service $21 is *functionally* the same as BIOS service $21. Hence, the following statements are equivalent:

```
Intr( $21, Regs )
```

and

```
MsDos( Regs )
```

Dzens of individual DOS functions are available in DOS service $21. Place the number of the desired function in the AH register prior to executing the `MsDos` procedure.

A Note on BIOS and DOS Service Numbers

Remember that all of the BIOS routines were developed by the hardware manufacturer and stored in ROM. When the PC is booted, the ROM addresses of the BIOS services are placed in a special 256-element array called the *interrupt vector table*. When your program calls a specific BIOS service, Turbo Pascal simply looks up its address in the interrupt vector table and then executes it.

DOS services are stored on disk, then loaded into memory when the PC boots. Individual DOS services also store their addresses in the interrupt vector table.

Understanding how the interrupt vector table works—the subject of Chapter 18—is the same as understanding how the operating system works.

Accessing BIOS Services

Ten BIOS services are useful for Turbo Pascal programming. The number of these services (in hex), together with the numbers of their individual functions (in hex), are listed in Table 16.3. This section briefly discusses each of these categories.

Table 16.3. *BIOS Services of IBM-Compatible Personal Computers*

Category	*Interrupt number*	*Function*	*Description*
Print-Screen	05	—	Print the Screen Display
Video	10	00	Set Video Mode
		01	Set Cursor Size
		02	Set Cursor Position
		03	Read Cursor Position and Size
		04	Read Light Pen Position
		05	Select Active Display Page (Text Mode)
		06	Scroll Window Up
		07	Scroll Window Down
		08	Read Character and Attribute at Cursor

Category	*Interrupt number*	*Function*	*Description*
		09	Write Character and Attribute at Cursor
		0A	Write Character
		0B	Set Color Palette
		0C	Write a Pixel
		0D	Read a Pixel
		0E	Teletype Style Character Output
		0F	Get Current Video State
		13	Write String (AT and EGA Only)
Equipment List	11	—	Identify PC Hardware Configuration
Memory Size	12	—	Determine Internal Memory Size
Disk	13	00	Reset Disk Drive
		01	Get Diskette Status
		02	Read Disk Sectors
		03	Write Disk Sectors
		04	Verify Sectors
		05	Format Diskette Track
		08	(AT only) Return the Current Drive Parameters
		09	(AT only) Initialize the Fixed Disk Table
		0A	(AT only) Read Long Sectors
		0B	(AT only) Write Long Sectors
		0C	(AT only) Seek a Cylinder
		0D	(AT only) Alternate Disk Reset
		15	(AT only) Read Disk Type
		16	(AT only) Read Disk Change Line Status
		17	(AT only) Set Disk Type for Format
Communications	14	00	Initialize Communications Port
		01	Send Character to Communications Port

continues

Table 16.3. continued

Category	*Interrupt number*	*Function*	*Description*
		02	Receive Character from Communications Port
		03	Get Communications Port Status
Cassette I/O	15	00	Turn Cassette Motor On
		01	Turn Cassette Motor Off
		02	Read 256-Byte Blocks from Cassette
		03	Write 256-Byte Blocks to Cassette
Extended PC/AT Support	15	80	Device Open
		81	Device Close
		82	Device Program Terminate
		83	Event Wait
		84	Get Joystick Switch Settings/ Read Inputs
		85	Systems Request Key Pressed
		86	Delay
		87	Move Block of Words
		88	Get Size of Extended Memory
		89	Go to Virtual Mode
		90	Device Busy Loop
		91	Set Flag/Complete Interrupt
Keyboard	16	00	Return Next Character from Keyboard
		01	Test Next Keyboard Character
		03	Return Current Keyboard Shift Status
Printer	17	00	Print Character
		01	Initialize the Printer
		02	Get Printer Status
Time-of-Day	1A	00	Read Clock Counter
		01	Set Clock Counter
		02	Read Real-Time Clock (AT Only)

Category	Interrupt number	Function	Description
		03	Set Real-Time Clock (AT Only)
		04	Read Date from Real-Time Clock (AT Only)
		05	Set Date of Real-Time Clock (AT Only)
		06	Set Alarm (AT Only)
		07	Reset Alarm (AT Only)

Print Screen (Interrupt $05)

Whenever you press the Shift and PrtSc keys simultaneously, the current contents of the screen (actually, the characters in video memory) are output to the printer.

The software routine that controls this process is contained in BIOS service number 5. The INT05 program in listing 16.1 demonstrates how to print the screen from a Turbo Pascal program. No options are available, so no function number needs to be specified. Nevertheless, the syntax of the `Intr` procedure must be obeyed; a dummy `Registers` record must still be included as a parameter.

Listing 16.1

```
program Int05;
uses Dos;
procedure PrintScreen;
var
   Regs : Registers;
begin
   Intr( 5, Regs );
end;
begin
   PrintScreen;
end.
```

Video Services (Interrupt $10)

The Video Service BIOS is extensively used by the Crt and Graphics standard units. `ClrScr`, `GotoXY`, and `Window` are examples of Turbo Pascal procedures that rely on these functions, as well as almost all color, high-resolution graphics, and screen highlighting routines.

Most of the Video Services BIOS functions are available in more convenient packages in standard Turbo Pascal subroutines. The few features that are not supported, such as reading the light pen, are not likely to be missed.

The `ClrScr` procedure in the Crt unit can be thought of as the combination of erasing the screen and repositioning the cursor. The INT10A program in listing 16.2 shows how these actions can be separated.

Listing 16.2

```
program Int10A;
uses Crt, DOS;
var
  i : integer;
procedure EraseScreen;
var
   Regs : registers;
begin
   with Regs do begin
      AH := $06;
      CH := 0;                  { Row of upper left corner }
      CL := 0;                  { Column of upper left corner }
      DH := 25-1;               { Row of bottom right corner }
      DL := 80-1;               { Column of bottom right corner }
      BH := 7;                  { Attribute byte for blank lines }
      Intr( $10, Regs );
   end;
end;
procedure ReturnCursor;
var
   Regs : registers;
begin
   with Regs do begin
      AH := 2;
      BH := 0;                  { Page }
      DH := 0;                  { Row }
```

```
            DL := 0;               { Column }
            Intr( $10, Regs );
        end;
    end;
    begin
        ClrScr;
        for i := 1 to 300 do
            write( i );
        GotoXY( 40, 5 );
        Delay( 1000 );
        EraseScreen;
        write( '*' );   { Output an asterisk at the cursor location }
        Delay( 1000 );
        ReturnCursor;
        readln;
    end.
```

The `EraseScreen` procedure, like its name implies, erases the screen but *does not* change the current cursor position in the process. When the program executes, the top half of the screen fills with numbers, and the cursor is placed in the center of the display. Notice that the cursor does not move when the screen is erased. The `ReturnCursor` procedure is what finally resets the cursor to the upper left corner.

One other potentially useful application of the Video Services BIOS can be found in Function 01, which sets the size of the cursor.

Recall that the monochrome and EGA displays use text characters that are 14 pixels high, and that the default CGA text is 8 pixels high. Most of the time, the cursor appears as an underline, using only the bottom two pixel rows. Function 01 reshapes the cursor by changing its top and bottom rows. If, for example, you use it on a system with a monochrome screen and you set the top line to 0 and the bottom line to 13, the cursor changes to a solid block.

To use Function 01, set the CH and CL registers to the desired upper and lower lines, respectively. The parameters are small, so only the bottom four bits of each register are needed to contain the selected values. If you set the sixth bit in the CH register, you can make the cursor disappear. The INT10B program in listing 16.3 does just that.

Listing 16.3

```
program Int10B;
uses Crt, DOS;
procedure SetCursorType( StartingLine, StoppingLine : byte );
var
   Regs : registers;
begin
   with Regs do begin
      AH := $01;
      CH := StartingLine;
      CL := StoppingLine;
      Intr( $10, Regs );
   end;
end;
begin
   ClrScr;
   SetCursorType( $20, $00 );
   readln;
end.
```

By itself, INT10B is not exciting. It erases the screen, blanks out the cursor, and waits for you to press the Enter key. Consider, however, that in some applications (such as displaying a help screen) you can improve the quality of the display by temporarily erasing the cursor.

To reset the cursor, you should have first saved its original shape. The INT10C program (listing 16.4) demonstrates how to obtain this information by using Function 3.

Listing 16.4

```
program Int10C;
uses Crt, DOS;
var
   StartingLine,
   StoppingLine,
   WhereIsY,
   WhereIsX    : word;
procedure GetCursorInfo;
var
   Regs : registers;
begin
```

```
    with Regs do begin
       AH := $03;                     { Read cursor position and size }
       BH := $00;                     { Default page number           }
       Intr( $10, Regs );             { BIOS interrupt $10            }
       StartingLine := CH;            { Top line in cursor            }
       StoppingLine := CL;            { Bottom line in cursor         }
       WhereIsY     := DH + 1;        { WhereY                        }
       WhereIsX     := DL + 1;        { WhereX                        }
    end;
end;
begin
    GotoXY( 38, 12 );   { Initial position for test }
    GetCursorInfo;
    ClrScr;
    writeln( 'The top line of the cursor is at:    ', StartingLine );
    writeln( 'The bottom line of the cursor is at: ', StoppingLine );
    writeln;
    writeln( '(X, Y) position:  (', WhereIsX, ', ', WhereIsY, ')' );
    readln;
end.
```

When INT10C executes, it produces the following output:

```
The top line of the cursor is at:    6
The bottom line of the cursor is at: 7
(X, Y) position:  (38, 12)
```

Notice that function 3 returns the top and bottom cursor lines in the CH and CL registers, respectively. In addition, the DH register contains the current cursor row, and the DL register contains the current cursor column. Hence, Function 3 is the equivalent of calling both `WhereX` and `WhereY`.

Equipment List (Interrupt $11)

The Equipment List Service BIOS is a convenient way to determine which peripherals are installed in your PC. It reports the number of printers, serial ports, and diskettes; whether a game adapter or math coprocessor is installed; the initial video mode of the system; and the size of the memory on the PC's motherboard.

No individual functions are available in the Equipment List Service BIOS, so the initial value of the AH register is ignored.

The INT11A program in listing 16.5 is designed to report on the configuration of the PC that runs it. All information is returned in the AX register; the large comment in the program explains how the individual bits can be interpreted.

Listing 16.5

```
program Int11A;
uses Dos;
var
   GamePort,
   Coprocessor       : Boolean;
   PrinterCount,
   RS232PortCount,
   DisketteCount,
   StartMode,
   Kbytes_RAM        : byte;
procedure EquipmentData( var NumberOfPrinters      : byte;
                         var GamePortAvailable     : Boolean;
                         var NumberOfRS232Ports    : byte;
                         var NumberOfDiskettes     : byte;
                         var InitialVideoMode      : byte;
                         var MotherboardRAM        : byte;
                         var CoprocessorAvailable : Boolean   );
var
   Regs : Registers;
begin
   Intr( $11, Regs );
{
   Bits returned in the AX register:
        ***AH*** ***AL***
        76543210 76543210
        -------- --------
   AX = PPUGRRRU FFVVMMCI
   U    Unused
   PP   Number of printers installed
   G    1 if a game adapter is installed; 0 otherwise
   RRR  Number of RS-232 ports installed
   FF   Number of floppy-disk drives minus 1 (0 = one drive)
   VV   Initial video mode
        01 = 40 x 25 color
        10 = 80 x 25 color
```

```
         11 = 80 x 25 monochrome
   MM    RAM on motherboard (0 = 16K, 1 = 32K, 2 = 48K, 3 = 64K)
   C     1 if a math coprocessor is installed; 0 otherwise
   I     1 if diskette installed; 0 otherwise
}
   with Regs do begin
      NumberOfPrinters          := (AH and $C0) shr 6;
      GamePortAvailable         := (AH and $10) = $10;
      NumberOfRS232Ports        := (AH and $0E) shr 1;
      if Odd( AL ) then
         NumberOfDiskettes      := ((AL and $C0) shr 6) + 1
      else
         NumberOfDiskettes      := 0;
      InitialVideoMode          := (AL and $30) shr 4;
      CoprocessorAvailable      := (AL and $02) = $02;
      MotherboardRAM            := (((AL and $0C) shr 2) + 1) * 16;
   end;
end;
begin
   EquipmentData( PrinterCount, GamePort, RS232PortCount,
                  DisketteCount, StartMode,
                  Kbytes_RAM, Coprocessor );
   writeln( 'Equipment Status Report' );
   writeln( '=======================' );
   writeln;
   writeln( 'Game port available?       ', GamePort );
   writeln( 'Number of printers:        ', PrinterCount );
   writeln( 'Number of RS232 ports:     ', RS232PortCount );
   writeln( 'Number of floppy drives:   ', DisketteCount );
   writeln( 'Initial video mode:        ', StartMode );
   writeln( 'RAM on motherboard:        ', Kbytes_RAM, 'K' );
   writeln( 'Coprocessor available?     ', Coprocessor );
end.
```

The `EquipmentData` procedure is clumsy to use. A more practical application of the Equipment List Service BIOS can be found in the INT11B program in listing 16.6. Here, the `DisketteCount` function returns the number of floppy diskettes, and the `Coprocessor` function returns a Boolean value to indicate whether a math coprocessor is installed.

Listing 16.6

```
program Int11B;
uses Dos;
function DisketteCount : byte;
var
   Regs : Registers;
begin
   Intr( $11, Regs );
   with Regs do begin
      if Odd( AL ) then
         DisketteCount := ((AL and $C0) shr 6) + 1
      else
         DisketteCount := 0;
   end;
end;
function Coprocessor : Boolean;
var
   Regs : Registers;
begin
   Intr( $11, Regs );
   Coprocessor := (Regs.AL and $02) = $02;
end;
begin
   writeln( 'Equipment Status Report' );
   writeln( '=======================' );
   writeln;
   writeln( 'Number of floppy drives: ', DisketteCount );
   writeln( 'Coprocessor available?   ', Coprocessor );
end.
```

Memory Size (Interrupt $12)

The Memory Size Service BIOS reports how many contiguous 1K byte blocks of memory are installed in your PC. No individual functions are available, so the initial value of the AH register is ignored.

The INT12 program in listing 16.7 reveals the amount of internal memory in your PC.

Listing 16.7

```
program Int12;
uses Dos;
function MemorySize : word;
var
   Regs : Registers;
begin
   Intr( $12, Regs );
   MemorySize := Regs.AX;
end;
begin
   writeln( 'The internal memory of your PC is ',
            MemorySize, 'K bytes.' );
end.
```

On the PC AT, BIOS service $15, function $88 returns in the AX register the amount of *extended* memory, in 1K bytes.

Disk Services (Interrupt $13)

The Disk Service BIOS contains a variety of functions that transfer data between the CPU and the disks. These functions are decidedly *not* trivial. Do not even *think* about executing them directly; even one mistake can cause a disastrous loss of data.

Communications Services (Interrupt $14)

The Communications Service BIOS contains functions that enable your PC to transfer data serially. This is the software that supports modems on the COM1 and COM2 ports.

Cassette I/O and Extended PC/AT Support Services (Interrupt $15)

BIOS service number $15 contains the routines that support cassette tape I/O on the PC. For obvious reasons, these functions have no value for most programmers; in fact, some later model PCs no longer include them.

Of considerably greater interest, however, is the fact that IBM uses service $15 also for specialized AT support routines. Consult the *PC/AT Technical Reference Manual* for further information.

Keyboard Services (Interrupt $16)

The Keyboard Service BIOS is used to manage input from the console. Function 00 returns the first character in the input buffer. Function 01 returns the next character but does not remove it from the buffer. Function 03 copies the keyboard status byte in $0040:$0017 to the AL register.

In some ways, Function 01 corresponds to the Turbo Pascal `KeyPressed` function. If a keystroke is available, the zero flag is cleared, the ASCII value of the keystroke is returned in AL, and the scan code is returned in AH. The INT16 program in listing 16.8 shows how it can be used.

Listing 16.8

```
program Int16;
uses Dos;
var
   i : byte;
   S : string;
   ch : char;
   ScanCode, ASCIIcode : byte;
function CharacterReady : Boolean;
var
   Regs : Registers;
begin
   Regs.AH := $01;
   Intr( $16, Regs );
   CharacterReady := Regs.Flags and FZero = 0;
end;
procedure NextCharacter( var ScanCodeValue, ASCIIcodeValue : byte );
```

```
var
   Regs : Registers;
begin
   Regs.AH := $01;
   Intr( $16, Regs );
   if Regs.Flags and FZero = 0 then begin
      ScanCodeValue  := Regs.AH;
      ASCIIcodeValue := Regs.AL;
   end else begin
      ScanCodeValue  := 0;
      ASCIIcodeValue := 0;
   end;
end;
begin
   while not CharacterReady do;    { Waiting for keystroke }
   NextCharacter( ScanCode, ASCIIcode );
   read( ch );
   writeln( 'I read "', ch, '"' );
   writeln( 'Scan code: ', ScanCode, '   ASCII code: ', ASCIIcode );
end.
```

INT16 uses Function 01 twice—the first time to wait patiently for a keystroke, and the second time to learn which key was pressed. Note that the `NextCharacter` procedure can correctly identify the key *before* it is read.

Printer Services (Interrupt $17)

The Printer Service BIOS allows Turbo Pascal to interface with the printers attached to the PC. Three functions are available. Function 00 prints a single character. Function 01 initializes the printer. Neither of these is particularly interesting.

Function 02, however, is a different matter. It tests the *availability* of a printer. With it, you can avoid those annoying delays caused by not knowing whether a printer is on-line. The INT17 program in listing 16.9 demonstrates how to test the status of a printer.

Listing 16.9

```
program Int17;
uses Dos;
function PrinterReady( Printer : byte ) : Boolean;
var
   Regs : Registers;
begin
   Regs.AH := $02;
   Regs.DX := Printer;    { 0=LPT1, 1=LPT2, 2=LPT3 }
   Intr( $17, Regs );
   PrinterReady := (Regs.AH and $80 = $80) and     { Test if ready      }
                   (Regs.AH and $10 = $10) and     { Test if selected   }
                   (Regs.AH and $08 = $00);        { Test if I/O error }
end;
function PrinterOutOfPaper( Printer : byte ) : Boolean;
var
   Regs : Registers;
begin
   Regs.AH := $02;
   Regs.DX := Printer;    { 0=LPT1, 1=LPT2, 2=LPT2 }
   Intr( $17, Regs );
   PrinterOutOfPaper := Regs.AH and $20 = $20;
end;
begin
   if PrinterReady( 0 ) then    { Check LPT1 }
      begin
         writeln( 'LPT1 is online' );
         if PrinterOutOfPaper( 0 ) then
            writeln( '...but it''s out of paper' );
      end
   else
      writeln( 'Printer not ready' );
end.
```

If `PrinterReady` returns `False`, the `PrinterOutOfPaper` test is undefined.

Althogh these functions are simple, they are probably the two most useful BIOS routines you will ever use directly.

A Precaution about INT17
Note that because of the absence of standards in the printer industry, Function $02 of BIOS service $17 may return different values for different printers even though they have the same status. If the INT17 program does not work correctly on your system, check the technical manual for your printer and adjust the program accordingly.

Time-of-Day Services (Interrupt $1A)

The Time-of-Day Service BIOS is used primarily to control the settings of the real-time clock in the AT. See the *PC/AT Technical Reference Manual* for further information.

A Note on Other BIOS Services

Many other BIOS services are not mentioned here, but unless you are an experienced systems programmer, you will never need (or want) to access them.

You should *never* randomly call an interrupt. However, because accidents—in the form of typographical errors—occur frequently, you should know something about what might happen so that you can figure out how to prevent recurring problems.

Whenever you write a program that uses interrupts, save it to disk before you run it. As obvious as that sounds, it is the best way to generate an "audit trail" you can later follow to discover your mistake.

If you do make an error, the odds are that nothing bad will happen. Most of the 256 possible slots in the interrupt vector table are not used; because no subroutine exists, calling a nonexistent service will "hang" your system until you reboot—probably by turning the machine completely off.

Other interrupts can cause bizarre results. In early versions of the BIOS, service $18 brings up the PC's ROM BASIC program—the version of BASIC that runs when DOS has not yet been loaded. Enjoy the session while it lasts; you will have to reboot to end it.

BIOS service $19 is a "warm" reboot—an annoying but harmless event. Consider, however, what might happen if you make a mistake while trying to run it yourself. If you forget to type the dollar sign in front of the number $19, hexadecimal 19 (which is decimal 25) becomes decimal 19 (which is hexadecimal $13). This simple error causes the Disk Service BIOS to execute, and—depending on the initial contents of the registers—can result in the need to reformat your hard disk.

Accessing DOS Services

Recall that the *number* of a BIOS service is actually a reference to the element of an array of addresses called the interrupt vector table. The disk operating system, commonly called DOS, also stores addresses in the interrupt vector table. Although IBM reserves all of the vectors from $20 through $3F for DOS, only a few of these are used. Table 16.4 summarizes how these interrupts are currently employed.

Table 16.4. *MS-DOS Interrupt Services*

Interrupt number	*Description*
20	Terminate Program
21	Primary DOS Functions
22	Terminate Routine Address
23	Control-C Handler Address
24	Critical Error Handler Address
25	Absolute Disk Read
26	Absolute Disk Write
27	Terminate and Stay Resident
2F	Print Spooling
28 to 2E	Unused but reserved
30 to 3F	Unused but reserved

This section explains what these services offer and how they can be used.

The DOS Services

Only nine DOS services are currently available through the interrupt vector table.

Interrupt $20 was the original program termination service. Since DOS Version 2.0, however, the preferred method is to use DOS Service $21, Function $4C.

Interrupts $22, $23, and $24 are not ordinary DOS routines and are not intended to be called directly. Rather, they serve as convenient pigeon holes for storing addresses. DOS fills them before it runs a program. $22 is the address of the next routine to run after the program terminates normally. $23 is the address of the routine to run if Ctrl-C is pressed while the program runs. $24 is the address of the routine to run in case the program terminates because of a run-time error. By keeping these three addresses in one convenient place, DOS ensures that it can regain control of the PC after a program ends.

Interrupts $25 and $26 directly access individual disk sectors. They are not intended to be used by ordinary applications programs.

Interrupt $27 is used by terminate-and-stay-resident (TSR) programs.

Interrupt $2F is primarily designed to support the PRINT.COM utility under DOS 3.X, but it can handle almost every other print spooler as well.

None of these DOS services contains more than a single function, yet over 80 individual DOS functions exist. All of the rest are found in the one major service accessed through Interrupt $21. In fact, so many functions are in service $21 that Turbo Pascal provides a separate procedure for using it: `MsDos`.

The DOS services are documented in the IBM *PC-DOS Technical Reference Manual*. Table 16.5 contains a listing of all DOS services and component functions by category. Table 16.6 reorganizes the same list into numeric sequence.

***Table 16.5.** MS-DOS Services by Category*

Category	*Interrupt*	*Function*	*Description*
Character Input	21	01	Character Input with Echo
	21	03	Auxiliary Input
	21	07	Direct Character Input without Echo

continues

Table 16.5. continued

Category	*Interrupt*	*Function*	*Description*
	21	08	Character Input without Echo
	21	0A	Buffered Input
	21	0B	Check whether Character Waiting
	21	0C	Flush Buffer, Then Read Input
Character Output	21	02	Character Output
	21	04	Auxiliary Output
	21	05	Printer Output
	21	06	Direct Console I/O
	21	09	Output a Character String
Disk Management	21	0D	Disk Reset
	21	0E	Select Default Drive
	21	19	Get Current Drive
	21	1B	Get File Allocation Table for Default Drive
	21	1C	Get File Allocation Table for Specified Drive
	21	2E	Set/Reset Verify Flag
	21	36	Get Disk Free Space
	21	54	Get Verify Flag
	21	68	Flush Buffer
File Management	21	0F	Open File with File Control Block (FCB)
	21	10	Close File with File Control Block (FCB)
	21	11	Find First File
	21	12	Find Next File
	21	13	Delete File
	21	16	Create File with File Control Block (FCB)
	21	17	Rename File
	21	1A	Set Disk Transfer Area (DTA) Address
	21	23	Get File Size
	21	2F	Get Disk Transfer Area (DTA) Address
	21	3C	Create File
	21	3D	Open File
	21	3E	Close File
	21	41	Delete File
	21	43	Get/Set File Attributes

Category	*Interrupt*	*Function*	*Description*
	21	45	Duplicate File Handle
	21	46	Force Duplication of File Handle
	21	4E	Find First File
	21	4F	Find Next File
	21	56	Rename File
	21	57	Get/Set Date/Time of File
	21	5A	Create Temporary File
	21	5B	Create New File
	21	5C	Lock/Unlock File Region
Information	21	14	Sequential Read
Management	21	15	Sequential Write
	21	21	Random Read
	21	22	Random Write
	21	24	Set Random Record
	21	27	Random Block Read
	21	28	Random Block Write
	21	3F	Read File or Device
	21	40	Write File or Device
	21	42	Move File Pointer
	25		Absolute Disk Read
	26		Absolute Disk Write
Directory	21	39	Create Subdirectory
Management	21	3A	Remove Subdirectory
	21	3B	Change Current Directory
	21	47	Get Current Director
Process	21	00	Terminate Program
Management	21	31	Terminate and Stay Resident
	21	4B	Load and Execute a Program
	21	4C	Terminate Process with Return Code
	21	4D	Get Return Code of Child Process
	21	59	Get Extended Error Information
	20		Terminate Program
	27		Terminate and Stay Resident
Memory	21	48	Allocate Memory Block
Management	21	49	Free Memory Block
	21	4A	Resize Memory Block
Miscellaneous System	21	25	Set Interrupt Vector
Management	21	26	Create New Program Segment Prefix (PSP)

continues

Table 16.5. continued

Category	*Interrupt*	*Function*	*Description*
	21	29	Parse File name
	21	2	Get System Date
	21	2	Set System Date
	21	2C	Get System Time
	21	2D	Set System Time
	21	30	Get DOS Version Number
	21	33	Get/Set Control-Break Check Flag
	21	35	Get Interrupt Vector
	21	38	Get/Set Current Country
	21	44	Device I/O Control
	21	5E	Get Network Machine/Printer Name
	21	5F	Get/Make Assign List Entry
	21	62	Get Program Segment Prefix Address
	21	65	Get Extended Country Information
	21	66	Get/Set Global Code Page
	21	67	Change Handle Count
	22		Terminate Routine Address
	23		Control-C Handler Address
	24		Critical Error Handler Address

Table 16.6. *MS-DOS Services in Numerical Order*

Interrupt number	*Function number*	*Description*
20		Terminate Program
21	00	Terminate Program
21	01	Character Input with Echo
21	02	Character Output
21	03	Auxiliary Input
21	04	Auxiliary Output
21	05	Printer Output
21	06	Direct Console I/O
21	07	Direct Character Input without Echo
21	08	Character Input without Echo
21	09	Output a Character String
21	0A	Buffered Input
21	0B	Check whether Character Waiting
21	0C	Flush Buffer, Then Read Input

Interrupt number	*Function number*	*Description*
21	0D	Disk Reset
21	0E	Select Default Drive
21	0F	Open File with File Control Block (FCB)
21	10	Close File with File Control Block (FCB)
21	11	Find First File
21	12	Find Next File
21	13	Delete File
21	14	Sequential Read
21	15	Sequential Write
21	16	Create File with File Control Block (FCB)
21	17	Rename File
21	19	Get Current Drive
21	1A	Set Disk Transfer Area (DTA) Address
21	1B	Get File Allocation Table for Default Drive
21	1C	Get File Allocation Table for Specified Drive
21	21	Random Read
21	22	Random Write
21	23	Get File Size
21	24	Set Random Record
21	25	Set Interrupt Vector
21	26	Create New Program Segment Prefix (PSP)
21	27	Random Block Read
21	28	Random Block Write
21	29	Parse File name
21	2A	Get System Date
21	2B	Set System Date
21	2C	Get System Time
21	2D	Set System Time
21	2E	Set/Reset Verify Flag
21	2F	Get Disk Transfer Area (DTA) Address
21	30	Get DOS Version Number
21	31	Terminate and Stay Resident
21	33	Get/Set Control-Break Check Flag
21	35	Get Interrupt Vector
21	36	Get Disk Free Space
21	38	Get/Set Current Country
21	39	Create Subdirectory
21	3A	Remove Subdirectory
21	3B	Change Current Directory

continues

Table 16.6. continued

Interrupt number	*Function number*	*Description*
21	3C	Create File
21	3D	Open File
21	3E	Close File
21	3F	Read File or Device
21	40	Write File or Device
21	41	Delete File
21	42	Move File Pointer
21	43	Get/Set File Attributes
21	44	Device I/O Control
21	45	Duplicate File Handle
21	46	Force Duplication of File Handle
21	47	Get Current Directory
21	48	Allocate Memory Block
21	49	Free Memory Block
21	4A	Resize Memory Block
21	4B	Load and Execute a Program
21	4C	Terminate Process with Return Code
21	4D	Get Return Code of Child Process
21	4E	Find First File
21	4F	Find Next File
21	54	Get Verify Flag
21	56	Rename File
21	57	Get/Set Date/Time of File
21	59	Get Extended Error Information
21	5A	Create Temporary File
21	5B	Create New File
21	5C	Lock/Unlock File Region
21	5E	Get Network Machine/Printer Name
21	5F	Get/Make Assign List Entry
21	62	Get Program Segment Prefix Address
21	65	Get Extended Country Information
21	66	Get/Set Global Code Page
21	67	Change Handle Count
21	68	Flush Buffer
22		Terminate Routine Address
23		Control-C Handler Address
24		Critical Error Handler Address
25		Absolute Disk Read
26		Absolute Disk Write
27		Terminate and Stay Resident

Using DOS Services

The list of DOS functions in table 16.5 reads like the index of the Turbo Pascal *Library Reference*. Because compilers, like all programs designed to run on the PC, must rely heavily on DOS services, it is no surprise that almost all of the DOS functions have found their way into Turbo routines.

When Borland first introduced Turbo Pascal, the `MsDos` procedure was a necessary part of almost every major programming application. Today, it is used principally in those few situations when execution speed is more important than programming convenience.

Calling DOS Services from Turbo Pascal

The rules for using `MsDos` are the same as those for `Intr`. The specific function number is placed in the AH register prior to calling the procedure. Any necessary parameters are placed in the appropriate registers. Any results generated by the procedure are returned in the registers. A few examples will illustrate how `MsDos` operates.

The INT21_9 program in listing 16.10 shows how you can use Function 09 of DOS Service $21. Function 09 displays a string of characters beginning at the current cursor location. Rather than using an ordinary Turbo Pascal `string` type, however, Function 09 can handle only a sequence of `char`-type characters, the last of which must be a dollar sign.

Listing 16.10

```
program Int21_9;
uses Dos;
var
   S : string;
procedure ShowString( var DisplayString : string );
var
   Regs : Registers;
begin
   Regs.AH := $09;
   Regs.DS := Seg( DisplayString );
   Regs.DX := Ofs( DisplayString ) + 1;
```

continues

Listing 16.10 continued

```
   MsDos( Regs );
end;
begin
   S := 'Hello, world!' + '$';
   ShowString( S );
end.
```

As you can tell from a quick examination of the `ShowString` procedure, the DS and DX registers must contain the segment and offset, respectively, of the first character in the string. `ShowString` adds 1 to the offset of `DisplayString` to bypass the string's size byte. When INT21_9 executes, the dollar sign is *not* displayed.

The INT21_ 2A program in listing 16.11 performs the same DOS call (Function $2A) as the `GetDate` procedure. After Function $2A is invoked, the DH register contains the month, the DL register contains the day, and the CX register contains the year.

Listing 16.11

```
program Int21_2A;
uses Dos;
procedure TodayIs;
var
   Regs : Registers;
begin
   Regs.AH := $2A;
   MsDos( Regs );
   with Regs do begin
      write( 'Current date:  ' );
      if DH < 10 then write( '0' );
      write( DH, '/' );
      if DL < 10 then write( '0' );
      writeln( DL, '/', CX - 1900 );
   end;
end;
begin
   TodayIs;
end.
```

The INT21_30 program in listing 16.12 duplicates the workings of the `DosVersion` function.

Listing 16.12

```
program Int21_30;
uses Dos;
procedure IdentifyVersion;
var
   Regs : Registers;
begin
   Regs.AH := $30;
   MsDos( Regs );
   writeln( 'Now running DOS Version ', Regs.AL, '.', Regs.AH );
end;
begin
   IdentifyVersion;
end.
```

The INT21_36 program in listing 16.13 uses Function $36 to obtain information about the formatting characteristics of a specified disk.

Listing 16.13

```
program Int21_36;
uses Dos;
procedure DiskFreeSpace( DriveCode : byte );
var
   Regs                 : Registers;
   SectorsPerCluster,
   AvailableClusters,
   BytesPerSector,
   ClustersPerDrive,
   Capacity,
   Free                 : LongInt;
begin
   Regs.AH := $36;
   Regs.DL := DriveCode;
   MsDos( Regs );
   SectorsPerCluster := Regs.AX;    { If bad DriveCode, AX = -1 ($FFFF) }
   AvailableClusters := Regs.BX;
```

continues

Listing 16.13 continued

```
    BytesPerSector     := Regs.CX;
    ClustersPerDrive   := Regs.DX;
    writeln( 'Sectors Per Cluster = ', SectorsPerCluster:10 );
    writeln( 'Available Clusters  = ', AvailableClusters:10 );
    writeln( 'Bytes Per Sector    = ', BytesPerSector:10    );
    writeln( 'Clusters Per Drive  = ', ClustersPerDrive:10  );
    Capacity := SectorsPerCluster * BytesPerSector * ClustersPerDrive;
    Free     := SectorsPerCluster * AvailableClusters * BytesPerSector;
    writeln( 'Capacity            = ', Capacity:10          );
    writeln( 'Free                = ', Free:10              );
end;
begin
    DiskFreeSpace( 0 );
end.
```

Using Assembly Language in Turbo Pascal

There is one final means of exploiting the power and speed of the PC: through assembly language programming. And, like all "final" means, assembly language is to be used only as a last resort.

Using Assembly Language with the *Inline* Procedure

The most direct way of using assembly language is to insert it in a Turbo Pascal program using the `Inline` procedure. `Inline` accepts any number of parameters, each of which corresponds to a hexadecimal value representing the results of the assembly operation—that is, the final 8086 machine code. A few examples will illustrate how to use `Inline`.

The INT05 program in listing 16.1 used the `Intr` procedure to execute the Print Screen Service BIOS. To achieve the same results with the `Inline` procedure, you would use the following code:

```
procedure PrintScreen;
begin
  Inline
    ($CD/$05);
end;
```

The two hex characters $CD and $05 are the actual 8086 machine code instructions that trigger an Interrupt 05.

A slightly more complicated situation arises when a value must be returned as a result of the execution of a procedure or function. The INT12 program in listing 16.7 used the `Intr` procedure to determine the size of internal memory in 1K blocks. To implement this interrupt in the form of an assembly language function, you would use the following code:

```
function MemorySize : integer;
  Inline
    ($CD/$12/          { int  12h          ; BIOS Equip Service }
     $89/$46/$04);     { mov  [bp +4],ax    ; Return size (x 1K) }
```

Here, five hexadecimal machine language instructions must be sent to the CPU. The equivalent assembly language source statements are shown in the comments on the right side. Recall that the BP register contains the current working offset of the stack segment. Hence, the instruction

```
mov    [bp+4],ax
```

copied the contents of the AX register (the result of the BIOS call) to the top of the stack—something that Turbo Pascal manages for you automatically.

These two examples show that a relatively trivial operation in Turbo Pascal can be excruciatingly painful to perform in assembly language. After all, not only do you need to understand how to translate your commands from Turbo Pascal to assembly language, but you also need to know how to translate assembly language to machine code.

It is impossible to teach assembly language in the space of a few pages. It is equally challenging to explain how to write machine-code instructions. Just to illustrate the difficulties, consider the following example. The single assembly language instruction `MOV` (for *move*) corresponds to a simple assignment operation in Turbo Pascal. While the two characters := achieve the desired result in Turbo Pascal, you need to choose among 22 unique hexadecimal machine-code formats! Either two or three bytes would need to be generated; thankfully, the exact rules do not matter for now.

Using the *Inline* Assembler

The `Inline` procedure, which was introduced by Turbo Pascal Version 4.0, limits itself to very short sequences of assembly language instructions. Turbo Pascal Version 6.0 introduces the inline assembler, which enables Turbo Pascal routines to contain the much clearer mnemonic assembly language code. The inline assembler is invoked using the `asm` statement. The general syntax of the `asm` statement is

```
asm
   <assembly statements>
end;
```

The general syntax for the assembly statement is

```
[Label ":"] < Prefix > [ Opcode [ Operand <"," Operand > ] ]
```

You separate assembly language statements from each other with semicolons, new lines, or a Pascal comment. Although the inline assembler is by no means a replacement for the full-fledged Turbo Assembler product, it supports enough mnemonics and instructions to make it a suitable tool for implementing assembly routines in Turbo Pascal programs.

The inline assembler is an excellent tool for teaching assembly language. It also makes it easier to code small, but critical, routines in assembly language. Going into the details of the inline assembler is beyond the scope of this book, but here are a few examples to give you a general idea.

The first example is the inline assembler version of the `MemorySize` function implemented earlier using the `Inline` procedure:

```
function MemorySize : integer;
begin
    asm
            int  12H
            mov  @Result,ax
    end;
end;
```

The inline assembler enables you to use the predefined `@Result` inside an `asm` statement to return the result of a function.

The second example, the `UpperCase` function, returns the uppercase characters of a string:

```
function UpperCase(Str : string) : string;
begin
  asm
```

```
    cld                 { Clear scan direction flag, to scan forward }
    lea    si,Str       { Load the effective address of Str in SI }
    les    di,@Result   { Load address of returned result in DI }
    SEGSS  lodsb        { Load DS:SI into AL, to store the string length
                          in register AL }
    stosb               { Store AL (the string length) in ES:DI, which
                          is byte 0 of the resulting string }
    xor    ah,ah        { Set AH to 0 because string length is < 256 }
    xchg   ax,cx        { Swap AX and CX registers.  CX now contains the
                          string length }
    jcxz   @3           { Jump to the end if the string is empty }
  @1:                   { Start the case-conversion loop }
    SEGSS  lodsb        { Load the next character in AL register }
    cmp    al,'a'       { Compare the current character with 'a'? }
    jb     @2           { Jump to @2 if the current character is
                          below 'a' }
    cmp    al,'z'       { Compare the current character with 'z'? }
    ja     @2           { Jump to @2 if the current character is
                          above 'z' }
    sub    al,20H       { Character is in ['a'..'z'], then
                          shift its ASCII code by subtracting $20 }
  @2:
    stosb               { Store the character in AL back in the string }
    loop   @1           { End of the case-conversion loop }
  @3:
  end;
end;
```

If you think this function is similar to the one on page 305 of the *Programmer's Guide*, you are right. The version in the *Programmer's Guide*, however, has a bug: the `jb` and `ja` instructions should be interchanged for the function to work properly.

The `asm` statements show labels—namely, `@1`, `@2`, and `@3`—that are local to the `asm` statement. In addition, the `asm` block makes a reference to the Pascal identifier `Str`. In general, the routines that contain `asm` statements can declare local Pascal variables and make references to them. The assembly language instructions in the `UpperCase` function are explained by the accompanying Pascal comments.

You can derive a `LowerCase` function easily from the `UpperCase` function. You need to change the following three `asm` statements:

asm *statements in* Uppercase	*Replace with*
`cmp al,'a'`	`cmp al,'A'`
`cmp al,'z'`	`cmp al,'Z'`
`sub al,20H`	`add al,20H`

Other Ways of Incorporating Assembly Language

Separate assembly language programs can be combined with Turbo Pascal by a process called *linking*, similar to the way the Turbo Pascal run-time libraries are linked with your program during compilation. The assembly language source program must first be assembled into object file (OBJ) format with an assembler. The object file is then linked with your Turbo Pascal program using the `{$L}` compiler directive. After the assembled routines are declared in your Turbo program with the reserved word `external`, they can be used like ordinary Turbo Pascal routines.

When To Use Assembly Language

Because Turbo Pascal provides the `Intr` and `MsDos` procedures, as well as the `Port`, `PortW`, `Mem`, `MemW`, and `MemL` arrays, there is really only one reason to consider using assembly language in a Turbo Pascal program: speed. Even then, assembly language provides only a minor improvement—often on the order of just a few clock cycles. Remember: Turbo Pascal is fast enough and powerful enough for almost every programming application.

Summary

In this chapter, you learned how Turbo Pascal allows you to directly access the BIOS and DOS services of your PC, and you saw how to directly incorporate assembly language instructions in your programs.

You learned that BIOS and DOS services are called just like ordinary Turbo Pascal procedures. The `Intr` procedure is used to call BIOS services, and the `MsDos` procedure is used to call DOS services. Many of the more useful BIOS and DOS routines were demonstrated.

You learned that the rules for using `Intr` and `MsDos` are the same. The specific function number is placed in the AH register prior to calling the procedure. Registers are used to pass parameters to the BIOS and DOS services, and any results are returned in the registers.

You learned that assembly language may be incorporated in your Turbo Pascal program using either the `inline` procedure or the `asm` statement. The `inline` procedure requires that the machine instructions be represented by their hexadecimal code numbers. The `asm` statement enables you to include mnemonic assembler instructions that are easier to write and clearer to read.

You also learned that external object files can be linked with Turbo Pascal through the use of the `{$L}` compiler directive. After the assembled routine is declared in your Turbo program with the reserved word `external`, it can be used like an ordinary Turbo Pascal procedure or function.

CHAPTER 17

The 8087 and External Devices

Long before IBM sold the first Personal Computer, the corporation had already taken the unprecedented step of publishing its technical specifications. IBM's design philosophy was called *open architecture*. IBM believed that if you knew how its new machine worked, you could more rapidly design, develop, and market products that relied on the PC and consequently increase the sales potential of the PC itself. Early editions of the *Technical Reference Manual* even contained the complete listing of the BIOS software.

IBM's open architecture is probably the biggest reason why the PC enjoys its current popularity. Other manufacturers were quickly able to introduce high-quality, competitively priced add-on memory, peripherals, and software. Today's PC supports such diverse products as modems, graphics plotters, laser printers, compact disk storage devices, and local area networks. PCs are connected to robots on assembly lines, laboratory equipment, and speech generation and recognition equipment.

Yet, even the engineers who designed the PC could not have predicted the range of products that emerged and flourished in the years since. The twofold question is: How were the new products able to adapt themselves to the PC, and how was the PC able to cope with them?

The answer is that both the computer's internal architecture and the operating system *expect* to support a generic piece of equipment called a *device*. Anything that can conform to the definition of a device can successfully interface with the PC. In this chapter, you learn how Turbo Pascal can access these strange machines through data ports and special software.

Accessing Data Ports

Turbo Pascal provides the predefined arrays `Port` and `PortW` so that you can access the computer's input and output data ports. Reading from or assigning to the `Port` and `PortW` arrays has the same effect as reading from or assigning to the I/O ports themselves.

A *port* is a special channel used by the CPU to communicate with its support circuitry. Each port is identified by a 16-bit value called the *port address*. Almost all of the PC's peripherals (including everything from fixed disks through any installed game adapter cards) communicate with the CPU through one or more ports. Therefore, by accessing the ports individually, you can directly communicate with any external hardware device.

Transferring Data

When `Port` or `PortW` appears on the left side of an assignment statement, the compiler assumes that you want to *move* data to the specified port. At all other times, the compiler assumes that you want to *read* data from the specified port. The `Port` and `PortW` array index corresponds to the port address.

The `Port` array transfers one byte of data at a time. `PortW` transfers a full word. Because most peripheral devices are designed to accommodate the 8-bit data bus of the PC, it is unlikely that you will ever use `PortW`.

The VANISH program in listing 17.1 uses the `Port` array to send instructions directly to the adapter card—either color or monochrome—and disable the PC's screen. The `Color` constant is set to either `True` or `False`, depending on whether your PC uses a color or monochrome adapter.

Listing 17.1

```
program Vanish;
uses Crt;
const
   Color = True;
```

```
var
   ch : char;
begin
   if Color then begin               {********* COLOR **********}
      Port[ $3D8 ] := $25;           {*    Disable the screen   *}
      repeat until KeyPressed;       {*    Wait for keypress    *}
      Port[ $3D8 ] := $2D;           {*    Restore the screen   *}
   end else begin                    {******* MONOCHROME *******}
      Port[ $3B8 ] := $21;           {*    Disable the screen   *}
      repeat until KeyPressed;       {*    Wait for keypress    *}
      Port[ $3B8 ] := $29;           {*    Restore the screen   *}
   end;                              {**************************}
   ch := ReadKey;                    {* Clear keyboard buffer   *}
end.                                 {**************************}
```

The VANISH program blanks the screen until a key is pressed. Blanking is not the same as erasing; a blanked screen is prevented from displaying the contents of video memory, but the video memory is unaffected. When the screen is restored, the original screen image returns.

Blanking has practical applications. For example, some graphics programs blank the screen while images are drawn. Restoring the screen has the effect of making the graphics display appear instantaneous.

The Danger of Accessing Ports

Never randomly experiment with a port! Some ports, for example, activate events when read, not just when written. The PORT1 program in listing 17.2 accesses port $3D9, which controls the background color of text mode. Even though the program only reads the value of the port, it is possible that the background color will change as a consequence.

Listing 17.2

```
program Port1;
begin
   writeln( Port[ $3D9 ] )
end.
```

Similar side effects exist with other ports. Unless you are careful, you can easily destroy data on your disks. For a complete list of ports, the devices they service, and the values they return, consult the *IBM PC Technical Reference Manual*.

Eliminating Snow on the Screen

When you move data directly to the video memory of a CGA color adapter card, you are liable to see snow on the screen. Snow is the result of the competition between two screen output instructions—in this case, the "normal" display signal and your own direct memory write.

All images appearing on the screen must constantly be updated, or *refreshed*, 60 times per second. On a monochrome screen, a single beam moves in a left-to-right and top-to-bottom motion, establishing the content of each pixel. A color screen uses three beams—one for each primary color.

When the beam reaches the right side of a line, the beam is temporarily turned off while it moves to the left side of the next line. Similarly, when the beam reaches the bottom right corner of the screen, it is temporarily disabled while it resets itself to the upper left corner. These periods of inactivity are called horizontal and vertical *blanking*, respectively. A blanking interval is also known as a *retrace*. Direct video writes during the horizontal and vertical blanking periods will not conflict with the normal screen update process. As a result, no snow appears.

To detect a retrace, access port $3DA. If bit 0 is set, the screen is in horizontal blanking. If bit 3 is set, the screen is in vertical blanking. By continuously testing this port and examining these bits, you can tell when your direct video write should begin.

The NOSNOW1 program in listing 17.3 performs a direct write to video memory for all the characters in a string. Each character is written only after the horizontal retrace is complete.

Listing 17.3

```
program NoSnow1;
const
   VideoSegment  = $B800;
   Blank         = 1;      { 1 = Horizontal (Bit 0), 8 = Vertical (Bit 3) }
var
   Position : byte;
procedure FlickerFree( Column, Row : word;  Message : string );
var
```

```
   i : byte;
   Offset : word;
begin
   Offset := (160 * Row) + (2 * Column);
   for i := 1 to Length( Message ) do begin
      while (Port[ $3DA ] and Blank =  Blank) do;    { Wait until clear }
      while (Port[ $3DA ] and Blank <> Blank) do;    { Wait until set }
      Mem[ VideoSegment : Offset ] := ord( Message[ i ] );
      Inc( Offset, 2 );
   end;
end;
begin
   for Position := 5 to 20 do
      FlickerFree( Position, Position, 'Hello, world!' );
end.
```

The `FlickerFree` procedure writes a single character at the beginning of a horizontal blanking period. The statement

```
while (Port[ $3DA ] and Blank = Blank) do;
```

prevents the program from proceeding until one horizontal blanking period ends (that is, until bit 0 is cleared). Similarly, the statement

```
while (Port[ $3DA ] and Blank <> Blank) do;
```

waits for the next horizontal blanking to begin (when bit 0 is set).

Because horizontal blanking lasts only 18.5 microseconds, you barely have time to write one character. In fact, because the blanking interval is so brief, this technique might not work at all unless the code is written in assembly language. Consequently, it may be necessary to use the vertical blanking interval by changing the `Blank` constant to 8. Because by comparison vertical blanking lasts an incredibly long time (1500 microseconds), you can further modify the program to allow several characters to be written during a *single* vertical blanking interval.

In the NOSNOW2 program in listing 17.4, the `FlickerFree` procedure waits for the vertical retrace to begin, then writes out the entire string.

Listing 17.4

```
program NoSnow2;
const
   VideoSegment = $B800;
```

continues

Listing 17.4 continued

```
   Blank         = 8;         { 1 = Horizontal (Bit 0), 8 = Vertical (Bit 3) }
var
   Position : byte;
procedure FlickerFree( Column, Row : word;  Message : string );
var
   i : byte;
   Offset : word;
begin
   Offset := (160 * Row) + (2 * Column);
   while (Port[ $3DA ] and Blank =  Blank) do;     { Wait until clear }
   while (Port[ $3DA ] and Blank <> Blank) do;     { Wait until set }
   for i := 1 to Length( Message ) do begin
      Mem[ VideoSegment : Offset ] := ord( Message[ i ] );
      Inc( Offset, 2 );
   end;
end;
begin
   for Position := 5 to 20 do
      FlickerFree( Position, Position, 'Hello, world!' );
end.
```

If coordinating direct memory writes with the vertical blanking interval still is not sufficient to remove flicker, one other trick remains for you to try.

1. Using the techniques in NOSNOW1 and NOSNOW2 (listings 17.3 and 17.4), wait for a blanking interval to begin.
2. Blank the entire screen, as shown in the VANISH program (listing 17.1).
3. Execute all of your direct memory write statements.
4. Wait for another blanking interval to begin.
5. Redisplay the screen.

With a little experimenting, you can create fast screen updates with no annoying snow.

Using Devices

To DOS, anything outside main memory is a *device*. The keyboard, screen, disk drives, modem, and printer are examples of devices. If your PC has an internal clock (such as on an AST SixPak Plus memory card), the clock itself is considered a device. Optical disks, network connector cards, and graphics plotters are also devices.

A device is not limited to external hardware physically connected to your PC. If your machine is configured for a RAM disk (that is, if you use internal memory to imitate a disk drive), the RAM disk is a device.

There are two broad categories of devices. *Block devices* are disks. Everything else is a *character device*. Disks, files, and directories were discussed in Chapters 13 and 14. In this section, you learn how to develop Turbo Pascal programs that access the character devices installed in your PC.

DOS Devices

Normally, when you use DOS, you access the devices attached to your PC with the reserved file names shown in table 17.1.

***Table 17.1.** DOS Device File Names*

Name	*Description*
AUX	The first asynchronous communications port (same as COM1)
COM1	The first asynchronous communications port (same as AUX)
COM2	The second asynchronous communications port
CON	For input, CON is the keyboard; for output, CON is the screen
LPT1	The first parallel printer port (same as PRN)
LPT2	The second parallel printer port
LPT3	The third parallel printer port
PRN	The first parallel printer port (same as LPT1)

You are probably intimately familiar with DOS devices already. For example, to change the system printer (LPT1) from its default setting of 80 columns to the larger size of 132 columns, you would use the DOS command:

```
MODE LPT1: 132
```

Similarly, to display a text file on the screen, you could redirect output from the console (CON) to the printer (PRN), as follows:

```
TYPE TEXTFILE.TXT > PRN
```

Although it is not shown in table 17.1, DOS also provides for a nonexistent device called NUL. The NUL device, which is rarely used, is handy only in those unusual circumstances when you do not want a real device to be used. For example, if you have a batch file that contains the instruction:

```
TYPE TEXTFILE.TXT > PRN
```

but you do not want printer output, you can either delete the line or change it to

```
TYPE TEXTFILE.TXT > NUL
```

DOS Device Drivers

Each physical device is different and requires a unique set of control commands. Yet, under DOS, all of these devices can be accessed identically.

For each device configured in your PC, the operating system includes a separate piece of controlling software called a *device driver* that serves as an interface between DOS and the peripheral. A device driver includes all the low-level, machine-specific code that manages the actual piece of hardware, but it also allows DOS to control the device with just a few standardized commands.

An individual device driver may be stored in a separate file on disk, but is loaded into memory after the system is running and before COMMAND.COM is loaded. Hence, a device driver may be part of the operating system, but it is not necessarily part of the DOS files.

Because of the existence of device drivers, DOS provides the same input and output software services for all external devices. Because Turbo Pascal uses DOS extensively, it must follow along. Consequently, the compiler interfaces with every device in the same way and cannot differentiate the exact type of physical device it is accessing.

Devices in Turbo Pascal

One of the reasons that DOS character devices can be treated so similarly is because of the common way they transfer data. All devices communicate with the CPU one byte at a time, sending and receiving their data in ASCII format. Suppose, for example, that you want to output the number $9AE5 to the printer. Even though $9AE5 is stored internally in binary format, you would probably want the number to list out as the string

```
39653
```

Consequently, the two-byte binary value is converted to the five individual ASCII characters for 3, 9, 6, 5, and 3—that is, bytes $33, $39, $36, $35, and $33.

Similarly, when you use a modem to receive data over a phone line, you probably use a protocol that groups every nine bits into one ASCII byte and one parity bit. If the parity test is successful, the ASCII data from the modem is converted to binary form for internal storage and later processing by the PC.

Not surprisingly, the ASCII-binary conversion that occurs when your program communicates with a device is identical to the conversion that occurs when you are processing text files. In fact, the text file is Turbo Pascal's mechanism for communicating with devices. You use `write` and `writeln` as the principal output procedures, and `read` and `readln` as the principal input procedures.

A *physical* character device may be any piece of hardware you can imagine. But to Turbo Pascal, it will always be a text file.

Using Devices as Turbo Pascal Text Files

Turbo Pascal provides predefined file names that correspond to the standard DOS devices. For the sake of simplicity, the file names used by the compiler correspond closely with those used by DOS itself.

To use one of the devices, declare a text file identifier, `Assign` it to one of the file names listed in table 17.2, and open it for input or output with `Reset` or `Rewrite`.

Table 17.2. Turbo Pascal Device File Names

Name	*Description*
AUX	The first asynchronous communications port (same as COM1)
COM1	The first asynchronous communications port (same as AUX)
COM2	The second asynchronous communications port
CON	Keyboard or screen
LPT1	The first parallel printer port (same as PRN)
LPT2	The second parallel printer port
LPT3	The third parallel printer port
NUL	The nonexistent device
PRN	The first parallel printer port (same as LPT1)
"	Standard input or output

For example, to open one file as the printer and another file as the keyboard, you can use the code demonstrated in the DEVICE1 program in listing 17.5. Be sure your printer is on-line before running the program.

Listing 17.5

```
program Device1;
var
   Printer, Console : Text;
   S : string;
begin
   Assign( Printer, 'PRN' );
   Rewrite( Printer );
   Assign( Console, 'CON' );
   Reset( Console );
   readln( Console, S );    { This is coming from the keyboard }
   writeln( Printer, 'This is going to the printer.' );
   writeln( Printer, S );
   Close( Printer );
   Close( Console );
end.
```

The *Printer* Standard Unit
Remember that the `Printer` standard unit declares the `Lst` variable as a text file, assigns `Lst` to the PRN device with the `Assign` procedure, and opens the file for output with `Rewrite`. Consequently, if your program includes a `uses Printer;` declaration, you can output to the printer by writing directly to the `Lst` file.

The CON device can be used for either input or output, as demonstrated in the DEVICE2 program in listing 17.6.

Listing 17.6

```
program Device2;
var
   Keyboard, Screen : Text;
   S : string;
begin
   Assign( Keyboard, 'CON' );
   Reset( Keyboard );
   Assign( Screen, 'CON' );
   Rewrite( Screen );
   readln( Keyboard, S );
   writeln( Screen, S );
   Close( Keyboard );
   Close( Screen );
end.
```

With only a few obvious exceptions (not being able to read from the printer, for example) DOS devices behave exactly like files. In fact, the procedures, functions, and syntax of Turbo Pascal are the same for a DOS device as they are for any normal text file.

Standard Input and Output

The System unit includes the two predefined text files `Input` and `Output`. You will find them declared in the SYSTEM.INT unit header file that came with your Turbo Pascal distribution disks.

`Input` and `Output` are called the *standard* input and output files, respectively. These files are automatically opened and available throughout the execution of a Turbo Pascal program. The two file identifiers are both Assigned to CON, but Input is opened with Reset, and Output is opened with Rewrite.

Whenever a file parameter is omitted from a read or write procedure, the compiler assumes that you are referring to Input or Output. For example, the following instructions are equivalent:

```
readln( x )                    readln( Input, x )
writeln( x )                   writeln( Input, x )
```

Note that every time one of your programs accessed the keyboard or the screen, Turbo Pascal processed the instructions invisibly as text files!

You can *specifically* open Input and Output by referencing the null file in an assignment statement. For example, the following code opens Output as the text file StdOut:

```
Assign( StdOut, '' );
Rewrite( StdOut );
```

All data written to the StdOut file will now be sent to Output. The CRTR1 program in Chapter 10 (listing 10.4) demonstrates the advantages of this technique.

DOS File Handles

When a Reset, Rewrite, or Append procedure is executed, the compiler passes DOS the name of the physical file identified in the Assign procedure. After DOS successfully opens a file, it returns a 16-bit number called a *file handle*. From that point forward, DOS always references the open file by its handle. (An unopened file always has a handle of –1.) Consequently, when the compiler wants to access a file, it must communicate with DOS using the handle rather than the file name.

In effect, the DOS file handle acts like the Turbo Pascal file identifier variable. Your program can use the same identifier to access several physical files (after each is appropriately closed and reopened). Similarly, DOS can use the same handle to reference several physical files. (Like Pascal, DOS must also close and reopen a file before the handle can be reused.)

By default, DOS allows only eight file handles to be active at a time. To change this value, include the instruction:

```
FILES=nn
```

in the CONFIG.SYS file. Under MS-DOS Version 3.0, the maximum number of file handles is 255. In Chapter 1, you learned that Turbo Pascal requires 20 files to be configured (that is, `FILES=20`).

Turbo Pascal *always* opens five standard DOS character devices. Each of these devices, together with their associated file handles, is listed in table 17.3.

Table 17.3. *Standard Files*

Handle	*Device name*	*Opened to*
0	Standard input	CON
1	Standard output	CON
2	Console device	CON
3	Communications	COM1/AUX
4	Printer	LPT1/PRN

DOS allows Turbo Pascal to have only 15 files open simultaneously. These 15 files are the difference between the system configuration total of 20 files and the 5 standard files shown in table 17.3.

Typed and Untyped File Variables

Whenever a file is opened in a Turbo Pascal program, the compiler creates a data record containing the information it needs to manage the file. If the Turbo Pascal file identifier variable is `FilVar`, the data record for the file can be found at the memory location `@FilVar`.

This data record takes one of two forms. The form of records for text files is slightly different than the one created for typed and untyped files. Although text file data records are more interesting, they are also more complicated. Data records for text files are covered a bit later in the chapter. The data records for typed and untyped files are smaller and less complicated, so I will begin with them.

Every open typed and untyped file has an associated 128-byte data record defined as `FileRec` in the Dos standard unit. `FileRec` is laid out as shown here.

```
FileRec = record
            Handle   : Word;
            Mode     : Word;
            RecSize  : Word;
            Private  : array[1..26] of Byte;
            UserData : array[1..16] of Byte;
            Name     : array[0..79] of Char;
          end;
```

The `Handle` field contains the file handle assigned by DOS. Remember that its value is –1 ($FFFF) until the file is opened. The `Mode` field contains one of the four values listed in table 17.4.

Table 17.4. *File Mode Constants*

Constant	*Hex value*	*Decimal value*	*Meaning*
`fmClosed`	$D7B0	55,216	File is closed.
`fmInput`	$D7B1	55,217	File is a text file open for input.
`fmOutput`	$D7B2	55,218	File is a text file open for output.
`fmInOut`	$D7B3	55,219	File is open for both input and output.

The Turbo Pascal *Programmer's Guide* colorfully describes these numbers as "magic" values. The `Mode` field of typed and untyped files may be either `fmClosed` or `fmInOut`. As you will see shortly, the `Mode` field of a text file can be `fmClosed`, `fmInput`, or `fmOutput`. If the `Mode` field contains any other number, the file variable has not yet been initialized.

`RecSize` equals the size—in bytes—of each data element in the file. Although the `Private` field is currently unused, future releases of the compiler will probably need it. The `UserData` field is available if you want to store any file-specific data. You can use it to store one or more pointers in case you need more than 16 bytes.

The `Name` field contains the file name in ASCIIZ format. In other words, `Name` is not a Turbo Pascal string data type, but a sequence of ASCII characters ending with a null character (#0).

To show you how a file record is used, the FILE0 program in listing 17.7 creates a small data file.

Listing 17.7

```
program File0;
type
   TestRecord = record
                   A : real;          { 6 bytes }
                   B : integer;       { 2 bytes }
                   C : byte;          { 1 byte  }
                end;                  { 9 bytes total }
var
   TestFile : file of TestRecord;
   TestData : TestRecord;
   i : byte;
begin
   Assign( TestFile, 'FileData.Tst' );
   Rewrite( TestFile );
   with TestData do begin
      A := 100.0;
      B := 100;
      C := 100;
   end;
   for i := 1 to 20 do
      write( TestFile, TestData );
   Close( TestFile );
end.
```

When FILE0 executes, it creates the FILEDATA.TST file, consisting of 20 records of nine bytes each. You can examine the file record for FILEDATA.TST using the FILE1 program in listing 17.8.

Listing 17.8

```
program File1;
uses Dos;
type
   TestRecord = record
                   A : real;
                   B : integer;
                   C : byte;
                end;
var
```

continues

Listing 17.8 continued

```
   InFile : file of TestRecord;
   InRec  : ^FileRec;
   i      : byte;
begin
   Assign( InFile, 'FileData.Tst' );
   Reset( InFile );
   InRec := @InFile;
   with InRec^ do begin
      write( 'File name:      ' );
      i := 0;
      while Name[ i ] < > #0 do begin
         write( Name[ i ] );
         Inc( i );
      end;
      writeln;
      writeln( 'Handle:        ', Handle );
      writeln( 'Record size:   ', RecSize );
      write( 'Mode:           ' );
      case Mode of
         $D7B0 : writeln( 'Closed' );
         $D7B1 : writeln( 'Open for input' );
         $D7B2 : writeln( 'Open for output' );
         $D7B3 : writeln( 'Open for both input and output' );
      end;
      write( 'Private area: ' );
      for i := 1 to 26 do write( Chr( Private[ i ] ) );    writeln;
      write( 'User area:      ' );
      for i := 1 to 16 do write( Chr( UserData[ i ] ) );   writeln;
   end;
   Close( InFile );
end.
```

FILE1 produces the following output:

```
File name:     FileData.Tst
Handle:        5
Record size:   9
Mode:          Open for both input and output
Private area:
User area:
```

The `Name` field contains the file name just as it appeared in the `Assign` statement, complete with the same pattern of upper- and lowercase letters. The `Handle` field is 5, the first available value after the standard devices are opened and their handles (0 through 4) are assigned. The 9-byte record size corresponds to `SizeOf( TestRecord )`. Both the `Private` and `UserData` fields are blank.

How the File Data Type Record Is Used

Assume that `DataRecs` is a file identifier variable. When you use `DataRecs` in an input or output statement, such as

```
Read( DataRecs, x, y, z )
```

or

```
Write( DataRecs, x, y, z )
```

you are passing the file identifier variable to the `read` and `write` procedures as one of the parameters. The `read` and `write` procedures can access the file record at `@DataRecs` to obtain information such as the following:

- The file handle, to pass along to DOS
- The file mode, to ensure that a `read` or `write` is a legal operation on the file
- The record size, to determine how many characters should be input or output at one time
- The file name, to pass along to any error messages

All things considered, you are passing along an impressive amount of information. And as you will see next, a text file record type contains even more data.

Text File Variables

When a text file is opened in a Turbo Pascal program, the compiler creates a 256-byte data record defined as `TextRec` in the Dos standard unit. `TextRec` is laid out as shown here.

```
TextBuf = array[0..127] of Char;
TextRec = record
          Handle     : Word;
          Mode       : Word;
          BufSize    : Word;
          Private    : Word;
          BufPos     : Word;
          BufEnd     : Word;
          BufPtr     : ^TextBuf;
          OpenFunc   : Pointer;
          InOutFunc  : Pointer;
          FlushFunc  : Pointer;
          CloseFunc  : Pointer;
          UserData   : array[1..16] of Byte;
          Name       : array[0..79] of Char;
          Buffer     : TextBuf;
       end;
```

The `Handle`, `Mode`, `UserData`, and `Name` fields are the same for a text file as for typed and untyped files. The `Private` field also has the same purpose, except it is defined as a word instead of an array.

Several additional fields are also evident. The `BufSize`, `BufPos`, `BufEnd`, `BufPtr`, and `Buffer` fields manage the text file buffering process. By default, the text file buffer is in the `Buffer` field. `BufPtr` points to a buffer whose size is given by `BufSize`. `BufPos` is the buffer location of the next character to be processed. `BufEnd` holds the number of characters in the buffer. If the `SetTextBuf` procedure is used to designate a different text file buffer, these fields change accordingly.

`OpenFunc`, `InOutFunc`, `FlushFunc`, and `CloseFunc` point to the DOS device driver software. These fields are discussed in more detail next.

The FILE2 program in listing 17.9 can be used to examine its own text file record.

Listing 17.9

```
program File2;
uses Crt, Dos;
var
   InFile : Text;
   InRec  : ^TextRec;
   Data   : string;
   i      : byte;
```

```
begin
   Assign( InFile, 'File2.PAS' );
   Reset( InFile );
   InRec := @InFile;
   with InRec^ do repeat
      ClrScr;
      Readln( InFile, Data );
      write( 'File name:     ' );
      i := 0;
      while Name[ i ] < > #0 do begin
         write( Name[ i ] );
         Inc( i );
      end;
      writeln;
      writeln( 'Handle:          ', Handle );
      write( 'Mode:            ' );
      case Mode of
         $D7B0 : writeln( 'Closed' );
         $D7B1 : writeln( 'Open for input' );
         $D7B2 : writeln( 'Open for output' );
         $D7B3 : writeln( 'Open for both input and output' );
      end;
      writeln( 'Private area: ', Private );
      write( 'User area:     ' );
      for i := 1 to 16 do write( Chr( UserData[ i ] ) );   writeln;
      writeln( 'Buffer size:  ', BufSize );
      writeln( 'Buffer pos:   ', BufPos );
      writeln( 'Buffer end:   ', BufEnd );
      writeln( 'Buffer:       ' );
      writeln( '==========================================' );
      for i := 0 to 127 do write( Buffer[ i ] );   writeln;
      writeln( '==========================================' );
      readln;
   until Eof( InFile );
   Close( InFile );
end.
```

FILE2 displays the contents of the text file record as each data record is read. The first display is shown in figure 17.1.

When you press the Enter key, the next record is read and a new screen is displayed. With each new record, notice that the `BufPos` value increases until all of the characters in the buffer are assigned to the `Data` string. Then, the next 128 bytes from the file are placed in the buffer, and the `BufPos` field is reset.

Fig. 17.1. Output produced by the FILE2 program.

```
File name:    File2.PAS
Handle:       8
Mode:         Open for input
Private area: 0
User area:
Buffer size:  128
Buffer pos:   16
Buffer end:   128
Buffer:
==========================================
program File2;
uses Crt, Dos;
var
   InFile : Text;
   InRec  : ^TextRec;
   Data   : string;
   i      : byte;
begin

==========================================
```

Text File Device Drivers

Although the set of built-in device drivers is more than adequate for most programming applications, new drivers are frequently needed as a result of special hardware and software requirements.

For example, in Chapter 11, the Borland Graphics Interface (BGI) files are used as device drivers for the graphics adapter cards. Other peripherals that usually require their own device driver include:

- RAM disks
- Mouse drivers
- Expanded memory managers
- Joysticks
- Modems and other communications hardware

Similarly, new device drivers may be required to support special software applications. For example, in the configuration instructions in Chapter 1, you are told to include the line

```
DEVICE = ANSI.SYS
```

in your CONFIG.SYS file. ANSI.SYS is actually a device driver that offers more sophisticated keyboard and screen management capabilities than does the standard console driver. Also recall that in the discussion of the text screen in Chapter 10, it was noted that the Crt standard unit contains its own customized screen and keyboard interface routines—actually, device drivers in disguise.

Turbo Pascal enables you to develop your own text-file device drivers. For ordinary disk files and the predefined devices listed in table 17.2, the four pointer fields in the text file record (`OpenFunc`, `InOutFunc`, `FlushFunc`, and `CloseFunc`) reference the built-in subroutines that manage the file opening, closing, and I/O processes—in other words, the DOS device drivers. By redirecting these pointers to functions of your own design, Turbo Pascal enables you to implement your own device drivers.

Developing a Customized Device Driver

Your device driver will need at least five major subroutines: one routine each for `OpenFunc`, `InOutFunc`, `FlushFunc`, and `CloseFunc` to point to, plus a customized assignment procedure that initiates the driver. Although your program can call them any name you want, here we will adopt the generic names used by the Turbo Pascal *Programmer's Guide*: `Open`, `InOut`, `Flush`, `Close`, and `Assign`.

Except for `Assign`, each function should be compiled in the force far calls state, that is, with the `{$F+}` compiler directive active.

Each of these five subroutines is explained in turn. Just reading about them can be confusing at first, so you should probably look ahead to see how they are implemented in the generalized device driver program in listing 17.10.

When you access the standard DOS device drivers, you always use the `Assign` procedure. This action associates a file identifier variable with one of the *reserved* file names such as CON, PRN, and LPT1. Because the compiler will not accept new reserved words, your customized device driver will have to operate a bit differently—specifically, with a *customized* `Assign` procedure, similar to the way the CRT device driver is accessed with the `AssignCrt` procedure.

Here, the customized `Assign` procedure is shown as `AssignDriver` in listing 17.10.

The *Assign* Procedure

The customized `Assign` procedure must perform the following tasks:

1. Accept the name of the text file identifier variable.
2. Set the `OpenFunc` and `CloseFunc` pointer variables to the address of your customized `Open` and `Close` functions, respectively.
3. Because the file has not yet been opened, the `Mode` field should be set to `fmClosed` and the `Handle` field should be set to –1 ($FFFF).
4. Establish the text file buffer. Any memory region can be used, but be sure to identify it to the compiler by assigning a pointer to the buffer to the `BufPtr` field and assigning the size of the buffer to the `BufSize` field.
5. Because run-time error messages might try to reference the text file by name, the `Name` field should be cleared. Remember that `Name` is an ASCIIZ string; consequently, all you have to do is set its first character to the null character (#0).

The *Open* Function

The `Open` function is shown as `DriverOpen` in listing 17.10. The `Open` function is called by the `Reset`, `Rewrite`, and `Append` procedures. Remember, though, that although `Append` is a valid text-file opening procedure, most peripheral devices are either read only or write only.

The customized `Open` function should perform the following tasks:

1. The `Mode` field should be set to either `fmInput` or `fmOutput`, depending on whether the file was opened with `Reset` or `Rewrite`. If the file was opened with `Append`, it initially has a mode of `fmInOut` and should be handled as follows:
   a. If appending has a special meaning for the physical device, the device should be positioned to its current end of file. Normally, however, you assume that files opened with `Append` will be used exclusively for output.
   b. Because text files cannot have a mode of `fmInOut`, `Mode` should be reset to `fmOutput`.
2. The `InOutFunc` and `FlushFunc` pointer variables should be set to reference functions that depend on whether the file was opened for input or output.

3. If no errors occurred during the execution of the function, `Open` should return a value of 0.

The *InOut* Function

The `InOut` function is shown as `DriverInput` and `DriverOutput` in listing 17.10. The `InOut` function is called by the `read`, `readln`, `write`, `writeln`, `Eof`, `Eoln`, `SeekEof`, `SeekEoln`, and `Close` procedures.

You probably will not use the same `InOut` function for *both* input and output. The `Open` function selects an appropriate function when it sets the `InOutFunc` pointer variable. Each input and output function should be designed to transfer one byte at a time between the buffer and the text file.

If no errors occurred during the execution of the function, `InOut` should return a value of 0.

The *Flush* Function

The `Flush` function is not shown in listing 17.10. The `Flush` function is called by the `Flush` procedure after each `read`, `readln`, `write`, and `writeln`. You probably will not need a separate `Flush` function. It has little or no value during input operations and can probably be replaced with `InOut` for output operations. This is demonstrated in the sample programs that follow.

The *Close* Function

The `Close` function is shown as `DriverClose` in listing 17.10. The `Close` function is called by the `Close` procedure. `Close` can be called also by `Reset`, `Rewrite`, and `Append` if the file they reference is currently open.

`Close` should execute all appropriate file cleanup routines. If no errors occurred during execution of the function, `Close` should return a value of 0.

A General Text File Device Driver

The `Driver` unit in listing 17.10 is a model you can use for your own device driver file. All necessary control code is shown, and all areas that either expect or allow your customized code are identified.

Listing 17.10

```
unit Driver;
   {**************************************************
   *   General Turbo Pascal text file device driver   *
   **************************************************}
interface
     uses Dos;
     procedure AssignDriver( var DriverFile : Text;
                                 FileName   : string );
implementation
{$R-,S-   Disable range and stack checking }
     {*************************************
     *   All unit-wide types, constants,   *
     *   and variables are defined here    *
     *************************************}
     const
        MoreInputAvailable : Boolean = True;   { An end-of-file test }
     function DriverCharacterInput : char;
     begin
        {********************************
        *   Return the next character   *
        ********************************}
     end;
     procedure DriverCharacterOutput( ch : char );
     begin
        {********************************
        *   Output the next character   *
        ********************************}
     end;
{$F+}
     function DriverInput( var DriverFile : TextRec ) : integer;
     var
        BufIndex : word;
     begin
        with DriverFile do begin
           BufIndex := 0;
           while MoreInputAvailable and (BufIndex < BufSize) do begin
              BufPtr^[ BufIndex ] := DriverCharacterInput;
              Inc( BufIndex );
           end;
           BufPos := 0;
           BufEnd := BufIndex;
```

```
   end;
   DriverInput := 0;
end;
function DriverOutput( var DriverFile : TextRec ) : integer;
var
   BufIndex : word;
begin
   with DriverFile do begin
      BufIndex := 0;
      while BufIndex < BufPos do begin
         DriverCharacterOutput( BufPtr^[ BufIndex ] );
         Inc( BufIndex );
      end;
      BufPos := 0;
   end;
   DriverOutput := 0;
end;
function DriverIgnore( var DriverFile : TextRec ) : integer;
begin
   DriverIgnore := 0;
end;
function DriverClose( var DriverFile : TextRec ) : integer;
begin
   {*******************************
   *   Closing routines go here   *
   *******************************}
   DriverClose := 0;
end;
function DriverOpen( var DriverFile : TextRec ) : integer;
begin
   with DriverFile do begin
      if Mode = fmInput then begin
         {*************************************
         *   Opening input routines go here   *
         *************************************}
         InOutFunc := @ DriverInput;
         FlushFunc := @ DriverIgnore;
      end else begin
         if Mode = fmInOut then begin
         {*************************************
         *   Opening Append routines go here   *
         *   (if Append has special meaning)   *
         *************************************}
         end;
```

continues

Listing 17.10 continued

```
                {*************************************
                 *    Opening output routines go here    *
                 *************************************}
                 Mode       := fmOutput;
                 InOutFunc := @ DriverOutput;
                 FlushFunc := @ DriverOutput;
              end;
          end;
          DriverOpen := 0;
      end;
{$F-}
      procedure AssignDriver;    { var DriverFile : Text;
                                        FileName    : string }
      var
          DriverRecord : ^TextRec;
      begin
          {*************************************
           *  Special initiation code goes here  *
           *************************************}
          DriverRecord := @ DriverFile;
          with DriverRecord^ do begin
             Handle     := $FFFF;
             Mode       := fmClosed;
             BufSize    := SizeOf( Buffer );
             BufPtr     := @ Buffer;
             OpenFunc   := @ DriverOpen;
             CloseFunc := @ DriverClose;
             Name[ 0 ] := #0;
          end;
      end;
end.
```

Note that because DRIVER.PAS is a unit, you must compile it to disk to create a TPU file.

The customized `Assign` procedure is named `AssignDriver`. Notice that it accepts two parameters: the text file identifier and the name of a disk file.

The customized `Open` and `Close` functions are named `DriverOpen` and `DriverClose`, respectively. `DriverOpen` determines which `InOut` and `Flush` functions should be used, based on whether the file is opened for input or output.

The `DriverIgnore` function is used when you do not want a function to perform any activity. For example, the `FlushFunc` variable points to `DriverIgnore` when the file is open for input.

Read-Only and Write-Only Files

As it is shown, the `Driver` unit is designed to be used for both input and output. Some text file devices (such as the keyboard) are read only, whereas others (such as the system printer) are write only. The drivers for those devices should be modified appropriately.

If the device is read only, make the following modifications:

1. Remove the `DriverCharacterOutput` procedure and the `DriverOutput` function.

2. In the section marked `Opening output routines go here` in the `DriverOpen` function, insert the statement `RunError( 105 )`. This causes the program to end with run-time error 105 (`File not open for output`). Assign `@ DriverIgnore` to both the `InOutFunc` and `FlushFunc` pointers.

If the device is write only, make the following modifications:

1. Remove both the `DriverCharacterInput` and `DriverInput` functions.

2. In the section marked `Opening input routines go here` in the `DriverOpen` function, insert the statement `RunError( 104 )`. This causes the program to end with run-time error 104 (`File not open for input`). Assign `@ DriverIgnore` to the `InOutFunc` pointer.

Not only do these changes help to ensure proper data transfer between your program and the device it accesses, but they also considerably reduce the size of the driver unit.

Using a Customized Device Driver

The `Cypher` unit in listing 17.11 is a device driver that supports text file encoding and decoding. The customized assignment procedure is called `AssignCypher`.

Listing 17.11

```
unit Cypher;
interface
     uses Dos;
     procedure AssignCypher( var DriverFile : Text;
                                 FileName   : string );
implementation
{$R-,S-   Disable range and stack checking }
     var
        WorkFile     : file of char;
     function DriverCharacterInput : char;
     var
        ch : char;
     begin
        read( WorkFile, ch );
        if ch = #0 then
           DriverCharacterInput := #255
        else
           DriverCharacterInput := Pred( ch );
     end;
     procedure DriverCharacterOutput( ch : char );
     var
        EncryptedCharacter : char;
     begin
        if ch = #255 then
          EncryptedCharacter := #0
        else
           EncryptedCharacter := Succ( ch );
        write( WorkFile, EncryptedCharacter );
     end;
{$F+}
     function DriverInput( var DriverFile : TextRec ) : integer;
     var
        BufIndex : word;
     begin
        with DriverFile do begin
```

```
         BufIndex := 0;
         while not Eof( WorkFile ) and (BufIndex < BufSize) do begin
            BufPtr^[ BufIndex ] := DriverCharacterInput;
            Inc( BufIndex );
         end;
         BufPos := 0;
         BufEnd := BufIndex;
      end;
      DriverInput := 0;
end;
function DriverOutput( var DriverFile : TextRec ) : integer;
var
   BufIndex : word;
begin
   with DriverFile do begin
      BufIndex := 0;
      while BufIndex < BufPos do begin
         DriverCharacterOutput( BufPtr^[ BufIndex ] );
         Inc( BufIndex );
      end;
      BufPos := 0;
   end;
   DriverOutput := 0;
end;
function DriverIgnore( var DriverFile : TextRec ) : integer;
begin
   DriverIgnore := 0;
end;
function DriverClose( var DriverFile : TextRec ) : integer;
begin
   Close( WorkFile );
   DriverClose := 0;
end;
function DriverOpen( var DriverFile : TextRec ) : integer;
begin
   with DriverFile do begin
      if Mode = fmInput then begin
         Reset( WorkFile );
         InOutFunc := @ DriverInput;
         FlushFunc := @ DriverIgnore;
      end else begin
         Rewrite( WorkFile );
```

continues

Listing 17.11 continued

```
                Mode       := fmOutput;
                InOutFunc  := @ DriverOutput;
                FlushFunc  := @ DriverOutput;
             end;
          end;
          DriverOpen := 0;
       end;
{$F-}
       procedure AssignCypher;      { var DriverFile : Text;
                                          FileName   : string }
       var
          DriverRecord : ^TextRec;
       begin
          Assign( WorkFile, FileName );
          DriverRecord := @ DriverFile;
          with DriverRecord^ do begin
             Handle    := $FFFF;
             Mode      := fmClosed;
             BufSize   := SizeOf( Buffer );
             BufPtr    := @ Buffer;
             OpenFunc  := @ DriverOpen;
             CloseFunc := @ DriverClose;
             Name[ 0 ] := #0;
          end;
       end;
end.
```

Note that because CYPHER.PAS is a unit, you must compile it to disk to create a TPU file.

When the `AssignCypher` driver is used, text files opened for output "scramble" their data before writing to the disk. This data can be correctly understood only by another text file that uses the `AssignCypher` driver and is opened for input.

The ENCRYPT program in listing 17.12 uses the `Cypher` unit to scramble its output file. ENCRYPT accepts a "secret message" from the keyboard, encodes it by substituting the next higher ASCII value for each character, and writes the message to disk. The program ends when a blank line is entered.

Listing 17.12

```
program Encrypt;
uses Crt, Cypher;
var
   CodeFile      : Text;
   SecretMessage : string;
begin
   AssignCypher( CodeFile, 'Secret.TXT' );
   Rewrite( CodeFile );
   ClrScr;
   writeln( 'Enter your message:' );
   repeat
      readln( SecretMessage );
      writeln( CodeFile, SecretMessage );
   until Length( SecretMessage ) = 0;
   Close( CodeFile );
end.
```

When ENCRYPT is executed, it displays `Enter your message:` and awaits data entry. A typical session is shown in figure 17.2.

Fig. 17.2. The original message you enter in the ENCRYPT program.

```
Enter your message:
Hello!  This message is being processed by a customized device driver that
converts keyboard input to an encrypted data file.  Each character will be
stored as the successor of the actual character.  That is, "a" becomes "b",
"b" becomes "c", and so on.
```

After the program ends, you can examine the file it produced by entering the command:

```
DUMP SECRET.TXT
```

The results of the file dump are shown in figure 17.3.

***Fig. 17.3.** The encoded file produced by the ENCRYPT program.*

```
secret.txt                        Page 1 of 1                      260 bytes

49666D6D 70222121 55696A74 216E6674 74626866 216A7421 Ifmmp"!!Uijt!nfttbhf!jt!
63666A6F 68217173 70646674 74666521 637A2162 21647674 cfjoh!qspdfttfe!cz!b!dvt
75706E6A 7B666521 6566776A 64662165 736A7766 73217569 upnj{fe!efwjdf!esjwfs!ui
62750E0B 64706F77 66737574 216C667A 63706273 65216A6F bu♫♂dpowfsut!lfzcpbse!jo
71767521 75702162 6F21666F 64737A71 75666521 65627562 qvu!up!bo!fodszqufe!ebub
21676A6D 662F2121 46626469 21646962 73626475 66732178 !gjmf/!!Fbdi!dibsbdufs!x
6A6D6D21 63660E0B 74757073 66652162 74217569 66217476 jmm!cf♫♂tupsfe!bt!uif!tv
64646674 74707321 70672175 69662162 64757662 6D216469 ddfttps!pg!uif!bduvbm!di
62736264 7566732F 21215569 6275216A 742D2123 62232163 bsbdufs/!!Uibu!jt-!#b#!c
6664706E 66742123 63232D0E 0B236323 21636664 706E6674 fdpnft!#c#-♫♂#c#!cfdpnft
21236423 2D21626F 65217470 21706F2F 0E0B0E0B          !#d#-!boe!tp!po/♫♂♫♂
```

Remember that the DUMP program, which was discussed in Chapter 13, "File Handling," displays the hexadecimal value of each byte in the file in the six columns on the left. The corresponding character contents are displayed in the larger right column. The first five characters are *Ifmmp*. Subtracting one letter from each of these characters gives *Hello*, the first word in the encoded message.

The DECODER program in listing 17.13 can be used to read the contents of the file more directly. Again, the `AssignCypher` driver is used, but this time the file is opened for input. When DECODER executes, the original message (shown in fig. 17.2) is displayed on the screen.

Listing 17.13

```
program Decoder;
uses Crt, Cypher;
var
   CodeFile      : Text;
   SecretMessage : string;
begin
   ClrScr;
   AssignCypher( CodeFile, 'Secret.TXT' );
```

```
   Reset( CodeFile );
   while not Eof( CodeFile ) do begin
      readln( CodeFile, SecretMessage );
      writeln( SecretMessage );
   end;
   Close( CodeFile );
aend.
```

Accessing Other Devices

Most of the time, the character input and output routines in a customized text file device driver are considerably more complicated than those shown in the `Cypher` example. Some devices (such as a game adapter board) are accessed using the `Port` or `PortW` arrays. Other devices (such as a printer) are accessed with DOS or BIOS calls. Some inline assembly language coding is usually required.

Nevertheless, as the `Cypher` example clearly shows, customized text file device drivers offer an easy way to implement a variety of high-performance applications and at the same time eliminate the need for special code in the body of the main program.

Using the 8087 Coprocessor

The 8086-family processor is designed to handle all numeric data and operations in its 16-bit registers. Consequently, real numbers, which range in size from the 4-byte `single` type through the 10-byte `extended` type, must be processed "in pieces" to fit.

Although the accuracy of the final result is not compromised, even a simple Turbo Pascal statement such as the addition of two real numbers can generate dozens of machine-language instructions, including:

- Translating each floating-point number to a fixed-point format
- Segregating each number into word-sized components
- Adding numbers at the word level

Floating-point operations require considerably more time to execute than their integer counterparts.

On the other hand, the 8087-family coprocessor is designed to accommodate floating-point numbers and instructions. Its register is 10 bytes long and consequently can manipulate even an `extended` real-number type in a single operation. In addition, the 8087 coprocessor can *directly* produce transcendental results, including all common trigonometric and logarithmic functions.

The 8087 is called a *co*processor with the 8086 because *both* chips monitor the instructions being sent to the CPU. The 8087 intercepts any instructions meant for it while allowing 8086 instructions to pass untouched. Similarly, the 8086 ignores instructions meant for the 8087, except for calculating any memory addresses the 8087 might need. The 8086 and 8087 operate simultaneously and thus together can execute the awaiting instructions faster than the 8086 alone.

This section shows how to use Turbo Pascal to take advantage of the power of the 8087.

8087 Data Types

Simply, Turbo Pascal defines a *real number* as any number that contains a decimal point. There are five forms of real numbers, as listed in table 17.5.

***Table 17.5.** Real-Type Numbers in Turbo Pascal*

Type	*Size*	*Ranges of allowed values*	*Significant digits*
Real	6 bytes	2.9×10^{-39} to 1.7×10^{38}	11–12
Single	4 bytes	1.5×10^{-45} to 3.4×10^{38}	7–8
Double	8 bytes	5.0×10^{-324} to 1.7×10^{308}	15–16
Extended	10 bytes	3.4×10^{-4932} to 1.1×10^{4932}	19–20
Comp	8 bytes	$-2^{63} + 1$ to $2^{63} - 1$	19–20

Real numbers compress very large values into a very small number of bytes using a format similar to that of scientific notation. But while scientific notation uses base 10, floating-point types store the binary representations of a sign (+ or –), an exponent, and a base value:

$$(+/-)\ \text{base} \times 2^{\text{exponent}}$$

The bit layout does not matter. Notice, though, that both the base value and the exponent are stored as binary numbers; this is why the table of reals shows ranges that seem so unusual.

The {*$N*} Numeric Processing Directive

Even if an 8087 is installed in the system, a Turbo Pascal program does not automatically generate the code to use it. For a program to take advantage of a numeric coprocessor, the `{$N+}` compiler directive must be enabled at the beginning of the program.

If numeric processing is enabled, the compiler tries to invoke the 8087 coprocessor whenever it encounters an instruction involving an operation on one or more real numbers. If the numeric processing option is disabled with `{$N-}`, the program executes just as if no 8087 is present.

The {*$E*} 8087 Emulation Directive

The `{$E}` 8087 emulation directive controls whether floating-point emulation software is to be included in the EXE file of a compiled program.

Emulation software is code that acts just as if the 8087 is present. Whereas a real number operation might be handled by the coprocessor in a single step, the emulation software converts the operation to data and instructions that the 8086 can handle, then reassembles the answers when the operation is finished. Emulation software produces the same results as a coprocessor, but with far less speed. The standard `Real` number type is routinely processed with emulation software on the 8086.

In the default `{$E+}` state, the compiled program contains all the software necessary to emulate the operation of an 8087 coprocessor. All IEEE floating-point types are supported, including the single, double, extended, comp, and real data types. If 8087 emulation is disabled with `{$E-}`, the only software emulation that Turbo Pascal will include in the compiled program is code to support the 6-byte standard real.

Enabling the 8087

The {$N} numeric processing and {$E} 8087 emulation directives are most often used together to achieve the right combination of speed and program portability. Table 17.6 summarizes the four possible combined settings. Remember that the default state is {$E+,N-}.

Table 17.6. Directive Combinations

Options	*Actions the compiler takes*
{$E+,N+}	If an 8087 coprocessor is detected, it will be used for all floating-point operations; otherwise, software emulation will be used. Consequently, programs compiled in this state can run on any machine, regardless of whether an 8087 is available. All IEEE real number types are supported.
{$E+,N-}	Numeric processing is disabled. Even if an 8087 coprocessor has been installed, Turbo Pascal uses only software emulation. All IEEE real number types are supported.
{$E-,N+}	No software emulation is available for any real number other than the 6-byte real type. Therefore, if your program uses any other IEEE real numbers (single, double, extended, or comp), an 8087 coprocessor *must* be present.
{$E-,N-}	Only the standard 6-byte real type is allowed, and its implementation is accomplished with software emulation. Even if an 8087 coprocessor is installed, it will be ignored. The program cannot use any single, double, extended, or comp numbers, *even if an 8087 coprocessor is present*.

Summary

In this chapter, you learned that the IBM open architecture design has fostered the introduction of a wide variety of add-in hardware. You saw that there are three ways that this hardware can be accessed: through ports, device drivers, and—for the 8087 coprocessor—special software.

You learned that a port is a channel between the CPU and its support circuitry. Almost all peripherals communicate with the CPU through one or more ports. The predefined arrays `Port` and `PortW` access the computer's input and output data ports. Programs that demonstrated the use of ports were presented.

You learned that—to DOS—anything outside main memory is considered a device and must be controlled by device driver software. Using this software, DOS controls each device with standardized commands. You learned that Turbo Pascal programs communicate with DOS devices through text files. You saw how the driver unit can be used as a model for creating your own device drivers, and you saw an example of a practical device driver in the `Cypher` unit, which supports text file encoding and decoding.

You learned that the 8087-family coprocessor is specifically designed to accommodate floating-point numbers and instructions. The 8087 handles five Turbo Pascal data types: real, single, double, extended, and comp. The `{$N}` numeric processing directive determines whether the 8087 is used. The `{$E}` 8087 emulation directive controls whether floating-point emulation software is to be included in the EXE file of a compiled program.

CHAPTER 18

Interrupt Service Routines

Probably for as long as you have known about computers, you have been hearing the phrase, "Computers can do only one thing at a time."

This is not completely true. Even though the CPU focuses only on a single task, a great deal of activity might be taking place in the computer. Keys may be pressed, a printer may be producing a report, a disk may be spinning, a modem may be communicating with another computer over a phone line, and the screen may be filling with characters. If your machine has Turbo Lightning installed, you hear a beep whenever you misspell a word. And, as soon as you press a certain hot key, your favorite memory-resident program appears.

The CPU cannot be in complete control of all this activity. However, your PC is designed in such a way that every legitimate claim for attention, such as a key being pressed, generates an interrupt signal that informs the CPU that it should temporarily suspend whatever it is doing (no matter what it is) and see what the fuss is about. The interrupt signal is well named; most of the time the CPU deals with the interruption quickly and then returns to its original pursuit.

Most interrupts automatically trigger the operation of a specific DOS or BIOS routine. (When you used the `MsDos` and `Intr` procedures in Chapter 16, you were requesting Turbo to execute interrupt routines.) When the routine terminates, the CPU returns to its original task.

Your PC can track up to 256 sources of interruption, so the CPU can stay aware (or more properly, can be made aware) of a great deal of activity and can react accordingly.

Interrupts are generated so frequently (every single keypress generates an interrupt, for example) that programmers usually do not even want to know about them. But sometimes, as with the `MsDos` and `Intr` procedures, you may want to run one of the interrupt routines yourself. Other times, as discussed in this chapter, you may want to create your own interrupt routines. Turbo Pascal provides a full set of procedures that enable you to accomplish all these tasks.

Types of Interrupts

Interrupts can be initiated by either hardware or software.

Hardware interrupts are generated by physical devices. Interrupts 0 through 5 are called by the processor. For example, Interrupts 1 and 3 are used for debugging. Interrupt 0 occurs when division by zero is detected. Interrupt 2 halts the system if a memory parity error is detected.

Interrupts 8 through $0F are generated by other hardware in the PC. For example, Interrupt 9 is triggered by each keypress. On the AT, another eight hardware interrupts have been reserved in $70 through $7F.

Software interrupts do not really interrupt anything. They are called directly as part of the natural flow of a program. Your Turbo Pascal application may generate an interrupt. You can call any one of the BIOS services by using the Turbo Pascal `Intr` procedure. You can also access any one of DOS's services by using the `MsDos` procedure, which is nothing more than the execution of Interrupt $21.

The Interrupt Vector Table

Interrupts are always identified by number (from 0 through 255) instead of by name or address. Each subroutine is called an *interrupt handler* or an *interrupt service routine* (ISR).

By common agreement, all PCs use a standardized set of interrupt numbers for each specific task. Beginning at the bottom of memory (segment $0000 and offset $0000), DOS stores a table of pointers to every interrupt handler. Each pointer is four bytes (two words) long. The first word contains the offset, and the second word contains the segment.

There are 256 possible entries, so this table, called the *interrupt vector table*, is 1K in size. When an interrupt is initiated, the CPU goes to the interrupt vector table, gets the appropriate address, and calls that routine.

(In engineering, a *vector* is something that defines both direction and magnitude. The term is frequently used by systems programmers to refer to addresses because to move to a new address you need to know which direction to face and how far to go.) Interrupts are listed in table 18.1. If two interrupts are received at the same time, the one with the lower number is executed first.

Table 18.1. *The Interrupt Vector Table*

Interrupt	*Cause*
$00	Divide by zero
$01	Single stepping (for use by debuggers)
$02	Non-maskable interrupt (NMI)
$03	Break point trap (for use by debuggers)
$04	Overflow
$05	Print screen
$06	Invalid opcode
$07	Processor extension not available
$08	System timekeeper
$09	Keyboard input interrupt
$0A	Reserved for MS-DOS
$0B	Asynchronous communications (COM2)
$0C	Asynchronous communications (COM1)
$0D	Fixed disk controller
$0E	Floppy disk controller
$0F	Printer controller
$10	Video display
$11	Equipment configuration check
$12	Memory size check
$13	Floppy disk, fixed disk driver (PC/XT)
$14	RS-232 communications port driver
$15	Cassette I/O, PC/AT auxiliary functions
$16	Keyboard driver
$17	Printer driver
$18	ROM BASIC entry code
$19	Bootstrap loader
$1A	Set/read real-time clock
$1B	Ctrl-Break handler

continues

Table 18.1. continued

Interrupt	*Cause*
$1C	Timer tick (18.2 times per second)
$1D	Pointer to video parameter table
$1E	Pointer to disk parameter table
$1F	Pointer to graphics character table for ASCII codes 128–255
$20	Program terminate (obsolete)
$21	MS-DOS function caller
$22	Terminate address for called programs
$23	Ctrl-C address
$24	Critical-error handler
$25	Absolute disk read
$26	Absolute disk write
$27	Terminate and stay resident (obsolete)
$28–$2E	Reserved for MS-DOS
$2F	Print spooler
$30–$3F	Reserved for MS-DOS
$40	Floppy disk driver (PC/XT)
$41	Fixed disk parameter table
$42–$43	Reserved for MS-DOS
$44	PC*jr* graphics character table (codes 0–FFh)
$45–$5F	Reserved for MS-DOS
$60–$67	User-definable
$68–$7F	Unused
$80–$85	Reserved for BASIC
$86–$F0	BASIC interpreter
$F1–$FF	Unused

An address in the interrupt vector table is the memory location of a subroutine you want to execute. This is how the CPU knows what you want it to do after you get its attention.

The Turbo Pascal procedure `GetIntVec` returns the address of a given interrupt. With this procedure (here, as part of the INTTAB1 program, listing 18.1), you can see the contents of the entire interrupt vector table.

Listing 18.1

```
program IntTab1;
uses DOS;
type
```

```
   String2 = string[ 2 ];
   String4 = string[ 4 ];
var
   i,j,k,
   IntNumber : byte;
   VectorAddress : pointer;
function HexNybble( Number : byte ) : char;
begin
   if Number < 10 then HexNybble := Chr( 48 +Number )
      <10            else HexNybble := Chr( 55 +Number );
end;
function HexBytes( Number : byte ) : String2;
begin
   HexBytes := HexNybble( Number div 16 ) +
            HexNybble( Number mod 16 );
end;
function HexWords( Number : word ) : String4;
begin
   HexWords := HexBytes( Hi(Number) ) + HexBytes( Lo(Number) );
end;
begin
   for i := 0 to 3 do begin
      for j := 0 to 15 do begin
         for k := 0 to 3 do begin
            IntNumber := i*64 + j + k*16;
            GetIntVec( IntNumber, VectorAddress );
            write( HexBytes( IntNumber ):7,
                   HexWords( Seg( VectorAddress^ ) ):5,
                   HexWords( Ofs( VectorAddress^ ) ):5 );
         end;
         writeln;
      end;
      readln;
   end;
end.
```

When INTTAB1 executes, it produces four "pages" of 64 interrupts. The first page is shown in figure 18.1.

If you run a program that attempts to divide by zero, the processor generates Interrupt 0. The CPU suspends execution and, according to figure 18.1, calls the subroutine that starts in segment $284D at offset $00CE. When that subroutine finishes, the CPU returns to its original activity.

Fig. 18.1. *The addresses of the first 64 interrupt service routines.*

```
00 284D 00CE     10 0DA1 003D     20 0E94 2814     30 F308 7EEA
01 0070 07D3     11 F000 F84D     21 0E94 26EB     31 0000 0000
02 F000 E2C3     12 F000 F841     22 05B4 028F     32 0000 0000
03 0070 07D3     13 C800 01CF     23 284D 00D5     33 0000 0000
04 0070 07D3     14 F000 E739     24 284D 009D     34 0000 0000
05 F000 FF54     15 F000 F859     25 00F3 0A78     35 0000 0000
06 F000 FF23     16 F000 E82E     26 00F3 0AC6     36 0000 0000
07 F000 FF23     17 0E94 2565     27 00F3 32AB     37 0000 0000
08 F000 FEA5     18 F000 E720     28 00F3 087D     38 0000 0000
09 0E94 56FB     19 C800 014E     29 050C 02D1     39 0000 0000
0A F000 FF23     1A F000 FE6E     2A 0000 0000     3A 0000 0000
0B F000 FF23     1B 27EB 012F     2B 0000 0000     3B 0000 0000
0C F000 FF23     1C F000 FF53     2C 0000 0000     3C 0000 0000
0D C800 01BE     1D F000 F0A4     2D 0000 0000     3D 0000 0000
0E F000 EF57     1E 0000 0522     2E 05B4 0343     3E 0000 0000
0F 0070 07D3     1F F000 0000     2F 0000 0000     3F 284D 00C6
```

A quick glance reveals that a large number of entries in the interrupt vector table are empty. The rest of the table is almost completely unused.

Your PC might use different addresses. Some systems, for example, recognize that the interrupt vector table is intended to list subroutines that normally end with a return instruction. Instead of defining nil pointers as all zeros, these systems use the address of a subroutine containing nothing other than a return so that a call to an undefined interrupt will not hang up the machine.

Calling an Interrupt

Your Turbo Pascal program can execute any interrupt through the use of the `Intr` procedure. Its general form is as follows:

```
Intr( IntNumber, Regs );
```

`IntNumber` is the number of the interrupt selected from the interrupt vector table. `Regs` is a data structure of the following type:

```
Registers = record
              case Integer of
                  0: (AX,BX,CX,DX,BP,SI,DI,DS,ES,Flags: Word);
                  1: (AL,AH,BL,BH,CL,CH,DL,DH: Byte);
            end;
```

Many interrupts have subordinate functions or options; some interrupts return values upon completion. Although actual register use varies for each interrupt, the `Regs` record is always the mechanism used to pass arguments between your program and the called interrupt.

One of the most useful BIOS routines is Interrupt 5, the Print Screen function. Program INTSCR (listing 18.2) uses the `for` loop to fill the screen with numbers, then invokes Print Screen with the `Intr` procedure. Notice that for this call, no parameters are passed between the program and the BIOS code.

Listing 18.2

```
program IntScr;
uses Dos;
var
   i : word;
procedure PrintScreen;
var
   Regs : Registers;  { Dummy only }
begin
   Intr( 5, Regs );
end;
begin
   for i := 0 to 702 do write( i );
   PrintScreen;
end.
```

When the instruction is called, the processor looks up the address of the interrupt routine in the interrupt vector table. Because the table starts at the lowest point in memory (segment 0, offset 0) and consists of one segment and one offset word for each entry, you can determine the address of an interrupt routine by multiplying the number of the interrupt by 4. The address of the Interrupt 5 ISR is stored at $0000:$0014 (decimal 20). The processor then jumps to this location and executes the code of the interrupt routine. When the routine finishes, control is returned to the next line in the program.

Replacing an Interrupt

When Intel originally announced its design for the 8086, the company reserved the first 32 interrupts for its own use. Not all were used in the final product, so IBM felt it could redefine the usage of interrupts $05 to $1F. Intel continued to treat those interrupts as reserved, so conflicts inevitably arose that resulted in compatibility problems, especially for the 80286 and 80386.

For software to remain *downward compatible* (that is, for a program designed for the 80386 to run successfully on the 8086 as well), the IBM interrupt usage must be followed even when it conflicts with the design of the chip. For example, Intel included a sophisticated new opcode in its design of the 80286 (now used in the AT) that generates an Interrupt 5 whenever an index is outside the limits of an array. IBM uses Interrupt 5 for the Print Screen function, however, so when the new function is used on the 80286 and the range error occurs, the screen is printed.

Programs that rely on the advanced features of the 80286 and 80386 must replace each unwanted interrupt handler with a customized version.

However, it is not just sophisticated applications that install customized interrupts. In a normal Turbo Pascal application, division by zero aborts the program with a run-time error. (According to Murphy's Law, a program will terminate only after a significant amount of time has been invested in processing data but prior to the time when the final results are printed or saved to disk.)

Program ZERO1 (listing 18.3) demonstrates this phenomenon. It forces a division by zero prior to the completion of its processing.

Listing 18.3

```
program Zero1;
var
   Zero : byte;
begin
   Zero := 0;
   writeln( 10 div 2 );
   writeln( 1 div Zero );
   writeln( 30 div 4 );
   writeln( 72 div 7 );
end.
```

When ZERO1 executes, it produces the following:

```
5
Runtime error 200 at 0000:0045.
```

The third and fourth divisions are never performed. In ZERO1, the program's termination is not disastrous, but you can imagine how frustrating it would be if it occurred before you had time to print a report or save the file.

Division by zero is undefined, which means that there is no right answer. Essentially, the CPU is notifying you in the only way it can that your program contains a serious error that demands your immediate attention.

Although division by zero is fatal, it is not catastrophic. When the CPU encounters the situation, it generates Interrupt 0. By gaining control of that interrupt handler, you can arrange for a softer error message and still retain control of the program. You do this by writing your own interrupt routine and substituting it for the ISR that would otherwise be used by default. Writing interrupt routines is usually a systems task, but Turbo Pascal makes it easy.

An interrupt routine is written like an ordinary Turbo Pascal procedure, with two main differences. First, the reserved word `interrupt` must be used immediately after the header declaration. Second, every interrupt procedure must be declared with register parameters. The format of a customized handler is as follows:

```
procedure CustomISR( Flags,CS,IP,AX,BX,CX,DX,SI,DI,DS,ES,BP : word );
interrupt;
begin
.
.
.
   ...code...
.
.
.
end;
```

Some or all of the parameters can be omitted, beginning with `Flags` and moving toward `BP`, depending on which registers are needed. For example, if you need only the BX register, you might define the `procedure` declaration as follows:

```
procedure CustomISR( BX,CX,DX,SI,DI,DS,ES,BP : word );
```

If no registers are used to exchange data, no registers need to be declared as parameters. The examples in this book include all registers as a matter of form.

If your ISR is generated by a hardware interrupt, it cannot include any Turbo Pascal input, output, or dynamic memory allocation procedures, nor can it include any BIOS or DOS calls.

You probably want to modify the interrupt handler only for the duration of your program, so you should save the original address before installing your routine. Then, when your program terminates, you can restore the original address.

You use the Turbo Pascal procedure `GetIntVec` to retrieve the current address of an interrupt handler. Similarly, you use the `SetIntVec` procedure to modify the contents of the interrupt vector table.

Program ZERO2 (listing 18.4) demonstrates how to use the minimum amount of code to save the original Interrupt 0 address, replace it with the address of a customized handler, and restore the original address when the program terminates.

Listing 18.4

```
program Zero2;
uses Dos;
var
   Zero      : byte;
   SaveInt0 : pointer;
procedure ZeroDivide( Flags,CS,IP,AX,BX,CX,DX,SI,DI,DS,ES,BP : word );
interrupt;
begin
   writeln( 'You just divided by zero!' );
end;
begin
   GetIntVec( $00, SaveInt0 );
   SetIntVec( $00, @ZeroDivide );
   Zero := 0;
   writeln( 10 div 2 );
   writeln( 172 div zero );
   writeln( 30 div 4 );
   writeln( 72 div 7 );
   SetIntVec( $00, SaveInt0 );
end.
```

When ZERO2 executes, it produces the following:

```
5
You just divided by zero!
172
7
10
```

Notice that instead of aborting when the division by zero is encountered, the program simply displays a warning message. The division did not occur, so the original value of 172 is returned.

Installing an Interrupt

As you will see in the following example, there is little difference between replacing an interrupt handler and installing one of your own.

One thing to do is to identify a free address in the interrupt vector table. If you review the results of the INTTAB1 program (listing 18.1), you will notice that almost every entry in the table is available. Arbitrarily, select interrupt $3A. (A more general approach would be to pick a starting point, then slide up the table until you find an open address.)

The SCRISR1 program (listing 18.5) demonstrates how parameters can be passed to an ISR. The `ScreenISR` procedure can be used either to save or to restore up to three screen images. If `ScreenISR` is called with a 1, 2, or 3 in the AX register, the current screen image is saved in buffer position 1, 2, or 3. Any position number can be used; no special sequence is implied. If `ScreenISR` is called with a 4, 5, or 6 in the AX register, the program restores screens 1, 2, or 3, respectively.

Listing 18.5

```
program ScrISR1;
uses Crt,Dos;
const
   VideoSeg = $B800;
var
   i           : word;
   Regs        : Registers;
   VectorSave  : pointer;
   VideoArray  : array [ 1..3 ] of array [ 0..1999 ] of word;
procedure ScreenISR( Flags,CS,IP,AX,BX,CX,DX,SI,DI,DS,ES,BP :
                     word );
interrupt;
var
   i : word;
begin
   case AX of
```

continues

Listing 18.5 continued

```
      1..3 : for i := 0 to 1999 do
               VideoArray[ AX, i ] := MemW[ VideoSeg : i ];
      4..6 : for i := 0 to 1999 do
               MemW[ VideoSeg : i ] := VideoArray[ AX-3, i ];
   end;
end;
begin
   GetIntVec( $3A, VectorSave );
   SetIntVec( $3A, @ScreenISR );
   for i := 0 to 702 do write( i );
   Regs.AX := 1;
   Intr( $3A, Regs );
   GotoXY( 1, 10 );
     write( '                                        ' );
   GotoXY( 1, 11 );
     write( ' Status message line 1 appearing here ' );
   GotoXY( 1, 12 );
     write( ' Status message line 2 appearing here ' );
   GotoXY( 1, 13 );
     write( '                                        ' );
   Readln;
   Regs.AX := 4;
   Intr( $3A, Regs );
   Readln;
   SetIntVec( $3A, VectorSave );
end.
```

When SCRISR1 executes, it begins by filling the screen with digits. Then the current screen image is saved by a call to the `ScreenISR` procedure, after which the message in figure 18.2 is displayed.

After you press the Enter key, a second call to `ScreenISR` restores the original pattern of digits as in figure 18.3.

Disabling an Interrupt

When you boot your PC, the address for the overflow handler, Interrupt 4, is set to point to a procedure return instruction (technically, an IRET opcode). In other words, when an overflow interrupt is generated, the CPU performs a procedure call that does nothing other than return control to the next line of code in the original program.

Fig. 18.2. Original display provided by the SCRISR1 program.

```
01234567891011121314151617181920212223242526272829303132333435363738394041424344
45464748495051525354555657585960616263646566676869707172737475767778798081828384
85868788899091929394959697989910010110210310410510610710810911011111211311411511
61171181191201211221231241251261271281291301311321331341351361371381391401411421
43144145146147148149150151152153154155156157158159160161162163164165166167168169
17017117217317417517617717817918018118218318418518618718818919019119219319419519
61971981992002012022032042052062072082092102112122132142152162172182192202212222
23224225226227228229230231232233234235236237238239240241242243244245246247248249
25025125225325425525625725825926026126226326426526626726826927027127227327427527
                                      892902912922932942952962972982993003013023
 Status message line 1 appearing here 316317318319320321322323324325326327328329
 Status message line 2 appearing here 234334434534634734834935035135235335435535
                                      693703713723733743753763773783793803813823
83384385386387388389390391392393394395396397398399400401402403404405406407408409
41041141241341441541641741841942042142242342442542642742842943043143243343443543
64374384394404414424434444454464474484494504514524534544554564574584594604614624
63464465466467468469470471472473474475476477478479480481482483484485486487488489
49049149249349449549649749849950050150250350450550650750850951051151251351451551
65175185195205215225235245255265275285295305315325335345355365375385395405415425
43544545546547548549550551552553554555556557558559560561562563564565566567568569
57057157257357457557657757857958058158258358458558658758858959059159259359459559
65975985996006016026036046056066076086096106116126136146156166176186196206216226
23624625626627628629630631632633634635636637638639640641642643644645646647648649
65065165265365465565665765865966066166266366466566666766866967067167267367467567
6677678679680681682683684685686687688689690691692693694695696697698699700701702
```

Fig. 18.3. Restored image in the SCRISR1 program.

```
01234567891011121314151617181920212223242526272829303132333435363738394041424344
45464748495051525354555657585960616263646566676869707172737475767778798081828384
85868788899091929394959697989910010110210310410510610710810911011111211311411511
61171181191201211221231241251261271281291301311321331341351361371381391401411421
43144145146147148149150151152153154155156157158159160161162163164165166167168169
17017117217317417517617717817918018118218318418518618718818919019119219319419519
61971981992002012022032042052062072082092102112122132142152162172182192202212222
23224225226227228229230231232233234235236237238239240241242243244245246247248249
25025125225325425525625725825926026126226326426526626726826927027127227327427527
62772782792802812822832842852862872882892902912922932942952962972982993003013023
03304305306307308309310311312313314315316317318319320321322323324325326327328329
33033133233333433533633733833934034134234334434534634734834935035135235335435535
63573583593603613623633643653663673683693703713723733743753763773783793803813823
83384385386387388389390391392393394395396397398399400401402403404405406407408409
41041141241341441541641741841942042142242342442542642742842943043143243343443543
64374384394404414424434444454464474484494504514524534544554564574584594604614624
63464465466467468469470471472473474475476477478479480481482483484485486487488489
49049149249349449549649749849950050150250350450550650750850951051151251351451551
65175185195205215225235245255265275285295305315325335345355365375385395405415425
43544545546547548549550551552553554555556557558559560561562563564565566567568569
57057157257357457557657757857958058158258358458558658758858959059159259359459559
65975985996006016026036046056066076086096106116126136146156166176186196206216226
23624625626627628629630631632633634635636637638639640641642643644645646647648649
65065165265365465565665765865966066166266366466566666766866967067167267367467567
6677678679680681682683684685686687688689690691692693694695696697698699700701702
```

If, after careful thought, you want to disable an interrupt completely, the safest way is to replace the address of the unwanted interrupt with the default address of the overflow ISR. To disable the interrupt resulting from division by zero, define a pointer variable (here, `AddrWork`) and use the commands:

```
GetIntVec( $04, AddrWork );
SetIntVec( $00, AddrWork );
```

After these lines are executed, a division by zero will produce an unpredictable algebraic result, but it will not cause your program to abort.

The DISABLE1 program (listing 18.6) uses this technique to disable the Print Screen function temporarily.

Listing 18.6

```
program Disable1;
uses Dos;
var
   i          : word;
   SaveInt5 : pointer;    { Global }
procedure DisablePrintScreen;
var
   AddrInt4 : pointer;
begin
   GetIntVec( $05, SaveInt5 );
   GetIntVec( $04, AddrInt4 );
   SetIntVec( $05, AddrInt4 );
end;
procedure EnablePrintScreen;
begin
   SetIntVec( $05, SaveInt5 );
end;
begin
   for i := 0 to 702 do write( i );    { Fills the screen }
   writeln;
   writeln( 'Print Screen is enabled' );
   readln;
   DisablePrintScreen;
   writeln( 'Print Screen is disabled' );
   readln;
   EnablePrintScreen;
   writeln( 'Print Screen is enabled' );
   readln;
end.
```

When DISABLE1 executes, it fills the screen with numbers, then displays the first of its status messages, `Print Screen is enabled`. At this point, you can still send the screen image to the printer. After you press the Enter key, Interrupt 5 is disabled by having its vector rerouted to an empty routine. Print Screen will not operate during this phase. When you press the Enter key again, Interrupt 5 is restored. Press the Enter key once more to end the program.

Concerns about Redefining Interrupt Routines

Before you consider redefining every troublesome interrupt, there are a few things to keep in mind.

Every interrupt gets the CPU's full attention. Therefore, every interrupt must be able to tell the CPU precisely what it should do, then enable it to return smoothly to its original activity. A poorly written program (or one that has not been completely debugged) will probably "hang" the PC and force you to reboot or turn off the machine.

If you execute the wrong interrupt, you may encounter more serious problems, such as accidental damage to disk files, if not to the entire disk. Some problems are subtle; for example, you might unknowingly modify a portion of RAM that you will not use for another hour.

The bottom line is this: Take care when you work with interrupts. Think through the entire application. Test it incrementally. Do not include any potentially damaging line of code (a disk write, for example) until you have seen the results on the screen or printer. And most importantly, make backups frequently!

Summary

In this chapter, you learned that an interrupt is a signal that causes the CPU to suspend whatever it is doing and execute the code in one of 256 predefined procedures. Each of these procedures is called an interrupt service routine (ISR). The addresses of the ISRs are stored in the interrupt vector table, which begins at the bottom of the PC's memory.

You learned that interrupts can be triggered by either hardware or software. Hardware interrupts are generated by physical devices, such as the keyboard. Software interrupts are called directly by Turbo Pascal programs through the use of the `Intr` and `MsDos` procedures.

Most ISRs consist of standard DOS or BIOS routines. You learned, however, that Turbo Pascal provides several tools that you can use to create your own interrupt procedures. You saw that the addresses in the interrupt vector table can be changed to reference specially modified procedures in your own program. You can now install your own custom ISRs, and you now know how to replace or disable existing ISRs.

CHAPTER 19

Memory-Resident Programs

When Borland introduced SideKick in 1984, it was a turning point for the software industry. From that moment on, the use of the previously little-known set of *terminate-and-stay-resident (TSR)* DOS commands became the standard for programming convenience.

Although most commercial applications of TSRs incorporate extremely sophisticated memory management techniques that only people with systems-level programming skills can fully understand, the basic principles of TSRs are easy to follow.

This chapter discusses how you can use Turbo Pascal to write and install several simple but practical memory-resident programs.

Introduction to TSR Programs

DOS keeps a pointer to the memory address where it can load a program. When you run a series of programs, each one, in turn, begins at this same location.

In Chapter 12, you learned that the program segment prefix (PSP) contains the address of the top of the program's memory. Consider what would happen if, while a program was running, it copied its top-of-memory address into the special pointer that stores the location where DOS loads programs. Quite simply, DOS would be fooled into loading every subsequent program into the memory area *immediately above* the original program. Consequently, the original program would remain in memory while all subsequent programs are executed.

This is exactly what happens in a terminate-and-stay-resident program. TSRs replace the beginning program vector with the top-of-memory pointer. Every program executed after the TSR runs is loaded in the higher memory area and consequently does not overlay the memory used by the TSR program.

When you load several memory-resident programs (SideKick and Turbo Lightning, for example), each one uses this technique in turn, stacking one program on top of the other.

Using a TSR Program

Now that you have tricked DOS into preserving the TSR's memory area, you are faced with the challenge of how to access it.

As in all Turbo Pascal programs, the basic useful unit is the procedure. When you first run the TSR program, you could use the `@` operator to determine the address of the desired procedure, then write that address to a file. Any program you run later could read that file and execute the procedure with a far call. For each additional procedure and variable you want to access, you simply enlarge the data file by one record. In essence, the file is storing a table of pointers.

Now make one simplification. Instead of going to all the trouble of creating and then reading a pointer table, use one that is already available: the interrupt vector table. That way, if the procedure you want to make memory resident is written in the form of an interrupt service routine (ISR), any later program could access it with the `Intr` procedure.

An example should help. Chapter 18 showed that the SCRISR1 program could be used to save screen images. With a few changes, you can make the `ScreenISR` procedure memory resident.

Using the *Keep* Procedure

The Turbo Pascal `Keep` procedure terminates a program and allows it to stay resident in memory. Additionally, `Keep` takes a word-sized parameter and passes it to DOS in the form of a program exit code.

When `Keep` is called, it copies the top-of-memory pointer from the PSP into the vector that DOS uses to track the start of free memory. This effectively turns the top-of-memory location for the program that executed `Keep` into the bottom-of-memory for all subsequent programs.

By default, a Turbo Pascal program occupies all available free memory, so the top-of-memory pointer is set to the highest memory location in the PC. Consequently, any program that calls the `Keep` procedure must use the `{$M}` compiler directive to minimize heap usage. If you forget this step, you will have to reboot the computer.

For the same reason, you cannot run a would-be TSR program from the integrated environment. *Your* program, not TURBO.EXE, must determine the contents of the PSP. Always compile a TSR program to disk, exit the TURBO.EXE compiler completely, and execute the TSR program directly from DOS. Do not run a TSR program in Turbo's DOS shell.

`Keep` causes the entire program to remain resident. All global data, procedures, and program code are preserved. Therefore, the code required to insert the ISR into the interrupt vector table must be in a separate procedure from the ISR (or in the main program body).

*Keep*ing a Program

The SCRISR2 program (listing 19.1) contains the interrupt service routine and the code required to install it in memory. Arbitrarily, choose Interrupt $3A as the vector the ISR will use. Make sure that the vector you select on your machine is available; once installed, the ISR remains lodged in memory until you reboot. Unlike the self-contained SCRISR1 program in the preceding chapter, the $3A vector here is not being "borrowed" during the run of the program; it is being seized for the duration of your session on the PC. Compile SCRISR2 to disk and execute the program from DOS. Do *not* execute the program through Turbo's DOS shell.

Listing 19.1

```
program ScrISR2;
{$M 1024, 0, 0 }
uses Dos;
const
   VideoSeg = $B800;
```

continues

Listing 19.1 continued

```
var
   VideoArray : array [ 1..3 ] of array [ 0..1999 ] of word;
procedure ScreenISR( Flags,CS,IP,AX,BX,CX,DX,SI,DI,DS,ES,BP :
                     word );
interrupt;
var
   i : word;
begin
   case AX of
      1..3 : for i := 0 to 1999 do
                VideoArray[ AX, i ] := MemW[ VideoSeg : i ];
      4..6 : for i := 0 to 1999 do
                MemW[ VideoSeg : i ] := VideoArray[ AX-3, i ];
   end;
end;
begin
   SetIntVec( $3A, @ScreenISR );
   Keep( 0 );
end.
```

`SetIntVec` places the starting address of the `ScreenISR` procedure into the interrupt vector table. `Keep` terminates the program with an error code of zero (normal termination). Remember that although only the `ScreenISR` procedure responds to an interrupt, the entire program remains in memory. Consequently, the `VideoArray` screen array can be stored as a global variable outside the procedure.

The SCRISR3 program (listing 19.2) fills the screen with numbers, performs an Interrupt $3A to save the screen, displays messages, then performs a second Interrupt $3A to restore the screen. When it executes (assuming that the SCRISR2 program has already run), its output is identical to the SCRISR1 program in the preceding chapter.

Listing 19.2

```
program ScrISR3;
uses Crt,Dos;
var
   i    : word;
   Regs : Registers;
begin
```

```
    for i := 0 to 702 do write( i );
    Regs.AX := 1;
    Intr( $3A, Regs );
    GotoXY( 1, 10 );
      write( '                                    ' );
    GotoXY( 1, 11 );
      write( ' Status message line 1 appearing here ' );
    GotoXY( 1, 12 );
      write( ' Status message line 2 appearing here ' );
    GotoXY( 1, 13 );
      write( '                                    ' );
    Readln;
    Regs.AX := 4;
    Intr( $3A, Regs );
end.
```

Categories of TSRs

A TSR is classified as being either *active* or *passive*, depending on how you activate it.

Passive TSRs execute as part of the normal flow of a program. The `ScreenISR` procedure was passive; it ran only because it was explicitly called by another application.

The more interesting TSRs are active. Active TSRs are either constantly running or invoked by a combination of keystrokes (commonly called *hot keys*) that have no meaning to the current program. An active TSR will usually—but not always—suspend the execution of the program running in the foreground.

Creating a Clock TSR Program

Your PC keeps time with a 1.19318 MHz clock. This frequency was chosen so that 64K (65,536) pulses, or *ticks*, occur each hour. Each tick generates an Interrupt 8.

In other words, your PC undergoes an Interrupt 8 approximately 18.2 times per second. Fortunately, the PC is so fast, you will never notice such a trivial inconvenience.

When each Interrupt 8 occurs, its ISR increments the four bytes beginning with memory location $0040:$006C. The word beginning at $0040:$006E contains the hour, and the word beginning at $0040:$006C contains the number of ticks in the current hour. The last action taken by the Interrupt 8 ISR is the generation of an Interrupt $1C, commonly called the *timer tick*.

When your PC first boots, Interrupt $1C does not have an ISR; the entry in the interrupt vector table points to a return instruction. By installing your own ISR in Interrupt $1C, you can gain control of your PC 18.2 times per second!

Using the Timer Interrupt

This process is best illustrated with an example. The CLOCK program (listing 19.3) displays a clock in the upper right corner of the screen in HH:MM:SS format. It first initializes the `Hour`, `Minute`, and `Second` variables, then installs the `ShowTime` ISR at Interrupt $1C. From then on, `ShowTime` is called 18.2 times per second and increments the `TimerTick` counter at the same rate. After every eighteenth tick, the `Second` counter is incremented. After the sixtieth increment of `Second`, the `Minute` counter is incremented. Finally, after the sixtieth increment of `Minute`, the `Hour` counter is incremented. The time is written directly to video memory once a second. Compile CLOCK to disk, and execute it directly from DOS. Do *not* execute the program through Turbo's DOS shell option.

Listing 19.3

```
program Clock;
{$M 1024, 0, 1024 }
uses Dos;
const
   VideoSeg = $B800;
var
   Hour, Minute, Second, Sec100, TimerTick : word;
procedure ShowTime( Flags,CS,IP,AX,BX,CX,DX,SI,DI,DS,ES,BP :
                          word );
interrupt;
begin
   Inc( TimerTick );
   if TimerTick = 18 then begin
      TimerTick := 0;
```

```
        Inc( Second );
        if Second = 60 then begin
           Second := 0;
           Inc( Minute );
           if Minute = 60 then begin
              Minute := 0;
              Inc( Hour );
              if Hour = 25 then Hour := 0;
           end;
        end;
        Mem[ VideoSeg : 144 ] := 48 + Hour div 10;
        Mem[ VideoSeg : 146 ] := 48 + Hour mod 10;
        Mem[ VideoSeg : 148 ] := ord(':');
        Mem[ VideoSeg : 150 ] := 48 + Minute div 10;
        Mem[ VideoSeg : 152 ] := 48 + Minute mod 10;
        Mem[ VideoSeg : 154 ] := ord(':');
        Mem[ VideoSeg : 156 ] := 48 + Second div 10;
        Mem[ VideoSeg : 158 ] := 48 + Second mod 10;
     end;
  end;
  begin
     TimerTick := 0;
     GetTime( Hour, Minute, Second, Sec100 );
     SetIntVec( $1C, @ShowTime );
     Keep( 0 );
  end.
```

Calling BIOS Routines

Writing directly to video memory is something of a pain. Why not just use ordinary Turbo Pascal routines like `GotoXY` and `write`?

The answer is that DOS routines are not reentrant. Instead of using the stack to save separate sets of data, each DOS routine stores data in the same set of global variables. If a routine is called and stores a return address, for example, and the ISR interrupts the CPU and calls the routine a second time, then the original return address is overwritten, the first routine transfers control of the program to the wrong location, and the system probably crashes.

When the CLOCK program is run, the `ShowTime` ISR executes 18.2 times per second, or 65,536 times in an hour. If you called a routine like

GotoXY or write that often, the odds are high that sometime during the program's run, the GotoXY or write would try to use a DOS routine that is already in use.

In general, then, an active TSR must ensure that it does not call a BIOS function that is being executed by the program running when the TSR takes control. Several technical means exist to accomplish this, but you can avoid the problem by writing directly to video memory.

Note that this problem arises only when the TSR—like the CLOCK program—is triggered by a hardware interrupt. Software interrupts called from and controlled by your program are different; every line of code prior to the Intr call must be complete before the Intr instruction is reached. Therefore, in a software interrupt, you can use any DOS, BIOS, or Turbo Pascal procedure you want because you can be confident that the routine you want is not currently in use in another part of your machine. Just do not allow your ISR to call itself.

Accessing the Timer

Because the CLOCK program rounds the 18.2-ticks-per-second rate, you may object to the resulting 40-seconds-per-hour error. Unlike the BIOS limitation, this is a problem you can do something about. The revised program, CLOCK0 (listing 19.4), accesses the system clock by reading the four timer bytes beginning at $0040:$006C. (In principle, the mod 24 and mod 60 operations are superfluous, but they help you to avoid the inevitable one- or two-seconds-per-hour rounding error.) Compile CLOCK0 to disk, and execute it directly from DOS. Do *not* execute it through Turbo's DOS shell option.

Listing 19.4

```
program Clock0;
{$M 1024, 0, 1024 }
uses Dos;
const
   VideoSeg = $B800;
var
   TimerTick : byte;
   Hour      : word;
   Minute,
   Second    : longint;
```

```
procedure ShowTime( Flags,CS,IP,AX,BX,CX,DX,SI,DI,DS,ES,BP :
                    word );
interrupt;
begin
   Inc( TimerTick );
   if TimerTick = 18 then begin
      TimerTick := 0;
      Hour   := MemW[ $40:$6E ] mod 24;
      Minute := MemW[ $40:$6C ];
      Minute := ((Minute * 5) div 5461) mod 60;
      Second := MemW[ $40:$6C ];
      Second := ((Second * 5) div 91) mod 60;
      Mem[ VideoSeg : 144 ] := 48 + Hour div 10;
      Mem[ VideoSeg : 146 ] := 48 + Hour mod 10;
      Mem[ VideoSeg : 148 ] := ord(':');
      Mem[ VideoSeg : 150 ] := 48 + Minute div 10;
      Mem[ VideoSeg : 152 ] := 48 + Minute mod 10;
      Mem[ VideoSeg : 154 ] := ord(':');
      Mem[ VideoSeg : 156 ] := 48 + Second div 10;
      Mem[ VideoSeg : 158 ] := 48 + Second mod 10;
   end;
end;
begin
   TimerTick := 0;
   SetIntVec( $1C, @ShowTime );
   Keep( 0 );
end.
```

Note that `Minute` is multiplied by 5, then divided by 5461. Similarly, `Second` is multiplied by 5, then divided by 91. This seemingly insane process is an integer approximation of the number of ticks in a minute and second, given that there are 65,536 ticks in an entire hour.

$$\frac{65{,}536}{60} \approx\approx \frac{5{,}461}{5} \quad \text{and} \quad \frac{65{,}536}{60 \times 60} \approx\approx \frac{91}{5}$$

In this technique, the errors are not cumulative. You will use this idea again shortly.

Notice also that even though the `ShowTime` procedure is called 18.2 times per second, you change the clock display only once every 18 ticks.

Adding an Alarm

You can add a simple alarm feature to make the clock produce a tone at a predetermined time. The ALARM program (listing 19.5) gives a sample. Compile ALARM to disk, and execute it directly from DOS. Do *not* execute it through Turbo's DOS shell option.

Listing 19.5

```
program Alarm;
{$M 1024, 0, 1024 }
uses Dos, Crt;
const
   VideoSeg = $B800;
var
   HourW, MinuteW, SecondW, Sec100W,
   TimerTick, AlarmHour, AlarmMinute : word;
   Hour, Minute, Second              : longint;
procedure ShowTime( Flags,CS,IP,AX,BX,CX,DX,SI,DI,DS,ES,BP :
                    word );
interrupt;
begin
   Inc( TimerTick );
   if TimerTick = 18 then begin
      TimerTick := 0;
      Hour   := MemW[ $40:$6E ] mod 24;
      Minute := MemW[ $40:$6C ];
      Minute := ((Minute * 5) div 5461) mod 60;
      Second := MemW[ $40:$6C ];
      Second := ((Second * 5) div 91) mod 60;
      Mem[ VideoSeg : 144 ] := 48 + Hour div 10;
      Mem[ VideoSeg : 146 ] := 48 + Hour mod 10;
      Mem[ VideoSeg : 148 ] := ord(':');
      Mem[ VideoSeg : 150 ] := 48 + Minute div 10;
      Mem[ VideoSeg : 152 ] := 48 + Minute mod 10;
      Mem[ VideoSeg : 154 ] := ord(':');
      Mem[ VideoSeg : 156 ] := 48 + Second div 10;
      Mem[ VideoSeg : 158 ] := 48 + Second mod 10;
      if (Hour   = AlarmHour   ) and
         (Minute = AlarmMinute) and
         (Second = 1          ) then begin
            Sound( 392 ); Delay( 300 );
            Sound( 296 ); Delay( 200 );
```

```
            NoSound;
         end;
   end;
end;
begin
   TimerTick := 0;
   GetTime( HourW, MinuteW, SecondW, Sec100W );
   writeln( 'The time is now ', HourW, ':', MinuteW );
   repeat
      write( 'Set the hour:    ' );
      readln( AlarmHour );
   until AlarmHour in [ 0..23 ];
   repeat
      write( 'Set the minute: ');
      readln( AlarmMinute );
   until AlarmMinute in [ 0..59 ];
   writeln( 'Alarm clock will ring at ', AlarmHour, ':',
            AlarmMinute );
   SetIntVec( $1C, @ShowTime );
   Keep( 0 );
end.
```

ALARM acts like the CLOCK0 program except it prompts for the alarm time in hours and minutes and produces a tone when the alarm goes off.

> The CLOCK, CLOCK0, and ALARM programs all write to the screen by moving data directly to video memory. Consequently, you may need to incorporate the snow eliminator techniques illustrated in NOSNOW1 and NOSNOW2, listings 17.3 and 17.4, respectively.

Calling an Active TSR

After a passive TSR is installed, it does nothing except wait for an interrupt. An active TSR, on the other hand, either runs continuously or must forever be testing for a triggering event.

So far you have seen how passive TSRs and continuously running TSRs work. Now it is time to consider how a TSR can be triggered.

Using Predefined Interrupts

Through your keyboard, you have immediate access to three interrupts: PrintScreen (Interrupt 5), Ctrl-Break (Interrupt $1B), and Ctrl-C (Interrupt $23). Each can be redefined for your purposes.

Remember that Ctrl-C and Ctrl-Break are two different animals. The original purpose of Ctrl-C was to interrupt a process "softly," after the next `write` statement. Ctrl-Break was intended to be more brutal; the interruption occurs immediately, without regard for what the main program is doing at the time of the call. The Ctrl-C and Ctrl-Break ISRs are too important to modify. The PrintScreen interrupt, however, can be redefined harmlessly.

If you are like most PC users, you may want to capture a screen image on disk instead of sending it to the printer. For example, you may want to include the screen image of a menu along with the program's documentation. Or you may want to include the image of a spreadsheet as part of a memo. Such a feature is also useful if you write a book on Turbo Pascal and need a general tool to illustrate the output of your programming examples.

The SNAP program (listing 19.6) redefines the PrintScreen vector, Interrupt 5. After SNAP is installed, the PrintScreen command (Shift-PrtSC) copies the current screen image into `VideoArray` and increments the `Image` counter. SNAP is designed to hold only three screens, but you could modify your version to accommodate more. Compile SNAP to disk, and execute it directly from DOS. Do *not* execute it through Turbo's DOS shell option.

Listing 19.6

```
program Snap;
{$M 1024, 0, 1024 }
uses Dos;
const
   VideoSeg = $B800;
var
   i,
   Image       : word;
   VideoArray : array [ 0..2 ] of array [ 0..1999 ] of byte;
procedure TakeThePicture( Flags,CS,IP,AX,BX,CX,DX,SI,DI,DS,ES,BP :
                          word );
interrupt;
begin
   if Image < 3 then begin
      for i := 0 to 1999 do
```

```
         VideoArray[ Image, i ] := Mem[ VideoSeg : 2*i ];
      Inc( Image );
   end;
end;
begin
   Image := 0;
   SetIntVec( $05, @TakeThePicture );
   SetIntVec( $3A, @Image );
   SetIntVec( $3B, @VideoArray );
   writeln( 'Snap program now installed' );
   Keep( 0 );
end.
```

Notice that this program is redefining three vectors. Interrupt 5 contains the address of the `TakeThePicture` procedure; when PrintScreen is invoked, `TakeThePicture` is executed. The address of `Image` is stored in vector $3A and the address of `VideoArray` is stored in vector $3B. After SNAP is installed, any program you run later can use the $3A and $3B vectors to determine how many screens you saved and what they contained when you saved them.

Accessing TSR Data

The SNAP program managed to save information in the memory area of the TSR program. The DEVELOP program (listing 19.7) retrieves the data. DEVELOP picks up the addresses from the $3A and $3B vectors, points to the `Image` variable, and checks to see if any screens were saved. If screens are available, the program appends them to the file called `ScreenFile`. (DEVELOP creates the file if it does not already exist.) Its final act is to reset the `Image` counter to 0 so that even more screens can be captured. Notice that a screen image is actually a continuous series of bytes. To make the screens more manageable, DEVELOP adds end-of-line markers to the file (through the `writeln`) every 80 characters.

Listing 19.7

```
program Develop;
uses Dos;
type
   ArrayType = array [ 1..3 ] of array [ 0..1999 ] of byte;
```

continues

Listing 19.7 continued

```
var
   Image       : ^word;
   VideoArray  : ^ArrayType;
   i,
   Screen      : word;
   Pntr        : pointer;
   ScreenFile  : text;
   FileName    : string;
begin
   GetIntVec( $3A, Pntr );
   Image := Pntr;
   GetIntVec( $3B, Pntr );
   VideoArray := Pntr;
   case Image^ of
        0 : writeln( 'No screens were found!' );
     1..3 : begin
               FileName := 'Scrn.DAT';
               Assign( ScreenFile, FileName );
               {$I-} Append( ScreenFile ); {$I+}
               if IOResult <> 0 then
                  Rewrite( ScreenFile );
               for Screen := 1 to Image^ do
                  for i := 0 to 1999 do begin
                     write( ScreenFile,
                            chr( VideoArray^[ Screen, i ] ) );
                     if (i + 1) mod 80 = 0 then
                        writeln( ScreenFile );
                  end;
               writeln( Image^, ' screens were written to ',
                        FileName );
               Image^ := 0;    { reset }
               Close( ScreenFile );
            end;
     else   writeln( 'The SNAP program hasn''t been installed.' );
   end;
end.
```

Consider what you just did. The program used two open slots in the interrupt vector table to store the addresses of TSR variables, then used a second program to read and modify them. With this technique, you can devise applications that allow several independent memory-resident programs to communicate with one another.

Notice, though, that you did not combine the functions of the two programs, immediately putting the screen image to disk. Here again, the program ran into a problem with hardware interrupts. You cannot be sure what (if any) DOS or BIOS interrupt is running when PrintScreen is invoked. Consequently, you cannot use Turbo Pascal routines, like `write` and `writeln`, that rely heavily on DOS and BIOS services. The `TakeThePicture` ISR in SNAP contains only nonrecursive, nonreentrant code.

Defining Hot Keys

Redefining PrintScreen, Ctrl-Break, and Ctrl-C usually has limited appeal. For one thing, these three interrupts have other valid (and perhaps more useful) applications. It is quite conceivable (and, of course, inevitable) that you will want both an immediate printed copy and a disk version of the same screen image. The challenge is to find a way to use other keys as triggers.

Remember how the CLOCK program used the Timer Tick (Interrupt $1C) to tally up the passing seconds. You can take advantage of the frequency of the Timer Tick interrupt to scan for the presence of certain key combinations.

Chapter 9 showed how the Keyboard Status byte at $0040:$0017 contains bits that indicate the state (pressed or not pressed) of the various toggle keys. If you test for certain bit combinations in an ISR that is executed as a result of the Timer Tick interrupt, you have a means of detecting when users press hot keys.

The SNAP1 program (listing 19.8) installs the `TestHotKey` procedure in vector $1C. As a result, `TestHotKey` tests, at the rate of 18.2 times per second, whether the Alt key and Right-Shift key have both been pressed. If these two keys are pressed simultaneously, the screen image is saved. (If this pair is not convenient for you, feel free to use any other combination.)

When you activate the routine, you will undoubtedly hold the keys down longer than 1/18.2 seconds. Consequently, the keys should be ignored for a short period of time after the save is complete. By comparing the `TimeNow` and `TimeHold` variables, you ensure that the screen copying process is performed no faster than once every 91 ticks, which works out to around five seconds. (Of course, you should also test for when the hour changes, but as a practical matter, this can be ignored.)

Compile SNAP1 to disk, and execute it directly from DOS. Do *not* execute it through Turbo's DOS shell option. You can execute the DEVELOP program to copy any captured screens to disk.

Listing 19.8

```
program Snap1;
{$M 1024, 0, 1024 }
uses Dos;
const   VideoSeg = $B800;
var
   i,
   Image       : word;
   VideoArray  : array [ 0..2 ] of array [ 0..1999 ] of byte;
   TimeHold    : integer;
   TimeNow     : integer absolute $0040:$006C;
procedure TestHotKey( Flags,CS,IP,AX,BX,CX,DX,SI,DI,DS,ES,BP :
                      word );
interrupt;
begin
   if Image < 3 then
      if abs(TimeNow-TimeHold) > 91 then { 18.2 * 5 }
         if Mem[ $0040 : $0017 ] and $09 = $09 then begin
                                                   { Alt-R Shift }
            for i := 0 to 1999 do
               VideoArray[ Image, i ] := Mem[ VideoSeg : 2*i ];
            Inc( Image );
            TimeHold := TimeNow;
         end;
end;
begin
   Image := 0;
   TimeHold := TimeNow;
   SetIntVec( $1C, @TestHotKey );
   SetIntVec( $3A, @Image );
   SetIntVec( $3B, @VideoArray );
   writeln( 'Snap program now installed' );
   Keep( 0 );
end.
```

Commercial TSR Programs

If you have a commercial memory-resident (TSR) program on your PC, you might have noticed that you were able to invoke it even while running the programs in this chapter. Clearly, TSR programs such as SideKick and

Turbo Lightning use some triggering method other than overwriting the Interrupt $1C vector.

Most commercially available memory-resident programs intercept the keyboard BIOS at Interrupt 9. They do this by replacing the entry in the interrupt vector table with the address of one of their own procedures, which identifies the key or keys being pressed. At the end of the procedure, the TSRs chain to the original BIOS routine.

In a similar fashion, commercial TSR programs intercept other interrupts and test when nonreentrant BIOS routines are executing. The TSR then "pops up" only when all BIOS routines are in a safe state.

As you might imagine, this is a complicated process beyond the scope of this book. Nevertheless, you can see from the examples presented in this chapter how—with few restrictions—Turbo Pascal can be used to implement extremely useful memory-resident programs.

Summary

In this chapter, you learned how to develop terminate-and-stay-resident (TSR) programs.

In Chapter 12, you learned that the program segment prefix (PSP) contains a pointer to the address of the highest memory location used by the program. The Turbo Pascal `Keep` procedure copies the contents of this top-of-memory field into the special pointer that DOS uses to store the memory location where a program is loaded. As a result, every program that runs after the `Keep` procedure has executed will be loaded into the memory area immediately above the TSR program. Consequently, the TSR program remains in memory while all subsequent programs are executed.

Because the `Keep` procedure causes the entire TSR program to remain resident, all global data, procedures, and program code are preserved. You saw that the addresses of these procedures and data can be stored in the interrupt vector table and accessed by any later program.

You learned that a TSR is either passive or active depending on how it is activated. A passive TSR executes only when specifically called by another Turbo Pascal program. An active TSR is either constantly running or invoked by pressing a special combination of keystrokes called hot keys. You learned how active TSRs test for hot keys. Several useful programs that demonstrate these features were presented.

CHAPTER 20

Object-Oriented Programming

There is an old saying about life that applies equally well to programming: "If the only tool you have is a hammer, you tend to think of all problems as nails."

By now, you know that one of the most powerful software development tools is structured programming. But even the best tool cannot be used in every situation.

Structured programming forces you to express problems in terms of control structures: sequence, selection, and repetition operations. Even procedures and functions are viewed as free-standing, self-contained control structures. Little or no attention is paid to the design of the program's data.

In the real world, however, data structure is as important as data flow. Almost any problem can be viewed as a collection of logical entities that exchange information with one another.

Object-oriented programming is a technique in which you can directly represent entities as a hierarchy of *objects* and the information exchange as a set of *methods*. An object-oriented program balances control and data structures and consequently is a more natural model of the problem it is intended to solve.

This chapter is an introduction to object-oriented programming (OOP). Do not worry if the ideas take time to sink in. Eventually, they will.

Newcomers have less difficulty with OOP concepts than do experienced programmers. This situation is similar to the way in which people whose first computer language is Pascal have less trouble understanding structured design than do people who learned first to program in BASIC. After a little practice, you will probably discover that object-oriented programming is far easier and more intuitive than the traditional Pascal design techniques you have been using.

Structured Design and Object-Oriented Programming

At this point, you are probably confused. After all, structured programming was the reason that Pascal was developed, and the value of structured programming can clearly be measured by the enormous popularity enjoyed by the first five releases of Turbo Pascal.

So why do we need object-oriented programming? This section begins to answer that question by considering some of the disadvantages of the structured approach.

Limitations of Structured Design

Imagine that you have been assigned to computerize the way your company tracks the costs of carpentry, painting, and other building repair work. In the present system, any department manager can request these services by submitting a work order to the Central Construction department. Ideally, the costs associated with completing the work order should be charged back to the requesting department.

There are three components of work order charges: labor, materials, and overhead. Labor expenses are determined by the Payroll department. Material expenses are tallied by the Warehouse. Overhead expenses are calculated by the Central Construction department. Finally, the labor, material, and overhead expense components are totaled by the Property Accounting department.

You kick off your project by interviewing the supervisors of the Payroll, Warehouse, Central Construction, and Property Accounting departments. Each supervisor, in turn, summarizes the mechanics of the services performed in his or her area:

- *Input*. "At the beginning of each day, week, or month, we get the such-and-such form from the so-and-so department." You are directed to stacks of documents, such as time cards, work order forms, and material requisitions.
- *Processes*. The services of each department are outlined. "We multiply the quantity used by the unit cost."
- *Output*. "When we are done," each supervisor says, pointing toward stacks of summary reports, "we send these forms over to so-and-so."

At the end of your interviews, you know exactly what data elements each department receives, exactly what actions each department takes, and exactly what data elements each department generates.

Remembering the principles of structured design, you set out to define record layouts that correspond closely with the results of the interviews. Simple, you say. A small number of giant records can hold all the data elements, and one giant program (essentially, a single database manager) can consolidate all the individual activities. You put it all together, present it to the supervisors, and recommend that Property Accounting maintain the entire system.

You sit back, waiting for compliments, but instead you are deluged with complaints. In your centralized design, every record contains fields that all the departments consider confidential and proprietary. Consequently, no department is willing to allow any other department to access any of the records in the database. The Payroll department cannot add a new employee or change a confidential hourly pay rate, the Warehouse department cannot reconcile its monthly inventories, the Central Construction department cannot enter work order progress reports. The Property Accounting department does not want to be responsible for entering and editing data supplied by the other departments. In short, no one likes it.

You followed the traditional approach: you talked with all the users to identify what information they need, what data manipulations they perform, and what information they provide. You consolidated all the data and structured the design around how it flows. What went wrong?

Simply, the consolidated data structure overlooked the fact that each department is responsible not only for performing its own processes, but also for *maintaining its own data*. From a programming standpoint, it is improper to assume that all data can be regarded as global.

Advantages of Object-Oriented Design

In the real world, a system is not a single entity with separate processes acting on common data. Instead, a real-world system is a collection of separate entities, or objects, each of which performs its own processes on its own data. In other words, an *object* is a set of private data elements and the public procedures and functions that act on those data elements.

Think of an object as a department in a company. Each department is responsible for maintaining the quality and integrity of the information it produces and protects. Personnel from another department cannot just wander over and adjust numbers. Information from another area is officially received and acknowledged only when a memo, form, or other report is sent.

Another common real-world object is your checking account. Your bank balance, which is unquestionably private data, can be changed only when you make a deposit, write a check, or pay bank charges. All of these events are carefully controlled: you fill out deposit slips, sign all your checks, and receive bank statements.

Object-oriented programming is a design philosophy that recognizes the relationship between data (variables, constants, and types) and processes (procedures and functions). In structured programming, you approach a problem by asking, "What data structure should I use?" In object-oriented programming, you ask, "What kinds of objects describe the process?"

Developing Programs with Objects

It is important to remember that the word *object* does not mean a three-dimensional physical being. Rather, an object is anything that you want to define with both data and subroutines. *Object-oriented design* is simply the process of identifying objects and the data and processes that are natural for those objects.

For example, suppose that you want to use object-oriented design to develop a program that displays different shapes on the screen, but you do not know which shapes you might want to draw. Using an object-oriented approach, all you need to do is think about the general requirements of the program. In other words, think of a shape *as an object*. What data and processes are common to all shapes?

First, all shapes need data to define position and size. For example, a circle has a center point and a radius; a rectangle can be described with upper left and lower right coordinates. Consequently, each object must contain the data elements peculiar to the selected shape. In addition, the shape object should contain a general-purpose routine to `Initialize` the data.

Second, shapes have basic style characteristics, such as color and fill pattern. Hence, the shape object needs data to store these characteristics, and it needs a routine, which could be called `SelectStyle`, to select these characteristics.

Third, the shapes must be produced. A convenient name for a routine that does this is `Draw`.

So, in general, displaying any shape object consists of calling the three routines `Initialize`, `SelectStyle`, and `Draw`. It does not matter what shape you choose, although different parameters might be required depending on the desired shape.

Even before Borland introduced Version 5.5, objects could be developed in Turbo Pascal through the use of units. Let us use this technique to consider how you can implement the two shape objects `circle` and `rectangle`.

Unit `Object1` in listing 20.1 defines all the necessary data and the `Initialize`, `SelectStyle`, and `Draw` procedures for producing a doughnut-like circle. Notice that `Initialize` is called with three parameters: the X-coordinate and Y-coordinate of the center point of the circle and the radius of the circle. `Initialize` also defines a default value for the `Color` variable. `SelectStyle` requires only the desired drawing color. The `Draw` procedure displays the circle.

Listing 20.1

```
unit Object1;
interface
   var
      x, y          : integer;
      Radius, Color : word;
   procedure Initialize( Xcoord, Ycoord : integer; RadSize : word );
   procedure SelectStyle( ColorChoice : word );
   procedure Draw;
implementation
```

continues

Listing 20.1 continued

```
   uses Graph;
   procedure Initialize;
   begin
      x := Xcoord;
      y := Ycoord;
      Radius := RadSize;
      Color := GetMaxColor;
   end;
   procedure SelectStyle;
   begin
      Color := ColorChoice;
   end;
   procedure Draw;
   var
      Ring : word;
   begin
      SetColor( Color );
      for Ring := 2 * (Radius div 3) to Radius do
         Circle( x, y, Ring );
   end;
end.
```

The Object2 unit in listing 20.2 defines all the necessary data and the Initialize, SelectStyle, and Draw procedures for producing a filled rectangle. Notice that this version of Initialize is called with four parameters: the X- and Y-coordinates of the upper left and lower right corners. Initialize also defines default values for the Pattern and Color variables. The new version of SelectStyle requires two parameters: the fill pattern and the desired color. The Draw procedure displays the rectangle.

Listing 20.2

```
unit Object2;
interface
   var
      x1, y1, x2, y2 : integer;
      Pattern, Color : word;
   procedure Initialize( UpLeftX, UpLeftY, LowRightX, LowRightY : integer );
   procedure SelectStyle( PatternChoice, ColorChoice : word );
   procedure Draw;
```

```
implementation
   uses Graph;
   procedure Initialize;
   begin
      x1 := UpLeftX;
      y1 := UpLeftY;
      x2 := LowRightX;
      y2 := LowRightY;
      Pattern := SolidFill;
      Color := GetMaxColor;
   end;
   procedure SelectStyle;
   begin
      Color := ColorChoice;
      Pattern := PatternChoice;
   end;
   procedure Draw;
   begin
      SetFillStyle( Pattern, Color );
      Bar3D( x1, y1, x2, y2, 0, TopOff );    { No depth and no top }
   end;
end.
```

The SHAPEOBJ program in listing 20.3 uses the `Object1` and `Object2` units to display a circle and a rectangle, respectively. Notice that even though both units have `Initialize`, `SelectStyle`, and `Draw` procedures, each routine can be identified easily by prefacing the name of the routine with the name of the unit. For example, the statement

```
Object1.Draw;
```

executes the `Draw` procedure in the `Object1` unit.

Listing 20.3

```
program ShapeObj;
uses Graph, Object1, Object2;
var
   Driver, Mode : integer;
begin
   {*********************}
   { Initialize graphics }
   {*********************}
```

continues

Listing 20.3 continued

```
   Driver := Detect;
   InitGraph( Driver, Mode, 'C:\TP' );
   {******************}
   { Display a circle }
   {******************}
   Object1.Initialize( GetMaxX div 5, GetMaxY div 2,   { Center }
                       GetMaxX div 5 );                { Radius }
   Object1.SelectStyle( Blue );
   Object1.Draw;
   {*********************}
   { Display a rectangle }
   {*********************}
   Object2.Initialize( 3 * (GetMaxX div 5),      { Upper left x }
                       GetMaxY div 4,            { Upper left y }
                       4 * (GetMaxX div 5),      { Lower right x }
                       3 * (GetMaxY div 4) );    { Lower right y }
   Object2.SelectStyle( CloseDotFill, Green );
   Object2.Draw;
   {********************}
   { Terminate graphics }
   {********************}
   readln;
   CloseGraph;
end.
```

The images produced by the SHAPEOBJ program can be seen in figure 20.1.

Using the Object Type Declaration

Through the use of units, each shape object consists of private memory with a public interface. However, using a separately compiled program unit to define an object has its disadvantages. Fortunately, beginning with Version 5.5, Turbo Pascal allows objects to be directly defined as distinct data types.

Fig. 20.1. Output produced by the SHAPEOBJ program.

Declaring Objects

An *object declaration* in Turbo Pascal can be regarded as a special form of record structure that contains both data and the algorithms that operate on the data. You declare an object by using the reserved word `object` in place of the word `record`.

For example, the circular object can be defined as follows:

```
CircleShape = object
   x, y          : integer;
   Radius, Color : word;
   procedure Initialize( Xcoord, Ycoord : integer; RadSize :
                         word );
   procedure SelectStyle( ColorChoice : word );
   procedure Draw;
end;
```

Similarly, the rectangular object can be defined in this manner:

```
RectangleShape = object
   x1, y1, x2, y2 : integer;
   Pattern, Color : word;
   procedure Initialize( UpLeftX, UpLeftY, LowRightX,
                         LowRightY : integer );
   procedure SelectStyle( PatternChoice, ColorChoice : word );
   procedure Draw;
end;
```

You have probably noticed the similarities between the declarations of these two objects and the format of the interface sections of the `Object1` and `Object2` units. Each object consists of data followed by the headers of the subroutines that operate on the data. In object-oriented programming terminology, combining data with procedures and functions in the same declaration is called *encapsulation*.

You can use an object type just like you use an ordinary record. The `Object1` and `Object2` identifiers can be declared as a `CircleShape` object and a `RectangleShape` object, respectively, through the following standard formats:

```
var
   Object1 : CircleShape;
   Object2 : RectangleShape;
```

The definition of an object is frequently called a *class*. `Object1` and `Object2` are called *instances* of the `CircleShape` and `RectangleShape` classes, respectively.

To avoid any confusion from using identical procedure names, the individual `Initialize`, `SelectStyle`, and `Draw` procedures for `CircleShape` are renamed

```
procedure CircleShape.Initialize;
procedure CircleShape.SelectStyle;
procedure CircleShape.Draw;
```

and the `Initialize`, `SelectStyle`, and `Draw` procedures for `RectangleShape` are renamed

```
procedure RectangleShape.Initialize;
procedure RectangleShape.SelectStyle;
procedure RectangleShape.Draw;
```

The complete program is shown in the SHPOBJ2 program, listing 20.4.

Listing 20.4

```
program ShpObj2;
uses Graph;
{===============================================================}
type
   CircleShape = object
      x, y          : integer;
      Radius, Color : word;
      procedure Initialize( Xcoord, Ycoord : integer; RadSize :
                            word );
      procedure SelectStyle( ColorChoice : word );
      procedure Draw;
   end;
   RectangleShape = object
      x1, y1, x2, y2 : integer;
      Pattern, Color : word;
      procedure Initialize( UpLeftX, UpLeftY, LowRightX,
                            LowRightY : integer );
      procedure SelectStyle( PatternChoice, ColorChoice : word );
      procedure Draw;
   end;
{===============================================================}
procedure CircleShape.Initialize;
begin
   x := Xcoord;
   y := Ycoord;
   Radius := RadSize;
   Color := GetMaxColor;
end;
procedure CircleShape.SelectStyle;
begin
   Color := ColorChoice;
end;
procedure CircleShape.Draw;
var
   Ring : word;
begin
   SetColor( Color );
   for Ring := 2 * (Radius div 3) to Radius do
      Circle( x, y, Ring );
end;
```

continues

Listing 20.4 continued

```
{===============================================================}
procedure RectangleShape.Initialize;
begin
   x1 := UpLeftX;
   y1 := UpLeftY;
   x2 := LowRightX;
   y2 := LowRightY;
   Pattern := SolidFill;
   Color := GetMaxColor;
end;
procedure RectangleShape.SelectStyle;
begin
   Color := ColorChoice;
   Pattern := PatternChoice;
end;
procedure RectangleShape.Draw;
begin
   SetFillStyle( Pattern, Color );
   Rectangle( x1, y1, x2, y2 );
   Bar( x1 + 1, y1 + 1, x2 - 1, y2 - 1 );
end;
{===============================================================}
var
   Driver, Mode : integer;
   Object1 : CircleShape;
   Object2 : RectangleShape;
begin
   {*********************}
   { Initialize graphics }
   {*********************}
   Driver := Detect;
   InitGraph( Driver, Mode, 'C:\TP' );
   {******************}
   { Display a circle }
   {******************}
   Object1.Initialize( GetMaxX div 5, GetMaxY div 2,  { Center }
                       GetMaxX div 5 );               { Radius }
   Object1.SelectStyle( Blue );
   Object1.Draw;
   {*********************}
   { Display a rectangle }
```

```
    {********************}
    Object2.Initialize( 3 * (GetMaxX div 5),      { Upper left x }
                        GetMaxY div 4,            { Upper left y }
                        4 * (GetMaxX div 5),      { Lower right x }
                        3 * (GetMaxY div 4) );    { Lower right y }
    Object2.SelectStyle( CloseDotFill, Green );
    Object2.Draw;
    {*******************}
    { Terminate graphics }
    {*******************}
    readln;
    CloseGraph;
end.
```

Accessing an Object's Fields

You access a data element in an object in the same way you access a field in an ordinary record. You can use either a `with` statement or a `dot` qualifier. For example, the single statement

```
with CircleShape do begin
   x      := GetMaxX div 5;
   y      := GetMaxY div 2;
   Radius := GetMaxX div 5;
   Color  := Blue;
end;
```

is identical to the four statements

```
CircleShape.x      := GetMaxX div 5;
CircleShape.y      := GetMaxY div 2;
CircleShape.Radius := GetMaxX div 5;
CircleShape.Color  := Blue;
```

Using Methods

In general, objects communicate with one another by exchanging messages. A message might be a request for information, or it may impart information. In object-oriented programming, a message is sent or received through the object's procedures and functions. Each one of these procedures and functions is called a *method*.

Although you can directly access any data field in any object whenever you want, the rules of object-oriented programming state that all data fields should be accessed *only* through the object's procedures and functions. In other words, appropriate procedures and functions should be developed for all initialization, modification, input, output, and comparison operations that the object's data must perform.

If this seems overly protective, remember that an object is, in essence, *private* data accessed by *public* subroutines.

Think back to the previous example of how several departments process work order charges. Special forms and reports were used to pass information from one department to another. Each form and report probably contains dates, names, descriptions, costs, and other information that might be useful to another department. Each department is an object, protecting and controlling private data, and exchanging information only through formal methods.

When you divide a problem into objects that contain both data and methods, your program more accurately represents the real-world event you want to describe. As a result, object-oriented programs are generally easier to understand and develop than procedural programs. But without an example, it is difficult to see the advantages of protecting an object's data so fiercely.

Consider the following riddle. A farmer needs to cross a river to take a fox, a chicken, and a sack of grain to market. A sudden flood has washed away the only available bridge. Fortunately, the farmer has a rowboat. Unfortunately, the farmer will have to make several crossings because the rowboat is large enough to transport only one of his products at a time. However, if the farmer leaves the fox and chicken together unattended, the fox will eat the chicken. Similarly, if the chicken is left alone with the grain, the chicken will eat the grain. What steps should the farmer take to ferry all three products across the river without losing any of them?

Spend a minute trying to envision how you would develop a *traditional* Pascal program to solve this problem. You would probably first try to solve the riddle on paper, then "reverse engineer" a program to fit your solution.

The CROSSING program in listing 20.5 solves the riddle with an object-oriented approach. The fox, chicken, and grain are all instances of an object called `Parcel`. Notice that `Nothing` is also defined as an instance of `Parcel`; after all, the farmer may want to cross the river without any cargo.

Listing 20.5

```
program Crossing;
const
   Left    = True;
   Right   = False;
   LastOne : byte = 0;   { Identifies the last parcel taken }
type
   Parcel = object
      Side        : Boolean;       { Current bank of river }
      ParcelCode  : byte;          { Unique code for each parcel }
      Instruction : string;        { Movement message }
      procedure Init( ShoreLine : Boolean;
                             ID : byte;
                        Package : string );
      procedure PickItUp;
      procedure PutItBackDown;
      function CurrentSide : Boolean;
      function WasNotLastParcelTaken : Boolean;
      procedure TakeItAcrossRiver;
   end;
procedure Parcel.Init;
begin
   Side        := ShoreLine;           { Initialize the side }
   ParcelCode  := ID;                  { Identifies the parcel }
   Instruction := 'Take ' + Package;   { Prepares the message }
end;
procedure Parcel.PickItUp;
begin
   Side := not Side;                   { Change sides }
end;
procedure Parcel.PutItBackDown;
begin
   Side := not Side;                   { Change sides }
end;
function Parcel.CurrentSide : Boolean;
begin
   CurrentSide := Side;                { Report current side }
end;
procedure Parcel.TakeItAcrossRiver;
begin
   writeln( Instruction );             { Display the message }
```

continues

Listing 20.5 continued

```
   LastOne := ParcelCode;              { Note which one was moved }
end;
function Parcel.WasNotLastParcelTaken : Boolean;
begin
   WasNotLastParcelTaken := ParcelCode <> LastOne;
end;
var
   Fox, Chicken, Grain, Nothing : Parcel;
   FarmerSide : Boolean;
procedure FarmerCrossesRiver;
begin
   if FarmerSide = Left then write( 'Left to right: ' )
                        else write( 'Right to left: ' );
   FarmerSide := not FarmerSide;
end;
function SafeChoice : Boolean;
begin
  SafeChoice := not ( ((Fox.CurrentSide = Chicken.CurrentSide) and
                       (Chicken.CurrentSide <> FarmerSide) ) or
                      ((Chicken.CurrentSide = Grain.CurrentSide) and
                       (Grain.CurrentSide <> FarmerSide)) );
end;
procedure Initialize;
begin
   Nothing.Init( Left, 0, 'nothing' );
   Fox.Init(     Left, 1, 'the fox' );
   Chicken.Init( Left, 2, 'the chicken' );
   Grain.Init(   Left, 3, 'the grain' );
   FarmerSide := Left;
end;
function Done : Boolean;
begin
   Done := (Fox.CurrentSide     = Right) and
           (Chicken.CurrentSide = Right) and
           (Grain.CurrentSide   = Right);
end;
begin
   Initialize;
   repeat
      FarmerCrossesRiver;
      if SafeChoice and Nothing.WasNotLastParcelTaken then
```

```
          Nothing.TakeItAcrossRiver
        else begin
          Fox.PickItUp;
          if SafeChoice and Fox.WasNotLastParcelTaken then
            Fox.TakeItAcrossRiver
          else begin
            Fox.PutItBackDown;
            Chicken.PickItUp;
            if SafeChoice and Chicken.WasNotLastParcelTaken then
              Chicken.TakeItAcrossRiver
            else begin
              Chicken.PutItBackDown;
              Grain.PickItUp;
              if SafeChoice and Grain.WasNotLastParcelTaken then
                Grain.TakeItAcrossRiver
              else begin
                writeln( 'Failure' );
                Halt;
              end;
            end;
          end;
        end;
    until Done;
    writeln( 'SUCCESS' );
end.
```

The most important data field in the object is the `Side` boolean field, which is set to `True` when the item is on the left bank of the river and `False` when the item has crossed over to the right bank. The `CurrentSide` function can be used to examine the `Side` field whenever you want.

The general initialization procedure `Initialize` and the individual `Init` routines begin the program by placing the farmer and all of the items on the left bank of the river. The program ends successfully when the `Done` function detects that all three of the farmer's products have crossed to the right bank. The `SafeChoice` function monitors where everything is located and reports any unsafe combinations.

The `PickItUp` procedure allows the `SafeChoice` function to examine what would happen if the farmer selects an item. If the choice is bad, the `PutItBackDown` procedure restores things to the way they were. If the choice is good, the `TakeItAcrossRiver` procedure allows the item to be rowed across.

Obviously, after an item has been taken across the river in one direction, you do not want the same item transported back again in the next move. The `LastOne` global variable and the `WasNotLastParcelTaken` function work together to ensure that such inefficient (but safe) moves are not made.

The final data item in the object is the `Instruction` field. It contains the name of each item and is used only for reporting which move has been made.

In the main body of the program, a repeat loop is used to represent each crossing of the rowboat. Every pass of the loop identifies another item that is safely moved. If no safe items can be found, the `Failure` message is displayed, and the program halts. The loop ends only when all items have been transported across.

When the CROSSING program executes, it produces the following correct instructions:

```
Left to right: Take the chicken
Right to left: Take nothing
Left to right: Take the fox
Right to left: Take the chicken
Left to right: Take the grain
Right to left: Take nothing
Left to right: Take the chicken
SUCCESS
```

Notice how the program could be developed naturally because we used methods. We did not need to understand how to *solve* the problem. Instead, it was more important to understand how to *describe* the problem.

Breaking a problem down into entities and relationships has long been a common technique for developing structured programs and has proved to be a particularly useful technique for database design. Unlike procedural programs, however, object-oriented programs allow entities and relationships to be directly expressed with objects and methods. This feature lets an object-oriented program closely model the real-world problem it is designed to solve.

Developing an Object Hierarchy

Almost any nontrivial real-world problem can be envisioned as a collection of objects communicating with one another through a set of methods. One common result of this approach is the recognition of natural relationships between objects. You know, for example, that a fox and a sack of grain have few *intrinsic* similarities, yet the CROSSING program (listing 20.5) focused on one characteristic that foxes and sacks of grain share, namely, their physical location. Object-oriented design almost always reveals the *key* similarities and differences among the real-world entities you want to model. Often, an understanding of these similarities and differences helps you identify relationships among the *structures* of the objects.

Most programmers know the frustration of trying to adapt old code to fit a new application. Even though the old code operates perfectly in the previous program, some changes must be made for the new program, then a new testing and debugging cycle must begin.

Object-oriented programming eases the pain of application development; you can *build* on earlier work rather than modify it. Even if an existing object does not quite fit, you can quickly create a new object by specifying only the differences.

A Basic Window Object

Suppose that you need to develop some basic window management routines. Because every window has private data (such as coordinates) and routines that use the data (such as the `Window` procedure itself), you decide to use an object-oriented programming approach.

The window object, called `Pane`, will contain the minimum number of data fields and methods needed to save the image of the screen, create a window, and restore the screen when the window closes. (You may want to review the WIND2 program in listing 10.16.)

Start by identifying the required data fields. Before you open the window, you will save the original screen image in a field called `SnapShot`. Then, because every window is defined by its upper left and lower right corners, `Pane` contains four fields for the `UpLeftX`, `UpLeftY`, `LoRightX`, and `LoRightY` coordinates. Finally, if you want to be able to open several windows simultaneously, and especially if you want the windows to be able to overlap, `Pane` should include data fields containing the coordinates of the prior window. The word-sized fields `UpperLeft` and `LowerRight` store the results of `WindMin` and `WindMax`, respectively.

Next, consider the methods that `Pane` needs. A data initialization routine, `InitWindowData`, establishes the window boundary coordinates. An `OpenWindow` routine opens the window. Finally, a `CloseWindow` routine restores the original screen image and returns to the prior window.

The WINDOBJ program in listing 20.6 demonstrates how a program can use the `Pane` object to produce windows. Notice that the `VideoMemory` array is set to point to either the monochrome or color memory segment, depending on the value of the byte at $0040:$0049.

Listing 20.6

```
program WindObj;
uses Crt;
type
   ScreenImage   = array [ 0..1999 ] of word;
var
   VideoMemory   : ^ScreenImage;
type
   Pane = object
      SnapShot : ScreenImage;
      UpLeftX, UpLeftY, LoRightX, LoRightY : byte;
      UpperLeft, LowerRight : word;
      procedure InitWindowData( ULX, ULY, LRX, LRY : byte );
      procedure OpenWindow( ULX, ULY, LRX, LRY : byte );
      procedure CloseWindow;
   end;
procedure Pane.InitWindowData;
begin
   UpLeftX := ULX;
   UpLeftY := ULY;
   LoRightX := LRX;
   LoRightY := LRY;
   SnapShot := VideoMemory^;
   UpperLeft := WindMin;
   LowerRight := WindMax;
end;
procedure Pane.OpenWindow;
begin
   InitWindowData( ULX, ULY, LRX, LRY );
```

```
    Window( UpLeftX, UpLeftY, LoRightX, LoRightY );
end;
procedure Pane.CloseWindow;
begin
    VideoMemory^ := SnapShot;
    Window( Lo( UpperLeft ) + 1, Hi( UpperLeft ) + 1,
            Lo( LowerRight ) + 1, Hi( LowerRight ) + 1 );
end;
var
    Wind1, Wind2 : Pane;
procedure FillScreen( Back, Front : byte );
var
    Index : byte;
begin
    TextBackground( Back );
    TextColor( Front );
    for Index := 1 to 255 do write( Index );
    NormVideo;
end;
begin
    ClrScr;
    if Mem[ $0040:$0049 ] = 7 then              { Test screen type   }
       VideoMemory := Ptr( $B000, $0000 )       { Monochrome screen }
    else
       VideoMemory := Ptr( $B800, $0000 );      { Color screen       }
    Wind1.OpenWindow( 25, 5, 55, 20 );
    FillScreen( Black, White );
    Wind2.OpenWindow( 5, 10, 75, 15 );
    FillScreen( White, Black );
    GotoXY( 1, 1 ); write( 'Press enter... ' ); Readln;
    Wind2.CloseWindow;
    GotoXY( 1, 1 ); write( 'Press enter... ' ); Readln;
    Wind1.CloseWindow;
end.
```

When WINDOBJ executes, it produces the overlapping windows shown in figure 20.2.

Creating a Framed Window

Now suppose that you want a single program that produces two types of windows: the original `Pane` style and a slightly fancier version with a double-lined border. The code for the new window will be developed as an object called `Frame`.

Fig. 20.2. Output produced by the WINDOBJ program.

```
                    8991001011021031041051061071081
                    0911011111121131141151161171181 1
                    9120121122123124125126127128129
                    1301311321331341351361371381391
                    40141142143144145146147148149 15
Press enter... 5137138139140141142143144145146147148149150151152153154 1
5515615715815916016116216316416516616716816917017117217317417517617717 8
1791801811821831841851861871881891901911921931941951961971981992002012 0
2203204205206207208209210211212213214215216217218219220221222223224225 2
2622722822923023123223323423523623723823924024124224324424524624724824 9
250251252253254255
                    2213214215216217218219220221222
                    2232242252262272282292302312322
                    3323423523623723823924024124224
                    32442452462472482492502512522 53
                    254255
```

What data fields and methods does `Frame` need? Quite simply, `Frame` needs the same fields and methods as `Pane` plus a new routine, which we call `MakeBorder`, to draw the border design. A revised `OpenWindow` procedure, unique to the `Frame` object, is also required.

All of `Pane`'s data fields and methods can be included as part of the `Frame` declaration by referencing `Pane` in the object header, as follows:

```
Frame = object( Pane )
   procedure MakeBorder;
   procedure OpenWindow( ULX, ULY, LRX, LRY : byte );
end;
```

In this declaration, `Frame` is said to *inherit* all of `Pane`'s fields and methods. In other words, any field or method defined in the `Pane` object is available to any instance of the `Frame` object. Only the two new procedures—`Frame.MakeBorder` and `Frame.OpenWindow`—need to be specially defined.

The `OpenWindow` procedure defined in the `Frame` object is actually named `Frame.OpenWindow`, and the original `OpenWindow` procedure is still called `Pane.OpenWindow`. This capability to use similarly named methods at different levels in an object hierarchy is called *polymorphism*. The compiler automatically invokes the correct `OpenWindow` procedure for every instance of every object.

The WINDUNIT unit in listing 20.7 contains the complete code for creating windows using `Pane` and `Frame`.

Listing 20.7

```
unit WindUnit;
interface
   type
      ScreenImage   = array [ 0..1999 ] of word;
      Pane = object
         SnapShot : ScreenImage;
         UpLeftX, UpLeftY, LoRightX, LoRightY : byte;
         UpperLeft, LowerRight : word;
         procedure InitWindowData( ULX, ULY, LRX, LRY : byte );
         procedure OpenWindow( ULX, ULY, LRX, LRY : byte );
         procedure CloseWindow;
      end;
      Frame = object( Pane )
         procedure MakeBorder;
         procedure OpenWindow( ULX, ULY, LRX, LRY : byte );
      end;
implementation
   uses Crt;
   var
      VideoMemory   : ^ScreenImage;
   procedure Pane.InitWindowData;
   begin
      UpLeftX := ULX;
      UpLeftY := ULY;
      LoRightX := LRX;
      LoRightY := LRY;
      SnapShot := VideoMemory^;
      UpperLeft := WindMin;
      LowerRight := WindMax;
   end;
   procedure Pane.OpenWindow;
   begin
      Pane.InitWindowData( ULX, ULY, LRX, LRY );
      Window( UpLeftX, UpLeftY, LoRightX, LoRightY );
      ClrScr;
   end;
```

continues

Listing 20.7 continued

```
   procedure Pane.CloseWindow;
   begin
      VideoMemory^ := SnapShot;
      Window( Lo( UpperLeft ) + 1, Hi( UpperLeft ) + 1,
              Lo( LowerRight ) + 1, Hi( LowerRight ) + 1 );
   end;
{====================}
   procedure Frame.MakeBorder;
   var
      Work : byte;
   begin
      Window( 1, 1, 80, 25 );
      for Work := UpLeftX to LoRightX do begin  { Horizontal lines }
         GotoXY( Work, UpLeftY );    write( #205 );
         GotoXY( Work, LoRightY );   write( #205 );
      end;
      for Work := UpLeftY to LoRightY do begin    { Vertical lines }
         GotoXY( UpLeftX, Work );    write( #186 );
         GotoXY( LoRightX, Work );   write( #186 );
      end;
      GotoXY( UpLeftX, UpLeftY );    write( #201 );  { Upper left }
      GotoXY( UpLeftX, LoRightY );   write( #200 );  { Lower left }
      GotoXY( LoRightX, UpLeftY );   write( #187 );  { Upper right }
      GotoXY( LoRightX, LoRightY );  write( #188 );  { Lower right }
      Inc( UpLeftX );          { Position the window in the border }
      Inc( UpLeftY );
      Dec( LoRightX );
      Dec( LoRightY );
   end;
   procedure Frame.OpenWindow;
   begin
      Pane.InitWindowData( ULX, ULY, LRX, LRY );
      Frame.MakeBorder;
      Window( UpLeftX, UpLeftY, LoRightX, LoRightY );
      ClrScr;
   end;
{====================}
begin
   { Determine video memory segment }
   if Mem[ $0040:$0049 ] = 7 then
      VideoMemory := Ptr( $B000, $0000 )   { Monochrome }
```

```
   else
      VideoMemory := Ptr( $B800, $0000 );  { Color }
end.
```

The WINDUSE1 program in listing 20.8 uses WINDUNIT to produce two windows. Notice that `Wind1` is declared as type `Pane`, and `Wind2` is declared as type `Frame`. Consequently, the call to `Wind1.OpenWindow` invokes `Pane.OpenWindow`, and the call to `Wind2.OpenWindow` invokes `Frame.OpenWindow`.

Listing 20.8

```
program WindUse1;
uses Crt, WindUnit;
var
   Wind1 : Pane;
   Wind2 : Frame;
procedure MakeBackdrop;
var
   work  : word;
begin
   LowVideo;
   for work := 1 to 2000 do write( '.' );
   NormVideo;
end;
procedure FillScreen( Contents : string );
var
   Index : byte;
begin
   HighVideo;
   for Index := 1 to 255 do write( Contents );
   NormVideo;
end;
begin
   MakeBackdrop;
   Wind1.OpenWindow( 10, 3, 35, 22 );
   FillScreen( 'Pane  ' );
   Wind2.OpenWindow( 45, 3, 70, 22 );
   FillScreen( 'Frame  ' );
   GotoXY( 1, 1 ); write( 'Press enter... ' ); Readln;
   Wind2.CloseWindow;
   GotoXY( 1, 1 ); write( 'Press enter... ' ); Readln;
   Wind1.CloseWindow;
end.
```

When WINDUSE1 is executed, it produces the windows shown in figure 20.3.

Fig. 20.3. Output produced by the WINDUSE1 program.

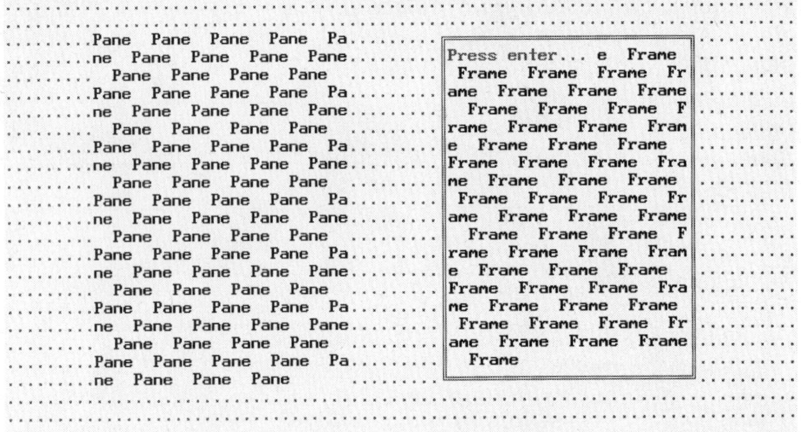

Creating a Tombstone Window

There is no practical limit to the number of hierarchically arranged object definitions. In fact, the more you work with object-oriented programming, the more you will find yourself developing small sections of code that serve as building blocks for later applications.

Consider one final window example. Suppose that you do not want to make any more changes to WINDUNIT, but you need to develop a window with a one-line heading at the top. (Look ahead to figure 20.4 for an example of this style.) The `Frame` object defined in WINDUNIT is close to what is required. All you need to add is a routine to produce the heading, which we call `MakeBanner`, and a customized `OpenWindow` procedure. You define the new object, called `TombStone`, as follows:

```
TombStone = object( Frame )
   procedure MakeBanner( Message : string );
   procedure OpenWindow( Message : string;
                         ULX, ULY, LRX, LRY : byte );
end;
```

Because TombStone is a descendent of Frame, the new object automatically inherits all the characteristics of its parent. In other words, TombStone inherits all the data fields and methods from Pane (its grandparent) plus all the data fields and methods from Frame (its parent).

The WINDUSE2 program in listing 20.9 contains the code needed to implement the TombStone object.

Listing 20.9

```
program WindUse2;
uses Crt, WindUnit;
type
{==============================}
{ Define the TombStone object }
{==============================}
   TombStone = object( Frame )
      procedure MakeBanner( Message : string );
      procedure OpenWindow( Message : string;
                            ULX, ULY, LRX, LRY : byte );
   end;
{==================================}
{ Define procedures for TombStone }
{==================================}
procedure TombStone.MakeBanner;
var
   Blanks : string[ 80 ];
   Work   : byte;
begin
   TextBackground( White );
   TextColor( Black );
   FillChar( Blanks, 80, ' ' );
   Blanks[ 0 ] := chr( LoRightX - UpLeftX + 1 );
   GotoXY( UpLeftX, UpLeftY );
   write( Blanks );
   GotoXY( (LoRightX + UpLeftX - Length( Message ) + 1) div 2,
           UpLeftY );
   write( Message );
   NormVideo;
   GotoXY( UpLeftX, UpLeftY + 1 );    { Prepare to make separator }
   for Work := UpLeftX to LoRightX do     write( #196 );
   GotoXY( UpLeftX - 1, UpLeftY + 1 );    write( #199 );
```

continues

Listing 20.9 continued

```
   GotoXY( LoRightX + 1, UpLeftY + 1 );   write( #182 );
   Inc( UpLeftY, 2 );
end;
procedure TombStone.OpenWindow;
begin
   Pane.InitWindowData( ULX, ULY, LRX, LRY );
   Frame.MakeBorder;
   Tombstone.MakeBanner( Message );
   Window( UpLeftX, UpLeftY, LoRightX, LoRightY );
   ClrScr;
end;
{================================}
{ Now continue with the program }
{================================}
procedure MakeBackdrop;
var
   work  : word;
begin
   LowVideo;
   for work := 1 to 2000 do write( '.' );
   NormVideo;
end;
procedure FillScreen( Contents : string );
var
   Index : byte;
begin
   HighVideo;
   for Index := 1 to 255 do write( Contents );
   NormVideo;
end;
var
   Wind1 : Pane;
   Wind2 : Frame;
   Wind3 : TombStone;
begin
   MakeBackdrop;
   Wind1.OpenWindow( 5, 3, 25, 22 );
   FillScreen( 'Pane ' );
   Wind2.OpenWindow( 30, 3, 50, 22 );
   FillScreen( 'Frame ' );
   Wind3.OpenWindow( 'Any Banner', 55, 3, 75, 22 );
   FillScreen( 'TombStone ' );
```

```
    GotoXY( 1, 1 ); write( 'Press enter... ' ); Readln;
    Wind3.CloseWindow;
    GotoXY( 1, 1 ); write( 'Press enter... ' ); Readln;
    Wind2.CloseWindow;
    GotoXY( 1, 1 ); write( 'Press enter... ' ); Readln;
    Wind1.CloseWindow;
end.
```

The output produced by WINDUSE2 is shown in figure 20.4.

***Fig. 20.4.** Output produced by the WINDUSE2 program.*

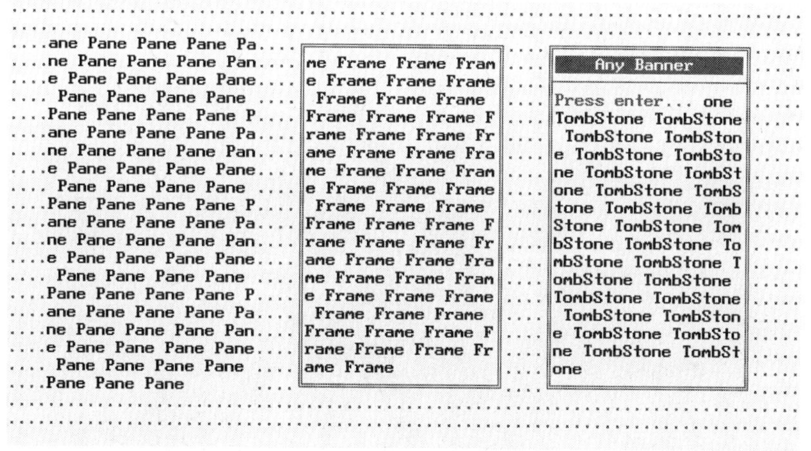

Inheritance encourages the development of small, reusable objects; after all, smaller sections of code are more likely to be reused than larger ones. Each method should be short, performing a single, clearly defined task. The more functionality you pack into a single procedure or function, the more likely that it will be inappropriate for solving future problems.

Large libraries are typical in object-oriented systems because they contain proven, off-the-shelf techniques that can be used as building blocks for many different applications.

Static and Dynamic Methods

In the window examples, you saw how the `Pane`, `Frame`, and `TombStone` objects had customized `OpenWindow` procedures. Any instance of `Pane` invokes Pane.OpenWindow, any instance of Frame invokes Frame.OpenWindow, and any instance of TombStone invokes TombStone.OpenWindow.

Similarly, all methods called by an OpenWindow procedure (namely, Pane.InitWindowData, Frame.MakeBorder, and TombStone.MakeBanner) were completely and unambiguously identified. Although OpenWindow was redefined for each object, InitWindowData, MakeBorder, and MakeBanner were never changed.

But what happens if the calling routine remains unchanged for several objects, but the *methods* called by the routine are redefined at each level?

Using Static Methods

Consider the related objects First and Second, as defined in the SHOWVIR1 program in listing 20.10.

Listing 20.10

```
program ShowVir1;
type
   First = object
      x : integer;
      procedure Init( Start : integer );
      procedure Retrieve;
      procedure Display;
   end;
   Second = object( First )
      y : integer;
      procedure Init( Start : integer );
      procedure Retrieve;
   end;
procedure First.Init;
begin
   x := Start;
end;
procedure First.Retrieve;
begin
   writeln( 'First.Retrieve ', x );
end;
procedure First.Display;
```

```
begin
   Retrieve;
end;
procedure Second.Init;
begin
   y := Start;
end;
procedure Second.Retrieve;
begin
   writeln( 'Second.Retrieve ', y );
end;
var
   Alpha : First;
   Beta  : Second;
begin
   Alpha.Init( 50 );
   Beta.Init( 100 );
   Alpha.Display;
   Beta.Display;
end.
```

Notice that the `Display` method calls the `Retrieve` procedure. The `Alpha.Display` statement in the main body of the program causes `First.Retrieve` to execute. But which version of `Retrieve` will be executed by `Beta.Display`?

Executing the program produces the following output:

```
First.Retrieve 50
First.Retrieve 0
```

So `Beta.Display` invoked `First.Retrieve` even though the `Second.Retrieve` method was the one we intended to call.

This is an example of a *static* method. When the compiler produced the executable code for the `Display` procedure, it automatically called the `Retrieve` procedure defined on the same level as `Display`. In general, calling methods are always assumed to reference routines at their own level, not the level of the instance itself. If the called method is not found on the current level, each ancestor object is searched. Methods defined in descendent objects are ignored.

In the language of object-oriented programming, this process is called *early binding*, and the called routine is said to be *bound* to the calling method at compile time.

Using Virtual Methods

Called methods can be redefined at any level in the object hierarchy by declaring those methods to be *virtual*. Simply add the keyword `virtual` immediately after the method declarations. For example, if each `Retrieve` procedure is virtual, as follows:

```
procedure Retrieve; virtual;
```

the `Retrieve` routine called by `Display` will be determined at run time. As you might expect, the object-oriented programming term for this process is *late binding*.

Any method can be made virtual. However, all occurrences of the method in all levels must also be made virtual. Virtual versions of the `Retrieve` routines are demonstrated in the SHOWVIR2 program in listing 20.11.

Listing 20.11

```
program ShowVir2;
type
   First = object
      x : integer;
      constructor Init( Start : integer );
      procedure Retrieve; virtual;
      procedure Display;
   end;
   Second = object( First )
      y : integer;
      constructor Init( Start : integer );
      procedure Retrieve; virtual;
   end;
constructor First.Init;
begin
   x := Start;
end;
procedure First.Retrieve;
begin
   writeln( 'First.Retrieve ', x );
end;
procedure First.Display;
```

```
begin
   Retrieve;
end;
constructor Second.Init;
begin
   y := Start;
end;
procedure Second.Retrieve;
begin
   writeln( 'Second.Retrieve ', y );
end;
var
   Alpha : First;
   Beta  : Second;
begin
   Alpha.Init( 50 );
   Beta.Init( 100 );
   Alpha.Display;
   Beta.Display;
end.
```

When SHOWVIR2 executes, it produces the following results:

```
First.Retrieve 50
Second.Retrieve 100
```

You may have noticed another change in the SHOWVIR2 program: in the `Init` data initialization routine, the reserved word `procedure` was replaced with the reserved word `constructor`.

A *constructor* is a routine that automatically performs the setup code that supports virtual methods. Consequently, a constructor must be called before any virtual method can be used. Furthermore, a constructor must be called for every instance of an object that uses a virtual method.

> During program development, you can activate the Range Checking compiler option `{$R+}` to ensure that all constructor calls have been properly performed. After your program has been debugged, you can reset the option to its default state `{$R-}`.

Declaring Dynamic Objects

So far, all of the examples have used static instances of object types. However, objects can also be dynamically allocated on the heap and referenced with pointers, just like ordinary record types.

Using Dynamic Objects without Virtual Methods

Memory space for a dynamic object can be allocated on the heap by using the `New` procedure and can be returned to the heap by using `Dispose`.

The WINDUSE3 program in listing 20.12 demonstrates how the original WINDUSE1 program (listing 20.8) can be revised to use dynamic objects. Notice that *no* changes need to be made to the methods in WINDUNIT.

Listing 20.12

```
program WindUse3;
uses Crt, WindUnit;
var
   Wind1 : ^Pane;
   Wind2 : ^Frame;
procedure MakeBackdrop;
var
   work  : word;
begin
   LowVideo;
   for work := 1 to 2000 do write( '.' );
   NormVideo;
end;
procedure FillScreen( Contents : string );
var
   Index : byte;
begin
   HighVideo;
   for Index := 1 to 255 do write( Contents );
   NormVideo;
end;
```

```
begin
   New( Wind1 );      { Allocate space for Wind1 }
   New( Wind2 );      { Allocate space for Wind2 }
   MakeBackdrop;
   Wind1^.OpenWindow( 10, 3, 35, 22 );
   FillScreen( 'Pane   ' );
   Wind2^.OpenWindow( 45, 3, 70, 22 );
   FillScreen( 'Frame  ' );
   GotoXY( 1, 1 ); write( 'Press enter... ' ); Readln;
   Wind2^.CloseWindow;
   GotoXY( 1, 1 ); write( 'Press enter... ' ); Readln;
   Wind1^.CloseWindow;
   Dispose( Wind2 );    { Deallocate Wind1 }
   Dispose( Wind1 );    { Deallocate Wind2 }
end.
```

Using Dynamic Objects with Virtual Methods

If a dynamic object contains a virtual method, the object's constructor call must be performed after the `New` procedure allocates space but before any method calls are made.

To simplify this rule, the `New` procedure has been modified to allow the constructor call as a second parameter. For example, if the `Alpha` and `Beta` objects in the SHOWVIR2 program (listing 20.11) are redefined to be dynamic, as follows:

```
var
   Alpha  : ^First;
   Beta   : ^Second;
```

the following statements will allocate heap space for the objects, invoke the virtual method manager, and initialize the data fields:

```
New( Alpha, Init( 50 ) );
New( Beta,  Init( 100 ) );
```

By itself, the `Dispose` procedure will deallocate any heap space for a dynamic object. One extra activity, however, is required to discontinue the use of the virtual method management code; a special procedure, called a *destructor*, must be executed as the second parameter of the `Dispose` operation.

Not surprisingly, a destructor is structured like a constructor, but the reserved word `destructor` is used instead of the reserved word `constructor`. The destructor method normally contains all the steps you must take to deallocate the dynamic object. If no special action is required, the `destructor` routine may be left empty; nevertheless, it must still be invoked.

For example, a destructor named `Done` is invoked for the `Alpha` and `Beta` objects by executing the following statements:

```
Dispose( Alpha, Done );
Dispose( Beta,  Done );
```

The revised version of the SHOWVIR2 program is shown in its entirety as SHOWVIR3 in listing 20.13.

Listing 20.13

```
program ShowVir3;
type
   First = object
      x : integer;
      constructor Init( Start : integer );
      procedure Retrieve; virtual;
      procedure Display;
      destructor Done;
   end;
   Second = object( First )
      y : integer;
      constructor Init( Start : integer );
      procedure Retrieve; virtual;
   end;
constructor First.Init;
begin
   x := Start;
end;
procedure First.Retrieve;
begin
   writeln( 'First.Retrieve ', x );
end;
procedure First.Display;
begin
   Retrieve;
end;
```

```
destructor First.Done;    { Empty, but must still be called }
begin
end;
constructor Second.Init;
begin
   y := Start;
end;
procedure Second.Retrieve;
begin
   writeln( 'Second.Retrieve ', y );
end;
var
   Alpha : ^First;
   Beta  : ^Second;
begin
   New( Alpha, Init( 50 ) );
   New( Beta,  Init( 100 ) );
   Alpha^.Display;
   Beta^.Display;
   Dispose( Alpha, Done );
   Dispose( Beta,  Done );
end.
```

When SHOWVIR3 is executed, it produces the same output as the SHOWVIR2 program. Notice that a destructor may be inherited by descendent object types just like any ordinary method.

Summary

In this chapter, you learned that almost any problem can be viewed as a collection of logical entities that exchange information with one another. In object-oriented programming (OOP), entities are directly represented as a hierarchy of objects, and the information exchange is represented as a set of methods. Because object-oriented programming regards control and data structures with equal importance, it is a more natural and intuitive problem-solving model than traditional structured programming techniques.

You learned that an object is declared as a single Turbo Pascal structure encapsulating both data and the methods (that is, the procedures and functions) that operate on the data. Each use of an object is called an instance of the object.

You learned that objects sharing similar features can be arranged hierarchically, with descendent objects inheriting the characteristics of their ancestors. New data and methods may be defined at each stage in the hierarchy. Whenever an object defines a method with the same name as an ancestor method, the new method is the one invoked by all further descendents. This feature of redefining methods to suit the specific needs of a new object is called polymorphism. Through inheritance and polymorphism, objects can be used as building blocks that simplify the development of larger applications.

You saw that confusion is possible when a call is made to a method that has been redefined. When a method is static, its selection is determined at compile time in a process called early binding. A method may optionally be declared virtual, allowing its selection to be determined at run time in a process called late binding.

You learned how instances of objects can be dynamically allocated on the heap. If there are any virtual methods, a constructor is required. If there is a dynamic virtual object, you need to use a destructor.

Finally, you learned that proficiency with object-oriented programming can come only with experience.

CHAPTER 21

Advanced Object-Oriented Programming

This chapter looks at more advanced topics in object-oriented programming. You learn about private data files and methods that limit the access of critical parts of an object type. You learn also about abstract object types that allow you to declare abstract functionality to be inherited by descendent object types. This chapter also discusses how to extend object types, a common techinique used in nontrivial OOP applications such as Turbo Vision. Object-oriented design and containment are also covered.

6.0

Private Object Fields

When objects were introduced in Turbo Pascal Version 5.5, all data fields and methods were public. The programmer was politely asked to use methods rather than directly access data fields. Moreover, many applications needed supporting routines. Without the ability to hide these routines, it became hazardous to let the client programs access them. Turbo Pascal Version 6.0 has rectified this weakness. The reserved word `private` is used to separate public data fields and methods from private ones. Now you can enforce the hands-off rule for data fields and auxiliary methods. Data hiding of object components affects the descendent objects and the instances of the objects. The rules for private object components follow:

1. The private data fields and methods of an object are accessible to descendent objects declared in the same module (program or library unit).

2. The private data fields and methods are inaccessible to the instances of the object and the instances of its descendent objects. This prevents a client program from accessing the private object components by using a descendant object.

3. In the `object` declaration, list all fields and methods to be private after the reserved word `PRIVATE`. There is no separate `END` to indicate the end of the `PRIVATE` block.

Listing 21.1 shows the source code of a library unit that declares an object type that represents a dynamic array of strings. Designing a dynamic string array using objects achieves two goals. One, you can encapsulate the data structures maintaining the dynamic array and the routines that manage them. Two, you can create descendents of the dynamic array object type that inherit a good portion of its methods, eliminating redundant coding.

Listing 21.1

```
unit DynArr;
interface
{$R-,X+,V-}
const DUMMY_STRING = '$1$2$3$4$5$6$7$8$9$0';
type
  Tstring = array[ 1..1 ] of string;
  Pstring = ^Tstring;
  StringArray = object
     constructor Init( MaxArraySize : word );
     destructor Done;
     function GetMaxSize : word;
     function GetWorkSize : word;
     function IsArraySorted : boolean;
     function Store( S : string; Index : word ) : boolean;
     function Recall( Index : word ) : string;
     procedure Sort;
     function Search( Key : string ) : word;
   private
     MaxSize : word;
     ArrayIsSorted : boolean;
     DataPtr : Pstring;
     procedure Qsort( Left, Right : word );
     function LinearSearch( Key : string ) : word;
```

```
     function BinarySearch( Key : string ) : word;
end;

implementation

constructor StringArray.Init( MaxArraySize : word );
var i : word;
    s : string;
begin
   MaxSize := MaxArraySize;
   GetMem( DataPtr, MaxSize * sizeOf( string ) );
   s := DUMMY_STRING;
   for i := 1 to MaxSize do
      DataPtr^[ i ] := s;
   ArrayIsSorted := False;
end;

destructor StringArray.Done;
begin
   FreeMem( DataPtr, MaxSize * sizeOf( string ) );
end;

function StringArray.GetMaxSize : word;
begin
   GetMaxSize := MaxSize
end;

function StringArray.GetWorkSize : word;
var i : word;
    notFound : boolean;
begin
   i := 1;
   notFound := True;
   while ( i <= MaxSize ) and notFound do begin
     if recall( i ) <> DUMMY_STRING then Inc( i )
        else notFound := False;
   end;

   if notFound then GetWorkSize := MaxSize
      else GetWorkSize := i-1;
end;
```

continues

6.0

Listing 21.1 continued

```
function StringArray.IsArraySorted : boolean;
begin
   IsArraySorted := ArrayIsSorted
end;

function StringArray.Store( S : string; Index : word ) : boolean;
begin
   if ( Index > 0 ) and ( Index <= MaxSize ) then begin
   DataPtr^[ Index ] := S;
   ArrayIsSorted := False;
   Store := True;
end
  else
     Store := False;
end;

function StringArray.Recall( Index : word ) : string;
begin
   if ( Index > 0 ) and ( Index <= MaxSize ) then begin
      Recall := DataPtr^[ Index ];
   end
   else
     Recall := DUMMY_STRING;
end;

procedure StringArray.Sort;
begin
   if not ArrayIsSorted then begin
     Qsort( 1, GetWorkSize );
     ArrayIsSorted := True;
   end;
end;

procedure StringArray.Qsort( Left, Right : word );
var i, j : word;
     x, w : string;
begin
   i := Left;
   j := Right;
   x := Recall( ( Left+Right ) div 2 );
   repeat
       while Recall( i ) < x do Inc( i );
       while x < Recall( j ) do Dec( j );
```

```
        if i <= j then begin
          w := Recall( i );
          Store( Recall( j ), i );
          Store( w, j );
          Inc( i ); Dec( j );
        end;
    until i > j;
    if Left < j then Qsort( Left, j );
    if i < Right then Qsort( i, Right );
end;

function StringArray.Search( Key : string ) : word;
begin
   if ArrayIsSorted then Search := BinarySearch( Key )
                    else Search := LinearSearch( Key );
end;

function StringArray.LinearSearch( Key : string ) : word;
var i : word;
    notFound : boolean;
begin
   i := 1;
   notFound := True;
   while ( i <= MaxSize ) and notFound do
      if Recall( i ) <> Key then Inc( i )
                            else notFound := False;
   if notFound then LinearSearch := 0
               else LinearSearch := i;
end;

function StringArray.BinarySearch( Key : string ) : word;
var low, high, median : word;
begin
   low := 1;
   high := GetWorkSize;
   repeat
      median := ( low+high ) div 2;
      if Key < Recall( median ) then high := median-1
                                else low := median+1;
   until ( Key = Recall( median ) ) or ( low > high );
   if Key = Recall( median ) then BinarySearch := median
                             else BinarySearch := 0;
end;

end.  {DynArr}
```

6.0

The dynamic string array has the following properties:

- Its lowest and highest index values are 1 and the maximum array size, respectively.
- The instances of `StringArray` are filled with copies of the `DUMMY_STRING` constant. This dummy string indicates whether an array element is occupied by meaningful data.
- The array should be sequentially populated with data, starting with data at index 1. This enables the array to maintain a clear separation between occupied and vacant array elements. This partition, called the working size, is needed in array-related operations, such as sorting and searching, where garbage data must be excluded.

The private section contains all the data fields and the auxiliary methods. The object type uses the following data fields:

- The `MaxSize` field stores the maximum size of the dynamic array.
- The `ArrayIsSorted` data field stores the order status of the array.
- The `DataPtr` field is the pointer to the heap memory storing the array of strings.

The `Init` constructor is used to allocate heap space for the dynamic array and initialize all elements of the array to `DUMMY_STRING`. The `Done` destructor recovers the heap space associated with the instances of the `StringArray` object type. The `GetMaxSize` and `IsArraySorted` methods return the values of the `MaxSize` and `ArrayIsSorted` fields, respectively. The `GetWorkSize` function returns the working size of the array.

The `Store` method stores a string in the designated index. The boolean result returned by the method indicates whether the data was stored. Boolean false values are returned when the designated index is 0 or greater that the maximum array size.

The `Recall` method returns the string stored at the specified index. The function returns the `DUMMY_STRING` constant if the specified index is out of range.

The `Sort` method sorts the array elements using the QuickSort algorithm. The `Sort` method does not perform the actual sorting. Instead, it sends a `Qsort` message to invoke the recursive `Qsort` method. (In object-oriented programming terms, the `Sort` method calls the `Qsort` method.) The `Qsort` method is placed in the private section, because it is an auxiliary method that should not be accessed by the instances of the `StringArray` object.

The `Search` method looks for a given string in the array. It returns the index of the matching string, or 0 if no match is found. The `Search` method is implemented in a rather abstract form. The method performs no search; it sends a `LinearSearch` or a `BinarySearch` message based on the value of the `ArrayIsSorted` data field. The `LinearSearch` method searches sequentially through the unsorted array elements. By contrast, the `BinarySearch` method uses the more efficient binary search algorithm to search through the sorted array element. The `LinearSearch` and `BinarySearch` methods are private because they are auxiliary.

If you examine listing 21.1 you will notice that the `Qsort`, `LinearSearch`, and `BinarySearch` methods access the array elements through the `Store` and `Recall` methods. This provides more streamlined data access, and makes it easier to create descendent objects that use alternate storage schemes. Such objects would need only new versions of the `Store` and `Recall` methods (and probably the `GetWorkSize` method). More about this in the next section.

The `DynArr` library unit, shown in listing 21.1, uses a number of directives, including the new `$X` directive. When the `$X` directive is switched on, you can discard the results of a Turbo Pascal function. This makes a function work like a procedure when its returned value is not really needed.

Abstract Objects

The elements of the `StringArray` object type are stored in the heap area. Alternate storage schemes can place the data in extended memory, expanded memory, or even data files. The last form is commonly called ***virtual storage*** (no relation to virtual methods) when disk space is used to emulate memory.

Suppose you want to create the `VMStringArray` as a descendent object of `StringArray`, such that it stores the array elements in a random-access file. The first scheme that might come to mind is one that starts with the `StringArray` as the base object type and `VMStringArray` as its descendent. However, there are a few drawbacks to this approach. If you make `StringArray` ***the*** base object type, you are basically saying that the heap storage scheme is the root of all other storage schemes. This denies the important object abstraction that plays an important role in object-oriented programming and polymorphism. In addition, the `DataPtr` data field is of little use to the descendent object types that do not use the heap.

The solution is to create an abstract object type, which we will call `AbstractStringArray`. The abstract type should have no instances of its own. Instead, it provides the specification for the main and common functionality of the descendent objects. There are two schools of thought regarding what should go in abstract types. The first trend says that the methods should be void of any statements. The second trend states that abstract types should be allowed to contain methods that will be inherited by a significant number of descendent objects (why avoid using inheritance?).

Listing 21.2 contains the `AbsArr` library unit that declares the `AbstractStringArray`, `StringArray`, and `VMStringArray` object types. The declaration of the `AbstractStringArray` resembles that of `StringArray` in listing 21.1. The differences follow:

1. The `GetWorkingSize`, `Store`, and `Recall` methods are declared virtual.

2. The `AbstractStringArray` object type has no `DataPtr` data field.

The descendent object types need to declare their own version of these methods to fit the implemented storage scheme. The `Sort` and `Search` methods are inherited because they access the array elements using the virtual `Store` and `Recall` methods. The `Sort`, `Qsort`, `Search`, `LinearSearch`, and `BinarySearch` methods contain fully functioning code, ready to be inherited. The other methods contain a single statement or no statements.

Listing 21.2

```
unit AbsArr;

interface
{$R-,X+,V-}

const DUMMY_STRING = '$1$2$3$4$5$6$7$8$9$0';

type
   Tstring = array[ 1..1 ] of string;
   Pstring = ^Tstring;

   AbstractStringArray = object
      constructor Init( MaxArraySize : word );
      destructor Done;
```

```
      function GetMaxSize : word;
      function IsArraySorted : boolean;
      function GetWorkSize : word; virtual;
      function Store( S : string; Index : word ) : boolean;
               virtual;
      function Recall( Index : word ) : string; virtual;
      procedure Sort;
      function Search( Key : string ) : word;
    private
      MaxSize : word;
      ArrayIsSorted : boolean;
      procedure Qsort( Left, Right : word );
      function LinearSearch( Key : string ) : word;
      function BinarySearch( Key : string ) : word;
   end;

   StringArray = object( AbstractStringArray )
      constructor Init( MaxArraySize : word );
      destructor Done;
      function GetWorkSize : word;  virtual;
      function Store( S : string; Index : word ) : boolean;
               virtual;
      function Recall( Index : word ) : string; virtual;
    private
      DataPtr : Pstring;
   end;

   VMStringArray = object( AbstractStringArray )
      constructor Init( VMfilename : string );
      destructor Done;
      function GetWorkSize : word;  virtual;
      function Store( S : string; Index : word ) : boolean;
               virtual;
      function Recall( Index : word ) : string; virtual;
    private
      VMfile : file of string;
    end;

implementation

constructor AbstractStringArray.Init( MaxArraySize : word );
begin
```

continues

Listing 21.2 continued

```
   { do nothing }
end;

destructor AbstractStringArray.Done;
begin
   { do nothing }
end;

function AbstractStringArray.GetMaxSize : word;
begin
   GetMaxSize := MaxSize
end;

function AbstractStringArray.GetWorkSize : word;
begin
   GetWorkSize := 0;
end;

function AbstractStringArray.IsArraySorted : boolean;
begin
   IsArraySorted := ArrayIsSorted
end;

function AbstractStringArray.Store( S : string;
                                    Index : word ) : boolean;
begin
   Store := False;
end;

function AbstractStringArray.Recall( Index : word ) : string;
begin
   Recall := '';
end;

procedure AbstractStringArray.Sort;
begin
   Qsort( 1, GetWorkSize );
   ArrayIsSorted := True;
end;

procedure AbstractStringArray.Qsort( Left, Right : word );
```

```
var i, j : word;
    x, w : string;
begin
   i := Left;
   j := Right;
   x := Recall( ( Left+Right ) div 2 );
   repeat
       while Recall( i ) < x do Inc( i );
       while x < Recall( j ) do Dec( j );
       if i <= j then begin
         w := Recall( i ); Store( Recall( j ), i );
         Store( w, j ); Inc( i ); Dec( j );
       end;
   until i > j;
   if Left < j then Qsort( Left, j );
   if i < Right then Qsort( i, Right );
end;

function AbstractStringArray.Search( Key : string ) : word;
begin
   if ArrayIsSorted then Search := BinarySearch( Key )
                    else Search := LinearSearch( Key );
end;

function AbstractStringArray.LinearSearch( Key : string ) : word;
var i : word;
    notFound : boolean;
begin
   i := 1;
   notFound := True;
   while ( i <= MaxSize ) and notFound do
      if Recall( i ) <> Key then Inc( i )
                             else notFound := False;
   if notFound then LinearSearch := 0
               else LinearSearch := i;
end;

function AbstractStringArray.BinarySearch( Key : string ) : word;
var low, high, median : word;
begin
   low := 1;
   high := GetWorkSize;
```

continues

Listing 21.2 continued

```
   repeat
      median := ( low+high ) div 2;
      if Key < Recall( median ) then high := median-1
                                else low := median+1;
   until ( Key = Recall( median ) ) or ( low > high );
   if Key = Recall( median ) then BinarySearch := median
                             else BinarySearch := 0;
end;

{ *************** object StringArray ************** }

constructor StringArray.Init( MaxArraySize : word );
var i : word;
    s : string;
begin
   MaxSize := MaxArraySize;
   GetMem( DataPtr, MaxSize * sizeOf( string ) );
   s := DUMMY_STRING;
   for i := 1 to MaxSize do
      DataPtr^[ i ] := s;
   ArrayIsSorted := False;
end;

destructor StringArray.Done;
begin
   FreeMem( DataPtr, MaxSize * sizeOf( string ) );
end;

function StringArray.GetWorkSize : word;
var i : word;
    notFound : boolean;
begin
   i := 1;
   notFound := True;
   while ( i <= MaxSize ) and notFound do
     if recall( i ) <> DUMMY_STRING then Inc( i )
                                    else notFound := False;
   if notFound then GetWorkSize := MaxSize
               else GetWorkSize := i-1;
end;

function StringArray.Store( S : string; Index : word ) : boolean;
```

```
begin
   if ( Index > 0 ) and ( Index <= MaxSize ) then begin
     DataPtr^[ Index ] := S;
     ArrayIsSorted := False;
     Store := True;
   end
   else
     Store := False;
end;

function StringArray.Recall( Index : word ) : string;
begin
   if ( Index > 0 ) and ( Index <= MaxSize ) then begin
     Recall := DataPtr^[ Index ];
   end
   else
     Recall := DUMMY_STRING;
end;

{ *************** object VMStringArray ************** }

constructor VMStringArray.Init( VMfilename : string );
begin
   Assign( VMfile, VMfilename );
   ReWrite( VMfile );
   MaxSize := 0;
   ArrayIsSorted := False;
end;

destructor VMStringArray.Done;
begin
   Close ( VMfile );
   Erase( VMfile );
end;

function VMStringArray.GetWorkSize : word;
begin
   GetWorkSize := MaxSize;
end;

function VMStringArray.Store( S : string; Index : word ) :
         boolean;
```

continues

Listing 21.2 continued

```
var i : word;
begin
   if ( Index > 0 ) then begin
     Dec( Index );
     If MaxSize > 0 then begin
       Seek( VMfile, MaxSize-1 );
       for i := MaxSize-1 to Index do
         Seek( VMfile, i );
     end
     else
       for i := 0 to Index do
         Seek( VMfile, i );
       Seek( VMfile, Index );
       Write( VMfile, S );
       if ( Index+1 ) > MaxSize then
         MaxSize := Index+1;
       ArrayIsSorted := False;
       Store := True;
     end
     else
       Store := False;
end;

function VMStringArray.Recall( Index : word ) : string;
var s : string;
begin
   if ( Index > 0 ) and ( Index <= MaxSize ) then begin
     Dec( Index );
     Seek( VMfile, Index );
     Read( VMfile, s );
     Recall := s;
   end
   else
     Recall := DUMMY_STRING;
end;

end.  { AbsArr }
```

The `StringArray` type declares the `Init` constructor, the `Done` destructor, and the virtual methods `GetWorkSize`, `Store`, and `Recall`. In addition, the `DataPtr` data field is declared in the private section. The `MaxSize` and `ArrayIsSorted` data fields are inherited.

The `VMStringArray` object type is also declared as a descendent of the `AbstractStringArray` object type. It declares its constructor, destructor, and own version of the virtual methods `GetWorkSize`, `Store`, and `Recall`. The role of the constructor is to open the random-access file that will store the array elements. No memory or disk space is allocated. This enables the instances of `VMStringArray` to dynamically grow without a preset maximum array size. They are limited, however, by the available disk space.

The `Done` destructor erases the data file, enabling the disk to recuperate its space (much like regaining heap space with `StringArray` objects). The `Store` and `Recall` methods access the array elements in the data file. `VMStringArray` declares a private data field, `VMfile`. This is the handle of the data file, declared as `file of string`. The `GetWorkSize` method systematically returns the value of `MaxSize`, because the working and maximum array sizes are the same in the `VMStringArray` type.

Listing 21.3 contains the source code for the TESTARR.PAS program, which tests the `StringArray` and `VMStringArray` object types. The program tests the instance of each object type in a similar way:

1. The instance of the array object type is instantiated.
2. The strings of a five-member array, `X`, are stored in the dynamic array.
3. The elements of the dynamic array are recalled and displayed on the screen. The `GetWorkSize` message is sent to obtain the working size, which is used in the `For` loop that displays the array members.
4. The elements of the `X` array provide the search strings to look up dynamic array elements. The bottom line of the screen tells you which string is being sought. When found, the `*` character is placed to the right of the matching string (at screen column 40).
5. The dynamic array is sorted, and steps 2 and 3 are repeated.
6. The instance of the dynamic array is removed by sending it a `Done` message.

Listing 21.3

```
program TestArr;

{$M 16384, 0, 655360}
{$V-,X+}

uses dos, Crt, AbsArr;

const MAX_SIZE = 5;
      DELAY_TIME = 500;

type NameArray = array[ 1..MAX_SIZE ] of string;

const X : NameArray =
          ( 'Paris', 'London', 'Madrid', 'Cairo', 'Dublin' );
var A : StringArray;
    B : VMStringArray;
    i, j : word;
    Akey : char;

procedure ClrBottomLine;
  begin
    Gotoxy(1,25);
    Clreol;
  end;

procedure PressAnyKey;
   begin
     ClrBottomLine;
     Write ( 'Press any key...' );
     Akey := Readkey; Clrscr;
   end;

procedure WriteStar(j: word);
   begin
      if j > 0 then begin Gotoxy( 40, j ); Write ( '*' ); end;
   end;

procedure SearchForStr(msg: string; j: word; s: string);
   begin
      ClrBottomLine;
      Write( 'Searching '+msg, s );
      Delay( DELAY_TIME );
```

```
      WriteStar(j);
    end;

begin
  Clrscr;
  A.Init( MAX_SIZE );
  for i := 1 to MAX_SIZE do
    A.Store( X[ i ], i );
  for i := 1 to MAX_SIZE do
    Writeln( i:2, '  ', A.Recall( i ) );
  for i := 1 to MAX_SIZE do begin
    j := A.Search( X[ i ] );
    SearchForStr('unsorted array on heap: 'j,X[i]);
  end;
  PressAnyKey;

  A.Sort;
  for i := 1 to MAX_SIZE do
    Writeln( i:2, '  ', A.Recall( i ) );
  for i := 1 to MAX_SIZE do begin
    j := A.Search( X[ i ] );
    SearchForStr('sorted array on heap: 'j,X[i]);
  end;
  PressAnyKey;
  A.Done;

  B.Init( 'VM.DAT' );
  for i := 1 to MAX_SIZE do
    B.Store( X[ i ], i );
  for i := 1 to MAX_SIZE do
    Writeln( i:2, '  ', B.Recall( i ) );
  for i := 1 to MAX_SIZE do begin
    j := B.Search( X[ i ] );
    SearchForStr('unsorted array on disk: 'j,X[i]);
  end;
  PressAnyKey;

  B.Sort;
  for i := 1 to MAX_SIZE do
    Writeln( i:2, '  ', B.Recall( i ) );
  for i := 1 to MAX_SIZE do begin
    j := B.Search( X[ i ] );
```

continues

Listing 21.3 continued

```
      SearchForStr('sorted array on disk: 'j,X[i]);
    end;
    PressAnyKey;
    B.Done;
end.
```

Where do you put an abstract object type in a hierarchy? The preceding example might suggest that an abstract object type naturally belongs only at the root of a hierarchy. This is not necessarily true. An abstract object type may be placed anywhere in the hierarchy as long as two or more descendent object types can inherit its methods. This eliminates redundant methods that might otherwise appear in sibling object types.

Extending Objects

Structured programming stresses reusability of code; object-oriented programming adds extendibility of code. This makes object-oriented programming languages superior to structured languages when programming sophisticated systems, such as Microsoft Windows applications.

The extendibility of objects lets you design applications at multiple levels. The base levels define the *engine* or *core* object hierarchy; the terminal levels define the *user interface* object hierarchy. This gives you the easy choice of reusing the core levels and designing a new user interface, or extending the current one.

Here is a simple example of using object extendibility to create core and interface level object types. Consider a simple clock. It has an internal timing mechanism (the core) and a display (the interface). Let us model a simple clock using Turbo Pascal objects. The `TimeObj` unit, shown in listing 21.4, declares a core `Ttime` object type. The object type simply reads the system time and creates a string that represents the time.

Listing 21.4

```
unit TimeObj;

interface

uses Dos;
```

```
type
   Ttime = object
      procedure GetSystemTime;
      function TimeStr : string;
   private
      Hour,
      Minute,
      Second,
      Sec100   : word;
      function ConcateTime( N, ModVal : word;
                            LeadingZero : boolean ) : string;
   end;

implementation

   const LeadingZeroYes : BOOLEAN = TRUE;
         LeadingZeroNo : BOOLEAN = FALSE;

procedure Ttime.GetSystemTime;
begin
   GetTime( Hour, Minute, Second, Sec100 )
end;

function Ttime.TimeStr : string;
begin
   TimeStr := ConcateTime( Hour, 12, LeadingZeroNo )  + ':' +
              ConcateTime( Minute, 60, LeadingZeroYes ) + ':' +
              ConcateTime( Second, 60, LeadingZeroYes );
end;

function Ttime.ConcateTime( N, ModVal : word;
                            LeadingZero : boolean ) : string;
var s : string;
begin
   s := '';
   N := N mod ModVal;
   if N < 10 then begin
     Str( N:1, s );
    if LeadingZero then s := '0' + s
                   else s := ' ' + s;
   end
```

continues

Listing 21.4 continued

```
    else
      Str( N:2, s );
      ConcateTime := s
end;

end.
```

The user interface part is shown in listing 21.5. The `ShowTime` unit declares the `TimeShow` object type as a descendent of `Ttime`. The `Show` method displays the time at the current cursor location—the simplest interface. The `Display` method places the time at the designated screen coordinates. The `ShowInBox` method displays the time in a single-line box. The box is erased by calling `ClearBox`. `TimeShow` is in a separate library unit to indicate that the user interface part need not be defined along with the core object types. Of course, this assumes a good core design.

Listing 21.5

```
unit ShowTime;

interface

uses Crt, TimeObj;

type
   TimeShow = object( Ttime )
     procedure Show;                   { display at current cursor }
     procedure Display( x, y : byte );       { display at screen }
                                             {   location  (X,Y) }
     procedure ShowInBox( x, y : byte ); { display upper left    }
                                        { corner of box at (X,Y) }
     procedure ClearBox;
   private
     x1, x2, y1, y2 : byte;
end;

implementation

procedure TimeShow.Show;
begin
   GetSystemTime;
   Write( TimeStr )
```

```
end;

procedure TimeShow.Display( x, y : byte );
begin
   GetSystemTime;
   gotoxy( x, y );
   Write( TimeStr );
end;

procedure TimeShow.ShowInBox( x, y : byte );
var s : string;
    strlen : byte absolute s;  { quick way to get string length }
    i : byte;
begin
   x1 := x; y1 := y;              { x1,y1 are used by ClearBox }
   GetSystemTime;
   s := TimeStr;
   if s[ 1 ] = ' ' then delete( s, 1, 1 );
   gotoxy( x, y ); Write( #218 );          { upper left corner }
   for i := 1 to strlen+2 do
     Write( #196 );                       { top horizontal line }
   Write( #191 );                          { upper right corner }
   gotoxy( x, y+1 ); Write( #179, ' ', s, ' ', #179 );
                                                { vertical line }
   gotoxy( x, y+2 ); Write( #192 );        { lower left corner }
   for i := 1 to strlen+2 do
     Write( #196 );                     { bottom horizontal line }
   Write( #217 );                          { lower right corner }
   x2 := WhereX; y2 := WhereY;    { x2,y2 are used by ClearBox }
end;

procedure TimeShow.ClearBox;
var x, y : byte;
begin
   for y := y1 to y2 do begin
     gotoxy( x1, y );
     for x := x1 to x2 do
       Write( ' ' );
   end;
   writeln;

end;

end.
```

Listing 21.6 shows the source code for the TIMER.PAS program. The program clears the screen and displays the time at the upper right corner of the screen. Pressing any key stops the timer and clears the screen. The timer is simulated using a `repeat until` loop that sends the `ShowInBox` message to the instance `T` of object type `TimeShow`.

Listing 21.6

```
program Timer;

uses Crt, ShowTime;

var
   T : TimeShow;
   C : char;
begin
   Clrscr;
   repeat
     T.ShowInBox( 65, 2 );
     Delay( 900 );       { reduces cursor "noise" }
   until Keypressed;
   while Keypressed do C := Readkey;
   T.ClearBox;
end.
```

The clock application is designed using two library units and a program. The core object `Ttime` is located in unit `TimeObj`. The interface object `TimeShow`, a descendent of `Ttime`, is in unit `ShowTime`. The client application, TIMER.PAS, uses an instance of the interface object type, `TimeShow`.

Object-Oriented Design

Object-oriented design (OOD) constitutes the early phases of developing object-oriented applications. This design stage identifies the object types and object variables that you seek to model and how they relate and interact with each other. The various stages of object-oriented design lead to specifying the various object types, their data fields, and their methods. Because objects do not exist alone, OOD lets the designer establish the hierarchy of object types as well as the object type interaction.

Turbo Pascal and most object-oriented implementations of Pascal have implemented linear (or single) inheritance. Under this inheritance scheme, an object type has at most one parent object type. The hierarchy of object types is a single chain. Other languages, such as C++ and Eiffel, support multiple inheritance, where an object type is allowed to have more than one parent object type. Multiple inheritance is more difficult to implement and, in the minds of some OOP experts, is vulnerable for misuse. You need not worry about multiple inheritance because it is not implemented in Turbo Pascal 6.0.

The basic bond along a single inheritance hierarchy is the *IsA* relationship. Looking at the object types of unit `AbsArr`, you can see that the heap-based array, `StringArray`, *is an* array, and so is the disk-based `VMStringArray` type. In general, each child object type *is a* special refinement of its parent type.

A second relationship can be used in modeling objects. It is the *HasA* relationship. It plays a role in both multiple inheritance and containment. Turbo Pascal Version 6.0 does not implement inheritance, but you can apply containment to Turbo Pascal object types. As the name might suggest, *containment* is when an object type contains data fields that are themselves object variables. These object fields need not be part of the host object's hierarchy.

One example of containment is a car. You can declare an object type that models it. A car is made up of sophisticated components with their own functionality, such as the engine, electrical system, heating/cooling system, and body. These parts can be represented by separate object types. The result is that the car ***has a*** body, ***has an*** engine, ***has an*** electrical system, and so on. You cannot say that a car *is a* body, *is an* engine, or *is an* electrical system. The *HasA* relationship is the sound way to describe a complex object. The next section looks at a simple example of containment.

Containment

The last set of programs offered a small hierarchy of objects to represent a clock. Suppose that you want the clock to display both the date and the time. The `Ttime` object type provides the core level for the clock. Listing 21.7 contains the `DateObj` unit that exports the `Tdate` object type. `Tdate` is similar to `Ttime`—it obtains the system date and provides a string image of the date. Given these two object types, how do you declare an interface object type? The matter is complicated by the fact that `Ttime` and `Tdate` are not part of the same hierarchy. This means that the clock interface object type is neither a date nor a time, but contains both (the *HasA* relationship). Containment could have been avoided by declaring a single date-and-time object type, but the date and time object types are separate for the sake of the example.

Listing 21.7

```
unit DateObj;

interface

uses Dos;

type
   Tdate = object
     procedure GetSystemDate;
     function DateStr : string;
   private
     Year,
     Month,
     Day,
     DayOfWeek  : word;
     function ConcateDate( N, ModVal : word;
                           LeadingZero : boolean ) : string;
   end;

implementation
const  LeadingZeroYes : Boolean = TRUE;
       LeadingZeroNo : Boolean = FALSE;
procedure Tdate.GetSystemdate;
begin
   GetDate( Year, Month, Day, DayOfWeek );
   Year := Year mod 1900;
end;

function Tdate.DateStr : string;
begin
   DateStr := ConcateDate( Month, 13, LeadingZeroNo )  + '/' +
              ConcateDate( Day, 32, LeadingZeroYes )    + '/' +
              ConcateDate( Year, 100, LeadingZeroNo );
end;

function Tdate.ConcateDate( N, ModVal : word;
                            LeadingZero : boolean ) : string;
```

```
var s : string;
begin
   s := '';
   N := N mod ModVal;
   if N = 0 then N := 1;
   if N < 10 then begin
     Str( N:1, s );
     if LeadingZero then s := '0' + s
                     lse s := ' ' + s;
     end
     else
       Str( N:2, s );
     ConcateDate := s
end;

end.
```

Listing 21.8 shows the `ClockObj` unit that declares the `TClock` object type. Its public methods are `ShowInBox` and `ClearBox`, resembling those of object type `TimeShow`. The private data fields contain two special members: `ClockTime` (a `Ttime` object) and `ClockDate` (a `Tdate` object). The instances of the `TClock` object type can obtain the system date and time indirectly through the functionality of the `ClockTime` and `ClockDate` data fields. Containment enables `TClock` to gain access to the functionality of two unrelated object types, without making `TClock` a child of either object type!

Listing 21.8

```
unit ClockObj;

interface

uses Crt, TimeObj, DateObj;

type
   TClock = object
     procedure ShowInBox( x, y : byte );
     procedure ClearBox;
   private
     x1, x2, y1, y2 : byte;
```

continues

Listing 21.8 continued

```
    ClockTime : Ttime;
    ClockDate : Tdate;
  end;

implementation

procedure TClock.ShowInBox( x, y : byte );
var s : string;
    strlen : byte absolute s;  { quick way to get string length }
    i : byte;
begin
   x1 := x; y1 := y;
   ClockTime.GetSystemTime;
   ClockDate.GetSystemDate;
   s := ClockDate.DateStr + ' ' + ClockTime.TimeStr;
   if s[ 1 ] = ' ' then delete( s, 1, 1 );
   gotoxy( x, y ); Write( #218 );           { upper left corner }
   for i := 1 to strlen+2 do
      Write( #196 );                       { top horizontal line }
   Write( #191 );                           { upper right corner }
   gotoxy( x, y+1 ); Write( #179, ' ', s, ' ', #179 );
                                                 { vertical line }
   gotoxy( x, y+2 ); Write( #192 );          { lower left corner }
   for i := 1 to strlen+2 do
      Write( #196 );                    { bottom horizontal line }
   Write( #217 );                           { lower right corner }
   x2 := WhereX; y2 := WhereY; { define x2,y2 so that ClearBox }
                                          { knows what to erase }
end;

procedure TClock.ClearBox;
var x, y : byte;
begin
   for y := y1 to y2 do begin
     gotoxy( x1, y );
     for x := x1 to x2 do
       Write( ' ' );
   end;
   writeln;    { return cursor to left }
end;

end.
```

With the `TClock` object type defined, listing 21.9 shows the TIMER2.PAS program. The program displays the date and time in a box on the screen, until a key is pressed.

Listing 21.9

```
program Timer2;

uses Crt, ClockObj;

var
   T : TClock;
   C : char;

begin
   Clrscr;
   repeat
     T.ShowInBox( 50, 2 );
     Delay( 900 );     { reduces cursor "noise" }
   until Keypressed;
   while Keypressed do C := Readkey;
   T.ClearBox;
end.
```

Summary

This chapter discussed advanced topics in object-oriented programming. You learned about hiding object components using the `private` keyword. You learned about the concept of abstract object types, and extending objects through inheritance.

You learned that you can create an object-oriented application using multilevel objects. Finally, you learned about containment and how it enables an object type to tap simultaneously into separate object hierarchies.

CHAPTER 22

6.0 Turbo Vision

Turbo Pascal Version 6.0 offers two major updates: a new integrated development environment (IDE) and Turbo Vision. The two are related; Turbo Vision constitutes the building blocks of the new IDE. Turbo Vision is a powerful software tool that can be used to implement professional and consistent user interfaces. To learn about the capabilities of Turbo Vision you need only to explore the various aspects of the integrated environment and its pull-down menus, status line, windows with and without scrolling bars, and dialog boxes with input lines, check boxes, and radio buttons. Turbo Vision is in the caliber of well-crafted third-party Turbo Pascal toolboxes.

Turbo Vision is by no means a trivial software toolbox. This is reflected by the sophisticated user interface of the integrated environment. Extensively covering Turbo Vision in one chapter is possible only for readers who have the stomach to read a 400-page chapter. Instead, this chapter answers some of the most obvious and general questions about Turbo Vision:

1. What is Turbo Vision?
2. What can Turbo Vision do for my applications?
3. What are the main components of Turbo Vision?
4. What does a source code Turbo Vision application look like?

What Is Turbo Vision?

Turbo Vision is a user-interface toolbox built on a sophisticated object-oriented hierarchy. It is a vehicle for developing text-based window applications, such as the Turbo Pascal integrated environment. Turbo Vision object types are incorporated in your application by extending them. Because this process involves a highly developed set of object types, your applications end up sharing a common user-interface style. Experience with Macintosh computers has shown that this approach makes such applications (and consequently the computer brand itself) easier to use. Like Macintosh programs, Turbo Vision applications are event-driven. This is perhaps the most important distinction between Turbo Vision and most of the third-party Turbo Pascal user-interface toolboxes.

Turbo Vision Capabilities

Turbo Vision gives your applications the desktop look—a background against which character-based windows are displayed, moved around, and stacked, much like paper documents on a physical office desk. You can incorporate the following Turbo Vision user-interface components in your applications:

A main menu bar with pull-down menus. The menu options highlight the shortcut-key characters and may have hot keys associated with them. You can also nest pull-down menus, and thus avoid the use of long pull-down menus.

A status menu bar at the bottom of the screen. This lists the available keys and their functions. For example, `Alt-X Exit` is typically displayed in Turbo Vision applications to indicate that you can quickly exit the program by pressing Alt-X.

Non-scrollable windows. These windows display information. They can be moved and closed.

Scrollable windows. With these windows—which are the most sought-after type of window—you can view a portion of a document using the vertical and horizontal scroll bars.

The vertical scroll bar enables you to move the document up and down. The scroll bar has a text position indicator (a box character) that indicates roughly what portion of the document you are viewing. As you move through the document, the indicator moves accordingly. If you use a mouse, you can navigate more flexibly. You can click on the scroll bar above or below the text position indicator to jump the viewed text up or down, respectively. You can click the mouse also at either end of the scroll bar (where the thick arrowhead characters are located) to scroll through the text upward or downward. Finally, you can drag the text position indicator with the mouse (by moving the mouse to the indicator, holding down the left mouse button, then moving the mouse up or down) to zoom in on any area of the text. (When you release the left mouse button, text in the window is updated.)

The horizontal scroll bar is similar to the vertical scroll bar. It enables you to scroll a document to the left or to the right.

Dialog boxes. These are the interactive parts of a Turbo Vision application. Dialog boxes contain text labels, radio buttons, check boxes, pushdown buttons, and input lines. These components can be used in various combinations to produce dialog boxes that vary in the level of interaction. The simplest dialog box is the one found in the `About` option of the system main menu. This type of dialog box displays a message and offers one button (usually, the OK button) that you press after reading the message. A more sophisticated type of dialog box is the one used by the `Add Watch` debug option. Such a dialog box contains an input line and several pushdown buttons.

The \TP\TVDEMOS directory contains a number of Turbo Vision applications and their building-block units. The programs follow:

- FILEVIEW.PAS is a file viewing program that uses scrollable windows. You may find yourself using this program daily, especially because it enables you to view multiple files.
- GENFORM.PAS generates *.TVF form files for the TVFORMS.PAS program. These form files are read and interpreted by TVFORMS.PAS to implement dialog box-based entry forms.
- GENRDEMO.PAS generates resources for TVRDEMO.PAS.
- TVBGI.PAS is a demo program that illustrates the capability to invoke the high-resolution graphics BGI system from a Turbo Vision application.
- TVDEMO.PAS demonstrates various aspects of Turbo Vision and offers a file browser (using scrollable windows). In addition, there are options that pop-up a puzzle, a calculator, a calendar, and an ASCII table.
- TVEDIT.PAS is a file editing program that uses scrollable windows. You can use this program for simple editing. Its advantage is its capability to open and edit multiple documents. TVEDIT is another candidate for daily use.

- TVFORMS.PAS demonstrates how dialog boxes can be used to implement form entry systems. It opens and interprets the *.TVF form files. Borland provides two form files, one for phone numbers and one for part numbers.
- TVHC.PAS is a Turbo Vision help file compiler. It converts a script file into a HLP help file and a PAS unit that exports the command constants.
- TVRDEMO.PAS is similar to TVDEMO.PAS, except it uses resource files and overlays to build the application. The resource files are created by the GENRDEMO.PAS program.
- TVTXTDMO.PAS is a simple file viewer. The program automatically scrolls through the viewed file, then lets you browse through it.

The preceding programs use these library units:

- ASCIITAB.PAS exports an object that displays the ASCII table.
- CALC.PAS exports an object that shows a four-function calculator.
- CALENDAR.PAS exports an object that displays a calendar.
- DATACOLL.PAS exports the `TDataCollection` object.
- DEMOCMDS.PAS exports only demonstration command constants. These constants are used by the other Turbo Vision demo units and programs.
- DEMOHELP.PAS exports only demonstration help constants. These constants are used by the various Turbo Vision demo units and programs.
- FIELDS.PAS exports two input field object types that extend `TInputLine`.
- FORMCMDS.PAS exports only command constants only. These constants are used by the TVFORMS.PAS program.
- FORMS.PAS exports the `TForm` object type, which creates a form entry window using a dialog box.
- FVIEWER.PAS exports the `TFileViewer` object for scrolling through text files. The TVDEMO.PAS example program uses the `TFileViewer` object type.
- GADGETS.PAS exports visible heap and clock objects.
- GENPARTS.PAS exports the data types used by GENFORM.PAS to generate the PARTS.TVF file, which is used by TVFORMS.PAS.

- GENPHONE.PAS exports the data types used by GENFORM.PAS to generate the PHONENUM.TVF file, which is used by TVFORMS.PAS.
- GRAPHAPP.PAS provides BGI support for Turbo Vision programs. The TVBGI.PAS example programs uses this unit.
- HELPFILE.PAS exports objects used by the TVHC.PAS Turbo Vision help compiler.
- LISTDLG.PAS exports objects that manage various list boxes. The TVFORMS.PAS program uses this unit.
- MOUSEDLG.PAS exports objects used in adjusting the mouse through a dialog. This unit is used by TVDEMO.PAS and TVRDEMO.PAS.
- PUZZLE.PAS exports object types that display a simple puzzle. This unit is used by TVDEMO.PAS.

You may want to use some of the preceding library units in your applications. These units are valuable extensions to the Turbo Vision object hierarchy.

The following two batch files are used to assist the Turbo Vision demonstration files:

- GENFORMS.BAT is a batch file that creates the two forms data files, PHONENUM.TVF and PARTS.TVF.
- MKRDEMO.BAT is a batch file that generates TVRDEMO.EXE, the overlaid version of TVDEMO.EXE. The TVRDEMO.EXE program also uses resource files.

You are encouraged to compile and run the preceding Turbo Vision demonstration programs to get an idea of what Turbo Vision applications can do. Figure 22.1 shows a session with the FILEVIEW.PAS program. The program lets you browse into one or more files anywhere in your system. In addition, the `Windows` option lets you manage the viewed windows, especially if you have no mouse. Using a mouse with this utility enhances navigation though the various options.

Figure 22.2 shows a file editing session with TVEDIT.PAS. The lower window is the active window, and its contents are being edited. The TVEDIT.PAS program supports basic editing keystrokes, like the ones found in the IDE editor. Cutting and pasting is also supported. These features make TVEDIT.PAS an attractive editor in its own right.

Figure 22.3 shows the TVFORMS.PAS program while a phone number entry is being edited. This program illustrates how Turbo Vision applications can be used in form entry.

Fig. 22.1. *A sample session with the FILEVIEW.PAS program.*

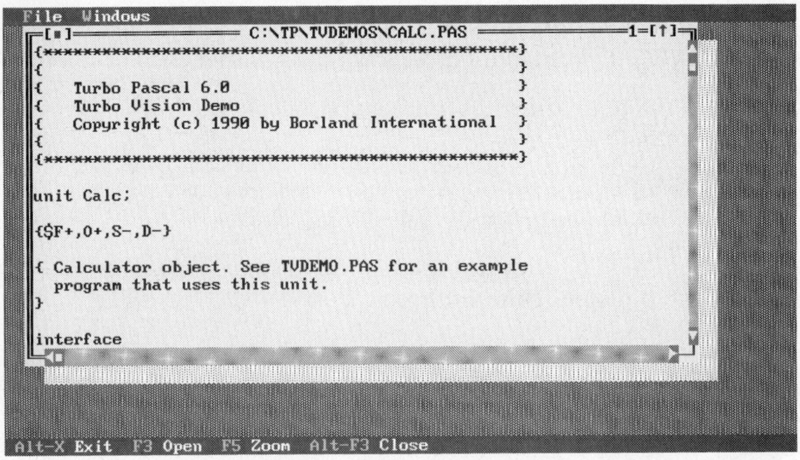

```
 File  Windows
 [■]============ C:\TP\TVDEMOS\CALC.PAS ============1=[↑]
 {*********************************************}
 {                                             }
 {   Turbo Pascal 6.0                          }
 {   Turbo Vision Demo                         }
 {   Copyright (c) 1990 by Borland International }
 {                                             }
 {*********************************************}

 unit Calc;

 {$F+,O+,S-,D-}

 { Calculator object. See TVDEMO.PAS for an example
   program that uses this unit.
 }

 interface

 Alt-X Exit  F3 Open  F5 Zoom  Alt-F3 Close
```

Fig. 22.2. *A sample session with the TVEDIT.PAS program.*

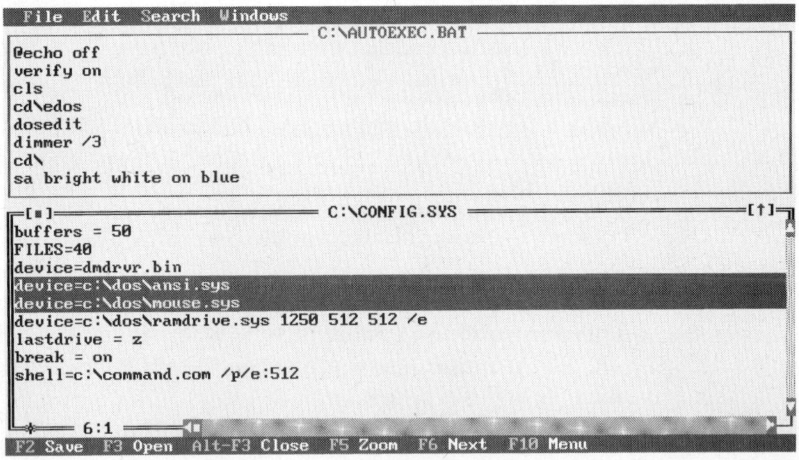

```
 File  Edit  Search  Windows
 ------------------ C:\AUTOEXEC.BAT ------------------
 @echo off
 verify on
 cls
 cd\edos
 dosedit
 dimmer /3
 cd\
 sa bright white on blue

 =[■]============== C:\CONFIG.SYS ==============[↑]
 buffers = 50
 FILES=40
 device=dmdrvr.bin
 device=c:\dos\ansi.sys
 device=c:\dos\mouse.sys
 device=c:\dos\ramdrive.sys 1250 512 512 /e
 lastdrive = z
 break = on
 shell=c:\command.com /p/e:512

 ==== 6:1 ====
 F2 Save  F3 Open  Alt-F3 Close  F5 Zoom  F6 Next  F10 Menu
```

Figure 22.4 shows the puzzle, calculator, calendar, and ASCII table windows while running TVDEMO.PAS. These tools can be popped up from menu selections. They need not be TSRs. Moreover, when TVDEMO.PAS terminates, these tools are removed with it.

Fig. 22.3. A sample session with the TVFORMS.PAS program.

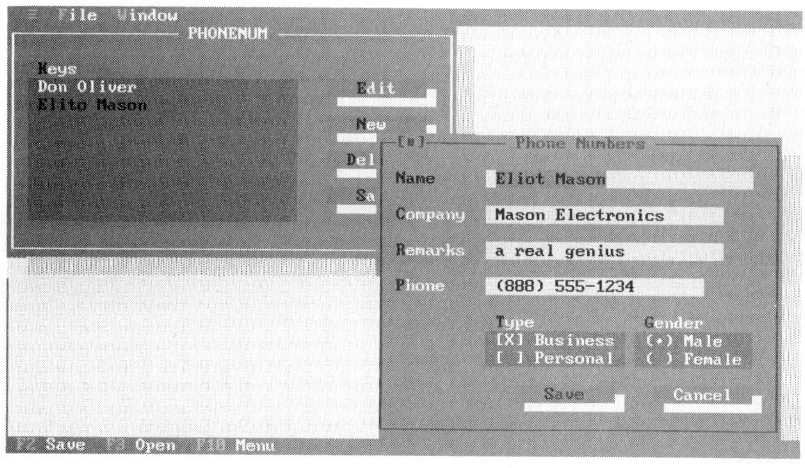

Fig. 22.4. A sample session with the TVDEMO.PAS program.

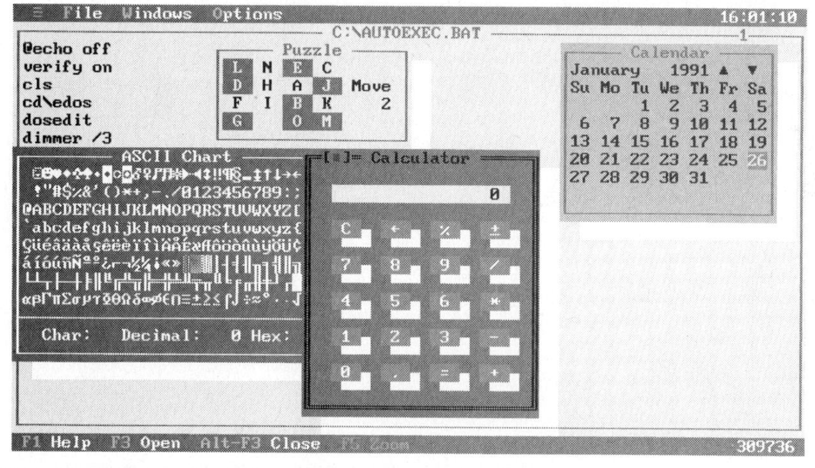

The Turbo Vision Hierarchy

The Turbo Vision hierarchy, shown in figure 22.5, is an excellent example of how object-oriented programming offers a divide-and-conquer strategy superior to structured programming. The various methods of the object types declared in the Turbo Vision hierarchy play different roles based on their nature.

Fig. 22.5. *The Turbo Vision hierarchy.*

```
+ TObject
     +   TView
            - TBackground
            - TButton
            + TCluster
                 - TCheckBoxes
                 - TRadioButtons
            - TFrame
            + TGroup
                 - TDeskTop
                 - TProgram
                        - TApplication
                 + TWindow
                        - TDialog
                        - THistoryWindow
            - THistory
            - TInputLine
            + TListViewer
                 - TMenuBar
                 - TMenuBox
            + TScroller
                 + TTextDevice
                        - TTerminal
            - TScrollBar
            + TStaticText
                 - TLabel
                 - TParamText
            - TStatusLine
     + TCollection
            + TSortedCollection
                 + TStringCollection
                        - TResourceCollection
     + TStream
            + TDosStream
                  -TBufStream
            - TEmsStream
     - TResourceFile
     - TStringList
     - TStrListMaker
```

To begin with, Turbo Pascal implements static and virtual methods. Virtual methods are vital in implementing polymorphic behavior, which plays a key role in how Turbo Vision variables react to messages. Static methods are used when the program requires monomorphic behavior (that is, a consistent response, which is achieved by calling the same sequence of Pascal routines). In addition, there are abstract methods, with varying levels of abstractness. The level depends on what the object types are passing down to their descendent. For example, the methods of TObject are highly abstract, because TObject is a bare-bone object type and the root of the Turbo Vision hierarchy. By contrast, the methods of TCluster are not highly abstract, because they are methods common to the descendants of TCluster.

The two main categories of Turbo Vision object types are Views and nonViews (mute) objects. The family of Views object types begins with TView. Views share the common characteristics of being rectangular views (hence the name Views).

Views are classified into two categories: groups and terminal views. Groups are highly interactive views that animate the desktop area of a Turbo Vision application. The TGroup object type is the root of the group subhierarchy. Terminal views are descendents of the TView that (a) have no descendents in the Turbo Vision hierarchy, and (b) offer fairly complete visible components.

Mute objects perform behind-the-scene tasks and offer auxiliary support to the Views objects. For example, collections manage lists of data used by scrolling views and list boxes.

A Turbo Vision applications contains a set of Turbo Vision instances. These instances work together by being connected and interacting with each other. The connection between various instances is expressed in terms of ownership—instance A owns instance B when B is placed inside A. For example, a button (an instance of TButton) is owned by a dialog box (an instance of TDialog) when the button appears inside the dialog box. Turbo Vision instances interact with each other by generating and handling events. Events are emitted by the keyboard, the mouse, or by other methods. Handling these events breathes life into a Turbo Vision application, making it event-driven.

Streams

Streams are object types that handle the input and output of object instances. Streams perform important services to the Turbo Vision hierarchy and applications. The concept of streams in Turbo Pascal has been borrowed from the C++ language, and for very good reasons. Streams are superior to the traditional I/O intrinsics (Read, ReadLn, Write, WriteLn, BlockRead, and BlockWrite) because they can handle complex objects (especially those with virtual methods and their addresses) more easily. This also permits streams to handle instances of future objects. The power of a stream lies in its capability to provide polymorphic object-oriented I/O.

The Streams I/O services parallel those of traditional file I/O. Streams support both sequential and random-access I/O. Using streams is as easy as regular file I/O. A stream must be initialized (the equivalent of opening a file) before you can read and write object instances to it.

How can streams handle the file I/O for various object types, especially when Turbo Pascal does not support the `file of object` type? The answer lies in a mechanism called registration. This involves the declaration of a registration record type that looks like the following:

```
PMyStreamRec = ^TMyStreamRec;
TMyStreamRec = record
     ObjType : Word;
     VmtLink : Word;
     Load : Pointer;
     Save : Pointer;
     Next : Word;
end;
```

`ObjType` is the unique object type ID number that you must supply (with careful planning). `VmtLink` is the link to the virtual method table (VMT), which handles virtual methods. The `Load` and `Store` fields are pointers to the `Load` and `Save` methods that are consistently used by the Turbo Vision object types for stream I/O. You can use streams in your own OOP, non-Turbo Vision applications, as long as you make your streamable object types descendents of `TObject`.

Resources

The concept of resources was popularized by the Apple Macintosh computer. Resources enable an application to display alternate views without changing the program's code! For example, the same set of pull-down menus can appear in French for the French-speaking computer user, and in English for the English speaking user, while the code for menus remains the same. Resources could be nicknamed "prefabricated views."

Turbo Vision implements resources that are stored in streams using unique names. Resources are usually generated by separate programs that create the different alternate views and save them in a resource file. The regular Turbo Vision application then selectively reads the resources it needs. TVRDEMO.PAS is a modified version of TVDEMO.PAS that uses resources to implement the same functionality of TVDEMO.PAS. Turbo Vision provides a highly flexible resources management system. Unlike the other Turbo Vision object types, the resource-related types are adequate and need not be extended to become more useful.

The Turbo Vision Object Hierarchy

This section describes the members of the Turbo Vision hierarchy and a few related object types. Publicly declared parts of the object types are included for two reasons (the private parts, if any, are omitted by Borland): to give you a feel for the extent of functionality of each object type, and to provide a quick reference.

A sophisticated hierarchy like Turbo Vision is bound to use auxiliary constants, records, object types, and variables. Among such numerous items are the `TPoint` and `TRect` object types. These two independent objects play an important role in the Turbo Vision hierarchy. The `TPoint` object type keeps track of the (X, Y) coordinate of a point:

```
TPoint = object
  X, Y : Integer;
end;
```

Turbo Vision uses a slightly different numbering system for screen coordinates. Normally, the coordinates of the upper left corner of the screen are (1,1), the first screen row and column. Turbo Vision looks at the screen as a rectangular grid of square blocks. The edges of these blocks—not the blocks themselves—are numbered. Thus, the character at the upper left corner of the screen is defined by the (0,0) and (1,1) coordinates, the upper left and lower right edges of the character, respectively.

The `TRect` object type is more elaborate than `TPoint`. It defines and manages the data for a rectangular area, defined by the `A` and `B` `TPoint` fields. `A` stores the upper left corner coordinates of the rectangular area; `B` holds the lower right coordinates. The Views object types use the `TRect` methods to set up a view and manage its movement. The `TRect` type is declared as follows:

```
TRect = object
  A, B : TPoint;
  procedure Assign( XA, YA, XB, YB : Integer );
  procedure Copy( R : TRect );
  procedure Move( ADX, ADY : Integer );
  procedure Grow( ADX, ADY : Integer );
  procedure Intersect( R : TRect );
  procedure Union( R : TRect );
  function Contains( P : TPoint ) : Boolean;
  function Equals( R : TRect ) : Boolean;
  function Empty : Boolean;
end;
```

The root of the Turbo Vision hierarchy is `TObject`. It declares three methods, but no data fields. The `Init` constructor is the first of a series of constructors declared by the Turbo Vision object types. Each descendent object type must invoke the `Init` of its parent as part of the constructor action. Thus, while `TObject.Init` is rarely called explicitly, it is always called by the instances of its descendent object types.

The `Free` method disposes the object's instance and calls the `Done` destructor. The `Done` destructor recovers the heap space of the dynamic object. Unlike `Init`, the `Done` destructor must be entirely overridden. The `TOBject` and its pointer type, `PObject`, are declared as follows:

```
PObject = ^TObject;
TObject = object
  constructor Init;
  procedure Free;
  destructor Done; virtual;
end;
```

The preceding style of declaring a type and its pointer is obeyed by all the descendent objects, including the ones you plan to add. The following naming conventions are used:

- The letter *T* is used as the first letter of the object type name.
- The letter *P* is used as the first letter of the object's pointer type.

The `TView` object type is the parent of the Views object types. `TView` is an abstract type for its descendents. Nevertheless, it is a well-developed object type that contains a number of data fields and methods. Although `TView` has two constructors, it is rarely instantiated. Most of its static methods are either inherited or overridden by descendent objects. The `TView` methods provide to the `TView` descendents a variety of services, such as event handling, view-size management, command control, view output, and mouse management.

The `Owner` data field establishes an ownership link of the view. This tells the Turbo Vision system which instance of a `TGroup` descendent owns the view. The `Next` and `Owner` data fields assist in maintaining the links among the active views of an application. The virtual `Draw` method is among the most important methods. It enables a view to display itself. All `TView` descendents implement their own `Draw` methods to sustain polymorphic behavior. The `TView` object type and its pointer type, `PView`, are declared as follows:

```
PView = ^TView;
TView = object( TObject )
  Owner : PGroup;
```

```
Next : PView;
Origin : TPoint;
Size : TPoint;
Cursor : TPoint;
GrowMode : Byte;
DragMode : Byte;
HelpCtx : Word;
State : Word;
Options : Word;
EventMask : Word;
constructor Init( var Bounds : TRect );
constructor Load( var S : TStream );
destructor Done; virtual;
procedure BlockCursor;
procedure CalcBounds( var Bounds : TRect; Delta : TPoint );
                      virtual;
procedure ChangeBounds( var Bounds : TRect ); virtual;
procedure ClearEvent( var Event : TEvent );
function CommandEnabled( Command : Word ) : Boolean;
function DataSize : Word; virtual;
procedure DisableCommands( Commands : TCommandSet );
procedure DragView( Event : TEvent; Mode : Byte;
                    var Limits : TRect;
                        MinSize, MaxSize : TPoint );
procedure Draw; virtual;
procedure DrawView;
procedure EnableCommands( Commands : TCommandSet );
procedure EndModal( Command : Word ); virtual;
function EventAvail : Boolean;
function Execute : Word; virtual;
function Exposed : Boolean;
procedure GetBounds( var Bounds : TRect );
procedure GetClipRect( var Clip : TRect );
function GetColor( Color : Word ) : Word;
procedure GetCommands( var Commands : TCommandSet );
procedure GetData( var Rec ); virtual;
procedure GetEvent( var Event : TEvent ); virtual;
procedure GetExtent( var Extent : TRect );
function GetHelpCtx : Word; virtual;
function GetPalette : PPalette; virtual;
procedure GetPeerViewPtr( var S : TStream; var P );
function GetState( AState : Word ) : Boolean;
procedure GrowTo( X, Y : Integer );
procedure HandleEvent( var Event : TEvent ); virtual;
```

```
procedure Hide;
procedure HideCursor;
procedure KeyEvent( var Event : TEvent );
procedure Locate( var Bounds : TRect );
procedure MakeFirst;
procedure MakeGlobal( Source : TPoint; var Dest : TPoint );
procedure MakeLocal( Source : TPoint; var Dest : TPoint );
function MouseEvent( var Event : TEvent;
                     Mask : Word ) : Boolean;
function MouseInView( Mouse : TPoint ) : Boolean;
procedure MoveTo( X, Y : Integer );
function NextView : PView;
procedure NormalCursor;
function Prev : PView;
function PrevView : PView;
procedure PutEvent( var Event : TEvent ); virtual;
procedure PutInFrontOf( Target : PView );
procedure PutPeerViewPtr( var S : TStream; P : PView );
procedure Select;
procedure SetBounds( var Bounds : TRect );
procedure SetCommands( Commands : TCommandSet );
procedure SetCursor( X, Y : Integer );
procedure SetData( var Rec ); virtual;
procedure SetState( AState : Word; Enable : Boolean ); virtual;
procedure Show;
procedure ShowCursor;
procedure SizeLimits( var Min, Max : TPoint ); virtual;
procedure Store( var S : TStream );
function TopView : PView;
function Valid( Command : Word ) : Boolean; virtual;
procedure WriteBuf( X, Y, W, H : Integer; var Buf );
procedure WriteChar( X, Y : Integer; C : Char; Color : Byte;
                     Count : Integer );
procedure WriteLine( X, Y, W, H : Integer; var Buf );
procedure WriteStr( X, Y : Integer; Str : String;
                    Color : Byte );
end;
```

The `TBackground` object type is part of the terminal views. Compared to other views, it is rarely called directly by a Turbo Vision application. The `TBackground` declaration follows:

```
PBackground = ^TBackground;
TBackground = object( TView )
```

```
    Pattern : Char;
    constructor Init( var Bounds : TRect; APattern : Char );
    constructor Load( var S : TStream );
    procedure Draw; virtual;
    function GetPalette : PPalette; virtual;
    procedure Store( var S : TStream );
  end;
```

The TButton object type displays a small shadowed box with a title. When multiple TButton instances are displayed, you can change the default button by using the tab key. The default button is selected by pressing the space bar or Enter key, or by clicking the button with a mouse. This generates an event that must be handled by the Turbo Vision system. The AmDefault data field indicates whether the button is the default. The TButton declaration follows:

```
PButton = ^TButton;
TButton = object( TView )
  Title : PString;
  Command : Word;
  Flags : Byte;
  AmDefault : Boolean;
  constructor Init( var Bounds : TRect; ATitle : TTitleStr;
                    ACommand : Word; AFlags : Word );
  constructor Load( var S : TStream );
  destructor Done; virtual;
  procedure Draw; virtual;
  procedure DrawState( Down : Boolean );
  function GetPalette : PPalette; virtual;
  procedure HandleEvent( var Event : TEvent ); virtual;
  procedure MakeDefault( Enable : Boolean );
  procedure Press; virtual;
  procedure SetState( AState : Word; Enable : Boolean ); virtual;
  procedure Store( var S : TStream );
end;
```

The TButton type inherits a good deal of data fields and methods from its parent, TView. The majority of TButton methods are virtual (even though TButton is a terminal view), which gives you flexibility in extending the object type.

The TCluster type is an abstract object type with TRadioButtons and TCheckBoxes as its descendents. TCluster declares the data fields and methods common to its descendents to avoid redundant code.

The TRadioButtons and TCheckBoxes form a control group with similar behavior: check boxes and radio buttons can be marked. The difference is that you can select only one radio button (which automatically deselects the current one), but you can select multiple check boxes. For the radio buttons, new control marks are made by using the cursor keys, selecting a highlighted letter, or mouse clicks. For the check boxes, new control marks are made by pressing the space bar, selecting a highlighted letter, or mouse clicks.

The Value data field permits your program to associate a value with the selected control. The Mark, Press, and MovedTo methods manage the marking of the controls, using the Sel index data field. TCluster is declared next:

```
PCluster = ^TCluster;
TCluster = object( TView )
  Value : Word;
  Sel : Integer;
  Strings : TStringCollection;
  constructor Init( var Bounds : TRect; AStrings : PSItem );
  constructor Load( var S : TStream );
  destructor Done; virtual;
  function DataSize : Word; virtual;
  procedure DrawBox( Icon : String; Marker : Char );
  procedure GetData( var Rec ); virtual;
  function GetHelpCtx : Word; virtual;
  function GetPalette : PPalette; virtual;
  procedure HandleEvent( var Event : TEvent ); virtual;
  function Mark( Item : Integer ) : Boolean; virtual;
  procedure Press( Item : Integer ); virtual;
  procedure MovedTo( Item : Integer ); virtual;
  procedure SetData( var Rec ); virtual;
  procedure SetState( AState : Word; Enable : Boolean ); virtual;
  procedure Store( var S : TStream );
end;
```

The TRadioButton and TCheckBoxes object types are declared in the following:

```
PRadioButtons = ^TRadioButtons;
TRadioButtons = object( TCluster )
  procedure Draw; virtual;
  function Mark( Item : Integer ) : Boolean; virtual;
  procedure MovedTo( Item : Integer ); virtual;
  procedure Press( Item : Integer ); virtual;
```

```
    procedure SetData( var Rec ); virtual;
  end;

  PCheckBoxes = ^TCheckBoxes;
  TCheckBoxes = object( TCluster )
    procedure Draw; virtual;
    function Mark( Item : Integer ) : Boolean; virtual;
    procedure Press( Item : Integer ); virtual;
  end;
```

The `TFrame` object type is an auxiliary terminal view controlled by `TView`. `TFrame` draws the window frames that contain the close-window and move-window icons. `TFrame` is declared as follows:

```
PFrame = ^TFrame;
TFrame = object( TView )
  constructor Init( var Bounds : TRect );
  procedure Draw; virtual;
  function GetPalette : PPalette; virtual;
  procedure HandleEvent( var Event : TEvent ); virtual;
  procedure SetState( AState : Word; Enable : Boolean ); virtual;
end;
```

The `TGroup` type and its descendents play a vital role in managing the visible components of the Turbo Vision desktop. This group controls and updates the current subviews using a dynamic linked list. This list is constantly updated, in response to keyboard or mouse action, to indicate which views have become visible, partially visible, or hidden behind others. The `Last` and `Current` data fields are used to control the list. The `Last` field points to the last element of the dynamic list; the `Current` data field signals whether the instance of `TGroup` is selected (a nil value indicates that the field is not selected). The `Insert` method plays an important role in inserting visible objects inside each other and establishing ownership of instances. The `TGroup` object type is declared next:

```
PGroup = ^TGroup;
TGroup = object( TView )
  Last : PView;
  Current : PView;
  Phase : ( phFocused, phPreProcess, phPostProcess );
            Buffer : PVideoBuf;
  constructor Init( var Bounds : TRect );
  constructor Load( var S : TStream );
  destructor Done; virtual;
  procedure ChangeBounds( var Bounds : TRect ); virtual;
```

```
  function DataSize : Word; virtual;
  procedure Delete( P : PView );
  procedure Draw; virtual;
  procedure EndModal( Command : Word ); virtual;
  procedure EventError( var Event : TEvent ); virtual;
  function ExecView( P : PView ) : Word;
  function Execute : Word; virtual;
  function First : PView;
  function FirstThat( P : Pointer ) : PView;
  procedure ForEach( P : Pointer );
  procedure GetData( var Rec ); virtual;
  function GetHelpCtx : Word; virtual;
  procedure GetSubViewPtr( var S : TStream; var P );
  procedure HandleEvent( var Event : TEvent ); virtual;
  procedure Insert( P : PView );
  procedure InsertBefore( P, Target : PView );
  procedure Lock;
  procedure PutSubViewPtr( var S : TStream; P : PView );
  procedure Redraw;
  procedure SelectNext( Forwards : Boolean );
  procedure SetData( var Rec ); virtual;
  procedure SetState( AState : Word; Enable : Boolean ); virtual;
  procedure Store( var S : TStream );
  procedure Unlock;
  function Valid( Command : Word ) : Boolean; virtual;
end;
```

The `TDesktop` object type provides the standard visible desktop, with the menu bar and the status line at the top and bottom screen lines, respectively. The `Tile` and `Cascade` methods are responsible for displaying multiple windows in a tile or cascade fashion, respectively. The declaration for `TDeskTop` follows:

```
PDeskTop = ^TDeskTop;
TDeskTop = object( TGroup )
  Background : PBackground;
  constructor Init( var Bounds : TRect );
  procedure Cascade( var R : TRect );
  procedure HandleEvent( var Event : TEvent ); virtual;
  procedure InitBackground; virtual;
  procedure Tile( var R : TRect );
  procedure TileError; virtual;
end;
```

The TProgram object type is an important ancestor and a basic template for all Turbo Vision applications. It provides a set of virtual methods that define the essential tasks of a program. Perhaps the most important one is Run, which executes the program. The InitDesktop, InitMenuBar, InitScreen, and InitStatusLine virtual methods are involved in initializing various parts of a Turbo Vision application. The TProgram object type is declared as follows:

```
PProgram = ^TProgram;
TProgram = object( TGroup )
  constructor Init;
  destructor Done; virtual;
  procedure GetEvent( var Event : TEvent ); virtual;
  function GetPalette : PPalette; virtual;
  procedure HandleEvent( var Event : TEvent ); virtual;
  procedure Idle; virtual;
  procedure InitDeskTop; virtual;
  procedure InitMenuBar; virtual;
  procedure InitScreen; virtual;
  procedure InitStatusLine; virtual;
  procedure OutOfMemory; virtual;
  procedure PutEvent( var Event : TEvent ); virtual;
  procedure Run; virtual;
  procedure SetScreenMode( Mode : Word );
  function ValidView( P : PView ) : PView;
end;
```

TApplication is the object type that will be connected to all Turbo Vision applications. You declare object types that are descendents of TApplication. These new types will own TMenuBar, TstatusLine, and TDeskTop subviews. The declaration of TApplication follows:

```
PApplication = ^TApplication;
TApplication = object( TProgram )
  constructor Init;
  destructor Done; virtual;
end;
```

A new application object type, for example, MyProgram, is typically declared as follows:

```
PMyProgram = ^TMyProgram;
TMyProgram = object( TApplication )
  procedure HandleEvent(var Event: TEvent); virtual;
  procedure InitMenuBar; virtual;
  procedure InitStatusLine; virtual;
end;
```

The InitMenuBar and InitStatusLine methods build the menu bar and the status line specific to TMyProgram. HandleEvent responds to the events of the TMyProgram variables. Other methods are included as needed.

The main section of a custom Turbo Vision program contains at least the following three statements:

1. The first statement instantiates the object variable MyProgram.
2. The second statement sends MyProgram a Run message (the TProgram.Run method is invoked).
3. The third message removes the instance of TMyProgram using the Done destructor.

The main program section follows:

```
var MyProgram : TMyProgram;
begin
  MyProgram.Init;
  MyProgram.Run;
  MyProgram.Done;
end.
```

The TWindow object type works with TFrame (through the Frame data field) in creating, displaying, and managing a window view. The Zoom and Close methods are used to zoom in on a window and close it, respectively. The HandleEvent method responds to the commands that move, resize, zoom, and close windows, and select the next or previous window. The last two commands are generated by pressing the Tab and Shift-Tab keys. TWindow is declared as follows:

```
PWindow = ^TWindow;
TWindow = object( TGroup )
  Flags : Byte;
  ZoomRect : TRect;
  Number : Integer;
  Palette : Integer;
  Frame : PFrame;
  Title : PString;
  constructor Init( var Bounds : TRect; ATitle : TTitleStr;
                    ANumber : Integer );
  constructor Load( var S : TStream );
  destructor Done; virtual;
  procedure Close; virtual;
  function GetPalette : PPalette; virtual;
  function GetTitle( MaxSize : Integer ) : TTitleStr; virtual;
```

```
    procedure HandleEvent( var Event : TEvent ); virtual;
    procedure InitFrame; virtual;
    procedure SetState( AState : Word; Enable : Boolean ); virtual;
    procedure SizeLimits( var Min, Max : TPoint ); virtual;
    function StandardScrollBar( AOptions : Word ) : PScrollBar;
    procedure Store( var S : TStream );
    procedure Zoom; virtual;
  end;
```

The `TWindow` type has two descendents: `TDialog` and `THistoryWindow`. `TDialog` creates a dialog box to interact with the application user. Dialog boxes may contain push-down buttons, radio buttons, check boxes, and input lines. Dialog boxes can be moved and closed, but they cannot be resized, because this would hide important information. The `TDialog` object type declares no data field of its own. It declares a constructor and three virtual methods—everything else is inherited. The declaration of `TDialog` follows:

```
PDialog = ^TDialog;
TDialog = object( TWindow )
  constructor Init( var Bounds : TRect; ATitle : TTitleStr );
  function GetPalette : PPalette; virtual;
  procedure HandleEvent( var Event : TEvent ); virtual;
  function Valid( Command : Word ) : Boolean; virtual;
end;
```

The `THistoryWindow` object type is the other descendent of `TWindow`. The history viewer is a special window that stores the most recent selections to reduce the amount of typing. The history window cannot be resized or zoomed. Typically, the history window first appears as a special input line with a grow icon next to it (the icon is a down-arrow symbol). When you click on the grow icon or press the down-arrow key, the history window expands to reveal the last few selections. You can scroll down the list to view and perhaps choose previous selections. The `Viewer` data field is a pointer to a dynamic list of strings representing your latest input. `THistoryWindow` is declared as follows:

```
PHistoryWindow = ^THistoryWindow;
THistoryWindow = object( TWindow )
  Viewer : PListViewer;
  constructor Init( var Bounds : TRect; HistoryId : Word );
  function GetPalette : PPalette; virtual;
  function GetSelection : String; virtual;
  procedure InitViewer( HistoryId : Word ); virtual;
end;
```

The task of THistoryWindow requires the help of two more object types, TInputLine and THistory. The THistory object type maintains the list of recent choices using a fixed heap size. When the storage space for the list is used up, the oldest selections are discarded. This makes the dynamic list behave like a first-in first-out queue. The THistory type works with the TInputLine and THistoryWindow types, as seen by the parameters of the Init constructor and InitHistoryWindow method. The declaration of THistory follows:

```
PHistory = ^THistory;
THistory = object( TView )
  Link : PInputLine;
  HistoryId : Word;
  constructor Init( var Bounds : TRect; ALink : PInputLine;
                    AHistoryId : Word );
  constructor Load( var S: TStream );
  procedure Draw; virtual;
  function GetPalette : PPalette; virtual;
  procedure HandleEvent( var Event : TEvent ); virtual;
  function InitHistoryWindow( var Bounds : TRect ) :
                              PHistoryWindow; virtual;
  procedure Store( var S : TStream );
end;
```

The TInputLine object type offers a basic line-input editor. It is typically owned by dialog boxes, and offers the user a way to type in a selection (such as a file name wild card when selecting a file). The HandleEvent method provides you with versatile input-line editing capabilities, such as marking and deleting blocks, inserting and overwriting characters, moving by a single character or words, and moving to the beginning or end of the line. You may display a default string that can be edited or overwritten by the user. There is a program-defined maximum size for the input line beyond which additional keystrokes are ignored. The TInputLine object type is declared as follows:

```
PInputLine = ^TInputLine;
TInputLine = object( TView )
  Data : PString;
  MaxLen : Integer;
  CurPos : Integer;
  FirstPos : Integer;
  SelStart : Integer;
  SelEnd : Integer;
  constructor Init( var Bounds : TRect; AMaxLen : Integer );
  constructor Load( var S : TStream );
```

```
    destructor Done; virtual;
    function DataSize : Word; virtual;
    procedure Draw; virtual;
    procedure GetData( var Rec ); virtual;
    function GetPalette : PPalette; virtual;
    procedure HandleEvent( var Event : TEvent ); virtual;
    procedure SelectAll( Enable : Boolean );
    procedure SetData( var Rec ); virtual;
    procedure SetState( AState : Word; Enable : Boolean ); virtual;
    procedure Store( var S : TStream );
end;
```

`TListViewer` is an abstract type that works with other objects that view a variety of lists. `TListViewer`, inherited by its descendents, `TListBox` and `THistoryViewer`, supports the following functions:

- Viewing a linked list of items
- Controlling one or two scroll bars, which in turn supports the scrolling of lists in one or two directions
- Using the keyboard or the mouse to select items
- Highlighting selected items
- Updating the view to accommodate resizing and scrolling

`TListViewer` displays dynamic lists, but cannot store and manage them. The task of storing the data is left to other object types. The declaration of `TListViewer` follows:

```
PListViewer = ^TListViewer;
TListViewer = object( TView )
  HScrollBar : PScrollBar;
  VScrollBar : PScrollBar;
  NumCols : Integer;
  TopItem : Integer;
  Focused : Integer;
  Range : Integer;
  constructor Init( var Bounds : TRect; ANumCols : Word;
                    AHScrollBar, AVScrollBar : PScrollBar );
  constructor Load( var S : TStream );
  procedure ChangeBounds( var Bounds : TRect ); virtual;
  procedure Draw; virtual;
  procedure FocusItem( Item : Integer ); virtual;
  function GetPalette : PPalette; virtual;
  function GetText( Item : Integer;
                    MaxLen : Integer ) : String; virtual;
```

```
    function IsSelected( Item : Integer ) : Boolean; virtual;
    procedure HandleEvent( var Event : TEvent ); virtual;
    procedure SelectItem( Item : Integer ); virtual;
    procedure SetRange( ARange : Integer );
    procedure SetState( AState : Word; Enable : Boolean ); virtual;
    procedure Store( var S : TStream );
  end;
```

The TListBox type is used by the File/Load menu option of the Turbo Pascal integrated environment. TListBox can display multiple columns of strings, with a horizontal scroll bar that lets you examine other columns. The methods inherited from TListViewer and TListBox allow you to select and highlight an item in the list using the keyboard or the mouse. The List data field is the pointer to the collection of items viewed. The TLisTBox methods store and manage the viewed data; the inherited methods of TListViewer do not perform these tasks. The declaration of TListBox follows:

```
PListBox = ^TListBox;
TListBox = object( TListViewer )
  List : PCollection;
  constructor Init( var Bounds : TRect; ANumCols : Word;
                    AScrollBar : PScrollBar );
  constructor Load( var S : TStream );
  function DataSize : Word; virtual;
  procedure GetData( var Rec ); virtual;
  function GetText( Item : Integer;
                    MaxLen : Integer ) : String; virtual;
  procedure NewList( AList : PCollection ); virtual;
  procedure SetData( var Rec ); virtual;
  procedure Store( var S : TStream );
end;
```

The THistoryViewer object type is the other descendent of TListViewer. Compared with its sibling type, TListBox, THistoryViewer implements simpler list views used in examining the most recent selections. THistoryViewer does not handle this task single-handedly. Instead, it works with THistory and THistoryWindow. The declaration of THistoryViewer follows:

```
PHistoryViewer = ^THistoryViewer;
THistoryViewer = object( TListViewer )
  HistoryId : Word;
  constructor Init( var Bounds : TRect;
                    AHScrollBar, AVScrollBar : PScrollBar;
                    AHistoryId : Word );
```

```
  function GetPalette : PPalette; virtual;
  function GetText( Item : Integer;
                    MaxLen : Integer ) : String; virtual;
  procedure HandleEvent( var Event : TEvent ); virtual;
  function HistoryWidth : Integer;
end;
```

The `TMenuView` type is an abstract object type created for its descendents, `TMenuBar` and `TMenuBox`, which implement pull-down and pop-up menus, respectively. To eliminate redundant code, `TMenuView` provides its descendents with common functionality. This includes the `FindItem` and `HotKey` methods, which return a pointer to the menu item selected with the shortcut and hot keys, respectively. The `TMenuView` declaration follows:

```
PMenuView = ^TMenuView;
TMenuView = object( TView )
  ParentMenu : PMenuView;
  Menu : PMenu;
  Current : PMenuItem;
  constructor Init( var Bounds : TRect );
  constructor Load( var S : TStream );
  function Execute : Word; virtual;
  function FindItem( Ch : Char ) : PMenuItem;
  procedure GetItemRect( Item : PMenuItem;
                         var R : TRect ); virtual;
  function GetHelpCtx : Word; virtual;
  function GetPalette : PPalette; virtual;
  procedure HandleEvent( var Event : TEvent ); virtual;
  function HotKey( KeyCode : Word ) : PMenuItem;
  function NewSubView( var Bounds : TRect; AMenu : PMenu;
                       AParentMenu : PMenuView ) :
                       PMenuView; virtual;
  procedure Store( var S : TStream );
end;
```

The `TMenuBar` object type offers the menu selection functionality promoted by Turbo Vision and applied to the main menu bar of the Turbo Pascal integrated environment. `TMenuBar` instances are horizontal menu bars whose options are selected using familiar techniques. `TMenuBar` inherits most of its functionality; it declares only two virtual methods, `Draw` and `GetItemRec`. The declaration of `TMenuBar` follows:

```
PMenuBar = ^TMenuBar;
TMenuBar = object( TMenuView )
  constructor Init( var Bounds : TRect; AMenu : PMenu );
  destructor Done; virtual;
```

```
    procedure Draw; virtual;
    procedure GetItemRect( Item : PMenuItem; var R : TRect );
                           virtual;
end;
```

The TMenuBox object type complements the action of its sibling, TMenuBar. TMenuBox displays the pull-down menus used by the integrated environment, for example. The menus of TMenuBox may also include submenus. TMenuBox instances use different colors to indicate the shortcut characters. On their own, TMenuBox instances give the effect of pop-up menus; when used with TMenuBar instances, they act as pull-down menus. Like TMenuBar, TMenuBox inherits most of its functionality from its parent object type. The TMenuBox declaration follows:

```
PMenuBox = ^TMenuBox;
TMenuBox = object( TMenuView )
    constructor Init( var Bounds : TRect; AMenu : PMenu;
                      AParentMenu : PMenuView );
    procedure Draw; virtual;
    procedure GetItemRect( Item : PMenuItem; var R : TRect );
                           virtual;
end;
```

The TScroller object type implements the interior view of a scrollable window with a vertical scroll bar, a horizontal scroll bar, or both. The HScrollBar and VScrollBar data fields are pointers to the ScrollBar types used to implement the horizontal and vertical scroll bars, respectively. When HScrollBar is assigned a nil value, the scrollable window has no horizontal scroll bar. A similar statement can be made about the VScrollBar data field. Normally, at least one of these two pointers is not nil. The Delta data field stores the position that indicates the relative position of the viewed text. The Limit data field specifies the maximum value for Delta.

```
PScroller = ^TScroller;
TScroller = object( TView )
  HScrollBar : PScrollBar;
  VScrollBar : PScrollBar;
  Delta : TPoint;
  Limit : TPoint;
  constructor Init( var Bounds : TRect;
  AHScrollBar, AVScrollBar : PScrollBar );
  constructor Load( var S : TStream );
  procedure ChangeBounds( var Bounds : TRect ); virtual;
  function GetPalette : PPalette; virtual;
  procedure HandleEvent( var Event : TEvent ); virtual;
  procedure ScrollDraw; virtual;
```

```
  procedure ScrollTo( X, Y : Integer );
  procedure SetLimit( X, Y : Integer );
  procedure SetState( AState : Word; Enable : Boolean ); virtual;
  procedure Store( var S : TStream );
end;
```

The `TTextDevice` object type is a simple descendent of `TScroller` that implements a scrollable TTY (teletype) viewer and device driver. It implements two virtual methods for reading and writing text to the emulated device. The main purpose of `TTextDevice` is to serve as a parent to object types that implement terminal drivers. The declaration of `TTextDevice` follows:

```
PTextDevice = ^TTextDevice;
TTextDevice = object( TScroller )
  Dummy : Word;
  function StrRead( var S : TextBuf ) : Byte; virtual;
  procedure StrWrite( var S : TextBuf; Count : Byte ); virtual;
end;
```

The `TTerminal` type implements a "dumb" terminal with a 64K buffer. Although `TTerminal` defines its own virtual `StrRead` and `StrWrite` functions, it declares a number of methods and four data fields to manage the circular-queue text buffer and its pointers. The declaration of `TTerminal` follows:

```
PTerminal = ^TTerminal;
TTerminal = object( TTextDevice )
  BufSize : Word;
  Buffer : PTerminalBuffer;
  QueFront, QueBack : Word;
  constructor Init( var Bounds :TRect;
  AHScrollBar, AVScrollBar : PScrollBar; ABufSize : Word );
  destructor Done; virtual;
  procedure BufDec( var Val : Word );
  procedure BufInc( var Val : Word );
  function CalcWidth : Integer;
  function CanInsert( Amount : Word ) : Boolean;
  procedure Draw; virtual;
  function NextLine( Pos :Word ) : Word;
  function PrevLines( Pos :Word; Lines : Word ) : Word;
  function StrRead( var S : TextBuf ) : Byte; virtual;
  procedure StrWrite( var S : TextBuf; Count : Byte ); virtual;
  function QueEmpty : Boolean;
end;
```

The `TScrollBar` object type manages the vertical or horizontal scrolling of a view. The position of the scroll indicator depends on the value of the `Value` data field in the range defined by the `Min` and `Max` data fields. The value of the `PgStep` data field indicates how much the `Value` field changes when the PgUp, PgDn, Ctrl-Left, or Ctrl-Right key is pressed. The `ArStep` data field specifies how much the `Value` field changes when you click the mouse on the scroll-arrow areas. The declaration of `TScrollBar` follows:

```
PScrollBar = ^TScrollBar;
TScrollBar = object( TView )
  Value : Integer;
  Min : Integer;
  Max : Integer;
  PgStep : Integer;
  ArStep : Integer;
  constructor Init( var Bounds : TRect );
  constructor Load( var S : TStream );
  procedure Draw; virtual;
  function GetPalette : PPalette; virtual;
  procedure HandleEvent( var Event : TEvent ); virtual;
  procedure ScrollDraw; virtual;
  function ScrollStep( Part : Integer ) : Integer; virtual;
  procedure SetParams( AValue, AMin, AMax, APgStep,
                       AArStep : Integer );
  procedure SetRange( AMin, AMax : Integer );
  procedure SetStep( APgStep, AArStep : Integer );
  procedure SetValue( AValue : Integer );
  procedure Store( var S : TStream );
end;
```

The `TStaticText` object type is assigned the task of displaying plain text in a view. The text can be centered or wrapped. The static text does not respond to the keyboard or the mouse. The declaration of `TStaticText` follows:

```
PStaticText = ^TStaticText;
TStaticText = object( TView )
  Text : PString;
  constructor Init( var Bounds : TRect; AText : String );
  constructor Load( var S : TStream );
  destructor Done; virtual;
  procedure Draw; virtual;
  function GetPalette : PPalette; virtual;
```

```
  procedure GetText( var S : String ); virtual;
  procedure Store( var S : TStream );
end;
```

The `TLabel` type is a descendent of `TStaticText`. It lets you select and highlight the text with the cursor keys, the mouse, or Alt key combinations. Using the `Link` data field, the instances of `TLabel` are connected with another control view. When a `TLabel` instance is selected, the associated controls are also selected, and vice versa. The declaration of `TLabel` follows:

```
PLabel = ^TLabel;
TLabel = object( TStaticText )
  Link : PView;
  Light : Boolean;
  constructor Init( var Bounds : TRect; AText : String;
                    ALink : PView );
  constructor Load( var S : TStream );
  procedure Draw; virtual;
  function GetPalette : PPalette; virtual;
  procedure HandleEvent( var Event : TEvent ); virtual;
  procedure Store( var S : TStream );
end;
```

The `TParamText` object type is a descendent of `TStaticText`. It displays formatted output, using a format string. The auxiliary `FormatStr` function (which you can use also in non-Turbo Vision applications) works like the `printf` function in the C language. The declaration of `TParamText` follows:

```
PParamText = ^TParamText;
TParamText = object( TStaticText )
  ParamCount : Integer;
  ParamList : Pointer;
  constructor Init( var Bounds : TRect; AText : String;
                    AParamCount : Integer );
  constructor Load( var S : TStream );
  function DataSize : Word; virtual;
  procedure GetText( var S : String ); virtual;
  procedure SetData( var Rec ); virtual;
  procedure Store( var S : TStream );
end;
```

The `TStatusLine` object type is used to display the status line at the bottom of the screen. This provides a context-sensitive list of available hot keys. It may also contain information on the status of the Ins, NumLock,

CapsLock, and ScrollLock keys, if the application requires it. The `Items` data field is a pointer to a list of records that specifies the options and their hot keys. The `Defs` data field monitors the context level. This enables `TStatusLine` to show certain options and hide others. The declaration of `TStatusLine` follows:

```
PStatusLine = ^TStatusLine;
TStatusLine = object( TView )
  Items : PStatusItem;
  Defs : PStatusDef;
  constructor Init( var Bounds : TRect; ADefs PStatusDef );
  constructor Load( var S : TStream );
  destructor Done; virtual;
  procedure Draw; virtual;
  function GetPalette : PPalette; virtual;
  procedure HandleEvent( var Event : TEvent ); virtual;
  function Hint( AHelpCtx : Word ) : String; virtual;
  procedure Store( var S : TStream );
  procedure Update; virtual;
end;
```

A *collection* represents a data structure that is more general (or abstract, if you like) than traditional arrays, lists, stacks, and so on. Collections came about as a result of creating a comprehensive data structure hierarchy in the object-oriented language SmallTalk. The `TCollection` object type implements a Turbo Vision collection and is a parent for more specialized object types, namely `TSortedCollection`, `TStringCollection`, and `TResourceCollection`. `TCollection` lets you store, insert, recall, and delete data. The data managed by `TCollection` can be of mixed types. The `Limit` data field specifies the current maximum number of items in the collection. This size can increase automatically in chunks of `Delta` elements, when the value of `Delta` is positive. Otherwise, the limit set by the constructor is fixed. The declaration of `TCollection` follows:

```
PCollection = ^TCollection;
TCollection = object( TObject )
  Items : PItemList;
  Count : Integer;
  Limit : Integer;
  Delta : Integer;
  constructor Init( ALimit, ADelta : Integer );
  constructor Load( var S : TStream );
  destructor Done; virtual;
```

```
  function At( Index : Integer ) : Pointer;
  procedure AtDelete( Index : Integer );
  procedure AtFree( Index : Integer );
  procedure AtInsert( Index : Integer; Item : Pointer );
  procedure AtPut( Index : Integer; Item : Pointer );
  procedure Delete( Item : Pointer );
  procedure DeleteAll;
  procedure Error( Code, Info : Integer ); virtual;
  function FirstThat( Test : Pointer ) : Pointer;
  procedure ForEach( Action : Pointer );
  procedure Free( Item : Pointer );
  procedure FreeAll;
  procedure FreeItem( Item : Pointer ); virtual;
  function GetItem( var S : TStream ) : Pointer; virtual;
  function IndexOf( Item : Pointer ) : Integer; virtual;
  procedure Insert( Item : Pointer ); virtual;
  function LastThat( Test : Pointer ) : Pointer;
  procedure Pack;
  procedure PutItem( var S : TStream; Item : Pointer ); virtual;
  procedure SetLimit( ALimit : Integer ); virtual;
  procedure Store( var S : TStream );
end;
```

The `TSortedCollection` object type implements a base type for sorted collections with unique or duplicate keys. The `Duplicates` data field is used to allow or prevent duplicate keys. The virtual `Compare` method is used when comparing the key data used for sorting the collection. The `Compare` function returns the following values:

– 1 when `Key1 < Key2`

0 when `Key1 = Key2`

+1 when `Key1 > Key2`

The virtual `KeyOf` method has the task of extracting the sort keys from the collected items. `TSortedCollection` descendents that you create must declare their own `Compare` method and possibly their own `KeyOf` method. The declaration of `TSortedCollection` follows:

```
PSortedCollection = ^TSortedCollection;
TSortedCollection = object( TCollection )
  Duplicates : Boolean;
  constructor Load( var S : TStream );
  function Compare( Key1, Key2 : Pointer ) : Integer; virtual;
  function IndexOf( Item : Pointer ) : Integer; virtual;
  procedure Insert( Item : Pointer ); virtual;
```

```
   function KeyOf( Item : Pointer ) : Pointer; virtual;
   function Search( Key : Pointer;
                    var Index : Integer ) : Boolean; virtual;
   procedure Store( var S : TStream );
end;
```

The `TStringCollection` object type manages collections of Turbo Pascal strings. A special version of the `Compare` method is implemented to accommodate string comparison. A string is removed from the collection by sending a `FreeItem` message. Stream I/O is performed by the `GetItem` and `PutItem` methods (as opposed to the usual `Load` and `Save` methods utilized by the rest of the Turbo Vision objects). The declaration of `TStringCollection` follows:

```
PStringCollection = ^TStringCollection;
TStringCollection = object( TSortedCollection )
  function Compare( Key1, Key2 : Pointer ) : Integer; virtual;
  procedure FreeItem( Item : Pointer ); virtual;
  function GetItem( var S : TStream ) : Pointer; virtual;
  procedure PutItem( var S : TStream; Item : Pointer ); virtual;
end;
```

The `TResourceCollection` object type works with `TResourceFile` to manage Turbo Vision resources. `TResourceCollection` administers the indexing of object instances. The declaration of `TResourceCollection` follows:

```
PResourceCollection = ^TResourceCollection;
TResourceCollection = object( TStringCollection )
  procedure FreeItem( Item : Pointer ); virtual;
  function GetItem( var S : TStream ) : Pointer; virtual;
  function KeyOf( Item : Pointer ) : Pointer; virtual;
  procedure PutItem( var S : TStream; Item : Pointer ); virtual;
end;
```

The `TStream` object type implements generic stream I/O. To implement more specialized streams, the virtual methods (`GetPos`, `GetSize`, `Read`, `Seek`, `Write`, and possibly `Flush`) must be overridden by descendent object types. This is the case with the `TDosStream`, `TEmsStream`, and `TBufStream` object types. The methods of `TStream` provide all the functionality needed to support stream I/O. The declaration of `TStream` follows:

```
PStream = ^TStream;
TStream = object( TObject )
  Status : Integer;
  ErrorInfo : Integer;
```

```
  procedure CopyFrom( var S : TStream; Count : Longint );
  procedure Error( Code, Info : Integer ); virtual;
  procedure Flush; virtual;
  function Get : PObject;
  function GetPos : Longint; virtual;
  function GetSize : Longint; virtual;
  procedure Put( P : PObject );
  procedure Read( var Buf; Count : Word ); virtual;
  function ReadStr : PString;
  procedure Reset;
  procedure Seek( Pos : Longint ); virtual;
  procedure Truncate; virtual;
  procedure Write( var Buf; Count : Word ); virtual;
  procedure WriteStr( P : PString );
end;
```

The `TDosStream` object type is a descendent of `TStream` that performs unbuffered stream I/O on DOS files. The `Mode` parameter in the `Init` constructor is used to determine the access mode of `FileName`. The predefined constants `stCreate`, `stOpenRead`, `stOpenWrite`, and `stOpen` (for both input and output) supply the arguments for the `Mode` parameter. The `TDosStream` type is declared as follows:

```
PDosStream = ^TDosStream;
TDosStream = object( TStream )
  Handle : Word;
  constructor Init( FileName : FNameStr; Mode : Word );
  destructor Done; virtual;
  function GetPos : Longint; virtual;
  function GetSize : Longint; virtual;
  procedure Read( var Buf; Count : Word ); virtual;
  procedure Seek( Pos : Longint ); virtual;
  procedure Truncate; virtual;
  procedure Write( var Buf; Count : Word ); virtual;
end;
```

The `TBufStream` object type extends `TDosStream` by incorporating a buffer. The four data fields of `TBufStream` manage the buffer and monitor its status. The `TBufStream` type overrides the `Flush` method as well as the virtual methods of its parent object type. The declaration of `TBufStream` follows:

```
PBufStream = ^TBufStream;
TBufStream = object( TDosStream )
  Buffer : Pointer;
```

```
    BufSize : Word;
    BufPtr : Word;
    BufEnd : Word;
    constructor Init( FileName : FNameStr; Mode, Size : Word );
    destructor Done; virtual;
    procedure Flush; virtual;
    function GetPos : Longint; virtual;
    function GetSize : Longint; virtual;
    procedure Read( var Buf; Count : Word ); virtual;
    procedure Seek( Pos : Longint ); virtual;
    procedure Truncate; virtual;
    procedure Write( var Buf; Count : Word ); virtual;
end;
```

The `TEmsStream` object type customizes `TStream` to implement streams that tap into EMS memory. The data members of `TEmsStream` provide the EMS handle, page count, stream size, and current location of the stream index. The declaration of `TEmsStream` follows:

```
PEmsStream = ^TEmsStream;
TEmsStream = object( TStream )
    Handle : Word;
    PageCount : Word;
    Size : Longint;
    Position : Longint;
    constructor Init( MinSize, MaxSize : Longint );
    destructor Done; virtual;
    function GetPos : Longint; virtual;
    function GetSize : Longint; virtual;
    procedure Read( var Buf; Count : Word ); virtual;
    procedure Seek( Pos : Longint ); virtual;
    procedure Truncate; virtual;
    procedure Write( var Buf; Count : Word ); virtual;
end;
```

The `TResourceFile` object type implements resource streams that can be indexed by unique names. These names are managed internally with the help of the `TResourceCollection` type. The `Put` and `Get` methods perform the stream I/O. The first parameter of the `Put` method, `Item`, is a pointer to `TObject`. This allows `Item` to point to instances of `TObject` or its descendents. The `Key` parameter is the key string used to store the resource. The `Get` method uses similar data types in its argument and return value. The declaration of `TResourceFile` follows:

```
PResourceFile = ^TResourceFile;
TResourceFile = object( TObject )
  Stream : PStream;
  Modified : Boolean;
  constructor Init( AStream : PStream );
  destructor Done; virtual;
  function Count : Integer;
  procedure Delete( Key : String );
  procedure Flush;
  function Get( Key : String ) : PObject;
  function KeyAt( I : Integer ) : String;
  procedure Put( Item : PObject; Key : String );
  function SwitchTo( AStream : PStream; Pack : Boolean ) :
          PStream;
end;
```

The `TStringList` type is responsible for accessing individual strings from streams by specifying unique indices. The range of the string index is the same range of values for the `Word` type (0 to 65,535). Storing strings in streams and retrieving them with the `Get` method permits Turbo Vision applications to externally manage a variety of messages while reducing the size of the EXE file. The `TStringList` declaration follows:

```
PStringList = ^TStringList;
TStringList = object( TObject )
  constructor Load( var S : TStream );
  destructor Done; virtual;
  function Get( Key : Word ) : String;
end;
```

The `TStrListMaker` object type complements `TStringList` by writing strings to a stream. Each string is associated with a unique numeric key.

`TStringMaker` works by gradually building the string list in memory. After the table is completed, it is written out to a stream. The constructor allocates the heap space required to store the string list. The declaration of `TStrListMaker` follows:

```
PStrListMaker = ^TStrListMaker;
TStrListMaker = object( TObject )
  constructor Init( AStrSize, AIndexSize : Word );
  destructor Done; virtual;
  procedure Put( Key : Word; S : String );
  procedure Store( var S : TStream );
end;
```

The declarations of the Turbo Vision object types are located in the *.INT files in the \TP\DOC directory. If you browse through these files, you will find additional object types that further extend Turbo Vision. The TVISION.DOC file provides you with the Turbo Vision updates not mentioned in the *Turbo Vision Guide*.

A Turbo Vision Example

Turbo Vision applications vary in length and content depending on the nature of the application. This section presents a Turbo Vision program of the kind that you will likely encounter early on. The program is similar to TVDEMO.PAS and is shown in listing 22.1. It is mainly a file browser that allows you to pop-up an ASCII table, a calendar, and a calculator. These tools are exported by a number of library units in the \TP\TVDEMOS directory. The program has three options in the main menu: File, Windows, and Tools. The File option has three pull-down selections: Open, New dir, and Exit. The Windows option has six selections: Resize/Move, Zoom, Next, Close, Tile, and Cascade. The Tools option has three selections: ASCII table, Calculator, and Calendar.

Listing 22.1

```
  program TurboVisionDemo;

  {$X+,M 16384,16384,655360}

uses
  Dos, Objects, Drivers, Memory, Views, Menus, Dialogs, StdDlg,
  MsgBox, App, Calendar, AsciiTab, HelpFile, DemoHelp, Calc;

const
  cmFileOpen    = 100;
  cmNewDir      = 101;
  cmGetCalc     = 102;
  cmGetASCII    = 103;
  cmGetCalendar = 104;
  hlNewDir      = cmNewDir;

type
  { TLinesCollection }
  PLinesCollection = ^TLinesCollection;
```

```
  TLinesCollection = object( TCollection )
    procedure FreeItem( P : Pointer ); virtual;
  end;

  { TLineScroller }
  PLineScroller = ^TLineScroller;
  TLineScroller = object( TScroller )
    Lines : PCollection;
    IsOK : Boolean;
    constructor Init( var Bounds : TRect;
                          AHScrollBar, AVScrollBar : PScrollBar;
                      var Filename : PathStr );
    destructor Done; virtual;
    procedure Draw; virtual;
    function Valid( Command : Word ) : Boolean; virtual;
  end;

  { TFileWindow }
  PFileWindow = ^TFileWindow;
  TFileWindow = object( TWindow )
    constructor Init( var Filename : PathStr );
  end;

  { TDemoApp }
  PDemoApp = ^TDemoApp;
  TDemoApp = object( TApplication )
    procedure HandleEvent( var Event : TEvent ); virtual;
    procedure InitMenuBar; virtual;
    procedure InitStatusLine; virtual;
    procedure OutOfMemory; virtual;
    { methods that support the application's commands }
    procedure FileOpen;
    procedure NewDir;
    procedure Tile;
    procedure Cascade;
    procedure GetAscii;
    procedure GetCalc;
    procedure GetCalendar;
  end;

{   ---------------- TLinesCollection ---------------- }
procedure TLinesCollection.FreeItem( P : Pointer );
```

continues

Listing 22.1 continued

```
begin
  DisposeStr( P );
end;

{    ---------------- TLineScroller ---------------- }
constructor TLineScroller.Init( var Bounds : TRect;
                                    AHScrollBar,
                                    AVScrollBar : PScrollBar;
                                var Filename : PathStr );
var
  ViewedFile : Text;
  Line : String;
  MaxWidth : Integer;

begin
  TScroller.Init( Bounds, AHScrollbar, AVScrollBar );
  GrowMode := gfGrowHiX + gfGrowHiY;
  IsOK := True;
  Lines := New( PLinesCollection, Init( 5,5 ));
  {$I-}
  Assign( ViewedFile, Filename );
  Reset( ViewedFile );
  if IOResult <> 0 then begin
    MessageBox( 'Cannot open file '+ Filename + '.',
                nil, mfError + mfOkButton );
    IsOK := False;
  end
  else begin
    MaxWidth := 0;
    while not Eof( ViewedFile ) and (not LowMemory) do begin
      Readln( ViewedFile, Line );
      if Length( Line ) > MaxWidth then
        MaxWidth := Length( Line );
      Lines^.Insert( NewStr( Line ));
    end;
    Close( ViewedFile );
  end;
  {$I+}
  SetLimit( MaxWidth, Lines^.Count );
end;

destructor TLineScroller.Done;
```

```
begin
  Dispose( Lines, Done );
  TScroller.Done;
end;

procedure TLineScroller.Draw;
var
  ZBuff : TDrawBuffer;
  ColorAttr : Byte;
  I : Integer;
  AString : String;
  StringPtr : PString;
begin
  ColorAttr := GetColor( 1 );
  for I := 0 to Size.Y - 1 do begin
    MoveChar( ZBuff, ' ', ColorAttr, Size.X );
    if Delta.Y + I < Lines^.Count then begin
      StringPtr := Lines^.At( Delta.Y + I );
      if StringPtr <> nil then
           AString := Copy( StringPtr^, Delta.X + 1, Size.X )
      else
           AString := '';
      MoveStr( ZBuff, AString, ColorAttr );
    end;
    WriteLine( 0, I, Size.X, 1, ZBuff );
  end;
end;

function TLineScroller.Valid( Command : Word ) : Boolean; begin
     Valid := IsOK;
end;

{    ---------------- TFileWindow ---------------- }
constructor TFileWindow.Init( var Filename : PathStr );
const
  WindowNumber : Integer = 1;
var
  R : TRect;
begin
  Desktop^.GetExtent( R );
  TWindow.Init( R, Filename, WindowNumber );
  Options := Options or ofTileable;
```

continues

Listing 22.1 continued

```
  Inc( WindowNumber );
  GetExtent( R );
  R.Grow( -1, -1 );
  Insert( New( PLineScroller, Init( R,
    StandardScrollBar( sbHorizontal + sbHandleKeyboard ),
    StandardScrollBar( sbVertical + sbHandleKeyboard ),
                    Filename )));
end;

{    ---------------- TDemoApp ---------------- }
procedure TDemoApp.FileOpen;
var
  FileTalk : PFileDialog;
  Filename : PathStr;
  WindowPtr : PWindow;
begin
  FileTalk := PFileDialog( ValidView( New( PFileDialog,
            Init( '*.*', 'Open a File', '~N~ame',
            fdOpenButton, 100 ))));
  if FileTalk <> nil then begin
    if Desktop^.ExecView( FileTalk ) <> cmCancel then begin
      FileTalk^.GetFilename( Filename );
      WindowPtr := PWindow( ValidView( New( PFileWindow,
                Init( Filename ))));
      if WindowPtr <> nil then Desktop^.Insert( WindowPtr );
    end;
    Dispose( FileTalk, Done );
  end;
end;

procedure TDemoApp.NewDir;
var
  DirTalk : PChDirDialog;
begin
  DirTalk := PChDirDialog( ValidView( New( PChDirDialog,
                    Init( 0, hlNewDir ))));
  if DirTalk <> nil then begin
    DeskTop^.ExecView( DirTalk );
    Dispose( DirTalk, Done );
  end;
end;
```

```
procedure TDemoApp.Tile;
var
  R : TRect;
begin
  Desktop^.GetExtent( R );
  Desktop^.Tile( R );
end;

procedure TDemoApp.Cascade;
var
  R : TRect;
begin
  Desktop^.GetExtent( R );
  Desktop^.Cascade( R );
end;

procedure TDemoApp.GetASCII;
var
  AsciiPtr : PAsciiChart;
begin
  AsciiPtr := New( PAsciiChart, Init );
  AsciiPtr^.HelpCtx := hcAsciiTable;
  Desktop^.Insert( ValidView( AsciiPtr ));
end;

procedure TDemoApp.GetCalc;
var
  CalcPtr : PCalculator;
begin
  CalcPtr := New( PCalculator, Init );
  CalcPtr^.HelpCtx := hcCalculator;
  if ValidView( CalcPtr ) <> nil then
    Desktop^.Insert( CalcPtr );
end;

procedure TDemoApp.GetCalendar;
var
  CalendarPtr : PCalendarWindow;
begin
  CalendarPtr := New( PCalendarWindow, Init );
  CalendarPtr^.HelpCtx := hcCalendar;
  Desktop^.Insert( ValidView( CalendarPtr ));
```

continues

Listing 22.1 continued

```
end;

procedure TDemoApp.HandleEvent( var Event : TEvent );
begin
  TApplication.HandleEvent( Event );
  case Event.What of
    evCommand :
      begin
        case Event.Command of
          cmFileOpen     : FileOpen;
          cmNewDir       : NewDir;
          cmCascade      : Cascade;
          cmTile         : Tile;
          cmGetASCII     : GetASCII;
          cmGetCalc      : GetCalc;
          cmGetCalendar : GetCalendar;
        else
          Exit;
        end;
        ClearEvent( Event );
      end;
  end;
end;

procedure TDemoApp.InitMenuBar;
var
  R : TRect;
begin
  GetExtent( R );
  R.B.Y := R.A.Y+1;
  MenuBar := New( PMenuBar, Init( R, NewMenu(
    NewSubMenu( '~F~ile', 100,
      NewMenu(
        NewItem( '~O~pen', 'F3', kbF3, cmFileOpen, hcNoContext,
        NewItem( '~N~ew dir', 'Alt-C', kbAltC, cmNewDir,
                hcNoContext,
        NewItem( 'E~x~it', 'Alt-X', kbAltX, cmQuit, hcNoContext,
      nil )))),
    NewSubMenu( '~W~indows', hcNoContext,
      NewMenu(
        NewItem( '~R~esize/Move','Ctrl-F5', kbCtrlF5, cmResize,
                hcNoContext,
```

```
        NewItem( '~Z~oom', 'F5', kbF5, cmZoom, hcNoContext,
        NewItem( '~N~ext', 'F6', kbF6, cmNext, hcNoContext,
        NewItem( '~C~lose', 'Alt-F3', kbAltF3, cmClose,
                hcNoContext,
        NewItem( '~T~ile', '', kbNoKey, cmTile, hcNoContext,
        NewItem( 'C~a~scade', '', kbNoKey, cmCascade,
                hcNoContext,
      nil ))))))),
    NewSubMenu( '~T~ools', hcNoContext,
      NewMenu(
        NewItem( '~A~SCII table', 'F7', kbF7, cmGetASCII,
                 hcNoContext,
        NewItem( '~C~alculator',  'F8', kbF8, cmGetCalc,
                hcNoContext,
        NewItem( 'Ca~l~endar'   ,  'F9', kbF9, cmGetCalendar,
                hcNoContext,
      nil )))),
    nil ))))));
end;

procedure TDemoApp.InitStatusLine;
var
  R : TRect;
begin
  GetExtent( R );
  R.A.Y := R.B.Y - 1;
  StatusLine := New( PStatusLine, Init( R,
    NewStatusDef( 0, 65535,
      NewStatusKey( '', kbF10, cmMenu,
      NewStatusKey( '~Alt-X~ Exit', kbAltX, cmQuit,
      NewStatusKey( '~F3~ Open', kbF3, cmFileOpen,
      NewStatusKey( '~F5~ Zoom', kbF5, cmZoom,
      NewStatusKey( '~Alt-F3~ Close', kbAltF3, cmClose, nil ))))),
    nil )));
end;

procedure TDemoApp.OutOfMemory;
begin
  MessageBox( 'Insufficient memory!', nil, mfError + mfOkButton );
end;

var
```

continues

Listing 22.1 continued

```
  DemoApp : TDemoApp;

begin
  DemoApp.Init;
  DemoApp.Run;
  DemoApp.Done;
end.
```

Listing 22.1 has the following main sections:

1. The constant declaration section lists the numeric codes representing the application's commands. All such constants begin with the letters *cm*, a convention used by Turbo Vision.
2. The data type declaration section contains the object types (and their pointers) that extend the Turbo Vision hierarchy to suit the needs of the demonstration program.
3. The bulk of the program contains the definitions of the methods for the various object types.
4. The variable declaration section.
5. The main program body.

You may be wondering how you would begin to write a nontrivial program like the one in listing 22.1. The answer lies with Turbo Vision's capabilities and how you want to channel them for your application.

Because Turbo Vision applications are object-oriented, you should start with the main object type—the application. Every Turbo Vision application has an application object type and its instance. For example, the program in listing 22.1 has the `TDemoApp` type and the `DemoApp` variable. The `DemoApp` variable is the owner of a menu bar, a status line, and desktop instances. The desktop contains (that is, owns) a window that views the file text lines. Scrolling through the file lines is a highly desirable feature, so the window should handle scrolling text. Thus, the viewing window is the owner of a text scroller. Finally, the scroller itself contains a collection of text lines. This cascading ownership can be summarized by the following:

Application → Desktop → Window → Scroller → Line collection

The Turbo Vision demonstration program requires the definition of new object types for all of these except the desktop, because its pointer, `Desktop`, is predefined.

The program defines the following object types:

- `TLinesCollection`. This simple extension to `TCollection` is needed to provide the application with the appropriate version of the virtual `FreeItem` method.
- `TLineScroller`, a descendent of the `TScroller` type. The `Lines` data field is a pointer to `TCollection` (and therefore, a pointer to its descendent, `TLinesCollection`). This pointer establishes the link between `TLineScroller` and `TLinesCollection`.
- `TFileWindow`. This object type is a simple extension of `TWindow`. It displays a scrollable window with the viewed file name as the window title. The window is linked to a scrolling view that displays the lines of the file.
- `TDemoApp`. This object type includes the methods required to set up the menu bar and status line, and respond to the custom application commands and messages.

Turbo Vision defines a number of commands (coded as `cmXXXX` constants), such as `cmQuit` and `cmZoom`. It reserves the integers 0 through 99 and 256 through 999 for its own use. This frees your application to define its own commands in the range 100 through 255 and 1000 through 65,535. The two sets allow the command of the first one to be disabled. The demonstration program needs to define the constants for the open file, new directory, ASCII table, calculator, and calendar related commands. The constant declaration section contains the identifiers that represent these commands.

Before looking at the methods of the participating object types, examine the main body of the program. There are only three statements: the first initializes the `DemoApp` variable, the second sends it a `Run` message, and the third removes it. This indicates that the main body of a Turbo Vision application is generally not crowded with statements, loops, and other constructs.

Now, let's look at the important methods of the program. Begin by looking at the methods of `TDemoApp`, the program object type.

The `InitMenuBar` method builds the menu bar for the demonstration program. Every descendent of `TApplication`, including `TDemoApp`, must define its own `InitMenuBar` method. Only three statements are in `InitMenuBar`. The most important one is the statement that builds the menu bar. The `MenuBar` pointer uses a `New` statement to dynamically create the menu bar.

A sequence of nested calls to the `NewMenu`, `NewSubMenu`, and `NewItem` functions builds the menu bar in a single statement. The first call to `NewMenu` simply triggers the menu creation. The first main menu option, File, appears as the first argument for the `NewSubMenu` call. The tilde characters around the letter *F* select the shortcut key, F, for this option. Inside the first `NewSubMenu`, a `NewMenu` call is used to build the various File options. Each option is inserted by invoking the `NewItem` function. Six arguments are required by this function:

- The first argument in `NewItem` is the selection name, `Open`. Again, the tilde characters are used to choose the shortcut key for the Open selection.
- The second argument is the string that represents the hot key. This is displayed along with the selection name. If the selection has no hot key, a null string is supplied.
- The third argument is a `kbXXXX` constant that represents the associated hot key. The `kbNoKey` constant is used when no hot key is related to the selection.
- The fourth argument is the command constant (`cmFileOpen` for the first one).
- The fifth argument contains the constants for the help context. `hcNoContext` is commonly used if the menu selections are not context sensitive, as is the case in the demonstration program.
- The last argument is a pointer to `TMenuItem`. The argument type matches the function return type, enabling chained `NewItem` calls.

Additional menu options are inserted by supplementary calls to `NewSubMenu`, `NewMenu`, and `NewItem`, as shown in listing 22.1.

The status line is created by the `InitStatusLine` methods. Like `InitMenuBar`, every Turbo Vision application object type must implement its own `InitStatusLine` method. The program assigns the status line to the `StatusLine` pointer by invoking a call to `New`. The status line is created by a call to `NewStatusDef` that contains a sequence of nested calls to the `NewStatusKey` function. The first two arguments of the `NewStatusDef` function specify the range of context sensitive help. The range of 0 through 65,535 indicates that the status line will remain visible at all help levels.

`NewStatusKey` is the function that inserts the status line item. It requires four arguments:

- The name of the hot key and a brief description of what it does. The tilde characters are used to highlight the hot key name.

- The kbXXXX constant that represents the hot key associated with the status line item.
- The cmXXXX constant representing the command (or event) generated by the hot key.
- The last argument is a pointer to TStatusItem. The argument type matches the function return type, enabling chained NewStatus calls.

The HandleEvent method is an integrated part of the nervous system of any Turbo Vision application. It receives and processes the events generated by the keyboard, the mouse, and other methods. The first statement in the HandleEvent method sends a TApplication.HandleEvent message to the instance of TDemoApp. This gives first preference to the other HandleEvent methods in the Turbo Vision hierarchy to respond to the generated event. This, in turn, enables TDemoApp.HandleEvent to concentrate on responding to "custom" application events.

Nested CASE statements isolate and handle any events that have not been handled by other HandleEvent methods. The inner CASE statement has seven clauses to deal with the File/Open, File/New dir, Windows/Tile, Windows/Cascade, Tools/ASCII table, Tools/Calculator, and Tools/Calendar menu selections. Events such as File/Exit, Windows/Zoom, and Windows/Close are handled by other HandleEvent methods invoked indirectly by the TApplication.HandleEvent message. The network of HandleEvent methods parallel the nervous system of Turbo Vision applications.

The TDemoApp methods that pop-up the ASCII table, calculator, and calendar tools are similar. They all have three statements that create the instance of the corresponding object type, set its help context level, and insert the instance in the desktop.

The FileOpen method creates a file-selection dialog box (like the one used by the integrated environment) and assigns it to the FileTalk pointer. The Desktop^.ExecView(FileTalk) message executes the dialog box, removes it from the screen, and returns a result. If that result is not cmCancel (an event generated by selecting the Cancel button), the FileOpen method opens a window, reads the contents of the file, and displays the leading lines in the window. As always, the newly created window is inserted in the desktop using the Desktop^.Insert(WindowTalk) message. As for the instance of the dialog box, it is removed at the end of the FileOpen method.

The `NewDir` method uses a dialog box for changing directories. The local variable `DirTalk` points to the instance of the dialog box. If it is successfully created, the dialog box is executed by sending a `Desktop^.ExecView(DirTalk)` message. The result of that function is discarded because the message basically performs the task of changing the directory (or keeping the current one). The dialog box instance is removed at the end of the `NewDir` method.

The `TFileWindow.Init` constructor is the only method of its type. It initializes an instance of `TFileWindow`; this also creates a scrollable window by inserting an instance of `TFileBrowser` with both vertical and horizontal scroll bars.

The `Init` constructor and `Draw` method of the `TLineScroller` object type play important roles. The `Init` constructor creates its instance by essentially reading the lines of the target file. In addition, the method sends the `TScroller.Init` message to initialize the parts inherited from the parent object type. Notice that the lines read from the file are inserted in the `Lines` data field (of type `PCollection`) using the `Insert` message. The `Draw` method is delegated the task of updating the viewed file as you scroll through its lines. The local variable `ZBuff` is a display buffer used by the scrollable view. The file lines are copied into that buffer before they are viewed. The limits of the for-do loop determine the current view size, taking into account possible window resizing. The `MoveChar` procedure fills the color attribute of a buffer line with a default color value. The file lines are retrieved from the line collection and copied into the `ZBuff` display buffer using the `MoveStr` procedure.

Summary

Learning to program with Turbo Vision is a process that requires new ways of planning and writing applications. If you find the mass of constants, variables, types, and methods in Turbo Vision overwhelming, the best approach is perhaps one in which you build and experiment with existing code (mostly, the various Turbo Vision demonstrations and utilities included in Turbo Pascal).

Part IV

Reference

Procedures and Functions

Abs

System

Purpose: Returns the absolute value of a variable. The result returned by the function has the same type as the argument, which may be any integer or real value.

Syntax:

```
Function Abs( X : AnyNumType ) : AnyNumType;
```

Example:

```
RootTerm :$eq Abs( Sqr(B) - 4.0*A*C );
```

Addr

System

Purpose: Returns the address of the specified object. The argument may be any variable, procedure, or function identifier. The result of the function is in the form of a pointer to the object. Note that the `@` operator produces the same result as the `Addr` function.

Syntax:

```
Function Addr( X : AnyDataObject ) : Pointer;
```

Example:

```
PointerVar := Addr( WorkItem );
```

Append — System

Purpose: Opens an existing text file for appending. The `FileIdentifier` variable must have been previously associated with an external file using the `Assign` procedure.

Syntax:

```
Procedure Append( var FileIdentifier : Text );
```

Example:

```
Assign( DataStorage, 'DATA.TXT' );
Append( DataStorage );
```

Arc — Graph

Purpose: Draws a circular arc of a specified `Radius` from starting angle `StAngle` to ending angle `EndAngle`, using `(X, Y)` as the center point. Angles are measured in degrees, running counterclockwise, with 0 degrees in the three o'clock position.

Syntax:

```
Procedure Arc( X, Y                  : Integer;
               StAngle, EndAngle,
               Radius                : Word );
```

Example:

```
Arc( 100, 100, 0, 90, 50 );
```

ArcTan — System

Purpose: Returns the angle, in radians, that has a tangent equal to the value of the argument.

Syntax:

```
Function ArcTan( X : Real ) : Real;
```

Example:

```
PIover4 := ArcTan( 1.0 );  { Returns 1/4 of pi }
```

Assign — System

Purpose: Assigns the name of an external file to a file variable. The `FileIdentifier` variable may be declared for any file type. `FileName` is a string containing the name of the external file.

Syntax:

```
Procedure Assign( var FileIdentifier;
                      FileName : String );
```

Example:

```
Assign( DataStore, 'DATA.TXT' );
```

AssignCrt — Crt

Purpose: Associates a text file with the CRT. The procedure is similar to the `Assign` standard procedure, but associates the text file directly with the CRT rather than associates a `FileIdentifier` variable with an external file.

Syntax:

```
Procedure AssignCrt( var FileIdentifier : Text );
```

Example:

```
AssignCrt( UserMessageFile );
```

Bar — Graph

Purpose: Draws a bar (that is, a filled-in rectangle) using the current fill style and color. The upper left corner of the bar is at `(X1, Y1)`, and the lower right corner is at `(X2, Y2)`.

Syntax:

```
Procedure Bar( X1, Y1, X2, Y2 : Integer );
```

Example:

```
Bar( 10, 10, 40, 100 );
```

Bar3D Graph

Purpose: Draws a three-dimensional bar (that is, a filled-in, three-dimensional rectangle) using the current fill style and color. The upper left corner of the bar is at (X1, Y1), and the lower right corner is at (X2, Y2). Depth is the number of pixels used to define the apparent thickness. If Top is True, a three-dimensional top appears on the bar. If Top is False, no top appears; Bar3D may be called again to stack another bar on top. Top can be set to one of the predefined constants: TopOn (True) or TopOff (False).

Syntax:

```
Procedure Bar3D( X1, Y1, X2, Y2 : Integer;
                 Depth : Word;
                 Top   : Boolean );
```

Example:

```
UpX := 30; UpY := 30; DownX := 50; DownY := 100;
Bar3D( UpX, UpY, DownX, DownY, (DownX-UpX) div 4,
       TopOn );
```

BlockRead System

Purpose: Reads one or more records from FileIdentifier into Buffer. Count or fewer records are read. The optional parameter Result contains the number of records written to the buffer.

Syntax:

```
Procedure BlockRead( var FileIdentifier : file;
                     var Buffer;
                     Count : Word
                     [; var Result : Word ] );
```

Example:

```
BlockRead( FromFile, Buf, SizeOf( Buf ), NumberRead );
```

BlockWrite System

Purpose: Writes one or more records from `Buffer` into `FileIdentifier`. `Count` or fewer records are transferred from memory. The optional parameter `Result` contains the number of records written to the buffer.

Syntax:

```
Procedure BlockWrite( var FileIdentifier : file;
                      var Buffer;
                      Count : Word
                      [; var Result : Word ] );
```

Example:

```
BlockWrite( ToFile, Buf, NumberRead, NumberWritten );
```

ChDir System

Purpose: Changes the current directory to the path specified in `NewPath`.

Syntax:

```
Procedure ChDir( NewPath : String );
```

Example:

```
ChDir( 'C:\TP\DATA' );
```

Chr System

Purpose: Returns the ASCII character for the specified ordinal number.

Syntax:

```
Function Chr( X : Byte ) : Char;
```

Example:

```
write( 'This is line 1.',
       Chr(13), Chr(10), 'This is line 2.' );
```

Circle Graph

Purpose: Draws a circle of a specified `Radius` using `(X, Y)` as the center point.

Syntax: `Procedure Circle( X, Y : Integer; Radius : Word );`

Example: `Circle( 100, 100, 50 );`

ClearDevice — Graph

Purpose: Clears the graphics screen using the current background color and moves the current pointer (CP) to (0, 0).

Syntax: `Procedure ClearDevice;`

Example: `ClearDevice;`

ClearViewPort — Graph

Purpose: Clears the current viewport. The fill color is set to the current background color, `Bar` is called using the dimensions of the viewport as its parameters, and the current pointer (CP) is moved to (0, 0).

Syntax: `Procedure ClearViewPort;`

Example: `ClearViewPort;`

Close — System

Purpose: Closes an open file of any type.

Syntax: `Procedure Close( var FileIdentifier : AnyFileType );`

Example: `Close( InputInfo );`

CloseGraph — Graph

Purpose: Shuts down the graphics system. `CloseGraph` restores the screen to the mode it was in before graphics was initialized and deallocates any heap memory used by the graphics scan buffer, drivers, and fonts.

Syntax: `Procedure CloseGraph;`

Example: `CloseGraph;`

ClrEol — Crt

Purpose: Clears all characters from the cursor position to the end of the line using the current setting of `TextBackground`. The cursor's position is not changed.

Syntax: `Procedure ClrEol;`

Example: `ClrEol;`

ClrScr — Crt

Purpose: Clears the current screen (or the current window, if one is active) using the current setting of `TextBackground`. The cursor is moved to (0, 0).

Syntax: `Procedure ClrScr;`

Example: `ClrScr;`

Concat — System

Purpose: Concatenates a sequence of strings. The final string gets truncated if it exceeds 255 characters. Note that the + operator produces the same result as the `Concat` function.

Syntax:

```
Function Concat( s1 [, s2, ..., sn ] : String )
                 : String;
```

Example:

```
FileName := Concat( 'C:\', 'DataFile', '.TXT' );
```

Copy

System

Purpose: Returns a substring of the `Original` string, beginning at `Index`, containing `Count` characters.

Syntax:

```
Function Copy( Original      : String;
               Index, Count : Integer ) : String;
```

Example:

```
Str := 'The quick brown fox';
New := Copy( Str, 11, 5 );      { "brown" }
```

Cos

System

Purpose: Returns the cosine of the argument. The input angle is measured in radians.

Syntax:

```
Function Cos( X : Real ) : Real;
```

Example:

```
C := Cos( AngleInRadians );
```

CSeg

System

Purpose: Returns the current value of the CS register, which contains the segment address of the current code segment.

Syntax:

```
Function CSeg : Word;
```

Example:

```
StartingCodeParagraph := CSeg;
```

Dec

System

Purpose: Decrements the value of any ordinal variable. If the optional parameter `n` is not specified, `X` is decremented by 1; otherwise, `X` is decremented by the value of `n`.

Syntax:

```
Procedure Dec( var X : OrdType [; n : LongInt ] );
```

Example:

```
Amount := 10;
Dec( Amount );      { Amount now equals 9 }
Dec( Amount, 3 );   { Amount now equals 6 }
```

Delay

Crt

Purpose: Delays program execution for a specified number of milliseconds.

Syntax:

```
Procedure Delay( MS : Word );
```

Example:

```
Delay( 500 );    { Delays half a second }
```

Delete

System

Purpose: Deletes `Count` characters from the `Original` string, beginning at `Index`.

Syntax:

```
Procedure Delete( var Original  : String;
                      Index,
                      Count     : Integer );
```

Example:

```
Str := 'Cat Dog Horse';
Delete( Str, 5, 4 );     { Returns "Cat Horse" }
```

DelLine

Crt

Purpose: Deletes the line containing the cursor. All lines below the cursor move up one row. A blank line appears at the bottom of the screen; the color of the blank line is defined by the current setting of `TextBackground`. The location of the cursor is unchanged.

Syntax:

```
Procedure DelLine;
```

Example:

```
DelLine;
```

DetectGraph Graph

Purpose: Checks the hardware and determines which graphics driver and mode to use. `GraphDriver` and `GraphMode` contain values that can then be passed to the `InitGraph` procedure.

Syntax:

```
Procedure DetectGraph( var GraphDriver,
                           GraphMode : Integer );
```

Example:

```
DetectGraph( grDriver, grMode );
```

DiskFree Dos

Purpose: Returns the number of free bytes on a specified disk drive. A `Drive` of `0` indicates the current drive, `1` indicates drive A, `2` indicates drive B, and so on. If `Drive` contains an invalid number, `DiskFree` returns `-1`.

Syntax:

```
Function DiskFree( Drive : Byte ) : LongInt;
```

Example:

```
RemainingOnFloppy := DiskFree( 1 );
```

DiskSize Dos

Purpose: Returns the total size in bytes on a specified disk drive. A `Drive` of `0` indicates the current drive, `1` indicates drive A, `2` indicates drive B, and so on. If `Drive` contains an invalid number, `DiskSize` returns `-1`.

Syntax:

```
Function DiskSize( Drive : Byte ) : LongInt;
```

Example:

```
FloppySize := DiskSize( 1 );
```

Dispose System

Purpose: Disposes a dynamic variable previously allocated by `New`. The memory referenced by `P` is returned to the heap. When using `Dispose` to deallocate space for a dynamic object containing virtual methods, `P` is the pointer to the object and `Destruct` is the name of the destructor for that object type.

Syntax 1:
```
Procedure Dispose( var P : Pointer );
```

Example:
```
Dispose( PtrVar );
```

Syntax 2:
```
Procedure Dispose( var P : ObjectPointer, Destruct );
```

Example:
```
Dispose( ObjectPtrVar, ShutDown );
```

DosExitCode Dos

Purpose: Returns the exit code of a subprocess. The low byte contains the code. The value of the high byte indicates the reason the subprocess terminated: `0` for normal termination, `1` for Ctrl-C, `2` for a device error, and `3` if the subprocess was terminated by the `Keep` procedure.

Syntax:
```
Function DosExitCode : Word;
```

Example:
```
writeln( 'Exit code: ', Lo( DosExitCode ) );
```

DosVersion Dos

Purpose: Returns the DOS version number. The low byte contains the major version number, and the high byte contains the minor version number.

Syntax:
```
Function DosVersion : Word;
```

Example:
```
writeln( 'Using DOS ', Lo( DosVersion ),
         '.', Hi( DosVersion ) );
```

DrawPoly Graph

Purpose: Draws the outline of a polygon containing `NumPoints` vertices, using the current line style and color. `PolyPoints` is an array of `PointType`, as shown here:

```
PointType = record
              X, Y : Integer;
            end;
```

Each `PointType` record contains the coordinates of a vertex of the polygon. For N vertices, `PolyPoints` must contain N + 1 `PointType` records; the first and last record must be identical.

Syntax:

```
Procedure DrawPoly( NumPoints : Word; var PolyPoints );
```

Example:

```
DrawPoly( SizeOf( Shape ) div SizeOf( PointType ),
          Shape );
```

DSeg System

Purpose: Returns the current value of the DS register, which contains the segment address of the data segment.

Syntax:

```
Function DSeg : Word;
```

Example:

```
StartingDataParagraph := DSeg;
```

Ellipse Graph

Purpose: Draws an elliptical arc from starting angle `StAngle` to ending angle `EndAngle`, using `(X, Y)` as the center point. `XRadius` and `YRadius` are the horizontal and vertical axes, respectively. Angles are measured in degrees, running counterclockwise, with 0 degrees at the three o'clock position.

Syntax:

```
Procedure Ellipse( X, Y                : Integer;
                   StAngle, EndAngle,
                   XRadius, YRadius    : Word );
```

Example:

```
Ellipse( 100, 100, 0, 90, 40, 20 );
```

EnvCount Dos

Purpose: Returns the number of strings contained in the DOS environment. Each environment string is in the form `EnvStr = EnvValue`.

Syntax:

```
Function EnvCount : Integer;
```

Example:

```
writeln( 'Your system has ', EnvCount, '
         environment strings.' );
```

EnvStr Dos

Purpose: Returns a specified environment string. The first string has an `Index` of 1. An empty string is returned if `Index` references a nonexistent environment string.

Syntax:

```
Function EnvStr( Index : Integer ) : String;
```

Example:

```
EnvListItem := EnvStr( 1 );
```

Eof System

Purpose: Returns the end-of-file status of a file. `Eof` is `True` if the current file position is beyond the last character in the file, or if the file is empty; otherwise, `Eof` is `False`. If no `FileIdentifier` is provided, the standard `Input` file is assumed.

Syntax:

```
Function Eof[ ( var FileIdentifier : AnyFileType ) ]
                                   : Boolean;
```

Example:

```
while not Eof( DataFile ) do begin
   readln( DataFile, InRec );
   writeln( InRec );
end;
```

Eoln System

Purpose: Returns the end-of-line status of a text file. `Eoln` is `True` if the current file position is at an end-of-line marker or if `Eof` is `True`; otherwise, `Eoln` is `False`. If no `Text` file `FileIdentifier` is provided, the standard `Input` file is assumed.

Syntax:

```
Function Eoln[ ( var FileIdentifier : Text ) ]
                                    : Boolean;
```

Example:

```
if Eoln( DataText ) then readln( DataText );
```

Erase System

Purpose: Erases an unopened external file.

Syntax:

```
Procedure Erase( var FileIdentifier : AnyFileType );
```

Example:

```
Assign( TempFile, 'Data.BAK' );
Erase( TempFile );
```

Exec Dos

Purpose: Executes the program specified in the `Path` string with the command line contained in `ComLine`. The `PathStr` and `ComStr` types are defined as follows:

```
PathStr = String[79];     { Full file path string }
ComStr  = String[127];    { Command line string }
```

Syntax:

```
Procedure Exec( Path : PathStr; ComLine : ComStr );
```

Example:

```
Exec( '\Command.COM', '/C DIR *.BAK' );
                         { Lists all backups }
```

Exit

System

Purpose: Exits immediately from the current block. When used in a subroutine, `Exit` ends the subroutine. When used in the main body of a program, `Exit` ends the program.

Syntax:

```
Procedure Exit;
```

Example:

```
Exit;
```

Exp

System

Purpose: Returns the exponential of the argument; that is, `Exp` returns the base of the natural logarithm, *e*, raised to the power of `X`.

Syntax:

```
Function Exp( X : Real ) : Real;
```

Example:

```
Power := Exp( Value );
```

FExpand

Dos

Purpose: Expands a file name into a fully qualified file name, consisting of the complete drive, path, and file name. The `PathStr` type is defined as follows:

```
PathStr = String[79];    { Full file path string }
```

Syntax:

```
Function FExpand( Path : PathStr ) : PathStr;
```

Example:

```
BigName := FExpand( 'app.pas' );
                { 'C:\TP\PROGRAMS\APP.PAS' }
```

FilePos

System

Purpose: Returns the current record number of an opened file. The value can range from 0 through `FileSize(FileIdentifier)`. `FilePos` cannot be used on a text file.

Syntax:
```
Function FilePos( var FileIdentifier ) : LongInt;
```

Example:
```
CurRecNum := FilePos( DataFile );
```

FileSize System

Purpose: Returns the number of components in an opened file. If the file is empty, `FileSize` returns 0. `FileSize` cannot be used on a text file.

Syntax:
```
Function FileSize( var FileIdentifier : AnyFileType )
                                       : LongInt;
```

Example:
```
RecordCount := FileSize( DataFile );
```

FillChar System

Purpose: Fills a variable `X` (declared to be of any type) with `Count` characters of `Ch`, which may be any ordinal type. No range checking is performed.

Syntax:
```
Procedure FillChar( var X     : AnyType;
                        Count : Word;
                        Ch    : AnyOrdType );
```

Example:
```
FillChar( NumVar, SizeOf( NumVar ), 0 );
```

FillEllipse Graph

Purpose: Draws a filled ellipse, centered at `(X, Y)`, having horizontal and vertical axes of `XRadius` and `YRadius`, respectively. The ellipse is drawn with the current fill style and fill color and is bordered with the current color.

Syntax:
```
Procedure FillEllipse( X, Y              : Integer;
                       XRadius, YRadius : Word );
```

Example:
```
FillEllipse( 100, 100, 50, 75 );
```

FillPoly Graph

Purpose: Draws and fills a polygon containing `NumPoints` vertices, using the current fill style and color. The border is drawn in the current line style and color. `PolyPoints` is an array of `PointType`, as shown in the following:

```
PointType = record
              X, Y : Integer;
            end;
```

Each `PointType` record contains the coordinates of a vertex of the polygon.

Syntax:

```
Procedure FillPoly( NumPoints : Word; var PolyPoints );
```

Example:

```
FillPoly( SizeOf( Shape ) div SizeOf( PointType ),
          Shape );
```

FindFirst Dos

Purpose: Searches the `Path` directory mask for the first file having the attributes specified by `Attr`. The `PathStr` and `SearchRec` types are defined as follows:

```
PathStr = String[79];      { Full file path string }
SearchRec = record
              Fill : Array[1..21] of Byte;
              Attr : Byte;
              Time : LongInt;
              Size : LongInt;
              Name : String[12];
            end;
```

The `SearchRec` record `F` is used as input for the `FindNext` procedure.

Syntax:

```
Procedure FindFirst(      Path : PathStr;
                          Attr : Word;
                      var F    : SearchRec );
```

Example:

```
FindFirst( '*.PAS', Archive, SRec );
```

FindNext — Dos

Purpose: Returns the next entry that matches the name and attributes specified in the `SearchRec` record `F`, obtained from a previous call to `FindFirst`. The `SearchRec` type is defined as follows:

```
SearchRec = record
              Fill : Array[1..21] of Byte;
              Attr : Byte;
              Time : LongInt;
              Size : LongInt;
              Name : String[12];
            end;
```

Syntax: `Procedure FindNext( var F : SearchRec );`

Example: `FindNext( SRec );`

FloodFill — Graph

Purpose: Fills a region containing the point `(X, Y)` and bounded by the `Border` color.

Syntax: `Procedure FloodFill( X, Y : Integer; Border : Word );`

Example: `FloodFill( 10, 25, Red );`

Flush — System

Purpose: Flushes the buffer of a text file that is open for output.

Syntax: `Procedure Flush( var FileIdentifier : Text );`

Example: `Flush( TextStuff );`

Frac

System

Purpose: Returns the fractional part of the argument.

Syntax:
```
Function Frac( X : Real ) : Real;
```

Example:
```
Decimals := Frac( 3.14159 ); { Returns  0.14159 }
```

FreeMem

System

Purpose: Disposes (that is, deallocates) a dynamic variable `P` of a given `Size` that was previously created by a call to the `GetMem` procedure.

Syntax:
```
Procedure FreeMem( var P : Pointer; Size : Word );
```

Example:
```
FreeMem( ScreenBuffer, ScreenSize );
```

FSearch

Dos

Purpose: Searches for a file given by `Path` in a list of directories given by `DirList`. The `PathStr` type is defined as follows:

```
PathStr = String[79];     { Full file path string }
```

Syntax:
```
Function FSearch( Path : PathStr;
                  DirList : String ) : PathStr;
```

Example:
```
FSearch( RequestedFile, GetEnv( 'PATH' ) );
```

FSplit

Dos

Purpose: Splits the file name specified by `Path` into its three components; the drive and directory are placed in `Dir`, the file name is placed in `Name`, and the file extension is placed in `Ext`. If a component is missing from `Path`, the corresponding output string will be empty. The `PathStr`, `DirStr`, `NameStr`, and `ExtStr` types are defined as follows:

```
PathStr = String[79];     { Full file path string }
DirStr  = String[67];     { Drive and directory string }
NameStr = String[8];      { File name string }
ExtStr  = String[4];      { File extension string }
```

Syntax:

```
Procedure FSplit(     Path : PathStr;
                  var Dir  : DirStr;
                  var Name : NameStr;
                  var Ext  : ExtStr );
```

Example:

```
FSplit( CompleteFileName, DirName, FileName, ExtName );
```

GetArcCoords Graph

Purpose: Returns the coordinates of the last `Arc` or `Ellipse` command as a record of the type `ArcCoordsType`, defined as follows:

```
ArcCoordsType = record
                  X, Y           : Integer;
                  Xstart, Ystart : Integer;
                  Xend, Yend     : Integer;
                end;
```

The center of the arc is at `(X, Y)`. Its starting and ending coordinates are `(Xstart, Ystart)` and `(Xend, Yend)`, respectively.

Syntax:

```
Procedure GetArcCoords( var ArcCoords : ArcCoordsType );
```

Example:

```
GetArcCoords( ArcData );
```

GetAspectRatio Graph

Purpose: Gets the effective resolution of the graphics screen. The aspect ratio can be computed by dividing the `Xasp` parameter by the `Yasp` parameter.

Syntax:

```
Procedure GetAspectRatio( var Xasp, Yasp : Word );
```

Example:

```
GetAspectRatio( Xasp, Yasp );
writeln( 'Aspect ratio is ', Xasp/Yasp );
```

GetBkColor Graph

Purpose: Returns the index into the palette of the current background color.

Syntax:

```
Function GetBkColor : Word;
```

Example:

```
writeln( 'Background color index is ', GetBkColor );
```

GetCBreak Dos

Purpose: Returns the state of Ctrl-Break checking in DOS. When checking is off (`Break = False`), DOS tests for Ctrl-Break only during I/O operations; when checking is on (`Break = True`), DOS tests for Ctrl-Break before every system call.

Syntax:

```
Procedure GetCBreak( var Break : Boolean );
```

Example:

```
GetCBreak( BreakTest );
writeln( 'Is Ctrl-Break checking on? ', BreakTest );
```

GetColor Graph

Purpose: Returns the color value passed to the previous successful call to `SetColor`.

Syntax:

```
Function GetColor : Word;
```

Example:

```
writeln( 'Current color index is ', GetColor );
```

GetDate Dos

Purpose: Returns the current date set in the operating system.

Syntax:

```
Procedure GetDate( var Year, Month, Day,
                       DayOfWeek : Word );
```

Example:

```
GetDate( Year, Month, Day, DayOfWeek );
writeln( 'Today is ',Month,'/',Day,'/',Year 1900 );
```

GetDefaultPalette Graph

Purpose: Returns the palette definition record of the type `PaletteType`, defined as follows:

```
PaletteType = record
                 Size   : Byte;
                 Colors : Array[0..MaxColors] of
                            ShortInt;
              end;
```

The palette contains the original colors initialized by `InitGraph`.

Syntax:

```
Procedure GetDefaultPalette( var Palette
                                : PaletteType );
```

Example:

```
GetDefaultPalette( PaletteRec );
```

GetDir System

Purpose: Returns the current directory `DirString` of a specified `DriveNumber`. A `DriveNumber` of 0 indicates the current drive, 1 indicates drive A, 2 indicates drive B, and so on.

Syntax:

```
Procedure GetDir( DriveNumber : Byte;
                  var DirString : String );
```

Example:

```
GetDir( 0, DirectoryName );
CurrentDrive := DirectoryName[ 1 ];
```

GetDriverName Graph

Purpose: Returns a string containing the name of the current driver.

Syntax:

```
Function GetDriverName : String;
```

Example:

```
OutText( 'Currently using driver ', GetDriverName );
```

GetEnv Dos

Purpose: Returns the value of a specified environment variable.

Syntax:
```
Function GetEnv( EnvVar : String ) : String;
```

Example:
```
writeln( 'Current path is ', GetEnv( 'path' ) );
```

GetFAttr Dos

Purpose: Returns the attributes of an unopened file. The file, `F`, can be tested for an individual attribute by logically `AND`ing the `Attr` parameter with one of the following predefined constants:

```
ReadOnly  = $01;
Hidden    = $02;
SysFile   = $04;
VolumeID  = $08;
Directory = $10;
Archive   = $20;
AnyFile   = $3F;
```

Syntax:
```
Procedure GetFAttr( var F : AnyFileType;
                    var Attr : Word );
```

Example:
```
Assign( StoredData, ExternalFileName );
GetFAttr( StoredData, FileAttribute );
if FileAttribute and ReadOnly <> 0 then
   writeln( ExternalFileName, ' is write-protected' );
```

GetFillPattern Graph

Purpose: Returns an array containing the fill pattern set by the most recent call to `SetFillPattern`. The `FillPatternType` record type is defined as follows:

```
FillPatternType = Array[1..8] of Byte;
                  { User-defined fill style }
```

Syntax:
```
Procedure GetFillPattern( var FillPattern :
                            FillPatternType );
```

Example:
```
GetFillPattern( PatternStyleArray );
```

GetFillSettings Graph

Purpose: Returns the last fill pattern and color set by a previous call to `SetFillStyle`. The `FillSettingsType` record type is defined as follows:

```
FillSettingsType = record     { Predefined fill style }
                       Pattern : Word;
                       Color   : Word;
                   end;
```

Syntax:

```
Procedure GetFillSettings( var FillInfo :
                                FillSettingsType );
```

Example:

```
GetFillSettings( PatternAndColor );
```

GetFTime Dos

Purpose Returns the date and time a file `F` was last written. `Time` may be unpacked and read with the `UnpackTime` procedure.

Syntax:

```
Procedure GetFTime( var F : AnyFileType;
                    var Time : LongInt );
```

Example:

```
GetFTime( StoredData, LastUpdate );
```

GetGraphMode Graph

Purpose Returns the current graphics mode.

Syntax:

```
Function GetGraphMode : Integer;
```

Example:

```
writeln( 'Current mode: ', GetModeName( GetGraphMode ) );
```

GetImage Graph

Purpose: Saves a bit image of a portion of the screen into a buffer. The specified region is bounded by a rectangle with an upper left corner of `(X1, Y1)` and a lower right corner of `(X2, Y2)`. The buffer is defined by the `BitMap` variable.

Syntax:

```
Procedure GetImage( X1, Y1, X2, Y2 : Integer;
                    var BitMap );
```

Example:

```
Size := ImageSize( UpX, UpY, DownX, DownY );
GetMem( BufferArea, Size );
GetImage( UpX, UpY, DownX, DownY, BufferArea^ );
```

GetIntVec Dos

Purpose: Returns the address stored in a specified interrupt vector.

Syntax:

```
Procedure GetIntVec( IntNo : Byte;
                     var Vector : Pointer );
```

Example:

```
GetIntVec( $05, PrintScreenISR );
```

GetLineSettings Graph

Purpose: Returns a `LineInfo` record containing the current line style, pattern, and thickness as set by `SetLineStyle`. The `LineSettingsType` record type is defined as follows:

```
LineSettingsType = record
                     LineStyle : Word;
                     Pattern   : Word;
                     Thickness : Word;
                   end;
```

Syntax:

```
Procedure GetLineSettings( var LineInfo :
                           LineSettingsType );
```

Example:

```
GetLineSettings( LineDataRec );
```

GetMaxColor Graph

Purpose: Returns the highest color that can be passed to the `SetColor` procedure.

Syntax:

```
Function GetMaxColor : Word;
```

Example:

```
Color := GetMaxColor;
```

GetMaxMode Graph

Purpose: Returns the maximum mode number for the currently loaded driver.

Syntax:

```
Function GetMaxMode : Integer;
```

Example:

```
ModeNumber := GetMaxMode;
```

GetMaxX Graph

Purpose: Returns the rightmost column (`X` resolution) of the current graphics driver and mode.

Syntax:

```
Function GetMaxX : Integer;
```

Example:

```
RightSide := GetMaxX;
```

GetMaxY Graph

Purpose: Returns the bottommost row (`Y` resolution) of the current graphics driver and mode.

Syntax:

```
Function GetMaxY : Integer;
```

Example:

```
BottomLine := GetMaxY;
```

GetMem System

Purpose: Creates a new dynamic variable of the specified `Size` and places the address of the block in the pointer variable `P`.

Syntax:

```
Procedure GetMem( var P : Pointer; Size : Word );
```

Example:

```
Size := ImageSize( UpX, UpY, DownX, DownY );
GetMem( BufferArea, Size );
GetImage( UpX, UpY, DownX, DownY, BufferArea^ );
```

GetModeName Graph

Purpose: Returns a string containing the name of the specified graphics mode.

Syntax:

```
Function GetModeName( GraphMode : Integer ) : String;
```

Example:

```
writeln( 'Current mode: ',
         GetModeName( GetGraphMode ) );
```

GetModeRange Graph

Purpose: Returns the lowest and highest valid graphics modes for a given driver.

Syntax:

```
Procedure GetModeRange(     GraphDriver    : Integer;
                        var LoMode, HiMode : Integer );
```

Example:

```
GetModeRange( CGA, Lowest, Highest );
```

GetPalette Graph

Purpose: Returns the current palette and its size in the `Palette` record. The `PaletteType` record is defined as follows:

```
PaletteType = record
                Size   : Byte;
                Colors : Array[0..MaxColors] of
                           ShortInt;
              end;
```

Syntax: `Procedure GetPalette( var Palette : PaletteType );`

Example: `GetPalette( PaletteInfo );`

GetPaletteSize Graph

Purpose: Returns the size of the palette color lookup table.

Syntax: `Function GetPaletteSize : Integer;`

Example:

```
writeln( 'There are ', GetPaletteSize, '
         colors available.' );
```

GetPixel Graph

Purpose: Gets the color of the pixel at `(X, Y)`.

Syntax: `Function GetPixel( X, Y : Integer ) : Word;`

Example: `PixelColor := GetPixel( 40, 25 );`

GetTextSettings Graph

Purpose: Returns the current text font, direction, size, and justification as set by `SetTextStyle` and `SetTextJustify`. The `TextSettingsType` record is defined as follows:

```
TextSettingsType = record
                       Font      : Word;
                       Direction : Word;
                       CharSize  : Word;
                       Horiz     : Word;
                       Vert      : Word;
                   end;
```

Syntax:

```
Procedure GetTextSettings( var TextInfo :
                           TextSettingsType );
```

Example: `GetTextSettings( TextOptions );`

GetTime Dos

Purpose: Returns the current time set in the operating system.

Syntax:

```
Procedure GetTime( var Hour, Minute, Second, Sec100 :
                        Word );
```

Example:

```
GetTime( Hour, Minute, Second, Sec100 );
writeln( 'It''s now ', Hour, ':', Minute, ':', Second );
```

GetVerify Dos

Purpose: Returns the state of the verify flag in DOS. When the flag is off (`Verify = False`), disk writes are not verified. When the flag is on (`Verify = True`), all disk writes are verified.

Syntax:

```
Procedure GetVerify( var Verify : Boolean );
```

Example:

```
GetVerify( Verify );
writeln( 'Are disk writes being verified? ', Verify );
```

GetViewSettings Graph

Purpose: Returns the current viewport and clipping settings, as set by `SetViewPort`. The `ViewPortType` record is defined as follows:

```
ViewPortType = record
                  X1, Y1, X2, Y2 : Integer;
                  Clip           : Boolean;
               end;
```

The active viewport consists of the rectangle with upper left coordinates `(X1, Y1)` and lower right coordinates `(X2, Y2)`. Clipping in the viewport is indicated by the state of the `Clip` field.

Syntax:

```
Procedure GetViewSettings( var ViewPort :
                              ViewPortType );
```

Example:

```
GetViewSettings( ViewPortData );
```

GetX Graph

Purpose: Returns the X-coordinate of the current pointer (CP).

Syntax:
```
Function GetX : Integer;
```

Example:
```
XLocation := GetX;
```

GetY Graph

Purpose: Returns the Y-coordinate of the current pointer (CP).

Syntax:
```
Function GetY : Integer;
```

Example:
```
YLocation := GetY;
```

GotoXY Crt

Purpose: Positions the cursor at `(X, Y)`.

Syntax:
```
Procedure GotoXY( X, Y : Byte );
```

Example:
```
GotoXY( 40, 12 );   { Centers the cursor }
```

GraphDefaults Graph

Purpose: Resets the graphics settings for the viewport; palette; draw and background colors; line style and pattern; fill style, color, and pattern; active font; text style; text justification; and user character size.

Syntax:
```
Procedure GraphDefaults;
```

Example:
```
GraphDefaults;
```

GraphErrorMsg Graph

Purpose: Returns an error message string for the specified `ErrorCode`.

Syntax:
```
Function GraphErrorMsg( ErrorCode : Integer ) : String;
```

Example:
```
ErrorCode := GraphResult;
writeln( 'Error: ', GraphErrorMsg( ErrorCode ) );
```

GraphResult Graph

Purpose: Returns an error code for the last graphics operation, after which the error code is reset to 0.

Syntax:
```
Function GraphResult : Integer;
```

Example:
```
ErrorCode := GraphResult;
writeln( 'Error: ', GraphErrorMsg( ErrorCode ) );
```

Halt System

Purpose: Stops program execution and returns to the operating system. The optional parameter `ExitCode` specifies the exit code of the program. When `ExitCode` is omitted, `Halt(0)` is assumed.

Syntax:
```
Procedure Halt[ ( ExitCode : Word ) ];
```

Example:
```
Halt( ExitNo );
```

Hi System

Purpose: Returns the high-order byte of the argument, which may be either an `Integer` or a `Word`.

Syntax:
```
Function Hi( X : IntWord ) : Byte;
```

Example:
```
writeln( 'Using DOS ', Lo( DosVersion ), '.',
         Hi( DosVersion ) );
```

HighVideo Crt

Purpose: Displays subsequent screen output in high-intensity characters.

Syntax:

```
Procedure HighVideo;
```

Example:

```
HighVideo;
```

ImageSize Graph

Purpose: Returns the number of bytes required to store a portion of the screen. The selected region is in the form of a rectangle, with upper left coordinates of `(X1, Y1)` and lower right coordinates of `(X2, Y2)`.

Syntax:

```
Function ImageSize( X1, Y1, X2, Y2 : Integer ) : Word;
```

Example:

```
Size := ImageSize( UpX, UpY, DownX, DownY );
GetMem( BufferArea, Size );
GetImage( UpX, UpY, DownX, DownY, BufferArea^ );
```

Inc System

Purpose: Increments the value of any ordinal variable. If the optional parameter `n` is not specified, `X` is incremented by 1; otherwise, `X` is incremented by the value of `n`.

Syntax:

```
Procedure Inc( var X : OrdType [; n : LongInt ] );
```

Example:

```
Amount := 10;
Inc( Amount );       { Amount now equals 11 }
Inc( Amount, 3 );    { Amount now equals 14 }
```

InitGraph Graph

Purpose: Initializes the graphics system and switches the hardware to graphics mode. If `InitGraph` is called when `GraphDriver` is equal to `Detect`—a predefined constant of 0—the procedure automatically selects and initializes an appropriate graphics driver and mode. Otherwise, if `GraphDriver` is not equal to 0, `InitGraph` loads the graphics driver and mode corresponding to the values of `GraphDriver` and `GraphMode`. The `PathToDriver` string contains the name of the directory containing the graphics driver files. If `PathToDriver` is empty, the driver files must be in the current directory.

Syntax:

```
Procedure InitGraph( var GraphDriver  : Integer;
                     var GraphMode    : Integer;
                         PathToDriver : String );
```

Example:

```
grDriver := Detect;
InitGraph( grDriver, grMode, 'C:\TP' );
```

Insert — System

Purpose: Inserts a `Source` string into a `Target` string, beginning at the `Index` position. If the resulting string would exceed 255 characters, it is truncated after the 255th character.

Syntax:

```
Procedure Insert(     Source : String;
                  var Target : String;
                      Index  : Integer );
```

Example:

```
Target := 'abchijklmnopqrstuvwxyz';
Insert( 'DEFG', Target, 4 );
   { "abcDEFGhijklmnopqrstuvwxyz" }
```

InsLine — Crt

Purpose: Inserts an empty line at the cursor position using the current setting of `TextBackGround`. All lines below the cursor are moved down one row. The contents of the bottom line are lost.

Syntax:

```
Procedure InsLine;
```

Example:

```
InsLine;
```

InstallUserDriver Graph

Purpose: Installs a vendor-added device driver called `DriverFileName` to the BGI device driver table. The pointer to an accompanying autodetect function (if any) is given by `AutoDetectPtr`.

Syntax:

```
Function InstallUserDriver( DriverFileName : String;
                            AutoDetectPtr  : Pointer )
                                           : Integer;
```

Example:

```
grDriver := InstallUserDriver( 'NewThing.BGI', Nil );
InitGraph( grDriver, grMode, 'C:\TP' );
```

InstallUserFont Graph

Purpose: Installs a new font called `FontFileName` that is not built into the BGI system.

Syntax:

```
Function InstallUserFont( FontFileName : String )
                                       : Integer;
```

Example:

```
NewFont := InstallUserFont( 'OddShape.CHR' );
grDriver := Detect;
InitGraph( grDriver, grMode, 'C:\TP' );
SetTextStyle( NewFont, HorizDir, 1 );
```

Int System

Purpose: Returns the integer part of a real-type argument.

Syntax:

```
Function Int( X : Real ) : Real;
```

Example:

```
WholeA := Int( 3.14159 );    { Returns 3.0 }
WholeB := Int( -3.14159 );   { Returns -3.0 }
```

Intr

Dos

Purpose: Executes BIOS interrupt number `IntNo`. Any parameters are passed with a record of type `Registers`, defined as follows:

```
Registers = record
              case Integer of
                 0 : (AX,BX,CX,DX,BP,SI,DI,DS,ES,Flags
                   : Word);
                 1 : (AL,AH,BL,BH,CL,CH,DL,DH
                   : Byte);
            end;
```

Syntax:

```
Procedure Intr( IntNo : Byte; var Regs : Registers );
```

Example:

```
Intr( 5, Regs );   { Same as pressing Shift-PrtSc }
```

IOResult

System

Purpose: If I/O checking is disabled with `{$I-}`, `IOResult` returns and resets the value of the internal error flag for the last I/O operation. A value of zero indicates success; nonzero indicates that an error occurred. Whenever an error occurs while I/O checking is disabled, all subsequent I/O operations are ignored until `IOResult` is called and the internal error flag is cleared.

Syntax:

```
Function IOResult : Word;
```

Example:

```
Assign( InFile, FileNameString );
{$I-} Reset( InFile ) {$I+};
if IOResult < > 0 then
   writeln( FileNameString, ' wasn''t found!' );
```

Keep

Dos

Purpose: Ends the current program and makes it—in its entirety—stay resident in memory. `ExitCode` corresponds to the exit code parameter used in the `Halt` procedure.

Syntax: `Procedure Keep( ExitCode : Word );`

Example: `Keep( 0 );`

KeyPressed Crt

Purpose: Returns `True` if a key has been pressed on the keyboard; otherwise, `KeyPressed` returns `False`. Special keys (such as Shift, Ctrl, and Alt) are ignored.

Syntax: `Function KeyPressed : Boolean;`

Example:

```
if KeyPressed then
   ProcessTheKeystroke;
```

Length System

Purpose: Returns the dynamic length of the `Str` string.

Syntax: `Function Length( Str : String ) : Integer;`

Example:

```
GotoXY( (80 - Length(Message)) div 2, 10 );
write( Message );    { Centered in row 10 }
```

Line Graph

Purpose: Draws a line from `(X1, Y1)` to `(X2, Y2)` using the line style and thickness set by `SetLineStyle` and the color set by `SetColor`.

Syntax: `Procedure Line( X1, Y1, X2, Y2 : Integer );`

Example:

```
Line( 0, 0, GetMaxX, GetMaxY );    { Draw a big X on }
Line( 0, GetMaxY, GetMaxX, 0 );    {     the screen   }
```

LineRel Graph

Purpose: Draws a line to a point located a relative distance from the current pointer (CP) using the line style and thickness set by `SetLineStyle` and the color set by `SetColor`. If `(X, Y)` is the position of the CP, then `LineRel(Dx, Dy)` is equivalent to `Line(X,Y,(X + Dx),(Y + Dy))`.

Syntax:

```
Procedure LineRel( Dx, Dy : Integer );
```

Example:

```
LineRel( 20, 40 );    { -----------------------------}
LineRel( 20, -40 );   { These 3 lines form a triangle }
LineRel( -40, 0 );    { ---------------------------- }
```

LineTo Graph

Purpose: Draws a line from the current pointer (CP) to `(X, Y)` using the line style and thickness set by `SetLineStyle` and the color set by `SetColor`.

Syntax:

```
Procedure LineTo( X, Y : Integer );
```

Example:

```
LineTo( GetMaxX, 0 );  { Draws line to }
                       { upper right corner }
```

Ln System

Purpose: Returns the natural logarithm of the argument, which must be positive.

Syntax:

```
Function Ln( X : Real ) : Real;
```

Example:

```
LogValue := Ln( Num );
```

Lo System

Purpose: Returns the low-order byte of the argument, which may be either an `Integer` or a `Word`.

Syntax: `Function Lo( X : IntWord ) : Byte;`

Example:

```
writeln( 'Using DOS ', Lo( DosVersion ), '.',
         Hi( DosVersion ) );
```

LowVideo Crt

Purpose: Causes all subsequent screen output to use low-intensity characters.

Syntax: `Procedure LowVideo;`

Example: `LowVideo;`

Mark System

Purpose: Copies the current value of `HeapPtr` to the pointer variable `P`.

Syntax: `Procedure Mark( var P : Pointer );`

Example: `Mark( HeapHold );`

MaxAvail System

Purpose: Returns the size, in bytes, of the largest contiguous free block in the heap, corresponding to the size of the largest dynamic variable that can be allocated at the time.

Syntax: `Function MaxAvail : LongInt;`

Example: `TopItemSize := MaxAvail;`

MemAvail System

Purpose: Returns the sum, in bytes, of all free blocks in the heap.

Syntax: `Function MemAvail : LongInt;`

Example: `HeapSpaceFree := MemAvail;`

MkDir — System

Purpose: Creates a subdirectory specified by `SubName`.

Syntax: `Procedure MkDir( SubName : String );`

Example: `MkDir( 'C:\TP\WORKAREA\TEMP' );`

Move — System

Purpose: Copies `Count` contiguous bytes beginning with the first byte of `Source` to the first byte of `Destination`. The `Source` and `Destination` variables may be of any type. No range checking is performed.

Syntax: `Procedure Move( var Source, Destination; Count : Word );`

Example: `Move( X, Y, SizeOf(X) );`

MoveRel — Graph

Purpose: Moves the current pointer (CP) a relative distance from its starting location. If `(X, Y)` is the original position of the CP, then `MoveRel(Dx, Dy)` is equivalent to `MoveTo(X + Dx, Y + Dy)`.

Syntax: `Procedure MoveRel( Dx, Dy : Integer );`

Example: `MoveRel( 50, 50 );`

MoveTo — Graph

Purpose: Moves the current pointer (CP) to `(X, Y)`.

Syntax: `Procedure MoveTo( X, Y : Integer );`

Example: `MoveTo( 100, 200 );`

MsDos　　　Dos

Purpose: Executes a DOS function call from BIOS interrupt number $21. Any parameters are passed with a record of type `Registers`, declared as follows:

```
Registers = record
                        case Integer of
                        0 : (AX,BX,CX,DX,BP,SI,DI,DS,ES,Flags
                          : Word);
                        1 : (AL,AH,BL,BH,CL,CH,DL,DH
                          : Byte);
            end;
```

Syntax: `Procedure MsDos( var Regs : Registers );`

Example:

```
Regs.AH := $30;
MsDos( Regs );
writeln( 'Running DOS ', Regs.AL, '.', Regs.AH );
```

New　　　System

Purpose: Allocates enough space in the heap for a dynamic variable. When used as a procedure, `New` allocates a variable of the type pointed to by `P`. Next, the procedure sets `P` equal to the location of the new variable, which can then be referenced as `P^`. When used as a function, `PointerTypeID` is the type of the variable to be allocated, and the memory location of the new variable is returned by the `New` function.

Syntax 1: `Procedure New( var P : Pointer );`

Example: `New( ByteVar );`

Syntax 2: `Function New( PointerTypeID ) : Pointer;`

Example:

```
type
   ByteType = ^byte;
var
   ByteVar : ByteType;
begin
   ByteVar := New( ByteType );
```

When using the procedure form of `New` to allocate space for a dynamic object containing virtual methods, `P` is a pointer to the object, and `Construct` is the name of the constructor for that object type. When used as a function, `ObjectPointerTypeID` is the type identifier for the object, and the memory location of the object is returned by the `New` function.

Syntax 3:

```
Procedure New( var P : ObjectPointer, Construct );
```

Example:

```
New( ObjectPtr, InitObj );
```

Syntax 4:

```
Function New( ObjectPointerTypeID, Construct ) :
         Pointer;
```

Example:

```
type
   ObjectType = ^Obj;
var
   ObjectPtr : ObjectType;
begin
   ObjectPtr := New( ObjectType, InitObj );
```

NormVideo — Crt

Purpose: Selects the original text attribute read from the cursor location when the program began. Usually, all subsequent screen output appears in characters of normal intensity.

Syntax:

```
Procedure NormVideo;
```

Example:

```
NormVideo;
```

NoSound — Crt

Purpose: Turns off the internal speaker.

Syntax:

```
Procedure NoSound;
```

Example:

```
NoSound;
```

Odd

System

Purpose: Returns `True` if the argument is an odd number; otherwise, `False` is returned.

Syntax:

```
Function Odd( X : LongInt ) : Boolean;
```

Example:

```
if Odd( Value Shl Bit ) then
   writeln( 'Bit number ', Bit, ' is set.' );
```

Ofs

System

Purpose: Returns the offset of the specified object.

Syntax:

```
Function Ofs( X : AnyType ) : Word;
```

Example:

```
DataLocation := Ofs( Object );
```

Ord

System

Purpose: Returns the ordinal number of any ordinal-type value.

Syntax:

```
Function Ord( X : OrdType ) : LongInt;
```

Example:

```
Ch := 'm';
writeln( Ch, ' is letter number ',
         Ord( UpCase(Ch) ) - 64 );
```

OutText

Graph

Purpose: Outputs `TextString` to the location of the current pointer (CP).

Syntax:

```
Procedure OutText( TextString : String );
```

Example:

```
OutText( 'Message string' );
```

OutTextXY Graph

Purpose: Outputs `TextString` to the location `(X, Y)`.

Syntax:

```
Procedure OutTextXY( X, Y : Integer;
                     TextString : String );
```

Example:

```
OutTextXY( 100, 50, 'Message string' );
```

OvrClearBuf Overlay

Purpose: Clears the overlay buffer, forcing all subsequent calls to overlay routines to be reloaded from the overlay file or from expanded memory (EMS).

Syntax:

```
Procedure OvrClearBuf;
```

Example:

```
OvrClearBuf;
```

OvrGetBuf Overlay

Purpose: Returns the current size of the overlay buffer.

Syntax:

```
Function OvrGetBuf : LongInt;
```

Example:

```
writeln( 'The overlay buffer was ', OvrGetBuf, '
         bytes long.' );
OvrSetBuf( OvrGetBuf + IncrementAmount );
writeln( 'It is now ', OvrGetBuf, ' bytes long.' );
```

OvrGetRetry Overlay

Purpose: Returns the current size of the overlay buffer probation area, as previously set by `OvrSetRetry`.

Syntax:

```
Function OvrGetRetry : Longint;
```

Example:

```
ProbationSize := OvrGetRetry;
```

OvrInit

Overlay

Purpose: Initializes the overlay manager and opens the overlay file called `FileName`.

Syntax:

```
Procedure OvrInit( FileName : String );
```

Example:

```
OvrInit( 'SpredSht.OVR' );
```

OvrInitEMS

Overlay

Purpose: If an expanded memory (EMS) driver and adequate expanded memory are detected, `OvrInitEMS` loads the overlay file into EMS and closes the overlay file on disk.

Syntax:

```
Procedure OvrInitEMS;
```

Example:

```
OvrInitEMS;
```

OvrSetBuf

Overlay

Purpose: Resets the size of the overlay buffer.

Syntax:

```
Procedure OvrSetBuf( Size : LongInt );
```

Example:

```
writeln( 'The overlay buffer was ', OvrGetBuf, '
         bytes long.' );
OvrSetBuf( OvrGetBuf + IncrementAmount );
writeln( 'It is now ', OvrGetBuf, ' bytes long.' );
```

OvrSetRetry

Overlay

Purpose: Sets the size of the overlay buffer probation area to `ProbationSize` bytes.

Syntax:

```
Procedure OvrSetRetry( ProbationSize : Longint );
```

Example:

```
OvrInit( 'MAINPROG.OVR' );
OvrSetBuf( BufferSize );
OvrSetRetry( BufferSize div 3 );
```

PackTime Dos

Purpose: Converts a `DateTime` record into a four-byte, packed date-and-time `LongInt` used by `SetFTime`. No range checking is performed on the fields. The `DateTime` record is defined as follows:

```
DateTime = record
               Year, Month, Day, Hour, Min, Sec : Word;
           end;
```

Syntax:

```
Procedure PackTime( var T : DateTime; var P : LongInt );
```

Example:

```
PackTime( CurrentMoment, ClockField );
```

ParamCount System

Purpose: Returns the number of parameters passed to the program on the command line.

Syntax:

```
Function ParamCount : Word;
```

Example:

```
if ParamCount > 0 then
   for i := 1 to ParamCount do
      writeln( 'Parameter', i:2, ' is ', ParamStr( i );
```

ParamStr System

Purpose: Returns a specified command-line parameter. `ParamStr` will be empty if `Index` is greater than `ParamCount`. Beginning with Version 3.0, `ParamStr(0)` returns the path and file name of the executing program. Under earlier DOS versions, `ParamStr(0)` returns an empty string.

Syntax:

```
Function ParamStr( Index : Word ) : String;
```

Example:

```
if ParamCount > 0 then
   for i := 1 to ParamCount do
      writeln( 'Parameter', i:2, ' is ', ParamStr( i );
```

Pi — System

Purpose: Returns the value of pi (3.14159265358979 32385).

Syntax:

```
Function Pi : Real;
```

Example:

```
Circumference := Diameter * Pi;
```

PieSlice — Graph

Purpose: Draws and fills a pie slice of a specified `Radius`, centered at `(X, Y)`, from starting angle `StAngle` to ending angle `EndAngle`. Angles are measured in degrees, running counterclockwise, with 0 degrees in the three o'clock position. The outline of the pie slice is drawn with the current color. Its interior is drawn with the pattern and color defined by `SetFillStyle` or `SetFillPattern`.

Syntax:

```
Procedure PieSlice( X, Y                 : Integer;
                    StAngle, EndAngle,
                    Radius               : Word );
```

Example:

```
PieSlice( 100, 100, 0, 90, 50 );
```

Pos — System

Purpose: Searches for the substring `SubStr` in the string `Str`. If found, `Pos` returns the index of the first occurrence of `SubStr` in `Str`. If not found, `Pos` returns `0`.

Syntax:

```
Function Pos( SubStr, Str : String ) : Byte;
```

Example:

```
ActiveString := '    12.345';  { Replace blanks with 0s }
while Pos( ' ', ActiveString ) > 0 do
   ActiveString[ Pos( ' ', ActiveString ) ] := '0';
```

Pred

System

Purpose: Returns the predecessor of the argument, which can be any ordinal type. The result is the same type as the argument.

Syntax:

```
Function Pred( X : OrdType ) : OrdType;
```

Example:

```
XminusOne := Pred( X );
```

Ptr

System

Purpose: Converts a segment base and an offset address to a pointer compatible with all pointer types.

Syntax:

```
Function Ptr( Seg, Ofs : Word ) : Pointer;
```

Example:

```
MemPtr := Ptr( $40, $13 );
writeln( 'There are ', MemPtr^, ' bytes of
         internal memory.' );
```

PutImage

Graph

Purpose: Copies the contents of `BitMap` into the rectangular region of the screen having an upper left corner of `(X, Y)`. The `BitMap` buffer was originally created by `GetImage`; it contains the bit image to be displayed, in addition to the height and width of the region. The `DisplayOption` parameter determines how each bit is displayed; it can be set to one of the following predefined constants:

```
CopyPut = 0;
XORPut  = 1;
OrPut   = 2;
AndPut  = 3;
NotPut  = 4;
```

Syntax:

```
Procedure PutImage(      X, Y          : Integer;
                     var BitMap;
                         DisplayOption : Word );
```

Example:

```
Size := ImageSize( 0, 0, GetMaxX, GetMaxY );
GetMem( BufferArea, Size );
GetImage( 0, 0, GetMaxX, GetMaxY, BufferArea^ );
PutImage( 0, 0, BufferArea^, NotPut );    { Inverts the }
                                          {   screen    }
```

PutPixel — Graph

Purpose: Sets the pixel at `(X, Y)` to the color of `PixelColor`.

Syntax:

```
Procedure PutPixel( X, Y : Integer; PixelColor : Word );
```

Example:

```
PutPixel( 100, 100, Red );
```

Random — System

Purpose: Returns a random number. If `Range` is not specified, `Random` returns a real-type random number in the range $0 \leq x < 1$. When `Range` is used, `Random` returns a word-type random number in the range $0 \leq x <$ `Range`. The `Randomize` procedure should be called at the beginning of the program to initialize the random number generator.

Syntax 1:

```
Function Random : Real;
```

Example:

```
if Random < 0.5 then writeln( 'Heads' )
                else writeln( 'Tails' );
```

Syntax 2:

```
Function Random( Range : Word ) : Word;
```

Example:

```
writeln( 'The values of the dice are ',
         Random(6)+1, ' and ', Random(6)+1 );
```

Randomize — System

Purpose: Initializes the predefined variable `RandSeed`—the seed of the built-in random number generator—with a random value taken from the system clock.

Syntax:
```
Procedure Randomize;
```

Example:
```
Randomize;
```

Read — System

Purpose: Reads one or more values from a file into one or more variables. `FileID`, if specified, may be a text or typed file. If `FileID` is omitted, the standard text file `Input` is assumed. When your program reads from a text file, each individual variable must be a char, integer, real, or string type. When the program reads from a typed file, each individual variable must be of the same type as the file itself.

Syntax:
```
Procedure Read[( [var FileID : FileType;]
                 v1 [,v2,...,vn] )];
```

Example:
```
Read( DataFile, Name, Address, City, State, Zip );
```

ReadKey — Crt

Purpose: Reads a character from the keyboard without echoing it to the screen. If a key has already been pressed, `ReadKey` immediately returns the character; otherwise, `ReadKey` waits for the next key to be pressed. Extended keys (such as F1, PgUp, and Alt-P) are returned as two characters: the first is null (#0), and the second is the extended key code. Hence, the value returned by `ReadKey` must be tested; if null, a second `ReadKey` routine must be executed.

Syntax:
```
Function ReadKey : Char;
```

Example:
```
Entry := ReadKey;
If Entry = #27 then    { Escape key }
   DoEscapeStuff;
```

Readln System

Purpose: Executes the read procedure, then skips to the next line of the file. `FileID`, if specified, must be a text file; if omitted, the standard text file `Input` is assumed. Each individual variable must be a char, integer, real, or string type.

Syntax:

```
Procedure Readln[( [var FileID : Text;]
                          v1 [,v2,...,vn] )];
```

Example:

```
Readln[( DataFile, Name, Address, City, State, Zip )];
```

Rectangle Graph

Purpose: Draws a rectangle using the current line style and color. The upper left corner is at `(X1, Y1)` and the lower right corner is at `(X2, Y2)`.

Syntax:

```
Procedure Rectangle( X1, Y1, X2, Y2 : Integer );
```

Example:

```
Rectangle( 0, 0, GetMaxX, GetMaxY );    { Boxes the }
                                        {   screen  }
```

RegisterBGIdriver Graph

Purpose: Registers a user-loaded or linked-in BGI driver with the graphics system. If an error occurs while the system is loading the driver, the function returns a negative number; otherwise, the function returns the internal driver number.

Syntax:

```
Function RegisterBGIdriver( Driver : Pointer )
                                   : Integer;
```

Example:

```
Assign( CGADriver, 'CGA.BGI' );
Reset( CGADriver, 1 );
GetMem( CGAPointer, FileSize( CGADriver ) );
BlockRead( CGADriver, CGAPointer^,
           FileSize( CGADriver) );
if RegisterBGIdriver( CGAPointer^ ) < 0 then
   writeln( 'Error in loading driver' );
```

RegisterBGIfont Graph

Purpose: Registers a user-loaded or linked-in BGI font with the graphics system. If an error occurs while the system is loading the font, the function returns a negative number; otherwise, the function returns the internal font number.

Syntax:

```
Function RegisterBGIfont( Font : Pointer ) : Integer;
```

Example:

```
Assign( TripFont, 'TRIP.CHR' );
Reset( TripFont, 1 );
GetMem( FontPointer, FileSize( TripFont ) );
BlockRead( TripFont, FontPointer^,
           FileSize( TripFont ) );
if RegisterBGIfont( FontPointer^ ) < 0 then
   writeln( 'Error in loading driver' );
```

Release System

Purpose: Returns the top of the heap to the location pointed to by `P`, which was assigned during the execution of the most recent `Mark` procedure.

Syntax:

```
Procedure Release( var P : Pointer );
```

Example:

```
Release( HeapTop );
```

Rename System

Purpose: Renames an unopened external file to `NewName`.

Syntax:

```
Procedure Rename( var F; NewName : String );
```

Example:

```
Assign( SwitchFile, 'Orig.TXT' );
Rename( SwitchFile, 'New.TXT' );
```

Reset — System

Purpose: Opens an existing file. If `F` is declared as a text file, `Reset` opens it for input only. If `F` is declared as a typed or untyped file, `Reset` opens it for both input and output. The optional `RecSize` parameter, which can be used only if `F` is declared as an untyped file, specifies the record size used for data transfers; if `RecSize` is omitted, `Reset` uses a default record size of 128 bytes.

Syntax:

```
Procedure Reset( var F: file [; RecSize : Word ] );
```

Example:

```
Assign( InFile, 'Data.TXT' );
Reset( InFile );
```

RestoreCrtMode — Graph

Purpose: Restores the screen to its mode before `InitGraph` initialized graphics. `RestoreCrtMode` is used after `SetGraphMode`.

Syntax:

```
Procedure RestoreCrtMode;
```

Example:

```
RestoreCrtMode;
```

Rewrite — System

Purpose: Creates and opens a new file. If `F` is declared as a text file, `Rewrite` opens it for output only. If `F` is declared as a typed or untyped file, `Rewrite` opens it for both input and output. The optional `RecSize` parameter, which can be used only if `F` is declared as an untyped file, specifies the record size used for data transfers. If `RecSize` is omitted, `Rewrite` uses a default record size of 128 bytes.

Syntax:

```
Procedure Rewrite( var F: file [; RecSize : Word ] );
```

Example:

```
Assign( OutFile, 'Data.TXT' );
Rewrite( OutFile );
```

RmDir — System

Purpose: Removes an empty subdirectory specified by `EmptyDir`.

Syntax:

```
Procedure RmDir( EmptyDir : String );
```

Example:

```
RmDir( 'C:\TURBO\DATA\TEMP' );
```

Round — System

Purpose: Rounds a real-type value to an integer-type value.

Syntax:

```
Function Round( X : Real ) : LongInt;
```

Example:

```
Three := Round( 3.14159 );
```

RunError — System

Purpose: Halts program execution and generates a run-time error. If the optional parameter `ErrorCode` is omitted, the run-time error number is assumed to be 0.

Syntax:

```
Procedure RunError[ ( ErrorCode : Word ) ];
```

Example:

```
if Mode = fmInput then
   RunError( 104 );      { File not open for input }
```

Sector — Graph

Purpose: Draws and fills an elliptical sector from starting angle `StAngle` to ending angle `EndAngle`, using `(X, Y)` as the center point. `XRadius` and `YRadius` are the horizontal and vertical axes, respectively. `Angles` are measured in degrees, running counterclockwise, with 0 degrees at the three o'clock position. The outline of the sector is drawn in the current color. The interior of the sector is filled with the pattern and color specified by `SetFillStyle` or `SetFillPattern`.

Syntax:

```
Procedure Sector( X, Y                 : Integer;
                  StAngle, EndAngle,
                  XRadius, YRadius     : Word );
```

Example:

```
Sector( 100, 100, 0, 45, 30, 50 );
```

Seek — System

Purpose: Moves the current position of an opened file `F` to the specified component `CompNumber`. The file variable `F` may reference a typed or untyped file, but not a text file. For a typed file, the component is the same data object as the type of the file. For an untyped file, the component is a record whose size defaults to 128 bytes, but may be changed by the optional record-size parameter of the `Reset` or `Rewrite` procedure that opens it. The first component of the file is always number 0.

Syntax:

```
Procedure Seek( var F; CompNumber : LongInt );
```

Example:

```
Seek( RandomFile, RecordKey );
```

SeekEof — System

Purpose: Returns the end-of-file status of a text file. `SeekEof` behaves like `Eof`, except it ignores all blanks, tabs, and end-of-line markers. If the optional file parameter `F` is omitted, `SeekEof` is assumed to reference the standard `Input` file.

Syntax:

```
Function SeekEof[ ( var F : Text ) ] : Boolean;
```

Example:

```
while not SeekEof( DataFile ) do begin
   readln( DataFile, InLine );
   writeln( DataFile, InLine );
end;
```

SeekEoln System

Purpose: Returns the end-of-line status of a text file. `SeekEoln` behaves like `Eoln`, except blanks and tabs are ignored. If the optional file parameter `F` is omitted, `SeekEoln` is assumed to reference the standard `Input` file.

Syntax:

```
Function SeekEoln[ ( var F : Text ) ] : Boolean;
```

Example:

```
while not SeekEoln( DataFile ) do begin
   read( DataFile, CharItem );
   ProcessTheCharItem;
end;
```

Seg System

Purpose: Returns the segment of a specified object.

Syntax:

```
Function Seg( X : AnyType ) : Word;
```

Example:

```
DataLocation := Seg( Object );
```

SetActivePage Graph

Purpose: Selects `Page` as the active page for graphics output.

Syntax:

```
Procedure SetActivePage( Page : Word );
```

Example:

```
SetActivePage( 1 );
```

SetAllPalette Graph

Purpose: Changes all palette colors as specified. `Palette` is an untyped parameter, but it usually conforms to the `PaletteType` record, defined as follows:

```
PaletteType = record
                 Size   : Byte;
                 Colors : Array[0..MaxColors] of
                          ShortInt;
              end;
```

The `Size` byte is the length of the active part of the structure; that is, `SetAllPalette` processes only the first `Size` bytes of the `Colors` array. Each active byte may have a value from –1 through 15; if the byte is –1, the color is unchanged. Changes to the palette are seen immediately on the screen.

Syntax:

```
Procedure SetAllPalette( var Palette );
```

Example:

```
SetAllPalette( PaletteRecord );
```

SetAspectRatio Graph

Purpose: Changes the default aspect ratio of the current graphics mode. The value must be specified as a fraction of whole numbers; the system computes the aspect ratio by dividing the `Xasp` parameter by the `Yasp` parameter. The `GetAspectRatio` procedure can be used to obtain the current aspect ratio.

Syntax:

```
Procedure SetAspectRatio( Xasp, Yasp : Word );
```

Example:

```
SetAspectRatio( Xaspect, Yaspect );
```

SetBkColor Graph

Purpose: Sets the current background color to `ColorNum`—a value from 0 through 15. The selected color must be in the range allowed by the current graphics driver and mode. `SetBkColor(0)` always sets the background color to black.

Syntax:

```
Procedure SetBkColor( ColorNum : Word );
```

Example:

```
if Color in [ 0 .. Palette.Size ] then
   SetBkColor( Color );
```

SetCBreak — Dos

Purpose: Sets the state of Ctrl-Break checking in DOS. If `SetCBreak` is called when `Break` is `False`, DOS will check for Ctrl-Break only during I/O operations. If `SetCBreak` is called when `Break` is `True`, DOS will check for Ctrl-Break at every system call.

Syntax:

```
Procedure SetCBreak( Break : Boolean );
```

Example:

```
SetCBreak( True );
```

SetColor — Graph

Purpose: Sets the current drawing color to `ColorNum`—a value from 0 through 15. The selected color must be in the range allowed by the current graphics driver and mode. Valid values of `ColorNum` range from 0 through `GetMaxColor`.

Syntax:

```
Procedure SetColor( ColorNum : Word );
```

Example:

```
if Color in [ 0 .. GetMaxColor ] then
   SetColor( Color );
```

SetDate — Dos

Purpose: Sets the current date in the operating system. `Year` must be in the range 1980 through 2099, `Month` in the range 1 through 12, and `Day` in the range 1 through 31. If an invalid date is specified, the request is ignored.

Syntax:

```
Procedure SetDate( Year, Month, Day : Word );
```

Example:

```
SetDate( 1981, 5, 4 );   { May 4, 1981 }
```

SetFAttr Dos

Purpose: Sets the attributes of the unopened file `F`. The desired attributes are chosen by using a value of `Attr` equal to the sum of an appropriate combination of the following predefined constants:

```
ReadOnly  = $01;
Hidden    = $02;
SysFile   = $04;
VolumeID  = $08;
Directory = $10;
Archive   = $20;
AnyFile   = $3F;
```

Syntax:

```
Procedure SetFAttr( var F : AnyFileType; Attr : Word );
```

Example:

```
Assign( WorkFile, ExternalFileName );
SetFAttr( WorkFile, ReadOnly );
```

SetFillPattern Graph

Purpose: Selects a user-defined fill `Pattern` and `Color`. The pattern is formed as an 8 × 8 grid of pixels corresponding to the 64 bits contained in the `FillPatternType` array, defined as follows:

```
FillPatternType = Array[1..8] of Byte;
```

Syntax:

```
Procedure SetFillPattern( Pattern : FillPatternType;
                          Color   : Word );
```

Example:

```
SetFillPattern( CustomPattern, Red );
```

SetFillStyle Graph

Purpose: Sets the fill pattern and color. The `Pattern` parameter may be chosen from the following predefined constants:

```
EmptyFill     = 0;  { Uses the background color }
SolidFill     = 1;  { Uses a solid fill color }
LineFill      = 2;  { --- fill pattern }
LtSlashFill   = 3;  { /// fill pattern }
```

```
SlashFill        = 4;  { /// fill pattern with }
                       { thick lines }
BkSlashFill      = 5;  { \\\ fill pattern with }
                       { thick lines }
LtBkSlashFill    = 6;  { \\\ fill pattern }
HatchFill        = 7;  { Light hatch fill pattern }
XHatchFill       = 8;  { Heavy crosshatch fill pattern }
InterleaveFill   = 9;  { Interleaving line fill pattern }
WideDotFill      = 10; { Widely spaced dot fill pattern }
CloseDotFill     = 11; { Closely spaced dot fill }
                       { pattern }
UserFill         = 12; { User-defined fill pattern }
```

`ColorNum` must be in the range allowed by the current graphics driver and mode; valid values range from 0 through `GetMaxColor`.

Syntax:

```
Procedure SetFillStyle( Pattern, ColorNum : Word );
```

Example:

```
SetFillStyle( HatchFill, Red );
```

SetFTime Dos

Purpose: Sets the date and time an open file was last written to. The `Time` parameter can be created by using the `PackTime` procedure.

Syntax:

```
Procedure SetFTime( var F : AnyFileType;
                        Time : LongInt );
```

Example:

```
PackTime( CurrentMoment, ClockField );
SetFTime( ActiveFile; ClockField );
```

SetGraphBufSize Graph

Purpose: Allocates `BufSize` bytes on the heap for the graphics buffer used for scan and flood fills. The default buffer size is 4K. The `SetGraphBufSize` procedure must be called before the call to `InitGraph`.

Syntax:

```
Procedure SetGraphBufSize( BufSize : Word );
```

Example:

```
SetGraphBufSize( 8192 );   { Doubles the buffer to 8K }
```

SetGraphMode Graph

Purpose: Sets the system to the specified graphics `Mode` and clears the screen. All other graphics settings are reset to their defaults. `SetGraphMode` can be used to change the mode in the current graphics session or can be used after `RestoreCrtMode` to return to graphics in a new `Mode`.

Syntax:

```
Procedure SetGraphMode( Mode : Integer );
```

Example:

```
SetGraphMode( CGAHi );
```

SetIntVec Dos

Purpose: Sets interrupt vector `IntNo` to point to the address specified by `Vector`.

Syntax:

```
Procedure SetIntVec( IntNo : Byte; Vector : Pointer );
```

Example:

```
SetIntVec( 5, @ NewPrtScProc );
```

SetLineStyle Graph

Purpose: Sets the current `LineStyle`, `Pattern`, and `Thickness`. The `LineStyle` parameter controls the pattern of segments and spaces that form the line. Standard styles can be selected from the following predefined constants:

```
SolidLn    = 0;
DottedLn   = 1;
CenterLn   = 2;
DashedLn   = 3;
UserBitLn  = 4;
```

If `UserBitLn` is chosen, the line style takes the form of the sequence of bits in the `Pattern` byte; otherwise, the value of `Pattern` is ignored. The `Thickness` parameter chooses whether the line is normal or thick, depending on the choice of the following predefined constants:

```
NormWidth  = 1;
ThickWidth = 3;
```

Syntax:

```
Procedure SetLineStyle( LineStyle, Pattern, Thickness :
                        Word );
```

Example:

```
SetLineStyle( DashedLn, 0, ThickWidth );
```

SetPalette Graph

Purpose: Changes the setting of the `ColorNum` entry in the palette to `NewColor`. The choice of `ColorNum` must be in the range allowed by the current graphics driver and mode; valid values range from 0 through `GetMaxColor`.

Syntax:

```
Procedure SetPalette( ColorNum : Word;
                      NewColor : ShortInt );
```

Example:

```
SetPalette( 2, Red );
```

SetRGBPalette Graph

Purpose: Modifies the palette entry `ColorNum` for the IBM 8514 and VGA drivers. The choice of `ColorNum` must be in the range allowed by the graphics driver: 0 through 255 for the IBM 8514, and 0 through 15 for the VGA. `RedValue`, `GreenValue`, and `BlueValue` enable the user to control the intensities of the three CRT color guns.

Syntax:

```
Procedure SetRGBPalette( ColorNum,
                         RedValue,
                         GreenValue,
                         BlueValue    : Integer );
```

Example:

```
SetRGBPalette( Green, $FC, $14, $14 );
                         { Changes Green to Red }
```

SetTextBuf System

Purpose: Assigns an I/O buffer of `Buf` to an unopened text file. The default buffer size is 128 bytes. If the optional `Size` parameter is specified, the buffer is set to the first `Size` bytes of `Buf`. If the `Size` parameter is omitted, the buffer size is assumed to be `SizeOf(Buf)` bytes.

Syntax:

```
Procedure SetTextBuf( var F : Text;
                      var Buf [; Size : Word ] );
```

Example:

```
Assign( BigText, ExternalFileName );
SetTextBuf( BigText, BufferPtr^ );
Reset( BigText );
```

SetTextJustify Graph

Purpose: Sets the text justification for strings output by `OutText` and `OutTextXY`. The `Horizontal` parameter selects left, center, or right justification based on the choice of one of the following predefined constants:

```
LeftText   = 0;
CenterText = 1;
RightText  = 2;
```

The `Vertical` parameter selects bottom, center, or top justification based on the choice of one of the following predefined constants:

```
BottomText = 0;
CenterText = 1;
TopText    = 2;
```

Syntax:

```
Procedure SetTextJustify( Horizontal, Vertical : Word );
```

Example:

```
SetTextJustify( LeftText, CenterText );
```

SetTextStyle Graph

Purpose: Sets the current text `Font`, `Direction`, and character `Magnification` factor. The `Font` is selected from one of the following predefined constants:

```
DefaultFont   = 0;
TriplexFont   = 1;
SmallFont     = 2;
SansSerifFont = 3;
GothicFont    = 4;
```

The `Direction` of the output may be left-to-right or bottom-to-top, depending on the use of one of the following predefined constants:

```
HorizDir   = 0;        { left to right }
VertDir    = 1;        { bottom to top }
```

The `Magnification` factor determines the size of the text.

Syntax:

```
Procedure SetTextStyle( Font, Direction,
                        Magnification : Word );
```

Example:

```
SetTextStyle( GothicFont, HorizDir, 4 );
```

SetTime Dos

Purpose: Sets the current time in the operating system. Military time is used, with `Hour` ranging from 0 through 23, `Minute` and `Second` from 0 through 59, and `Sec100` from 0 through 99.

Syntax:

```
Procedure SetTime( Hour, Minute, Second, Sec100 :
                   Word );
```

Example:

```
SetTime( 12, 0, 0, 0 );   { 12:00 noon }
```

SetUserCharSize Graph

Purpose: Varies the character width and height for stroked fonts. Any factors may be used, but they must be expressed as fractions of whole numbers. The horizontal factor is given by `MultX div DivX`, and the vertical factor by `MultY div DivY`.

Syntax:

```
Procedure SetUserCharSize( MultX, DivX, MultY, DivY :
                           Word );
```

Example:

```
SetUserCharSize( 3, 2, 4, 1 );  { 1.5x wide by }
                                { 4.0x high    }
```

SetVerify Dos

Purpose: Sets the state of the verify flag in DOS. When the flag is off (`Verify = False`), disk writes are not verified. When it is on (`Verify = True`), all disk writes are verified.

Syntax:

```
Procedure SetVerify( Verify : Boolean );
```

Example:

```
SetVerify( True );
```

SetViewPort Graph

Purpose: Sets the size and location of the window to use for graphics output. The upper left corner of the window is positioned at `(X1, Y1)`, and the lower right corner is positioned at `(X2, Y2)`. Clipping is controlled by setting the `Clip` parameter, which can be either of the following predefined constants:

```
ClipOn  = true;
ClipOff = false;
```

Syntax:

```
Procedure SetViewPort( X1, Y1, X2, Y2 : Integer;
                       Clip           : Boolean );
```

Example:

```
SetViewPort( 25, 25, 100, 100, ClipOn );
```

SetVisualPage Graph

Purpose: Sets the visual graphics page number.

Syntax:

```
Procedure SetVisualPage( Page : Word );
```

Example:

```
SetVisualPage( 1 );
```

SetWriteMode Graph

Purpose: Sets the writing mode for line drawing. The `WriteMode` parameter determines the binary operation used to place the line on the screen, as follows:

```
CopyPut         = 0;     { MOV }
XORPut          = 1;     { XOR }
```

`CopyPut` uses an ordinary assembly language `MOV` instruction, overwriting the contents of the screen. `XORPut` uses an `XOR` instruction, which activates pixels when the screen is blank and deactivates pixels when the screen is lit.

Syntax: `Procedure SetWriteMode( WriteMode : Integer );`

Example: `SetWriteMode( XORPut );`

Sin System

Purpose: Returns the sine of the argument, which is expressed in radians.

Syntax: `Function Sin( X : Real ) : Real;`

Example: `SinValue := Sin( Pi/4 );   { Sin(45 degrees) }`

SizeOf System

Purpose: Returns the number of bytes occupied by the argument, which can be any variable reference or type identifier.

Syntax: `Function SizeOf( X : AnyType ) : Word;`

Example: `MemReqd := SizeOf( DataArray );`

Sound

Crt

Purpose: Causes the internal speaker to generate a tone of `Hz` hertz (cycles per second).

Syntax:

```
Procedure Sound( Hz : Word );
```

Example:

```
Sound( 550 );
```

SPtr

System

Purpose: Returns the current value of the SP register, which contains the offset of the stack pointer in the stack segment.

Syntax:

```
Function SPtr : Word;
```

Example:

```
StackPointerOffset := SPtr;
```

Sqr

System

Purpose: Returns the square of the argument, which can be any integer-type or real-type expression. The result returned by `Sqr` is the same type as the argument.

Syntax:

```
Function Sqr( X : AnyType ) : AnyType;
```

Example:

```
SideC := Sqrt( Sqr(SideA) + Sqr(SideB) );
```

Sqrt

System

Purpose: Returns the square root of the argument, which must be non-negative.

Syntax:

```
Function Sqrt( X : Real ) : Real;
```

Example:

```
SideC := Sqrt( Sqr(SideA) + Sqr(SideB) );
```

SSeg

System

Purpose: Returns the current value of the SS register, which contains the segment address of the stack segment.

Syntax:

```
Function SSeg : Word;
```

Example:

```
StackSegmentAddress := SSeg;
```

Str

System

Purpose: Converts a numeric value to a string `Str`. The number, `X`, may be any integer-type or real-type expression. The optional string `Width` and `Decimals` are integer-type expressions having the same formatting effect as a call to the `write` procedure.

Syntax:

```
Procedure Str( X [ : Width [ : Decimals ] ];
               var Str : String );
```

Example:

```
Str( NumberValue, OutString );
OutText( OutString );
```

Succ

System

Purpose: Returns the successor of the ordinal-type argument.

Syntax:

```
Function Succ( X : OrdType ) : OrdType;
```

Example:

```
Ch := Succ( 'B' );   { Returns "C" }
```

Swap

System

Purpose: Swaps the high- and low-order bytes of the argument, which can be either an integer or a word. The value returned by `Swap` has the same type as the argument.

Syntax:

```
Function Swap( X : IntWord ) : IntWord;
```

Example:

```
Flipped := Swap( $4567 );   { Returns $6745 }
```

SwapVectors Dos

Purpose: Swaps interrupt vectors prior to a call to the `Exec` procedure.

Syntax:

```
Procedure SwapVectors;
```

Example:

```
SwapVectors;      { Saves interrupt vectors }
Exec( ProgName, ComLine );
SwapVectors;      { Restores interrupt vectors }
```

TextBackground Crt

Purpose: Selects the background `Color` from one of the following predefined constants:

```
Black          = 0;
Blue           = 1;
Green          = 2;
Cyan           = 3;
Red            = 4;
Magenta        = 5;
Brown          = 6;
LightGray      = 7;
```

Syntax:

```
Procedure TextBackground( Color : Byte );
```

Example:

```
TextBackground( Red );
```

TextColor Crt

Purpose: Selects the foreground character `Color` from one of the following predefined constants:

```
Black          = 0;
Blue           = 1;
Green          = 2;
Cyan           = 3;
Red            = 4;
Magenta        = 5;
Brown          = 6;
LightGray      = 7;
DarkGray       = 8;
LightBlue      = 9;
LightGreen     = 10;
```

```
LightCyan      = 11;
LightRed       = 12;
LightMagenta   = 13;
Yellow         = 14;
White          = 15;
```

A blinking effect can be achieved by adding the constant:

```
Blink          = 128;
```

Syntax: `Procedure TextColor( Color : Byte );`

Example: `TextColor( Green + Blink );`

TextHeight Graph

Purpose: Returns the height of a string in pixels. The value is calculated from the current font size and multiplication factor.

Syntax: `Function TextHeight( TextString : String ) : Word;`

Example: `Tall := TextHeight( 'Press Enter to terminate...' );`

TextMode Crt

Purpose: Selects a specific text `Mode` from the following list of predefined constants:

```
BW40        = 0;   { 40 x 25 B/W on Color Adapter }
CO40        = 1;   { 40 x 25 Color on Color Adapter }
BW80        = 2;   { 80 x 25 B/W on Color Adapter }
CO80        = 3;   { 80 x 25 Color on Color Adapter }
Mono        = 7;   { 80 x 25 on Monochrome Adapter }
Font8x8     = 256; { Add-in for ROM font }
```

The `Font8x8` value is added to one of the other options to use the additional lines available on VGA and EGA screens (43 and 50 lines, respectively). When `TextMode` is called, the screen is reset to its default values.

Syntax: `Procedure TextMode( Mode : Integer );`

Example: `TextMode( CO80 );`

TextWidth Graph

Purpose: Returns the width of a string in pixels. The value is calculated from the length of the string, the current font size, and the current multiplication factor.

Syntax:

```
Function TextWidth( TextString : String ) : Word;
```

Example:

```
Wide := TextWidth( 'Press Enter to terminate...' );
```

Trunc System

Purpose: Truncates a real-type value to an integer-type value.

Syntax:

```
Function Trunc( X : Real ) : LongInt;
```

Example:

```
Num := Trunc( 3.999 );    { Returns "3" }
```

Truncate System

Purpose: Truncates the file by deleting all records beyond the current file position.

Syntax:

```
Procedure Truncate( var F : AnyFileType );
```

Example:

```
Truncate( WorkFile );
```

UnpackTime Dos

Purpose: Converts the four-byte, packed date-and-time `LongInt` `Squish` returned by `GetFTime`, `FindFirst`, or `FindNext` into `Legible`, an unpacked `DateTime` record, defined as follows:

```
DateTime = record
               Year, Month, Day, Hour, Min, Sec : Word;
           end;
```

The values of the individual fields are not range checked.

Syntax:

```
Procedure UnpackTime( Squish : LongInt;
                      var Legible : DateTime );
```

Example:

```
UnpackTime( SmallSize, ReadRec );
with ReadRec do
   writeln( Month, '/', Day, '/', Year-1900 );
```

UpCase System

Purpose: Converts a character to uppercase.

Syntax:

```
Function UpCase( ch : Char ) : Char;
```

Example:

```
Repeat
   write( 'Continue?  (Y/N) ' );
   readln( Ans )
until UpCase(Ans) in [ 'N', 'Y' ];
```

Val System

Purpose: Converts the original string value `Orig` to its numeric representation `Final`. If the string cannot be converted, `Code` contains the index of the first troublesome character. No trailing spaces are allowed.

Syntax:

```
Procedure Val( Orig : String;  var Final;
               var Code : Integer );
```

Example:

```
Val( ParamStr(1), SelectedValue, TroubleItem );
```

WhereX Crt

Purpose: Returns the X-coordinate of the current cursor position, relative to the current window.

Syntax:

```
Function WhereX : Byte;
```

Example:

```
Over := WhereX;
```

WhereY — Crt

Purpose: Returns the Y-coordinate of the current cursor position, relative to the current window.

Syntax:

```
Function WhereY: Byte;
```

Example:

```
Down := WhereY;
```

Window — Crt

Purpose: Defines a text window on the screen. The window is in the form of a rectangle, with upper left coordinates `(X1, Y1)` and lower right coordinates `(X2, Y2)`.

Syntax:

```
Procedure Window( X1, Y1, X2, Y2 : Byte );
```

Example:

```
Window( 1, 1, 80, 25 );
          { Resets screen to original size }
```

Write — System

Purpose: Writes one or more values to a file. `FileID`, if specified, must be a text or typed file. If the file identifier is omitted, the standard `Output` file is assumed.

Syntax:

```
Procedure Write[( [var FileID : FileType;]
                       v1 [ ,v2, ..., vn ] )];
```

Example:

```
Write( DataFile, WorkLine );
```

Writeln

System

Purpose: Executes the `write` procedure, then outputs an end-of-line marker to the file. `FileID`, if specified, must be a text file. If the text file identifier is omitted, the standard `Output` file is assumed.

Syntax:

```
Procedure Writeln[( [var FileID : Text;]
                    v1 [ ,v2, ..., vn ] )];
```

Example:

```
Writeln( TextFileID, WorkLine );
```

Compiler Directives

Although the Pascal language forces each line of your program to have one clear meaning, the Turbo compiler can generate the machine-level output code in various ways. These different options are selected with compiler directives.

There are three categories of directives: switch, parameter, and conditional. *Switch directives,* as their name implies, switch particular code-generation options on or off. *Parameter directives* specify external file names and memory sizes. *Conditional directives* conditionally select which parts of a program to compile and which parts to ignore.

Compiler directives can be implemented in the integrated environment by selecting the desired directive with the Options/Compiler menu. Although many more directives exist than can be specified in this manner, this is the best way to establish your preferences for program defaults.

Alternatively, directives can be embedded in your source code or given in the command line of the command-line compiler. When given in the command line of the command-line compiler, the form must be

```
/$ <directive>
```

When included in your source code, the directive is written as part of a comment. In such a case the dollar sign is the first character following the opening comment delimiter, followed immediately by the symbol that designates the directive. If any blanks or other characters appear before the dollar sign, the compiler treats the entire line as an ordinary comment and ignores any directives it contains.

Although all these methods achieve the same result, you should remember that good programming entails good documentation; the preferred way to select a directive is to include it as part of the source code in your program. Further, you may want directives to be turned on or off in the same program as the situation requires; this can be accomplished only with the embedded directive method.

Many of your programs will not need to use any directives. However, when properly understood, directives can simplify the debugging of troublesome programs and considerably improve the speed and efficiency of your finished product.

Switch Directives

With switch directives, you can choose from several code-generation options. Switch directives may be either *global*, meaning that the entire compilation is affected, or *local*, meaning that the effect exists only until the next use of the same directive. In other words, after a global directive is set, it cannot be changed, whereas local directives can be switched on or off as often as needed. Global directives must be declared immediately after the initial `program` or `unit` line. Local directives may appear anywhere in the program.

Several switch directives can be specified in the same comment line by separating them with commas, as follows:

```
{$ A+,B-,C+,... <any desired comment>}
```

`A`, `B`, and `C` may be any directive. The `+` indicates that the directive is enabled; the `-` indicates that the directive is disabled. Any spaces appearing before a directive on a line cause the remainder of the line to be treated as a comment, and any additional directives are ignored.

A Align Data

Syntax: `{$A+}` or `{$A-}`

Default: `{$A+}`

Type: Global

Menu: Options/Compiler/Word Align Data

With the Align Data directive you can choose between byte and word alignment when you store variables and typed constants. The directive has no effect on the functional operation of the program.

Alignment refers to the starting memory address. For example, when a segment must be *aligned* to a paragraph boundary, the memory address of the first byte in a segment must be evenly divisible by 16. Similarly, a *word-aligned* variable is one in which the memory address of the first byte in which the variable is stored is evenly divisible by 2.

In the default state `{$A+}`, every variable and typed constant requiring two or more bytes is stored in a memory location that begins on an even address. Because some memory locations may be skipped, the resulting EXE file may be a *few* bytes larger than it would be if the option were not used. The Align Data directive affects only individual variables; it has no impact on compound variables such as the fields in a record or the elements of an array.

When word alignment is disabled with `{$A-}`, all data items are stored continuously in memory, without any consideration for their individual sizes or beginning addresses.

Some processors, such as the 8088, have only an 8-bit data bus and, consequently, always fetch data a single byte at a time. Word alignment offers no efficiency improvements for those machines. Other processors, such as the 8086 and the 80286, have a 16-bit data bus and can fetch a word in a single operation. Therefore, word alignment can considerably enhance the performance of most PCs.

B Boolean Evaluation

Syntax: `{$B+}` or `{$B-}`

Default: `{$B-}`

Type: Local

Menu: Options/Compiler/Complete Boolean Eval

The Boolean Evaluation directive allows the option of evaluating a Boolean expression only as far as necessary to determine the result of the entire expression.

In the following code:

```
W := 3;
X := 4;
CondA := False;
if ( W < X ) or ( Y > Z ) then begin
   Proc1;
   Proc2;
end;
if CondA and CondB then
   Proc3;
```

the `Proc1` and `Proc2` procedures are always executed because 3 is less than 4; the values of the `Y` and `Z` variables are irrelevant. Similarly, because `CondA` is `False`, `Proc3` cannot be executed no matter what the state of `CondB`.

In the default `{$B-}` state, the compiler generates code containing exits that allow the program to end the Boolean evaluation after the result of the entire expression becomes evident. Although in this example the `{$B-}` directive still creates code to compare `Y` and `Z` and to evaluate `CondB`, during program execution those code segments are simply bypassed because they would have no effect on the condition of the entire sentence. This feature is commonly known as *short circuit Boolean evaluation.*

If the `{$B+}` directive had been enabled in the example, the entire Boolean expression would have been evaluated, even though in each case the final result could have been determined in the first clause.

Using the `{$B+}` directive results in slightly smaller output files because programs compiled in the default `{$B-}` state contain extra conditional jump instructions. However, the adverse effects of the larger program size and the additional condition tests are usually trivial. Depending on the structure of a Boolean expression, the default `{$B-}` directive may significantly improve the speed with which the program executes. For example, if the following statement is executed repeatedly:

```
if (A > B) or ((((C+ D)>E) and (F< G)) or ((not H)
    and (I > J))) then
```

considerable execution time will be saved if the default `{$B-}` directive is used and `A` is almost always greater than `B`. In general, whenever you use the `{$B-}` directive, you should remember to arrange the clauses of a Boolean expression to optimize program efficiency.

One negative consequence of the `{$B-}` directive is that using functions as Boolean operands can produce strange results. For example, consider the SWITCHB program (listing 1).

Listing 1

```
program SwitchB;
var
   GlobalX : integer;
function BumpUp : integer;
begin
   inc( GlobalX );
   BumpUp := GlobalX;
end;
begin
   GlobalX := 37;
   writeln( '1: GlobalX = ', GlobalX );
   if ( 4 > 2 ) or ( BumpUp > 67 ) then           { Test 1 }
      writeln( '2: GlobalX = ', GlobalX );
{$B+}
   if ( 4 > 2 ) or ( BumpUp > 67 ) then           { Test 2 }
      writeln( '3: GlobalX = ', GlobalX );
{$B-}
   if ( 4 > 2 ) or ( BumpUp > 67 ) then           { Test 3 }
      writeln( '4: GlobalX = ', GlobalX );
end.
```

When executed, the program results in the following:

```
1: GlobalX = 37
2: GlobalX = 37
3: GlobalX = 38
4: GlobalX = 38
```

Because 4 is always greater than 2, the `if` statements of Tests 1 and 3 were completely determined by the first clause. In Test 2, however, the `{$B+}` directive forced the `if` statement to evaluate the second clause unnecessarily. As a consequence, the `BumpUp` function was invoked and the global variable `GlobalX` was changed.

D Debug Information

Syntax: `{$D+}` or `{$D-}`

Default `{$D+}`

Type: Global

Menu: Options/Compiler/Debug Information

When the Debug directive is enabled with `{$D+}`, the Turbo Pascal debugger can relate a program's source code to the machine code produced by the compiler. The Debug directive is what allows the TURBO.EXE integrated development environment to respond to a run-time error by automatically returning to the editor and highlighting the offending source code.

In addition, the Debug directive provides the information needed for Turbo's built-in debugger to allow a program to run freely, to be single-stepped, or to run until a user-defined breakpoint is reached—all while displaying the effect of the program's statements.

The Debug directive is usually enabled in conjunction with the Local Symbol directive `{$L+}`. The Local Symbol directive allows the debugger to track individual local symbols, whereas the Debug directive can relate those symbols to specific lines of program code.

Use of the Debug directive increases the size of an output file, but the resulting information is in a separate location from the normal machine code. Consequently, it has no effect on execution speed.

E Emulation

Syntax: `{$E+}` or `{$E-}`

Default: `{$E+}`

Type: Global

Menu: Options/Compiler/Emulation

The Emulation directive controls whether floating-point emulation software is included with a compiled program.

In the default `{$E+}` state, the compiled program contains all the software necessary to emulate the operation of an 8087 coprocessor. The program may use any floating-point data types, including `single`, `double`, `extended`, and `comp`.

If 8087 emulation is disabled with `{$E-}`, the only software emulation that Turbo Pascal includes in the compiled program is code to support the 6-byte `real` data type. The program may still use the `single`, `double`, `extended`, and `comp` data types, but if it does, it can run only on a PC in which a math coprocessor has been installed.

The EXE file for a program is considerably smaller when a program is compiled with the Emulation directive disabled. Furthermore, the program runs faster because it does not include additional software to dynamically decide which machine code will handle which operation. Nevertheless, such a program is not portable. The directive should be disabled only when you are certain that the program will always run on a PC in which a coprocessor has been installed.

F Force Far Calls

Syntax: `{$F+}` or `{$F-}`

Default: `{$F-}`

Type: Local

Menu: Options/Compiler/Force Far Calls

The Force Far Calls directive determines whether the code generated for making procedure and function calls uses the near or far call model.

Far calls allow the program to reference a subroutine anywhere in memory. Both the segment and offset values must be specified; four bytes are required to contain the address. Near calls can reference a subroutine only in the current segment; only the two-byte offset is specified.

All of the code in a single unit resides in the same segment. Different units place their code in different segments. In the default state (when the directive is disabled), the compiler automatically determines whether a procedure or function call is referencing a routine outside the current segment (which results in a far call) or if the routine is in the current segment (which results in a near call).

When the directive is enabled with `{$F+}`, *all* calls use the far model.

By themselves, the extra two bytes used by the segment address may seem negligible; however, during execution, code must be generated to save, replace, and restore the segment registers. Further, the compiler believes that the routine is in another segment, so any variable parameter used by the routine is referenced by both its segment and offset addresses. Because of these inefficiencies, the Force Far Calls directive should be used sparingly.

With Turbo Pascal 6.0, you can declare a function or procedure as far by including `FAR` after the header. For example:

```
FUNCTION HeapError(Size: WORD): INTEGER; FAR;
```

6.0

G — Generate 80286 Code

Syntax: `{$G+}` or `{$G-}`

Default: `{$G-}`

Type: Local

Menu: Options/Compiler/286 Instructions

The Generate 80286 Code directive determines whether the Turbo Pascal compiler emits 80286 code.

When the directive is disabled with `{$G-}` (the default), the compiled program contains only 8086 instructions. Such a program can run on any PC with a 80x86 processor. By contrast, when the directive is enabled with `{$G+}`, the compiled program contains 80286 instructions that enhance code generation; however, you need a PC with an 80286 processor or better.

I — Input/Output Checking

Syntax: `{$I+}` or `{$I-}`

Default: `{$I+}`

Type: Local

Menu: Options/Compiler/I/O Checking

The I/O Checking directive controls whether code is generated to test for input and output errors.

When the directive is enabled with `{$I+}`, the compiler automatically tests every I/O procedure and function. If any problem is detected, the program immediately ends with a run-time error.

When the directive is disabled with `{$I-}`, a single I/O error suspends all further input and output activity but will not cause program termination. In this case, I/O errors can be detected—and I/O processing restored—by calling the `IOResult` function. If `IOResult` returns zero, the operation was successful; a nonzero value corresponds to an error code that the program can use to determine an appropriate response. Note that when I/O checking is disabled, the `IOResult` function *must* be called after every individual input and output statement.

Consider the simple integer squaring program SWITCHI1 (listing 2).

Listing 2

```
program SwitchI1;
var
   Selection : integer;
begin
   write( 'Please enter an integer value: ' );
   readln( Selection );
   writeln;
   writeln( 'The square of ', Selection, ' is ', Sqr( Selection )
     );
end.
```

If an integer value is entered for the `Selection` variable, the program responds with its square. If a letter, real number, or some other noninteger value is entered, the program terminates with the message: `Error 106: Invalid numeric format`.

This inconvenience can be avoided by disabling the I/O Checking directive with `{$I-}`. The `IOResult` function can then be used to determine if an error has occurred, as shown in SWITCHI2 (listing 3).

Listing 3

```
program SwitchI2;
var
   Selection : integer;
   IOAction  : integer;
begin
   repeat
      write( 'Please enter an integer value: ' );
```

continues

Listing 3 continued

```
{$I-}
     readln( Selection );
{$I+}
     IOAction := IOResult;
     if IOAction <> 0 then
        writeln( 'Please try again.' );
  until IOAction = 0;
  writeln;
  writeln( 'The square of ', Selection, ' is ', Sqr( Selection ) );
end.
```

In this program, if a noninteger value is entered, the `IOAction` variable will contain a nonzero error code (actually, it will be 106, just as before).

By developing your own error-processing routines, you can make your programs virtually "crash proof" from inadvertent (or deliberate) I/O errors.

L Local Symbol Information

Syntax: `{$L+}` or `{$L-}`

Default: `{$L+}`

Type: Global

Menu: Options/Compiler/Local Symbols

The Local Symbol directive determines whether local symbol information is included as part of the program's output.

For a debugger to examine and modify local variables, information about them (specifically, their names, types, and locations in the program) must be summarized in the same output file that contains the program's machine code.

When the Local Symbol directive is enabled with `{$L+}`, the Turbo Pascal integrated debugger can access a program's local variables. In addition, you can use the `Debug/Call Stack` menu option to analyze the parameters passed in procedure and function calls.

The Local Symbol directive is usually enabled with the Debug directive `{$D+}`. The Local Symbol directive allows the debugger to track individual local symbols, whereas the Debug directive can relate those symbols to specific lines of program code.

Use of the Local Symbol directive increases the size of an output file, but the resulting information is contained separate from the normal machine code. Consequently, it has no effect on execution speed.

N Numeric Processing

Syntax: `{$N+}` or `{$N-}`

Default: `{$N-}`

Type: Global

Menu: Options/Compiler/"8087/80287"

The Numeric Processing directive determines whether an installed 8087 coprocessor will be used to handle floating-point operations.

By default, the Numeric Processing directive is disabled. The program executes just as if no 8087 coprocessor is present—regardless of the configuration of the PC.

In the `{$N+}` state, the compiler tries to use the coprocessor whenever it encounters an instruction involving an operation on one or more real numbers. If no coprocessor is present, emulation software may be invoked, depending on the setting of the `{$E}` Emulation directive.

O Overlay Code Generation

Syntax: `{$O+}` or `{$O-}`

Default: `{$O-}`

Type: Global

Menu: Options/Compiler/Overlays Allowed

The Overlay Code Generation directive enables or disables the generation of the special code that allows a unit to be used as an overlay. This code consists of slightly different parameter-passing routines that are not as efficient as the default routines but have the same functionality.

The use of the `{$O+}` directive does not *force* the unit to be used as an overlay; it simply tells the compiler that the unit *can* be used as an overlay.

R Range Checking

Syntax: `{$R+}` or `{$R-}`

Default: `{$R-}`

Type: Local

Menu: Options/Compiler/Range Checking

The Range Checking directive enables or disables the generation of code designed to perform range checking in an executing program.

When you enable the Range Checking directive with `{$R+}`, Turbo Pascal generates code to ensure that each reference to the subscript of an array or string is in the defined bounds of the variable. In addition, the compiler ensures that each assignment to a scalar or subrange variable is in the appropriate range. If the range-checking code detects any out-of-bounds condition, the program will end with a run-time error.

Because code is generated for every occurrence of a limit condition, compiling with the Range Checking directive enabled results in a larger and slower program. Programs compiled without range checking, however, may exhibit unpredictable effects. Consider the SWITCHR program (listing 4).

Listing 4

```
program SwitchR;
var
   i : byte;
   X : array [ 1..3 ] of integer;
   Y : integer;
   Z : integer;
begin
   Y := 14;
   Z := 35;
   for i := 1 to 5 do X[ i ] := 0;
   writeln( 'Y = ', Y, ' and Z = ', Z );
end.
```

When executed, SWITCHR produces the following result:

```
Y = 0 and Z = 0
```

The `for` loop placed zeros in the first five elements of the `X` array. Because `X` was defined as having only three elements, however, the fourth and fifth entries overflowed the array and affected the values in the `Y` and `Z` variables. If the Range Checking directive had been enabled with `{$R+}`, the program would have terminated with the run-time error message `Error 201: Range check error.`

Note that the Range Checking directive is a run-time test only. If the SWITCHR program had contained a statement such as

```
writeln( X[ 5 ] );
```

the compilation would have terminated with the compile-time error message `Error 76: Constant out of range`, no matter how the Range Checking directive had been set.

Range-checking errors generally produce far more subtle problems than those demonstrated here. Consequently, it is a good idea to turn on the Range Checking directive until a program is completely debugged.

S Stack Overflow Checking

Syntax: `{$S+}` or `{$S-}`

Default: `{$S+}`

Type: Local

Menu: Options/Compiler/Stack Checking

The Stack Checking directive enables or disables the generation of code to check whether a stack-overflow condition is encountered.

In the default `{$S+}` state, the compiler generates code to calculate—*prior* to a function or procedure call—whether sufficient stack space remains to contain both the passed parameters and any local variables. In the SWITCHS program (listing 5), the stack size is set deliberately low with the `{$M}` option and recursive calls are made to the `Shrinker` procedure.

Listing 5

```
program SwitchS;
{$S+ Keep the default; that is, check stack size }
{$M 1024, 0, 1024   The stack and heap are relatively small. }
var
   BigInt : longint;
procedure Shrinker( StartNumber : longint );
begin
   if StartNumber > 0 then begin
      StartNumber := StartNumber - 1;
      Shrinker( StartNumber );
      writeln( StartNumber );
   end;
end;
begin
   readln( BigInt );
   Shrinker( BigInt );
end.
```

If you enter a number less than or equal to 62, the program displays all integers from 0 through 1 that are less than the selected number. If you enter a number greater than or equal to 63 (that is, if 64 or more procedure calls are made), the program ends with the message: `Error 202: Stack overflow error.`

If the Stack Checking directive had been disabled with `{$S-}`, the results would be unpredictable, but a system crash would be likely.

Note that the Stack Checking directive has no effect on the *contents* of the stack. The same amount of stack space is available regardless of whether the directive is enabled. Programs that rely heavily on recursion should be developed with the Stack Checking directive enabled. The directive should then be disabled only after the program has been thoroughly debugged. Alternatively, because the directive is local, it could be enabled for only a few functions or procedures.

V — Var-String Checking

Syntax: `{$V+}` or `{$V-}`

Default: `{$V+}`

Type: Local

Menu: Options/Compiler/Strict Var-Strings

The Var-String Checking directive determines whether strict type checking is performed on strings passed as variable parameters to functions and procedures.

In the default {$V+} state, formal and actual string parameters must be the same type. When the directive is disabled, a subroutine accepts strings of any size.

Although strong typing helps to ensure that variables are properly used, disabling Var-String Checking enables you to develop generic string routines. Consider the SWITCHV program (listing 6).

Listing 6

```
program SwitchV;
type
   String10 = string[ 10 ];
   String100 = string[ 100 ];
var
   Var1 : String10;
   Var2 : String100;
procedure StringUp( var TestString : String10 );
var
   i : byte;
begin
   writeln;
   writeln( 'Processing ''', TestString, '''' );
   writeln( 'It has a size of ', SizeOf( TestString ), ' characters' );
   writeln( 'It is ', Length( TestString ), ' characters long' );
   for i := 1 to Length( TestString ) do
      TestString[ i ] := UpCase( TestString[ i ] );
   writeln;
end;
begin
       Var1 := 'xyz';
       Var2 := 'abcdefghijklmnopqrstuvwxyz';
       StringUp( Var1 );
       writeln( Var1 );
{$V-}  StringUp( Var2 );
       writeln( Var2 );
end.
```

When executed, SWITCHV generates the following output:

```
Processing 'xyz'
It has a size of 11 characters
It is 3 characters long
XYZ
Processing 'abcdefghijklmnopqrstuvwxyz'
It has a size of 11 characters
It is 26 characters long
ABCDEFGHIJKLMNOPQRSTUVWXYZ
```

In the SWITCHV program, the `StringUp` procedure is designed to work on 10-byte strings. By disabling the Var-String Checking directive, however, a 100-byte string was successfully processed.

6.0

X Extended Syntax

Syntax: `{$X+}` or `{$X-}`

Default: `{$X-}`

Type: Global

Menu: Options/Compiler/Extended Syntax

The Extended Syntax directive determines whether the Turbo Pascal extended syntax is enabled or disabled.

When you enable the directive with `{$X+}`, a Turbo Pascal function can be treated just like a procedure. In other words, the value of the function can be discarded and need not be assigned. With the extended syntax, Turbo Pascal functions behave similarly to functions in the C language.

In some applications (for example, recursive calls to manage AVL-trees), the value returned by the function is meaningful only during the recursive calls—the initial call to the function has no real use for the result it returns.

The Extended Syntax directive works only with functions declared by the programmer; it cannot be used with built-in functions.

Parameter Directives

A procedure or function parameter passes information to a subroutine. A program parameter, however, passes information to the operating system. Program parameters are principally concerned with file names and DOS memory allocation requirements.

I Include File

Syntax: `{$I filename}`

Default: None

Type: Local

Menu: Options/Directories/Include Directories

The Include File directive instructs the compiler to insert the contents of the named file immediately after the occurrence of the directive.

The directive may appear anywhere in your program except in a `begin...end` statement block.

The default file name extension for include files is .PAS. A directory may be specified. If the file is not found, the compiler searches the directories named in the Options/Directories/Include Directories menu (or those specified with the `/I` option of the TPC command-line compiler).

Include files may be nested up to eight levels deep.

L Link Object File

Syntax: `{$L filename}`

Default: None

Type: Local

Menu: Options/Directories/Object Directories

The Link Object File directive identifies a file to be linked with the program or unit currently being compiled.

Files to be linked must be in proper Intel relocatable object file (OBJ) format. The default file name extension for link files is OBJ. A directory may be specified. If the file is not found, the compiler will search the directories named in the Options/Directories/Object Directories menu (or those specified with the `/O` directive of the TPC command-line compiler).

M Memory Allocation Sizes

Syntax: `{$M stacksize, heapmin, heapmax}`

Default: `{$M 16384, 0, 655360}`

Type: Global

Menu: Options/Compiler/Memory Sizes

The Memory Allocation Sizes directive specifies the amount of memory to be allocated for the program's stack and heap.

Default, minimum, and maximum sizes are shown in table 1. Only integer values are accepted.

***Table 1.** Sizes of Memory Allocations*

	Default	*Minimum*	*Maximum*
`stacksize`	16,384	1,024	65,520
`heapmin`	0	0	655,360
`heapmax`	655,360	`heapmin`	655,360

The Memory Allocation Sizes directive is global. It can appear only in the main module; the directive is ignored if you include it in a unit.

O Overlay Unit Name

Syntax: `{$O unitname}`

Default: None

Type: Local

Menu: No equivalent

The Overlay Unit Name directive tells the compiler which units are to be processed as overlays.

The directive must appear after the `unitname` is referenced by the `uses` clause. If the directive appears in a unit, or if it references the System unit, it is ignored.

Conditional Compilation Directives

Conditional compilation allows separate sections of a single program to be compiled, based entirely on user-defined conditions. This feature is particularly useful for debugging large programs and for tailoring a general program to fit a variety of specific applications or installations.

The conditionally compiled portions of code are placed in logical block structures that are entirely independent of any program logic. The basic format of a conditional compilation block is:

```
{$IFxxx}    The $IFxxx statement tests a condition.
  .
  .
  .         These statements are compiled only if the
  .         condition in the $IFxxx statement is True.
  .
  .
{$ELSE}     The optional Else designates alternate code.
  .
  .
  .         These statements are compiled only if the
  .         condition in the $IFxxx statement is False.
  .
  .
{$ENDIF}    One Endif is required for each If block.
```

Any legal Pascal statement, including directives, data, and program code, may appear in a conditional compilation block. The `{$IFxxx}` statements may be nested up to 16 levels deep, but each must be terminated with an `{$ENDIF}` statement. Whenever an `{$ELSE}` appears, it always refers to the most recently defined `{$IFxxx}`. If conditional compilation statements are used in an include file, you must ensure that each file has balanced pairs of `{$IFxxx}` and `{$ENDIF}` statements.

The `{$IFDEF}` and `{$IFNDEF}` statements evaluate predefined symbols or symbols defined by other conditional compilation statements. Symbols are defined and undefined (that is, set to `True` and `False`) with the following directives:

```
{$DEFINE SymbolName}
{$UNDEF SymbolName}
```

The `{$UNDEF}` directive cancels a previous definition; if `SymbolName` had not been previously defined, it would have automatically evaluated to `False`.

Conditional symbols can be defined also with the command-line compiler through the use of the `/D` directive. In the interactive development environment, conditional symbols can be defined with the Options/Compiler/Conditional Defines menu.

The predefined conditional symbols are listed in table 2.

Table 2. *Predefined Conditional Symbols*

Symbols	*Defined (True) When*
VER40	Current compiler version is 4.0
VER50	Current compiler version is 5.0
VER55	Current compiler version is 5.5
VER60	Current compiler version is 6.0
MSDOS	Current operating system is MS-DOS or PC DOS
CPU86	CPU is an Intel 80x86 processor
CPU87	80x87 coprocessor is present during compilation

For example, the Numeric Processing directive could be controlled with the following:

```
{$IFDEF CPU87}
{$N+}
{$ELSE}
{$N-}
{$ENDIF}
```

The `{$IFOPT}` statement evaluates as `True` or `False`, depending on whether the directive is enabled or disabled, as indicated. For example, if a program contained the directives just listed for enabling numeric processing, it could additionally allow 8087 emulation to be disabled as follows:

```
{$IFOPT N+}
{$E-}
{$ENDIF}
```

DEFINE

Syntax: `{$DEFINE name}`

The `DEFINE` directive both defines a conditional symbol for use by other directives and sets the symbol to Boolean `True`. If `name` has already been defined, the directive is ignored.

UNDEF

Syntax: `{$UNDEF name}`

The `UNDEF` directive removes the definition of a conditional symbol. In effect, the symbol is set to Boolean `False`. If `name` has already been undefined, the directive is ignored.

IFDEF

Syntax: `{$IFDEF name}`

The `IFDEF` directive compiles the section of code following the directive if the conditional symbol `name` has been defined using a `DEFINE` directive.

IFNDEF

Syntax: `{$IFNDEF name}`

The `IFNDEF` directive compiles the section of code following the directive if the conditional symbol `name` has not been defined with a `DEFINE` directive or if `name` has been undefined with an `UNDEF` directive.

IFOPT

Syntax: `{$IFOPT switch}`

The `IFOPT` directive compiles the section of code following the directive if the `switch` directive is enabled or disabled.

ELSE

Syntax: `{$ELSE}`

The `ELSE` directive compiles the section of code following the directive if the most recent `IFxxx` is not `True`.

ENDIF

Syntax: `{$ENDIF}`

The `ENDIF` directive marks the end of the most recent `IFxxx` or `ELSE` section.

Index

Symbols

A

B

D

E

F

G

H

I

J

K

L

M

P

Q

R

S

T

U

V

W

X-Z

Computer Books From Que Mean PC Performance!

Spreadsheets

1-2-3 Database Techniques $29.95
1-2-3 Graphics Techniques $24.95
1-2-3 Macro Library, 3rd Edition $39.95
1-2-3 Release 2.2 Business Applications . . . $39.95
1-2-3 Release 2.2 PC Tutor $39.95
1-2-3 Release 2.2 QueCards $19.95
1-2-3 Release 2.2 Quick Reference . . . . . . $ 8.95
1-2-3 Release 2.2 QuickStart, 2nd Edition . . . $19.95
1-2-3 Release 2.2 Workbook and Disk $29.95
1-2-3 Release 3 Business Applications $39.95
1-2-3 Release 3 Workbook and Disk $29.95
1-2-3 Release 3.1 Quick Reference . . . . . . $ 8.95
1-2-3 Release 3.1 QuickStart, 2nd Edition . . . $19.95
1-2-3 Tips, Tricks, and Traps, 3rd Edition . . . $24.95
Excel Business Applications: IBM Version . . $39.95
Excel Quick Reference . . . . $ 8.95
Excel QuickStart $19.95
Excel Tips, Tricks, and Traps $22.95
Using 1-2-3/G $29.95
Using 1-2-3, Special Edition $27.95
Using 1-2-3 Release 2.2, Special Edition . . . $27.95
Using 1-2-3 Release 3.1, 2nd Edition $29.95
Using Excel: IBM Version $29.95
Using Lotus Spreadsheet for DeskMate $22.95
Using Quattro Pro $24.95
Using SuperCalc5, 2nd Edition $29.95

Databases

dBASE III Plus Handbook, 2nd Edition $24.95
dBASE III Plus Tips, Tricks, and Traps $24.95
dBASE III Plus Workbook and Disk $29.95
dBASE IV Applications Library, 2nd Edition . $39.95
dBASE IV Programming Techniques $24.95
dBASE IV Quick Reference . . . . $ 8.95
dBASE IV QuickStart $19.95
dBASE IV Tips, Tricks,and Traps, 2nd Edition. $24.95
dBASE IV Workbook and Disk $29.95
Using Clipper $24.95
Using DataEase $24.95
Using dBASE IV $27.95
Using Paradox 3 . . . . $24.95
Using R:BASE $29.95
Using Reflex, 2nd Edition $24.95
Using SQL $29.95

Business Applications

Allways Quick Reference . . . . $ 8.95
Introduction to Business Software $14.95
Introduction to Personal Computers $19.95
Lotus Add-in Toolkit Guide $29.95
Norton Utilities Quick Reference . . . . $ 8.95
PC Tools Quick Reference, 2nd Edition . . . . $ 8.95
Q&A Quick Reference . . . . $ 8.95
Que's Computer User's Dictionary . . . . . . $ 9.95
Que's Wizard Book . . . . $ 9.95
Quicken Quick Reference . . . . $ 8.95
SmartWare Tips, Tricks, and Traps
2nd Edition $24.95
Using Computers in Business $22.95
Using DacEasy, 2nd Edition $24.95
Using Enable/OA $29.95
Using Harvard Project Manager $24.95
Using Managing Your Money, 2nd Edition . . $19.95
Using Microsoft Works: IBM Version $22.95
Using Norton Utilities $24.95
Using PC Tools Deluxe $24.95
Using Peachtree $27.95
Using PFS: First Choice $22.95
Using PROCOMM PLUS $19.95
Using Q&A, 2nd Edition $23.95
Using Quicken: IBM Version, 2nd Edition . . $19.95
Using Smart $22.95
Using SmartWare II $29.95
Using Symphony, Special Edition $29.95
Using Time Line $24.95
Using TimeSlips $24.95

CAD

AutoCAD Quick Reference . . . . $ 8.95
AutoCAD Sourcebook 1991 . . . . $27.95
Using AutoCAD, 3rd Edition $29.95
Using Generic CADD $24.95

Word Processing

Microsoft Word 5 Quick Reference . . . . . . $ 8.95
Using DisplayWrite 4, 2nd Edition $24.95
Using LetterPerfect $22.95
Using Microsoft Word 5.5: IBM Version,
2nd Edition $24.95
Using MultiMate $24.95
Using Professional Write $22.95
Using Word for Windows $24.95
Using WordPerfect 5 . . . . $27.95
Using WordPerfect 5.1, Special Edition . . . $27.95
Using WordStar, 3rd Edition $27.95
WordPerfect PC Tutor $39.95
WordPerfect Power Pack $39.95
WordPerfect Quick Reference . . . . $ 8.95
WordPerfect QuickStart $19.95
WordPerfect 5 Workbook and Disk $29.95
WordPerfect 5.1 Quick Reference . . . . . . $ 8.95
WordPerfect 5.1 QuickStart $19.95
WordPerfect 5.1 Tips, Tricks, and Traps . . . $24.95
WordPerfect 5.1 Workbook and Disk $29.95

Hardware/Systems

DOS Tips, Tricks, and Traps $24.95
DOS Workbook and Disk, 2nd Edition $29.95
Fastback Quick Reference . . . . $ 8.95
Hard Disk Quick Reference . . . . $ 8.95
MS-DOS PC Tutor $39.95
MS-DOS Power Pack $39.95
MS-DOS Quick Reference . . . . $ 8.95
MS-DOS QuickStart, 2nd Edition $19.95
MS-DOS User's Guide, Special Edition . . . $29.95
Networking Personal Computers, 3rd Edition $24.95
The Printer Bible $29.95
Que's PC Buyer's Guide $12.95
Understanding UNIX: A Conceptual Guide,
2nd Edition $21.95
Upgrading and Repairing PCs $29.95
Using DOS $22.95
Using Microsoft Windows 3, 2nd Edition . . $24.95
Using Novell NetWare $29.95
Using OS/2 . . . . $29.95
Using PC DOS, 3rd Edition $24.95
Using Prodigy $19.95
Using UNIX $29.95
Using Your Hard Disk $29.95
Windows 3 Quick Reference . . . . $ 8.95

Desktop Publishing/Graphics

CorelDRAW Quick Reference . . . . $ 8.95
Harvard Graphics Quick Reference . . . . . . $ 8.95
Using Animator $24.95
Using DrawPerfect $24.95
Using Harvard Graphics, 2nd Edition $24.95
Using Freelance Plus $24.95
Using PageMaker: IBM Version, 2nd Edition . $24.95
Using PFS: First Publisher, 2nd Edition $24.95
Using Ventura Publisher, 2nd Edition $24.95

Macintosh/Apple II

AppleWorks QuickStart $19.95
The Big Mac Book, 2nd Edition $29.95
Excel QuickStart $19.95
The Little Mac Book . . . . $ 9.95
Que's Macintosh Multimedia Handbook . . . $24.95
Using AppleWorks, 3rd Edition $24.95
Using Excel: Macintosh Version $24.95
Using FileMaker $24.95
Using MacDraw $24.95
Using MacroMind Director $29.95
Using MacWrite $24.95
Using Microsoft Word 4: Macintosh Version . $24.95
Using Microsoft Works: Macintosh Version,
2nd Edition $24.95
Using PageMaker: Macinsoth Version,
2nd Edition $24.95

Programming/Technical

Assembly Language Quick Reference . . . . . $ 8.95
C Programmer' sToolkit $39.95
C Quick Reference . . . . $ 8.95
DOS and BIOS Functions Quick Reference . . $ 8.95
DOS Programmer's Reference, 2nd Edition . . $29.95
Network Programming in C $49.95
Oracle Programmer's Guide $29.95
QuickBASIC Advanced Techniques $24.95
Quick C Programmer's Guide $29.95
Turbo Pascal Advanced Techniques $24.95
Turbo Pascal Quick Reference . . . . $ 8.95
UNIX Programmer's Quick Reference . . . . $ 8.95
UNIX Programmer's Reference $29.95
UNIX Shell Commands Quick Reference . . . $ 8.95
Using Assembly Language, 2nd Edition $29.95
Using BASIC $24.95
Using C $29.95
Using QuickBASIC 4 . . . . $24.95
Using Turbo Pascal $29.95

For More Information,
Call Toll Free!

1-800-428-5331

All prices and titles subject to change without notice. Non-U.S. prices may be higher. Printed in the U.S.A.

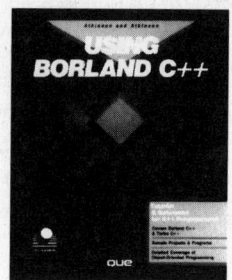